THE

ANNUAL REGISTER
Vol. 227

A friendly greeting between Ronald Reagan, President of the USA, and Mikhail Gorbachev, General Secretary of the Communist Party of the USSR, as they meet in Geneva on 19 November 1985.

Victims of an Arab terrorist attack at the El Al desk in Rome airport on 27 December 1985 which, with a like outrage at Vienna airport on the same day, killed 17 people, crowning a year outstanding in the history of contemporary terrorism.

THE
ANNUAL REGISTER

A Record of World Events
1985

Edited by
H. V. HODSON

Assisted by
VERENA HOFFMAN

FIRST EDITED IN 1758
BY EDMUND BURKE

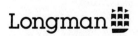

R909. 82

THE ANNUAL REGISTER 1985
Published by Longman Group Limited, Longman House,
Burnt Mill, Harlow, Essex CM20 2JE, United Kingdom

Distributed exclusively in the United States and Canada by Gale Research Company,
Book Tower, Detroit, Michigan 48226, USA

ISBN 0-582-50329-9 (Longman)
    0-8103-2043-6 (Gale)

Library of Congress Catalog Card Number: 4–17979

British Library Cataloguing in Publication Data
The Annual Register—1985
   1. History—Periodicals
   909.82′8′05   D410

ISBN 0-582-50329-9

Set in Times Roman by
COMPUTERISED TYPESETTING SERVICES, LONDON
and Printed in Great Britain at
THE BATH PRESS, AVON

CONTENTS

FRONTISPIECES

A friendly greeting between Ronald Reagan, President of the USA, and Mikhail Gorbachev, General Secretary of the Communist Party of the USSR, as they met in Geneva on 19 November 1985.

Victims of an Arab terrorist attack at the El Al desk in Rome airport on 27 December 1985 which, with a like outrage at Vienna airport on the same day, killed 17 people, crowning a year outstanding in the history of contemporary terrorism.

ACP	Africa—Caribbean—Pacific
AID	Agency for International Development
ASEAN	Association of South-East Asian Nations
AR	Annual Register
AWACS	Advanced Warning and Communications Systems
CAP	Common Agricultural Policy
CARICOM	Caribbean Common Market
CBI	Confederation of British Industry
CHOGM	Commonwealth Heads of Government Meeting
CIA	Central Intelligence Agency
COMECON	Council for Mutual Economic Assistance
ECA	Economic Commission for Africa (UN)
ECE	Economic Commission for Europe (UN)
ECOSOC	Economic and Social Council (UN)
ECOWAS	Economic Community of West African States
ECUs (MECUs)	(Million) European Currency Units
EEC	European Economic Community (Common Market)
EFTA	European Free Trade Association
EMS	European Monetary System
ESCAP	Economic and Social Commission for Asia and the Pacific (UN)
EURATOM	European Atomic Energy Community
FAO	Food and Agriculture Organization
GATT	General Agreement on Tariffs and Trade
GCC	Gulf Cooperation Council
GDP/GNP	Gross Domestic/National Product
IAEA	International Atomic Energy Agency
IBRD	International Bank for Reconstruction and Development
ICAO	International Civil Aviation Organization
ICBM	Inter-Continental Ballistic Missile
IDA	International Development Association
ILO	International Labour Organization
IMF	International Monetary Fund
LDCs/MDCs	Less/More Developed Countries
MBFR	Mutual and Balanced Force Reductions
NATO	North Atlantic Treaty Organization
OAS	Organization of American States
OAU	Organization of African Unity
OECD	Organization for Economic Cooperation and Development
OPEC	Organization of Petroleum Exporting Countries
PLO	Palestine Liberation Organization
SALT	Strategic Arms Limitation Talks
SACEUR	Supreme Allied Commander Europe
SDI	Strategic Defense Initiative
START	Strategic Arms Reduction Talks
SWAPO	South-West Africa People's Organization
TUC	Trades Union Congress
UN	United Nations
UNCTAD	United Nations Conference on Trade and Development
UNDP	United Nations Development Programme
UNESCO	United Nations Educational, Scientific and Cultural Organization
UNHCR	United Nations High Commission for Refugees
UNRWA	United Nations Relief and Works Agency
VAT	Value Added Tax
WEU	Western European Union
WHO	World Health Organization

CONTRIBUTORS

EXTRACTS FROM PAST VOLUMES   **W. N. Medlicott,** CBE, DLitt, MA, FRHistS, Stevenson Professor of International History Emeritus, University of London

PART I
UNITED KINGDOM   **H. V. Hodson,** Formerly Editor, *The Sunday Times*

SCOTLAND   **Maurice Baggott,** Principal, Scottish Industrial Communications

WALES   **Peter Stead,** Lecturer in History, University College of Swansea

NORTHERN IRELAND   **Brian M. Walker,** MA, PhD, Lecturer in Political Science, The Queen's University, Belfast

PART II
USA   **James Bishop,** Editor, *The Illustrated London News*

CANADA   **David M. L. Farr,** Professor of History, Carleton University, Ottawa

LATIN AMERICA   **Peter Calvert,** AM, MA, PhD, Professor of Comparative and International Politics, University of Southampton

THE CARIBBEAN   **Neville C. Duncan,** PhD, Senior Lecturer, Faculty of Social Sciences, University of the West Indies

PART III
USSR   **Peter Frank,** Senior Lecturer in Soviet Government and Politics, University of Essex

GERMAN DEMOCRATIC REPUBLIC   **Jonathan Fenby,** Bonn correspondent of *The Economist*

POLAND   **Z. J. Blazynski,** Writer and broadcaster on Polish and communist affairs

CZECHOSLOVAKIA   **Vladimir V. Kusin,** PhD, Deputy Director, Radio Free Europe research and analysis, Munich

HUNGARY   **George Schöpflin,** Joint Lecturer in East European Political Institutions, London School of Economics and School of Slavonic and East European Studies, University of London

ROMANIA   **George Fodor,** South-East European Service, BBC

BULGARIA   **Rada Nikolaev,** Head of Bulgarian research section, Radio Free Europe

YUGOSLAVIA   **F. B. Singleton,** MA, Formerly Chairman, Postgraduate School of Yugoslav Studies, University of Bradford

ALBANIA   **Anton Logoreci,** BSc(Econ), Writer and broadcaster on communist affairs

MONGOLIA   **Alan Sanders,** FIL, Soviet Regional Editor, BBC Monitoring Service

PART IV

FRANCE	**Martin Harrison,** Professor of Politics, University of Keele
FEDERAL REPUBLIC OF GERMANY	**Jonathan Fenby,** Bonn correspondent of *The Economist*
ITALY	**Muriel Grindrod,** OBE, Writer on Italian affairs; formerly Assistant Editor, *The Annual Register*
BELGIUM, NETHERLANDS, LUXEMBOURG	**J. D. McLachlan,** Managing Director, Marketing, FT Business Information Ltd
REPUBLIC OF IRELAND	**Louis McRedmond,** MA, BL, Head of Information in Radio Telefis Eireann, the Irish broadcasting service
NORDIC COUNTRIES	**Hilary Allen,** BSc (Econ), DPhil, Writer on Nordic affairs
AUSTRIA	**Angela Gillon,** Researcher in West European affairs
SWITZERLAND	**Hermann Böschenstein,** DPh, Historian and editor
SPAIN, PORTUGAL	**G. A. M. Hills,** BA, DLit, Writer and broadcaster on Iberian current affairs and history
GIBRALTAR, MALTA	**D. G. Austin,** Emeritus Professor of Government, University of Manchester
GREECE	**Richard Clogg,** MA, King's College, University of London
TURKEY	**A. J. A. Mango,** BA, PhD, Orientalist and writer on current affairs in Turkey and the Near East
CYPRUS	**Thomas O'Dwyer,** Director of the Levant Bureau and professional writer specializing in Cypriot and East Mediterranean affairs

PART V

ISRAEL	**Noah Lucas,** PhD, Chairman, Department of Political Theory and Institutions, University of Sheffield
ARAB WORLD, EGYPT, JORDAN, SYRIA, LEBANON, IRAQ	**Christopher Gandy,** Formerly UK diplomatic service; writer on Middle Eastern affairs
SAUDI ARABIA, YEMEN ARAB REPUBLIC, PDRY	**R. M. Burrell,** Lecturer in the Contemporary History of the Near and Middle East, School of Oriental & African Studies, University of London
ARAB STATES OF THE GULF	**George Joffe,** Consultant Editor for Middle East and North Africa, Economist Publications Ltd.; journalist and broadcaster on North Africa and the Middle East
SUDAN	**Ahmed al-Shahi,** DPhil, Lecturer in Social Anthropology, Department of Social Studies, University of Newcastle-upon-Tyne
LIBYA, TUNISIA, WESTERN SAHARA, ALGERIA, MOROCCO	**Robin Bidwell,** Secretary, Middle East Centre, Cambridge University

PART VI

ETHIOPIA, SOMALIA, DJIBOUTI	**Christopher Clapham,** MA, DPhil, Senior Lecturer in Politics, University of Lancaster
KENYA, TANZANIA, UGANDA	**William Tordoff,** MA, PhD, Professor of Government, University of Manchester
GHANA	**D. G. Austin** (see GIBRALTAR)

NIGERIA	**Martin Dent,** Senior Lecturer, Department of Politics, University of Keele
SIERRA LEONE, THE GAMBIA, LIBERIA	**Arnold Hughes,** BA, Lecturer in Political Science, Centre of West African Studies, University of Birmingham
CHAPTER 3 (SENEGAL to EQUATORIAL GUINEA)	**Kaye Whiteman,** Editor-in-Chief, *West Africa*

PART VII

CHAPTER I (ZAÏRE to ANGOLA)	**Robin Hallett,** MA, Writer and lecturer on African affairs
ZAMBIA, MALAWI	**Robin Hallett** (see above)
ZIMBABWE	**R. W. Baldock,** BA, PhD, Senior Editor, Yale University Press; writer on African affairs
NAMIBIA, BOTSWANA, LESOTHO, SWAZILAND, SOUTH AFRICA	**Gerald Shaw,** MA, Chief Assistant Editor, *The Cape Times*, Cape Town

PART VIII

IRAN	**Keith McLachlan,** BA, PhD, Senior Lecturer in Geography with reference to the Near and Middle East, School of Oriental and African Studies, University of London
AFGHANISTAN, INDIA, BANGLADESH, NEPAL	**Peter Lyon,** BSc (Econ), PhD, Reader in International Relations and Secretary, Institute of Commonwealth Studies, University of London
PAKISTAN	**Salman A. Ali,** Formerly Pakistan diplomatic service
SRI LANKA	**James Jupp,** MSc(Econ), PhD, Senior Fellow, Australian National University
SEYCHELLES, MAURITIUS	**Jane Davis,** Lecturer, Department of International Politics, The University College of Wales, Aberystwyth
MALAGASY, COMORO STATE	**Kaye Whiteman** (see Part VI, Ch.3)

PART IX

BURMA, THAILAND, INDONESIA, PHILIPPINES, VIETNAM, KAMPUCHEA, LAOS	**A. S. B. Olver,** MA, Specialist in South-East Asian affairs
MALAYSIA, BRUNEI, SINGAPORE	**Michael Leifer,** BA, PhD, Reader in International Relations, London School of Economics and Political Scienee
CHINA, TAIWAN	**Brian Hook,** Senior Lecturer in Chinese Studies, University of Leeds
HONG KONG	**A. S. B. Olver** (see above)
JAPAN	**Reginald Cudlipp,** Director, Anglo-Japanese Economic Institute
SOUTH AND NORTH KOREA	**Richard Sim,** Consultant and political analyst on Far Eastern affairs

PART X

AUSTRALIA — **Geoffrey Sawer,** AO, LLD, DLitt, BA, LLM, Emeritus Professor of Law, Australian National University

PAPUA NEW GUINEA — **Michael Oliver,** Chairman, Department of Political and Administrative Studies, University of Papua New Guinea

NEW ZEALAND, SOUTH PACIFIC — **Roderic Alley,** PhD, School of Political Science and Public Administration, Victoria University of Wellington

PART XI

UNITED NATIONS — **Frances Boyd,** MA, Editor of United Nations Association publications; writer on international and UN affairs

COMMONWEALTH — **Derek Ingram,** Editor of *Commonwealth* and author and writer on the Commonwealth

EUROPEAN COMMUNITY — **Michael Berendt,** Expert on affairs of the European Communities

COUNCIL OF EUROPE — **Sir John Rodgers,** Bt, DL, MA, FRSA, Former President, Political Affairs Commission, Council of Europe and Vice-President of the Assembly of WEU

WEU, EFTA, OECD — **H. V. Hodson** (see United Kingdom)

NORTH ATLANTIC ASSEMBLY — **James P. Cross,** Information Officer, North Atlantic Assembly

NORDIC COUNCIL — **Hilary Allen** (see Part IV, Nordic countries)

COMECON — **Michael Kaser,** MA, Reader in Economics, Oxford University, and Professorial Fellow of St Antony's College, Oxford

AFRICAN ORGANIZATIONS — **Kaye Whiteman** (see Part VI, Ch.3)

S.E. ASIAN ORGANIZATIONS — **A.S.B. Olver** (see Part IX, Burma etc.)

CARIBBEAN ORGANIZATIONS — **Neville C. Duncan** (see Part II, Caribbean)

OAS, SELA — **Peter Calvert** (see Part II, Latin America)

SOUTH PACIFIC INSTITUTIONS — **Roderic Alley** (see Part IX, New Zealand)

NON-ALIGNED MOVEMENT — **Peter Willetts,** PhD, Lecturer in International Relations, The City University, London; author of *The Non-Aligned in Havana*

PART XII

ARMAMENTS AND DEFENCE — **Jane Davis** (see Part VIII, Seychelles etc.)

PART XIII

RELIGION — **Geoffrey Parrinder,** MA, PhD, DD, Emeritus Professor of the Comparative Study of Religions, University of London

PART XIV

CHAPTERS I and 2 — **John Newell,** Editor, Science, Industry and Agriculture, BBC External Services

TECHNOLOGY — **Michael Cross,** Technology correspondent, *New Scientist*

ENVIRONMENT — **Lloyd Timberlake,** Editorial Director, *Earthscan*

PART XV

INTERNATIONAL LAW   **Christine Gray,** Lecturer in Law, St Hilda's College, Oxford

EUROPEAN COMMUNITY LAW   **N. March Hunnings,** LLM, PhD, Editor, *Common Market Law Reports*

LAW IN THE UK   **C. T. Emery,** MA, LLB, Lecturer in Law, University of Durham

PART XVI

OPERA   **Rodney Milnes,** Deputy Editor, *Opera*

DANCE-BALLET   **Mary Clarke,** Editor, *The Dancing Times*

THEATRE   **Giles Gordon,** Theatre Critic, *The House Magazine;* theatre reviewer for *The Observer* and *Punch*

NEW YORK THEATRE   **Edward G. Greer,** Associate Professor, Drama Department, Syracuse University, USA

MUSIC   **Francis Routh,** Composer and author; founder-director of the Redcliffe Concerts of British Music

CINEMA   **Roger Manvell,** PhD, DLitt, Director, British Film Academy 1947–59; Visiting Fellow, University of Sussex; Professor of Film, Boston University

TV & RADIO   **Raymond Snoddy,** Writer on communications and broadcasting, *The Financial Times*

ART   **Marina Vaizey,** MA, Art critic, *The Sunday Times*

ARCHITECTURE   **Jonathan Glancey,** Editor, *The Architect*

FASHION   **Anne Price,** Fashion writer

LITERATURE   **David Holloway,** Literary Editor, *The Daily Telegraph*

PART XVII

SPORT   **Tony Pawson,** Sports writer, *The Observer*; cricket, football and fly-fishing international

PART XVIII

CHAPTERS 1 to 4   **Peter Riddell,** Political Editor, *The Financial Times*

STATISTICS   **Sue Cockerill,** Statistical Department, *The Financial Times*

INDEX   **Richard German,** Professional indexer

PREFACE

THE apex of world diplomacy in 1985 was the Reagan-Gorbachev meeting in November. Its immediate achievements were few, but it was preceded and followed by a more hopeful atmosphere in arms control talks between the superpowers. The conflict over intermediate-range nuclear weapons in Europe (Cruise, Pershing and the Russian SS range) gave way in prominence to even sharper confrontation over the Strategic Defense Initiative. Was it a threat of destabilizing nuclear deterrence and escalating superpower competition to a still higher level, or the way to a world rid of the nuclear arms menace? Many Europeans had their doubts. The year saw further growth of the Green movement, primarily ecological in its aims but strongly anti-nuclear in both the armaments and power-supply contexts—perhaps destabilizing in another way.

At less stratospheric levels 1985 was a year of widespread violence. While war in Lebanon cost fewer lives, it still smouldered and flamed. Palestinian revolt was one cause among many of the terrorist acts which made lead stories in the world's media (see EDITORIAL). The Gulf war continued its slaughter. Oppression under tyrannical governments was the lot of hundreds of millions. In South Africa the boil of black subordination broke in human blood and political pus: even the white-minority Government was constrained to admit that apartheid had to end. If that end came nearer, some gain in human rights could be recorded.

Economically it was a year of improvement for Western industrialized nations, for the drought-ridden sub-Sahara and some other developing countries, but not for those dependent on exports of primary products, whose prices fell, widening further the gulf between rich and poor, nor for the hitherto-prospering oil producers, as the market slumped. The 'new international economic order' seemed more of a chimera than ever.

Such is the story told in detail in the Annual Register 1985. No significant changes have been made in the arrangement of its contents. The range of documents is perhaps even more comprehensive and important than ever.

ACKNOWLEDGEMENTS

The Advisory Board again gratefully acknowledges its debt to a number of institutions for their help with sources, references, documents, figures and maps. The Board, and the bodies which nominate its members, disclaim responsibility for any opinons expressed or the accuracy of any facts recorded in this volume.

THE ANNUAL REGISTER

200 years ago

1 November 1785, *Arabia*. We are informed that Arabia has again produced a prophet and a warrior, who is beginning with success the career of the impostor Mahomet. This man has already collected a large body of disciples and followers from the various tribes of Arabs. He forbids his disciples from pilgrimage to or at the tomb of Mahomet, asserting that the power of that prophet is now superseded by his mission. He has framed several new laws in addition to his predecessor's, which he says the depravity of mankind has rendered necessary, and that he has long since been appointed by the Supreme Power to work a reformation. He keeps his troops in the most exact discipline, and has already seized on several strong posts. It is suspected that his first step will be to fall on the caravan from the Porte to Mecca. The event of this pretender is uncertain, but he bids fair for success.

150 years ago

28 July 1835, *Fieschi's machine gun*. The king [Louis Philippe] reviewed a large body of troops and national guards. As he was riding along the Boulevard du Temple. . . an explosion, like a discharge of musquetry, took place from the window of an adjoining house. The effect was terrific. . . the police seized the assassin in the act of letting himself down by a rope from a back window of the apartment. . . The machine consisted of between twenty and thirty gun barrels arranged horizontally, side by side upon a frame, the back part of which could be raised or lowered, according to the angle required to reach the space in the street below which was to be swept. Each barrel was loaded with several bullets, and a heavy charge of powder. A train of gunpowder connected the touch-holes, and the explosion of one discharged them all. Five of the barrels had burst, and wounded the assassin severely in the head. . . All parties joined in expressing their abhorrence of so atrocious an attempt.

100 years ago

26 January 1885, *Gordon's death at Khartoum*. When the full measure of the disaster was at length realised, and the heroic efforts made by General Gordon to hold out until the arrival of the British troops became known, there was on all sides a loud and bitter cry raised against the Cabinet, the War Office, and Lord Wolesley. The Cabinet was accused of helpless indecision, or of being guided only by the expediency of the hour, putting off from day to day its consent to any relief expedition; the War Office had stinted men and materials; and at the last moment Lord Wolesley, goaded to make an effort to save Gordon from the treachery by which he was menaced, despatched an inadequate force across a trackless desert, swarming with hostile Arabs. From all sides the cry, 'Too late!' arose.

50 years ago

7–9 December 1935, *Hoare-Laval discussions in Paris*. When the alleged proposals were reported in England, they at first created a feeling of stupefaction in all those who had been relying on the British Government to uphold the authority of the League of Nations. There could be no doubt that, if the terms were only half as favourable to Italy as they were reported to be, the aggressor, so far from being punished, was being rewarded, and Great Britain had completely reversed the policy which she had so far been pursuing in relation to the Italo-Abyssinian dispute. In many quarters the report was received with blank incredulity, and hopes were entertained that the truth would be found to be something entirely different.

ANNUAL REGISTER

FOR THE YEAR 1985

EDITORIAL

THE temptation is strong to call 1985 the year of the terrorist. Certainly, the piratical and murderous seizure of the Italian cruise liner *Achille Lauro*, the hijacking of an Egyptian passenger aircraft which led to over 50 deaths, and the massacres by gunfire at Rome and Vienna airports, not to mention—if indeed it was a terrorist act—the destruction of an Air India jumbo jet at a cost of 327 lives, were spectacular landmarks in the history of international terrorism, and the year saw many other death-dealing terrorist assaults. But political terrorism has afflicted the world for a very long time, and will continue to do so, perhaps mounting to a still higher peak; and a few dramatic instances may distract and pervert a critical appraisal of political terrorism in all its forms.

Many activities have been labelled 'terrorist' which a cool, detached judgment would call something else. And many activities which deserve the name have escaped being classed as terrorist because they have been committed by established governments or their agencies. The essence of terrorism, by whomsoever committed, is not the motive or character of its perpetrators but its method, the method of terror, the terrifying of people and the institutions they represent into doing things which if not put in fear they would not do. That is a means which can be directed to widely different ends. Political terrorism obviously excludes protection rackets, blackmail, kidnapping and other forms of criminal intimidation whose motive is financial gain or other non-political ends, though political terrorists have not been averse to emulating such crimes: they need money for their operations, and are not scrupulous as to how they get it.

It may be open to question whether to dismiss from the class of terrorist action deliberate political assassinations. The murder of an Austrian archduke at Sarajevo in July 1914 was not designed to terrorise other archdukes, nor was the assassination of Mrs Indira Gandhi by her Sikh bodyguard in October 1984 designed to intimidate her successors or Indian Cabinet Ministers at large. It was a specific act of revenge for the storming of the Golden Temple of the Sikhs on her orders. What then should we say about the Brighton bombing of October 1984, which was manifestly intended to kill the Prime Minister and other members of the Cabinet? The facts that the target was not a single person but several, and that people other than the prime targets were killed or injured, are not by themselves decisive. In 1947 Premier U Aung San and six other members of the Government of Burma were slain by a gunman as they sat in Council session; the multiple target did not shift the crime from the class of political assassination to that of terrorism. We rightly call the Brighton bombing terrorist, however, because it was part of a series of operations by an organization openly steeped in terrorism: the aim was not the elimination of particular figures but ultimate political objectives, to be furthered by frightening political leaders and parties into policies which they would otherwise have refused.

The policies and actions of the IRA, and of the equally violent and murderous INLA, raise another problem in definition. In war—that is, in international war generally recognized as such, whether or not formally declared—many things are done which in other circumstances would rank as terrorist crimes; indeed the whole object of warfare could be said to be to use whatever violent or other means are deemed necessary to terrify the opposing forces or governments or peoples into surrendering. Thus the saturation bomb attacks on cities like Coventry or Dresden in World War II were undoubtedly major acts of terrorism; the supreme act of terrorism was committed at Hiroshima. But such military actions in wartime are excused, if not always justified, by their being incidental to an overriding aim, that of ending, with victory or at least without defeat, a war of which opposing violence is the essence.

The IRA and like-minded violent Republicans in Ireland claim that they are at war. They regard the agents of the United Kingdom regime in Northern Ireland, especially the army and the police, as forces of an occupying power. In acting against those forces they claim the legitimacies of international warfare. They call themselves 'Armies' and give their officers and contingents military titles; when captured they demand the rights of prisoners-of-war. Those pretensions are quite false. The notion of an international war in Northern Ireland has no historical or constitutional base whatever. The Union Government exercised from Belfast has a legitimacy deeper-founded in history than the Republican Government exercised from Dublin. The southern successor state to the united Ireland which existed before 1921 never claimed to be at war with Britain after the Anglo-Irish treaty was concluded. Both the two Governments in Ireland treat the IRA and other violent movements as their internal foes. How then can there be a war in Ireland? Agents of those movements act, not like soldiers, but like assassins and saboteurs. The armed actions of the IRA and INLA are aimed not only at military and police establishments and personnel, but also at politicians, judges, anyone deemed a collaborator with the forces of law and order, and even the public at large. They seek, not a military victory, but a political denouement.

The same principles apply to other countries disturbed by insurrectionary violence. Though civil wars are a particular kind of war, they are wars, and actions taken in the course of them which would otherwise be called terrorism may well be regarded as something different. The question is: when does an insurgency, or the armed violence of an ardent minority, become a civil war? If on both sides there are organized forces capable of engaging each other, not necessarily in big battles but in inter-force actions, or if the insurgency is so coherent, widespread and effective that the state military forces have to engage in warlike activities in order to contain it, or if it holds substantial areas or major towns where the writ of the state forces do not run, then we can say that a civil war exists and the judgment of what is terrorism requires new criteria. In a civil war, as in any other war, the actions of both sides have to be judged by the same standards and, where justified, given the same opprobrious names. In 1985, by the criteria set out above, there were civil wars in Angola, in Namibia, in El Salvador, perhaps in Nicaragua, but not yet, in, say, Chile or, the most conspicuous candidate of all, South Africa.

The distinction between political terrorism and other forms of violence for political ends evidently turns, in part, upon whether the action is levied directly or indirectly against the agents of whatever structures the violent actors seek to replace or destroy. When an angry crowd confronts a force of police—at a strike picket, on an inner-city street, in a South African township—and violent actions are exchanged, those actions cannot be called terrorism on the part of either side. They are aimed directly against the opponents, and their purpose is not terror but self-defence, retaliation or the other side's on-the-spot defeat.

Violent action against the police or by the police can, however, take very different shapes from such battles. It may be, as so often in Northern Ireland, the murder or attempted murder of individual policemen or posses of police, or of isolated military personnel, or of people believed to be helping the police or military, not because of what they are doing at the time, or are believed to be intending to do, but simply because they are police or military or their supposed allies. Such action against one man or a few men is, in effect, aimed indirectly against the whole force or the whole regime that they represent, in other words is meant to frighten and thus coerce whole classes of people. That is terrorism. So, too, was the attempt of some striking miners in Britain in 1984–85 to terrorise others who were working, as a threatening example to others.

The forces of government can commit terrorism too. You do not have to be a card-carrying terrorist to perform acts of terrorism. If, in any country or in any situation, the police or military set out, by their violence against some persons, to intimidate and cow others not present, or if they exert violence indiscriminately against groups of people, whether or not those people severally are, or are supposed about to be, acting in a violently unlawful manner, then they are committing terrorism as surely as any Bader-Meinhoff gangster or Libyan hit-man. Most regimes commit deeds of that sort sometimes; alien, imperial or otherwise dictatorial regimes commit them most often. Far from being ashamed of their terrorist methods, they may consciously applaud their effectiveness. A little blood-letting here and now, they say, may save much death and destruction later. Even the notorious massacre in the Jallianwalabagh at Amritsar in 1919 was justified by General Dyer and his many British defenders in India on precisely those grounds. In 1985, the instant eye of television exposed many apparent acts of terrorism by South African government forces as well as by their foes. Israel's actions in Lebanon have frequently been of a terrorist kind. Neither the Israeli Government has sought to legitimate its methods by declaring war against the invaded nation and its people, nor the South African Government by acknowledging the existence of a revolutionary civil war.

Another, basically similar, way of identifying political terrorism is to say that it involves what are journalistically called innocent people. What are they supposed to be innocent of? The point is, not that they are innocent, but that they are not known to be guilty of any offence except being there. It is more accurate to call them 'third parties'—neither the attackers nor the political objects of the attack. They may be hostages, or people who get in the way of some otherwise-directed action, or just people at large, victims of the terrorists' illusion that whole governments, whole nations, can be intimidated by the killing of a dozen shoppers or church-goers or airport occupants, or that the competitive capitalist system, with its banks and factories, its multinational corporations, its indifference, can be grievously wounded by an explosion at a bank or a company headquarters which just as indifferently happens to kill or maim some 'innocent' passers-by.

So the identifying marks of political terrorism are these: its method and intention are to intimidate people beyond those presently attacked; its objectives are not direct and immediate, but indirect and distant from the scene; it is not action in a recognised international or civil war; the victims, by design or inevitable consequence, are or include 'third parties', identified neither with the terrorists nor with their ultimate objectives. That analysis seems restrictive, narrowing the field by excluding certain kinds of violence often wrongly called terrorist, as well as intimidatory acts performed in the course of war—international or civil—where the only 'third parties' are neutral nationals who may get caught, so to say, in the cross-fire. But the analysis also reveals that terrorism is all around us, throughout the world. It is not confined to revolutionary fanatics. It may be committed by governments, military forces, police, embattled workers, ruthless employers, sectional interests. It is a permanent feature of organized society, which inevitably has enemies within for whom some of the organs of society are themselves perceived as enemies. It is commonly a feature of efforts at destabilizing a disliked regime, as in many actual governmental interventions in the affairs of other nations.

There is danger in isolating political terrorism from other violent

crime and subjecting it to peculiar laws and penalties. Capital punishment for terrorists is often a popular cry in countries where it has been
abolished for murder; but there is neither less nor more evil in killing
people for political aims than in killing them for money, sex or power.
The honorable tradition of giving sanctuary to those accused of political
offences should not be compromised; if, however, the offence, ade-
quately proven by evidence, includes murder or grievous bodily harm,
the political epithet is of no account, provided that there is assurance of
fair trial. A sense of proportion is also needed; innocent lives are far less
endangered by terrorists than by drunken drivers.

Action to prevent, deter or punish political terrorism is, like action
against any other class of crime, an unending process, more or less
successful from time to time, in particular places and cases, but never
conclusive. The ultimate causes of crime are complex and profound, lying
deep in private and public morality, in the imperfections of society and
the sinfulness of mankind. Those fundamental causes have to be
attacked, but their conquest will take a very long time, and meanwhile
society has to be protected, whether against terrorists or against rapists,
thieves, extortioners, racketeers or murderers. The counter-action,
against terrorists and common criminals alike, consists essentially in
anticipation, protection, detection and deterrent punishment; in short, it
depends upon efficient policing, including penetration and other under-
cover methods, and on a fair but swift and stern system of justice.

International terrorism calls for the projection of such measures
beyond national frontiers. Political terrorism can be called international
when either its perpetrators do not belong to the country where it takes
place, or it is committed in international waters or air-space, or its
ultimate objective is of a transnational kind. Such terrorist crimes are the
phenomenon that produces the most dramatic incidents for the world's
press and broadcasters to report. Tighter security at airports and other
checkpoints, closer international collaboration between police forces,
pledges by governments to try and punish or extradite terrorists and not
to allow hijacked aircraft to refuel, more effective extradition treaties—
these and other such measures can deter some forms of terrorism and
immobilize some kinds of terrorist. The greater the perceived risk to the
would-be actor, the less the risk to others of becoming his victim, and that
is all to the good, just as it is good that citizens and banks and shops
should take stronger precautions against burglars, bank robbers and
shop-lifters, and the police be well equipped and trained to detect and
capture them. But we know well that the impulse to crime, whether of the
one sort or of the other, is not eliminated by such defences, which it will
strive to circumvent, perhaps by finding some fresh less-protected target.

International terrorism claims its own justification in the state of
hostility between nations and in the oppression and fear that mar relations between certain peoples. Its exponents often claim that they are

compelled into violent acts for want of any peaceful means of attaining
their legitimate ends. That excuse will not wash in open democracies—
for instance in the United Kingdom and the Irish Republic. It certainly
has force in such cases as those of the blacks in South Africa or the
displaced Palestinians with whom Israel will not treat. But it has no effect
on the definition of terrorism or on its condemnation as such. Nor has the
excuse of retaliation or revenge. The retaliator in kind tars himself with
the same brush as his attackers. Real causes do not justify evil methods.

With the sole exception of the Gulf war, no declared or mutually
acknowledged international war exists at the present time between member states of the United Nations. A number of Arab countries are,
indeed, in a state of permanent hostility to Israel; a Soviet army occupies
Afghanistan; in Kampuchea, in Central America, in Angola, Mozambique and Namibia, armed conflicts proceed in which outside powers
have intervened. Thus in many theatres, though there is no international
war, there is no international peace. But none of this sets up that
condition of all-out war which excuses, though it may not justify, action
of an inherently terrorist nature committed or promoted internationally.
Yet such action is widespread and notorious. It cannot be said that
countries which commit, connive at or condone it, including some judg-
matically self-righteous, have their hands clean, or set a shining example
to the perpetrators or promoters of acts of terrorism against themselves,
their citizens or their interests.

Those acts are plentiful and menacing enough. Besides such flagrant
examples as aircraft hijacks, seizure of hostages or mass bombings, many
emigré communities live in fear of murder by agents of the home governments or racial groups that they oppose. All this is wickedness, assault on
basic human rights, an affront to civilized life; and it has to be countered
accordingly. To guard against it and to apprehend and punish the perpetrators is manifestly an international as well as a national duty. Worldwide collaboration to that end is far from complete, though it is being
strengthened. Certain governments notoriously aid, promote or even
order terrorist crimes or flagrantly harbour their perpetrators. If, in the
use of terrorist methods for political ends, no country is entirely innocent,
some are clearly more guilty than others and should be brought to book.
But unilaterally to condemn them and punish their peoples is international lynch law. The civilised world desperately needs a regime of
international criminal law, embracing not only terrorism but also genocide and other grave assaults on human life and liberty—a code of
international criminal law, a world court of criminal justice and an agreed
system of enforcing its judgments by appropriate penalties or sanctions.
That is the ideal towards which the contemporary impact of international
political terrorism bids the world's statesmen aspire.

London, January 1986

I THE UNITED KINGDOM

Chapter 1

STRIKES OFF AND ON

AT the start of 1985 the strike in the coal industry (see AR 1984, pp. 8–19), which had begun in March 1984, showed no sign of ending through a settlement between the National Coal Board (NCB) and the National Union of Mineworkers (NUM). The latest negotiations had broken down at the end of October, and the Board was relying on a progressive return to work by NUM members still on strike. This proceeded slowly until the last week in February, but by the end of that month the Board could claim that over half of the 170,000 miners on its books were now working; Mr Ian MacGregor, the NCB's chairman, had said that when this happened he would regard the strike as over. On 8 January the highest peak demand for electricity ever recorded was met without any trouble, and through the whole winter there were no power cuts.

Meanwhile further attempts at settlement by negotiation had been launched. When 'talks about talks' failed at the end of January, the pit deputies' union, Nacods, returned to the front of the stage, joining the NUM in demanding immediate negotiations without the NCB's precon-ditions, which, they claimed, 'would effectively negate' the agreement that had averted a Nacods strike in the previous October (see AR 1984, pp. 13–14). The Prime Minister was caused to affirm in the House of Commons that the Nacods agreement would be honoured in full.

Now Mr Norman Willis, general secretary of the Trades Union Con-gress (TUC), renewed an attempt at mediation. Proposals which he had negotiated with the NCB were rejected on 20 February by NUM del-egates, who voted to continue the strike. Thereupon sourness entered the relations between the NUM and the TUC; Mr Willis declined to attend a miners' rally in London on 24 February at which Mr Arthur Scargill, president of the NUM, whistling into the wind, appealed for more support from other unions. In the following week over 9,000 striking miners returned to work.

At last, a few days short of a year after it had begun, the strike ended. On 3 March an NUM delegate conference, boycotted by the working coalfields, voted by a narrow margin for a general return to work on 5 March without any agreement with the NCB. The Union's executive had been evenly split, but had advised a continuance of the strike. The conference's call for a general amnesty for the 700-odd miners who had been dismissed during the strike was at once rejected by the NCB. Its area managers would treat cases on their merits, but it would not re-employ, Mr MacGregor declared, miners convicted of deliberate sabotage or violence against fellow workers, the police or the public. 'We have to see that there are no rewards for that.' And in a letter to all miners he gave warning that there would be no pay rises until the NUM's overtime ban, which had preceded the strike itself, was lifted. The Labour Party leader, Mr Neil Kinnock, said on 4 March that an amnesty for those guilty of serious crimes was impossible—for which pronouncement he was pelted by students at a London college of further education.

In most areas the return to work was undemonstrative, but in South Wales miners marched to the collieries in procession with banners and bands. In Scotland and Kent there were votes to stay out until an amnesty was granted; Kent miners travelled to Yorkshire to picket the pits, to no effect. In the Kent field the drift back was slow, but the Scots quickly changed their minds. The NCB reported that 94·5 per cent of NUM workers were at work by 6 March.

'The dispute goes on', declared Mr Scargill; 'we will continue the fight against pit closures and job losses.' But his claim that the strike had been a victory for the miners' solidarity could not blot out its total defeat. Mrs Thatcher confessed a sense of 'overwhelming relief': 'there would,' she said, 'have been neither freedom nor order in Britain if we had given in to violence'. Mr MacGregor looked to the future. 'We need to restore coal production to former levels, to regain coal markets we have lost, and to plan ahead to ensure that Britain has the high-volume, low-cost coal industry which alone will guarantee a secure future.' British miners, he said, were the finest work-force in the world: NCB management had learnt to communicate directly with the people under their control.

The cost of the strike to the nation had been high. Mr Nigel Lawson, in his Budget speech on 19 March, revealed that it had added £2,750 million to government expenditure and £1,850 million to the losses of the Coal Board, had worsened the balance of payments by £4,000 million and cut the country's economic output by 1 per cent. The cost to other nationalized industries, it emerged, had also been heavy: to British Steel at least £300 million, to British Rail £250 million and to the electricity supply industry £2,200 million, which the Government agreed to fund, thus obviating a dreaded 'Scargill surcharge' to consumers. Costs to the NCB continued to pile up after the return to work; many pits had been severely damaged by neglect, some beyond recovery; it would take time to recapture lost markets. Nevertheless, the Board reported as early as 22 April that coal deliveries were less than 4 per cent below normal.

The NCB pressed on relentlessly with its policy of cutting manpower and concentrating on the more profitable pits. Although the earlier closures were imposed without recourse to the review procedure there was little active union opposition, most displaced miners being content to accept the tempting redundancy terms on offer. On 2 April a delegate conference of the NUM, against the advice of Mr Scargill, voted 122 to 74 in favour of lifting the ban on overtime working which had been in force for 17 months, and soon afterwards the NUM and NCB agreed on a backdated wage settlement. The colliery review procedure would now go into operation, though management would continue to shut pits where economic output was no longer possible after a year's deterioration. Despite the handicap, in some areas, of bad blood between those who had worked during the strike and the bitter-enders, efficient operation was restored and indeed increased in the great majority of pits.

It was now Nacods that was disgruntled and threatening over the delay in applying the new review procedure. Its general secretary declared that 'we have been lied to by Ian MacGregor and Mrs Thatcher'. The Nacods leaders called for a ban on overtime, which was applied on 17 May, with considerable effect on mine output. A total strike was threatened, but on 4 June the NCB agreed with Nacods that no further redundancies or transfers of workers would be imposed until colliery closures had gone through the pre-October procedure pending establishment of the new system, and the Nacods overtime ban was then lifted.

By mid-June the NCB had announced actual job losses and others pending within two years to a total of 18,000, added to 12,000 miners who had left the industry during the strike. The prospective cut of 30,000 in the pre-strike work-force thus exceeded by 50 per cent the intended figure of 20,000 which had provoked the year-long strike. On 7 June the Board announced the impending shut-down of the Cortonwood pit in Yorkshire whose threatened closure had been the trigger setting the national strike in motion. The decision now met no active protest.

Immediate political reactions to the strike's end were muted by the fact that, while the Government avoided shouts of triumph, the Labour Party was split between an equivocal leadership and militants who had wanted all-out support for the miners and blamed the lack of it for their defeat. The expected electoral advantage gained for the Government seemed soon to evaporate. Inter-party heat rose when the Prime Minister, Mrs Thatcher, speaking on 6 April in Malaysia during a visit to the Far East (see p. 39), boasted that the Government had 'seen off' the miners, and referred to people like the NUM leaders as 'the enemy within'. Mr Gerald Kaufman retorted by calling her 'the enemy abroad'. Mr Kinnock accused the Prime Minister of 'clumsy arrogance'. An unrepentant Mrs Thatcher said in Singapore on 8 April: 'Despite cruel intimidation, the working miners insisted on their right to continue to work, and they found they had an employer and a Government prepared to stand up for them. I hope and believe the lesson will not be lost on others.'

The failure of the miners' strike, seen from either side of the political divide, was an event of crucial importance in the history of British industrial relations. It could be ascribed to a number of causes. The NUM's deliberate evasion of a national ballot (see AR 1984, p. 8) not only resulted in whole areas staying out of the strike and in legal actions and heavy fines, but also undermined support from other unions, the Labour Party and the public. Backing by other unions, notably those in road and rail transport which could have stopped the movement of coal and other vital supplies, was more verbal than real. The steel unions and those concerned with electricity supply refused to act in sympathy, and in road transport the supportive Transport and General Workers' Union failed to prevent the NCB from organizing 800,000 lorry journeys to replace rail in moving coal. The Central Electricity Generating Board had a comprehensive plan in readiness for national coordination of fuel supplies from oil, nuclear power and imported coal as well as coal from working pits. And the Government as well as the NCB was determined not to give way to a demand which would have meant perpetual subsidy by the rest of the community of an industry producing part of its output at a cost far above any price it could fetch; while the Labour Opposition's ability to trade on public sympathy for miners and their families, on trade union solidarity and on resentment against massive, forceful police action was greatly weakened by the violence and intimidation committed by many striking miners in scenes shown on television screens. Taking all these things together, the strike was doomed to failure.

Interest now focused on two issues, the NUM's attempt to secure TUC and Labour Party backing for its demand that all miners dismissed for offences arising from the strike should be reinstated, and that all fines and other financial penalties imposed on the union during the strike should be made good by a Labour Government (see pp. 25–26), and the intention of miners in anti-strike areas to form a breakaway union.

Champions of a new moderate union were encouraged when on 7 August the High Court refused to grant an injunction preventing them from defying the national union leadership. To grant it, said the judge, would be contrary to common sense and justice. This happened shortly after the leaders of the Nottinghamshire and South Derbyshire miners and the small Durham-based Colliery and Allied Trades' Association (CATA) had agreed to ballot their members on the creation of a Union of Democratic Miners (UDM). Mr Scargill and others in the NUM executive denounced this move as a betrayal of national solidarity and a plan for a 'company union'. Their fierce campaign against it failed to convince miners in the dissident groups; for all three voted to join the UDM, by very large majorities in Nottinghamshire and CATA, by a narrow margin in Derbyshire. Like the NUM itself, the UDM under its draft constitution would be a league of semi-autonomous regional or occupational unions.

The UDM got a head-start in competition with the NUM by reaching in October a fresh pay settlement with the NCB comprising a basic rise of 6·9 per cent and extra earnings based on productivity, while the NUM was inhibited from negotiating by the NCB's insistence on prior acceptance that productivity and efficiency would be an element in pay, a policy repellent to the union's leadership. Not until 5 December did the NUM executive vote to accept that condition, Mr Scargill and his fellow hardliners dissenting. Shortly afterwards the NCB offered the NUM the same terms as it had agreed with the UDM, which the union refused because a clause would have reduced the pension rights of miners who had struck. But the failure of the year-long stoppage, the closure of many pits without protest and the creation of a rival union—now proselytising in all areas—had left the NUM in a chastened mood. A written undertaking to participate in relating pay to productivity and efficiency was at last given by the NUM executive, against the minority vote of Mr Scargill and his close associates, on 6 December, the day on which the UDM gained its statutory status as a trade union.

Creation of the UDM confronted the TUC and the Labour Party with a menacing dilemma. All trade-union tradition militated against recognition of a 'breakaway union'; but the TUC was already at grave risk of a split caused by the insistence of two powerful unions, those of the electricians and engineering workers, contrary to TUC conference policy, on accepting government money for postal ballots—decisions confirmed in December by overwhelming votes of their members. On 17 December the TUC's general council signalled a prudent change of direction by calling a special conference of head officers of member unions to review policy towards all industrial relations law passed under the Conservative Administration. Perhaps the TUC saw the spectre of a rival national congress embracing dissident unions and the UDM.

To concede any legitimacy to the UDM would be anathema to Mr Scargill and his henchmen, but there were signs that his personal dominance of the NUM was weakening even in loyal areas. Thus on 28 October the NUM executive voted by 11 to 7, against his will, to purge the contempt of court which had resulted in sequestration of its assets and receivership (see AR 1984, p. 16). On 14 November a High Court judge lifted the sequestration order after accepting a sworn statement by Mr Scargill and his two chief allies which the judge evidently thought fell short of true repentance. He asked 'What has been the price of this folly?' and answered that in fines and costs of sequestration and receivership it had cost the union more than £1,400,000.

The cause of regaining employment for all miners dismissed for offences committed during the strike, though not forsaken, had clearly become unrealistic. By contrast, the pursuit by the criminal law of alleged offenders in the course of picket-line violence proved an almost unredeemed fiasco.

On 15 July 13 miners charged with riot outside the Yorkshire headquarters of the NUM in June 1984 were acquitted by a jury at Sheffield Crown Court. Two days later the Crown dropped its case against 14 Yorkshire miners charged with riot and unlawful assembly in a particularly violent picket-line incident at Orgreave colliery, and during the next three weeks the prosecution of 87 other miners arising out of the same or similar incidents was abandoned. A like sequence occurred at Nottingham Crown Court in September and October—a jury acquittal of eight men charged with riotous assembly and affray at Mansfield colliery in June 1984, followed by the dropping of cases against a total of 135 other defendants, most of whom were bound over for a year. The case for continued prosecutions had virtually collapsed, not necessarily because the charges were ill-founded but rather because they could not be proved by reliable evidence and identification more than a year after the event, and because juries were manifestly reluctant to convict for crimes alleged to have been committed in incidents better forgotten now that the strike was long over. On 16 May, by a majority verdict, two South Wales miners were found guilty of murdering a taxi-man driving two miners to work during the strike, but on appeal the crime was reduced to manslaughter (see p. 46).

Apart from the coal strike, the most grievous industrial dispute in 1984 concerned schoolteachers. Their largest union, the National Union of Teachers (NUT), began selective strike action in February and in this policy was soon afterwards joined by the less militant union of women teachers and assistant schoolmasters (NAS/UWT). A High Court injunction obliged the NUT to hold ballots before striking, but the support of the members was never in doubt. They were demanding a sufficient pay rise (a figure of 30 per cent was unofficially mentioned) to bring teachers' salaries to their previous relationship with other workers' pay, in face of an offer of 4 per cent, the figure on which Treasury grants to local education authorities for 1985–86 had been based. The offer was later raised to 5 per cent, on conditions. The Secretary of State for Education, Sir Keith Joseph, repeatedly affirmed that more money might be available after 1985–86 if the teachers agreed to restructuring of the pay system, periodical assessment of merit and the incorporation in their employment contracts of certain duties like supervising pupils at lunchtime which the unions held were voluntary. But he insisted that no more Treasury money could be offered during the current year.

Although the financial limits were being set by the Government the actual employers were the local education authorities, which however sympathetic to the teachers could not pay more without either robbing other local services or raising rate demands at their peril. Teachers' pay had been settled nationally by a tripartite body called the Burnham Committee, the complexion of which was changed, on the employers' side, by Labour and Alliance advances at the local elections in May (see p. 24). The direct victims of the unions' action, however, were neither the Government nor the employing authorities but the pupils at school and the schools themselves, where indiscipline and truancy mounted. This excited bitter recrimination, Ministers accusing the unions of cowardice in acting with the maximum effect upon the children at minimum risk of losing their own pay or jobs, the teachers retorting that it was the Government that by its meanness and intransigence was putting the education and welfare of children in jeopardy. For months the unions intensified their selective strike action and spread it round the country.

In the background to the dispute was a reformist Secretary of State's vision of the long-term future. In a White Paper on education policy for the twenty-first century (Cmnd. 9469), published on 26 March, Sir Keith Joseph laid strong emphasis on higher standards and on constant appraisal of teaching merits. Education must be directed towards 'the opportunities of a technological and competitive world'. School governors should include more parents. A short-term measure was the introduction of a new examination at A/S level (qualification for higher education). The general secretary of the NUT, while supporting some elements of the White Paper, called its overall effect depressing. 'Higher standards', he declared, 'cannot be achieved with poorer facilities and a dose of centralist rhetoric.' Teachers would unite against being legally obliged to accept assessment.

Sir Keith followed his exercise on schools with a Green (consultative) Paper on higher education, published on 21 May. Universities were adjured to encourage the entrepreneurial spirit and to beware of 'anti-business snobbery'. They had to raise standards of teaching, to work more efficiently and concentrate research in strong departments, while facing a cut in government funding of 2 per cent per annum (in real terms) for three years. Some institutions would need to be closed or merged during the next ten years in line with the fall in numbers of young people of university age—an expectation challenged by critics who held that the demographic factor would be outweighed by increasing numbers seeking and qualified for higher education. Mr Giles Radice, MP, Labour's spokesman on education, called the Green Paper 'a miserable flop'; the cut in resources, he proclaimed, was equivalent to the closing of a medium-sized university every year. The chairman of the committee of vice-chancellors and principals declared: 'This is not the way to improve our competitiveness and quality of life.' Attack swelled on the alleged philistinism and narrow vision of the Government in pressing for a switch from the humanities to more 'practical' subjects. 'Barbaric', Mr Enoch Powell, MP (a former classics lecturer), called it.

Pay settlement with the teachers was not made easier by the Cabinet's decision, announced on 18 July, to implement recommendations of the Top Salaries Review Body which would give permanent secretaries of government departments a phased rise of nearly 32 per cent and under-secretaries over 15 per cent, with corresponding increases for the higher ranks of the armed forces and 16·3 per cent for judges. Labour's employment spokesman in the Commons called it 'a kick in the teeth for teachers'. Many Tory MPs were also outraged; it was pushing the loyalty of the Conservatives in the constituencies too far, said one. In vain did

Ministers argue that the cost was very small compared with that of a rise of teachers' pay by a percentage point, and that the rises were necessary for recruitment, retention and motivation of men and women of the highest calibre when earnings in private industry were far higher. Do not the same considerations apply, asked the critics, to school teachers who will educate those men and women of the future?

The rises required no parliamentary vote save in the case of the Lord Chancellor in his judicial capacity, though the actual holder of that office, Lord Hailsham, declined to take the increase. On a Commons motion about the Lord Chancellor's salary on 23/24 July no fewer than 48 Conservatives voted with the Opposition and others abstained. The Government's majority fell to only 17, and might have disappeared if all available Labour MPs had voted. Ministers were palpably shaken, still more so when on 29 July the House of Lords, while approving the Lord Chancellor's potential rise, carried by 140 votes to 135 an amendment deploring the Government's 'insensitivity' in announcing such an enviable scale of enhancement at that time. Typical of cross-bench reaction was Lord Denning's remark that many judges would think it wrong that they should have 16 per cent when the teachers were being offered 5 per cent.

In the autumn term the teachers' strike action, suspended in high summer, was renewed, after their unions had rejected a revised offer of 5·4 per cent in July, and in August an informal offer of 6·9 per cent for the remainder of 1985–86. On 5 August Sir Keith put a figure on his promise of more money from 1986–87 onwards—an extra £1,250 million over four years, on condition that the teachers called off their action and agreed to a new job definition and a revised pay structure. But he refused to release any of the £1,250 million to raise pay in the rest of 1985–86. The NUT was insisting that the increase in pay must at least match the current rise in national average earnings (7·5 per cent) and furthermore must include an element towards restoring the level, compared with other workers, recommended by the Houghton report in 1980. 'Back to Houghton', Sir Keith told the Conservative Party conference on 9 October, meant a return to the pay leapfrogging of the 1970s—a sure recipe for inflation and massive unemployment.

Towards the end of 1985 there were hopes of some movement in the dispute after the NUT had lost its overall majority on the employees' side of the Burnham Committee because of its reduced numbers. When, however, in mid-December the unions formulated a demand for 9·9 per cent by the end of March 1986 the Secretary of State said this showed they were more interested in posturing than in a settlement; there would be no increases without strings. So, as the year ended, damaging action in the schools began to match in duration the year-long miners' strike.

A call by the rail unions for a one-day sympathetic strike on 17 January had been only partially effective; in such strikes, under recent

Conservative legislation, the unions were no longer exempt from civil suits. Later that month BR warned the unions that thousands of jobs were at risk unless labour productivity improved. On 2 April the unions accepted a 5 per cent wage rise after BR had dropped a condition of higher productivity, but that issue was strenuously pressed in further negotiations. When the National Union of Railwaymen (NUR) called a 24-hour strike on London's Underground on 20 May, against a policy of running more one-man trains, London Transport obtained from the High Court an injunction banning the action as illegal for want of a ballot. The NUR executive decided to defy the ban, but of its 15,000 members concerned only 6,000 obeyed the call, and the strike was called off late on the same day. Government supporters hailed the event as further evidence that union leaders were out of touch with their members. On 30 May the NUR and the engine drivers' union Aslef accepted the extended solo manning on London Transport trains which they had denounced.

BR's announcement on 24 June of plans to introduce more driver-only trains, and on 12 July of its intention to proceed with productivity measures unilaterally in the absence of agreement with the unions, were followed by unofficial strikes or non-cooperative action by guards in several areas and the consequent suspension or dismissal of large numbers. The NUR called for a national strike of guards, and in conformity with the law held a ballot which its leaders confidently predicted would decisively favour strike action. The result was announced on 28 August. Of the 11,000 guards 80 per cent voted, giving a majority of 4,815 to 4,360 against strike action. Thus fortified, BR management refused to reinstate the guards who had been dismissed until the unions negotiated a series of productivity reforms. More local disruptive action followed, until on 19 September the NUR agreed to allow one-man running of certain passenger and freight trains and to discuss further cost-saving measures, and in return BR took back the 251 dismissed guards.

Another occasion on which the law operated to prevent a strike occurred when in March the largest civil service union, the CPSA, proposed to call a strike with the support of branch meetings instead of a ballot. Threatened with legal action, the union executive voted by a narrow majority to obey the law. A ballot on a one-day strike was accordingly held and resulted in a wafer-thin majority against striking. In April a large number of Post Office sorters stopped work in protest against the impact of new technology and plans to use more part-time workers, defying a High Court injunction against their union. The union, however, declared the strike unofficial, and on 4 May the terms of a comprehensive settlement were agreed and the disruption petered out.

Chapter 2

UNEMPLOYMENT AND ECONOMIC POLICIES

IN December 1984 the number of registered unemployed was 3,219,400; in December 1985 it was 3,273,089. Although the numbers in employment rose during the year by over 300,000, the obdurate persistence of over three million officially listed as unemployed was again a dominant feature of the economy. The Opposition proclaimed the real extent of unemployment to be much worse, adding around half a million people taken off the register by government training and special employment measures and several hundreds of thousands eliminated by changes in the registration rules. On the other hand, a Department of Employment survey published in October showed, by sample analysis, that 940,000 of those on the register in fact had jobs of some sort or were not really seeking work. The survey also indicated that roughly as many people not registered as unemployed might be drawn into the labour market if they saw opportunities for suitable work.

The failure to reduce unemployment greatly exercised many Conservative politicians as well as their electorate. Of these, the most persistently critical was the former Prime Minister, Mr Edward Heath. In a lecture to the London Business School on 27 November, the main thrust of which was an attack on the Government's privatization policy (see pp. 27–29), he repeated the warning he had given in the Budget debate in March that unemployment created a 'national emergency'; British people, he declared, would show contempt for leaders who clung to their ideologies with no heed to the nation's needs. He particularly scorned the Government's intention to use any budgetary surplus for cutting taxation: one man's tax cut, he said, might mean loss of another man's opportunity of employment.

Another ex-Minister, Mr Francis Pym, was prominent in the formation of a new Conservative group, taking the name Centre Forward (CF), whose principal aim was to promote policies to relieve unemployment. Defending his action Mr Pym, in a speech at Cambridge on 14 May, recalled that, although he claimed a lot of common ground with the party leadership in the economic field, unemployment was now three times higher than before the Conservatives came to power. He told the Tory backbench 1922 Committee that CF was not a party within a party and would not whip its members. CF subsequently achieved little publicity. While other prominent Tory ex-Ministers like Mr James Prior, Mr Geoffrey Rippon and Mr St John Stevas continued to criticise Government policy, the dissident voice that struck the public's ear most forcibly was that of Lord Stockton, the former Prime Minister Harold Macmillan. The policies of deflation and expenditure cuts, he said in the House of Lords on 14 November, were now barren and must be reversed; and he repeatedly spoke of the tragedy of dividing the country into two nations, one active and prosperous, the other jobless and poor. Within the Cabinet itself, Mr Peter Walker again sounded a warning bell. The Conservative Party faced serious reverses, he said on 31 March, if it failed to tackle unemployment; and on 1 May, in a speech at Cambridge, he called on the Government of which he was a member to review its priorities in that interest.

Challenged on this apparent palace revolt, Mrs Thatcher observed that Mr Walker was not the only Minister very much concerned about unemployment. In a radio interview on 24 May she promised that the Government would act to create more jobs if unemployment was not falling within a year. The Budget measures (see below) and the expansion of the youth training scheme, she said, would take a year to work through. Generally, the views expressed by Ministers were that their own policies were right, were succeeding in raising productivity and efficiency on which depended industry's ability to create more jobs, were encouraging new and small businesses and would be continued.

Mr Nigel Lawson's Budget, opened on 19 March, had been preceded by rumours of an extension of VAT to a variety of goods and services hitherto exempt, such as books and newspapers, and of the imposition of income tax on pension funds by one route or another. If these notions had been deliberately floated to test public opinion, the adverse reaction must have persuaded the Chancellor of the Exchequer to stay his hand; for VAT was newly imposed only on advertising in newspapers and magazines, and pension funds were left alone. Personal allowances against income tax were raised by about 10 per cent, at a cost of £430 million, taking about 800,000 families out of the income tax net, and thresholds for higher tax rates were raised in line with inflation. Duties on alcohol, tobacco and petrol, and taxes on motor vehicles, were raised as expected. Development land tax, long decrepit as a revenue-raiser, was abolished. On the expenditure side the most notable announcement was the provision of £1,000 million more for special employment measures (youth training, and community service for the long-term unemployed). The contingency reserve, which had proved its necessity in the Falklands war and the coal strike, was raised by £2,000 million to £5,000 million. Overall, the Chancellor forecast a cut in the Public Sector Borrowing Requirement (PSBR) from £10,500 million to £7,000 million. His estimates were based on expectations of an increase of $3\frac{1}{2}$ per cent in national output in 1985, continuance of unemployment at around 3 million, and inflation rising to 6 per cent then falling to 5 per cent per annum.

While public reaction to the Budget was muted, it was fiercely denounced by the Opposition. 'This stagnant Chancellor,' said Mr Kinnock, 'has turned his back on millions of his fellow citizens who are unemployed or poor. . . . He was prepared to find £2,500 million to fight the miners, so why was he not prepared to do that to fight unemployment?' Some dissident Conservatives took the same line, more mildly. Describing the Budget as inadequate in face of still-rising unemployment, Mr Pym said: 'Responsible financial management does not itself constitute an economic strategy.' Mr Lawson retorted to his Labour and SDP critics that 'all we hear is the tired nostrums of the '60s and '70s which led us into inflationary disaster, low productivity and low growth', from which he said the Thatcher Government had liberated the economy.

On 6 November the Chancellor of the Exchequer made his autumn financial statement. He prudently put no figure on an expected fiscal outturn which would enable him to cut taxation in 1986, but his tone was confident. The annual inflation rate, after a late-1985 peak, would fall to 3·75 per cent by the last quarter of 1986; growth would be 3 per cent in 1986; unemployment would fall to about 3 million. Public expenditure would increase by £5,000 million over the next two years, during which receipts from sale of state industries would rise to £9,500 million from the previously predicted £4,500 million. The social security budget for 1986–87 was raised by £1,000 million and there would be £350 million more for roads, £300 million more for agencies of law and order, and £57 million more for overseas aid. The Chancellor insisted that this expansion was not a U-turn towards reflation, but, perchance with general election prospects in mind, he and other Ministers were conspicuously laying more emphasis on government spending on public-sector infrastructure and welfare services and less on budgetary economy. Thus in her speech at the Lord Mayor's banquet in November the Prime Minister positively boasted of her Government's 'colossal programme' of public investment. The altered tenor of Ministers' speeches, even if intended only to improve the Government's propagandist image, seemed to imply a certain deflection of policy in order to live up to their own pretensions.

Ministerial utterances in the autumn also conspicuously emphasised the need to keep down wage increases in the interest of competitiveness and consequently of employment. In July the Government had announced that legislation on Wages Councils (which fixed minimum wages and conditions in a number of industries open to exploitation of cheap labour) would be introduced in the next session; reforms in the interest of increasing work opportunities for the young and unskilled would include abolition of controls on employment of persons under 21. More generally, Ministers were alarmed by the steady rise of earnings faster than inflation—a further contribution to the contrast between an employed population better off than ever and an impoverished other nation of unemployed and disadvantaged. In evidence to a Commons select committee on 26 November the Chancellor of the Exchequer expressed the hope that private-sector pay settlements would come down to those in the public sector (where the line had been held overall at a little above the rate of inflation). Lower wage deals, he said, were likely to lead to more investment and more employment. In taking this line he concurred with the employers' organization the CBI, whose director-general, Sir Terence Beckett, speaking at its annual conference in November, called for ending the notion of an annual pay round and for adopting the principle of 'nowt for nowt'.

On the Opposition side there was also a change of emphasis. In a speech on 2 June Mr Hattersley, Labour's deputy leader, described party policy changes since the general election as 'a reunion with reality'. The leader himself, Mr Kinnock, told a union conference on 24 June that the party was 'seeking a modern system for full employment', different from that of the previous three decades—which included the Labour Governments of Mr Wilson and Mr Callaghan. In August the Labour Party and the TUC published a joint policy declaration entitled 'A New Partnership: a New Britain' embodying a fresh pact between the political and industrial wings of the movement. A great deal of it necessarily dealt with industrial relations law, stressing workers' rights to a voice in company policies. There was no specific mention of incomes policy, but in launching the publication Mr Kinnock insisted that a Labour Government would not allow money released in order to enlarge employment to be dissipated on other expenditure of short-term value—which presumably included inflationary wage rises. Shortly before the party conference in September, Mr Hattersley promised in a speech at Ilford that a Labour Government would not 'begin with the bang of over-ambitious expansion and end with the whimper of deflation and contraction'.

Part of Labour's new economic recipe was a plan, published on 19 September, to repatriate British capital which had been invested abroad and redirect it into home industry and commerce: tax concessions would be withdrawn from companies and individuals having more than a certain fraction, say 5 per cent, of their assets overseas, the returning money to go into a national investment bank providing long-term finance for British industry. (It was estimated that in June 1985 British equity investment abroad alone totalled over £42,000 million.) Yet another shift in party attitudes was signalled when Mr Hattersley, in a speech on 16 October, stressed the virtues of industrial democracy and share-owning; in the public sector there would be no return to 'centrally-controlled state monopolies'—an implicit total retreat from the traditional socialist doctrine of seizing 'the commanding heights'.

Thus under its centrist leadership the Labour Party seemed to be moving tacitly, though perhaps deliberately, towards an economic policy not far removed from that of the Liberal/SDP Alliance. The SDP conference in early September overwhelmingly approved an Alliance plan for the economy embracing £1,000 million a year more for local authority expenditure and a £5,000 million overall budgetary expansion, coupled with a firm monetary policy and a strategy for incomes. A week later the Alliance plan was approved by the Liberal Assembly, at which the party's economic spokesman insisted that pay policy was the key.

On various aspects of economic policy the Government had to withstand criticism not only from the Opposition and dissident Tories but also from 'cross-bench' sources. The CBI, while demanding in the short run lower interest rates and stable exchange rates which did not overvalue the pound, also called for a substantial increase in spending on the economic infrastructure. A CBI document published in November framed a long-term strategy directed, among other targets, at eliminating 'involuntary unemployment', which it described as 'a cancer feeding on society': to achieve its aims over 25 years would require an annual growth rate of 4 per cent. On 15 October the House of Lords select committee on overseas trade, headed by Lord Aldington, chairman of Sun Alliance, and including other leading businessmen, published a highly critical report. Unless, it said, there were an immediate change in policy towards manufacturing industry there would be further contraction, an adverse balance of payments requiring severe deflation, higher unemployment and an irreplaceable loss of gross domestic product. Tight money and high-valued sterling were the first targets of attack, but urgent action was needed from everyone concerned. Mr Hattersley commented that the committee was only confirming what Labour had been saying for years. For the Government, however, Mr Leon Brittan, Secretary of State for Trade and Industry, retorted that the report gave 'a totally biased and misleading view of the performance and prospects of our economy', failing to point out that in manufacturing industry, since the trough of the recession, output had risen by 11 per cent, investment by 39 per cent and productivity by 31 per cent, and that the volume of manufactured exports stood at record levels.

In July, a unanimous report of the National Federation of Housing Associations (charitable bodies serving the provision of low-cost housing), of which the Duke of Edinburgh was the active chairman, had recommended a radical change in government rent subsidies, substituting a needs-related housing allowance not only for existing housing benefit and the housing element in supplementary benefit but also for tax relief on mortgage interest, which should be slowly and carefully phased out. In the Commons immediately after the report's publication Mrs Thatcher declared: 'So long as I am here mortgage tax relief will continue.' Although Labour demanded that the relief be confined to standard rate of tax and to a lower ceiling of mortgage debt, the beneficiaries of the relief among the electorate of all classes were so many that no opposition party now stood for its abolition.

However, it was also a focus of criticism in a much wider-ranging publication, the report of a Commission on Urban Priority Areas set up in 1983 by the Archbishop of Canterbury, published on 3 December. Claiming that the Church of England ought to be the conscience of the nation, the commission held that economic policies had to be judged morally by their outcome; its members were 'united in the view that the costs of present policies, with the continuing growth of unemployment, are unacceptable'. They recommended a series of measures to alleviate the plight of people in the inner cities: *inter alia*, increased child benefit, more benefit for the long-term unemployed, higher rate support grants for local authorities, especially for inner cities and their overspills, more funds for the Government's 'urban programme', job-creating capital projects, restored support for public housing for rent, and a fundamental examination of subsidies to public and private housing, in which respect, the commission argued, mortgage tax relief helped the better-off at the expense of the poor. The proposals as a whole obviously required a massive, but unspecified, increase in public expenditure. The first governmental response came from an anonymous Cabinet Minister who dismissed the report as 'marxist', an unlikely description of the work of a body of distinguished churchmen, economists, officials and others. Although the opprobrious epithet was not repeated, Government spokesmen continued to treat the document as a politically hostile manifesto, the work of clerics who were ignorant of the real constraints of politics and economics and ought to stick to their religious last.

Chapter 3

LOCAL GOVERNMENT STRAINS

In July the Local Government Bill abolishing the Greater London Council (GLC) and other metropolitan county councils (see AR 1984, pp. 19–20) received the Royal Assent. At its last stage in the House of Lords the Government appeased some of the Bill's critics by moving an amendment providing for a post-abolition joint committee of London boroughs for overall planning and development; an amendment extending a similar provision to the other metropolitan counties was defeated by 35 votes. The Bill had not escaped its expected mauling by the Lords at earlier stages. Indeed as regards London its main purpose survived by a margin of only four votes on 30 April on an amendment to establish a new London metropolitan authority; and on 7 and 9 May the Government was defeated three times on amendments setting up new metropolitan authorities for roads maintenance, landscape protection and waste disposal. At report stage in the Lords on 10 June a further amendment, relating to strategic planning for public transport, highways and traffic in the metropolitan counties, was rejected by only one vote. When the Bill returned to the House of Commons the Government's intentions were substantially restored. Nevertheless, not only had critics of the measure made a demonstration against fragmentation of responsibility for major functions in London and other big cities, but the Upper House had shown again that it had teeth against a powerful party majority even though its bites could be caused to heal.

Central and local government remained in sharp conflict over both the restriction of rate support grants and 'rate-capping' (fixing a legal upper limit for rate poundage). Most penalized councils were Labour-controlled, but the Conservative chairman of Buckinghamshire county council, speaking on 9 April, called the Government's system of rationed support grants and financial penalties for overspending 'unjust and unreasonable'. Rate-capping orders were passed on 25 February (see AR 1984, p. 19). Three months into the financial year Mr Patrick Jenkin, Secretary of State for the Environment, said that 107 English councils were overspending against government targets by a total of £278 million, and had suffered £550 million penalties in withheld grants.

More than a dozen Labour councils, led by Greater London, at first refused to fix rates for 1985–86. But on 10 March, thanks to a split in Labour ranks, the GLC voted to adopt a legal budget; and its leader, Mr Ken Livingstone, urged other capped authorities to do the same, while keeping open the option of overspending in order to preserve jobs and services. Amid bitter recrimination between right and left factions of Labour, one by one other rebellious councils followed.

Two recalcitrants remained—Lambeth, in South London, and Liverpool. On 16 June Liverpool city council, dominated by Labour's far left, fixed a rate while approving by 49 votes to 42 an illegal budget deficit and insisting that no services or jobs would be cut. On 28 June district auditors served Liverpool and Lambeth councillors with notices of personal surcharges totalling £233,000 because of their delays in legalizing expenditure, and warned that these penalties would mount. On 3 July Lambeth council gave way, setting a legal rate and leaving Liverpool isolated.

As the time approached when Liverpool council would run out of money, its far-left leaders tried to engineer a direct political confrontation with the Government. Instead the active participants in the struggle became the council majority, the local and national Labour Party, unions of council workers and the TUC, while the Government, which had given firm notice that no more money from the centre could be hoped for, watched the internecine warfare with ironic satisfaction, tempered with expressions of sympathy for the sufferings of the people of Liverpool dependent on council services. To anticipate, indeed to precipitate, a confrontation crisis, the council announced that it was issuing three-month redundancy notices to all employees. On 16 September local union leaders called for an indefinite strike of council workers against the job cuts that impended if Liverpool were not bailed out, but the union memberships were divided, the strike was called off, and a substitute one-day strike on 25 September was poorly supported. In his keynote speech to the Labour Party conference on 1 October Mr Kinnock denounced the

Liverpool council majority for bringing about 'grotesque chaos'. 'You can't play politics with people's jobs and people's services,' he said.

On 20 October leaders of the Labour Party and the TUC launched an effort to solve Liverpool's financial problem, whereupon the council withdrew the redundancy notices. Four financial experts from Labour-controlled authorities examined the city's finances and on 29 October produced a package of measures including the mobilization of reserves and a rise of 11 per cent in rates. Welcoming the plan Mr Kinnock said that political dogma must give way to realism; but Mr Derek Hatton, deputy leader of the council, a supporter of Militant Tendency, whose unremitting, repetitious eloquence became all too familiar to British television viewers and radio listeners, declared that the proposals were playing into the Government's hands. On 2 November the Liverpool leaders rejected a revised package, framed by the leader of Sheffield council on behalf of the Labour-controlled Association of Metropolitan Authorities. Mr Kinnock became more hostile than ever. 'I and my colleagues in Labour local authorities, in Parliament and in the trade unions completely disown those people who are prepared to use 31,000 workers and helpless people as hostages,' he said, and he added: 'People cannot have confidence in our commitment to democratic procedures, particularly Parliament and the rule of law, while we have in our midst a powerful minority whose sole aim is to engage in revolutionary confrontation.'

On 22 November, within days of city bankruptcy, Liverpool councillors capitulated, accepting a financial plan based largely on restoring the city's borrowing credit by capitalizing funds in its house repair and maintenance account as base for an international banking consortium credit of £30 million, and by borrowing £3 million from other Labour-controlled councils, the loan facilities being conditional upon a pledge to act lawfully in future. Mr Hatton predictably laid the blame for his faction's discomfiture upon the 'treachery' of national Labour Party and some trade union leaders. Thus the immediate crisis for Liverpool was averted, but the financial expedient was obviously only a temporary one, and another budgetary crisis in 1986 cast its long shadow.

Mr Kinnock clearly had the majority of Labour's National Executive Committee (NEC) and the parliamentary party behind him, though a few, among whom Mr Eric Heffer (a Liverpool MP) and the way-out Mr Tony Benn were the most prominent, protested that he had betrayed a socialist authority. But he now faced a consequent problem—how to deal with supporters of Militant Tendency (MT), that trotskyite group which the Labour right and centre had always regarded as an illegitimate 'party within the party' (see AR 1982, pp. 25–26, and 1983, p. 11), whose tactics had been so damagingly exemplified in Liverpool. Some Labour moderates openly called for all MT supporters to be expelled from the party, but the prospect of what the left called a 'witch hunt', involving the identification of thousands of goats among the sheep in the Labour fold, was too much for the leadership. The opportunity of the Liverpool collapse, however, had to be seized. On 27 November the NEC voted to suspend the Liverpool district Labour party while its conduct was investigated by a nine-man team, under allegations of malpractice, intimidation and corruption. The Liverpool leaders protested with their usual vehemence, but they could not escape the fact of an overwhelming vote in the NEC, 21 to 5, which showed that they had lost the goodwill of all but a far-left nucleus in the unions as well as Parliament. 'The MT is a maggot in the body of the party', Mr Kinnock said; 'we are seeing Militant on the way out and democratic socialism very much on the way in.'

On 18 December the Government published details of rate support grants to be made in 1986–87. While the aggregate would rise by 3·5 per cent to £11,800 million, and the ratio of central grant to assumed local authority spending would remain at 46·4 per cent overall, there was a clear shift of some £300 million from the shire counties and districts to city areas. Ministers claimed this to be a fair adjustment of aid to need; the Opposition denounced it as an attempt to influence the urban elections in May 1986, and the total as grossly inadequate to vital local government services; representatives of the largely Conservative shire authorities protested, predicting big rate rises. In the financial relations between the centre and localities it was clearly all too easy to please nobody.

Chapter 4

GOVERNMENT AND OPPOSITION

DURING 1985 Mrs Thatcher's popularity declined, along with her Government's, if the opinion polls were to be believed. Labour's stock rose relatively through the spring and summer until one poll in July put it nine points ahead of the Conservatives (42 per cent against 33 per cent, with the Liberal-SDP Alliance at 23 per cent). Later polls brought the showing of the two larger parties and of the Alliance much closer together.

In the local elections in shire counties on 3 May the total voting figures were Conservatives 36 per cent, Labour 31, Alliance 27, others 4. The switch of votes since the 1983 general election had been mainly from Conservative to Labour, and marginally to the Alliance; but in terms of seats won the Alliance did far better, making a net gain of 129 seats. The Tories lost control of nine counties. On the eve of a by-election in Brecon and Radnor on 4 July, a former Conservative seat, a Mori poll predicted a runaway victory for Labour from the Alliance (Liberal) by 46 to 28 per cent of the votes, the Tories getting only 24 per cent. In fact, the Alliance candidate won by the narrow margin of 35·8 per cent against 34·4 per cent for Labour, while the Conservative trailed at 27·7 per cent (see p. 47).

The win was a big boost for the Alliance, though it had probably been helped by some tactical voting by Conservatives. But the 'Scargill factor' also played a part. Labour MPs returning from the constituency reported that voters were scared of the party's connection with Mr Scargill and the extreme left personified by Mr Tony Benn. A few days before the by-election, at an NUM conference, Mr Scargill had declared that only industrial action would succeed in changing the direction of policy, and demanded that a Labour Government should free all convicted miners, remove all senior NCB personnel and call in the unions to manage the industry 'by the people, for the people'—meaning, presumably, the people working in it. The next day Mr Kinnock dismissed the Scargill line as 'fantasy', but the electoral damage had evidently been done.

Indeed Mr Kinnock spent much effort during the year trying to distance himself and the Labour Party leadership from the radical left. His task focused on three particular issues: 'black sections' of local Labour parties, the NUM's sweeping post-strike demands (see p. 10) and the conduct of the left-wing Liverpool city council (see pp. 22–24).

Some 35 constituency parties had formed 'black sections', designed to give separate representation to so-called blacks, who in current jargon included people of Asian as well as African or Caribbean stock. Champions of black sections claimed that they were necessary to overcome neglect of ethnic minorities and to give them a stronger voice in Labour councils. But by no means all black party members were of one mind, and the campaign was vehemently denounced by the party's leader and deputy leader as racist and contrary to Labour's principle of treating all citizens alike, whatever their race or colour. At the party conference on 30 September, the call to create black sections was defeated by a five-to-one vote; by a similar majority the delegates endorsed a statement from the NEC approving 'positive discrimination' in favour of ethnic minorities in employment, housing and welfare services. Meanwhile 'blacks' had been adopted as Labour parliamentary candidates in several Labour-held or marginal constituencies, and an Asian had been elected deputy general secretary of one of the largest trade unions.

At the party conference Mr Kinnock used the opportunity of his speech as leader to denounce all those—and specifically the Liverpool councillors—who made impossible promises 'pickled into rigid dogma' and could 'end in the grotesque chaos of a Labour council hiring taxis to scuttle round the city to hand out redundancy notices'. (At these words, Mr Eric Heffer walked out of the conference hall.) Mr Kinnock's speech, the theme of which was the overriding need to win power, was hailed by his supporters as a masterpiece, and it impressed many people in other parties; but it could not save him from defeat on the issue of re-imbursement of legally-mulcted miners' union funds. The NUM's motion was carried by 55 to 45 per cent of the card vote. To little avail did the leader tell the conference that 'if we were ever to endorse the idea of retrospective reimbursement we would harm our chances because people would be confused about our attitudes to the rule of law'. The party leadership was comforted by the fact that the winning margin fell far short of the two-thirds majority needed for automatic inclusion in the party's election manifesto, which Mr Kinnock declared he would never allow. The conference's reception of Mr Scargill was conspicuously less enthusiastic than it had been a year earlier (see AR 1984, p. 18). Not he, as in 1984, but beyond doubt Mr Kinnock, was the 'man of the conference' at Bournemouth. Elections to the NEC left the balance in his favour unchanged; more important, his personal prestige was greatly enhanced.

The Liberal and SDP conferences were remarkable for the cohesion of the two-party alliance. Friction over apportionment of seats to be fought and who should lead an Alliance Government was put aside in an atmosphere of unity and optimism. To loud applause the SDP leader Dr David Owen, whose esteem in the eyes of the television-viewing public was further enhanced during the year, told the Liberal Assembly that he, for one, no longer aimed at holding the balance of power in Parliament; more and more people, he believed, were feeling that the Alliance could form the next Government. 'A sense of national unity,' he declared, 'is the prerequisite for economic recovery.'

Through the summer the press was forecasting a radical reconstitution of Mrs Thatcher's Cabinet, but when she announced the changes on 2 September they included only two removals and one voluntary retirement, that of Lord Gowrie, Chancellor of the Duchy and Minister for the Arts. Mr Patrick Jenkin left the Department of the Environment for the back benches and was succeeded by his former Minister for Local Government, Mr Kenneth Baker. The most unexpected appointment was that of Mr Douglas Hurd to the Home Office, from Northern Ireland, the most expected that of Mr Norman Tebbit as chairman of the party, with a Cabinet seat as Chancellor of the Duchy, a forceful if abrasive figure, replacing the pleasant but unemphatic Mr John Gummer. Mr Tom King took over Northern Ireland, Mr Leon Brittan Trade and Industry, Mr John MacGregor the Chief Secretaryship to the Treasury (*vice* Mr Peter Rees, who was left out) and Lord Young of Graffham Employment, with Mr Kenneth Clark as his Commons aide. Lord Hailsham (Lord Chancellor), Sir Keith Joseph (Education), Mr Norman Fowler (Social Services), Mr Nigel Lawson (Exchequer) and Mr Peter Walker (Energy) stayed in their places (see DOCUMENTS). Overall, the reshuffle was seen as giving the Cabinet a more determined and vigorous face, without changing its balance within the party. Mr Walker remained its only 'licensed wet'.

Parliament was prorogued on 30 October and the new session was opened by Her Majesty on 6 November. The Queen's Speech, though promising a heavy programme of legislation, contained little that was unexpected, except perhaps the Government's adoption of a controversial measure to allow shops in England and Wales, as already in

Scotland, to open at all hours, including Sundays. The Government's overriding concern for law and order was reflected in notice of a Public Order Bill to strengthen police powers, give statutory definition to common law offences like riot and affray, and create the statutory offence of disorderly conduct. The Speech strongly reaffirmed the Government's restrictive financial strategy, which would be buttressed by a cost-saving review of social security and by the sale of more state assets. The fiscal object, the Government declared, was to reduce the burden of income tax. In the field of education, the Government planned to enable the Secretary of State to compel local authorities to assess their teachers regularly and systematically.

In the immediate debate that followed the Prime Minister said that her Government utterly rejected a policy of reflation. Production and investment, she said, were at an all-time high; 675,000 new jobs had been created in the last two years, more than anywhere else in the EEC. Labour's reckless spending promises would require savage increases of taxation on working people, and would instantly cause rapid inflation. Upholding the rule of law was the crucial issue facing the country. The inner cities must be helped, as her Government had done, but 'the solution must ultimately lie in a strengthening of our traditional sources of discipline and authority: the family, the church, the school, responsible community and civic leadership and support for the police'.

The Leader of the Opposition would not claim, he said in reply, that unemployment was the sole cause of crime in Britain, still less that there were excuses for crime; but was a 40 per cent rise in crime in six years of increased hopelessness brought about by unemployment a pure coincidence? An awful change in our time had been the emergence of 'crime for some sort of brutal, vicious entertainment'. Intolerable conduct, Mr Kinnock concluded, was a problem for parents, teachers and every responsible citizen as well as for government; but none could succeed unless the Government adopted policies to get at the roots of violent behaviour. The financial stragegy, he said, was a recipe for further rundown of the economy; high interest rates were crippling business; public spending cuts deprived communities of vital services. British taxpayers, whom the Prime Minister wished to solace, were also parents worried about schools and about cuts in house-building and improvement grants; calls for more generous relief of suffering in the Third World, for more houses, for lower unemployment, were national demands. Connoisseurs of parliamentary debate thought that in style and effectiveness Mr Kinnock had the better of the exchange.

In face of blistering attacks by its political enemies and some of its friends on the ethos of selling nationalized industries and enterprises to the private sector, the Government relentlessly pursued its programme of 'privatization'. Shares in the British Oil Corporation (Britoil), floated on 7 August, were four times oversubscribed and went to an immediate premium of 30p on the sale price of 185p. Despite the weak market for oil after Opec abandoned fixing minimum prices, the shares still stood at 210p at the end of the year, after going as high as 243p. British Telecom, privatized in 1984 (see AR 1984, p. 21), registered pre-tax profits of £1,480 million in that year, up nearly 50 per cent; at the end of 1985 its shares, floated at 130p, stood at 192p, after touching 208p. In May the Government announced plans to 'privatize' the British Gas Corporation, whose 1984 profits exceeded £1,000 million, 'as speedily as possible', a plan which the Labour spokesman Mr Stanley Orme, MP, said would create 'a massive new private monopoly out of publicly-developed assets', and which Mr Kinnock called 'fruit-machine economics'.

Privatization policy touched the fringe of a problem, the expansion of airport capacity, which, after festering for many years, was at last brought to a head. If a third London airport was to be built, the only remaining strong candidate was Stansted in Essex, where a small airport already existed. Growth of Stansted, however, had been strenuously opposed on environmental grounds. Many critics, too, particularly MPs from the North and Midlands, deplored further expansion in the south-east and called for more investment in regional airports; others questioned the need for any more London capacity, disputing estimates of future traffic. The decision announced by the Secretary of State for Transport, Mr Nicholas Ridley, on 15 June was to enlarge capacity at Stansted from two million passengers per annum to 7 to 8 million, beyond which limit further parliamentary approval would be necessary; to spend £2 million on a road link between Stansted and the motorway system; and at the same time to encourage the growth of regional airports, which Mr Ridley claimed was no real alternative to expansion in the south-east. The British Airports Authority would be privatized, and every airport would become a public limited company, subject to official regulation. The Government's announcement was greeted with the expected outcry from Opposition MPs, non-commercial residents in East Anglia and sympathetic environmentalists; 17 Conservative MPs voted against a motion, carried by a large majority, approving the White Paper on airports policy.

In July the Secretary of State for Defence told Parliament that legislation would be introduced to enable the royal dockyards to be handed over to commercial management—this in face of criticism by two Commons select committees. On its second reading on 2 December the Dockyard Services Bill secured a majority of 80, one Tory MP voting against it and a number of others abstaining. The Severn Bridge, the Mersey Tunnel and other crossings might be privatized, said Mr Ridley on 3 July, but his order doubling the Severn Bridge tolls, doubtless as a prelude to privatization, was ruled null and void by the High Court in December for want of due weight to objections. A worse legal setback was suffered by the proposed sale of the Trustee Savings Banks to the public, planned for February 1986 (see AR 1984, p. 22). On 12 November the Court of

Session at Edinburgh ruled, in a case brought by some TSB depositors, that in Scotland those banks did indeed belong to their depositors. Anticipating similar action elsewhere in the kingdom, the Government postponed the intended sale *sine die*. On the other hand, its hope of eventually privatizing British Steel was revived by the announcement on 9 December that BSC had made a pre-tax profit of £21 million in the first half of its financial year, the first time it had been in the black since 1974. Closer at hand appeared the sale of British Airways, which announced a pre-tax profit of £201 million in the six months to September, up £12 million.

The Labour Party was, of course, opposed to privatization in principle, and committed to reversing it, but Mr Kinnock disappointed the left when on 29 December he stated that renationalization was far from having top priority in Labour's spending plans. He warned that shares in privatized businesses held by financial institutions would be taken back at the original purchase price, with no allowance for inflation.

The Earl of Stockton, the former Prime Minister Harold Macmillan, voiced a thought in many minds, not confined to the Opposition, when in a speech in the House of Lords he likened the sale of state assets to finance current expenditure to selling off the family silver to pay the tradesmen's bills. He was not against privatization, he subsequently explained, only against using the proceeds as income, rather than to finance investment. That was also the cry of all opposition parties. Ministers were quite unmoved by these strictures.

On 3 June the Secretary of State for Social Services, Mr Norman Fowler, revealed the outcome of the overall review of the social security system which he had initiated in the previous year (see AR 1984, p. 22). Publication had been preceded by confident forecasts that the Government intended to abolish state earnings-related pensions, known by the rebarbative acronym Serps, contribution-based supplements to the basic old-age pension. Under Mr Fowler's plan, Serps would be phased out by about the year 2000: no existing beneficiaries would be affected. Housing benefit, at present costing £4,300 million p.a., would be reformed. Supplementary benefits (means-tested) would be abolished, along with extra payments for special needs, and replaced with a new system of income support. In order to eliminate the 'poverty trap', the present family income support system would give way to a new 'family credit' paid through the wage packet. Child benefit would remain, but might not be fully indexated. 'Earnings rules' applied to pensioners, single-parents, the disabled and the unemployed would be eased. A new computerized system for delivering benefit would come into operation in April 1987.

While Conservative MPs were relieved that the severest economies predicted were absent from the plan, the expected outcry from the Labour Opposition and champions of those affected was loud and bitter. 'The themes,' said Mr Michael Meacher, MP, Labour's frontbench spokesman, 'are more means-testing, further cuts, penalizing the pensioners, the unemployed and the low-paid in order to enrich further the already rich.' Critics claimed that cuts in housing benefit would adversely affect some five million pensioners and others on low incomes.

Mr Fowler's pension proposals were also attacked ferociously by spokesmen for industry and commerce, on which would fall the burden of replacing state earnings-related pensions with private contributory schemes. Sir Terence Beckett, director-general of the CBI, claimed that the policy would cost industry £3,000 million, and on 18 September the CBI in conference cheered its president when he said the Serps plan should be 'thrown on the bonfire'. Dr David Owen, the SDP leader, was among those who called for all-party agreement on pensions policy, as had been secured for the present system, because it affected people's lives and prospects through many parliaments.

On 16 December Mr Fowler presented his definitive plan. Most features of the earlier proposals remained, including the replacement of suplementary benefit by a system of income support, favouring families, single parents, pensioners and the disabled; changes in housing benefit to save £450 million, even the poorest being required to pay 20 per cent of local rates; and a new family credit, which would double to 400,000 the number of poor families helped and end the worst of the poverty trap. Maternity and death grants would go, but a cash-limited Social Fund would be able to make means-tested maternity grants and loans for funeral expenses and such needs as furniture and bedding. The White Paper estimated that 3,800,000 claimants to welfare benefit would lose, while nearly 2,200,000 people would gain. The greatest change from the June proposals concerned Serps, which would be retained, with no sacrifice for existing beneficiaries, but would be radically pruned, so that by AD 2033 its cost would be halved, from £25,000 million to £13,000 million. Incentives would be given to private occupational pension schemes. The changes in the social security system would start going into effect in April 1988.

Recommending his plan to the House of Commons Mr Fowler said the Government wanted to see a simpler and financially secure system of social security, more people independent in retirement, more effective help to those who really needed it, especially the families of the low-paid and unemployed with children. For Labour, Mr Meacher said that the package was much less about reform than about benefit cuts, totalling around £750 million. While Labour welcomed the Government's retreat from abolishing Serps, they utterly condemned their emasculation.

Several incidents concerning espionage or the misuse of secret documents caused public and parliamentary concern during the year. On 9 May the Security Commission's report on the case of Michael Bettaney, an MI5 officer who had been convicted in 1984 of attempting to spy for the Soviet Union, caustically criticized the conduct of that section of the secret service for continuing to employ him on counter-espionage when he was known to be an alcoholic and suspected of being a spy, and for faults in management and training. The simultaneous appointment of Sir Antony Duff, an eminent diplomat, as head of MI5 was intended to effect reforms, including a channel for complaint by officers who had strong feelings about what they were asked to do. That last point was highly germane to the case of Clive Ponting, a senior official at the Ministry of Defence, who had been charged in October 1984 with offences under the Official Secrets Act in connection with the *Belgrano* affair (see AR 1984, p. 26). At his trial, prosecuting counsel said it was not alleged that Mr Ponting's disclosures had endangered national security; the trial was about lying, not spying. In his own evidence Mr Ponting said he acted as he did because 'Ministers were sending to Parliament a document that was deliberately misleading'. On 11 February Ponting was acquitted and awarded costs against the Crown estimated at £50,000. The catch-all Section 2 of the Official Secrets Act was in tatters.

A parliamentary row followed on Labour allegations that the decision to prosecute Ponting had been a political one. The Prime Minister told Mr Kinnock that Ministers had no role whatever in a decision taken by the Director of Public Prosecutions. 'Your charge is utterly untrue', she wrote. 'If you cannot substantiate it—and you cannot—I must demand that you withdraw it and apologise unreservedly and immediately.' Mr Kinnock, with the backing of the Shadow Cabinet, refused to do so. In a Commons debate on the *Belgrano* affair on 18 February the Government's defence was vigorously put by Mr Heseltine, Secretary of State for Defence, who accused Mr Ponting of duplicity in urging Mr Tam Dalyell, MP, to put questions to Ministers which a few days earlier he had himself advised them not to answer. The Minister of State, Mr John Stanley, said that in an attempt to allay 'Belgranomania' Ministers might have actually disclosed too much. Even Mr Ponting, he said, had not claimed a connection between the sinking and a Peruvian peace plan. An Opposition amendment, affirming that Ministers has misled the House, was rejected by 350 votes to 202. On 26 February Sir Robert Armstrong, head of the civil service, sent out a note of guidance to all departments, in which he said: 'Civil servants are servants of the Crown. For all practical purposes the Crown in this context means the Government of the day.' The general secretary of the association of top-grade civil servants commented: 'It is as if Ponting had never happened.'

Another blow to prosecutions under the Official Secrets Act was dealt by the acquittal, on 24 and 28 October, of all defendants in a trial of seven RAF men, formerly serving in a communications centre in Cyprus, who were accused of disclosing secret information to foreign agents. The trial had lasted four months, and was believed to have cost over £4 million. Officials were still convinced that there had been a serious leak of communications secrets in Cyprus, but the jury evidently believed that the defendants' alleged confessions, which were the bulwark of the prosecution's case, had been extorted by wrongful means. A leading barrister was appointed to head an inquiry into the interrogation methods used by RAF police and security officials.

On 19 December the Government published a Financial Services Bill which had been awaited with some anxiety by the City of London since a White Paper in January had foreshadowed a radical reform. The Bill, together with an immediately preceding White Paper on banking supervision and a promised Bill on building societies, was intended to create a new regime at once of freer competition and tighter regulation in the interest of the public. The background to these moves was the exposure of certain major frauds or misconduct in the worlds of banking and insurance (see AR 1984, p. 24). The chief insurance swindles, revealed in 1982 and 1984, concerned two syndicates of Lloyds underwriters. The Government had strengthened Lloyds' internal supervisory and punitive powers in the Lloyds Act 1982; in face of the later scandal they insisted, against vigorous Opposition demands for statutory external control, that this system of self-regulation must be given a chance to prove itself.

The banking scandal was of a different order. Johnson Matthey Bankers (JMB) had been brought to the brink of collapse in 1984 with an apparent deficiency of nearly £250 million. The Bank of England, fearful of domino-like repercussions, negotiated a rescue package, including a Bank indemnity of £75 million and a loan of £100 million. In a Commons statement on 20 June 1985 Mr Nigel Lawson, Chancellor of the Exchequer, after describing an 'appalling and bizarre record of incompetence and mismanagement', admitted that the Bank of England, as supervisor of banks, had been at fault in not acting soon enough. The Bank's supervisory department was to be fortified under a new chief. There was, said Mr Lawson, no *prima facie* evidence of fraud. On 17 July, however, he reported that the police were investigating 'serious and unexplained gaps' in JMB's records. Now began a virulent campaign by Mr Brian Sedgemore, a lawyer Labour MP, who lost no opportunity of blackguarding JMB's directors, its officers and clients, the present and preceding chairmen of Lloyds, the Governor of the Bank of England and even the Chancellor of the Exchequer, under protection of parliamentary privilege. Those whom he accused repeatedly denied his allegations, which included such lively details as a clandestine attempt by a JMB client to bribe him and corruption of JMB executives by the provision of call girls. On 11 November he was suspended from the service of the House for a week for refusing the Speaker's demand that he withdraw a charge against Mr Lawson of perverting the course of justice. Nevertheless, as facts emerged about JMB's loan book and certain transactions behind it, some of the mud he slung did seem to stick.

Mr Sedgemore's excesses apart, the nub of Opposition attack on the

Government's policy was that self-regulation of financial markets would become self-protection, and that the Bank of England, which would remain in charge of banking supervision, was itself part of the cosy club of City financiers. Mr Hattersley, Labour's deputy leader, talked of a 'crime wave' in the City, which would itself be the loser unless a thorough-going remedy were applied. 'Cleaning up the City', he said, 'has become a test of the Government's own probity'. The Ministerial case in reply was that 'wholly statutory regulation would be more bureaucratic, legalistic and slower to respond' than self-regulation, whose authority could be withdrawn if need arose.

The December White Paper proposed a Board of Banking Supervision (BBS), headed by the Governor of the Bank of England and two colleagues but including also outside bankers, an accountant and a lawyer. Withholding information required by the BBS, or supplying false or misleading information, would be a criminal offence. Under the Financial Services Bill the Secretary of State could devolve his comprehensive powers to regulate investment business, including commodity futures contracts and certain forms of insurance, to an agency which in turn could delegate authority to approved Self-Regulating Organizations (SROs) when it was satisfied that their rules and means of enforcement were at least as strong as its own. Criminal and civil sanctions would be available against breaches or evasions of SRO rules. All commentators agreed that proof of the pudding must await the system's success in ridding the City of London of the taint of fraud and cheating.

An extraordinary political episode, not unconnected with the City, enlivened the last days of Parliament before the Christmas recess. It concerned the future of Westland, Britain's only manufacturer of helicopters, which had been threatened with liquidation for lack of orders. On 13 December Westland's board announced that they had agreed in principle with United Technologies, an American company making Sikorsky helicopters, and Fiat, the Italian car firm, on a rescue deal whereby those companies, which already held an equity stake, would put in fresh capital, while remaining minority shareholders, and provide certain work; at the same time the board rejected a belated approach by a European consortium which had been engineered by Mr Heseltine, Secretary of State for Defence. So far from giving up, however, Mr Heseltine persisted in advocating the 'European solution', which he argued was essential if Britain and the rest of Europe were not to succumb to a United States' monopoly of helicopter technology. On 16 December Mr Brittan, Secretary for Trade and Industry, 'speaking for the Government as a whole' after what the press deduced had been a fierce Cabinet squabble, told the House that it was entirely for Westland shareholders to decide the issue, while making plain how sceptically he and others in the Cabinet viewed the European proposal.

Mr Heseltine held his ground, though it was understood that the

Prime Minister had severely rebuked him for publicly opposing his colleagues. After the European consortium, now joined by the British firms GEC and British Aerospace, had published an offer which on its face appeared more attractive than the 'American solution' to Westland's shareholders, creditors and workforce, the political and personal as well as the industrial and financial contest was seen to be still wide open when the year ended.

Footnote on the Press. For Fleet Street 1985 was a year of crisis. The chief catalyst of impending radical change was Mr Selim (Eddie) Shah, far-famed for his triumphant resistance to striking compositors in defence of his Stockport-based chain of give-away local newspapers (see AR 1983, pp. 32–33), who planned to launch early in 1986 a national newspaper produced entirely by new printing technology at a London site away from Fleet Street; it would employ a fraction of the numbers manning the older production system, even as modified by elements of the new technology which had been introduced against stubborn resistance by the printing unions. Another disturbing factor was the intention of Mr Rupert Murdoch to publish a new evening paper, the *London Post*, similarly produced at a purpose-built plant in Wapping in London's dockland, where he also planned to print his four national newspapers, including *The Times*.

A major victim of the sharpened competitive climate was the *Daily* and *Sunday Telegraph*, last bastion of the great press empire created in the first three decades of the century by the Berry brothers, Lords Camrose and Kemsley. The *Telegraph*, a family-owned property, had for many years been regarded as one of the most securely profitable newspaper concerns in the country, but a check to its circulation and a fall in advertising revenue coincided with the imperative need to find new capital for a modern production system to replace its grossly overmanned plant in Fleet Street. Its accounts showed a loss of over £16 million in the six months to September. On 11 December it announced that Mr Conrad Black, a Canadian businessman who had bought 14 per cent of the share capital earlier in the year, would enlarge his stake to a controlling 50·1 per cent and give his companies' guarantee to new borrowing. The Berry scion, Lord Hartwell, would remain chairman and editor-in-chief. Nevertheless, the purchase signalled the end of an era in Fleet Street.

Mr Black had followed the late Lords Beaverbrook and Thomson of Fleet from Canada into London newspaper proprietorship; Mr Murdoch had invaded from Australia, and yet another major press group was headed by the Czech-born Mr Robert Maxwell, whose struggle to cut the labour force of *Mirror* newspapers under threats of immediate closure produced some cliff-hanging situations in 1985.

Chapter 5

RIOTS AND REVERBERATIONS

On 9 and 10 September serious rioting broke out in the Handsworth district of Birmingham. On 28 September the accidental shooting of Mrs Cherry Groce, a black lady, by a policeman engaged with others in searching her house for her son, who was believed to be armed, sparked off a riot in Brixton, South London, scene of grave disorders in 1981 (see AR 1981, pp. 9–13). Among other casualties, a press photographer who had been struck by a lump of masonry died later in hospital. On 1 October the Toxteth district of Liverpool, also a victim of past rioting (see AR 1981, p. 10), was sealed off by police after a mob of some 300 had attacked a police station and set fire to cars. Worse was to come. On 6 October rioting youths advanced on police from a council housing estate known as Broadwater Farm in Tottenham, north London, and for two hours the police were unable to penetrate the area. One constable was killed by wounds from a knife and a machete while defending firemen who were trying to control a blazing building, and many other policemen were hurt. The rioters used as missiles not only bricks and broken-up paving stones but also petrol bombs, supplied by the dozen in milk crates, and forensic evidence revealed that at least three guns had been fired—none by the police.

Mr Enoch Powell, MP, had the satisfaction of recalling his notorious speech in 1968 in which he had said: 'I am filled with foreboding. Like the Roman, I seem to see "the river Tiber foaming with much blood"' (see AR 1968, p. 13). In the foreseeable future, he declared, one-third or more of the population of English cities would be black.

Although, however, all those four theatres of violence in 1985 were poor inner-city districts with a high proportion of black residents, the riots were not primarily racial. White as well as black youths took part in them. In Handsworth (as in Toxteth) the chief material victims were Asian shopkeepers, whose premises were attacked and looted; two Asians were burnt to death defending a sub-post-office. In all cases the prime targets of violence were the police, and in all cases the riots were sparked off by a particular police action. In Handsworth it was the arrest of a black youth for drug offences in an area infested by drug pushers; in Brixton it was the shooting of Mrs Groce; in Toxteth it was the arrest of four blacks charged with affray in an earlier incident; in Tottenham it was the death of a black lady who collapsed when police with a search warrant raided her home. Police officers, however, were not the only objects of mob violence. Firemen summoned to extinguish burning buildings and cars were also attacked. Furthermore, attacks on shops were accompanied by wholesale looting. In the Brixton riot 140 serious crimes were reported, including the rape of two white women.

The Home Secretary, Mr Hurd, persisted in emphasizing the element of naked criminality. He backed independent police inquiries into the several incidents and rejected Opposition demands for a full-scale study of causes on the lines of the Scarman report on the 1981 Brixton riots, 'Inquiries do not stop riots,' he said. He approved the use by police, if necessary, of tear gas and plastic bullets: these had been available at Tottenham but had not been used. At the Tory party conference on 10 October Mr Hurd praised the police and promised a new Public Order Bill (see p. 27). Labour spokesmen, on the other hand, charged the Government with neglect of the inner cities (though all the areas concerned had received large special grants for rehabilitation) and with deliberately causing high unemployment whose worst victims were young black people, reduced thereby to despair and alienation from society. Other defenders of the rioters blamed the 'insensitivity' of police tactics. Mr Norman Tebbit, chairman of the Conservative Party, retorted that it could not be said that 'unemployment is the cause of a hundred people falling on a single policeman and murdering him'. He in turn blamed 'large and influential elements' of the Labour Party who had verbally attacked the police force and other institutions protecting society.

Takers of this line were given splendid ammunition when Mr Bernie Grant, black Labour leader of the Harringey council in whose area Broadwater Farm fell, proclaimed: 'The police were to blame for what happened on Sunday night, and what they got was a bloody good hiding.' Mr Kinnock and Mr Hattersley at once publicly distanced themselves from Mr Grant, who was seeking nomination as a Labour candidate for Parliament, but his words were on the record and were no help to Labour.

While there was no direct connection between the inner-city riots and the ugly crowd behaviour which disfigured the latter months of the 1984–1985 football season (see Pt. XVII, SPORT), those troubles also demonstrated the existence of a violently lawless element among young people, especially in big cities, and they too aroused political heat. After Millwall football club fans had rioted at Luton in March the Prime Minister expressed her wish to see stiffer penalties, including gaol sentences, for soccer hooligans, and the Home Secretary, Mr Brittan, declared: 'Football riots are outbursts of savagery; they threaten the future of football and smear the country's good name abroad.' (Historically, he might have reflected, they were no novelty: five hundred years previously, the premier guild of merchants in the City of London had forbidden its apprentices to play football, a game already notorious for causing brawls, riots and murder.) After very mild reaction by the Football Association, a Police Federation spokesman asked; 'Do we have to wait for a policeman to die before real action is taken?' A disastrous fire in a thronged stadium at Bradford City's ground on 11 May, which left 53 people dead and hundreds injured, was not caused by rioting, but it did expose the very poor state of many sports grounds in respect of crowd safety and control. A judicial inquiry was set up under Mr Justice Popplewell to consider both the Bradford disaster and rioting at Birmingham City's football ground on the same day.

The climax came on 29 May when British fans at the European Cup final in Brussels launched an attack on Italian supporters which caused a stampede, killing more than 30 people (see p. 140). They had brought disgrace to their country and to football, said Mrs Thatcher; 'the whole of Britain is appalled'. That was no more than the truth. Public opinion manifestly regarded the punishment inflicted by UEFA, the governing body of the game in Europe, in barring all English clubs from European competitions as just and salutary. The chairman of the Sports Council, who was also chairman of Liverpool Football Club, described it as 'a very statesmanlike decision', which 'puts a lot of pressure—and rightly so—on English clubs to put their house in order as soon as possible'. 'There are no excuses,' said the Prime Minister, 'and we must not try to find any.' She promised a Bill to ban the possession of alcohol at football grounds or on football trains. Police would be given powers to limit attendances at matches where trouble might be expected. The Brussels catastrophe was added to Judge Popplewell's agenda. From the Government's point of view the football authorities were dragging their feet on the path to urgent reforms. When the Football Association's appeal board rescinded the light penalties imposed after the Millwall-Luton match in March the Minister for Sport, Mr Neil Macfarlane, called the decision 'absurd and alarming'.

Chapter 6

FOREIGN AND COMMONWEALTH AFFAIRS

ON the issue in the forefront of relations between the superpowers, that of the United States' Strategic Defense Initiative (SDI), or in press parlance Star Wars, the British attitude was expressed in the most cautionary terms. Speaking to the Royal United Services Institute on 15 March the Foreign Secretary, Sir Geoffrey Howe, urged the US Administration to proceed only with 'utmost deliberation', lest the risks outweigh the benefits to the world (for extracts from his speech, see DOCUMENTS). The Leader of the Opposition was blunter in his criticism; he told Nato officials in Brussels on 6 March that he was extremely hostile to SDI, which would start a new arms race.

When, on 3 October, Mr Gorbachev put forward his proposals for a 50 per cent cut in nuclear weapons (see Pt. XII), and called for direct talks with Britain and France on their 'rapidly growing' nuclear forces, the

British response was far softer than President Mitterrand's *non possumus*. While Britain's deterrent was equal to only about 3 per cent of the Soviet Union's strategic arsenal, said the Foreign Secretary, and Britain would therefore not consider cutting it until the two superpowers substantially cut their nuclear armaments, he would 'never say never' to opening arms talks with Moscow if and when they were formally proposed; he undertook to give the Gorbachev initiative serious and constructive consideration.

It was not a propitious moment for Soviet-British detente. On 12 September 25 Russians, diplomats and others, were expelled from Britain for spying activities exposed by a defector, Oleg Gordievsky, a high official of the KGB, counsellor of embassy in London since 1982. Two days later, an equal number of British officials, businessmen and journalists, presumably innocent, were expelled by the Soviet Government. Britain responded with six more expulsions, and the Soviet Union with another tit for tat. (A similar altercation had occurred in April; when two Russians were expelled, Moscow expelled three British officials, and three more Russians were then given their *congé*). 'We have consistently made clear,' said the Foreign Secretary on 15 September, 'our wish to have improved political and commercial relations with the Soviet Union and have worked hard for that. But this Soviet action, for which there is no justification whatever, is bound to set back that process.'

'I like Mr Gorbachev', Mrs Thatcher had said when she met him in December 1984 (see AR 1984, p. 45), and she was assumed not to have changed her mind when she talked with him at the funeral of General Secretary Chernenko in Moscow on 13 March. The personal nature of her stance in foreign affairs was again displayed when she said in a television interview on 17 February, on the eve of her departure for Washington, 'I am President Reagan's greatest fan.' Mr Hattersley, five days later, remarked: 'The reward for her open infatuation has been a slap in the face.' He was referring to the President's refusal to act to stop the rise in the exchange value of the dollar—a policy reversed in September (see Part XVIII and DOCUMENTS). In her speech to the US Congress on 20 February, which was received with a standing ovation, Mrs Thatcher expressed solid support for 'Star Wars', pleaded against protectionism and deplored American aid for IRA terrorism.

International terrorism came to the front of public attention when the Italian ship *Achille Lauro* was pirated by Palestinian gunmen on 7 October (see pp. 137 and 183). Direct British interest was confined to the fate of six British girls on board; when they were released on 13 October they said the gunmen had threatened to kill them and had abused Mrs Thatcher. That was hard on the Prime Minister, who had been bitterly criticized by Israel for her invitation, made while she was in Cairo and Amman in September, to two eminent members of the PLO, who were understood to have rejected terrorism, to join a Jordanian-Palestinian delegation to London. The two Palestinians turned up in London for the talks scheduled for 14 October, but when they refused to sign a public declaration renouncing terrorism and accepting Security Council Resolution 242 the meeting was called off. Next day, King Husain of Jordan absolved the British Government of all blame for the fiasco; a clear text of the desired declaration, he said, had been agreed in advance, and it was the PLO representatives who had gone back on their undertaking. The two Palestinians did have half-an-hour's talk with the Foreign Secretary, and the British Government's view that anti-terrorism PLO spokesmen must be included in peace talks was unchanged. Ministers prudently refrained from public comment on the rude American interception of an Egyptian plane carrying the *Achille Lauro* terrorists.

In April Mrs Thatcher spent 11 days on a tour of six countries in South-East Asia, all but one of them, Indonesia, members of the Commonwealth. Her first and longest call was Malaysia, whose dislike of British policy on university fees for overseas students and on authorized air flights to and from South-East Asia had led to prickly relations for the previous four years and a considerable loss of British trade. In Kuala Lumpur she clinched a settlement of the latter dispute. Anglo-Malaysian relations, she said, had been enormously improved by her visit. She hoped that Prime Minister Dr Mahathir Mohamad would revise his sceptical view of the Commonwealth and himself attend a Commonwealth heads of government meeting—which indeed he did at Nassau later in the year (see Pt. XI, Ch. 2). In Singapore a similar airlines controversy was put aside, and mutual cordiality reigned. Mrs Thatcher's visit to Jakarta was the first ever by a British Prime Minister, and no doubt did something to foster mutual goodwill, if nothing more. A call at Colombo fortified her in discussing Sri Lanka's Tamil problem with Mr Rajiv Gandhi in New Delhi; its chief direct impact upon Britain had been a minor flood of Tamils seeking entry, causing some painful official decisions on the question of political asylum. But her principal objective in India, in which she appeared to be successful, was to establish good personal relations with Mr Gandhi. The Prime Minister appeared tired at the end of her journey and many thought it had been too much of a strain, but her health, industry and vigour were soon seen to have been undiminished.

The importance attached by the Government to relations with India was signalled when Mrs Thatcher, on 14 October, the day after her 60th birthday, personally welcomed Mr Gandhi at Heathrow airport. Those relations had been injured by Indian wrath at the evil behaviour of some extreme Sikh groups in Britain at the time of Mrs Indira Gandhi's murder, and by the sufferings of Asian shopkeepers at the hands of black and white rioters in British cities (see p. 35). On 25 September the Home Secretary had told India's high commissioner and Pakistan's ambassador that the fight against inter-racial violence was a political priority for the

Government: Asians, said Mr Hurd, need have no fear. In anticipation of Prime Minister Rajiv's visit 12 Sikhs and three Kashmiris were detained under the Prevention of Terrorism Act 1978, and four Sikhs were later charged with conspiracy to murder him. Mr Gandhi, however, publicly asked that more should be done politically to curb enemies of his Government in Britain. Mrs Thatcher, at a banquet she gave for him, expressed willingness so to extend the Prevention of Terrorism Act as to make it easier to extradite fugitive terrorists from Britain. Expert British and Indian teams, it was revealed, were to study how to ensure that crimes committed in one country would be recognized as such in the other, and that extradition could not be evaded by claims that the offences were political. The two Prime Ministers also agreed on the scope which India's latest five-year plan would afford for British industry to participate through industrial collaboration and supply of technology.

Relations with another Commonwealth country, Nigeria, remained sour. The trial of four men involved in the kidnapping of the Nigerian fugitive Umaru Dikko (see AR 1984, p. 41) ended on 11 February, when a Nigerian intelligence officer was sentenced to 12 years' imprisonment, the Israeli organizer to 14 years and two other Israelis to ten years. During the trial at the Old Bailey the court was told that the Nigerian high commissioner himself had helped to organize and finance the attempt to shanghai Mr Dikko to Nigeria, where he was accused of enriching himself by corruption in public office, a charge which he strenuously denied. Lagos continued to demand his return. On a fence-mending visit there in September, the Foreign Secretary failed to secure the restoration of full diplomatic relations. Then on 7 October two British engineers who had been involved in preparing for flight a stolen light aircraft in June 1983 were sentenced in Lagos to 14 years' imprisonment. The Foreign and Commonwealth Office was 'appalled', it said, by sentences bearing no relation to the gravity of the alleged offence. Political and public opinion had no doubt that they had been imposed as leverage to secure the extradition of Mr Dikko.

With Commonwealth countries in general the main bone of contention was policy towards South Africa (see Pt. VII, Ch. 3). In a major policy speech on 23 July the Foreign Secretary urged upon the Pretoria Government a number of 'bold steps' towards constructive dialogue with elected representatives of the black community, including the unconditional release of Mr Nelson Mandela and other leaders of the African National Congress, an end to detention without trial and to discriminatory legislation like the pass laws and 'a commitment to some form of common citizenship'. Sir Geoffrey Howe expressed the Government's abhorrence of apartheid, but he affirmed their stern opposition to the economic sanctions which were being demanded by the Opposition and by most Commonwealth countries. Britain joined the US in abstaining from the Security Council's vote on sanctions on 26 July (see Pt. XI, Ch.

1), and on 10 September vetoed joint European Community economic and cultural sanctions. When the organizers of the international games for paraplegics banned the participation of South African crippled athletes the press and much of the public were shocked. A Tory MP called the deprivation 'absolutely despicable'. President Botha's eagerly awaited speech on 15 August evoked in Britain a 'surge of disappointment', so wrote *The Times*.

At the Commonwealth heads of government meeting in Nassau in October Mrs Thatcher's opposition to imposing trade sanctions seemed likely to isolate her Government in a minority of one. However, strenuous debate in private session produced a compromise (see Pt. XI, Ch. 3 and DOCUMENTS). The Commonwealth heads renewed the demands for reform in South Africa very much as the Foreign Secretary had expressed them in July, and agreed to certain 'new measures'—to save Mrs Thatcher's face not called 'sanctions'—on the lines of those already applied by the United States. The accord also envisaged a tightening of the economic screw if adequate progress towards ending apartheid was not achieved within six months, but in a Commons debate on 23 October Sir Geoffrey made clear that the Government was not committed to imposing, even then, sanctions designed, in the words of the Minister of State, Mr Rifkind, to do the maximum damage to South Africa's economy without regard for its people. For the Opposition, Mr Healey was at his most scathing. So-called constructive engagement, he said, was a hollow sham; President Botha had broken all the agreements he had made with Mrs Thatcher in June 1984 (see AR 1984, p. 41). The choice in South Africa, said Mr Healey, was between dialogue with the African National Congress and revolution: the only two people who refused to talk with the ANC were the President of South Africa and the Prime Minister of the United Kingdom. On that point Sir Geoffrey told Mr Kinnock: 'We do not engage in contact with organizations of this kind which are actually engaging in violence.'

Relations with two other countries with which Britain had quarrelled before 1985, Libya and Argentina (see particularly AR 1982, pp. 7–21; 1983 pp. 35–38; 1984, pp. 39–41 and 45–46), remained at arm's length. The mission of Mr Terry Waite, envoy of the Archbishop of Canterbury, to Tripoli was at last accomplished after several hitches, when on 5 February four British subjects imprisoned in Libya without apparent due cause were released and flew home; two more, serving life sentences for smuggling alcohol, were also freed. Reconciliation with Argentina was blocked by stiff British refusal to discuss sovereignty over the Falkland Islands, but on a visit to Brazil on 7 July the Foreign Secretary announced that the ban on Argentine imports into Britain would be lifted, and Ministers repeatedly expressed their wish to normalize Anglo-Argentine relations in other spheres. Mrs Thatcher was 'very deeply surprised', she said, by news of a meeting between the Leader of the Opposition and

President Alfonsín in Paris on 18 September, claiming that the Argentinians wanted only to discuss sovereignty. Mr Kinnock, however, declared that the sovereignty issue had not been raised in their talk: the question to which he had sought an answer was why Argentina did not formally end a state of hostilities with Britain.

Mr Tam Dalyell, MP, was relentless in his pursuit of the Government for its alleged dishonesty over the sinking of the Argentine warship *General Belgrano* (see AR 1982, pp. 12–13; 1983, p. 37; 1984, p. 26). The Commons select committee on foreign affairs, reporting on its investigation of the affair on 24 July, was obliged to publish majority and minority reports. The majority concluded that the sinking had been authorized for legitimate military reasons, not out of political design, and that there had been no cover-up, though they criticized Ministers for giving inadequate information to Parliament. The minority held that the link with the Peruvian peace plan, which the Government's critics alleged had been deliberately sabotaged by the sinking, was 'still an open question'; and they accused Ministers of 'sustained deception of Parliament' (see also p. 31). The new airport on the Falkland Islands, capable of handling the largest aircraft in the world, was officially opened by Prince Andrew in May. Significantly, the construction workers on site outnumbered the whole population of the islands. About 3,500 service personnel were also stationed in the Falklands—double their normal civilian population.

Another vexed issue of sovereignty entered a phase of relaxation. At midnight on 4 February Spain opened its frontier with Gibraltar (see AR 1984, p. 45), and on the following day the British Foreign Secretary said that the talk he had had with his Spanish opposite number had recorded 'a significant measure of success'; Sr Moran acclaimed 'a positive step forward'. Ministers repeatedly expressed their satisfaction at the admission of Spain, as well as Portugal, to the European Community.

Criticism of the alleged inadequacy of the Government's response to the famine in north-east Africa (see AR 1984, pp. 46–47) was sharpened by the publicity aroused by the efforts of the pop singer Bob Geldof to raise money for that cause. His first Live Aid 'global rock show' was held at the Wembley stadium, London, on 13 July; within a week British contributions had totalled £13·5 million, and the fund continued to grow while the British public watched with admiration Mr Geldof's worldwide money-raising triumph and his frank disdain of political excuses and bureaucratic red tape. In July the Minister for Overseas Development told the House of Commons that a further grant for lorry transport in Sudan brought the total government contribution to relief in that country since October 1984 to £23 million, while £44 million had been granted to Ethiopia. Parliamentary criticism was directed less at the total of this aid than at its inclusion in an unaugmented global aid budget.

Relations with the European Community were generally calm after the 1984 financial settlement at Fontainebleau and the release of budgetary repayments due to Britain (see AR 1984, pp. 42 and 344–5). When the Bill ratifying the Fontainebleau terms, primarily the increase of member states VAT contributions from 1 to 1·4 per cent, had its third reading in the Commons on 22 October, 17 Tory MPs voted against the Government, but the Bill passed by 307 votes to 190. The financial fight being appeased, British policy towards the Community concentrated on sharpening its mode of operation. At the meeting of EEC Foreign Ministers at Stresa on 4 June Sir Geoffrey Howe urged four ways of lubricating Community action as it approached further enlargement: i) greater use of majority voting under existing rules, ii) on issues not open to majority vote, more use of abstention rather than veto, iii) authority for Ministerial meetings to take decisions implementing policy objectives set by Community 'summits', iv) requirement that any member Government applying a veto on grounds of 'vital national interest' must explain those grounds to the Council of Foreign Ministers. Sir Geoffrey also called for European coordination of foreign policies to be fortified by a binding obligation to consult on major issues and by the establishment of a small permanent secretariat for foreign policy. The British view was that all these reforms could be adopted forthwith without the tortuous and dilatory process of amending the Treaty of Rome. When the Milan summit in July voted to call a conference on revising the Treaty Mrs Thatcher called the outcome 'just an excuse for not taking decisions'.

Britain's most striking gesture towards Europe, however, was the Prime Minister's pact with President Mitterrand at the Bonn summit in May to accelerate the project for a fixed cross-Channel link. The deadline for private enterprise bids was fixed for 30 October—'an historic moment', both national Ministers of Transport called it.

The 1984 agreement between Britain and China on the future of Hong Kong (see AR 1984, pp. 47, 309–10 and 515–24) was the prelude to a notable warming of relations between the two countries. During his visit to London in the first week of June Prime Minister Zhao Ziyang went well beyond the call of politeness in his praise of Britain and particularly of Mrs Thatcher, to whose foresight and vision, he said in a major speech to the Royal Institute of International Affairs (see DOCUMENTS), the success of the Hong Kong negotiations owed a great deal. Increased cooperation between an independent China, dedicated to the interests of the Third World, and a strong, united Europe, Zhao Ziyang declared, was vital for world peace; in which respect he attached particular import-ance to the Sino-British bridge. Agreements on cooperation in economic and nuclear technology were signed on 3 June, and the two Prime Ministers agreed to make strong efforts to increase mutual trade. The crowning gesture from Beijing was an invitation to the Queen to visit China in 1986, which after due deliberation Her Majesty accepted.

Chapter 7

SCOTLAND

SCOTLAND saw 1985 out in a spirit of cautious optimism after a year of contrasting records broken: record oil production, record inward investment, record rainfall and record unemployment.

Economic growth continued for the second year. Manufacturing output rose faster than the 4 per cent UK average. From 1983 to the second quarter of 1985 it increased by 6 per cent annually; conversely, unemployment at 340,000 had risen in a year by 1·9 per cent against 1·6 per cent nationally.

Investment in projects assisted by the Scottish Office rose to £917 million and inward investment in 1984-85 was £690 million. Most notable were Digital Equipment's £82 million semi-conductor plants, achieved in the midst of a worldwide recession in the sector, and the first full-scale manufacturing plant for genetically-engineered biotechnology products in Livingston, for US-based Damon Biotech. A Scottish Office report revealed that output of high-technology industries doubled in five years and that high-tech jobs represented 10 per cent of manufacturing employment. The year also saw the announcement of closure for General Instruments at Glenrothes, a victim of the semi-conductor recession, and redundancies in other electronics companies; even computer leader IBM cut output at its Greenock plant.

Traditional industries continued to shed labour. Mining industry manpower was cut by 4,000 to 9,000. Over 1,200 redundancies were announced by British Rail Engineering, and shipyard jobs were lost at the Scott-Lithgow oil-rig yard. Engineering did show signs of an upturn with sales of innovative new products, including wind turbine and oil engineering equipment. British Leyland announced major investment at their Albion axle works in Glasgow, and Pringles group were due to spend £5 million on a quality knitwear plant in Arbroath. Whisky sales and exports rose, but the main interest in the sector was in ownership. Guinness won control of Bells whisky. In another contested bid the Argyll Group, run by Scot Mr James Gulliver, offered £1,900 million for the Distillers Company.

The planned closure of Gartcosh strip mill by British Steel (BSC), combined with the loss by flooding of Scotland's only coking coal pit, was seen as a serious threat to the future of Ravenscraig steelworks and sparked a major rebellion in Scottish Conservative ranks. Many Scottish Conservatives urged a Government rethink. Mr Iain Lawson, chairman of the newly-formed Committee for the Communication of Conservative Policies, resigned and threatened to put up rival candidates in Conservative seats whose members favoured BSC. Cunningham South constituency party threatened resignation, but the biggest row followed replacement of the chairman of the Scottish Conservative backbench committee, Sir Hector Munro, a leading Gartcosh supporter, by Mr Bill Walker, with the aid of English MPs. The decision was subsequently overturned, but left its bitter mark.

The rebellion in Conservative ranks was the second in six months. Earlier in the year, Mr George Younger, Secretary of State for Scotland, was forced to find an extra £40 million in rates relief and concede rating reform to appease supporters threatening full-scale revolt. Unlike the rest of the UK, Scotland was legally required to revalue rated property every five years. After two postponements, revaluation took place in 1985, resulting in massive rises which fell particularly heavily on Conservative supporters. The reform proposal favoured in Scotland was a residents' tax on everyone over 18, the existing system being retained for business premises, with rates set nationally.

Scottish teachers continued their 17-month strike for an independent pay review, escalating action through the year. The Scottish Office remained unmoved despite part-time education in many schools and disruption threats to the Scottish Higher and Lower exams.

With no elections, the political atmosphere was generally quiet. The left-wing reselection challenge to Labour was defused, no sitting MP being ousted. Shadow Scottish Secretary Donald Dewar convincingly won reselection in a contest expected to be close. Local by-elections showed little sign of an Alliance upsurge; although the Nationalists, looking more united than in recent years, picked up a few seats, Labour remained dominant. Labour Councils bitterly fought government spending guidelines, the left-wing Edinburgh District Council coming close to illegality before conceding.

Edinburgh's left-wingers also threatened the 1986 Commonwealth Games in that city by insisting on display of an anti-apartheid poster at an athletics meeting featuring South African-born Zola Budd. TV coverage was cancelled for the event, and sponsors for the privately-funded event threatened to pull out, until the council agreed not to repeat the gesture at the Games.

Scotland's sporting successes included the British Open golf title, won by Sandy Lyle, and the National Village Cricket Cup, won by the village of Freuchie. Scots footballers gained a place in the World Cup, a success overshadowed by the death of team manager Jock Stein in September.

The year brought the wettest summer on record, causing damage to tourism and agriculture. In some places, hay production was only 15 per cent of normal and fruit growers had a disastrous season. Weather was blamed for a number of fishing disasters.

The Russian spy purge (see p. 38) forced the Scottish Secretary to pull out of a trade mission to Moscow in September. The Soviets then called off the annual informal peace talks known as the 'Edinburgh

Conversations'. Consternation greeted Cabinet papers which revealed consideration of a nuclear weapons test near Wick in the 1950s. Another ghost from the past—a High Court case in April in which two brothers claimed trial by combat under ancient Scottish law—failed to materialize when lawyers agreed that the option was no longer available.

Chapter 8

WALES

As the miners' strike dragged on, all the evidence suggested that within the NUM there was a growing tension between Mr Arthur Scargill and the South Wales leaders. Only 6 per cent of South Wales miners had voluntarily abandoned the strike, but what convinced the Welsh leaders that the strike had to be ended were the developments at Cynheidre colliery in Dyfed, where more than half of the 1,100-strong labour-force were back at work and where a working miners' movement was being promoted. When the official return to work came there were defiant scenes, especially at the Mardy pit in the Rhondda where not one miner had broken ranks, but in reality Welsh miners were bracing themselves for immediate and drastic changes. Between the end of the strike and the end of 1985 the NCB closed eleven pits in South Wales and reduced manpower by 25 per cent, but total output was now greater than before the strike and the coalfield moved towards profitability. Threatened industrial action over individual closures never materialized, but in electing a new area president the men opted for Mr Les Dutfield, a Rhondda 'Scargillite', rather than his 'Kinnockite' opponent. Only at Point of Ayr colliery in the separately-organized North Wales area did the Union of Democratic Miners (see p. 10) establish a significant base in Wales.

The main legacy of the strike in Wales was the case of the three miners who were accused of causing the death of a taxi-driver in November 1984 when a concrete block had been dropped from Rhymney Bridge on a car carrying a working miner. One of the accused was cleared of all charges but Dean Hancock and Russell Shankland, both 21-year-old miners of Rhymney, were found guilty of murder and sentenced to life imprisonment by Mr Justice Mann. Immediately some 800 miners withdrew their labour in protest against the sentence, and both the charge and the verdict were criticised by local MPs Ted Rowlands and Michael Foot. In October three judges in the Court of Appeal quashed the verdict of murder and sentenced the two miners to eight years' imprisonment for manslaughter. It was nevertheless conceded that confusion over the guidelines to judges concerning intent in distinguishing between murder and manslaughter necessitated a House of Lords ruling, and in December the Law Lords confirmed the lesser charge of manslaughter, suggesting that Mr Justice Mann had been unwittingly misled by the guidelines. The deceased taxi-driver's widow was 'disgusted' at this outcome.

The death of Mr Tom Hooson, Conservative MP for Brecon and Radnor since 1979, necessitated a by-election which was won, on 4 July, for the SDP-Liberal Alliance by Mr Richard Livesey with a majority of 559. As compared to the general election the Alliance's share of the vote had increased from 24 to 36 per cent, Labour's from 25 to 34 per cent, while in the Tories' worst by-election result for years their vote slumped from 48 to 28 per cent. The Labour camp were strongly of the view that they might have won had it not been for a speech by Mr Scargill in which he had demanded, in effect, that a Labour Government should give the mines to the NUM (see p. 25).

The death also occurred of the 91-year-old Mr Saunders Lewis, who had been described as 'the grandfather of Welsh nationalism and litera-ture' (see OBITUARY). Lewis's twenty plays had established him as the Welsh language's greatest modern writer, and in his political career he had been a founder and inaugural president both of Plaid Cymru and of the Welsh Language Society. He had always insisted that the well-being of the Welsh language was the main priority of Welsh nationalism, and the fact that Wales now had both a well-established system of bilingual schools and a flourishing structure of Welsh-language broadcasting ser-vices could be attributed to his vast influence. The vitality of Welsh broadcasting was reflected in BBC2's decision to make its first national transmission of a subtitled Welsh-language play; significantly, the play, *Penyberth* by William Jones, was based on the story of how Saunders Lewis and two other Welsh Nationalists had set fire to an RAF bomber station in 1936.

Chapter 9

NORTHERN IRELAND

THE Anglo-Irish Agreement of 15 November between the Governments of the United Kingdom and the Republic of Ireland came after lengthy negotiations which had not included any political representatives from Northern Ireland. Basically the Agreement recognised the existing status of Northern Ireland's constitutional position within the UK, but enabled the Irish Government to represent the nationalist minority at an inter-governmental council and laid the groundwork for greater cooperation on security (for text, see DOCUMENTS). Interpretations of the implica-tions of the deal differed greatly.

The Social Democratic and Labour Party (SDLP) enthusiastically backed the Agreement. Official recognition of the role of the Republic's Government was welcomed and hopes were expressed that various social and political reforms would follow. The Alliance Party (AP) declared reservations about the new arrangements, particularly because of the lack of consultation with local parties, but stated that it would allow time to see if the Agreement would bring benefits to the community. Sinn Fein (SF) opposed the measure on the ground that it accepted partition and that it promised reforms which they dismissed as valueless.

From the two main unionist parties there was a united and forthright condemnation of the Agreement. The Official Unionist Party (OUP) and the Democratic Unionist Party (DUP) both opposed it on the grounds that it gave a formal say to the Irish Government in the affairs of Northern Ireland, which they believed would lead to a serious weakening of Northern Ireland's position within the UK. On 23 November a large unionist rally in opposition to the new accord was held at the Belfast City Hall. In December the 15 Unionist MPs at Westminster vacated their seats in order to fight by-elections in protest at the Government's actions.

The Minister in charge of the implementation of the new policy, Mr Tom King, was appointed in early September as Secretary of State for Northern Ireland in place of Mr Douglas Hurd. After the announcement of the Anglo-Irish Agreement Mr King strongly defended its value. He gave assurances that this new accord did not weaken the Union, that it would help remove nationalist alienation from the state, and that it would assist in defeating terrorism. Such statements, however, had no effect on unionist opposition to the deal.

In May elections to the local councils the number of seats won by the various parties were OUP 190, DUP 142, SDLP 101, Sinn Fein 59, Alliance 34 and others 40. The presence of Sinn Fein representatives on the councils was strongly opposed by unionist councillors because of Sinn Fein's association with the Provisional IRA. Most unionist-controlled councils were suspended temporarily by their members as a protest against the attendance of Sinn Fein councillors.

The Northern Ireland Assembly continued to meet during the year. Besides serving as a plenary body, committees from the Assembly scrutinized administration of transferred matters in Northern Ireland. The SDLP, however, had still not agreed to attend the Assembly and the AP withdrew on 6 December. On 29 October a committee of the Assembly produced a report on devolution known as the Catherwood report. In early December the two unionist parties established a grand committee to examine the Anglo-Irish Agreement.

The economic position of the region had not improved during 1985. The seasonally adjusted figure for the number of people unemployed at the end of December stood at 125,700, a rise of 7,900 compared with 12 months previously. Molin's factory in Derry, which had been threatened with closure, was restructured in early 1985 on a cooperative basis with government assistance. The Lear Fan aircraft company at Newtownabbey collapsed in May. In March, however, Shorts, the Belfast aircraft builder, announced a number of important orders, including a deal with the Brazilian company Embraer to build 130 Tucano training planes for the RAF.

During 1985 the number killed as a result of political violence came to 55, compared to 64 in 1984. Of the members of the security forces murdered by the Provisional IRA or the Irish National Liberation Army, no fewer than 23 were members of the Royal Ulster Constabulary. Mortar attacks on police stations led to serious loss of life. An assault on Newry police station on 28 February killed nine officers. Another notable feature of deaths during 1985 was the high number of Catholics murdered by republican terrorists because of links with the security forces or with the construction of police stations.

Various other matters aroused special interest. Cases in the courts against Dominic McGlinchy and James Shannon, both of whom had been extradited from the republic to face terrorist charges, failed to bring convictions, and McGlinchy had to be sent back, but demands continued for greater ease of extradition between north and south. Attempts to control loyalist marches in July and August led to violent confrontation between marchers and police. Informers or 'supergrasses' continued to be used in the courts against members of paramilitary organizations and so also did criticism of their role. In July the evidence of William 'Budgie' Allen was thrown out by the judge as unreliable but in December the evidence of Harry Kirkpatrick brought convictions against 27 men.

On a more positive note, 1985 witnessed wide community support for some top local sportsmen. Barry McGuigan won the world featherweight boxing championship in June, and Dennis Taylor won the world snooker championship in April; throughout the province their achievements were greeted with great pride. The cultural scene continued to flourish. Besides the widely-recognised work of Northern poets, playwrights and novelists, the visual arts also gave evidence of a healthy artistic life.

II THE AMERICAS AND THE CARIBBEAN

Chapter 1

THE UNITED STATES OF AMERICA

THE third successive year of economic recovery prompted a general sense of well-being among most Americans in 1985, though the rate of growth was slower than in either of the previous two years. There were frustrations, too, both at home and abroad, that seemed to contradict the sense of confidence and purpose reflected by President Reagan when he said, in the inaugural address at the start of his second term of office, that Americans believed that 'there are no limits to growth and human progress, when men and women are free to follow their dreams.' As he pointed out, tax rates had been reduced, inflation cut (the rate was 3·6 per cent for 1985) and more people were employed than ever before. What the President did not know, when he addressed the nation at the beginning of the year, was that by its end the United States would also have a trade deficit of more than $140,000 million, the largest in its history, and would be plagued by a budget deficit of equally massive proportions, while the President's package of tax reforms, the major domestic proposal for his second term of office, would survive only by the grace of his political opponents, and then not in the form he wanted.

At home the year may also be remembered for the death of the actor Rock Hudson, which drew attention to the spread of the disease AIDS (see Pt. XIV, Ch. 1), for which there was no known cure and of which there were more than 14,000 registered cases in the USA in 1985, and for less grim statistics such as the breaking of Ty Cobb's 1928 record of 4,192 major league baseball hits by Pete Rose of the Cincinnatti Reds, and the $142 million paid by Mr Samuel Newhouse for the *New Yorker* magazine. 1985 was also the year when the traditional formula for the making of the world's best-selling soft drink, Coca-Cola, was abandoned in favour of a new Coke, only to be reinstated three months later by popular demand as Coca-Cola Classic.

Overseas there was success for America's policy of bringing the Soviet Union back to the negotiating table. Arms talks were resumed in Geneva, and the President met the new Soviet leader, Mr Mikhail Gorbachev, at a summit conference in the same city. Though not much of substance came of it, the Administration took comfort from the fact that the two men had met, had talked amicably, and had agreed to meet again. The US was also encouraged by a lessening of tension in most of Central America, though not in Nicaragua, and by the support it received from at least some of its allies for the President's 'Star Wars' programme. But terrorist activities in the Middle East were a nagging anxiety for much of the year, as American citizens were often the target and there was little that their Government seemed able to do about it.

HOME AFFAIRS. Because of the bitter cold in Washington the traditional parade and inauguration ceremonies were abandoned for the first time since Andrew Jackson's inauguration in 1829. In his second inaugural address on 21 January Mr Reagan said the time had come for a new American emancipation—'a great national drive to tear down economic barriers and liberate the spirit of enterprise in the most distressed areas of our country.' He emphasised his concern to control government spending, to balance the budget and to simplify the tax system, ambitions which he expounded in greater detail two weeks later when he sent his budget to Congress and went before the joint Houses to deliver his State of the Union address.

Speaking to Senators and Congressmen on his seventy-fourth birthday Mr Reagan proclaimed that in his first term a great industrial giant had been reborn. There had been 25 months of economic growth, a three-year inflation average of 3·9 per cent, and the creation of more than seven million new jobs in the last two years. His second term would see the completion of 'a second American revolution of hope and opportunity'. Among his proposals for bringing this about were the creation of enterprise zones providing tax incentives in depressed urban areas, support for job training, tuition tax credits and health vouchers. The best way to reduce deficits, he said, was through economic growth, and the best way to reduce government spending was by increasing the general prosperity. He made particular pleas to Congress to approve his defence budget, including allocations for the MX intercontinental ballistic missiles and for research under the Strategic Defense Initiative or 'Star Wars' programme, which he described as investments in peace and freedom, and he surprised his audience by introducing two 'heroes' who, he said, epitomised American values, and who were sitting alongside his wife in the visitors' gallery—one a female refugee from Vietnam who was now a West Point cadet, the other a woman from Harlem who cared for the children of heroin addicts.

In his budget message for fiscal 1986, sent to Congress on 4 February, the President had forecast total spending of $973,700 million and revenues of $793,700 million, leaving a deficit of $180,000 million (compared with the 1985 deficit of $222,000 million). In effect overall spending was to be frozen at the 1985 level, because the budgeted increase of $15,000 million would be entirely consumed by interest on the debt. The President asked for military spending to be increased by $30,000 million but for spending on domestic programmes to be cut by $39,000 million—a challenge to Congress that was to preoccupy them for most of the year. Though they had a new man in the Administration to deal with it—on 8

January James A. Baker, the White House Chief of Staff, had become Secretary of the Treasury in a straight switch of jobs with Mr Donald Regan—there was little that any well-meaning go-between could hope to achieve. Congress believed that the President's commitments to reduce the deficit, cut spending everywhere except in defence and not raise taxes presented an impossible scenario, and one which they could not work to when trying to prepare their own version of a budget.

The first public indication of the conflict came in March when the President vetoed a Bill which would have provided credit relief to farmers. He accused Congress of failing at its first major opportunity to hold the line against federal spending, and said there was no justification for this expenditure at a time of large federal deficits. 'Just as your families don't have a blank cheque for whatever your needs may be, neither can government—and that means taxpayers—bail out every farmer hopelessly in debt or every bank that made imprudent or speculative loans,' he said. The farmers responded by sending delegations to Washington to draw attention to their plight, caused primarily by the fall in exports following the rise of the dollar. The strength of their political lobby, boosted by a rash of bankruptcies in the conservative farm belt, was reflected at the end of the year when a new Farm Bill, setting farm support spending at its highest level, was put through Congress after an eight-day conference session and signed into law by the President, who described it as on balance a step forward for American agriculture by moving it closer to a market-oriented industry.

Another American institution that escaped the President's budget axe was the country's inter-city train system, known as Amtrak, which Mr Reagan had suggested was an expensive anachronism not worth its subsidy. He proposed that its passenger service, the only inter-city passenger rail service in the country, should cease operating at the end of September, when his new budget came into force. The Senate refused to go along with this, voting to keep Amtrak on the rails by restoring its subsidy of $684 million for the coming year, but reducing it by stages in subsequent years.

Much of the congressional debate in the early part of the year, as in 1984, was centred on the MX intercontinental ballistic missile (ICBM). Under a compromise arrangement between the House and the Senate $1,500 million had been allocated for the construction of a further 21 MX missiles, provided assent for the release of the funds was given by both Houses after 1 March 1985. This was not readily forthcoming until the President summoned the chief US negotiator at the Geneva arms talks, Mr Max Kampelman, to emphasize the importance of the missiles to the American negotiating position. Both Houses agreed to release the funds at the end of March, but they refused to meet the President's request in his new budget for a further 48 missiles, with the ultimate objective of building 223 in all. The Administration's plan was to house 100 of these in the permanent silos currently occupied by the Minuteman missiles, but Congress held that these were too vulnerable. They decided to limit the maximum deployment of MX missiles to 50 unless they were housed in more mobile and less obvious positions, to which at this stage the Administration was not prepared to agree.

Meanwhile efforts to make progress on the main economic issues of the budget ran into all sorts of political difficulties. At the end of June Mr Peter Domenici, the chairman of the Senate budget committee, suspended talks between Congress and the Administration designed to reach agreement on spending cuts, the six-month effort collapsing mainly because of party differences, as Republicans in the Senate insisted on maintaining the level of defence expenditure and Democrats in the House of Representatives demanded cuts. On 29 July the President rejected another attempt by the Senate to introduce a series of measures designed to cut the deficit in half by 1989, including an oil import fee, revisions in cost-of-living increases for social security pensioners and changes in tax indexing proposals. Mr Paul Volcker, chairman of the US Federal Reserve Board, told Congress that there had to be a way out of the impasse, though that way could not be by monetary policy alone. 'Either we have to increase our savings or reduce our deficits,' he said. 'We cannot increase savings, so we have to reduce the deficit.'

On 1 August the Senate and House of Representatives broke their own deadlock by approving a budget of $967,600 million, reducing the projected deficit by $55,500 million in fiscal 1986. The package allowed defence spending to keep up with inflation, cut some domestic programmes but left social security payments and benefits for the old and the poor largely untouched. The White House was cautious in its response, but officials made clear that the President intended to fight for deeper cuts in domestic spending than Congress had agreed, and that presidential vetoes on some appropriation Bills were to be expected. The crisis drifted on through the summer and into autumn, when the total US national debt approached the $2,000 billion mark and Congress was required to raise the federal borrowing limit or let the government run out of money.

At this point two Republican Senators, Mr Phil Gramm and Mr Warren Rudman, proposed an amendment, to which Senator Ernest Hollings, a Democrat, also lent his name, calling for a reform of the budget which would enforce a phased reduction of the deficit so that it was reduced to nothing by 1991. The amendment (to legislation providing for an increase in the borrowing limit) imposed automatic spending cuts when specified deficit ceilings were exceeded, half to be made in military spending and half in non-military, with pension and poverty programmes exempted. It was passed shortly before Congress adjourned for Christmas, and was signed into law on 12 December by the President, though he noted that the new law raised serious constitutional questions.

Not least of these were the Gramm-Rudman Act's apparent confusion between the powers of the executive and legislative branches of the American government and its denial to both of any discretion or decision over a substantial proportion of future federal spending. It seemed a desperate way of getting out of a budgetary dilemma, and one which promised to create a deal of trouble for both executive and legislature in the coming year. In the words of the Senate majority leader, Robert Dole, of Kansas: 'We've made history of some kind, and we'll see how it works next year.'

The preoccupation with the budget deficit nearly cost the President his plans for tax reform, which he regarded as the principal domestic measure of his second term. In his State of the Union address he reminded Congress that the Treasury Department had put forward 'an excellent reform plan' in the previous year (see AR 1984, pp. 65–66), and he urged Congress to pass in 1985 'a tax bill for fairness, simplicity and growth, making this economy the engine of our dreams and America the investment capital of the world.' On 29 May he sent to Congress his revised plans for tax reform, which were described as 'revenue neutral', meaning that they would raise as much as the current system and not add to the federal budget deficit. The key points in the President's package were:

A reduction in the number of federal income tax brackets from fourteen to three (15, 25 and 35 per cent);
Raising personal exemptions from $1,040 to $2,000;
Raising standard deductions for individuals from $2,390 to $3,000 and for couples from $3,450 to $4,000;
Withdrawal of state and local taxes as deductible items from federal income tax;
Reduction of top corporation tax rate from 46 per cent to 33 per cent;
Capital gains to be taxed as ordinary income but with 50 per cent excluded and with the rate reduced from 20 to 17·5 per cent;
Business deductions for sport, theatre and similar entertainment to be disallowed, and deductions for meals and travel reduced.

The response in Congress was desultory. By December no plan acceptable to the Administration had been debated and the whole idea was in danger of foundering. Rather than let this happen the President decided to put his weight behind an alternative Democrat-sponsored Bill proposed in the House of Representatives by Mr Dan Rostenkowski, chairman of the House Ways and Means Committee. In a personal letter to all 435 members of the House Mr Reagan said he strongly supported the Bill, though he had reservations about some parts of it, because it was an essential first step towards real tax reform. 'To fail to advance a Bill now will mean maintaining the *status quo*, a tax system with all its inequities, complexities and tendencies to discourage economic growth,' he wrote. 'This is not what I want. It is not what the American people want. And I trust it is not what the House wants.'

The Democratic Bill proposed to reduce the number of tax brackets to four instead of three, cutting the top rate from 50 per cent to 38 per cent. In addition it preserved some of the deductions the President had wanted to do away with (including mortgage payments on second homes and taxes paid to state and local governments) and imposed stiffer minimum taxes on corporations. The President's sudden support for a Bill that emasculated many of his own proposals angered his Republican supporters in the House, many of whom joined in a revolt to keep the Bill from being voted on by the full House.

Mr Reagan had to lobby hard to overcome this opposition within his own party and to meet a challenge from the Speaker of the House, Mr Tip O'Neill, who declared that he would not bring the Bill up again unless the President could personally guarantee that fifty Republicans would vote for it. Mr Reagan went Capitol Hill to address the Republicans and won enough of them round by promising to veto the Bill unless the Senate, when it came to consider the measure in 1986, cut the top rate to 35 per cent and protected incentives for business investment. On 17 December the House voted by 256 to 171 to pass the Bill, thus giving the President a chance of achieving some measure of tax reform in the coming year. At a ceremony in the White House on the following morning an exultant Mr Reagan cried: 'What's that I heard about lame duckery?'

It was a question that had been posed earlier in the year, and in much more personal terms, when the President went into hospital for an operation to remove a polyp from his bowel. The possibly serious nature of the condition was reflected in the fact that, before undergoing the operation, the President sent letters to the President *pro tempore* of the Senate, Senator Strom Thurmond, and to the Speaker of the House, Mr Tip O'Neill, formally transferring power to the Vice-President, Mr George Bush. The decision was in accordance with section 111 of the 25th Amendment to the Constitution, which came into law in 1967.

In his letter Mr Reagan said that he would be 'briefly and temporarily incapable of discharging the constitutional powers and duties' of his office, and that he was therefore transferring them to the Vice-President. At the same time, he wrote, he did not believe that the drafters of the 25th Amendment intended its application to situations such as this, and he did not mean to set a precedent binding on any future President. In Washington it was assumed that his main object was to prevent any repetition of the confusion that had briefly taken hold of the Administration after the attempt on his life in March 1981.

The letter was signed and sent on 13 July, and on that day the President had a major operation at the Bethesda Naval Hospital. The polyp was found to be cancerous, and a two-foot section of the colon was removed during surgery which appeared to be wholly successful. No spread of the cancer was found. Later the same day Mr Reagan wrote again to Senator Thurmond and Mr O'Neill to advise them that he was resuming his constitutional powers and duties as President. Mr Bush had been the nation's first Acting President and Commander-in-Chief for eight hours, but it was Mr Donald Regan, the White House Chief-of-Staff, who took day-to-day charge of running the Administration during the President's convalescence, which proved to be quite short. Once again Mr Reagan surprised everyone with his resilience and the speed of his recovery. He left hospital on 20 July and returned to the White House two days later. Early in August a small pimple removed from the side of his nose was found to be a form of skin cancer caused by exposure to the sun, but no further treatment was needed.

In addition to the highly unusual exchange of posts between Mr Donald Regan and Mr James Baker early in the year there were a number of other significant changes in the Administration during 1985. Mr William Clark, the Secretary of the Interior, confirmed his intention to leave the Government in January, and was replaced later in the year by Mr Donald Hodel, the Secretary of Energy; he in turn was succeeded by Mr John Herrington, who had served as director of personnel in the White House since 1983. The Secretary of Education, Mr Terrel Bell, who had resigned at the end of 1984, was succeeded by Mr William Bennett, formerly chairman of the National Endowment for the Humanities; and Mrs Jeane Kirkpatrick, who had resigned as Permanent Representative at the United Nations, was replaced by Mr Vernon Walters, former deputy director of the Central Intelligence Agency and a lieutenant-general in the US Army. Mr Raymond Donovan, the Secretary of Labour, who had been on unpaid leave since October 1984 after being arraigned on 137 counts in a criminal indictment charging him with grand larceny and falsifying business documents, resigned on 15 March after being ordered to stand trial on the charges. He was succeeded as Secretary of Labour by Mr William Brock, formerly US Special Trade Representative. Another member of the Administration who fell foul of the law, Mr Paul Thayer, resigned his post as Deputy Defense Secretary after admitting that he had lied to a grand jury about his part in a stock scandal. He was sentenced to four years' imprisonment and fined $5,000.

In July, following the sudden resignation of Mr David Stockman as Director of the Office of Management and Budget to take up a more lucrative business post, the President nominated Mr James Miller, chairman of the Federal Trade Commission, to take his place. Three months later the President lost another member of his Cabinet, Mrs Margaret Heckler, the Secretary of Health and Human Services, who was somewhat reluctantly persuaded to accept the appointment of ambassador to Ireland. It was reported that she had not been forceful enough in making the required cuts in social services, and had consequently run into difficulties with Mr Donald Regan, the White House Chief-of-Staff. Another member of the Administration who was also said to have clashed with Mr Regan was the National Security Adviser, Mr Robert C. McFarlane. Mr

McFarlane resigned his post on 4 December and was replaced by his deputy, Vice-Admiral John M. Poindexter. On the same day it was announced that the President had reluctantly agreed to a request from Mr James Beggs, Administrator of the National Aeronautics and Space Administration, to relieve him temporarily of his duties following charges that he had tried to defraud the government while a vice-president of General Dynamics, most of whose business was in government contracts.

Elsewhere within the lower echelons of government service 1985 was a year for uncovering espionage. 'Spies, Spies, Everywhere' cried *Time* magazine in December, reporting that ten Americans had been arrested during the year on charges of spying for a foreign country. The most celebrated case of the year, however, did not involve an American but a Russian, Vitaly Yurchenko, a KGB agent who apparently defected to the United States but then, three months later, made a well-publicized return to the Soviet Union, claiming that he had been kidnapped and tortured by the CIA. His behaviour naturally cast doubts on the reliability of the information he supplied to the Americans, but it was nonetheless he who fingered Mr Ronald Pelton, a communications specialist for the National Security Agency (NSA) for 14 years, who was arrested on 25 November and accused of selling highly confidential and sensitive material to the Russians. Federal officials believed he had done significant damage to the US national security, and possibly also to British secret communications and code-breaking activities because of the close ties that existed between the NSA and the British Government Communications Headquarters. Yurchenko was also said to have named a former CIA employee, Mr Edward Howard, as a Russian spy, but Howard fled the country before he could be arrested.

An earlier catch involved a retired naval officer, Commander Arthur Walker, who was found guilty in August on seven counts of selling military documents and passing secrets to the Soviet Union for more than a decade. He was later sentenced to life imprisonment and fined $250,000. Two other members of his family were alleged to have been involved in the same crimes, together with another man. In addition to those found working for the Soviet Union some moles were unearthed who were active on behalf of other countries. Mr Larry Wu-Tai Chin, a CIA intelligence analyst, was arrested in November and charged with spying for China since 1952. Mr Jonathan Pollard, a civilian analyst employed by the US Navy, was accused, with his wife, of passing military information to Israel. Miss Sharon Scranage, a clerk in the CIA, was sentenced to five years' imprisonment for spying for Ghana. Her Ghanaian lover, for whom she was working, and who was also convicted on similar charges, was expelled from the country in exchange for Ghanaians who had been accused of spying for the US. Meanwhile Mr Caspar Weinberger, the Defense Secretary, ordered new security controls on 50,000 military and civilian employees who had access to secret codes and cryptographic equipment.

The American space programme continued to make substantial and sometimes spectacular advances during the year, but not all of them were as well publicized as usual. For example, the space shuttle *Discovery*, launched successfully in January, was orbiting the Earth in silence and secrecy, and no information was given about what it was doing. Mission control at Houston stated that the shuttle was performing satisfactorily, but refused to comment on reports that it was on a military mission which would include the deployment of a spy satellite. There were no such inhibitions about publicity when the shuttle was launched again in April. Among its crew of seven was a congressional observer, Senator Jake Garn, a Republican from Utah, who was chairman of the Senate sub-committee which kept an eye on Nasa's expenses, and who thus became the first legislator to orbit the Earth. He also became the first politician to be able to give a press conference from space, saying to earth-bound journalists that if he were ten years younger he would rather be a working astronaut than a senator. During their otherwise successful mission, the crew failed in attempts to activate a disabled US Navy communications satellite. This was eventually done by a later *Discovery* flight, Nasa's twentieth shuttle mission, in September. Two astronauts repaired the disabled satellite after working on it in space for seven hours. The crew also launched three other communications satellites during their week-long mission, but one of these stopped working after two days and seemed to be a write-off. Late in the year a new space shuttle craft, the *Atlantis*, completed a successful maiden voyage in space. As it was on a military mission its payload was again not revealed, though some of the crew's building operations in space were recorded and shown on television, the aluminium structures they put together being the first tests towards the building of a permanent space station.

In September the US carried out its first successful test of an anti-satellite weapon in space. The detailed results were kept secret, but it was confirmed that a disused scientific satellite was hit and destroyed, at a height of 300 nautical miles, by the impact of the anti-satellite weapon (known as Asat) fired by an F15 fighter flying at about 40,000ft. Reporting the test to Congress, President Reagan said that the test was in accord with the Anti-Ballistic Missile Treaty of 1972, and was necessary to restore balance with the Soviet Union, which had possessed for many years the world's only operational anti-satellite system.

FOREIGN AFFAIRS. The first item on the agenda for the US in the new year was preparation for a meeting between Mr George Shultz, the Secretary of State, and Mr Andrei Gromyko, the Soviet Foreign Minister, scheduled to take place in Geneva on 7 January. The aim was to get Russian agreement to a resumption of the full arms talks which had been stalled for more than a year. When the President met Mr Shultz, Mr

Caspar Weinberger and Mr Robert McFarlane in Palm Springs, California, on New Year's Day it was decided that the Americans should propose that the arms talks should be in two sets—one for offensive weapons, the other for defensive systems. The US was prepared to be flexible, and would be willing to put its controversial Strategic Defense Initiative (SDI) or 'Star Wars' programme (see DOCUMENTS) on the table for general discussion, though it would not agree to suspend this research into futuristic space defensive weapons.

After two days of tough talking in Geneva Mr Shultz and Mr Gromyko agreed that the arms talks should be resumed, and that they should be divided into three groups—space weapons, strategic missiles and intermediate range missiles. The US and the Soviet Union would each send one delegation to the new talks, split into three sub-groups. In a joint statement the Americans and the Russians emphasised that they saw the three groups as inter-related, and that the objective of the talks would be to work out effective agreements to prevent an arms race in space and terminate it on earth, with the ultimate aim of 'the complete elimination of nuclear arms everywhere'. The Americans were pleased with the outcome, though their initial enthusiasm was subsequently modified as reports came in from Moscow about the Soviet interpretation of the extent of the linkage between the three groups of arms talks. The real problem was clearly was going to be the 'Star Wars' programme.

The President was emphatic about its importance in his State of the Union address. Aimed at finding a non-nuclear defence against ballistic missiles, it was, he believed, the most hopeful way of eliminating the threat of nuclear war. But he recognised that it was not well understood. 'Some say it will bring war to the heavens,' he said; 'but its purpose is to deter war, in the heavens and on earth. Some say the research would be expensive. Perhaps, but it could save millions of lives, indeed humanity itself. Some say if we build such a system, the Soviets will build a defence system of their own. They already have strategic defences that surpass ours, a civil defence system where we have almost none, and a research programme covering roughly the same areas of technology we're exploring. And finally, some say the research will take a long time. The answer to that is: "Let's get started".'

Some doubts about the SDI were expressed by America's allies, based partly on the difficulties it might impose on the arms talks and partly on a fear that it might reduce the US commitment to the defence of Europe. The President sought to allay these anxieties before the Geneva talks, first by sending Mr Weinberger to Europe to reassure the allies that the system would be as effective against intermediate-range missiles as against long-range missiles aimed at the US, and to emphasise that the Administration believed that SDI would help in the negotiations on arms cuts; and secondly by instructing the US delegation to go to Brussels on their way to Geneva to brief Nato officials along the same lines. Mr

Reagan also took the opportunity of a visit to Washington by the British Prime Minister to talk to her on the subject, winning from Mrs Thatcher her full support for the American position (see p. 38). In an address to a joint session of Congress on 20 February the Prime Minister endorsed the policy of negotiating through strength. 'If we are to maintain deterrence, as we must,' she said, 'it is essential that our research and capacity do not fall behind. That is why I fully support President Reagan's decision to pursue research into defence against ballistic nuclear missiles—the SDI. Indeed, I hope that our scientists will share in this research.' It was a welcome reassurance to Washington after the British Foreign Secretary, Sir Geoffrey Howe, had seemed to indicate some lack of enthusiasm for the project (see p. 37 and DOCUMENTS).

Before the arms talks began in Geneva on 12 March it was made clear by the US that it wanted first to ensure that existing arms treaties would be properly adhered to by the Soviet Union. The Administration had published three recent reports showing that the Russians seemed to be violating the agreements. In particular the US was concerned about the construction of a big phased-array radar station at Krasnoyarsk, in Siberia, which it believed was part of a plan to expand the existing anti-ballistic missile system in contravention of the 1972 ABM Treaty. The US also charged that the Soviet Union had been violating the 1972 convention on biological and toxic weapons in Afghanistan. But even as the Geneva talks began the news came from Moscow of the death of President Chernenko, and attention inevitably switched to the Soviet capital, where many world leaders assembled for the funeral and took the opportunity of brief encounters with the new leader, Mr Mikhail Gorbachev. The US was represented by Vice-President George Bush and Mr Shultz, and they passed on a proposal from the President that there should be a summit meeting between himself and Mr Gorbachev later in the year. The invitation was accepted, and this was taken by Washington as a welcome sign that the new man in the Kremlin wished to maintain the prospect of an improvement in East-West relations, although Mr Gorbachev's reply came after there had been angry exchanges between the two Governments following the shooting of an unarmed US major by a Russian guard in East Germany on 24 February. The exact circumstances of the incident were disputed by the two countries, but both were clearly determined not to let it sour negotiations.

With his acceptance of the invitation to a summit meeting Mr Gorbachev took the US Administration unawares by declaring an immediate Soviet freeze of missile deployment in Europe. He said the moratorium would cover both the deployment of SS-20 missiles and the stationing of missiles in response to the American deployment of Cruise and Pershing missiles, and would expire at the end of the year unless the US responded by suspending those developments. President Reagan, clearly taken aback by the new Soviet leader's swift seizure of the initiative, responded by rejecting the moratorium as an attempt to per- petuate the Soviet Union's current superiority and as part of a propa- ganda campaign to drive a wedge between the US and some of its Nato partners. The President had his own gesture to make in June, when he decided that the US would continue to abide by the SALT 2 agreement, which had not been ratified and which was due to expire at the end of the year, in order 'to go the extra mile' in restraining the arms race. The US would dismantle an old Poseidon nuclear submarine when a new Trident nuclear submarine was launched later in the year, in order to comply with the limit of 1,200 missile launchers with multiple warheads imposed by SALT 2.

In August the preparations for the summit, which had been fixed for November, seemed to be threatened by the discovery that the Russians were secretly using chemicals to track the movements of American diplomats in Moscow, chemicals which it was said could cause cancer. The State Department protested strongly and demanded an immediate halt to the practice. The US Administration denied that it was trying to sabotage the summit, which had more far-reaching issues to deal with, and said its only interest was to protect the health of US diplomats. Preparations for the meeting went on. Mr Shultz had a series of meetings with the new Soviet Foreign Minister, Mr Eduard Shevardnadze, finding him more affable and more relaxed than his predecessor, and a prelimin- ary format for the meetings was agreed without difficulty, although Mr Reagan repeatedly emphasised that he did not regard the SDI as a bargaining chip to be used in exchange for cuts in the Soviet nuclear arsenal. For the US, he said, the SDI was too important to be traded off.

More public preliminaries to the summit came in the autumn when world leaders gathered in New York for the fortieth session of the UN General Assembly. Mr Shevardnadze went to the White House on 27 September to put an alternative to the American plan, tabled at the arms talks in Geneva, that the total number of ballistic missile warheads should be reduced by one-third to about 5,000. The Soviet alternative was that there should be a 50 per cent cut by both superpowers in nuclear weapons capable of reaching each other's territory, coupled with a ban on all space weapons. It was also proposed that there should be direct talks between Russia and Britain and France on their nuclear forces. When he addressed the UN on 24 October Mr Reagan said he thought that within the Soviet proposals were seeds that should be nurtured. He hoped that both sides were now committed to dialogue, and he looked to a fresh start in the relationship between the US and the Soviet Union when he met Mr Gorbachev. He also called for a joint approach to ending the wars in Afghanistan, Nicaragua, Angola, Ethiopia and Cambodia.

Before the planned meeting Mr Reagan invited the leaders of America's principal allies to assemble in New York for a pre-summit conference. President Mitterrand of France refused, but the leaders of

Britain, West Germany, Italy, Canada and Japan were there, and Mr Reagan was reported afterwards to have been extremely pleased with the support he was given, though it was known that some of his allies were uneasy at the apparent move away from arms control as America's major objective. The US was inclined to concentrate on issues on which it seemed to have the advantage, such as regional conflicts, human rights and bilateral matters like cultural exchanges and the resumption of air links. But Mr Reagan made it clear that he was not going to Geneva to get agreement at any price, and he let it be known that he would be quite prepared to leave without much significant progress provided the dialogue could be continued.

In the event that was about what he had to settle for. He and Mr Gorbachev spent more than fifteen hours in a variety of meetings, of which five were spent on their own (with their interpreters) in what Mr Reagan subsequently described as 'our fireside summit', but little of substance was achieved. Both men agreed that their meeting had made the world a safer place, and a joint statement (see DOCUMENTS) pledged that the arms control negotiations would be speeded up and that there should be a 50 per cent cut in nuclear arms by each side, but did not go into the problem of what should be counted in the 50 per cent. There was agreement on cultural exchanges but, as Mr Reagan said in his report to Congress on 21 November, there was no meeting of minds on fundamentals. Probably the most significant accomplishment was the agreement that the two men should meet at least twice more—first in the USA, and then in the Soviet Union. Towards the end of December it was revealed that Mr Gorbachev had written to President Reagan offering to allow American inspectors to visit Soviet underground nuclear test sites, and urging the President to resume negotiations on the banning of all such tests. The US welcomed the offer. It had already issued an unconditional invitation to Soviet experts to visit American sites, a spokesman for the White House said, and Soviet agreement for reciprocal visits would certainly be welcome. At the same time the White House insisted that this was an entirely separate issue from the question of a nuclear test moratorium. At the end of the year it seemed that the atmosphere created by the summit had begun to dissipate, as the Russians accused the US of breaching the 1972 ABM Treaty in constructing a new 'phased-array' radar station in Greenland and in conducting an underground nuclear test in Nevada (which was not one of the treaty's named sites), while the US issued a new list of Soviet violations, and strongly denounced the continuing intervention in Afghanistan. Nonetheless the announcement that the two leaders would directly address each other's people on television on New Year's Day suggested that they wished to maintain an element of the goodwill achieved in Geneva in spite of lapses into the more conventional rhetoric.

For the United States an important development in the last month of the year was the signing of an agreement with Britain for participation in research aspects of the SDI. It was seen as a significant breakthrough in winning active allied cooperation in the project, and it was followed on 18 December by an equally welcome commitment from Bonn that West Germany would also take part, though in a less active manner.

A more persistent concern between the US and its allies throughout the year was the threat of protectionist trade legislation. The growing American trade deficit aroused increasing protectionist sentiment in Congress, and forced the President to order an inquiry into alleged unfair practices by some of America's trading partners. In September he asked for a list of possible counter-measures to be drawn up, although he said these would only be used as a last resort, and in December he vetoed restrictive legislation on textile imports because he did not want to trigger a wave of retaliatory action in other countries. In American eyes one of the worst offenders was Japan. When the Japanese Prime Minister, Mr Yasuhiro Nakasone, visited the US in January he undertook to work to open Japanese markets to American products in the hope of reducing the current imbalance of trade between the two countries, but this was not enough to stop the passage of Bills through Congress imposing tariffs and other barriers on some Japanese imports. Relations deteriorated later in the year as the Japanese promise to open its markets failed to materialize, and in September Mr Reagan warned that, although he would continue to support free trade, he would order retaliatory action against countries that restricted imports of American goods or gave their own exports an unfair advantage, by means of special subsidies or other devices, in the American market. In late December Japan agreed to make trade concessions worth $260 million to compensate the US for unfair trade practices, but there were many in Washington who doubted whether this would be enough to stem the protectionist tide in Congress, where several hundred restrictive trade Bills were still to be debated.

For Americans the most horrific episode of 1985 began on 15 June when a TWA Boeing 727 jet airliner with more than 100 Americans on board was hijacked by two Lebanese gunmen when on a scheduled flight from Athens to Rome. The plane was forced to fly to Beirut after the gunmen had stormed the cockpit and beaten several of the passengers. After releasing the women and children on board the pilot was then ordered to fly to Algiers and then back to Beirut, where one of the American passengers was shot dead. The hijackers demanded the release of 766 Shia internees held by Israel. President Reagan cut short his weekend at Camp David to preside over a meeting of the National Security Council, after which it was announced that the US would not negotiate with terrorists. It was also published in the American press, much to the Administration's alarm, that a unit of commandos known as the Delta Unit, specially trained in anti-terrorist operations, had been sent to the Mediterranean, though Administration spokesmen emphasised that the first priority was to secure the safe release of all the passengers. In Beirut, meanwhile, 39 American hostages were taken from the aircraft and hidden in the city, though five of them were paraded at a chaotic press conference in the airport transit lounge to declare that they and their fellow captives were alive and being well looked after.

It was a frustrating time for a President who had taken office at the end of the humiliating hostage crisis in Iran, and who found when confronted with a similar experience that he could do little more than had been done by his predecessor, Jimmy Carter. At a press conference in Washington Mr Reagan repeated that the US would never make concessions to terrorists, nor put pressure on other governments to give in to their demands. But he also said that the US limits had been reached, and announced that he was setting up a task force under Vice-President Bush to coordinate American and allied attempts to curb terrorists. 'We and our similarly threatened friends,' he said, 'must see what actions, military and otherwise, can be taken to end this increasingly violent and indiscriminate but purposeful affront to humanity.' When, after 18 days, the hostages were finally released, following the intervention of President Asad of Syria, and after Israel had freed some of the Shia internees, Mr Reagan repeated his call that the world should unite in taking decisive action against terrorists and the nations that sponsored and harboured them.

It was not the last experience of terrorism that America was to suffer during the year. When the Italian liner *Achille Lauro* was hijacked in October it was an American holidaymaker, Leon Klinghoffer, an elderly man confined to a wheelchair, who was shot and thrown overboard by the four gunmen who seized control of the ship. The gunmen, who appeared to be members of the PLO acting against orders, surrendered the liner to the Egyptian authorities but were themselves released by President Mubarak before he knew that they had killed a passenger. American fury turned to elation two days later when an Egyptian airliner flying the terrorists out of the country was intercepted by American fighters and forced to land in Sicily, but President Reagan's request for the extradition of the four men to America was turned down by the Italian Government (see p. 138). The US also failed to persuade the Italians to hold the man they believed to have master-minded the hijacking of the liner, Muhammad Abbas. Relations between the US and both Egypt and Italy were soured by these incidents. The Italian Prime Minister protested at the American attempts to force Italy to hand over the four terrorists, and President Mubarak accused the US of stabbing him in the back by intercepting a civilian Egyptian airliner. For its part the US Administration was incensed with both Italy and Egypt for failing to support its actions against international terrorism, though it was swift to express its support for Egypt in November when Egyptian commandos stormed a hijacked Egyptian airliner in Malta. It was later revealed that the US had offered to send its Delta Unit to help—an offer that President Mubarak turned down—and had intensified its own aerial and electronic surveillance of Libya, which the US regarded as a prime instigator of terrorism and haven for international terrorists.

As in previous years, relations with near neighbours in Central America were discomforting during most of 1985, though in El Salvador, at least, the American Administration was able to find some grounds for optimism. When President José Duarte visited Washington in May US officials found him considerably more relaxed, and though the civil war continued the Salvadorian armed forces seemed to have taken a firmer grip. Later in the year President Reagan was able to boast that it was one of his Administration's proudest accomplishments that it had turned round a desperate situation in Central America. Speaking at a Republican fund-raising dinner in California he said that this had happened slowly and quietly, with little recognition. 'When we got to Washington, the question on everyone's lips was "Will El Salvador fall to the Communists?" Today the question is "Will democracy win in Nicaragua?" And tomorrow the question will be "How soon?" '

There was some presidential hyperbole in the claim, at least as regards Nicaragua, where only American support for the Contra guerrilla movement kept the Sandinista regime from imposing one-party rule and, so the US Administration feared, exporting arms to revolutionary left-wing parties throughout Central America. The Administration's policy of providing covert aid to the Contras was not universally supported within the US, and the President was rebuffed when he asked Congress for $14 million to keep the action going against the Sandinistas. A sudden announcement by President Daniel Ortega of Nicaragua that he was declaring an arms freeze and reducing the number of Cuban military advisers in his country was seen by the US Administration as a token gesture designed to influence Congress, though President Reagan came up with a gesture of his own a few days later when he suggested that there should be a ceasefire in the fighting between the Contras and government forces, to be followed by peace talks in which the Church would act as mediator. The President further proposed that if the Sandinistas agreed to his plan the $14 million he wanted from Congress would be used for humanitarian purposes instead of military aid, for a period of 60 days; if there was no agreement after that time the fund could be used for arms.

Congress was not impressed with the proposal, and though the Senate voted by 53 to 46 in its favour on 23 April it was rejected in the House of Representatives later the same day by 248 votes to 180. The President was thus deprived of his $14 million, though he declared that he would return again and again to Congress with proposals to aid the Contras, and he ordered an immediate review of possible political, economic and other measures that might be taken to bring further pressure to bear on the Nicaraguan Government. On 1 May he signed an executive order, which did not require congressional approval, imposing a total embargo on

trade with Nicaragua, suspension of landing rights in the US for Nicaraguan ships and aircraft, and termination of the treaty of friendship,
commerce and navigation between the two countries. The President
declared that he had taken this action because the Sandinista Government had become a threat to the security of the region and to the security
and foreign policy of the United States. The Administration, he said, was
declaring a national emergency to deal with that threat. The US used its
veto in the UN Security Council later in the month to block a resolution
regretting the imposition of the trade embargo, and refused to respond to
a request from twenty-four Latin American nations to lift the embargo,
which they said was accentuating tension in Central America.

In the following month the Administration was pleased to discover
that opinion within Congress appeared to be swinging in favour of its
request for funds, largely because a visit to Moscow by President Ortega
had resulted in the signing of an economic aid agreement between the
Soviet Union and Nicaragua. Both Houses voted this time in favour of
allowing food, clothing and other 'non-lethal' aid to be sent to the
Contras, a sum of $27 million for this purpose being released in three
instalments over a nine-month period. The CIA and the Defense Department were barred from dispensing the aid, but Congress allowed the CIA
some continuing involvement in the conflict by agreeing that the agency
could carry out information-gathering operations.

President Reagan's Administration was slow to respond to events in
South Africa during the year, and certainly seemed to lag behind the
swell of public and congressional opinion. A visit to South Africa in
January by Senator Edward Kennedy, accompanied by a press corps
numbered in hundreds, drew public attention to what Mr Kennedy called
'the outrages of apartheid', and he was one of the sponsors of a number of
Bills put forward in the Senate for the imposition of sanctions against
South Africa and the abandonment of the Administration's policy of
'constructive engagement'. Mr Reagan tried for a while to defend his
attempts at quiet diplomacy against the calls for stronger action, but the
violence in South Africa during the summer prompted the House of
Representatives to pass a sanctions Bill in August and the Senate to
prepare a similar one, though this was not voted on before the summer
recess.

Faced with the prospect of a Bill he would probably have to veto the
President decided, before the Senate reassembled, to pre-empt the legislation. He signed an executive order imposing selective sanctions against
South Africa, including the banning of the sale of computers to the police
and security agencies enforcing apartheid, prohibition of the sale of
nuclear technology, the stopping of all loans to the South African government except those which would benefit all races, consultation with GATT
parties about halting the import of krugerrand gold coins, and enforcing
on American firms with more than 25 employees in South Africa a code of

conduct, known as the Sullivan principles, on the treatment of black workers. At the same time the President announced that he was sending back Mr Herman Nickel, the US ambassador to Pretoria who had been withdrawn three months earlier, with a letter to President Botha 'underlining our grave view of the current crisis and our assessment of what is needed to restore confidence abroad and to move from confrontation to negotiation.' Though he emphasised that the US believed apartheid to be wrong, and was united in hoping for the day when it would be no more, he said that the US was still trying to help South Africa, which was not a totalitarian society and which had begun the process of change. He said his policy towards the country now was one of 'active' constructive engagement.

The US found itself in some difficulty with Spain during the year because of that country's determination to reduce the number of American troops based there (see p. 162). Mr Reagan's visit to Madrid during his May journey through Europe was accompanied by almost continuous street demonstrations protesting at his presence and Spain's membership of Nato, but he promised while there that talks about the future of the American military presence would be started quickly. The first round of talks evidently did not move fast enough for the Spanish Prime Minister, Señor Felipe González, who warned that if a reduction of American troops did not take place through negotiations 'it will take place by decision of this Government.' In December, following two days of difficult talks in Madrid, the US agreed to negotiate on an 'adjustment' of its military presence during the first half of 1986. A joint statement noted that a phased reduction of the US military presence would be based 'on the assumption by Spain's armed forces of specific responsibilities and missions currently undertaken by the US', while maintaining the 'overall defence capability and level of security for both countries and their allies.'

Relations with China continued to move slightly forward and a shade backwards in 1985, as they had in most recent years. When President Li visited the US in July he had a constructive meeting with President Reagan which was reflected in the signing of a long-delayed agreement enabling American companies to take part in the development of China's nuclear power programme though not, as was emphasised on the American side, in its nuclear weapons programme. At the same time China was concerned at moves in Congress to reduce textile quotas, and as always its representatives raised the question of Taiwan. They brought it up again when Vice-President Bush visited Beijing in October. Mr Bush reported that he saw no new urgency among Chinese leaders on the Taiwan question, though there was no doubting Chinese frustration at the slow pace of American reductions in arms sales to Taiwan.

Following on its withdrawal from the UN Educational, Scientific and Cultural Organization in 1984, largely because of its extravagance, the

US in 1985 decided to try to instil a sense of fiscal responsibility in the UN itself. The initiative came from Senator Nancy Kassebaum, who sponsored an amendment to the Act authorizing money for the State Department to the effect that the US should cut its mandatory contribution to the UN budget from a quarter of the total to a fifth, unless the UN changed its Charter to give members a vote on budget matters proportionate to their contributions. The Kassebaum Amendment was accepted by Congress, though opposed by the Administration, and the State Department warned the UN in December that unless weighted voting on the UN budget was achieved by October 1986 the US would have to cut its contribution from 25 per cent to less than 20 per cent.

Chapter 2

CANADA

THE Progressive Conservative Party (PC) under Brian Mulroney passed its first year in office in 1985. Supported by a massive majority in the House of Commons (211 of 282 seats) after its dramatic election victory in September 1984, the new Government moved cautiously, even hesitantly, to implement its campaign promises. The Prime Minister was instrumental in setting the tone for the Administration. Personable and assured, Mulroney dominated his Cabinet, yet gave the impression of not pointing clear directions for his Government. He tended to retreat from unpopular decisions and failed to take a strong stand on issues which were found to be controversial. His deep desire to be popular across the country weakened his credibility and made him susceptible to pressures from a variety of interests.

In relations with the ten provinces Mulroney was more successful, devoting his considerable talents to conciliation rather than continuing the confrontational approach of his predecessor, Pierre Trudeau. Through this means he achieved important accords on resources utilization and energy pricing with provinces in the West and on the Atlantic coast. He used his Quebec background to smooth over points of friction between Quebec and the central government.

Not surprisingly, Mulroney's mixed record during his first year in office was reflected in the public opinion polls. The PCs enjoyed the confidence of 58 per cent of decided voters when they came to power, the once-dominant Liberals only 21 per cent. The socialist New Democratic Party (NDP) stood at 20 per cent. Fifteen months later the Conservatives and the Liberals found themselves tied in the opinion standings with 38·5 per cent each, the NDP moving little at 22 per cent. The Liberals moved ahead of the PCs in Ontario and Quebec, while the Conservatives remained strong in the Atlantic region and in the West.

An immediate objective of the Mulroney Government was to dismantle economic structures put in place by the previous Liberal regime. This emphasis reflected the new Administration's desire to give freer rein to private enterprise at home and to promote more trade and investment with the United States. Early in its term the Government had announced the termination of an agency set up in 1974 to screen foreign investment, mostly from the United States, entering Canada (see AR 1984, p. 78). This plan was carried out in 1985 and a new body was established to encourage, rather than scrutinize, foreign investment. In March the Government moved to clear away the structure of regulations in the energy field, the National Energy Program (NEP), another inheritance from the Trudeau years. The NEP, designed to foster a larger Canadian participation in the oil and gas industry, had never been popular in the Western oil-producing provinces and had been seen as discriminatory by the Reagan Administration. Now an agreement between Ottawa and Alberta, Saskatchewan and British Columbia, called the Western Accord, freed the price of Canadian oil, allowing it to move towards world levels. At the same time the federal Government removed many of its taxes and royalties on oil and natural gas. A new regime for natural gas prices was created, allowing the Western provinces to sell gas to the US at market prices, rather than at a previous artificial level based on the cost of shipping it to Toronto.

Another energy bargain was struck with Newfoundland on 11 February. This ended a long-standing dispute concerning the exploitation of off-shore hydrocarbon resources. Newfoundland was given equal representation with Ottawa, which owned the resources, on a management board set up to control the pace and manner of off-shore development. The new agreement, called the Atlantic Accord, also allowed Newfoundland to tax the resources as if they had been found on land. These measures went some distance towards relieving discontent with the central Government's economic policies which had existed in the West and in Atlantic Canada.

The Canadian economy performed more strongly in 1985 than had been expected. A growth rate of 4·5 per cent was realized, resulting in a gross national product of Can.$458,300 million at annual rates. Inflation continued at low levels, the consumer price index in November showing a 4 per cent increase over the previous twelve months. The recovery was based on a strong demand at home for automobiles, houses and home entertainment equipment, combined with export sales that declined over the summer but picked up sharply in the third quarter. The unemployment rate, which showed a downward tendency in the months following March, stood at 10·2 per cent in November.

Finance Minister Michael Wilson presented his first Budget on 23 May. Net spending was slightly reduced while revenues were increased, resulting in a forecast reduction of about Can.$1,100 million in the deficit for 1985–86. A special 10 per cent surtax on incomes of over Can.$30,000 was imposed for the next 18 months. A controversial plan to de-index, partially, federal old-age pensions and family allowances was outlined in the Budget. Senior citizens reacted strongly and on 27 June the Minister retreated from his scheme, while continuing the restraint on family allowances.

The new Government's legislative accomplishments in its first parliamentary session, running from 5 November 1984 to 28 June 1985, were unremarkable. Forty-nine Bills were approved, the majority being housekeeping measures drafted by the previous Administration. An important human rights measure was enacted. This concerned the removal of a section in the Indian Act which had deprived Indian women, but not Indian men, of their native status when they married non-Indians. Passage of the amendment meant that about 16,000 Indian women and 40,000 of their children gained the right to return to native reserves. The change had been strenuously opposed by the Indian bands, which feared it would lead to the overpopulating of the reserves.

Mulroney's Cabinet of 40 persons, the largest in Canada's history, experienced some changes during the year. The most prominent departure was that of the Minister of National Defence, Robert Coates, who offered his resignation on 12 February after his judgment had been questioned following a visit to a seedy night club near a Canadian forces base in West Germany. The Minister was replaced by one of Mulroney's strongest colleagues, Erik Nielson, who held the honorific title of Deputy Prime Minister and was in charge of a group looking into ways of cutting government spending. In September there were two more resignations, one temporary, one permanent. Marcel Masse, Minister of Communications, resigned from the Cabinet when he learned that he was under investigation for alleged improprieties in the reporting of election expenses. When Masse was cleared of the charges, he was reappointed to the Cabinet on 30 November. The other Minister, John Fraser from British Columbia, heading the fisheries department, admitted overruling his fisheries inspectors in permitting a consignment of rancid canned tuna fish to be placed on the market. The Minister had acted to safeguard jobs at a New Brunswick fish-packing plant but an outcry in Parliament compelled his resignation.

Two major provinces changed their political complexions in 1985. In Ontario the Progressive Conservative Party, after almost 42 years of uninterrupted power, was swept out of office by an alliance between the Liberal and New Democratic Parties. A new Conservative leader had been chosen in January. He took the party into a general election on 2 May in which it lost 20 seats. The two opposition parties combined to back a successful vote of no-confidence which led to the defeat of the PC government on 18 June. David Peterson, the Liberal leader, in accordance with an agreed plan of cooperation with the NDP, was sworn in as

Ontario's 20th premier on 26 June. Quebec saw the defeat of the separatist Parti Québécois (PQ) government, which had been in office since 1976. Its founder, René Lévesque, worn out by dissension within the party on whether or not to emphasize independence at the next election, resigned his post on 20 June. He was succeeded by a colleague, Pierre-Marc Johnson, who did his best to play down separation from Canada as an option for Quebec. Leading the PQ into an election on 2 December, the new premier suffered an humiliating defeat. His party won only 23 seats, while the Liberals under Robert Bourassa, the leader whom Lévesque had ousted as premier nine years before, captured the remaining 99. Bourassa formed a cabinet and took office as premier on 12 December.

In Alberta, where the Progressive Conservatives had governed since 1971, the premier, Peter Lougheed, stepped down, to be succeeded by a former cabinet colleague, Donald Getty, on 1 November. Getty's position was not in doubt as the PC held 75 of the 79 seats in the legislature. Newfoundland held an election on 2 April. Fresh from his success in negotiating the Atlantic Accord, Premier Brian Peckford called for a vote of confidence for his PC administration. He received it but not in full measure, his party winning 36 of the legislature's 52 seats, a decline from the 44 it had previously held. There was also a change of government in Yukon Territory, where the NDP took over control of the territorial legislature in voting held on 14 May. Antony Penikett became head of the elected administration in the federal territory, which did not yet possess the status of a province.

Canadians debated the benefits and costs of free trade with the United States during 1985. Purchasing 78 per cent of Canada's exports and supplying 70 per cent of its imports, the United States was Canada's dominant market. Protectionist measures before the US Congress threatened this trade. When Prime Minister Mulroney met President Reagan in Quebec City, 17–18 March, they discussed the subject, agreeing to ask officials to investigate and remove 'specific impediments to trade' between the two nations. Reagan assured Mulroney that he would work against the passage of protectionist legislation. Mulroney expressed his strong interest in what he called 'freer' or 'enhanced' trade. (Historically the phrase 'free trade' in relation to the United States had been politically sensitive in Canada, since to many it had implied a loss of political independence.) On 26 September Mulroney formally requested the President to secure approval from Congress for trade negotiations to commence.

While a royal commission on the future of the Canadian economy appointed by former Prime Minister Trudeau reported in favour of free trade, and a joint House of Commons-Senate committee took the same stand, Canadians were divided on the consequences of the move. Opposed was the trade union movement, while Ontario, the province containing most of Canada's manufacturing, was worried about the future of its industry. The other nine provinces were in favour of the plan, as were important elements in the business community. There were large questions to be resolved before negotiations started. Were the talks to include all aspects of commercial interaction or were sectors such as motor vehicles and parts, the subject of a successful trade agreement of 1965, to be excluded? What would be the status of sensitive cultural areas such as communications and book publishing? The United States wanted all aspects of trade and investment to be placed on the bargaining table while many Canadians felt there should be a selection before discussion. The provinces, controlling natural resources, were also anxious to be consulted in any negotiation. Under these circumstances the talks were expected to be protracted and complicated.

Air defence was another topic of conversation between the two North American countries in 1985. Canada allowed the continued testing of Cruise missiles over its northern territory in late February. It also agreed to join with the US in improving, at a cost of Can.$1,500 million, the two countries' northern radar warning system. It endorsed research on President Reagan's Strategic Defense Initiative (SDI) but declined to approve the development and deployment of the system. Government agencies were not to be permitted to participate in SDI research, although there was no official ban on private groups in Canada bidding for research contracts.

The legal status of the waters around Canada's Arctic islands, including the historic Northwest Passage, was also under active scrutiny in 1985. When the United States sent a coast-guard icebreaker *Polar Sea* through the ice-clogged passage in early August the Mulroney Government did not formally protest. However, on 10 September the Government issued a statement reaffirming Canada's claims to sovereignty in the Arctic archipelago. Noting Soviet submarine activity in the Arctic, as well as the *Polar Sea* voyage, the Government announced that as of 1 January 1986 straight baselines would be proclaimed around the islands, giving the enclosed waters a protected 'internal' status under international law. A large and powerful Class 8 icebreaker would be built to give Canada access to all parts of the vast archipelago. Military surveillance flights over the Arctic would be increased and there would be naval operations in the Eastern Arctic in 1986. While the statement welcomed Canada-US defence cooperation in the Arctic, it made clear that such cooperation would have to be based on a recognition by the United States of Canada's sovereignty in the area.

The Mulroney Government vigorously condemned apartheid in South Africa, in the Canadian Parliament and at the United Nations, where both Prime Minister Mulroney and External Affairs Minister Joseph Clark spoke at the autumn session of the General Assembly. Canada imposed trade sanctions against South Africa and agreed not to process uranium ore from Namibia beyond 1988, when current contracts expired. At the Commonwealth heads of government meeting at Nassau in October (see Pt. XI, Ch. 2, and DOCUMENTS), Mulroney played a notable role in bridging the gap between Britain and African and Asian members on a response to apartheid. Canada appointed a representative to the committee of 'eminent persons' charged with the task of opening a dialogue on racial questions with Pretoria.

Chapter 3

LATIN AMERICA

ARGENTINA—BOLIVIA—BRAZIL—CHILE—COLOMBIA—ECUADOR—PARAGUAY—
PERU—URUGUAY—VENEZUELA—CUBA—THE DOMINICAN REPUBLIC AND
HAITI—CENTRAL AMERICA AND PANAMA—MEXICO

ARGENTINA

ON 19 February, to general surprise, President Raúl Alfonsín dismissed the Minister of the Economy, Bernardo Grinspun, and appointed Secretary of Planning Juan Sourrouille in his place. After the IMF decided to cut off further financial aid in March, Sourrouille, in consultation with leading Argentine economists, prepared a dramatic new economic initiative, which came into effect on 14 June, by which time inflation, which had been 688 per cent to the end of 1984, had risen from an annualized rate of 800 per cent to over 1000 per cent. The centre-piece was the introduction of a new currency, the austral, and the simultaneous introduction of comprehensive wage and price controls. Meanwhile the choice by the Peronist opposition of the populist leader of the province of Buenos Aires, Herminio Iglesias, as party secretary in February resulted in the new leadership's being repudiated by the majority of Peronist senators, deputies and congressmen.

On 8 March, in a significant reorganization of the military establishment, an air force officer, Brigadier Teodoro Waldner, was promoted to head the joint chiefs of staff. Dissension in the armed forces arose from several causes, but above all from the continuing prosecution of nine senior military officers accused of crimes against humanity in the course of the 'dirty war' of 1977–79. On 25 October, in face of right-wing terrorist incidents, the President had to impose a 60-day state of siege. On 9 December ex-President Jorge Videla and Admiral Massera were sentenced to life imprisonment, and ex-President Viola, Admiral Armando Lambruschini and Air Force Brigadier Orlando Agosti to 17 years', 8 years' and $4\frac{1}{2}$ years' imprisonment respectively. General Leopoldo

Galtieri, Admiral Jorge Anaya and Air Force Brigadier General Basilio Lami Dozo, accused of mishandling the Falklands war, were acquitted on all charges. By then inflation had dropped from over 30 per cent a month to 2 per cent, and the Government had demonstrated at the mid-term elections held on 3 November that it had held on well to its public support. In an 84 per cent turnout, the ruling Radicals won 20 of the 24 electoral districts and obtained 43.5 per cent of the poll (against 48 per cent in 1983) and 130 seats, a gain of one seat in the Chamber of Deputies. The Peronists polled 34.5 per cent and won 104 seats, a loss of 8.

In March the Senate approved, by 23 votes to 22, the Peace and Friendship Treaty with Chile (see AR 1984, p. 81). Relations with the United Kingdom over the Falkland Islands remained frozen, despite the high priority attached to a settlement by Foreign Minister Dante Caputo, who in December 1984 had described British pledges to the islanders as 'arrogant'. During a three-day state visit to Washington in March, President Alfonsín blamed British 'intransigence' for lack of further negotiations, and tried to persuade President Reagan to exert pressure on Mrs Thatcher. Strong protests were voiced at the opening of Mount Pleasant airport on East Falkland in May. The British Government's decision in July unilaterally to lift its trade embargo was dismissed as irrelevant, though in conversations with the Leader of the Opposition, Mr Kinnock, in Paris in September, in the course of a 12-day visit to Western Europe, the President subsequently offered unilaterally to end the formal state of hostilities maintained by successive Argentine Governments since 1982, if talks with an open agenda could follow. At the United Nations in December, the omission of the word 'sovereignty' from the pro-Argentine resolution on the islands brought an even bigger majority than ever in its support.

BOLIVIA

Inflation in 1984 exceeded 2,700 per cent, and took a dramatic leap into five digits in January, while, with the economy in disarray, the moratorium on the national debt continued. An indefinite general strike called by the Bolivian Workers' Federation (COB) began on 8 March, led by miners demanding a truly socialist government, price controls and the nationalization of the banks and mines. On 20 March President Hernán Siles Zuazo deployed troops and tanks on the streets of La Paz in response to a call by Juan Lechín for the workers to prepare for armed struggle. Four days later the miners accepted a four-fold wage increase.

Elections postponed from 16 June to 14 July on account of the strike were overshadowed by rumours of impending coups and accusations of fraud on all sides. Former President Hugo Banzer Suárez, whose massive borrowing during his 1971–78 period of office was largely responsible for the country's serious economic position, obtained, as candidate of the right-wing Nationalist Democratic Action (ADN), 28·6 per cent of the popular vote to 26·4 per cent for the candidate of the centre-right wing of the Historic Nationalist Revolutionary Movement (MNR-H), Dr Victor Paz Estenssoro, President and leader of the Revolutionary Government of 1952–56. The candidate of the left-wing Movement of the Revolutionary Left (MIR) gained 8·8 per cent while the governing Intransigents (MNR-I) failed to gain 5 per cent. In the second ballot, however, the Congress on 5 August exercised its constitutional right to choose among the three leading candidates Dr Paz, who, with the support of the smaller parties, received 94 votes to only 51 for General Banzer, whose partisans then tried to storm the building. The armed forces stated that they would abide by the decision, and on 6 August Dr Paz took office in the first constitutional succession for 25 years, by which time inflation was running at 20,561 per cent annually. He immediately proclaimed a state of 'national disaster' and called for work, discipline and a campaign against corruption.

In face of a new general strike, a state of siege was imposed (19 August). On 29 August the Government, in the most drastic programme to fill an empty treasury yet attempted in Latin America, ended currency controls and scrapped subsidies. Exports of tin were down by a third in the first quarter of the year, and the world debt crisis in October helped at least to consolidate a crisis agreement with the ADN. Meanwhile the earnings from the cocaine trade were widely believed to be running at some $2,000 million a year, greater than all other exports put together.

BRAZIL

On 15 January the Electoral College chose the opposition candidate, Sr Tancredo Neves, by 480 votes to 180 over the military-backed candidate of the Social Democratic Party (PDS), Sr Paulo Maluf. In February the IMF cancelled the payment due in March, ending talks between Brazil and creditor banks. On 12 March Sr Neves announced a conservative Cabinet, in which his Brazilian Democratic Movement (PMDB) held 14 seats, his nephew, Francisco Neves Dornelles, former head of the Internal Revenue Service, taking the key post of Minister of Finance, and 39-year old João Sayad that of Planning. Four seats went to the new Liberal Front of the outgoing Vice-President, Sr Aureliano Chaves, who became Minister of Mining and Energy, and one to the PDS of which it was a splinter group.

But, in a malign turn of fate, on inauguration day the 75-year-old President-elect, whose personality and record of opposition had made the coalition possible, was taken into hospital suffering from neglected peritonitis. Hence the 55-year-old Vice-President, José Sarney, former chairman of the PDS, who had served the military government for 20 years, was sworn in as acting President. After a series of further operations the President-elect lapsed into a coma and died (see OBITUARY). In July Sr Dornelles announced a new package of cuts designed to reduce the public-sector deficit. Efforts to promote solidarity among the state governors, however, were vitiated by rising pressure among the rival contenders for office, led by Leonel Brizola, Governor of Rio de Janeiro, for direct elections to be brought forward to 1986, and a secession of deputies from the PMDB led by the Minister of Communications, Sr Antonio Carlos Magalhães. On 26 August Sr Dornelles resigned, his austerity programme undermined by the President's support for growth in a television address in July, and was replaced by a protégé of Sr Fayad, Sr Dilson Funaro, aged 52, president of the National Bank for Economic and Social Development. The president of the Central Bank, Antonio Carlos Lemgruber, who had just assured international bankers, in face of all the facts, that Brazil would not need any new loans in 1985 or 1986, also resigned.

Meanwhile audits ordered by the Minister of Industry and Commerce, Roberto Gusmão, uncovered evidence of extensive corruption in three major government agencies, the Brazilian Coffee Institute (IBC), the Sugar and Alcohol Institute (IAA) and the national tourist agency, Embratur. As elsewhere in Latin America the return to civilian rule was accompanied by a sharp increase in labour militancy. Brazil's first land reform law, signed on 10 October, projecting a four-year programme for the distribution of 106 million acres, fell short of what had been hoped, but was still a significant landmark. In the municipal elections on 15 November, the ruling PMDB won the mayoralties of 17 of the 23 state capitals, but Senator Fernando Henrique Cardoso, the eminent social scientist, was defeated for the mayoralty of São Paulo by the 69-year-old populist Jãnio Quadros, whose sudden resignation after only seven months as President in 1961 (see AR 1961, p. 195) had helped accelerate the breakdown of the Second Republic.

CHILE

The Government of General Augusto Pinochet (who was increasingly under criticism for nepotism and corruption) remained isolated, both at home and abroad, where the President's refusal to have dealings with the weak and divided Democratic Alliance (AD) was causing concern to the United States. In February, when the President renewed the state of siege imposed on 6 November 1984, and 240 university students were arrested, the resignation of the liberalizing Minister of the Interior, Sr Sergio Onofre Jarpa, was accepted. He was replaced by a non-political businessman, Sr Ricardo Garcia. Bomb incidents had become commonplace, and towards the end of March a number of murders, including that of the president of the Santiago Teachers Association, Sr Manuel Guerrero, pointed to the renewal of right-wing violence against suspected opponents of the regime. The government-controlled media minimized the significance of the major earthquake which struck more than 1,000 miles of the Pacific coastline around Valparaiso on 3 March; though it killed only 25 people, it destroyed more than 170,000 homes and was a substantial additional setback.

Despite pressure from Washington and the Vatican, the state of siege was renewed for 90 days on 6 May, only to be abruptly lifted the following month to facilitate agreement on the $7,800 million package agreement with Chile's creditor banks. In July the terrorists of the Manuel Rodríguez Patriotic Front (FPMR) turned their attention towards the United States, whose request for an extension of the runway on Easter Island was viewed in Chilean circles as the prelude to construction of a permanent base. Public opinion polls showed both fear of violence and lack of confidence in the Government. On 26 August representatives of eleven parties, supported by the Archbishop of Santiago, Cardinal Juan Francisco Fresno, signed a 'National Agreement for a Transition to Full Democracy' calling for the immediate restoration of civil liberties. The Government prevented the broadcast of the Cardinal's sermon on the twelfth anniversary of the coup of 1973, which had been preceded by protests on 5 and 6 September in which ten died and over 700 were arrested, while Church sources reported a new wave of kidnapping, apparently by 'death squads', in the shanty towns. At the beginning of November a 24-hour student strike coincided with a new wave of bombings, one aimed at the President himself.

COLOMBIA

The uneasy peace (see AR 1984, p. 86) did not last long. On 9 January General Miguel Vega Uribe was appointed Minister of Defence, with the task of eradicating the cocaine dealers, whose 'undeclared war' on the United States threatened even the life of its ambassador Lewis Tambs, and on 24 July resulted in the shooting in Bogotá of the examining magistrate investigating the assassination of the Minister of Justice. In February the Interior Minister, Sr Jaime Castro, made clear Government opposition to a reunion of the populist 19 April Movement (M-19) in their camp at Los Robles near Corinto, though in the 1984 talks it had conceded their right to retain arms. The M-19, whose leader, Ivan Marino Ospina, had been replaced by Alvaro Fayad, apparently in preparation for an electoral campaign, responded on 6 March by a 'temporary withdrawal' from the peace talks. For its part, the army, whose offensive on the M-19 base near Cali after the truce date had been halted by the President in December 1984, remained restive. Fire bombs in several major cities accompanied the Government's forceful response to a national one-day strike led by left-wing trade unions and backed by the M-19 and the pro-Soviet Revolutionary Armed Forces of Colombia (FARC), the largest guerrilla group. The FARC had gone furthest towards becoming a regular political party, renamed the Patriotic Union (UP), its candidate being Jacobo Arenas.

Then on 28 June the truce was finally broken by an M-19 attack on Génova (Quindío) in which 19 died. Further clashes at La Herrera (Tolima), Riofrío and Bolívar (Valle del Cauca) and elsewhere confirmed that M-19's commander, Carlos Pizarro León Gómez, had 'assumed the rupture of the truce by the army and the government'. The commander of the armed forces, General Augusto Moreno Guerrero, announced an all-out drive on the rebels, and on 29 August it claimed the life of Sr Marino Ospina in a raid on a flat in Cali. Neither Alvaro Gómez Hurtado, presidential candidate for the ruling Conservatives, nor Virgilio Barco for the Liberals was prepared to identify with the peace process, even before 6 November when troops using helicopter gunships and tanks gutted the interior of the Palace of Justice in the centre of Bogotá, killing the President of the Supreme Court, Dr Alfonso Reyes, and two of his colleagues, following its occupation by a group of the M-19, all of whom also perished.

Yet it was nature that had the last word in this dismal year, when before dawn on 14 November mudslides released by the eruption of the volcano Nevado del Ruiz, in the Department of Tolima, dormant since 1595, swept away the town of Armero with the loss of more than 25,000 lives (see also Pt. XIV, Chs 2 and 4). In the wake of these events the Government announced, on 24 November, the imposition of a national economic emergency.

ECUADOR

The newly-installed Government of President Leon Febres Cordero was challenged on 9–10 January by a 48-hour general strike, in which five died, and by pressure from Congress in February to approve a 66 per cent public-sector pay rise. The subsequent defection to the Government of seven opposition deputies, however, gave the Administration a one-vote majority, and in July the President reconvened Congress and secured a realignment which chose as its president the 29-year-old Averroes Bucaram, leader of the Concentration of Popular Forces (CFP), in place of his opponent Sr Raúl Baca. Meanwhile the development of a new guerrilla movement, the Alfaro Vive (AVC), linked to the M-19 of Colombia, was confirmed, when a kidnapped banker, Nahim Isaias, was killed along with four guerrillas on 6 September in a rescue attempt personally directed by the President, who acknowledged full responsibility. Abroad the Government's sudden withdrawal from the Lima Group and the breaking-off of diplomatic relations with Managua (11 October) were widely regarded as a move inspired by the United States and designed to put an end to the Contadora peace process in Central America. But with the successful rescheduling of the national debt in November the main continuing problem at home was the decline in Opec oil production and prices.

In March a massive brush fire started on Isabela Island in the Galápagos, possibly as the result of volcanic activity, and raged out of control for weeks, threatening with extinction the unique wildlife, including the giant turtles that had inspired Darwin's *Origin of Species*.

PARAGUAY

Reports that it was harbouring the Auschwitz prison-camp doctor, Dr Josef Mengele, who took Paraguayan citizenship in 1959, forced President Alfredo Stroessner to cancel a state visit to West Germany planned for July. But the discovery in June of what appeared to be Dr Mengele's body in Brazil, and evidence that it was in that country that he had been living, strengthened the position of the President and his Ministers.

The Government's own stand on human rights was weak. Opposition leaders of the Movimiento Popular Colorado (MOPOCO) were detained in January, and accusations of the use of torture were made against the Interior Ministry by the Radical Liberal Party (PLR) in February, when the Febreristas (PRF) held a legal public rally in Asunción. On 14 May the National Accord (AN) of the five principal opposition parties held a major rally in the capital to demand a return to democracy, and student movements became increasingly restive; protests against tuition fee increases were broken up on 20 June by police with electric prods. A concerted attack was made on the remaining independent media: a new weekly '*Nuestro Tiempo*' was immediately closed in July and Radio Ñandutí was closed in August and its director, Humberto Rubín, subsequently charged with subversion. When in September 'militants' backed the candidature of the President's secretary, Mario Abdo Benítez, for the vice-presidency of the ruling Colorado Party, this was seen as heralding the succession of the President's son Gustavo.

More detentions of MOPOCO leaders followed in the run-up to the municipal elections in October in which the ruling Colorado Party claimed 701,274 votes (88 per cent) to 61,481 (7·7 per cent) for the Liberal Party (PL), and 24,210 (3·0 per cent) for the PLR. The National

Accord boycotted the elections, which the Liberal Party leader, Joaquín Atilio Burgos, said had been characterized by 'scandalous fraud'.

PERU

The Sendero Luminoso (SL) opened 1985 with an attack on a Lima army club, a major attack on Cerro de Pasco on 28 January paralysed copper production, and the visit of Pope John Paul II was marked by a daring attack on 4 February which blacked out the capital. As electioneering began, the Government, with inflation in 1984 at 111·5 per cent, announced the introduction of a new monetary unit, the inti, worth 1,000 soles. On 5 March more than 300,000 public-sector workers went on strike, demanding default if necessary to maintain their salaries.

In the elections held on 14 April 36-year-old Alan Garcia of the Alianza Popular Revolucionaria Americana (APRA) gained 47·7 per cent of the vote, defeating the candidate of the United Left (IU), Alfonso Barrantes Lingan, who conceded victory and thus averted a run-off election. Hence on 28 July, despite continuing economic crisis, strikes and car-bombings, President Belaúnde became the first civilian President of Peru since 1912 to hand over power to an elected successor, and President Garcia the first member of APRA to assume the presidential office. In a bold initiative, he immediately offered an amnesty to the SL, and limited foreign debt repayments to 10 per cent of exports, while calling for renegotiation of the debt directly with his creditors, thus by-passing the IMF.

In the declaration of Lima, signed on 29 July by the Presidents of Argentina, Colombia, Bolivia, the Dominican Republic, Panama, Peru and Uruguay, and by representatives of Costa Rica, Cuba, Ecuador, Guatemala, Haiti, Honduras, Mexico, Nicaragua and Venezuela, other Latin American states backed the President's view that protectionist trade policies of the industrialized nations were responsible for the region's serious and worsening crisis. In August the sol was devalued, maximum interest rates fixed, salaries of public sector workers raised and unnecessary official expenditure curtailed. At the same time more than 1,400 people were detained in a new offensive against the SL, 31 senior police officers were dismissed (19 August) as part of a new attack on the cocaine trade, and the exploration contracts of three US oil companies were cancelled. In September the head of the joint chiefs of staff, Air Force General César Enrico Praelli, resigned shortly before the dismissal of two generals for involvement in peasant massacres. On 23 September the President told the UN General Assembly that Latin America faced the choice of 'debt or democracy'.

An attack by the SL on APRA headquarters on 7 October, in which three died, was followed by a new state of emergency in six Departments and the first reported defections from the movement. But Peru, with its loans declared 'value impaired' by the banks, was still in serious difficulties.

URUGUAY

President Gregorio Alvarez resigned on 11 February to pave the way for a return to civilian rule, and on 12 February the President of the Supreme Court, Dr Rafael Adieggo, was sworn in as interim President, while the army commander, General Hugo Medina, threatened a military coup if there were fresh trouble on the left. The new civilian Government of Dr Julio Sanguinetti took office as planned on 1 March after twelve years of military rule which left one of the highest per capita national debts in the world, unemployment at over 15 per cent and inflation at 50 per cent. The nine-member Cabinet had six members from the President's Colorado Party, with a 44-year-old economic liberal, Ricardo Zerbino, as Minister of Finance and the Economy. Of the Nationalists Enrique Iglesias agreed to serve as Foreign Minister and Raúl Ugarte as Minister of Public Health, and Juan Vicente Chiarino of the Catholic Civic Union as Minister of Defence.

Within hours the new President had legalized left-wing political groups. On 8 March the Chamber of Deputies approved by 86 votes to 5 an Amnesty Bill covering 267 political prisoners. The 193 released on 10 March included Raul Sendic, former Tupamaro leader, while 61 transferred to police custody pending review of murder charges included the founder of the Tupamaros, Jorge Manera Lluberas, and Antonio Mas Mas, who killed Dan Mitrione, the US police adviser (see AR 1970, p. 85).

The new Government immediately confronted a series of wage demands from the newly-legalized trade union confederations. On 26 August the President appealed on television for moderation, and a further strike on 19 September was unsuccessful, leading to a provisional agreement with the unions for a social compact in October. Meanwhile the President, who visited the United Nations at the end of September to appeal for restraint over the country's debt, was reported to have reached an agreement with General Medina for the exemplary punishment of the worst human rights violations, and the Nationalists supported the Government's plan to cut the armed forces by some 20 per cent.

VENEZUELA

Declining oil revenue continued to threaten the gains in international financial credibility achieved in September 1984. So the strict austerity programme of President Jaime Lusinchi was maintained despite complaints from the Venezuelan Workers Confederation (CTV), and the consumer price index, which had risen by 18·3 per cent in 1984, declined in the early part of the year through rigid application of price controls.

On 9 February it was announced that agreement had been reached with the Foreign Minister of Guyana, Rashleigh Jackson, on bilateral economic cooperation and on an invitation to the United Nations to mediate the long-running boundary dispute in which Venezuela had claimed some two-thirds of Guyana's national territory. Moves were made to lift restrictions on trade with Colombia, and on 14 June the two Presidents met on the Aracua River bridge to sign a series of agreements and confirm their common front on the Contadora initiative and the debt problem. The President, who remained cool toward Nicaragua, stated on 4 July that he intended to leave the nation's frontiers fully defined, and on 11 August he rejected the policy of repudiation of debts that had been advocated—but not followed—by President Fidel Castro of Cuba. On 1 October he met the President of Mexico and, in New York, US Secretary of State George Shultz.

CUBA

The return of 2,746 'excludables'—criminals and the mentally ill—sent to the United States after the 1980 Peruvian embassy crisis (see AR 1980, p. 85), began in January under an agreement signed in New York on 14 December 1984, by which the US agreed to take in return 3,000 political prisoners. President Castro continued to indicate his preparedness for improved relations with the new Reagan Administration, adding that Cuba was 'not impatient, nor anxious'. These moves were linked by commentators with the extraordinary session of the Central Committee held on 31 January which dismissed two senior officials of the department of political education. Subsequently, in reaction to Soviet quiescence in face of bellicose US statements on Nicaragua, President Castro neither attended the funeral of Konstantin Chernenko nor signed the book of condolences.

In June, shortly after Cabinet changes designed to replace old revolutionaries by young technocrats, the President made his first published reference to the succession, naming his 54-year-old brother, Raúl, Minister for the Revolutionary Armed Forces, as 'the best option'. Continuing stresses were shown by the decision on 3 July to postpone the Party Congress planned for December to February 1986. The visit of the Soviet Foreign Minister, Eduard Shevardnadze, at the end of October, moreover, was cool compared with those of the Presidents of Angola and Poland in the previous month, though the country remained heavily dependent on the Soviet Union, which was currently subsidizing its economy through fixed sugar contracts and the supply of oil for resale to the extent of some $4,100 million a year.

Economic growth in 1984 had been 7·4 per cent, but the country was heavily in debt, and President Castro took advantage of this to try to reassert his leadership in the region. In a rival summit to that of Cartagena, held from 31 July to 4 August, he urged other Latin American states to default, arguing that it would be in the interests of the creditors to do so, and dismissing President Garcia's plan of a debt ceiling as useless. Yet on 9 August banking sources confirmed that meanwhile both he and they had agreed to a rescheduling of Cuba's external debts to a total of some $85 million. In the last months of the year, however, drought damaged the sugar crop.

THE DOMINICAN REPUBLIC AND HAITI

On 24 January the Government of President Jorge Blanco in the DOMINICAN REPUBLIC implemented IMF-inspired price increases of up to 50 per cent on basic foods and 34 per cent on petrol, as troops stood by. At the third ministerial meeting of the eleven states of the Cartagena Group in Santo Domingo from 4 to 8 February, the President warned that the social pressures released by the debt crisis could yet undermine democracy, and a week later he announced a partial rollback in prices following two general strikes (28 January, 11 February) and rioting that left four dead. A third strike on 20 June was only partially successful, but on 9 July the President conceded a 32 per cent minimum pay rise to public service employees, whereupon the IMF threatened to withdraw its standby agreement. A 24-hour strike of judges on 2 July demanding a 70 per cent pay rise, which had forced the release of over 700 prisoners, continued. Though crop diversification had some success despite a prolonged drought, the crisis in sugar brought a sharp fall in export earnings.

HAITI's human-rights record was again certified by the Reagan Administration (though by no one else) as improving. 'Serious exceptions' included the assassination of two dissidents on 23 April and a third on 8 October, besides the disappearance of several more. In April prisoners arrested in November 1984 were released, but the revision of the 1983 constitution to create the post of Prime Minister and license political parties also enabled the President-for-life, whose position they had to accept, to depose mayors and nominate his successor. On 22 June a major demonstration occurred in Port-au-Prince. Widespread, independently-supported accusations of fraud followed the referendum on 22 July in which the Government claimed the changes were approved by 99·93 per cent of those voting. The following day an 80-year-old Belgian priest was beaten to death by the secret police, and three others expelled, leading to massive public protests backed openly by the Church. Roger

Lafontant, latterly Minister of Defence and Interior, was dismissed from the inner Cabinet, but at the year's end, following the death of school-children in demonstrations in November, the Government looked very insecure.

CENTRAL AMERICA AND PANAMA

The United States suspended bilateral talks with NICARAGUA in January, despite the inauguration of the new National Assembly and of President Daniel Ortega Saavedra on 9 and 10 January. The Government had offered amnesty to all (22 January) but refused to negotiate with the US-backed Nicaraguan Democratic Force (FDN) or 'Contras', whom President Reagan publicly hailed as 'our brothers' and likened to the US Founding Fathers. His Secretary of State, George Shultz, having earlier claimed it was the duty of the US to rescue the Nicaraguans from 'the endless darkness of communist tyranny', met President Ortega in Montevideo on 2 March. The arrest of a Costa Rican student by Nicaragua formed the pretext for Costa Rica, El Salvador and Honduras to boycott the meeting of the Contadora Group on 14 February in Panama (see AR 1984, p. 368).

On 31 May the killing of two Costa Rican border guards highlighted Costa Rican support of the Democratic Revolutionary Alliance (ARDE) of Eden Pastora, which after a major government offensive at the end of May sued for peace. On 5 June tension increased as Sandinista forces shot down two helicopters that had entered Nicaraguan airspace from Honduras; after further incursions of US jet aircraft, on 13 June President Ortega ended a five-month old voluntary moratorium on the importation of arms. On 19 July, the sixth anniversary of the Sandinista revolution, he claimed that it was the United States, not Nicaragua, that was supporting terrorism.

In HONDURAS the Government of President Roberto Suazo Córdova had been under heavy criticism for allowing both Contra and US military activity. On 24–26 August representatives of the Contadora Group met in Cartagena, Colombia, where they were joined, in a bid for wider Latin American support for the proposals initiated by President Alan Garcia of Peru, by representatives of the so-called 'Lima Group', the new demo-cratic Governments of Argentina, Brazil, Peru and Uruguay. At a fur-ther meeting in Panama on 12 September new Contadora proposals were published for a freeze on military forces and the entire removal of foreign military advisers from the region. The following day Honduran jet air-craft attacked positions inside Nicaragua, backing an attack by some 800 guerrillas. Honduras, claiming Nicaraguan provocation, then broke off diplomatic relations, bringing the two countries to the verge of the war for which US forces in Honduras had been openly planning. But, after much diplomatic activity, when on 12 November representatives of the five Central American states and Panama met in Luxembourg to sign a convention with the EEC they were joined by the Contadora states in signing a pledge to oppose 'terrorism' and work for the elimination of all foreign military forces in the region.

In the Honduran presidential elections on 24 November the 58-year-old Sr José Azcona, of the ruling Liberal Party but a newly-converted opponent of Sr Suazo, was declared the winner. Despite winning only 344,000 votes to the 515,000 cast for Sr Rafael Callejas, 42-year-old candidate of the more conservative National Party, the Liberals collectively had gained 51 per cent of the total poll to 45 per cent for the National Party candidates, who disputed the result as unconstitutional.

In EL SALVADOR, despite a new military offensive in Chalatenango in January, the civil war remained stalemated. Meanwhile the guerrillas of the Farabundo Martí Liberation Front (FMLN), in a major change of strategy, turned to a fresh offensive in the cities aimed at disrupting the elections. But on 31 March the President's Christian Democrats (PDC) and their allies won a surprise victory, taking 34 seats of the 60 in the National Assembly, and won over two-thirds of the 262 mayoralties, a result supported by the army, who disowned right-wing opposition. A wave of strikes followed and on 2 June six died when the President ordered troops into state hospitals. On 19 July the FMLN killed four US marines and 9 civilians in an attack on a restaurant in the capital. When in August the Government, whose security forces successfully tracked down and arrested the killers, implemented stricter wartime taxes and controls on imported goods, businesses closed in protest. The FMLN then abducted on 10 September the President's daughter, Sra Iñes Guadaloupe Duarte Durán, and demanded the return of 34 captives.

In GUATEMALA, where a further 957 were estimated to have died in civil violence in 1984, the forced resettlement of Indians in the highlands continued, while inflation, 23 per cent in 1984, climbed by the end of May to an annual rate of some 57 per cent. The quetzal, which had been at par with the US dollar since 1926, fell to $0·25 by June, when, as the Constituent Assembly completed work on the new constitution and electoral law, the Government of General Oscar Mejía Victores ceased to function in more than name. Violent protests between 29 August and 4 September led the Government to rescind unpopular price increases and publicly concede a return to democracy. On polling day, 3 November, the candidate of the Christian Democrats (DC), Sr Vinicio Cerezo Arévalo, only a week after his headquarters had been machine-gunned, emerged well in the lead over Sr Jorge Carpio of the National Union of the Centre (UCN), and looked set to take office as Guatemala's first civilian President for sixteen years.

In COSTA RICA the strong US pressure to remilitarize and join in the regional combat eroded the political support of President Luis Alberto

Monge's National Liberation Party (PLN). PANAMA's mediating role in the area was reduced by its economic weakness. On 12 August the head of the defence forces, General Manuel Antonio Noriega, warned President Nicolas Ardito Barletta that the economic situation was 'totally anarchic and out of control'. On 28 September the President, summoned by the General from the United Nations in New York, resigned under military pressure after a leading critic of the armed forces, Dr Hugo Spadaforo, had been found in Costa Rica murdered after torture. A 48-year-old businessman, Sr Eric Arturo Del Valle, was sworn in as President in his place.

MEXICO

Though the purchasing power of an average worker had fallen by some 50 per cent in 1984, when inflation was officially estimated at 59·2 per cent, the main challenge to the regime came from the right. The ruling party of the Institutionalized Revolution (PRI) was uneasy at prospects of losing state governorships to the National Action Party (PAN) at the mid-term elections on 7 July. Despite the request of President de la Madrid that the elections be held 'in a peaceful climate and with strict adherence to legality', the PRI officially won all 300 congressional seats and all seven state governorships contested, claiming a 3 to 1 victory in both Sonora and Nuevo León within an hour of the close of the poll. The result, regarded as incredible by foreign observers, who reported seeing widespread padding of electoral rolls and ballot-stuffing, did not tally with poll predictions and was followed by extensive rioting. The proportional allocation of the remaining 100 seats in the Chamber gave the PRI 292 seats overall and actually resulted in a loss of 13 seats for the PAN (38) and of 5 for the Mexican Unified Socialist Party (12).

On the economic front the Government was embarrassed by the continuing fall in the price of oil, which forced additional budget cuts in June, while in August even the 85-year-old leader of the Mexican Workers Confederation (CTM), Fidel Velazquez, elected for an eighth term, demanded an emergency wage increase.

Relations with the United States were frosty after the kidnapping on 7 February and murder of a US Drug Enforcement Agency (DEA) agent in Guadalajara had led to weeks of strict searches and the closing of some border crossings. Bilateral talks with US Secretary of State George Shultz on 25 July focused less on the Mexican call for the US to resume negotiations with Nicaragua than with Mexican-US relations, and on 28 August the Government resumed diplomatic relations with El Salvador, while rejecting the US policy of overthrowing the Nicaraguan Government. The difficulty of maintaining an independent foreign policy was, however, cruelly demonstrated when on 19 September the IMF announced that once again Mexico had failed to meet its targets and would be ineligible for new loans.

Within hours the worst natural disaster Mexico had suffered in the twentieth century, an earthquake measuring 8·1 on the Richter scale, had laid waste the centre of the capital. Steel-framed buildings in the main business district, including three hospitals and some three hundred hotels and public buildings, collapsed. The Economic Commission for Latin America estimated 7,000 dead, 30,000 injured, more than 100,000 homeless, and losses of some US$4,000 million. Despite pressure, the Government refused to ask for relief from its creditors, but did for the first time publicly accept aid from the United States. (See also Pt. XIV, Ch. 4.)

Chapter 4

THE CARIBBEAN

JAMAICA—GUYANA—TRINIDAD AND TOBAGO—BARBADOS—BELIZE—
GRENADA—THE BAHAMAS—THE WINDWARD AND LEEWARD ISLANDS—
SURINAME

JAMAICA

PRIME Minister Edward Seaga, in the face of mounting criticism of his economic policies and the growing unpopularity of his Government, explained that there was no alternative to his economic prescriptions. He said that the choice was 'not between pain and pleasure but between pain and greater pain'. For the past three years he had fully accepted the medicine offered by the IMF, applying policies involving continued deregulation of the economy, sharp cutbacks in public sector jobs and heavy tax packages in addition to austerity budgets. The process had led to very few achievements in the economy.

Mr Seaga referred to creditable performances in the building of other sectors of the economy over the past five years, which accounted for additional earnings of US$749 million foreign exchange, and also to the fact that a US$1,700 million loss in bauxite earnings had negated these gains. Because of a depressed world aluminium market and local dislocations in the industry, output was expected to be just over 6 million tonnes compared with 8·735 million tonnes in 1984. Mr Seaga pointed out that the number of new investment projects had averaged over a hundred a year for the past three years.

However, foreign investment levels had been disappointingly low. Additionally, external debt stood in excess of US$3,000 million, more than twice what it was in 1980 when he took over the government, and accounted for 32 per cent of foreign exchange earnings in 1984. With a new loan agreement for a twenty-month IMF credit of US$115 million to cover the period up to March 1987, Jamaica had now exhausted its permitted limit of 450 per cent of its quota with the Fund. Once again the government was able to obtain favourable treatment in having US$193·4 million of its foreign debt due in the current financial year rescheduled, and was granted a moratorium on a further US$197 million of debt falling due between 1 April 1987 and 31 March 1990, which would be consolidated into a single loan. Having failed another IMF test in September, and having complained at the Seoul meeting of the IMF that he had no quarrel with IMF strategies for Jamaica but only with its pace, Mr Seaga invited a joint mission which included Mr Jacques de la Rosière, a director of the IMF, and representatives of the World Bank and US Aid for International Development (USAID) to review the country's economic position.

The US Government committed US$135 million to Jamaica in the 1985–86 financial year. Throughout 1985 a number of events upset ministerial plans to record growth in Gross Domestic Product (GDP), which was now expected to show a decline of between 3·5 and 6 per cent for 1985. Although non-traditional exports showed an increase and tourism performed adequately, bauxite/alumina production and earnings continued their decline. A major shock came in February with the announced closure of Alcoa Minerals. It was later reopened under the direction of a state company after the Government had managed to secure a market for its output. Industrial unrest and increased oppositional politics added to the difficulties experienced by the Government.

Politically, a resurgent People's National Party (PNP), while carefully avoiding confrontational politics in the streets, put pressure on the Government to call a general election. Its argument was that the 1980 mandate ran out in 1985 and that the December 1983 elections, which it had boycotted, were invalid. Additionally, the PNP insisted on local government elections, which had been promised by July after being postponed from the previous year. The Government avoided this test of its popularity in 1985 by deciding to reduce the number of parish council seats from 278 to 120. After public outcry it agreed to put its proposal as a recommendation to the Electoral Advisory Committee, to abide by its decision and to call local government elections by 31 December. The Committee agreed to reduce the number of seats to 189 and the elections were never held. Continuing labour unrest reached its high point in late June when the six major Jamaican trade unions, including the Bustamante Industrial Trade Union, which was aligned with the Jamaica Labour Party and the Government, called a general strike. It was the first such strike in post-independent Jamaica but its obviously weak coordination allowed Mr Seaga to ride out the storm. Coming after the 15 and 16 January street demonstrations during which 7 persons were killed, it must have severely tested the resolve of the Government. A rapid slide in the Jamaican dollar to a rate of J$6·40 to one US$ forced the Government to intervene in the weekly auctions and stabilize the rate at J$5·50. Investment of US$58 million in the Kingston Free Zone by Hong Kong-based businessmen was expected to create 8,150 new jobs, and it was anticipated that another J$439 million would be invested in a tourism project. US$90 million were to be invested in expanding the cement plant and a Swiss finance company was to provide a US$450 million soft loan for a second cement plant in eastern Jamaica. The Government promised a price and income-tax reduction package which would cost a total of about J$380 million in revenue. The intention was to cut income tax to a flat 35 per cent rate on incomes, eliminating the system of graduating rates to the scale of income.

GUYANA

The sudden death of Life-President Linden Forbes Burnham on 6 August (see OBITUARY) led to the accession of Mr Hugh Desmond Hoyte to the presidency. Mr Burnham had ruled Guyana with an increasingly heavy hand since 1964. Any expectation that a liberalization of the political system would follow was quickly scotched by Mr Hoyte, who moved swiftly to consolidate his hold on power. By the end of September, he had been elected unopposed as leader of the Peoples' National Congress (PNC) and president-general of the Guyana Labour Union and had secured a pledge of loyalty from his nearest rival, Mr Hamilton Green, the Prime Minister and First Vice-President. He called an early general election on 9 December. The ruling PNC, once again, manufactured an overwhelming victory. The final votes showed the PNC receiving 228,718 votes, the Peoples' Progressive Party (PPP) 45,926 and the remaining five political parties 16,531 votes between them. Under the system of proportional representation, the PNC secured 42 parliamentary seats, the PPP 8, the United Force two and the Working Peoples' Alliance (WPA) one. The PPP and WPA had intended boycotting parliament but took up the seats offered.

These elections short-circuited talks on a 'government of national unity' between the PNC and the PPP. The latter had withdrawn from the elections on the day of the poll, declaring them to be obviously fraudulent. The opposition parties and the Guyana Council of Churches (GCC), as well as other civic groups, had earlier called for fair elections, an impartial electoral machinery and non-involvement of the army in the process. The only concessions made by the Government were to abolish postal voting and to place restrictions on overseas voting and voting by proxy. Both before and after the elections, GCC members were harassed by the Government. Substantial salary increases were announced for members of the Government and National Assembly, and the opposition-controlled Trades Union Congress (TUC) agreed to pay-increases for the public sector workers.

The Government was put under severe pressure when, first, the IMF decided to suspend further financial assistance to Guyana because of arrears on payments; then when the Caribbean Development Bank (CDB) reaffirmed a two-year ruling on the cessation of loans to Guyana; and when US Aid for International Development (USAID) closed its office in Guyana. Guyana owed the IMF US$19 million and the CDB US$7·5 million. USAID had allocated no new funds to Guyana since March 1982.

Nevertheless, the International Development Agency of the World Bank approved a US$8·8 million loan for expansion in the forestry industry, and the Inter-American Development Bank (IDB) approved loans totalling US$49·9 million for education, irrigation and an industrial recovery programme. The World Bank declared itself ready to assist Guyana, indicated that the Government should aim to restore 1975 levels of production by 1990, proposed a US$730 million projects package for foreign funding to meet that objective and pointed out that debt servicing amounted to 72 per cent of GNP in 1984. The Government itself announced an ambitious G$800 million agricultural development plan for 1986–89. Guyana was hurt by a decision of the Government of Trinidad and Tobago to suspend its oil credit facility to Guyana from 1 October, because of arrears in payment amounting to US$217 million. Oil supply was maintained to the end of December under an experimental barter arrangement whereby Guyana would supply Trinidad with 3,000 tonnes of rice per month. For the first half of 1985 oil imports cost 62·6 per cent of Guyana's export earnings of US$99 million. The 1985 budget envisaged a current account deficit of G$392 million. In January 1985 the external debt totalled US$1,230 million.

A thaw in relations with Venezuela appeared when Dr Isidro Morales Paul, Foreign Minister of Venezuela, visited Guyana. Venezuela agreed to buy 250,000 tonnes of bauxite from Guyana in 1985.

TRINIDAD AND TOBAGO

The major event of 1985 was the 33·3 per cent devaluation of the Trinidad & Tobago dollar. This was announced in the 1985–86 budget presentation to parliament on 17 December. The Prime Minister, Mr George Chambers, argued that it would result in substantial benefits to the country, bringing competitiveness to industry and tourism, and would attract foreign investment. The devaluation followed a fall in the world market price for oil which caused declining revenues in Trinidad & Tobago. While there were favourable performances by some state-owned companies

producing fertilizers, ammonia, methanol and steel, other state operations such as the telephone company, the water and sewerage authority,
the bus service and the port authority continued to lose money. In spite of
the government's putting TT$1,460 million into the sugar industry
between 1973 and 1984, the industry experienced serious cash flow
problems in 1985. The construction sector with nearly 80,000 persons
unemployed was virtually at a standstill.

External debt in June was TT$2,206 million, a 23·3 per cent increase
over the 1984 figure for the same period. Gross public debt was
TT$3,606·4 million. Foreign exchange reserves stood at TT$2,092·8 million in March. There were clear signs that the process of adjustment of
the economy had begun to have positive effects. In 1984 the fiscal deficit
was reduced to 6·7 per cent of GDP, the sugar output of 92,600 tonnes for
1985 was the best for four years, and by the third quarter the trade surplus
was over TT$1,051 million, more than double the TT$489·9 million
surplus for the same period in 1984.

A number of sizeable new investment projects included TT$150
million by the Trinidad & Tobago Oil Company, TT$400 million by the
American Oil Company, US$250 million for a new ammonia plant, and a
second methanol plant, a joint venture between the government and
Imperial Chemical Industries costing US$155 million. An industrial
agreement was imposed upon the Republic's 65,000 public servants by a
special civil service tribunal.

Politically, the three-party National Alliance, at its first Congress in
July, elected Mr A. N. R. Robinson as its leader, Mr Basdeo Panday as
his deputy and Dr Beau Tewarie as party chairman. In September this
National Alliance, along with the Organization for National Reconstruction, officially launched the National Alliance for Reconstruction
(NAR), with Mr Robinson as the leader. An opinion poll had earlier
indicated that the NAR would win an election, garnering 59 per cent of
the votes against 17 per cent for the ruling People's National Movement
(PNM), and declared Mr Robinson the most popular political leader in
Trinidad & Tobago. The ANR promised to extend democracy by involving the public in decision-making; to keep the 'commanding heights of
the economy' in the hands of the state while transferring some of the
commercial enterprises to private investors, trade unions and cooperatives; and to work for Caribbean integration and stronger relations with
Latin America. It was the first time since 1956 that an opposition grouping appeared to have a real chance of dethroning the ruling PNM.

BARBADOS

Prime Minister J. M. G. M (Tom) Adams died unexpectedly in March
(see OBITUARY). He would be remembered mainly for his deftness in

handling the economy and for the part he played in the military invasion
of Grenada in 1983. Mr Bernard St John, who was deputy Prime Minister
at the time, was quickly appointed as Prime Minister. His party retained
the seat left vacant by Mr Adams's death, albeit in the face of a 12 per cent
swing against it. Early in the year controversy arose when the Inter-
American Development Bank (IDB) refused to accept the recommendation of the Barbados Government that a local construction firm be
awarded the contract to build a Bds$90 million, 20 km highway from the
West Coast to the airport for which the IDB was providing a Bds$45
million loan. On a new appeal for tenders a Canadian firm secured the
contract.

The manufacturing sector continued to be plagued by regional and
international constraints on trade, resulting in further lay-offs of workers.
The manufacturing sector had declined by 3·5 per cent in 1984. The 1984
harvest, at 100,400 tonnes, was slightly higher than in the previous year
but earnings were expected to register a decline. The Government took a
decision to guarantee a further Bds$10 million loan to the Barbados
Sugar Industry Ltd, and it confirmed a Bds$10 million subsidy to the
industry as a whole. Tourism put in a creditable performance but arrivals
were fewer than anticipated. The GDP was expected to grow by no more
than 1·5 per cent.

The new Prime Minister included in the 1985–86 budget a package of
tax concessions to manufacturers. Estimated expenditure was put at
Bds$829·9 million. By September the national debt was Bds$1,073·5
million but foreign exchange reserves remained steady throughout the
year, reaching Bds$342 million in September. The rate of inflation for
1984 had been 4·6 per cent, the lowest for 17 years. The unemployment
rate was 19·8 per cent. Earlier in the year a loan of US$19 million was
raised in the Japanese financial market to finance government capital
works programmes and for balance of payments support.

BELIZE

The Bel$213 million 1985 budget included a taxation package
intended to raise Bel$3 million. Foreign exchange reserves were Bel$12
million at the end of 1984. USAID provided a US$13 million loan on
supposedly concessionary terms but obliged the Government to remove
trade restrictions imposed in 1982, to import, within a year of each
disbursement, an equivalent amount of raw materials, intermediate
goods, spare parts, etc., from the US, to restructure state-owned statutory boards and to maintain the programmed levels of development
expenditure and public sector savings. USAID, with the US Export-
Import Bank, established a US$5 million trade credit arrangement, and
obtained a US$14 million loan from the IMF.

A consortium of investors headed by Coca-Cola Foods bought a major interest in 13 per cent of Belize's total land area in a US$6 million deal. The primary intention of the group was to grow oranges for shipment to Florida, taking advantage of favourable provisions under the Caribbean Basin Initiative (CBI).

The US had considerable leverage against Belize, whose sovereign integrity, in the face of Guatemalan claims to its territory, remained open to doubt. Additionally, the US market accounted for approximately 50 per cent of Belize's exports and imports. US entrepreneurs also owned much of the land and business enterprises. However, Guatemala's constituent assembly, which was working on a draft constitution to come into effect in 1986, omitted the claim in the previous constitution that Belize was a part of Guatemalan territory. Nonetheless, the Guatemalan Foreign Minister reaffirmed Guatemala's stand on not recognising Belizean independence. In relation to the 47,000 aliens who accounted for two–sevenths of Belize's population, the Government was determined to make it as difficult as possible for them to become nationals.

GRENADA

On 8 December the ruling New National Party, a merger of three parties, held its first convention. After much party in-fighting, Dr Francis Alexis was elected as deputy Prime Minister. Earlier in the year, a faction said to be led by Dr Alexis had complained of the authoritarian style of the Prime Minister, Mr Herbert Blaize, and of its lack of access to the decision-making process, and had intended moving a motion of no confidence in Mr Blaize's leadership at a Cabinet meeting.

The withdrawal of the remaining US and Eastern Caribbean troops took place during 1985. In their place the Grenadian government had a 560-member police force, including an 80-man-strong paramilitary Special Service Unit. On 4 February a Bill was passed in parliament validating all laws passed between March 1979 and November 1984. A commission was appointed to review the constitution and submitted its report. By the end of the year the Government had not announced any further steps to be taken.

An EC$249·9 million budget was presented in April. Recurrent expenditure was set at EC$123·2 million, while revenue was expected to amount to only EC$95 million. The US Government was reported to have been working on an aid allocation which was lower than the US$57·3 million committed in 1984. The Government also announced a reduction of import duties, company tax and personal income tax rates. Unemployment was near 40 per cent of the work-force, and the national debt was put at EC$160·5 million. The Industrial Development Corporation announced that the Government had approved 17 hotel construction, expansion and renovation projects which were expected to provide an extra 1,461 rooms and 1,600 new jobs.

THE BAHAMAS

New taxation to yield Bh$25 million was a feature of the 1985 budget of Bh$421·8 million. Public debt servicing accounted for 25 per cent of the recurrent expenditure of Bh$421·8 million. No less than 60 per cent of the entire recurrent budget was appropriated for personal emoluments to more than 14,000 public officials. Tourism earnings were expected to exceed US$900 million in 1985 and to reach US$1,000 million in 1987. Ninety per cent of earnings went back to the US as payment for goods and services. Hotel employers and workers signed a five-year pay agreement, ending a 10-month dispute involving 6,000 members of the Hotel Catering and Allied Workers' Union. There were new investments totalling US$152 million for a water supply, telephone upgrading, a battery-cell manufacturing plant, a brewery, a hotel, a low-cost housing project and a radio system. The Bahamas became the 21st and last country to qualify for benefits under the Caribbean Basin Initiative. The Bahamas and Haiti signed a treaty pertaining to illegal Haitians in the Bahamas.

THE LEEWARD AND WINDWARD ISLANDS

Good performances in the tourism and agricultural sectors, with growing improvement in the manufacturing sector, led to a solid year of growth in the economy of ST LUCIA, expected to reach 5 per cent of GDP. 68,000 tonnes of bananas were sold to the UK and stop-over tourist arrivals were expected to exceed 94,000. The economy was reported to be on a take-off path. Among St Lucia's greatest problems were the rising cost of its public service, whose emoluments accounted for 55 per cent of the total recurring expenditure (EC$136 million in 1985), and a birth rate which at 33 per thousand was the highest of any country in the Western Hemisphere.

In DOMINICA unemployment, housing, the poor state of the roads and the future of the banana and tourism industries were the major issues in the general election campaign. The Dominica Freedom Party (DFP) of Prime Minister Miss Mary Eugenia Charles won 15 of the 21 seats in the Assembly with an increased popular vote. Former Prime Minister Patrick John and a former deputy commander of the Defence Force were each sentenced to 12 years' imprisonment for conspiring to overthrow the Government in 1981.

In ST VINCENT good performances in the banana and tourism industries, inducing an anticipated 3·1 per cent growth in the GDP, could not ease the difficulties facing the economy. With unemployment at 40 per cent, it was announced that the sugar industry would be closed after the 1985 crop, putting 1,200 workers out of jobs. The arrowroot industry was on the verge of collapse, with a 3-year production stockpile of 3·7 million lbs. and debts of EC$8·5 million.

In ANTIGUA & BARBUDA, despite an EC$201 million budget which introduced no new taxes, the Government was obliged, six months later, to increase a range of taxes and licence fees. It also ordered a wage freeze for public employees. A US$30 million combined power and desalination plant was to be set up with Japanese funding.

The Prime Minister of ST KITTS, Dr Kennedy Simmonds, presented his first budget since taking over the finance portfolio. His Government reached a final settlement with the former sugar industry owners whose lands were compulsorily acquired by the previous Administration. They would be paid EC$22 million over the next five years, with an interest rate of 6·5 per cent. The tourism sector performed remarkably well and growth of 5 per cent in GDP was expected.

The Premier of MONTSERRAT, Mr John Osborne, found his narrow 4–3 margin of seats in the Assembly, after the defection of his party's deputy leader in 1984, a difficult basis on which to take policy initiatives. Rumours of further defection and the formation of another opposition party did not help.

SURINAME

The Prime Minister, Mr Wim Udenhout, announced on 1 January a new Cabinet consisting of 12 members. It was the first step by the military regime to work toward the restoration of democratic rule. The 31-member National Assembly had 14 members nominated by the military, 11 by the trade unions and 6 by the private sector. Its major function was to draft a new constitution for a return to civilian rule by March 1987. Rendered ineffective by the resignation of three of the country's four trade union federations in April, and reorganized in June, signalling the end of the tripartite arrangement, the Government announced a new Cabinet having no ties with political groups and answerable to no such group. By September, Lieut.-Colonel Desi Bouterse permitted the right-wing Suriname National Party of a former Prime Minister, Mr Henck Arron, and the United Reform Party led by Mr Jaggernath Lachmon, both of the pre-1980 military coup Assembly, to resume open political activity.

So far, none of these efforts satisfied the Netherlands Government, which saw them as not meeting its conditions about elections and the composition of the Assembly in order for there to be a resumption of dialogue over the suspended 'independence' aid programme. Meanwhile, the Surinamese Government took the matter to the World Court at The Hague, accusing the Netherlands of hypocrisy since it subsequently invested SF150 million in Suralco, the Suriname bauxite and alumina company.

Suriname rejected an IMF package whose stringent terms included a recommendation for a 30 per cent devaluation of its currency. The Government, instead, with a foreign debt of US$20 million, opted for continuing its austerity programme. The 1985 budget estimates were reduced from SF740 million to SF480 million. Additionally the Government recalled 50 of its 150 diplomats based overseas. Imports were restricted to a value of US$167 million in 1985, compared with US$250 million in 1984 and US$417 million in 1983.

Foreign exchange earnings from bauxite represented only a third of what they used to be in 1982. The Tamberedjo oilfield was producing 1,300 barrels of oil per day (b/d) and was expected to produce up to 5,000 b/d in two years' time, from estimated reserves of 203 million barrels of oil. Foreign exchange savings could be as much as 50 per cent. A visit to Libya by Lieut.-Colonel Desi Bouterse resulted in a US$100 million loan agreement. A visit to Colombia secured a US$15 million line of credit to finance imports, and the Brazilian Government provided a US$20 million line of credit and undertook a 50 per cent increase in Brazil's purchase of up to 130,000 tonnes per year.

III THE USSR AND EASTERN EUROPE

Chapter 1

THE USSR

On 10 March, Konstantin Ustinovich Chernenko, General Secretary of the Communist Party of the Soviet Union (CPSU) since 13 February 1984, Chairman of the Supreme Defence Council and President of the USSR, died at the age of 73. At an extraordinary plenum of the Central Committee (CC), held the next day, Mikhail Sergeevich Gorbachev was elected to succeed him as General Secretary. Aged 54 and the youngest member of the Politburo, he was the Soviet Union's fourth leader in only 27 months. After more than a decade of ailing gerontocracy, the USSR now had a comparatively youthful, energetic, dynamic personality at its head. By the end of the year, the new General Secretary had made considerable progress towards consolidating his domestic political position and had won worldwide recognition as a statesman worthy to lead a great superpower.

Apart from the vacancy caused by the death of Marshal Ustinov in December 1984, there had been no changes in the composition of the Politburo during Chernenko's thirteen months in office, and although some younger members had previously been brought in by Andropov a substantial portion (about half) consisted of old Brezhnevites who were resistant to innovation and might be expected to have reservations about the new leader. Gorbachev moved swiftly to widen his power-base. At the next CC Plenum (23 April) he brought two men directly into the Politburo without having first served as candidate members. Both were already CC secretaries: E. K. Ligachev (64) and N. I. Ryzhkov (56). Ligachev, a former first secretary of the Tomsk obkom (regional party committee) in Siberia, had been brought into the Secretariat by Andropov in April 1983 to head the crucially important cadres department; known to be tough, abstemious and anxious to weed out corruption in public life, he quickly assumed a central role in Gorbachev's discipline campaign and in his drive to rejuvenate the party and state apparatuses. Ryzhkov was also a former Andropov protégé, but, unlike Ligachev, he had never held party office prior to his appointment to the Secretariat in November 1982, when he was put in charge of the newly-created Economic Department. Once the director of the huge Uralmash engineering conglomerate in western Siberia, he held ministerial office from 1975 to 1982, most recently as deputy chairman of Gosplan, the state planning body. The third new member was V. M. Chebrikov (62), appointed chairman of the KGB by Andropov in December 1982, who was also raised from candidate to full membership. These promotions, as well as strengthening Gorbachev's position within the collective leadership, corresponded to several current priorities: replacement of personnel (Ligachev), economic planning (Ryzhkov) and discipline and security (Chebrikov).

At the same Plenum, 74-year-old Marshal S. I. Sokolov, Ustinov's successor as Minister of Defence, was accorded candidate membership of the Politburo (in constrast to his predecessor, who was a full member), while V. P. Nikonov (56), a former party obkom first secretary and republic-level minister of agriculture, was brought into the Secretariat to head the Agriculture Department, Gorbachev's own portfolio from 1978 to 1985.

Other than these organizational matters, the only item on the agenda at this Plenum concerned the convening of the Party's twenty-seventh Congress in February 1986, at which, it was announced, N. A. Tikhonov as Chairman of the Council of Ministers (Premier) would deliver the report on the main directions for economic and social development in the period 1986–90 and the outlook up to the year 2000—thus indicating that the 79-year-old Premier intended to hold on to office at least until Congress met.

Gorbachev's speech to the Plenum sketched out the main points of what was rapidly emerging as an agenda for action to rescue the Soviet Union from the inertia into which it had slipped in the previous ten to fifteen years. The overall goal was ambitious in the extreme: 'the scientific-technical renovation of production and attainment of the highest world level of productivity of labour' in the shortest possible time— Soviet industrial productivity then stood at 55 per cent of the best international standards (in agriculture it was much lower).

The Central Committee met again on 1 July on the eve of a session of the USSR Supreme Soviet. Once more, personnel change dominated the agenda. Precedent suggested that in order to become leader of the Soviet Union it was necessary *inter alia* to be both a full member of the CPSU Politburo and a member of the Secretariat. At the time of Chernenko's death only one person other than Gorbachev fulfilled those preconditions—G. V. Romanov (62), formerly in charge of the Leningrad party organization and currently the secretary with responsibility for the defence industries and thus closely identified with the military interest. It was widely believed that he had challenged Gorbachev for the succession, possibly with the support of V. V. Grishin (71), first secretary of the Moscow city party committee. Romanov's 'retirement' at the July Plenum on health grounds fooled no one, despite the rumours (no doubt officially inspired) that he was in a drying-out clinic for alcoholics. Gorbachev had moved quickly and decisively to remove his erstwhile rival and potential challenger for the leadership. The vacancy thus created in the Secretariat was filled by L. N. Zaikov (62), an industrial administrator *cum* party functionary from Leningrad. Another newly designated secretary (but not new to the Secretariat, where he already headed the construction department) was B. N. El'tsin (54), some-time party chief in Sverdlovsk, where he had established strong career links with Ryzhkov.

The least-expected promotion was that of E. E. Shevardnadze (57), until then first secretary of the Communist Party of Georgia, who was raised from candidate to full membership of the Politburo. Even more astounding was his appointment, at the Supreme Soviet meeting the next day, as Foreign Minister in place of Andrei Gromyko (75), who was elected Chairman of the Presidium of the USSR Supreme Soviet (President), the office left vacant by Chernenko's death. Gromyko had joined the diplomatic service in 1939, became ambassador to the USA in 1943 at the age of 34, and had been Foreign Minister uninterruptedly since 1957. Dour, intelligent and a brilliant executor, in 1973 he was brought by Brezhnev into the Politburo and thus into the policy-making process itself. In recent years, however, he seemed to be losing his touch. Large areas of the world were left relatively neglected (Africa and the Pacific in particular), while the all-important relationship with the US had reached apparent deadlock, the USSR adopting seemingly immovable positions from which it had proved difficult to extricate itself.

These appointments were surprising for two reasons. First, Shevardnadze was completely lacking in experience of international affairs; and, secondly, it had been widely expected that, like his three immediate predecessors, Gorbachev would himself take the presidency. Some 'sources' had suggested that he would assume the premiership in addition to the party general-secretaryship, but this would have violated the principle enunciated at the time of Khrushchev's ousting in 1964 that those two posts should never again be embodied in the same person. On the other hand, since 1977 it had become customary for the party leader also to take on the role of head of state—indeed, Gorbachev himself had once praised this practice. But the promotion of Shevardnadze and his appointment to the foreign ministry was an astute move. At a stroke Gorbachev both enhanced his own position in the Politburo (by moving in a supporter) and acquired close control over the foreign policy process. Gromyko, who had supported Gorbachev strongly for the succession, retained his membership of the Politburo (and thus involvement in the broad field of decision-making) and acquired an office to which high formal prestige and status are attached, yet suffered a diminution of political influence to the advantage of Gorbachev.

The fact that the main evening television news, scheduled to be extended to include a summary of Gorbachev's speech to the July Plenum, was curtailed, and that the speech was not published in the next day's press, gave substance to unofficial reports that there had been a 'shouting match' between the General Secretary and Tikhonov, who was being cast in the role of leader of the residual Brezhnevite faction. But on

27 September he, too, was obliged to beg Gorbachev to release him from office on the grounds of worsening health. His request was granted readily, and N. I. Ryzhkov was named as the new Prime Minister.

At the fourth and last Plenum of 1985, held on 16 October, Ryzhkov, as expected, resigned from the Secretariat and Tikhonov was routinely dropped from membership of the Politburo. The only newcomer to the central leadership on this occasion was N. V. Talyzin (56)—the recently-appointed successor to 74-year-old N. K. Baibakov as head of Gosplan—who was awarded candidate membership of the Politburo. It was yet another indication of the importance that Gorbachev attached to refashioning the role of central planning in his drive to modernize the economy.

Before the year was out, one more member was in effect dropped from the Politburo. For several months there had been repeated criticism in the press about the state of affairs in Moscow. In mid-November, V. I. Konotop (69), first secretary of Moscow obkom, was pensioned off and replaced by V. K. Mesyats (57), since 1976 Minister of Agriculture of the USSR and therefore well known to Gorbachev. Then on 25 December *Pravda* carried a terse announcement of the retirement of V. V. Grishin as first secretary of the city party committee and his replacement by B. N. El'tsin. Significantly, the report added that the General Secretary had taken part in the proceedings personally. In view of the fact that only in July had El'tsin been appointed to the Secretariat, the change of office bore signs of tough resistance within the Moscow committee and the necessity of putting a close supporter in office to get a grip on affairs in the capital.

In the foreign-policy realm the year began inauspiciously when a Soviet 'cruise' missile went out of control, crossed over Norwegian territory and landed in a frozen lake in Finland. But a few days later, on 6 January, Foreign Minister Gromyko and US Secretary of State Shultz met in Geneva and agreed that new disarmament talks should begin, in place of those broken off by the Soviet Union in November 1983 in response to the stationing of Cruise and Pershing missiles in Europe. It was decided that the resumed negotiations would focus on three issues: strategic weapons, intermediate weapons in the European theatre and space-based systems. Almost immediately, disagreement broke out between the two sides, the United States being willing to discuss the first two questions, but determined to proceed with its Strategic Defense Initiative (SDI), whereas the Soviets insisted that progress should be made in all three areas simultaneously. Indeed the cessation of SDI replaced the removal of American missiles from Europe as the principal bone of contention between the two sides.

Still, only thirty minutes after the official announcement of Chernenko's death Soviet officials informed their American counterparts that there was no reason to postpone the beginning of the disarmament talks due to open in Geneva the next day. In the months that followed, parallel to the formal negotiations, the Soviet Union mounted a skilful and at times quite sophisticated propaganda campaign which took the Americans by surprise and frequently had them on the defensive. For example, in early April, just as Western peace groups were about to mount their Easter campaigns, Gorbachev captured the world's head-lines by declaring unilaterally a moratorium on the deployment of medium-range missiles in Europe (see Pt. XII).

Relations were further exacerbated by a series of incidents that attracted maximum publicity. In March, US army Major Nicholson, on a permitted tour of inspection in East Germany, was shot dead by a Soviet soldier (see p. 60). In April, Britain expelled several Soviet embassy staff and in September sent home another 25 officials who had been exposed by Oleg Gordievsky, the former senior KGB resident in London; the Soviet Union retaliated by expelling 25 Britons from Moscow, where-upon six more Russians were sent home, followed by another six British diplomats, journalists and businessmen, before Mrs Thatcher decided to 'draw a line' under the affair (see p. 38). Then in November there was the bizarre case of Vitaly Yurchenko, the 'double defector', who claimed to have been abducted by the CIA in Italy and held drugged and captive in the United States, and then to have escaped, to tell his sensational story at press conferences in Washington and Moscow (see p. 57).

The new Foreign Minister Shevardnadze presented a more attractive image of the Soviet Union. Although clearly his master's voice, he soon showed himself to be personable, quick to learn and capable. His conduct at Helsinki at the end of July, when he delivered a speech to the gathering convened to mark the tenth anniversary of the Helsinki accords, impressed observers, as did his address to the United Nations in New York in September, when he condemned 'Star Wars' (SDI) and instead cleverly called for a 'Star Peace' involving international cooperation in space.

Gorbachev's first visit to the West as leader came in early October when he arrived in France. Once more he seized the initiative, this time by proposing a 50-per-cent reduction in long-range nuclear missiles in conjunction with a complete ban on space-based weapons systems, and separate negotiations on nuclear arms with France and Britain—an offer that was promptly declined by President Mitterrand, while the British expressed polite interest. More frivolously, the Western popular press dubbed his wife, Raisa, 'Gorbachev's secret weapon'—a mark of the public-relations success of the visit and a weapon that he was to deploy with spectacular effect again the next month (19–21 November) when he met President Reagan in Geneva.

The series of meetings between the leaders of the two superpowers produced no tangible results in the shape of agreement on any of the major issues (see DOCUMENTS). Yet the summit as a whole was deemed a success. This was because both men had gone to Geneva determined to seek a better understanding of each other as persons and of the other's country's point of view. The chemistry worked, not least because of a press blackout during the talks and the lengthy tête-à-tête conversations with only interpreters present. Both leaders agreed to instruct their representatives to speed up negotiations when the disarmament talks reconvened in Geneva in January 1986; the international atmosphere became more relaxed; agreement was reached on lesser questions such as the opening of consulates in Kiev and New York, cultural exchanges, research on nuclear fusion and air safety. It was encouraging, too, that Gorbachev accepted an invitation to visit the United States in 1986, and invited President Reagan to go to the USSR the year after. Neither side sought to disguise the fact that there were deep differences of opinion left unresolved, or that the dialogue had at times been 'sharp' and uncompromising. But at the year's end the 'spirit of Geneva'—to which the Soviet media and leadership made frequent reference—seemed still to have real substance. It was a good start.

Soviet self-confidence grew noticeably following Gorbachev's accession. While the US remained at the centre of Soviet diplomatic effort, greater attention was paid to Western Europe and the Middle East; and the USSR rediscovered its identity as an Asian power and began to take initiatives towards North Korea, Japan and the Asean countries. Trade with China expanded and the Sino-Soviet atmosphere became cautiously friendly; but political rapprochement remained as distant as ever, as the Chinese insisted upon the removal of the 'three obstacles', namely, Soviet support for Vietnam in Kampuchea, the large concentration of troops and weapons on the Sino-Soviet border and Soviet involvement in Afghanistan.

There had been signs at Geneva that the USSR might be willing to seek a solution to the war in Afghanistan, which entered its seventh year at the end of December, following the humiliating vote on 14 November in the UN General Assembly which by 122 votes to 19 (with 12 abstentions) condemned the Soviet Union. However, it was made clear by Moscow that any withdrawal of Soviet troops would depend upon there being a Government in Kabul friendly to the USSR, to which end Babrak Karmal was encouraged to 'widen the social base' and his Administration by bringing in elements from outside the ruling party.

The question of Afghanistan had been kept in the background during Prime Minister Rajiv Gandhi's visit to the USSR in May, although he was reported as having reiterated Indian disapproval at the Soviet presence there. The close Indo-Soviet relationship was emphasised by the signing of a new 15-year agreement on scientific and economic cooperation and the provision of a Soviet thousand-million-rouble credit.

In July there was mounting speculation that the USSR and Israel were about to resume diplomatic relations and that this would result in a massive exodus of Jews from the Soviet Union. The fact that it was strenuously denied by Moscow did not prevent another wave of rumour building up towards the end of the year, according to which France and Poland were to play the roles of broker and staging-post in any agreement that was reached. Meanwhile, the number of Jews permitted to emigrate remained small—well under 200 in most months.

Gorbachev had been appointed leader primarily to tackle the acute problem of the USSR's economic decline and the attendant malaise afflicting public morale and morality. With the military at his back, he had to ensure his country's security, and at the same time try to reach a modus vivendi with the United States which would permit a transfer of resources from the military sector of the economy to the civilian. While the disciplinary measures introduced by Andropov continued to have a beneficial effect, industrial performance overall still gave rise to anxiety. In several key sectors output was stagnant or had even declined. In agriculture, despite colossal investment, returns were poor. The results for the first nine months of 1985, published in October, showed chemicals, ferrous metallurgy, mineral fertilizers, timber and oil lagging behind the plan, together with consumer-oriented light industry. When the draft five-year plan for 1986-90 was published on 9 November it envisaged a growth in national income of 3·5 per cent a year, a less ambitious target than had been expected, given that earlier in the year Gorbachev had taken the unprecedented step of returning the draft plan for further revision and had said, in a speech in Leningrad in June, that a growth-rate of at least four per cent was essential.

Despite much debate, it remained unclear at the end of the year whether or not radical reform was imminent. During his visits to Leningrad, the Ukraine, Siberia and Kazakhstan (where on each occasion he went on a highly-publicized walkabout, usually accompanied by his wife), the emphasis of his set speeches and off-the-cuff remarks was on discipline, conscientious work-habits and scientific and technical innovation, the speeding-up of which was the leitmotif of 1985. The press was packed with stories of corruption, bribery, inefficiency, dismissal of officials and, in several cases, their execution. Nor was there any let-up in the campaign against alcoholism. The effect of all this was to reveal a tangle of problems even more complex than had been imagined when the old leadership was still in charge. Yet Gorbachev had little choice but to attempt to tackle them all simultaneously. Change of personnel assumed a pre-eminent place in his campaign, but, as he stressed over and over again, it was also a question of 'restructuring people's psychology'. In that context his own personal style was clearly important. On the other hand, there was little structural reform, although creation of a kind of 'super ministry' in November—the State Agro-Industrial Committee, headed by a Gorbachev protégé from Stavropol—may have indicated the kind of innovation the leadership had in mind.

The struggle between the political generations assumed surrogate form in the rivalry between Anatoly Karpov and Gary Kasparov for the world chess championship. On 15 February the match was abandoned with Karpov leading 5–3, but with Kasparov playing strongly. When it resumed in September, the contest took on political overtones, with Karpov, G. V. Romanov's son-in-law, pitted against the flamboyant Kasparov, who obviously enjoyed the support of his fellow Azeri, Geidar Aliev, a member of the Politburo and first deputy chairman of the Council of Ministers. On 9 November Kasparov, at the age of 22, became the youngest-ever world chess champion.

Earlier, in May, the Soviet Union took pride in marking the fortieth anniversary of its victory over Nazi Germany with a spectacular parade in Red Square in which were displayed not only some of the latest military hardware but also a number of wartime T-34 tanks and 'Katyusha' rockets. Gorbachev, who was just eleven years old when the Germans overran his native Stavropol, made a dignified speech to Soviet veterans on 5 May, but then caused deep offence by implying at a Kremlin reception that the Western powers had colluded with Hitler.

After the celebrations, the Soviet military found itself, in common with the party and state apparatuses, subjected to a high rate of turnover of leading personnel. Particularly notable was the retirement of A. Epishev (77) as head of the main political administration of the armed forces and his replacement by A. Lizichev, formerly commander of the Soviet group of forces in East Germany. In the same month, July, V. F. Tolubko (71) relinquished command of the strategic rocket forces; while in August it was acknowledged publicly that Gorbachev was head of the Supreme Defence Council. Admiral S. Gorshkov (75), for three decades commander-in-chief of the Soviet navy and the man generally credited with creating a powerful blue-water fleet, retired in December, Admiral V. Chernavin (57) taking his place.

The Soviet rock group 'Avtograf' made an appearance on the Live Aid show in July, although the concert was not shown on Soviet television. In the same month, the twelfth World Youth Festival was opened by Gorbachev in Moscow and devoted most of its activity to denouncing the wickedness of imperialism, although a few West European delegations managed with difficulty to raise issues such as human rights and the Soviet invasion of Afghanistan. October saw the award of the Nobel peace prize to the co-chairmen of the organization International Physicians for the Prevention of Nuclear War, Dr E. Chazov (USSR) and Dr B. Lown (USA), although there was some embarrassment when it was pointed out to the awarding committee that Dr Chazov (personal physician to the Politburo and a member of the Party's Central Committee) had been a signatory to a document denouncing the exiled Academician Andrei Sakharov.

Early in December, Sakharov's wife, Elena Bonner, was permitted to leave Russia for medical treatment in Italy and America. On 18 December, the middle-aged 'Angry Young Man', the poet Evgenii Evtushenko, made a brave speech to a writers' congress in Moscow in which he denounced censorship, Stalinism, the purges, the treatment of the peasants during collectivization and privilege (including that enjoyed by writers). None of these topics was mentioned in the version published by *Literaturnaya Gazeta*, but the fact that the speech was made at all offered some encouragement to those who hoped that Gorbachev might permit some relaxation in the field of culture—so far, about the only area which he had failed to purge of its elderly functionaries.

As the year drew to a close the focus of attention switched back to the Communist Party. All over the Soviet Union report-and-election meetings were being held at every level from factory floor upwards in preparation for the forthcoming Party Congress. On the agenda was discussion of the draft of the new Party programme (the fourth, previous ones having appeared in 1903, 1919 and 1961) and revisions to the Party's statutes. Unlike the Khrushchev-inspired programme, which had been moribund for years, the new version made few grandiose claims and set no firm timetable. These meetings also confirmed in office the key first secretaries, many of whom were new to their posts (out of 157 obkom first secretaries, 38 had been appointed since Gorbachev came to power).

In the last minutes of 1985, a self-confident but not self-satisfied Mikhail Gorbachev went on television to address the Soviet people. 'I think,' he said, 'that you will agree with me when I say that the departing year will remain in our memory as a year of strenuous labour, of hope, and of bold plans for the future'. It was an appropriate epitaph for Russia's 1985.

Chapter 2

GERMAN DEMOCRATIC REPUBLIC—POLAND—CZECHOSLOVAKIA—HUNGARY—
ROMANIA—BULGARIA—YUGOSLAVIA—ALBANIA—MONGOLIA

THE GERMAN DEMOCRATIC REPUBLIC

FOR the German Democratic Republic, 1985 was a year of domestic political consolidation, economic progress and tentative moves towards re-establishing inter-German relations after the break caused by the deployment of new American intermediate-range missiles in the Federal Republic. The 40th anniversary of the end of World War II in Europe did not cause the same heart-searchings in the East as it did in the West. East Berlin moved cautiously to assess its room for manoeuvre under the new leadership of Mr Mikhail Gorbachev in Moscow. The East German leader, Herr Erich Honecker, appeared to be laying the groundwork for his eventual successor while pursuing efforts to gain greater international recognition for his country.

The major political developments came towards the end of the year. During the autumn, the ruling party, the SED, carried out a review of its 2·2 million members in preparation for the party congress to be held the following spring. Almost 5,000 members were expelled or resigned and 3,000 more were put under review. On 22 November a major change was announced at the very top of the party. Herr Konrad Naumann, a hard-liner who had been particularly critical of what he called laxness towards artists and church critics of the regime, was dropped from the Politburo. Herr Herbert Häber, the Politburo's leading expert on West Germany, resigned at the same time. Ill health was given as the official reason in both cases. This appeared to be the truth as far as Herr Häber was concerned, but Herr Naumann's departure was seen as removing an awkward critic and enabling Herr Honecker to promote more trusted colleagues to top posts.

Herr Honecker's control was further strengthened at the beginning of December when the Defence Minister, General Heinz Hoffmann, died of a heart attack at the age of 75. His successor, General Heinz Kessler, aged 65, previously chief political officer of East Germany's forces, was close to Herr Honecker.

Both the ousting of Naumann and the appointment of Kessler appeared to be to the advantage of the Politburo's defence and security expert, Herr Egon Krenz. At the comparatively young age of 54, Krenz was generally regarded as Honecker's favourite candidate to succeed him when the 73-year-old leader should decide to step down.

Herr Honecker was active in 1985 in promoting East Germany's foreign relations, notably with a visit to Italy, the first official trip by an East German leader to a Nato country. He also had talks with Mr Gorbachev and other members of the new Soviet leadership, particularly during an extended visit to the Soviet Union in April. The French Prime Minister, M Laurent Fabius, went to East Germany in June for a visit which the East Germans saw as an important recognition of their place in Europe.

The most prominent political visitors from the West were, however, from the Federal Republic. While the possibility of Herr Honecker's visiting Bonn and his home region of the Saarland remained a matter for speculation all year, the East Germans went out of their way to play host to West German visitors, mainly from the opposition Social Democratic party. The Social Democratic parliamentary leader, Herr Hans-Jochen Vogel, visited East Berlin in May, and the party's chairman, former Chancellor Willy Brandt, was given the honours normally reserved for an actual head of government when he visited the Democratic Republic in September. Herr Oskar Lafontaine, the left-wing premier of the

Saarland, had talks with Herr Honecker in November. The SED and the Social Democrats agreed during the summer on a draft 'framework' pact to ban chemical weapons from German soil. At the end of the year, the two parties opened talks aimed at reaching a similar agreement to create a nuclear-free zone in Germany, extending to other Central European countries in due course. The real impact of such agreements with the out-of-power Social Democrats might be questioned, but the East Germans clearly saw advantages in building up their relationship with the West German party in advance of the 1987 national general election in the Federal Republic.

East German relations with the ruling coalition in Bonn moved more slowly. The West Germans agreed to finance repairs on the motorway leading from the West to Berlin through East Germany. Negotiations over a cultural agreement and joint anti-pollution measures ran into repeated problems. An East German Politburo member, Herr Herbert Mittag, visited West Germany for talks, and leading West German politicians of the centre-right went to the two trade fairs in Leipzig during the year. The East Germans announced the removal of remaining mines and automatic-firing guns from the border, but this was done only after the completion of a highly-effective double-fence system which cut to a trickle the number of refugees fleeing across the frontier without authorization.

Still, it was evident that both parts of Germany wanted to restore dialogue after the crisis over American missile deployment which caused Herr Honecker to cancel a planned visit to the West in 1984 at Moscow's urging (see AR 1984, pp. 111–12). The defections and arrests of a string of East German spies in West Germany during the summer and autumn was not allowed by either side to become a major irritant in inter-German relations. Nor was East Germany caused any lasting damage by the shooting of an American liaison officer, Major Arthur Nicholson, by a Soviet guard near Ludwigslust on 24 March. During July, two other incidents occurred involving the occupying Soviet forces. On 5 July a British airliner had to take evasive action when a Soviet MIG fighter flew dangerously close to it, and in mid-July American sources reported that Soviet troops had pursued and rammed an American liaison mission vehicle, injuring one of its occupants. Neither case was allowed to develop into a major incident.

Economically, the year began badly. Extreme cold weather froze supplies of lignite coal, a major energy source. One big power station, at Cottbus near the Polish border, had to interrupt its feed of electricity to the national grid. As the weather improved, however, East Germany asserted its claim to be a pace-setter among communist economies. National income rose by 4·4 per cent in the first nine months of 1985. Industrial production was up 4·5 per cent, slightly above target. Vehicles and electricity products led the way with output increases of 13·7 and 13·6 per cent respectively. Agriculture also had a good year. The record grain harvest reached 1·6 million tonnes. Fruit was so abundant that it was distributed free to schools in some parts of the country. Economic targets set in December provided for a 4·3 per cent rise in industrial output in 1986. The Prime Minister, Herr Willi Stoph, said that among 1986 innovations would be the installation of 17,000 office and personal computers. To finance industrial investment, East Germany arranged a $500 million new credit from United States and West European banks in March. The country was estimated to have hard-currency reserves of $4,500 million. At the end of December, East Germany and the Soviet Union signed a five-year trade agreement providing for exchanges worth about £100 million between 1986 and 1990. About 40 per cent of East German exports went to the Soviet Union and the agreement would ensure that Moscow remained by far the largest trading partner of the GDR.

The economy remained tightly controlled, but the number of people employed by private enterprises in the trades sector rose to nearly 260,000, according to the communist newspaper *Neues Deutschland*. Non-collectivized small farms played a role in the growth of agricultural output well beyond their 5 per cent share of arable land. At the end of the year, the East Germans undertook a sizeable deal to buy Ford cars produced in Saarland, as well as 900,000 tonnes of coal from Herr Lafontaine's state. Leading East German officials also had talks during the year with managers of some of West Germany's biggest industrial companies, such as the Krupp group, to explore the possibility of cooperative ventures.

POLAND

Neither the underground resistance nor Polish society's refusal to accept the basic premises of the Government's policies and actions disappeared or weakened. The authorities, while aware of those sentiments, professed to ignore them. Opposition appeals for dialogue and accommodation between government and society were rejected as anti-socialist and imperialist-inspired. The authorities assumed they alone had sufficient force to impose their decisions, albeit they showed restraint in public displays of force against continuing celebrations of various anniversaries, including the fifth anniversary of the August 1980 agreements (see AR 1980, p. 110).

Amendments made to the Penal Code·enlarged the scope of punishable political offences. The new law on 'special criminal liability' allowed for summary court proceedings without right to counsel. Amendments to trade union law rejected the principle of pluralism and strengthened the regime-sponsored unions, at factory and national levels. In numerous plants the workers boycotted the official unions and turned to elected workers' councils to represent their interests. The Party plenum warned the intelligentsia that they must 'accept the Party's leadership in all aspects of political life and struggle against any form of opposition'. The censorship office reverted to the pre-1980 practice of banning the works of certain authors and prohibiting some subjects. The publishing houses were told to remove non-conformist writers, and more paper would be allocated for 'pure socialist' literary works. The amendments to the higher education law (July) restricted student autonomy and gave the Minister extensive discretionary powers to interfere with the running of universities.

In November, 106 senior academic administrators and professors were removed from 14 major institutions of higher learning as politically unreliable. In February the Gdansk court sentenced three prominent Solidarity leaders, Wladyslaw Frasyniuk, Bogdan Lis and Adam Michnik, to $2\frac{1}{2}$ to $3\frac{1}{2}$ years' imprisonment for 'participating in activities of an illegal union'. Five members of the underground Confederation for an Independent Poland were arrested and charged with 'leadership of an illegal organization'.

The economic crisis continued. More basic foods were available in the shops but at higher prices. Price rises of food and energy averaging 35 per cent, smaller than originally planned, were introduced over four months. Some ration cards were withdrawn. To reduce the likelihood of strikes workers in a number of enterprises received substantial pay settlements and were warned that they risked immediate dismissal for engaging in stoppages.

In 1984 GNP rose by 5 per cent (16 per cent down on 1979) and consumption by 4 per cent (11 per cent down on 1979). Poland had to import 3·5 million tons of grain. The 1985 plan was put in jeopardy when wages rose by 19 per cent instead of the planned 12 per cent and industrial production by only 2·7 instead of 4 per cent. Inflation at 17 per cent was rising. Despite $29,200 million of foreign debt the necessary economic reforms ran aground through the familiar resistance of entrenched political and industrial bureaucracies. Seventeen countries rescheduled the repayment of $12,000 million owed to Western governments. That gave Warsaw a five-year period of grace until repayment was due, spread over 1991–97. According to a semi-official report 'at least half of society blamed government policies', and in an opinion poll conducted by the underground publication *Obecnosc* the Party was regarded as responsible for the crisis by 91 per cent respondents.

Relations between the Church and the state grew increasingly tense in the first half of the year as a result of an unprecedented escalation of anti-Church propaganda by mass media. In February the four murderers of Father Popieluszko (see AR 1984, p. 116) were sentenced by a Torun court to 14 to 25 years' imprisonment. The authorities' response was to purge the secret police. Officers were vetted for their allegiance to Jaruzelski. General Milewski, a Politburo member and Central Committee secretary in charge of security matters, was removed from both posts. Cardinal Glemp accused the communist media of having put the Church and Father Popieluszko in the dock alongside the accused secret police officers: 'the trial', he said, 'was used by the regime to show the guilt of Father Popieluszko and point to the Church as a source of guilt'. Terrorist attacks by 'unknown' assailants on young priests and people engaged in protest actions multiplied. The Episcopate asked the Government to end immediately the anti-Church campaign, which 'severely disrupted public peace', and proclaimed that the Church 'must have freedom to pass moral judgment even about political issues'. The bishops accused the mass media of a 'vicious, hostile and hateful' campaign against the Pope, who at an extremely frosty audience in November lectured Foreign Minister Olszowski on human rights, especially the sentencing of the three Solidarity leaders.

In June the papal nuncio Mgr Poggi arrived in Warsaw and the Primate met General Jaruzelski. Principles of Church-state relations were discussed and the 'conviction was expressed that the superior interests of the country required constant efforts to widen and consolidate the cooperation of Poles'. Cardinal Glemp visited Britain and the United States.

In the Sejm elections on 13 October 78·86 per cent of the electorate voted—a disastrously low turn-out by communist standards—for candidates chosen by the Patriotic Movement of National Rebirth (PRON) (see AR 1983, p. 110) and approved by the Party. According to Solidarity, which appealed for an election boycott, the attendance was 20 per cent lower than officially recorded. The authorities wanted a large turn-out to demonstrate the success of their attempts at 'normalization' and suggested that the Church had 'silently given its support for voting'. This was strongly denied by Cardinal Glemp.

Jaruzelski relinquished the premiership on 6 November and became head of state while retaining the leadership of the Party and of the National Defence Committee, the top security post. His successor Zbigniew Messner, an economist, affirmed that the new Government would pursue current policies and methods. It was necessary, he said, to strengthen central planning and control of the economy but simultaneously, in order to intensify production, the independence, initiative and responsibility of enterprises would also be strengthened. The number of Deputy Prime Ministers was reduced from eight to five. Thirteen out of thirty Ministers were removed—nine of them replaced by technocrats brought from the reliable military and Party establishment. In the Party, hardliner Stefan Olszowski resigned from the Politburo and was replaced as Foreign Minister by Marian Orzechowski. Kazimierz Barcikowski remained in the Politburo but resigned from the Central Committee secretariat. Marian Wozniak took over his post. The Sejm elections and personnel changes were heralded as reflecting 'normalization' of the country.

Against such official claims, the political clandestine opposition consisted of eighteen groups of which the TKK Solidarity (see AR 1984, p. 115) was the most important. Its leader claimed that 500,000 members were paying union dues and distributing underground newspapers, and 70,000 activists were working in a nationwide structure of clandestine committees. Solidarity, which in August had appealed for 'cooperative effort with the Government aimed at overcoming the dire economic problems', commissioned a report by eminent experts on the situation in the country. They argued that the East-West divide defined at Yalta did not 'force on us the choice of either passively adapting to the system or risking a complete breakdown of the existing order . . . In between the two extremes, there is a breathing-space for the ideas of Solidarity'. In October TKK advocated the gradual building of an 'independent society' in order to break the state monopoly of education, publishing and the media, and to facilitate self-help and self-organization by society. It could claim the most sophisticated underground press under communism, with numerous publishing houses and 600 book titles of about 7,000 copies each.

In the new Sejm, Professor Ryszard Bender hoped that 'parliament would appreciate the values of Solidarity and ensure that they were reflected in social practice'. In a speech to the Oxford Union, smuggled out of Poland, Walesa warned that because 'of repression and arrogance of the authorities there existed a permanent danger of a violent massive outbreak of workers' protests which could not be contained'.

Interior Minister Czeslaw Kiszczak admitted that the political underground exerted 'a negative influence on the internal situation', and Jaruzelski warned that 'a heated political struggle will continue'. At the Central Committee plenum on 21 December he insisted that the Party was not becoming too passive and tolerant; every member would be assessed ideologically. General Baryla, his trusted associate, became secretary of the Central Committee to help in strengthening ideological control. Jaruzelski reaffirmed the Party's exclusive right to shape the country's evolution and even hinted at the right to set limits to religious activities if 'political clericalism, fanaticism and intolerance continue'.

Slight cracks appeared in the Western isolation of the regime. Jaruzelski spoke at the UN General Assembly but was not seen by any member of the American Administration. On a one-day private visit to Paris he was received by President Mitterrand, the first Western statesman to do so since martial law was declared in Poland. The British Foreign Secretary on his official visit to Warsaw prayed at Father Popieluszko's grave and met Cardinal Glemp and prominent Solidarity advisers. Belgian, West German and Irish Foreign Ministers cancelled their official visits to Warsaw. The Italian Prime Minister refused to see Olszowski while he was in Rome on an official visit. On the other hand Herr Willy Brandt talked in Warsaw to Jaruzelski but refused to see Walesa. Poland tried to side-step the Western boycott by cultivating ties with socialists in West Germany.

CZECHOSLOVAKIA

If some of the Czechoslovak leaders had feared a ruffling of their feathers by Mikhail Gorbachev's putative reformism, they breathed with relief after Gustav Husák's visit to Moscow in May. The new Soviet General Secretary evidently valued the relative tranquillity of the Czechoslovak scene more than the elusive benefits of a new round of reform. Husák could then tell his party's Central Committee in mid-June that 'we will not take any of the roads based on market-orientated concepts. . . . We had bad experience with that kind of thing.' The changes arising from Gorbachev's 'dynamism' found only muted response in Czechoslovakia. No personnel changes occurred at the higher levels of the Party and the Government, and the impression was given that the campaigns against corruption and alcoholism, and for tighter work discipline, became reflected more in official rhetoric than in reality.

There was no shortage of statements and media items professing identification with the greater vehemence with which Soviet foreign and domestic policies were being conducted. If anything, Czechoslovakia distinguished itself by going always a little further than the Soviets, for example in the anti-revanchist campaign around the 40th anniversary of the end of World War II and in warning against expecting too much from the Reagan-Gorbachev summit in Geneva. The customary orthodox ideological line was vigorously confirmed at a conference in December to mark the 15th anniversary of a Communist Party document condemning the Prague Spring. The occasion was used to reiterate the validity of the so-called Brezhnev doctrine of limited sovereignty inside the Soviet bloc.

The national income grew by 3·2 per cent, a respectable achievement which was mainly due, however, to a change in the statistical computation introduced in the wake of two years of negative growth (1981 and 1982), a change which made an overall assessment of the seventh five-year plan (1981–85) well-nigh impossible. Beginning in 1983, the 'gross' national income was taken to include depreciation of capital stock. The harvest was good, for the second year in a row, and the country's net indebtedness to the West (probably $1,400 million) became insignificant because it was offset by unpaid Czechoslovak financial claims on the Third World. Czechoslovakia continued to run a sizeable deficit in its trade with the USSR, mainly because of rising Soviet raw material prices. Over 80 per cent of the country's trade was with other communist states, including more than 46 per cent with the USSR. The leeway for importa-tion of Western technology remained exceedingly small and imports from the West were kept to a bare minimum.

The related problem of how to modernize and 'intensify' an economy that appeared stuck in the 'extensive' groove was repeatedly answered by reference to the self-generating technical powers that were said to be immanent in the Soviet bloc. Actual progress was not encouraging, and the endeavour largely consisted of mobilizing 'the human factor' by way of appeals to 'a change in the old ways of thinking' and against 'old habits'. A great deal of editorial enthusiasm was drummed up for the Comecon programme of collective advancement in science and techno-logy, signed in Moscow in December, but even official pronouncements implied that defining the desiderata was a much easier task than fleshing up the programmatic text with real action.

The regime made no concessions to the surviving dissident com-munity or to the disaffected groups of the population, including the younger generation, but oppression was somewhat less severe than in previous years. The police appeared to have mastered the tactics of harassment and pre-emptive action to the point where not so many people had to be put on trial. Charter 77 issued almost thirty documents, a number of which concerned the question of war and peace, and the *samizdat* scene remained as lively as ever. When the regime's ideologist Vasil Bilak said some particularly preposterous things about the Prague Spring in his October interview with *Der Spiegel*, Alexander Dubček stepped out from enforced obscurity and countered him in a letter to three Czechoslovak newspapers. When they failed to publish it, his statement appeared in the Italian communist newspaper *l'Unita*. It seemed that a number of ex-communist dissidents set great store by the accession of Mikhail Gorbachev, believing that, even though progress must of necessity be slow, an opportunity for 'reformed communism' was once again opening up. These sentiments were not shared by the public at large, who had long viewed perspectives offered from Moscow with almost total scepticism.

Religious revival continued, especially among the young. While the petition to invite the Pope for the 1100th anniversary of the death of St Methodius in July had failed to move the authorities into issuing an official invitation, the commemoration was still an impressive event, with a congregation that some observers estimated at up to 150,000. Cardinal Agostino Casaroli attended on behalf of the Pontiff and it looked as if the more moderate international climate and the evident strength of religious feelings in the country would bring about an improvement in relations between the Church (and the Vatican) and the authorities. In the end no practical results transpired. Instead of relenting, the regime may have felt threatened by the fervour of popular sentiment into prolonging its obstinacy.

On the whole, the year was of a nature that President and Party leader Gustav Husák liked to describe as stable. Many observers found it difficult to distinguish between this kind of stability and stagnation.

HUNGARY

In both the political and the economic realms, the year proved to be a markedly poor one for Hungary. In politics, despite the seeming success of the thirteenth congress of the Hungarian Socialist Workers' Party in the spring, a gradual but unmistakable sense of drift and helplessness was perceptible. This lack of purposiveness, regardless of the rhetoric to the contrary, had its impact on economics, in the reluctance of the leadership to face up to ever-more-difficult decisions that could not be put off without even more damaging consequences.

The year actually began reasonably well, as the preparations for the congress seemed to show a measure of readiness to press forward with necessary changes. In the event, while the congress was remarkable for the openness with which criticsm was expressed, there was an absence of any determination to apply remedial measures. This was attributed to several factors.

First, there was the inherent conservatism of the party elite, which was reluctant to be prodded into changes that would affect its power and privileges. Second, there was the question of succession to the long-serving party leader, János Kádár (b. 1912). While rumours of Kádár's ill health had circulated for some time (but could not be confirmed), the implication that he could well leave the political scene in the 1980s began to be taken seriously by the elite. Several contenders emerged, albeit none of them overtly. The congress itself promoted Kádár to Secretary-General (from First Party Secretary) and elevated Károly Németh to be his deputy. This would place Németh in the position of interim successor. The real contenders for the succession—János Berecz, Károly Grósz, Imre Pozsgay, László Maróthy—would emerge in the aftermath, but were evidently mustering forces within the elite. This had the result that the divisions within the party likewise hindered decisiveness.

The third factor was the uncertainty over Soviet intentions. Although Gorbachev's determined moves to purge the Soviet party and state bureaucracies, together with his commitment to change, were welcome to Hungarian supporters of reform, his emphasis on discipline and coercion ran counter to this. Further, his success in reintegrating Comecon and formulating new joint investment schemes placed a major highly-unwelcome economic burden on Hungary at an already difficult time. Finally, Gorbachev's struggle to remove Grigory Romanov (see p. 98) had its repercussions in Hungary, in as much as Romanov was the leader of the Soviet delegation to the congress and instrumental in the elevation of Grósz, regarded as an unprincipled hardliner, to Hungary's Politburo.

The elections to parliament, widely advertised as a new move towards political reform, had rather contradictory results. Under the new regulations, except for a list of 35 seats reserved for top leaders and a few others, all of the country's 352 constituencies had to be contested by at least two candidates. The democratic opposition decided to test the regime's sincerity in its reform-mindedness and sought to nominate several of its own candidates. This took the authorities by surprise and they were forced to mobilize their forces (state employees, workers' militia) in order to pack the nomination meetings and thus prevent opposition candidates from reaching the nomination list. At the same time, a number of independent candidates not connected to the opposition did reach the list and some were actually nominated in the teeth of opposition from local elite coteries.

The election process also revealed that there was more than a measure of popular dissatisfaction with issues not touched on in the official media, notably poverty, environmental deterioration and, above all, the decline in the standard of living. It was also noteworthy that not one of the candidates from the official trade union movement (other than those on the reserved list) was elected. This was interpreted as a strong indication of popular irritation with the spinelessness of the unions.

Continued misgiving was also expressed at the authorities' persistence with the Gabčikovo-Nagymaros hydroelectric barrage scheme. Despite the economic and ecological evidence, which all pointed towards abandonment of the project, the Government announced its go-ahead in August. Subsequent reports hinted that the decision had a military-strategic background, namely that the barrage would provide a fixed link over the Danube, capable of carrying armour, and would connect Soviet bases in Western Hungary with those in the Börzsöny hills, just above the Danube bend where the barrage would be built.

On the economic side, 1985 was a very poor year indeed. There were all-round failures to meet plan targets—in national income, in material product, in agriculture and, most seriously, in exports. Whereas the plan had provided for a surplus of $661 million in trade with the hard-currency area, the actual figure was a deficit of about $2,200 million, thereby increasing Hungary's total indebtedness to around $9,000 million. This adversely affected the country's credit-worthiness on Western markets, although not to the extent of destroying it altogether. To make matters worse, Hungary's position in rouble-trade with its allies also deteriorated.

The reasons for the economic failure were partly contingent on the bad weather experienced in 1985—a very severe winter followed by poor summer growing conditions. The harsh winter forced the authorities to import 1·7 million tons of coal at a cost of $10 million and the poor summer undermined the harvest. All of this demonstrated again how close to the economic margin Hungary really was and how dependent it was on a few products.

Despite many years of discussion, there was little sign that either the party leadership or the economic managers were ready to change the way in which the economy was run. The persistence of protection for too many loss-making enterprises and the reluctance to apply profitability criteria and the discipline of the market ensured a high degree of mis-allocation of investment funds.

The year was also an active one for the democratic opposition. In addition to the attempt to nominate candidates in the elections, a meeting of 47 leading opposition figures was held in the summer at Monor, near Budapest, where the leaders of the different strands of opposition currents sought to find common ground and, as far as possible, create a common front. Some progress was made in this direction. Considerable quantities of *samizdat* were issued during the year, dealing with a wide range of topics.

ROMANIA

The exceptionally cold winter of 1984–85 hit Romania with the impact of a natural disaster. Much of the country's economic activity stopped. By March, the cost of the winter became apparent: massive losses in production, exports severely affected and currency earnings lost, while an extra million tonnes of oil had been imported to compensate for the shortfall in domestic coal and gas production.

The cost was even higher in terms of the psychological effect on the population of the hardships endured, combined with the harsh and callous attitude of the authorities. Throughout the country, heating was for several months completely discontinued in public buildings and cut off for most of the day in apartment blocks. It was forbidden by decree to switch on the light in more than one room at a time, and to use household electrical appliances. Lighting in public places, already much reduced, was cut by another 50 per cent; all private cars were banned from the road from January to the end of March. The morale of the population, already badly shaken by years of food shortages, collapsed.

In March, the Government had to decide whether to persist in its ambitions to put the country back on a course of intensive development—a 10 per cent growth rate had been envisaged for 1985—or to concentrate on healing the wounds left by the winter. The decision was to recoup the winter's losses by forcing the pace. It became clear in the following months that this was not being achieved and that more severe trouble was lying ahead. In August, a law was passed requiring all able-bodied citizens to work six days annually without pay for the state. In

September, a special law was introduced for three months covering all branches of the economy involved in energy production and exports, and providing for a two per cent cut in workers' wages for every unfulfilled percentage point in the production plan. In October, all coal-based power-plants in the country were militarized, the entire personnel coming under military penalties for failings in discipline or performance. Military commanders, assisted by a group of officers, were sent to each plant to supervise the civilian management. Later in the year there were reports that military units were on duty to maintain order in the countryside, and that they had clashed with peasants who tried to break into grain depots.

On 11 December the Defence Minister, General Constantin Olteanu, was replaced. Although a few days later he was appointed mayor and party chief of Bucharest, a not unimportant position, his removal from the headship of the army signalled President Ceauşescu's mistrust and dissatisfaction with the military establishment. In a speech to a meeting of army commanders Ceauşescu criticised the isolation of the military from the security forces and the people in general and said that 'our army prepares for defence and not for purposes alien to the people's interest', an odd remark to make amid signs that he was increasingly relying on the army's support. Possibly the military establishment, having been called upon to maintain the country's internal stability, tried to have a greater say in the making of policies as well, and was rebuffed. One month before Olteanu's replacement, Foreign Minister Stefan Andrei was sacked for allegedly disagreeing with the President.

Up to a point, these incidents showed how firmly Ceauşescu was still in control of the leadership, but they also showed that resistance to his policies was building up. This was the more significant in view of the widely-circulating speculations that his health was deteriorating and that during 1985 he had undergone cancer surgery. There were relatively brief periods when Ceauşescu was not seen in public at all, and most people who saw him in later months agreed that he looked gaunt and frail. Reports from Bucharest towards the end of the year, however, indicated that he was very active and apparently able to cope with a heavy schedule of work.

Nevertheless, the possibility of Ceauşescu's disappearance from Romania's political scene was now likely to be a major factor in the calculations both of people around him and of political circles abroad. His wife Elena, who during 1985 further consolidated her position as an unofficial Number Two of the regime, was regarded as a likely immediate successor. She was also seen, in the longer term, as likely to want to pave the way for Ceauşescu's son Nicu to succeed to the supreme leadership.

The replacement of Chernenko, with whom Ceauşescu had established a good relationship, by Gorbachev, with whom relations remained cool, in the Kremlin was an important setback for Romanian foreign policy. Romania's demands for cheap energy and raw material supplies from the Soviet Union were not included in the 15-year cooperation agreements concluded in 1985 among Comecon member-states. Relations with the US became also strained, with the emergence in the American Congress of influential pressure groups strongly critical of Romania's human rights record. Secretary of State George Shultz paid a visit to Bucharest in November to tell Ceauşescu that his country might lose its most-favoured-nation trading status with the US if the present state of affairs did not change. The number of unfavourable reports about Romania increased greatly in the Western press, and their critical tone sharpened. Relations with Hungary deteriorated further, following a very tough-worded campaign in the Romanian press against what were described as revisionist and irredentist Hungarian attitudes over Transylvania.

BULGARIA

Forced assimilation of the Turkish ethnic minority and deterioration of the economy were the main features of a grim year for Bulgaria. In January alarming reports from Turkey described government pressure on ethnic Turks (10 to 15 per cent of Bulgaria's population) to adopt Bulgarian instead of Islamic names. The brutality of the campaign provoked resistance, and numerous deaths were reported by relatives living in Turkey.

The 'Bulgarization' drive encompassed prohibitions on the public speaking of Turkish and intense propaganda against Muslim beliefs and customs. In March leading Communist Party figures visited minority areas to proclaim that the Muslims who had 'spontaneously' changed their names were not Turks, but descendants of Bulgarians forcibly converted during the centuries of Ottoman rule. It was emphasized that the Government would not negotiate with Turkey nor allow emigration.

After an initially cautious reaction, Turkey dispatched protest notes and offered to accept Muslims who wanted to leave Bulgaria. Subsequently Ankara began to minimize economic ties with Bulgaria and denounced its assimilation policy in various international forums.

While relations with Turkey deteriorated, contacts with Greece remained lively and friendly. Todor Zhivkov paid an official visit to Athens in July. Bulgaria and Greece reaffirmed their earlier proposals for the denuclearization of the Balkans, a project also supported by Romania but opposed by Turkey.

Relations with Yugoslavia were more problematical, despite a visit by Prime Minister Grisha Filipov to Belgrade in November. Yugoslavia continued to criticise Bulgaria over its Macedonian policies and complained at the chauvinistic style of centenary celebrations of Bulgaria's victory in the 1885 war against Serbia.

The accession to power of Mikhail Gorbachev in Moscow seemed to bring little rejoicing in Sofia. Although Zhivkov visited the USSR in June on his return from a Far Eastern tour and signed a programme for long-term economic and technological cooperation, the coordination of the two countries' new five-year plans proved difficult. In July the Soviet ambassador in Sofia, Leonid Grekov, criticised the Bulgarian economy surprisingly forcefully in an interview with the weekly *Pogled*. During his 'friendly visit' to Sofia in October Gorbachev uncovered what he described as 'a few sharp edges' in his talks with the Bulgarian leadership.

The insufficiency of Soviet oil and coal exports exacerbated the effects of a prolonged drought and a severe winter which had caused a critical energy shortage. Poor management, the inadequate maintenance of installations and public wastefulness were also blamed. An unprecedented shortfall from plan targets was reported for the first quarter. Provisional results for the year showed that industry expanded by 3·5 instead of the planned 5·2 per cent. Output in the mining, metallurgical and energy sectors fell. Agricultural production declined by 9 per cent and national income, instead of rising by 4.1 per cent, achieved only a 2·5 per cent increase. A number of prices were drastically increased on 1 October.

An immediate consequence of the crisis was the dissolution in May of the 'super-ministry' of Energy and Raw Material Resources and the demotion of its head, Todor Bozhinov, to the more modest post of Minister of Supplies. In October the chairman of the State Planning Committee, Stanish Bonev, was dismissed.

The 'new economic mechanism' (NEM) (see AR 1984, p. 125) came in for criticism in February during a plenum on scientific and technical progress. Zhivkov charged managers with evading effective reform. In the autumn four leading economists appealed in the daily *Trud* for amendment of the NEM to allow a freer play of market forces and to facilitate the autonomy of enterprises. Several leading articles in the party daily *Rabotnichesko Delo* were scathing of incompetent and corrupt managers and party functionaries.

A decree against young people 'not engaged in socially useful work' and measures to enforce discipline among secondary school pupils tightened controls over the young. Culture suffered a lean year, enlivened only by an acrostic against Zhivkov published in the weekly *Puls* and the .opening of an extravagant gallery of modern art. Measures were introduced to control video-recordings and discotheques.

The existence of opposition to the regime was shown by the continuation of the bomb outrages that began in 1984 (see AR 1984, p. 125). In March a train was blown up outside Sofia, killing nine people; 15

people died in arson incidents in street cars. Amendments to the Penal Code in May raised the penalties for acts of terrorism.

Bulgaria's image in the world continued to suffer. Charges of complicity with international terrorism and drug smuggling persisted, while in Rome the trial of Sergey Antonov and six other defendants suspected of involvement in the shooting of the Pope in 1981 began.

YUGOSLAVIA

There were few signs that the Long-Term Economic Stabilization Programme, launched in July 1983 (see AR 1983, p. 121) in an attempt to impose some social discipline on the economy, was achieving its objectives. One prominent Macedonian communist, Kiro Gligorov, stated that the programme had totally failed, and at a plenary session of the LCY (League of Communists) central committee held in April Nikola Stojanović identified the failure to implement the anti-inflationary measures approved in 1983 as one of the chief causes of the economic and political crises which faced the country. Inflation officially reached over 85 per cent, but unofficial estimates gave a much higher figure. The fall in living standards, which was put at 30 per cent over the previous four years, slowed down slightly, and there was an increase in the volume of exports to hard currency areas. However, the decline in the exchange value of the dinar and the galloping inflation rate meant that the overall balance of payments deteriorated. Unemployment reached over one million—over 15 per cent—which put Yugoslavia's rate well above the European average.

Prime Minister Milka Planinc made important journeys to the USA and USSR, where, bonnet in hand, she sought aid for the ailing economy. Her two-day visit to the UN in New York, which began on 27 May, was concerned mainly with questions related to Yugoslavia's role in the Non-Aligned Movement, but in Washington she met President Reagan, Secretary of State Shultz and directors of the IMF and World Bank. Promises of continuing aid were given, linked with warnings about the need for changes in the management of the economy. One change widely discussed was the aim to create a genuine Yugoslav common market and to break down the autarchic tendencies of the republics. Another was the desirability of encouraging private enterprise. Mrs Planinc's visit to Moscow in July involved talks with General Secretary Gorbachev and Premier Tikhonov, and resulted in a communique which spoke of 'frankness and mutual understanding' but produced no concrete proposals for economic assistance.

Yugoslavia's external debt increased from about $20,000 million to an estimated $24,000 million as a result of accumulated interest charges. The

IMF and Western bankers, prompted by their Governments, were sympathetic to Yugoslavia's plight, and a number of debt-rescheduling agreements were reached during the second half of the year. However, as the well-known Serbian leader, Ivan Stambolić, told the LCY central committee in April, it was an illusion that foreign aid could remedy the situation. By taking foreign credits 'we are only buying time'.

There was considerable disagreement amongst state and LCY leaders as to the best way out of the crisis. Stane Dolanc, the Slovene member of the federal Presidency, complained that the 'inflation of meetings' had become a political problem, and that people were tired of hearing the same issues being 'discussed and repeated a thousand times'. Urgent action was required.

The lines of action discussed, especially among intellectual critics in the universities, included an ending of the LCY's monopoly of political power. The LCY central committee, however, called for a tightening of discipline, and threatened expulsion even of members of the Presidium if they refused to accept majority decisions.

The reaction of the authorities to dissent varied from republic to republic. The group of Belgrade intellectuals whose trial was postponed in 1984 (see AR 1984, p. 127) received relatively light sentences when the trial was resumed in 1985. On the other hand, those accused of nationalism or of promoting religious extremism were more severely dealt with.

The province of Kosovo, with its Albanian-speaking majority, was seen as the most dangerous centre of nationalist agitation, and in December over 100 arrests were made when the authorities claimed to have uncovered a conspiracy to promote separatism and Albanian nationalism. Many of the accused were teachers and members of other professions who were graduates of Priština University. Trials of Albanian dissidents took place throughout the year and many of those accused were sentenced to terms of imprisonment. There were complaints at the Writers Congress held in Novi Sad in April that Serbs in Kosovo had been subject to persecution—even genocide—by members of the Albanian majority in the province.

Despite these problems, relations between the Yugoslavs and the post-Hoxha regime in Albania were expanded (see p. 123). Work on the rail link from Titograd to the Albanian border proceeded, and an official opening was expected early in 1986. The dispute with Bulgaria concerning the separate existence of the Macedonian nation, and a similar dispute with Greece, following a ban by the Athens Government on Slav-speaking Greek students attending Skopje University, had little effect on trade relations between Yugoslavia and its southern neighbours.

Yugoslavia's relations with the PLO, and in particular its action in permitting one of those accused of complicity in the *Achille Lauro* affair to pass through Belgrade, brought strong protests from Secretary of State Shultz during a visit in December.

The normal rotation of offices promoted Radovan Vlajković of Vojvodina to the post of federal President in May, and of Vidoje Žarkovic of Montenegro to the leadership of the LCY Presidium in October.

ALBANIA

Enver Hoxha, First Secretary of the Workers' (Communist) Party, died on 11 April, aged 76, having ruled his country with the utmost ruthlessness almost like his private domain for over forty years (see OBITUARY). Since 1948 he had suffered from diabetes, which had gradually affected his heart, kidneys and other organs. Two days after his death, he was succeeded as party leader by Ramiz Alia, the nominal head of state, who had served for many years as member of the Politburo and Hoxha's principal deputy.

The new leader lost no time in making it plain that he would pursue current policies with the same energy and tenacity that Hoxha had shown throughout his long career. This theme was reiterated on numerous occasions during 1985. Great efforts were made on Hoxha's birthday on 16 October, in particular, to extol his achievements as founder of the Communist Party, wartime guerrilla leader, statesman, diplomat and marxist-leninist thinker. This act of political glorification suggested that Alia and the other leaders, the real beneficiaries of Hoxha's draconian purges, hoped to ensure that the source of their legitimacy would not be eventually undermined as Stalin's and Mao Zedong's legacies had been in the Soviet Union and China.

Some of the country's acute economic and social problems were discussed during the year in official statements and newspaper articles. Alia admitted in June that oil and gas production had declined during previous years. The mining industry in general was in dire need of modern technology, expertise and greater efficiency. Albania's weak and inefficient economy suffered serious blows caused by severe winter conditions in the early months of the year and a prolonged summer drought. The Chairman of the People's Assembly referred in June to difficulties that had arisen in supplying people, particularly those living in the countryside, with consumer goods. According to some unconfirmed reports, meat and other items of food and consumer goods had to be rationed. People were also asked to save electricity and gas, both at home and at work.

As in previous years, the low morale, restlessness and alienation of many young people again preoccupied party and government officials. In February, a special seminar on youth problems of the capital disclosed that there were many school drop-outs, and that some young people had come under what officialdom regarded as harmful foreign cultural influences. In July, the leader of the country's youth organization said that the behaviour and attitudes of many young people were being influenced by foreign broadcasts, commercial advertising and personal contacts with tourists from abroad. There had also been a religious revival among the young, despite the fact that religious practices were made illegal in 1967.

Hoxha's policy of isolation from the outside world, designed to protect the people over whom he ruled from alien political, social and cultural contamination, was now working against the country's vital interests. Although neither he when alive nor his successors seemed prepared to open up to the world as a matter of principle, sheer economic necessity forced them to do their utmost to expand trade exchanges with other countries. This was a direct consequence of the lack of any foreign economic aid since the break-up of Albania's alliance with China in 1978. But trade relations, particularly with Western Europe, were hampered by the communist regime's reluctance to accept credits from foreign governments or banks.

Neverthless the country's relations with Greece steadily improved during 1985. The road link between the two countries, closed since 1940, was officially opened in January. It was also decided to establish a ferry service between the Greek island of Corfu and the Albanian port of Saranda. A trade agreement enabled Greece to build a chrome processing plant in Albania.

Relations with Italy also showed a marked improvement. In October, the Albanian Minister of Foreign Trade signed an economic agreement in Rome dealing with sea and air transport, telecommunications and mining. It envisaged, among other things, a ferry link between Brindisi and the Albanian port of Durres, and joint off-shore oil exploration.

Relations with Yugoslavia continued in the same frozen state as they had been in since the Albanian riots of Kosovo in 1981 (see AR 1981, pp. 127–9). The Albanian media were highly critical of the numerous trials of Albanians that were still being held in Kosovo and Macedonia (see p. 121). The Yugoslavs regarded such criticism as interference in their domestic affairs. Yet, despite their propaganda support for the Albanians in Yugoslavia over many years, the Albanian authorities did return to that country in October two Yugoslav citizens of Albanian origin who had escaped to Albania. The two defectors, according to the Yugoslavs, had been convicted of political offences.

MONGOLIA

In June, Jambyn Batmonh, General Secretary of the ruling Mongolian People's Revolutionary Party (MPRP) and Chairman of the Presidium of the People's Great Hural (President of Mongolia), announced at a plenum of the Central Committee that its 19th congress would open on 28 May 1986. Besides Batmonh's own report on domestic and foreign policy, the congress agenda would include a report by Premier Dumaagiyn Sodnom on the economy, the adoption of guidelines for the eighth five-year development plan (1986–90) and the election of a new Central Committee.

The plenum emphasised that, in the run-up to the congress, including local party elections and the selection of congress delegates, all party organizations must analyse their past efforts carefully and strive for concrete results in the leadership of economic construction and ideological work. In February, Batmonh had warned staff of the MPRP Central Committee of the need for a 'broad, farsighted and overall approach' to the solution of the 'urgent problems of the day'. 'Bureaucratism, formalism, abstraction and passive transmission (of responsibility) up the chain of command' must be replaced by a 'creative atmosphere', he said.

In comparison with the turnover of party officials and government Ministers of previous years, the leadership was relatively stable in 1985, only one senior figure having retired—Damdingiyn Gombojav, member of the Politburo and secretary of the MPRP Central Committee since 1981. A new Minister of Water Supply, Dzunduyn Janjaadorj, was appointed in June, on the retirement, due to illness, of Bavuudorjiyn Bars. The long-time administrator of the affairs of the Council of Ministers, 68-year-old Baldangiyn Badarch, and the Minister of Forestry and Woodworking Industry, Damdingiyn Tseden, aged 49, both died in November. On Dangaasurengiyn Saldan's appointment to be ambassador to Hungary and Austria, the chairmanship of the State Committee for Foreign Economic Relations was given to Punsalmaagiyn Ochirbat (January); Ochirbat's job as Minister of Fuel and Power Industry went to his deputy, Sodovyn Bathuyag. The Minister of Education, Chimediyn Sereeter, was appointed Chairman of the State Committee for Higher and Special Secondary Education (April), and the first deputy Minister, Byambyn Davaasuren, was promoted Minister. Meanwhile, Major-General Galsansandzayn Mahbariad, first deputy chief of the general staff, was appointed head of the civil defence directorate and deputy Minister of Defence (December).

Jambyn Batmonh told Mongolian army officers in May that they must improve their style of leadership. 'Young officers must be taught to carry out their service duties in an exemplary manner', he declared. Young people must be better prepared for military service and educated in a 'military-patriotic spirit'.

Batmonh visited Moscow in March for Konstantin Chernenko's funeral, and afterwards he and Mikhail Gorbachev reaffirmed the unchanging nature of the two countries' policy of strengthening their traditional friendship and 'deepening multifaceted cooperation'. In August, at the end of a holiday in the USSR, Batmonh met Gorbachev again, saying that Mongolia's alliance and friendship with the Soviet Union were 'stronger than they have ever been'.

The two leaders signed an economic, scientific and technical cooperation programme, outlining Soviet aid to Mongolia up to the year 2000 in developing such key sectors as agriculture, mining, fuel and power, construction, forestry and transport.

While in Moscow Batmonh said that Mongolia continued to pursue 'normalization of inter-state relations' with China and was also 'following with interest' the Sino-Soviet consultations on normalization. Earlier, Mongolia had insisted that normalization 'should not prejudice the interests of third countries' and opposed China's involvement in any discussion of the stationing of Soviet troops in Mongolia. Although there were some exchanges of low-level delegations as well as increases in trade and other contacts with China, the Mongolian press remained generally hostile to China over domestic political developments and particularly foreign policy.

The launching of a Mongolian 'food programme' was announced at the June plenum. Average consumption of basic foodstuffs was planned to rise through intensification of animal husbandry and expanded production of such basic crops as potatoes and green vegetables, whose annual output was to reach respectively 340,000 and 160,000 metric tons by the year 2000, 1984 production having been 122,900 and 34,200 metric tons respectively. Mongolia was self-sufficient in grain, and the harvest in 1985 set a new record of more than 800,000 metric tons. Concern about losses of livestock continued, however; no total figure was released, but the number of young animals surviving from birth during the year (8·4 million) was well below plan for the third year running.

Reporting on economic developments to the year-end session of the People's Great Hural, Vice-Premier Puntsagiyn Jasray, Chairman of the State Planning Commission, estimated the rise in gross production during 1985 at 6·6 per cent for industry (plan, 7·5 per cent) and 12·5 per cent for agriculture.

IV WESTERN, CENTRAL AND SOUTHERN EUROPE

Chapter 1

FRANCE—FEDERAL REPUBLIC OF GERMANY—ITALY—BELGIUM—
THE NETHERLANDS—LUXEMBOURG—REPUBLIC OF IRELAND

FRANCE

UNITY and tolerance featured prominently among President Mitterrand's hopes for France in 1985, but politically they were at a discount. If the public was wearied by three years of pre-election jousting, the politicians were tireless in their quest for advantage. Defeat of the left in the 1986 elections being already taken as read, speculation focused on whether or how the President could subsequently 'cohabit' with a right-wing Assembly. The institutional balance of the Fifth Republic would turn on the outcome.

Midway through his term the President's standing was at its lowest ebb. His austerity programme had alienated left support without pacifying the right; his achievements received little recognition. Even the weather seemed against him. The exceptionally bitter winter caused frost damage right down to the Riviera, leading to 145 deaths. In the March cantonal elections the Socialists won 25·01 per cent of the vote and the Communists 12·67 per cent. The Union for French Democracy took 19·28 per cent, the Rally for the Republic 16·87 per cent and the National Front 8·69 per cent. The left lost control of 10 of the 36 departments it held in metropolitan France. Although these results implied defeat at the parliamentary elections, they were better than the Socialists had feared. With 49·1 per cent of the vote the traditional right was still short of a popular majority; there was ground for hope—and for manoeuvre.

Unsentimentally drawing the lesson of the cantonals, the Government moved speedily to alter the electoral law. The Assembly was increased from 491 members to 577, reducing the number of sitting members at risk, and the system of single-member constituencies with two ballots was replaced by proportional representation based on departmental (county) constituencies with a single ballot and a minimum of 5 per cent of the vote to win a seat. The change precipitated the resignation of the Minister of Agriculture, M Michel Rocard, who was replaced by M Henri Nallet from the President's personal staff. The opposition alleged that the Bill sacrificed stable majority government to partisan advantage, and that, to thwart the 'respectable' right, it guaranteed seats to the extreme-right National Front.

Aware of M Mitterrand's hopes of dividing and conquering, the UDF and RPR pledged they would 'govern together and only together' and agreed joint proposals on cutting public expenditure and taxes, privatization, workers' participation, curbs on the unions, and limitations on immigration—while respecting human rights. In June the Liberal Convention brought the three main opposition leaders together in a display of unity. But in reality they were in disarray. M Jacques Chirac and M Valéry Giscard d'Estaing favoured some form of cohabitation with M Mitterrand after the election; M Raymond Barre was hostile. All three opposed the Socialist Government, but each was manoeuvering with an eye to the 1988 presidential election.

Unsure of outright victory in March 1986, the opposition was uncertain about its relationship with the National Front, on whose support it might depend to govern. With its strident patriotism and hostility to immigrants the Front had appreciable popular support in areas of high immigration. But the killing of a North African at Menton stirred a movement of sympathy, culminating in an anti-racist festival that attracted some 300,000 people in Paris in June. Nor did the Front's leader, M Jean-Marie Le Pen, appear a more attractive ally after his embarrassing libel actions against papers that recalled his attitude to torture during the Algerian war. M Chirac made it clear that M Le Pen would not make an acceptable coalition partner.

In February, at the 25th Congress of the Communist Party, the customary public endorsement of the leadership line could not entirely smother disquiet at the party's continuing decline. The Congress confirmed both the party's unwavering hostility to the Socialists and its political isolation.

With the prospect of electoral defeat Socialist morale flagged; the ambitious began vying for the succession to M Mitterrand. The Prime Minister, M Laurent Fabius, and the party's general secretary, M Lionel Jospin, squabbled publicly over the conduct of the election campaign and Socialist strategy. M Fabius' star waned over his handling of the *Rainbow Warrior* affair (see p. 130 and Pt. X, Ch. 2), an unfortunate television confrontation with M Chirac and his implied criticism of the President's decision to receive General Jaruzelski. Concern over the Government's poor showing led M Mitterrand to intervene more actively on its behalf than would have been expected of a President who might shortly have to coexist with Ministers of a very different ideological stamp intent on seeing, in M Jacques Chaban-Delmas' words, that the President might preside—but the Government would govern.

Meanwhile M Mitterrand was seeking to build on consensus in defence and foreign affairs, emphasising presidential prerogatives and extending his role in senior appointments. His most striking coup, in

December, was to award a Franco-Italian group the contract for a fifth television channel on exceedingly favourable terms, apparently designed to thwart privatization of the existing channels and to ensure that at least one service would remain sympathetic to him after the elections. Opposition leaders threatened to rescind the contract on taking power.

Extremists again left their murderous mark. The far-left Action Directe assassinated the director of international affairs at the Defence Ministry in January, attempted to kill the controller-general of the armed forces in July and attacked four bodies having links with South Africa in September. In March 18 people were injured by a bomb at the International Jewish Film Festival in Paris. In December unattributed bombs in two Paris department stores injured 35 people. Corsica had a quieter year following public revulsion over the murder of a leading pro-French activist. In the Basque country there were sporadic reprisals on nationalists by the anti-terrorist Liberation Group.

It was a relatively good year for the economy. Inflation was down to 4·7 per cent—fractionally above the target of 4·5 per cent but the best figure since 1968. Consumer purchasing power rose by 0·3 per cent, contributing to a 1·5 per cent growth in GDP, though industrial production was slow to respond. Capital spending was running 4·4 per cent above the depressed 1984 level at the end of the year. Trade and external debt figures improved, the former into a slight surplus after a £600 million deficit in 1984. The one major blot remained unemployment. Although jobs were being created faster than they were lost it was little changed at 10·8 per cent of the work-force.

Despite the approach of the election austerity continued. The Government pressed forward with industrial modernization and tight budgeting. The 1986 Budget made further expenditure cuts in real terms; expenditure increased by 3·6 per cent for an expected 6·1 per cent rise in GDP, reducing state spending from 23·3 per cent of GDP to 21·3 per cent. Capital expenditure was to fall by about 10 per cent. The other casualties were housing, transport, agriculture and industry. Spending on education, culture, research, justice, defence and law and order was relatively unscathed. Income tax was reduced by 3 per cent but there were increases in nationalized industry prices and social security contributions.

Among the biggest public-sector headaches was Renault, which accounted for half the nationalized industry deficit of £2,100 million for 1984—steel making up much of the remainder. In January M Bernard Henault was sacked from the chairmanship and replaced by M Georges Besse, who had successfully turned round Pechiney. The company successfully weathered a strike against job losses by the Communist-led Confédération Générale du Travail (CGT) in October. Like an earlier incident in June when there were violent clashes over the 'reconquest' of the SKF factory at Ivry, after an occupation had been ended by the police, the CGT's activism was seen as further evidence of Communist hostility to the Socialists. Generally, though, it was a year of relative industrial calm.

DEFENCE AND FOREIGN AFFAIRS. When France's sixth missile submarine, *Inflexible*, entered operational service in May, M Mitterrand's presence was symbolic testimony to the country's continuing commitment to nuclear forces. Armed with 16 M4 MIRV missiles of 4,000 km range, *Inflexible* more than doubled the navy's complement of nuclear warheads. The 1985 Budget was to provide for another strategic-missile submarine and a nuclear-powered aircraft carrier. In the autumn, visits by both the President and the Prime Minister to Mururoa Atoll again emphasised continuity and consensus in defence. However, in July the retiring chief of staff, General Lacaze, expressed anxiety at the state of France's defences. Advocating development of the neutron bomb, chemical weapons and a space defence system, he warned that economies in operating expenses were threatening efficiency. With a fifth of the defence budget committed to the nuclear force it might be necessary to shelve plans for M5 MIRVs in the submarine fleet and delay a new land-based missile system, and to cut conventional military programmes by a quarter. In November General Philippe Arnold was relieved of his divisional command for criticizing the state of the armoured forces.

The need for economy might also explain the continuing move away from the 'Fortress France' attitudes of de Gaulle's day towards greater European defence cooperation and the extension of the French nuclear umbrella to West Germany. Supported by all parties except the Communists, the new line meant that for most practical purposes France had returned to a full position within Nato. However, its determination to maintain an independent stance was reiterated in November when M Paul Quilès, the Defence Minister, said France's defences must take account of 'Star Wars' developments and advocated greater priority for the navy and ground-based missiles.

Diplomatically a routine year was marred by several unhappy episodes. January brought withdrawal of the ambassador to India and the expulsion of a military attaché after the disclosure that France had received classified documents from both the Prime Minister's office and the Defence Ministry in New Delhi. The incident compromised France's flourishing arms trade with India. At the Bonn summit in May President Mitterrand refused both to associate France with the Strategic Defense Initiative (SDI) and to set a date for trade negotiations until the Americans had taken effective action on the monetary front. This ruffled feathers in Bonn, with which relations remained cool, but at home, where 'isolation' is customarily considered rather grand, it did the President no harm—especially as he also tenaciously defended French agriculture.

France showed a similarly independent spirit in June when M Fabius became the first important Western leader to meet Chairman Honecker in East Berlin, and in July when France broke European ranks in imposing sanctions on South Africa. More symbolic than practical, these were meant to emphasise traditional French concern for human rights. French hopes of a leading role in the new European combat aircraft were dashed in October, and the relative success of M Mitterrand's Eureka scheme for European technological cooperation (see pp. 393–4) was only minor recompense. In October there was satisfaction that Mr Gorbachev chose France for his first visit to Western Europe since becoming General Secretary, but M Mitterrand rejected his suggestion of negotiations over the French nuclear strike force. December brought another first, when the President received General Jaruzelski—a much-criticized visit indicating that 'realism' rather than 'human rights' was now the watchword. However, also in December, the twelfth Franco-African summit in Paris, with 35 governments represented, emphasised France's continuing links with the Third World.

But the diplomatic year was above all overshadowed by the *Rainbow Warrior* affair (see also Pt. X, Ch. 2). Though senior officers had been pressing for action against Greenpeace for some years, the Government reacted slowly to the fingers of suspicion. Four weeks elapsed before the President asked M Bernard Tricot, secretary-general to the presidency under de Gaulle, to investigate. Three weeks later he reported that there had been no governmental order to sink the vessel—unless he had been lied to. When the press revealed this had indeed happened the President ordered the Prime Minister to discover the full truth. Two months after the sinking it was admitted that French agents, under orders, had sunk the ship. The Defence Minister, M Charles Hernu, resigned and the head of the security services was dismissed. But who had ordered the attack was not disclosed. The Government had to apologise to New Zealand and compensate Greenpeace and the dependants of the dead crewman. French opinion seemed little moved by this criminal fiasco, which focused more attention on French nuclear testing than Greenpeace could have achieved unaided. But the tests continued.

OVERSEAS DEPARTMENTS AND TERRITORIES. NEW CALEDONIA remained a major preoccupation. In January M Edgard Pisani arrived there with proposals for 'independence-association', to be put to a referendum in July and operate from January 1986. This plan for a form of internal autonomy in which France would continue to control defence and public order was attacked by the opposition as undermining France's position in the Pacific. Only the Socialists supported a Bill to extend the state of emergency in the island. Any chance the Pisani plan had of acceptance disappeared when police killed a Kanak leader in one of a series of violent incidents. A lightning visit by President Mitterrand did nothing to turn the situation. Pisani returned to Paris in March having failed to rally any section of island opinion. The Government put back the referendum until after the 1986 general election and dissolved the island's territorial assembly, replacing it with four regional councils which would form a new territorial assembly to decide on a plan for independence. Replaced as high commissioner by a less abrasive man, Pisani briefly entered the Government as Minister for New Caledonia. The Government's proposals were fought by both the parliamentary opposition and the Europeans in New Caledonia. In August the Constitutional Council ruled the proposed distribution of seats unconstitutional, leading to a hurried special parliamentary session to approve a revised scheme. On 29 September anti-independence parties in New Caledonia won 60·8 per cent of the vote to 35·1 per cent for supporters of independence, but the latter controlled three of the four regional councils. The opposition in Paris pledged itself to respect the wishes of the majority after the 1986 elections. It also fought unsuccessfully a Bill granting a partial amnesty which was adopted by 318 votes to 158 in December. (See also Pt. X, Ch. 3.)

The situation in the Caribbean was also volatile. In GUADELOUPE three people died in bomb attacks and in April a conference of 'the last French colonies' was held there, in face of official hostility, to discuss a strategy for destabilizing metropolitan authority in the remaining overseas departments and territories. In July police reinforcements had to be flown in from France following clashes with advocates of independence over the imprisonment of an 'independentist' leader. Calm returned after his hasty release. Opposition leaders repeatedly accused the Government of planning to 'scuttle' the remaining colonies. In rebuttal President Mitterrand paid an uneventful if heavily-guarded visit to the Antilles in December.

Earlier even the tiny archipelago of ST PIERRE et MIQUELON provided a storm in a teacup when a dispute between dockers and fish-processing workers led to the expulsion of the prefect from the islands and the hurried dispatch of a fact-finding mission. The incident reflected the continuing economic crisis in the islands, and the residents' resentment at what they saw as the indifference of Paris to their plight.

FEDERAL REPUBLIC OF GERMANY

The 40th anniversary of the end of World War II in Europe meant that 1985 was bound to be a difficult year for West Germany, still burdened by the guilt of the Nazi past but also anxious to claim credit for the longest-lived democratic experience in Germany's history. Controversy over the anniversary duly flared up, particularly over a visit by Chancellor Helmut Kohl and President Reagan in May to a military cemetery containing the graves of some SS soldiers. But 1985 is likely to be remembered rather for its political upsets and uncertainties, and its economic progress, than for the memories from the past which dominated the summer headlines. Despite a series of electoral and governmental problems, Herr Kohl remained firmly in the saddle at the end of the year and looked forward confidently to the next national election at the beginning of 1987. But the opposition Social Democrats also found new heart as they pulled up from their crushing defeat at the 1983 federal election. The smallest partner in the ruling coalition, the Free Democrats, staged a modest revival, but the environmental, anti-nuclear 'Greens' went through a protracted internal dispute about their political role which left them divided and weakened at the end of the year.

In foreign policy, the Government was bedevilled by arguments which raged for most of the year on the attitude to adopt towards participation in President Reagan's Strategic Defense Initiative (SDI). The Foreign Minister, Herr Hans-Dietrich Genscher, was frequently attacked by right-wing supporters of the Government for putting too great stress on maintaining the best possible relations with France and avoiding antagonizing East European governments, instead of following Washington's lead on East-West relations and space defence. In the EEC, Bonn pushed for greater political union but also used its veto power to protect its cereal farmers. Relations with France blew hot and cold. Herr Kohl insisted on the importance of maintaining close links with Paris, but displeased the French by siding with US policies on trade and defence which France opposed. Contacts with East Germany improved in small ways, but remained subject to the overall tenor of East-West relations. West Germany's role outside Europe remained a limited one, despite frequent trips to Africa and Asia by Herr Genscher and other Ministers. A long-standing scheme to supply tanks to Saudi Arabia was shelved because of Israeli objections, though West German companies began preliminary negotiations with the Saudis to build an ammunition factory there.

Economically, 1985 was a good year for West Germany, with inflation falling to 2 per cent and exports boosting a record trade surplus. Unemployment of around two million, 9 per cent of the workforce, remained the economic black spot, but by the end of the year the Government felt that it had a solid foundation for an election-winning performance in 1987, while the Social Democrats' main alternative economic policy was based on introducing an energy tax to pay for job-creating environmental measures.

The Government's optimism at the end of 1985 contrasted with an atmosphere of muddle and uncertainty which hung over it from March until the autumn. The year had begun with internal coalition squabbles over the SDI and policy towards East Europe which heralded the year-long skirmishes between Herr Genscher and the right wing of the Christian Democrats and their sister party, the Bavarian Christian Social

Union. But what shook the Bonn Government far more was the result of a state election in the Saarland in March. For the first time, the Social Democrats gained control of the state. The Social Democratic leader there, Herr Oskar Lafontaine, had waged a vehement left-wing campaign, advocating increased state aid for declining industries, nationalization of a local steel firm, removal of US medium-range nuclear-armed missiles deployed in West Germany and looser membership of Nato. The Christian Democrats could draw some comfort from their retention of power in city elections in West Berlin on the same day as the Saarland poll, but their victory in Berlin over a dispirited and divided local Social Democratic party had been taken for granted.

The Government's political worries deepened in May when the Social Democrats crushed the Christian Democrats in retaining power in North Rhine-Westphalia, West Germany's most heavily-populated state, containing about 30 per cent of the national electorate. The Christian Democratic score of 36 per cent of the vote was a particular blow to Herr Kohl because the party's leader in North Rhine-Westphalia, Herr Bernhard Worms, was generally regarded as a protégé of the Chancellor. The Social Democrats' overall majority in the four-party election immediately propelled their leader in the state, Herr Johannes Rau, to the forefront of national politics and made him his party's choice as its candidate for Chancellor in 1987.

Herr Rau's pragmatic, middle-of-the-road style, allied with his vote-winning skills, put him well ahead of Herr Kohl in mid-year opinion polls and reawakened Social Democratic hopes of returning to power in Bonn. But the Chancellor and his party regained ground towards the end of 1985 as the Social Democrats were confronted with internal party debates over defence and economic policy. One major problem which the main opposition party had to face was its attitude to the Greens. The ecological party did badly in state elections in 1985, failing to pass the 5 per cent score needed to win state parliament seats in either the Saarland or North Rhine-Westphalia. But opinion polls still gave them between 5 and 7 per cent of the national vote. This meant it would be extremely difficult for the Social Democrats, on their own, to win an overall majority in the next federal election. Still, Herr Rau insisted that there must be no form of cooperation with the Greens, whom he regarded as unreliable. But another Social Democratic state premier, Herr Holger Börner, agreed in the autumn to take a Green minister, Herr Joschka Fischer, into his government in Hesse in return for support from the ecologists in the state parliament. The formal swearing-in of Herr Fischer in December gave the centre-right parties an opportunity to sow doubts about how determined the Social Democrats would be to resist a pact with the Greens if it offered them the chance of national power.

The Greens themselves were bitterly divided all year between their 'realo' (realist) wing, which favoured cooperation with the Social

Democrats under appropriate circumstances, and the '*fundis*' (funda-mentalists) who believed such cooperation would be a betrayal of basic Green principles. The confusion in the party was underlined when, a few days after Herr Fischer had taken office in Hesse, a Green party congress voted by a two-to-one margin in support of *fundis* who had criticized him. The Greens' impact at the national level was reduced during the year when some of its leading members who had become the first Green members of parliament in 1983 gave up their seats in the Bundestag to other, less experienced party members under a 'rotation' rule enforced by the party's rank-and-file.

West Germany's other small party, the Free Democrats, had a more hopeful year. The party's poor electoral performances in 1984 had led to speculation that it might fall below the 5 per cent barrier in major elections, but it did better than many had expected in the 1985 state elections, including an 8 per cent score in West Berlin. In February, Herr Genscher stepped down as the Free Democrats' leader. Under his suc-cessor, Herr Martin Bangemann, the party went out of its way to present itself as the advocate of the free market economy, pressing for deregula-tion, higher growth and a speeded-up reduction of state intervention in business. Herr Bangemann, who had been appointed Economics Minis-ter in Bonn in 1984, won a personal success in December when Herr Kohl chose him to conduct negotiations with the US Government on West German participation in SDI research.

The Government's mid-year problems were sharpened by two events on which Herr Kohl had been counting for a personal boost. The major industrialized democracies held their annual summit in Bonn in May. This ended in disagreement between France and the other participants. France insisted on the need for an international monetary conference before a new GATT round to liberalize trade, while the US, in particular, wanted to go straight ahead with trade negotiations. Herr Kohl sided with President Reagan but was made uncomfortable by the gap which this opened up between Bonn and Paris. Coinciding with the summit, Mr Reagan paid an official visit to West Germany which turned sour when a storm blew up over a ceremony attended by the President and the Chancellor at a military graveyard in Bitburg, where SS men are among the dead. It was left to the West German President, Herr Richard von Weizsäcker, to make the most impressive 40th anniversary speech, in which he insisted that Germans should face the past squarely and should acknowledge their failure to resist Nazi tyranny and the holocaust of the Jews.

A fresh embarrassment to the Government came in August and September when a string of spy cases surfaced, mainly involving secre-taries in official positions in Bonn. The worst case was that of Herr Hans Joachim Tiedge, a senior counter-espionage official, who defected to East Germany in August. As a result of the spy cases, the West German intelligence and counter-espionage services were shaken up. But the Interior Minister, Herr Friedrich Zimmermann, declined to accept responsibility for the scandals, despite sustained opposition calls for his resignation. At the end of the year, the image of the intelligence services was further clouded by disclosures that they had undertaken work in the past for industrial firms and by the revelation that a deputy to Herr Zimmermann had used intelligence material to compile dossiers on leading members of the Green party.

The final months of 1985 saw some more positive developments. In November, West European countries meeting in Hanover agreed on a first list of projects for their high-technology programme known as Eureka. This satisfied Herr Genscher and eased Herr Kohl's relations with President Mitterrand, who had initiated the scheme. In December, the long battle over SDI participation was settled by a decision to send Herr Bangemann to Washington to draw up a framework agreement covering participation by West German firms in American-led space research. Internationally, the Geneva summit between President Reagan and the Soviet leader Mikhail Gorbachev was warmly welcomed in West Germany, with its particular sensitivity to the climate of East-West relations. While the East German leader, Herr Erich Honecker, did not pay his long-awaited visit to West Germany in 1985, relations between the two Germanys warmed from the chill brought on in 1984 by US missile deployment in the Federal Republic. Progress was slow, but the two Germanys edged towards concluding a cultural agreement, while Social Democratic leaders were particularly active in visiting East Germany (see p. 126).

But the main cause for cheer in the Federal Republic in 1985 was the economy. West Germany raised its growth rate to about 2·5 per cent. While some other countries wanted faster expansion in order to boost their exports to the Federal Republic, the economic expansion was strong enough to encourage West German industry into a series of moves that significantly altered the business landscape. The vehicle maker, Daimler-Benz, took over three other big firms—MTU in aero-engines, Dornier in aerospace and AEG in electrical and electronic goods—to become the country's biggest industrial company. The Flick group, previously West Germany's largest private firm, was bought by the Deutsche Bank, which then sold off Flick's main external shareholdings and planned to float the group's industrial assets on the stock market in 1986. Half-a-dozen substantial family firms issued shares to the public for the first time. West German stock markets boomed and moved some way towards growing from their previous minor status into financial centres more commensurate with the overall strength of the national economy. In December, the business world was heartened by a Cabinet decision to amend the country's labour laws to make it more difficult for trade unions to bring industry to a halt through selective strikes against components firms, as they did in the metal industry in 1984. The unions warned of a 'hot winter' of protests against the change.

Culturally, 1985 saw the death of the Nobel prize-winning novelist, Herr Heinrich Böll (see OBITUARY), and a bitter controversy over the planned staging in Frankfurt of an allegedly anti-semitic play by the late film director, Herr Rainer Werner Fassbinder, which was abandoned after demonstrations and political protests. For many West Germans, two of the most memorable events of the year came in July when 17-year-old Boris Becker won the men's singles tennis title at Wimbledon and in November when the Government, after much debate, decided not to impose a compulsory motorway speed limit.

ITALY

By the end of the year Italy's first Socialist Prime Minister, Bettino Craxi (52), had been in power for nearly two-and-a half years. His was the longest-lived Italian Government since World War II (the previous record belonged to Aldo Moro, February 1966 to June 1968). This was a remarkable feat for a Socialist whose own party accounted for only 11·4 per cent of the electorate. His other coalition partners were the Christian Democrats (still numerically the largest party), Social Democrats, Liberals and Republicans.

A test of the Government came in the five-yearly regional elections, held on 12–13 May and involving 120 regional councils. The Communists had high hopes of repeating their success in the European parliamentary elections of 1984, when they marginally overtook the Christian Democrats. But their challenge boomeranged. Their poll fell to 30·1 per cent of the total, as compared with the previous 34·5, while the Christian Democrat decline halted with a 35 per cent vote. The other smaller coalition parties also maintained their position. The overall effect was that in a number of big towns hitherto run by left-wing councils power-sharing arrangements now had to be made with the coalition parties. Most galling of all for the Communists, in Rome, which had had a Communist mayor for the past ten years, they were overtaken by the Christian Democrats.

The Government's next hurdle was a referendum, held on 9–10 June, on a demand by the Communists for restoration of the 4 percentage-point slice docked from pay-packets in 1984 when wage-indexation was suspended. They had collected more than the one-and-a-half million signatures needed to justify a referendum. The Government made unavailing efforts to avoid it, viewing it as a threat to its anti-inflation policy. But the result brought another defeat for the Communists: in a 78 per cent turn-out their proposal secured only 45·7 per cent of the votes.

These two setbacks within a month caused a good deal of heart-searching in the Communist Party. Alessandro Natta, its secretary since

Enrico Berlinguer's death in 1984, was blamed for his over-optimism and for his abrasive attacks on other parties, especially the Socialists. A special congress was planned for 1986 aiming to revitalize the party and bring it into closer touch with the masses.

Craxi's premiership had been carried on under the auspices of a fellow-Socialist, President Alessandro Pertini. But in July Pertini's seven-year term of office expired, and an unwritten tradition demanded that his successor should be a Christian Democrat. Pertini himself, now 88, declared in mid-June that he would not be standing again. He had been a very popular President, appealing to ordinary people with his unconventional ways and to the left with his fine wartime Resistance record. He had provided an uncontested example of personal probity in high office; and he had given the tired and quarrelsome Christian Democrats a rest from their permanent tenure of the premiership by choosing two Prime Ministers from the lay parties, Giovanni Spadolini (Republican) in 1981 and Craxi in 1983. And by his occasional interventions he had shown that the presidency could be a more influential office than its limited constitutional powers provided for.

The Christian Democrats sought as their candidate a respected figure who might also command support from the other parties, including the Communists. The party secretary, Ciriaco De Mita, skilfully steered his group towards making Senator Francesco Cossiga, the presiding officer of the Senate, their candidate. It proved a sound choice, for in the election, held on 24 June by both Houses of Parliament, he was chosen on the first ballot. It had taken 16 ballots to elect Pertini in 1978 and 23 to elect his predecessor in 1971. This consensus was in a way a tribute to the country's newly-acquired stability. Cossiga, aged 56 (and thus the youngest-ever President), though a former Prime Minister was something of an outsider who had kept aloof from Christian Democrat factional disputes. A Sardinian, he was related to the Communists' late leader Berlinguer and thus had good relations with that party. He had been a close friend of Aldo Moro and was Minister of the Interior at the time of Moro's kidnap and murder in 1978, after which he insisted on resigning, an unusual gesture among Italian politicians which won him much respect. That office gave him an insight into constitutional problems, and, himself a constitutional lawyer, he could be expected to further recent moves towards improving the constitution, especially in strengthening the executive.

In October the Government's handling of the *Achille Lauro* hijacking episode had political repercussions. On 7 October the cruise liner, from Genoa, was hijacked off Port Said by four Palestinian guerrillas who threatened to blow up the ship and kill the passengers if their demands were not met; a 69-year-old American passenger was in fact killed. But on 9 October the hijackers surrendered to the Egyptian authorities, who next day allowed them to leave for Tunis. Their plane, however, was intercepted by American Tomcat P14s and forced to land at the US-Italian military base of Sigonella in Sicily. President Reagan, who had obtained permission from Craxi for the airliner to land there, then asked for the hijackers to be sent to the USA for trial, but Craxi insisted they should be tried in Italy, since the *Achille Lauro* counted as Italian territory. They were later brought before the judicial authorities in Genoa. But two PLO officials who had also been on the plane with them were flown to Rome and then allowed to leave for Yugoslavia. One of the two was Abu Abbas, leader of the Palestinian Liberation Front, who was said to have masterminded the hijack plan. The US ambassador in Rome delivered a strong protest to Craxi, who argued that Italy had no grounds for arresting him.

The Defence Minister and Republican Party leader Giovanni Spadolini disagreed with Craxi's decision to release Abu Abbas—and indeed with the general trend of the Government's open-minded policy towards the PLO—and on 16 October he and his party's other two Ministers withdrew from the coalition. On 17 October Craxi gave Parliament a full account of the *Achille Lauro* affair and then tendered his Government's resignation, but President Cossiga promptly asked him to remain in office. Craxi, after consultations with the coalition party leaders, resurrected his old Government, in which the Defence Minister, Spadolini, had been pacified by promises of more collegial consultation among the governmental allies and by assurances that Mediterranean policy would always take into consideration the views of the EEC and Nato. Craxi's position was strengthened by this episode and his Government secured votes of confidence in the Chamber on 6 November (347–239) and in the Senate two days later (180–102).

The *Achille Lauro* affair also caused a temporary break in Italy's normally cordial relations with the USA. It was not until 19 October, when the US Under-Secretary of State John Whitehead came to Italy bearing a personal letter to Craxi from President Reagan, that the fences began to be mended. Craxi, who had at first thought of cancelling his planned visit to the USA, went there for the UN's 40th anniversary celebrations on 24 October and had a 'brittle' meeting with President Reagan, who went out of his way to stress US appreciation of Italy's steadfastness as a Nato partner.

In the year's first half, when Italy's turn came to hold the presidency of the EEC, it aimed to give the Community a weightier role in world affairs, especially in Middle Eastern policy. Italy also had to preside over the negotiations for the accession of Spain and Portugal to the EEC, a difficult role for the country which had most to fear from the economic effects of the southern extension of the Community. Italy was disappointed at the inconclusive outcome of the Milan summit of 28 June on European unity, a cause close to Italian hearts on which President Pertini had addressed the European Parliament in Strasbourg on 11 June; Italy pressed for maximum reforms in the EEC, especially increased consultative power for the Parliament, and only unwillingly accepted the less radical reforms agreed to in December (see Pt. XI, Ch. 3).

The Soviet Foreign Minister Andrei Gromyko visited Rome (25–28 February), the first such visit for six years. On 13 March President Pertini cut short a long-planned visit to Latin America to represent Italy in Moscow at President Chernenko's funeral. On 28–30 May Craxi and the Foreign Minister Giulio Andreotti visited Moscow, the first leaders from a Nato country to do so since Gorbachev became Soviet leader. On the way Craxi stopped off at Warsaw airport for talks with General Jaruzelski about human rights and East-West relations.

In a report to Parliament in August Craxi said that, while on the domestic front the Mafia was a greater cause of concern than the fading-out Red Brigades, he considered that the main terrorist threat to Italy now came from abroad, and from the possible extension to Italy and Europe of outside conflicts, especially in the Middle East. His forecast proved all too prophetic when on 27 December four Palestinian terrorists attacked the Israeli El Al check-in counter at Rome's airport with grenades and gunfire. Sixteen people died, including three of the gunmen killed in the ensuing battle with the Italian police.

The Government's economic measures brought inflation down to under 9 per cent, but a constant preoccupation was the huge budget deficit and the public spending requirement. Failure to heed repeated warnings about this from the Bank of Italy and the IMF resulted on 19 July—'Black Friday'—in a closure of the foreign exchange markets and a fall in the lira by almost 20 per cent against the dollar. EMS Finance Ministers agreed to a 6 per cent devaluation of the lira, and the Government hastily introduced a package of fiscal measures designed to reduce the deficit. Paralleling the financial deluge, also on 19 July, two reservoirs collapsed above the hamlet of Stava, in the Dolomites, releasing a 150-foot-high wall of mud and water which crashed through hotels and houses and killed over 200 people.

BELGIUM

As the year opened, the Government, nearing the end of its term of office, looked increasingly divided. However, on the vexed issue of deploying Cruise missiles in Belgium to fulfil an earlier commitment to Nato, the members of the coalition parties closed ranks during a crucial parliamentary vote of confidence. The Government won by 116 votes to 93, which in the circumstances amounted to a substantial majority for deployment. The debate over the missiles revealed very clearly that the Flemish Social Christians were not fully under the control of Prime Minister Martens, but in another sense the vote helped to push the coalition partners closer together, since the Socialists declared that their party would not join any future coalition unless it were committed to removing the missiles.

In the approach to the general election, the Prime Minister sought to extract as much credit as possible from having stuck to his austerity programme, through its various phases, over the previous three years and having led the country to economic redemption. By mid-year, the Liberal–Social Christian coalition had become increasingly preoccupied with the electoral prospects and its initiatives more and more took on the aspect of window-dressing rather than concrete action. In these circumstances it was hardly surprising that the bombing attacks in May by a far-left terrorist group on the employers' federation and other establishment targets made 'law and order' a major issue.

The Heysel stadium disaster caused by rioting British football supporters (see p. 37) produced major problems for the Government. After an inquiry into safety and security provisions, there were calls for the resignation of the Minister of the Interior, Mr Charles-Ferdinand Nothomb. His refusal split the coalition and Mr Martens then submitted the resignation of his Administration, which King Baudouin declined to accept. Though the opinion polls had indicated that the dominant Social Christian party would lose votes in the elections held on 13 October, the reverse was the case. Basically, the traditional mainstream parties held their positions, though the Liberals suffered in Flanders. The Social Christians even made some inroads into the opposition vote. Thus there was a consolidation of the majority in the 212-seat Lower Chamber held by Mr Martens' Social Christians and their coalition partner, the Liberals, who together ended up with two more seats and, psychologically very important, just over 50 per cent of the total vote.

The electorate clearly took the view that the economy was the most important issue, pushing the communal question relatively into the background. The environment was also an important electoral concern. These shifts were shown in losses by both the Walloon and the Flemish sectional parties, and by gains in Flanders and Wallonia by the Greens.

The Flemish wing of the Liberal Party—in Belgium very much a party of the right—lost ground as a result of stressing the need to cut public spending further (including state sector jobs and social security) and their assertion that job-creation should be on purely economic, not social, criteria. The Liberals also set their face sternly against anything other than very limited and temporary aid for businesses in difficulty, whatever the possible job losses. The Flemish Liberal leadership also made the point just before the election that the proven success of austerity policies had not been sold to the electorate strongly enough: in the case of their own party, the election results proved them right.

The Socialists gained ground in Flanders with their message that the burdens of austerity were being unfairly distributed, the workers suffering disproportionately. A clear-cut policy was put to the voters: the Socialists would create more jobs by work-sharing, and would ensure that the increased labour inputs generated by the business recovery were translated into new full jobs and not just into overtime and part-time working; by ensuring that fiscal receipts from taxpayers other than wage-earners were fairer, and properly collected, they claimed that the public debt problem would be diminished. The Socialists also declared that state aid to businesses in difficulty would be available in order to fund restructuring, with job preservation as an important objective. After allowance for the increase in parliamentary seats in Flanders from 121 to 124, it was clear that the voters were impressed by the Socialists' case, which won them a substantial increase of six seats, and backed off the hard line advocated by the Liberals, which cost them six seats.

After a long delay Mr Martens announced his new Government on 28 November, a month and a half after an election at which he secured an increased majority. In these circumstances, it was perhaps surprising that the new Government was virtually identical with its predecessor, the only significant change being the entry of Mr Verhofstadt, president of the Flemish wing of the Liberals, an economic fundamentalist, as Minister for the Budget.

New attacks on supermarkets by the so-called 'Brabant killers' caused a major security crisis that put considerable pressure on Mr Martens. In three raids in September and November 15 people were killed and as many more were wounded. In addition, the marxist terrorist group CCC made four bomb attacks on banks in November.

THE NETHERLANDS

The coalition of Christian Democrats and Liberals continued to be preoccupied with reducing public borrowing and restoring much-needed competitiveness to Dutch industry. Overall, official economic policy was broadly successful: industrial production increased, business investment was strong—partly directed towards productivity enhancement and partly adding new capacity—and unemployment gradually declined, providing part of the basis for a modest increase in personal consumption during the year. Nevertheless, the Government's popularity remained low, according to the opinion polls, leading the coalition to decide to continue in office with its narrow majority and not call an early election.

The Liberals' unpopularity was increased by publication of the report on the collapse of RSV, the state-owned shipbuilding firm, which strongly criticised the Liberal Minister for the Economy, Mr Gijs Aardenne. In February, during the parliamentary debate on the issue, opposition leaders pressed for Mr Aardenne's resignation, claiming that he had misled parliament over the firm's financial position. However, although some members of the coalition felt that his continuance in office might prove an electoral liability, Mr Aardenne mustered sufficient support to resist these calls.

The issue of whether to accept the siting of Cruise missiles in the Netherlands was the subject of continued national debate for much of the year. Opinion polls suggested that 60 per cent of the population was against taking the missiles. The Government sought to take a conciliatory line, and in April the Foreign Minister, Mr van der Broek, visited Moscow to urge the USSR to reduce its number of SS-20s before 1 November, otherwise the Netherlands would follow the other Nato members that had already agreed to take the missiles. The Government rejected an invitation from the US to join in research for the Strategic Defense Initiative programme, although no prohibition was placed on participation by individual Dutch companies.

Pope John Paul II visited the Netherlands in May and was greeted by violent demonstrations. Protesters ranged from some of the six million Dutch Catholics, anxious the restrain Vatican domination of the Dutch Church, to radical youth groups. Incidents varied from violent clashes between police and demonstrators in Utrecht to embarrassingly small crowds of well-wishers elsewhere, and the visit generally was regarded with disappointment by Vatican officials and leaders of the Dutch Church.

In the latter part of 1985, the political parties became increasingly engaged in manoeuvring in preparation for the next year's general election. In September, the coalition produced an electioneering budget that was by no means as stringent as the problematic condition of public finances required. The budget made some cuts in spending, including social security benefits and health care; but, although revenues were expected to rise, the deficit was still very large at an estimated 7.8 per cent of net national income, significantly above the target of 7.4 per cent. The Government did not cut income tax, as it had hoped to, but corporation tax was reduced, to provide a stimulus for industry.

Doubts whether Mr Joop den Uyl, the 65-year-old leader of the Labour Party, would stay on to fight the election were dispelled towards the end of the year when he announced that he would continue as leader.

LUXEMBOURG

Luxembourg's active role at the forefront of European developments in satellite television acquired additional momentum with the announcement in March of the formation of the European Satellite Corporation to launch a medium-power satellite to beam programmes to cable networks. Efforts to keep Luxembourg as one of the seats of the European Parliament achieved some success. The July and September sittings each year were to continue to be held in Luxembourg city, despite the efforts of Strasbourg and Brussels to be made the sole seat of Parliament.

The chosen response by the Prime Minister, Mr Santer, to the economic recession was to propose a significantly reflationary budget. The main thrust was to lighten the fiscal burden on individuals and on companies. Concessions on personal taxation and payroll tax gave encouragement to the increasingly important banking sector, which would shed LuxFr.500 million of tax in 1986. Together, those tax cuts were worth the equivalent of 1 per cent of GDP, according to the Prime Minister. Overall, the 1986 estimates balanced out exactly at LuxFr.77,600 million ($1,400 million), compared with an expected small surplus in 1985.

Although syndicated lending, which provided much of the basis for Luxembourg's expansion as an international financial centre, became much less important in 1985, the number of foreign banks located in the Grand Duchy reached a record level. Diversification of banking services, including development of private banking along Swiss lines, kept the sector profitable and attractive. The Government restated its policy to maintain a strong banking orientation and to secure Luxembourg's position as a financial centre.

REPUBLIC OF IRELAND

At the local elections held throughout the country in June the opposition Fianna Fail party took an impressive 45 per cent of the votes, while the Government parties, Fine Gael and Labour, could muster no more than a total of 37 per cent. The outcome, which gave Fianna Fail control of a number of county councils and municipal authorities, reflected the inability of the Administration led by Dr Garret FitzGerald to satisfy a variety of conflicting sectional interests while at the same time steering the Republic safely through a worldwide recession. High taxation could not be mitigated without curbs on public service pay, which in turn alienated vocal segments of the work-force such as teachers and transport employees. Agriculture could be helped only by forcing compromise deals on milk and beef out of a reluctant EEC; Irish farmers proved more ready to complain about the compromises than to welcome the deals. Inflation had been brought down to one of the lowest levels in Europe by 1985 but the stabilization of prices also involved record unemployment.

Perhaps the most dramatic aspect of Government policy was its impact on state enterprises. A warning had been sounded the previous year when the Government refused to rescue the Irish Shipping freight line from liquidation (see AR 1984, p. 154). Now the British-and-Irish car-ferry service and the Irish Steel smelting works were compelled to adopt draconian redundancy measures. The Bula lead-zinc mine, in which the state held a 49 per cent interest, was allowed to go into receivership. Teachers and civil servants resorted to symbolic one-day strikes in protest against the shelving of pay awards. The Government's single-minded assault on public expenditure paid tangible dividends. Not only did inflation fall below the British level but real incomes increased, helped further by the decline of mortgage and other interest rates. The modest but undoubted growth in consumer demand received an additional boost from strategically-calculated reductions in VAT, while the balance-of-payments deficit continued to fall—a rare combination of favourable phenomena in the Irish economy.

This was good household management in difficult circumstances but it offered little cause for optimism. Fortuitous advantages which arose in 1985 could not be guaranteed to recur, such as the drop in petrol prices or the excellent tourist season assisted by the strength of the American dollar. Objectively, the closure of firms in long-established industries like shoe-making or meat-processing might have been tolerated if credible alternatives were available. The subsidence in the international demand for microchips, however, caused the withdrawal of several foreign manufacturers from Ireland and showed that the hopes placed in new technology as the basis for future industrial expansion were certainly premature and probably exaggerated. The cost of foreign borrowing continued to absorb resources needed for investment at home. Unexpected emergencies also made inroads on a hard-pressed exchequer. Extensive flooding at the height of summer seriously depleted the farmers' fodder stocks, which the Government had to make good by purchases from abroad. The country's second-largest insurance company, the Insurance Corporation of Ireland, had to be taken over by the state when threatened with collapse on a scale too big to be handled by its owners, Allied Irish Banks.

The talks between the Irish and British Governments on the Northern Ireland question resumed early in the year. Press speculation fuelled suspicions that the ultimate agreement would be a 'sell-out'—the concept used both by Fianna Fail in the Republic and by Northern Unionists, meaning in the first case the Dublin Government's abandonment of the nationalist demand for the reunification of Ireland and, in the second case, the abandonment by London of the Unionist principle that Northern Ireland remain an integral part of the United Kingdom. Dr FitzGerald contented himself with repeating that the nationalist aspiration would not be renounced but that it was more immediately important to pursue peace in the North than Irish unity. In the event, the terms of the agreement published after the meeting between the two Prime Ministers at Hillsborough on 15 November (see DOCUMENTS) attracted widespread approval in the Republic. The Anglo-Irish Intergovernmental Conference, of which the Republic's Foreign Minister, Mr Peter Barry, would be co-chairman, was seen as an effective assurance that the interests of the Northern minority would not be overlooked in the decision-making process. Mr Haughey, leader of Fianna Fail, condemned the agreement on the ground that it would retard the achievement of a united Ireland, but end-of-year opinion polls showed that 60 per cent or more of the people rejected this judgment. Dr FitzGerald shot ahead of Mr Haughey in the popularity ratings and the Fianna Fail lead over the combined Government parties was substantially narrowed.

Notwithstanding the general improvement in Anglo-Irish relations signalled by the agreement, the Northern Ireland situation provoked many moments of tension. Sir John Hermon, chief constable of the Royal Ulster Constabulary, was reported to have cast doubts, during a visit to Canada, on the commitment of the Irish authorities to the maintenance of security. This caused deep annoyance to the Republic's Government, as also did the assertion by Mr Tom King, the Northern Ireland Secretary, that Dr FitzGerald had accepted at Hillsborough 'for all practical purposes and in perpetuity' that there would never be a united Ireland.

Two cases of acquittal by courts in Northern Ireland of persons extradited from the Republic on Northern warrants confirmed the popular resistance in the Republic to recurrent demands from Belfast and London for a wider application of the extradition laws: it was felt that this would be used by the Northern police to obtain custody of persons wanted for questioning even if substantive charges could not be successfully brought against them. Security measures added to the pressure on the Republic's exchequer and led to severe difficulties in prison administration. The decline in crimes of violence, burglary, car-theft and drug-dealing resulted from a law-enforcement campaign which put still more convicted criminals into the already over-crowded goals. Prison riots, attempted mass escapes and the destruction of a newly-opened prison on Spike Island in Cork harbour followed, as well as claims for better staffing and conditions by the prison officers' association.

Relatively low-keyed confrontation developed once more between the state and some elements in the Roman Catholic Church. A limited liberalization of the law relating to the availability of contraceptives drew criticism from the new Archbishop of Dublin, Dr Kevin McNamara. Archbishop McNamara, together with Bishop Jeremiah Newman of Limerick, also repeatedly denounced the arguments advanced by a number of politicians, editorial writers and pressure groups in favour of removing the constitutional ban on divorce. Fianna Fail opposition prevented a parliamentary committee from recommending that the question be submitted to the people in a referendum, but successive opinion polls, including one commissioned by the Roman Catholic hierarchy, suggested that some 45 per cent of voters would like to see the ban removed. Dr FitzGerald declared himself against a referendum until a clear majority could be detected in favour of change.

Meanwhile, the Foreign Minister, Mr Barry, in a speech delivered in the presence of Cardinal Casaroli, Papal Secretary of State, distinguished between the right of the Church to alert the consciences of its followers and the duty of the state to legislate in what it considered to be the best interests of the people. He claimed this to be in line with oral statements made during 1984 to the New Ireland Forum on behalf of the Roman Catholic bishops. None of the bishops who had addressed the Forum challenged the Minister's comment. This reinforced the growing belief that a number of the Catholic bishops disagreed with the rigid stance adopted by their more conservative colleagues.

Official party attitudes on the Northern Ireland and Church-state issues strained the loyalty of a number of members of parliament. Three members of Fine Gael lost the whip for some months when they voted against the Government on the contraception question. A Labour member left his party permanently on the same issue. Mr Desmond O'Malley, who had been expelled from the Fianna Fail parliamentary party the previous year for supporting the Government on the North (see AR 1984, p. 155), spoke against the Fianna Fail stand on contraception and was then expelled from the party organization. When Miss Mary Harney, another Fianna Fail member, was expelled for voting with the Government on the Anglo-Irish Agreement, she joined Mr O'Malley in forming a new party called the Progressive Democrats.

Questions concerning police investigation methods and the questioning of women witnesses by barristers in cases bearing on sexual relations caused much controversy during the prolonged sessions of a judicial inquiry into the violent deaths of two babies in County Kerry. Reports that statues of the Virgin Mary had been seen to move of their own volition in various parts of the country evoked a quasi-religious fervour in some people, embarrassed others, including the church authorities, and kept the newspapers supplied with sensational stories. A group of shopworkers picketed a Dublin supermarket for the greater part of the year in protest against the sale of South African produce. An Air India plane crashed into the Atlantic off the south west coast of Ireland in June, with the loss of 320 passengers and crew. The Live Aid effort to raise funds for the relief of African famine (see p. 42) was conceived and led by Dubliner Bob Geldof. The Republic of Ireland responded by making the biggest financial contribution proportionate to population of any country in the world—IR£8 million (£6·75 million sterling) from three-and-a-half million men, women and children.

Among the distinguished Irish citizens who died during the year were the Most Rev Dermot Ryan of the Vatican Curia, a former Archbishop of Dublin; Dr C. S. Andrews, former chairman of a number of public enterprises, including the transport service and the broadcasting authority; Alexis FitzGerald, economist, jurist and former policy adviser to the Government; and Shelah Richards, stage and television actress.

Chapter 2

DENMARK—ICELAND—NORWAY—SWEDEN—FINLAND—AUSTRIA—SWITZERLAND

DENMARK

Mr Poul Schlüter's four-party minority coalition Government retained a majority in the Folketing for its economic policy throughout 1985. This ensured the tight control of public expenditure and firm incomes policy necessary to achieve its aims of reducing inflation and eliminating the large budget and current account deficits. In his New Year speech, Mr Schlüter warned that the current account deficit was again increasing and that the Government would adopt the measures necessary to reduce it.

The immediate threat to the Government's strategy came from the negotiations for a new two-year collective wage agreement due to come into force on 1 March. The private-sector unions were demanding general wage increases, a two-hour reduction in the working week and substantial wage increases for the lowest-paid. The employers argued that this would lead to large increases in wage costs. The official mediator's intervention having failed to break the deadlock, large-scale strikes began on 24 March, and the employers responded with lock-outs. The most comprehensive industrial conflict in the private sector for many years, it halted industrial production, air traffic, docks, shipping and the distribution of oil, petrol and food supplies. On 30 March, while 100,000 people demonstrated outside, the Folketing majority supporting the Government's economic policy (the coalition parties and the Radical Liberals) passed a law imposing a settlement and ending the strike on 1 April, a step opposed by the three left-wing parties and the Progress Party. The settlement extended the existing collective wage agreements in the private and public sectors, which provided for wage rises of 3·5 per cent over a two-year period; it also gave a one-hour reduction in the working week with effect from 1 January 1987.

Other measures passed at the same time aiming to cut demand in a socially equitable way included an increase in corporate income tax from 40 to 50 per cent, compulsory five-year savings in non-interest-bearing accounts of 8 per cent of personal taxable incomes over DKr 150,000, a freeze on fees to the liberal professions, limitations on increasing profit margins, reductions in mortgage loan limits and restrictions on consumer credit. Widespread strikes affecting many services and industries continued for a fortnight after the passing of the new legislation, with demonstrations outside Parliament on 1 and 10 April. Spring public opinion polls showed that support for the Socialist People's Party and Social Democrats had increased to a level where they would secure an absolute parliamentary majority in an election.

Mr Schlüter's Government nevertheless held to its course. The 1986 draft budget, presented on 15 August, forecast a further fall in the budget deficit to DKr 26,000 million (or 4·2 per cent of GDP) compared to DKr 36,000 million in 1985 (and DKr 55,000 million in 1982). Despite a record current account deficit of DKr 12,700 million between January and June, the Government still aimed to eliminate the deficit by 1988.

The results of the mid-term local elections held on 19 November were not too discouraging for the coalition. Although the Socialist People's Party did very well and the Social Democrats also made gains, it was a good election for Mr Schlüter's Conservatives and their small coalition partner, the Christian People's Party. The other large coalition party, the Liberals, lost support and so did the fourth coalition party, the small Centre Democrats. The Radical Liberals, supporting the coalition on economic policy and the left-wing parties on foreign and defence policy, did badly, and the Progress Party very badly.

On 4 December the Government announced further measures to cut the current account deficit, estimated at DKr 22,000 million for 1985, and the 1986 budget deficit, now revised downwards to DKr 14,500 million. The measures included increases in energy taxes, restrictions on mortgages and cuts in public-sector construction projects. Despite this further tightening of fiscal policy, the economy was forecast to grow by 3 per cent in 1986, with further increases in private consumption and business investment.

On foreign and security policy the Government remained in a minority in the Folketing. In March the three left-wing parties and the Radical Liberals passed a resolution condemning the militarization of space and the American 'Star Wars' research programme and opposing Danish participation in such research. In May the majority criticised the Government for its allegedly inadequate presentation of the Folketing's views at a meeting of Nato Defence Ministers. On 14 November it passed a resolution, similar to one of 3 May 1984, which had instructed the Government to oppose the deployment of new missiles in Europe. The majority also instructed the Government to work actively for the establishment of a Nordic nuclear-free zone guaranteed by the United States and the Soviet Union.

By late December it appeared that the Social Democrats, and hence a majority of the Folketing, would reject the reforms agreed by EC heads of government at Luxembourg earlier in the month. The Social Democrats opposed the proposal to increase the influence of the European Parliament and argued that majority voting on internal market affairs would threaten Denmark's right to implement its own environmental legislation. The Foreign Minister, Mr Uffe Ellemann-Jensen, warned that rejection of the reforms would have an influence on whether Denmark remained in the EC in the longer term.

On the Faeroe Islands the new centre-left coalition led by Mr Atli Dam took office on 10 January, with a stringent economic policy to tackle the Faeroes' serious problems of increasing balance of payments deficits and a foreign debt equivalent to 62 per cent of GNP. An official report on the Faeroe Islands' economy published in the spring attributed these problems to a too-rapid expansion of investment and consumption, and recommended reductions in public expenditure, imports and consumption levels.

On 1 February Greenland finally left the European Community, following Ireland's ratification of the withdrawal treaty. Greenland immediately joined the preparations under way in Iceland and the Faeroes for the establishment of a West Nordic Parliamentary Council, a contact and advisory body of parliamentarians with particular emphasis on common concerns such as fishing, economic matters, culture and transport. The first annual meeting took place in Nuuk on 23–24 September.

ICELAND

Following the large wage rises won by Iceland's unions in the autumn of 1984 (see AR 1984, p.157), inflation rose steeply to around 60 per cent in early 1985. Opinion polls showed a sharp drop in support for the Government parties, the Independence Party and Progressives. There was also dissatisfaction with the Government's performance within the two parties themselves, but as yet there was insufficient pressure for change, whether in the form of a reshuffle, the formation of a new Government or an election.

On 8 February the Government announced a series of measures to deal with the economic situation. Some of the measures, such as the promised aid to home buyers and gradual phasing-out of income tax, aimed to ease the position of average wage-earners in order to reduce pressure for large nominal wage increases in the wage negotiations due in the autumn. Other measures aimed to cut public expenditure, rationalize the financial sector and reduce the already heavy burden of foreign debt. In April the Independence Party's national congress, brought forward from the autumn, renewed its pledge of support for the Government. Similar support was forthcoming at the same time from the Progressive Party's national executive.

Although covering the period to the end of December 1985, the 1984 wage agreements had given the unions the right to withdraw as of 1 September 1985. Negotiations for new agreements therefore began in the spring, with the Government seeking to avoid large wage increases, the employers refusing to consider the reintroduction of indexation, and the unions aiming to maintain their members' standard of living. By spring the rate of inflation was falling rapidly. On 15 June the private-sector employers and unions concluded an agreement for the period until December 1985 which gave wage increases of 12–16 per cent. Other unions soon reached similar agreements.

In late September dissatisfaction had mounted within the Independence Party at the coalition's handling of the economy, and in particular at the large deficit in the proposed 1986 budget. The party decided that its chairman, Thorsteinn Pálsson, should enter the Government and the other Independence Party Ministers be reshuffled. On 16 October Mr Pálsson replaced Mr Albert Gudmundsson as Minister of Finance, and Mr Gudmundsson became Minister of Industry. Mr Geir Hallgrímsson, former party chairman, would retire as Foreign Minister at the end of 1985 and be replaced by Mr Matthías Á. Mathiesen. On 12 November the new Finance Minister presented a revised 1986 budget with significant reductions in public expenditure and new foreign loans. Negotiations began for public- and private-sector collective agreements to replace those due to expire at the end of December. The unions proposed a comprehensive type of agreement, to which the Government should be a party, based on a standard-of-living guarantee instead of the old indexation system. The Government's initial response to this idea seemed positive.

On 24 October the women of Iceland took a 'free day' on the anniversary of a similar day ten years before. This nearly led to a government crisis when President Vigdís Finnbogadóttir, a strong supporter of women's rights and prominent in the earlier demonstration, hesitated to sign a law passed by the Allting in the early hours of that day forbidding a strike by Iceland Air's air hostesses. After a discussion with the acting Prime Minister, the President gave her signature while deploring that she be required to sign such a law on that particular day.

NORWAY

The Norwegian economy continued to grow strongly in 1985, stimulated by the three-party coalition's expansionary budget, easy credit and rising real wages. Growth in the mainland non-oil economy was particularly marked at around 4 per cent. Unemployment fell to around 2 per cent, inflation to under 6 per cent, and the current account again showed a large surplus, forecast at NKr 20,000 million. Rising government expenditure was covered by the state's North Sea revenues, estimated at NKr 46,000 million in 1985. However, by the summer there were signs of overheating in the economy. Rising wage costs threatened higher inflation and a further reduction of competitiveness in traditional export markets. Strong private demand was stimulating imports and widening the current account deficit (excluding oil and gas) to some NKr 64,000 million. Although covered by oil and gas exports, this large and increasing non-oil trade deficit highlighted Norway's ever-greater dependence on the North Sea, as did the 20 per cent which oil and gas revenues contributed to state income.

All the more important therefore were developments affecting the

North Sea. Negotiations to secure the guaranteed markets without which development could not proceed received a heavy blow in February when the British Government vetoed a £20,000 million agreement between Statoil and the British Gas Corporation for the sale to Britain in the early 1990s of gas from the Sleipner field. Without a market the development plans ready for implementation had to be postponed, opening up a threatened gap in future North Sea earnings and the immediate prospect of unemployment in offshore industries. In order to close the gap the Storting in June approved the development of Phase II of the Gullfaks oilfield. In May negotiations had also begun with a continental consortium for the sale of gas from the giant Troll field, though these negotiations were slowed down by disagreements over price, with Norway at a disadvantage in a weak gas market.

Despite the country's strong economic performance, Mr Kaare Willoch's coalition of Conservative Party, Centre Party and Christian People's Party lost their overall majority in the Storting election held on 9 September. Labour, led by Mrs Gro Harlem Brundtland, ran an effective campaign focusing primarily on deficiencies in the health and social sectors and proposing a NKr 20,000 million economic development plan utilizing oil revenues.

Labour was deprived of victory, however, by the peculiarities of the Norwegian electoral system, reform of which Labour had itself opposed, and by the Storting's decision in the spring, also opposed by Labour, to permit electoral alliances as an interim solution pending such reform. Labour rejected an electoral alliance with the Socialist People's Party, while the coalition parties concluded such alliances between themselves. In consequence, while individually the coalition parties lost votes, the Centre Party and Christian People's Party gained seats and the Government was able to remain in office, albeit as a minority Administration. The Liberal Party disappeared from the Storting, and Labour, the largest party, stayed in opposition, now ready however to examine electoral reform. The results of the election for the new, 157-seat Storting were as follows (with the 1981 results for the 155-seat Storting in brackets):

	seats		% of votes	
Labour	71	(66)	40·8	(37·3)
Socialist Left	6	(4)	5·5	(4·9)
Conservatives	50	(53)	30·4	(31·6)
Christian Peoples Party	16	(15)	8·3	(9·3)
Centre	12	(11)	6·6	(6·7)
Liberals	0	(2)	3·1	(3·9)
Progress Party	2	(4)	3·7	(4·5)
Others	0	(0)	1·6	(1·8)

As the Government parties held 78 seats and the two socialist parties together held 77, Carl I. Hagen's Progress Party was able to occupy a disproportionately important position despite having lost two seats. The Government parties having refused to accord the Progress Party a special status as part of the Storting's non-socialist majority, they were forced to seek a majority on each issue as it arose.

In the autumn budget debates this led to prolonged uncertainty about the Government's future. In October the Government presented an expansionary 1986 budget, with expenditure to increase by 12.6 per cent, twice as fast as prices, and especially fast in the controversial health and social security sector. Since government North Sea revenues were forecast to decline because of lower prices and a weaker US dollar, the budget showed a deficit (before loan transactions) compared to a surplus of some NKr 20,000 million in 1985. Faced by Progress Party threats to vote with the socialist parties, the Government was nevertheless forced to increase its social security appropriations despite warnings about inflation.

In foreign and security policy the minority Government's position was equally precarious. Although the Progress Party would vote with the Government, defections from the coalition's own ranks threatened to produce a situation similar to that in Denmark (see p. 148). Even before the election, in June, the Government had only narrowly won Storting approval for its position on the Strategic Defense Initiative, refusing to condemn research into 'Star Wars' technology as proposed by the socialist parties. However, in November, following the election, the Government finally agreed to vote in the UN Assembly for the revised Swedish-Mexican proposal to freeze nuclear arsenals, thereby bringing Norway into line with the other Nordic countries. The proposal for a Nordic nuclear-free zone was another deeply controversial security policy issue on which there were likely to be defections from the coalition parties to the socialist position.

The trial for espionage of Mr Arne Treholt, a senior Norwegian diplomat and prominent Labour Party member, took place between February and June without having any noticeable impact on the election campaign or result. The court found Mr Treholt guilty on the major charges of spying for the Soviet Union and Iraq and sentenced him to twenty years' imprisonment.

SWEDEN

As 1985 opened Mr Olof Palme's Social Democratic Government faced problems on both the political and economic fronts. Facing an election in September, the party was trailing behind the non-socialist parties in the public opinion polls. In February there was a no-confidence motion in Parliament against the Foreign Minister, Mr Lennart Bodström, following his alleged private denial that Soviet submarines had violated Swedish territorial waters after 1982. Although Mr Bodström survived the vote, commentators thought the impression of unreliability on security matters had damaged the Government's chances of re-election.

The Government's economic strategy of export-led growth, so successful in 1983–84 in recapturing market shares and eliminating Sweden's large current account deficit, was threatened by an inflation rate of 8 per cent, double the Government's target for December 1984, and by rapidly-rising labour costs, both of which were steadily eroding Sweden's regained international competitiveness. The Government had stopped the rise in public expenditure: although the 1985–86 budget presented on 10 January forecast a state deficit of SKr 63,500 million, this compared with SKr 86,600 million in 1982–83. But the Government faced serious problems on the wages front. Union agreement in principle to a voluntary 5 per cent norm for 1985 had been obtained in 1984, but was conditional on a 1985 inflation rate of 3 per cent and had still to be translated into agreements between unions and employers. The budget contained a promise of income tax reductions to ensure higher real incomes, provided that wage-cost rises were limited to 5 per cent and there was no serious deterioration in the external current account.

In February the industrial unions and employers reached a framework agreement within the 5 per cent norm which covered some 30 per cent of Sweden's labour force. This was based, however, on a forecast 3 per cent inflation and would ensure real wage increases. As the attainment of this inflation target looked increasingly unlikely, the Government on 8 March imposed a price freeze and a system of price controls. On 19 March the engineering employers and unions concluded an agreement within the 5 per cent norm and the Government announced that the general income tax rebate would be paid in June.

On 2 May, however, Sweden's civil servants, refusing to adhere to the 5 per cent norm and claiming compensation for falling behind the private sector, began a strike which closed airports and halted foreign trade and, when the employers responded with lock-outs, caused increasing disruption to Swedish life. On 14 May, faced by a heavy outflow of capital, the Government had to introduce crisis measures, including a 2 per cent rise in interest rates to 11.5 per cent, a tightening of hire-purchase controls and increases in some indirect taxes. In view of the recent private-sector agreements within the 5 per cent guideline, the Government was under pressure to maintain a firm line with the public-sector unions. On 20 May, however, following Mr Palme's intervention, a settlement was reached which, although not due to be implemented until early December, breached the 5 per cent ceiling. In the private sector, too, wage-drift at local level was breaching the guidelines negotiated centrally, leading to actual wage rises significantly higher than 5 per cent. At the same time, surging imports, provoked by strong private consumption, were taking the current account back into deficit, already at SKr 14,000 million by the end of August.

Despite the mounting economic problems, the Government's standing in the public opinion polls improved steadily during the spring and summer, so the Social Democrats' return to office following the election on 15 September did not come as a surprise. The major surprise of an election dominated by an increasingly ideological conflict between Mr Palme's Social Democrats and Mr Ulf Adelsohn's Moderates—between preserving the 'Swedish model' of welfare and 'freedom of choice'—was the extraordinary surge of support for the Liberals led by Mr Bengt Westerberg, a support taken mostly from the Liberals' allies, the Conservatives and The Centre (Centre Party in alliance with the Christian Democratic Alliance). The results were as follows (1982 results in brackets):

	seats		% of votes	
Social Democrats	159	(166)	45·0	(45·9)
Communists	19	(20)	5·4	(5·6)
Moderates	76	(86)	21·3	(23·6)
The Centre	44	(56)	12·5	(17·4)
Liberals	51	(21)	14·3	(5·9)
Others	0	(0)	1·5	(1·6)

Although confirmed in office, the Government's position was weakened. Previously, despite depending on the Communists for an absolute majority in the Riksdag, it had enjoyed a three-seat majority over the non-socialists. Now the non-socialists had 12 seats more than the Government, making Mr Palme even more dependent on Communist votes.

Following the election, Mr Palme made major changes to his Government. Among the more important, the Foreign Minister, Mr Bodström, was replaced by the influential Mr Sten Andersson, formerly Minister for Social Affairs; Mr Roine Carlsson, deputy Industry Minister, became Defence Minister; and a new post of Wages Minister was created, with responsibility for overseeing public-sector pay. This recognised the crucial importance of the forthcoming wage negotiations, particularly in the public sector, for the Government's aims of maintaining full employment, keeping the rise in prices and labour costs to the level in Sweden's main trading partners, and avoiding an increase in the tax burden.

In early December the electoral committee of the Centre Party voted Mr Thorbjörn Fälldin out of his post as leader and proposed as his replacement Mr Olof Johansson, the party's second vice-chairman. Commentators linked this controversial step not only to the party's bad showing in the election, but also to Mr Fälldin's commitment to a non-socialist alliance and the wish of some party members to take the party closer to the Social Democrats and play a more independent balancing role in Parliament. On 9 December Karin Söder, the party's first vice-chairman, was named chairman, with Mr Johansson remaining vice-chairman, until the party elected its new chairman in June 1986.

FINLAND

During 1985 the long-existing *de facto* split in the Finnish Communist Party began to be formalized when the majority, who already occupied all leading party posts, started to expel minority-controlled party organ-izations. By late January majority 'parallel' organizations had been estab-lished in the eight districts controlled by the minority. The party leadership continued preparations for the special congress originally proposed by the minority but in which they now refused to participate. The congress took place on 23 March and made two important changes to party rules, the first permitting the central committee to expel district organizations, the second increasing the proportion of party districts required to demand a special congress. Mr Aalto was confirmed as chairman and Mr Esko Vainionpää was elected general secretary. They made clear their intention of ending a situation in which the minority could oppose official policy through party organizations and through their own newspaper, *Tiedonantaja*. Mr Vainionpää also said that minor-ity candidates would not be included on party lists at the next election.

In September the leadership at last started the process of expulsion, in defiance of a letter dated 10 September from the central committee of the Soviet Communist Party warning that measures against the minority would damage relations between the two countries as well as the two parties. On 13 September the leadership presented an ultimatum to the minority district organizations: they were to return to party discipline and cease publication of their newspaper or face expulsion. The ultimatum was rejected, and on 13 October the eight districts were expelled. Indi-vidual members and local organizations within the districts were given longer to adhere to the majority line. The minority described the expul-sions as illegal and set up a national coordinating body to work for minority policy and for electoral alliances within the People's Democratic League. In November majority-controlled People's Democratic districts began expelling minority organizations and the possibility of minority candidates standing on People's Democratic lists seemed to have disappeared.

The prospect of two competing communist parties was already having an impact on the calculations of Finnish politicians. The year passed without any major disagreements threatening the existence of Mr Kalevi Sorsa's centre-left coalition of Social Democrats, Centre Party, Swedish

People's Party and Rural Party. However, most commentators speculated that the split would lead to heightened tension between the Social
Democrats and a majority Communist Party anxious to win support in
competition with a minority party; that this in turn would lead the Social
Democrats to adopt a more radical and aggressive posture; and that this
again would cause difficulties for the Social Democrats' relations with the
parties of the middle. The split was also widely expected to weaken the
left as a bloc in Finnish politics, and thus perhaps increase the likelihood
of the non-socialist parliamentary majority's being translated into a
centre-right coalition.

On the other hand some Centre Party strategists feared that sharper
rivalry between communists and social democrats, leading to a more
prominent social democratic 'profile', could eventually produce a situation like that in Norway and Sweden where the political debate was
increasingly dominated by large parties on the left and right. Partly in
response to this perceived threat the Centre Party leadership in November concluded agreements aimed at tightening links with the other parties
in the middle of the Finnish political spectrum. Under these agreements
the small Christian Party would establish formal organizational ties with
the Centre Party and the Swedish People's Party. These three parties and
the Liberals would try to establish electoral alliances for the 1987 parliamentary election, while the Centre Party, Liberals and Christian Party
would act as a bloc in any post-election coalition negotiations. The
Swedish People's Party, although retaining its independence in such
negotiations, would join in the middle group's internal discussions about
coalition formation.

Another important consideration for the Centre Party in establishing
these formal commitments for 1987 was believed to be the hope of
increasing support for its presidential candidate in 1988. Halfway through
President Koivisto's first term, speculation was already starting about
possible contestants, with the name of Mr Paavo Väyrynen, Centre Party
chairman and Foreign Minister, often mentioned. Discussion also continued about changing the method of electing the President following the
coalition's proposal of December 1984 that in future the electors should
have two votes, one for a presidential candidate, the other for a member
of the electoral college which, if no candidate received 50 per cent of the
direct vote, would elect the President according to the existing method.
By the autumn there was criticism of the proposal from within the
coalition parties themselves. In particular many social democrats now
favoured a direct election in two stages on the French model.

Despite the warnings of the Soviet Communist Party the quarrels of
Finland's communists did not appear to have damaged relations between
the two countries. In September the Government announced that
Finland was seeking to change its associate membership of Efta into full
membership. It denied that Finland's neutrality would be affected,

arguing that Finland had long been a *de facto* full member. Similarly it was argued that Finland's wish to participate in Eureka, the European high-technology programme (see pp. 393–4), was compatible with Finnish neutrality as Eureka research would serve only civil purposes and Finland already participated in similar research with the Soviet Union.

During 1985 the Finnish economy continued its recent record of steady growth and at last experienced a significant fall in inflation. By contrast with a forecast 5 per cent inflation in 1985 and 4 per cent in 1986, figures for the second half of 1985 showed a mere 1 per cent rise in prices. Prospects for future growth and prices were considered to depend crucially on demand in Finland's main foreign markets and on the centralized wage negotiations due to begin in January 1986 for a new two-year wage agreement.

AUSTRIA

The thirtieth anniversary of the signature of the Austrian State Treaty was duly celebrated in Vienna on 15 May at an occasion attended by the Foreign Ministers of all the signatory states. 1985 was also a good year in economic terms, with steady GDP growth (3 per cent in real terms), buoyant exports and an increase in industrial investment. Inflation and unemployment both continued low by the standards of Austria's OECD partners, the former at 3·2 per cent being on a downward trend and the latter at 4·7 per cent only gradually rising. The 1986 Budget presented to Parliament on 23 October accordingly envisaged some expansion in expenditure on education, science, environmental protection and housing, with an increased net budget deficit of 65,600 million Austrian schillings, against 60,410 million in 1985.

Economic policy-makers remained cautious, however, and this mood was reinforced at the end of the year by concern over unexpectedly high deficits registered by two of Austria's main nationalized companies. The Government had little option but to foot the bill, but announced its intention of introducing fundamental reforms with a view, apparently, to reducing the weight of the state sector in the economy—potentially a radical move, given the importance traditionally ascribed in Austria to the nationalized industries and the elaborate system of 'social partnership' fostered by them.

There were no major elections during 1985—apart from provincial elections in Upper Austria on 6 October which slightly increased the absolute majority of the People's Party (ÖVP)—and few ministerial changes in the governing Socialist (SPÖ) and Freedom Party (FPÖ) coalition. The SPÖ Building Minister Herr Karl Sekanina resigned unexpectedly on 22 February, vigorously denying improper use of trade union funds, and was succeeded by Dr Heinrich Ubleis. On 16 December Dr

Kurt Steyrer, the Health and Environment Minister, resigned to run as the SPÖ candidate in the presidential election due in May 1986; the former Foreign Minister and UN Secretary-General Dr Kurt Waldheim had previously announced his candidature on behalf of the ÖVP. Dr Steyrer was succeeded on 17 December by Herr Franz Kreuger, formerly head of the state radio and television service, and on the same day the State Secretary in the Federal Chancellery, Dr Franz Löschnak, was promoted to a new post as Minister in that department.

Although there was relatively little political change, the political climate was far from settled, and the major events of the year did nothing to resolve internal tensions within both SPÖ and FPÖ or to ease the task of the Federal Chancellor, Dr Fred Sinowatz, in managing his ill-assorted coalition. The Government's inability to carry forward its energy policy was particularly unfortunate, given the continuing challenge posed by the 'Greens' to Austria's political establishment.

The year opened with the coalition in considerable disarray over the siting of the Hainburg hydroelectric power plant, the target of unprecedented opposition on environmental grounds. On 3 January the constitutional court banned temporarily all work on the Hainburg site, thus effectively shelving the project. On 21 March there was a further reverse when a parliamentary initiative introduced by the Government failed to achieve the two-thirds majority necessary to authorize a new referendum to overturn the 1978 referendum, which had prevented the opening of the nuclear power station at Zwentendorf. It was subsequently decided that this power station should be dismantled. On 5 November an Ecology Commission appointed by the Government recommended that no further work should take place at Hainburg.

In foreign affairs Austria's bilateral diplomacy and painstaking work in such international forums as the Council of Europe, the Conference on Disarmament in Europe (CDE) and the CSCE cultural forum held in Budapest were overshadowed by two events which did considerable damage to Austria's image abroad. The first was the decision taken by the FPÖ Defence Minister Dr Friedhelm Frischenschlager to greet personally the ex-SS officer Walter Reder on his return from imprisonment for war crimes in Italy on 24 January. The FPÖ responded to SPÖ and ÖVP demands for the Minister's resignation by threatening to withdraw from the coalition. Dr Frischenschlager subsequently apologized for his 'mistake' (a move vigorously opposed by some right-wing FPÖ members), and an ÖVP censure motion against the Government was defeated on 1 February.

The outcome of that affair probably satisfied no one, at home or abroad, and in July further adverse publicity followed the discovery that many Austrian wines had been sweetened with a toxic chemical additive, diethylene-glycol, not dissimilar to substances used in anti-freeze. This scandal dealt a temporary blow to Austrian exports and resulted in the withdrawal from sale and destruction worldwide of very large quantities of Austrian wine, prompting the Government at a special session of Parliament at the end of August to pass Europe's strictest wine laws. The year ended unhappily with Austria once more in the news as a result of the horrific terrorist attack of 27 December on the El Al check-in counter at Vienna's Schwechat airport, which left 3 dead and over 40 injured.

SWITZERLAND

At the beginning of 1985 Parliament met for a special session to take protective measures in face of the bad condition of Swiss forests, mainly in the Alpine area where the forests protected many villages against avalanches. In spite of all the efforts of scientists to find the real reason for the sickness of the trees the specialists were still in disagreement as to the cause. Certainly the extremely hot summer of 1985 had a damaging effect on the woods.

At the end of the year the main topic of public and parliamentary debate was the steadily rising influx of so-called political refugees seeking asylum, though many of them really came to Switzerland for economic reasons. The number of such immigrants rose to about 30,000, including many Tamils claiming to be persecuted in Sri Lanka. Parliament agreed to a revision of the fairly generous legislation, but the churches of both Protestant and Catholic confessions and the left-wing parties fought for the country's traditional hospitality. When, however, in local elections in Geneva and Lausanne the 'Vigilants', a right-wing group with a clear xenophobic tendency, won nearly 30 seats for the first time, and when the people were told that more than 1,000 Tamils reached Swiss territory every month, public opinion, followed by the main parliamentary parties, asked for more severe screening.

Since 1974 the federal state had shown year after year an annual deficit of roughly SwFr. 1,000 million. In the context of the need to balance the budget—for the first time in 1986—by new taxes, reduction of federal subsidies and reform of the costs of the federal state and the 26 cantons, in a referendum on 10 March the people approved the cancelling of federal subsidies for primary schools (conducted by the cantons) by 802,869 votes to 570,047, and of similar subsidies for the health service by 726,622 votes to 644,943. But the third draft, concerning subsidies for the education of young people, was rejected by 716,576 votes to 649,896. On the same day a trade-union Initiative for four weeks' holidays for workers under 20 years of age and five weeks for those over 40 was rejected by 921,226 votes to 490,247.

In a second referendum on 9 June the subsidies for bread-cereals were cancelled by 790,681 votes to 594,786. On the same day a majority denied the cantons participation in the yield of the alcohol monopoly and the duty on the issue of shares and bonds. The Christian Democrats (Roman Catholics) launched a proposal to prohibit any abortion, even before three months of pregnancy. The people rejected this proposal massively, by more than one million votes against 450,000.

On 22 September a new civil law was adopted by 921,593 votes to 762,962. It gave women a much better matrimonial status, in accordance with the constitutional rule of equality between men and women. On the same day the people said 'yes' to a uniform federal beginning of the school year after the summer holidays. Until now some cantons had started the school year after Easter, some in the autumn. A proposal by the Department of Economics to subsidize middle-sized industrial firms for introducing new technology was rejected. In fact the Swiss economy had a much better year, including the machine and tool industries as well as the watchmakers. Tourism and agriculture were also satisfied. The unemployment figures fell back to less than one per cent. Banking and the chemical industry again had a record year.

The last referendum of 1985 brought to an end the passionate campaign of the league for the protection of animals calling for a complete prohibition of vivisection. The pharmaceutical industry won the battle by 1,099,864 votes to 459,567.

The Geneva meeting of President Reagan and General Secretary Gorbachev was a great success for Switzerland. The police forces were reinforced by 3,000 militia soldiers in order to secure the safety of the delegates. The summer brought a state visit by the King and Queen of Sweden, and just before Christmas a visit by Italy's President Cossiga to the Italian-speaking area confirmed Switzerland's friendly relations with its southern neighbour.

Meteorologically 1985 was a most exceptional year: extremely cold days in January and March, heavy snowfall with a great number of victims of avalanches, a cold early summer followed by an outstandingly hot period prolonged until late autumn, and a complete lack of snow at the beginning of the winter season.

Dr Alphons Egli succeeded Dr Furgler as President of the Confederation in 1986, all-but unanimously nominated by Parliament.

Chapter 3

SPAIN—PORTUGAL—GIBRALTAR—MALTA—GREECE—TURKEY—CYPRUS

SPAIN

On 12 June the Treaty of Accession of Spain into the EEC was signed, after prolonged and hard bargaining over the points still outstanding at the beginning of 1985. The low rate of progress in the final adjustment of

Spain's interests and those of the existing member countries during the first four months of the year severely tested the belief of many Spaniards that membership was likely to be beneficial, on balance, to the economic, social and political well-being of the country. A tendency appeared in the press to emphasize the negative consequences of Spain's membership: for example, that France would be able to market milk and other dairy products in Spain more cheaply than local producers: that the curtailment of Spain's wine production would impoverish thousands of smallholders; that Spain's manufacturing industries would have to face unprecedented competition; that there would be less fish to satisfy the Spanish palate. The signature was a relief to the leaders of all the major political parties, for all had been committed of old to the quest for membership.

For domestic reasons the right-wing Coalición Popular, headed by Manuel Fraga, argued that Spain could have got better terms. Elections for the autonomous parliament of Galicia were due in November. Galicia was the region where fear was strongest that entry into the EEC would affect its agriculture adversely, and where in previous elections the Coalición had always done quite well. This time it spared no effort to gain an overall majority, but in the event it just failed to do so, obtaining 34 of the 71 seats. The Socialists won 22. The nationalist Galician centre, a party with ideas similar to those of the Catalan Convergencia's Miquel Roca i Junent (see AR 1984, p. 168), won 11. Centrists allied to the ex-Premier Adolfo Suárez fared badly.

The Prime Minister, Felipe González, was under heavy pressure from the left of his own Socialist Party and others to hold the referendum on whether Spain should remain in Nato immediately and not in 1986 as promised. One opinion poll after another revealed that the majority of the electorate still did not share his view that membership was necessary to Spain's security. In the minds of many Spaniards Nato continued to be seen, not as an organization for the defence of the West, but as an instrument of US foreign policy, no facet of which was more abhorrent to them than President Reagan's policy towards Central and South America. González would have been well pleased had Reagan omitted Spain from his tour of Western Europe. He arrived when the memory was fresh of his imposition of sanctions on Nicaragua. His assurance that he was coming as 'a loyal and sincere friend of Spain' to salute its new democracy and not to exhort it to remain in Nato was widely disbelieved. The only politician to welcome him publicly was Manuel Fraga. Before and during the visit several hundred thousand persons took part in noisy demonstrations in the major cities, in which protest against US support for the 'contras' in Nicaragua was linked with demands for Spain's withdrawal from Nato.

Nothing would have helped González to sway Spaniards to his view on Nato more than to have been able to announce real progress towards Spain's recovery of sovereignty over Gibraltar. All restrictions on the passage of people and vehicles overland to and from the Rock were lifted on 5 February, ten days ahead of schedule. On the same day the Spanish Foreign Minister, Fernando Morán, had a meeting in Geneva with the British Foreign Secretary, Sir Geoffrey Howe. At this, 'all problems relating to Gibraltar, including the issue of sovereignty' were officially listed as subjects for future discussions. Either then, or soon afterwards at meetings of British and Spanish officials, Spain proposed consideration of a condominium, or alternatively a lease-back agreement as a possible interim arrangement; Britain proposed joint use of the Gibraltar airport for civilian air traffic. However, Britain's promise to the Gibraltarians not to change the status quo contrary to their 'freely and democratically expressed wishes' inhibited any definitive reply to either of the Spanish proposals. The airport was a military and not a civil installation, on land not ceded by the Treaty of Utrecht; and Spain had never accepted Britain's claim to that land on the grounds of prescription.

After a meeting of the same Ministers on 6 June, Morán expressed the opinion that Spain's full claim would be satisfied 'in less than 25 years'. The following day Sir Geoffrey said in Gibraltar that the wishes of the Gibraltarians could change, but that it was too early to say exactly how or when. Nothing was announced after a meeting on 5 December between Howe and a new Spanish Foreign Minister, Francisco Fernandez Ordóñez, which González could use to popularize Spain's membership of Nato.

However, five days later the US committed itself to discussions in the spring of 1986 on a phased reduction of its forces in Spain 'on the assumption by Spain's armed forces of specific responsibilities and missions currently undertaken by the US', and provided that 'the overall defence capability and level of security for both countries and their allies' were assured. The meaning was obvious: there would be a reduction in the unpopular US military presence in Spain if it remained in Nato, but not otherwise. With his hand thus strengthened, González announced that the referendum would definitely take place in March 1986.

The Government also faced opposition from its own left and beyond to its economic and social policies. Unemployment rose yet again, to 22 per cent. Only one in three of the unemployed were receiving social benefits. In August the Government sought to provide more money for them through a law reducing pensions. The law met with strong protests from the socialist UGT as well as the communist-led Workers' Commissions, but the Government was undeterred.

There were changes in the Cabinet on 3 July. The Foreign Ministry passed from Fernando Morán to Francisco Fernández Ordóñez, a one-time leader of the Social Democrat group in Adolfo Suárez's vanished Centre Democratic Union. The Minister of the Economy and Finance, Miguel Boyer, whose policy was more monetarist than socialist, was replaced by Carlos Solchaga, hitherto Minister for Industry.

Morán's departure had long been expected. He was by conviction an advocate of closer connections with North Africa and Latin America rather than with Europe. He was opposed to Spain's membership of Nato. With the signature of the Treaty of Accession to the EEC his work under González had been accomplished. A career diplomat, he was appointed in November Spain's ambassador to the UN.

Boyer's displacement had a background of personal and domestic problems and political ambitions. It was a surprise, and it caused consternation temporarily in Spanish and foreign financial circles. The Prime Minister promptly assured them that under the new Minister there was to be no change in economic or financial policies. Solchaga had been appointed to the Cabinet in the first place at Boyer's suggestion, and had been responsible for the harshly realistic restructuring of Spain's major industries. The budget for 1986 which Solchaga produced in October could have been Boyer's in the austerity it demanded of the population. It was designed to reduce the inflation rate from the current 9 per cent to 8, in spite of the introduction of VAT in keeping with EEC stipulations. It displeased the labour unions by imposing 7·2 per cent as the average figure for wage increases for 1986 in the civil service and state-owned enterprises, and 8·5 per cent in private firms. The wealthy were irritated by a slight increase in income tax, though this remained considerably lower than the West European average.

The Government was gratified in October by the findings of the Constitutional Court on the Abortion Law, passed in October 1983, but then referred to the Court as incompatible with the constitution's affirmation of the human right to life (see AR 1983, p. 162).

This law 'depenalized'—the word its text preferred to 'legalized'—abortion on victims of rape, or where a physician was of the opinion that the child might be born 'seriously mentally or physically handicapped' or where a doctor considered the mother's health at risk. The 12-man court, by 7 votes to 6 (the chairman having a double vote) ruled that the law was not incompatible with the constitution in principle, but only in detail. It proposed amendments which the Government accepted: two doctors, not one, would be required to judge the risk of deformity in the child or of health to the mother, and, to prevent abuses, abortions were to be carried out only in state-owned or state-controlled clinics. The law continued to be regarded as unworkable by most lawyers (rape, it was argued, would surely have to be proved first by the slow process of the law courts), and by the majority of doctors as contrary to the Hippocratic oath they had all taken, or as contrary to natural law. Fewer than 50 abortions were carried out under the law before the end of the year. In November the Government allocated one million dollars to a television campaign to popularize contraception and sterilization.

During most of the year terrorist activity was on a reduced scale. ETA lost much Basque public sympathy by assassinating in March the chief of the new Basque police force. It tried to damage Spain's tourist industry by giving warning in the spring of its intention to place bombs in the Mediterranean holiday resorts, and it did detonate a few in May, causing only superficial material damage. There was a slight fall in the number of tourists from Britain but a rise in the numbers from other countries. French cooperation in anti-terrorist action and the Spanish policy of pardoning terrorists who promised good behaviour continued to yield good results. However in December the body of a handcuffed ETA suspect was found drowned. According to the Civil Guard he had escaped while under detention. ETA avenged the death by killing two ex-members of the Civil Guard and kidnapping the manager of the Bilbao football team.

There were no rumours of subversive activity within the armed services, though there was some pressure for the pardoning of the officers serving sentences for their part in the attempted coup of 23 February 1981. The armed services were busy with their reorganization and re-equipment to bring them more into line with other Nato forces. The Government allocated $560 million to the purchase of ground-based anti-aircraft defence systems.

PORTUGAL

President Eanes's second term of office was due to end in January 1986. The constitution barred him from a third term, yet he had no desire to retire from politics, and there was a way whereby he might be able to continue to exercise political power. This was by taking over the leadership of a party on stepping down from the presidency. It had to be a new party; for as President he had not endeared himself to any in existence. Between his ideas and those of the centre democrat CDS or the communist PCP there was nothing in common. He had made enemies of all his Prime Ministers, socialist PSP and social democrat PSD alike. In his 1985 new year message he berated all those parties and the PSP-PSD governing coalition in particular. They had made of 1984, he said, 'yet another year of crisis . . . yet another of mortgaging (Portugal's) future'; the Government, he went on, had 'sabotaged the correct functioning of every one of the country's democratic institutions' by reserving to itself all important decisions.

The Government thereupon challenged Eanes to dismiss it if he really believed what he said. He did not take up the challenge, with good reason. Given the strengths of the parties in the 250-seat Assembly—101 PSP, 75 PSD, 44 PCP and 30 CDS—and the fact that no one was prepared to form a minority Government, dismissal of the coalition would have led to an immediate election. The new party was not as yet ready to take part in such a contest, and Eanes' term as President still had a year to go.

The new party emerged from its inaugural meeting on 24 February as the Democratic Renewal Party (PRD), with a programme establishing it to the left of the PSD, but to the right of the PSP. At its first congress on 15–16 June, it elected to its executive committee personal friends of Eanes. In the meantime there had been a fresh outbreak of dissension within the PSD. First, its national council was divided on whether the party leader, Carlos Mota Pinto, was exerting as much pressure as he could within the Government, of which he was Vice-Premier, on the socialist Prime Minister Mario Soares to liberalize the economy. Secondly, on 5 February, when Pinto argued in favour of a military man as the party's candidate for the presidency, others in the national council expressed preference for a civilian. Pinto made the issue a vote of confidence, lost by a large majority, and resigned both the party leadership and the vice-premiership. The council then appointed Rui Machete, the Minister of Justice, as acting leader pending the party's annual congress. Soares accepted him as his deputy. Carlos Pinto died suddenly on 7 May, seven days before the congress. Machete decided not to seek his confirmation as party leader, and the congress chose for the post a professor of economics and ex-Minister of Finance, Anibal Carvaço Silva.

Silva was notoriously an opponent of the agreement between Pinto and Soares which had established in 1983 the PSP/PSD coalition Government. Its survival was therefore now in jeopardy. In the Assembly on 24 May Silva led the PSD to vote in favour of a CDS motion demanding an immediate revision of the constitution. The combined PSD/CDS vote was not enough to carry the motion. Silva's decision was intended to warn Soares that the PSD would withdraw from the Government unless he made new concessions to it on economic, labour and agricultural affairs. Soares refused to do so, and on 4 June the PSD gave notice that it would abandon the coalition on 13 June, the day after the signature in Lisbon of the Treaty of Accession of Portugal to the EEC.

Soares was prepared to form a new Government of socialists and independents. The PSD, CDS and PCP were for the dissolution of the Assembly and a general election. Eanes refused Soares' offer and ruled that all Ministers, PSP and PSD alike, were to continue in office until after a general election had been held. To give the PRD as much time as possible to get ready, he delayed the dissolution of the Assembly to 12 July, after it had ratified the Treaty of Accession, and the holding of the election to 6 October.

The campaign was remarkable for the enthusiasm of Senhora Manuela Eanes, the President's wife, on behalf of the PRD, and the electioneering zeal of the new PSD leader, Anibal Carvaço Silva. Sra Eanes presented the PRD as genuinely concerned with the problems and aspirations of ordinary people, and not with political ideologies. Silva, whose parents ran a petrol station and a very small farm in the Algarve, projected himself as a dedicated family man determined to encourage private enterprise.

Both the PSD and the PRD did well. The PSD attracted a record 30 per cent of the votes. The PRD obtained 18 per cent, on this their first electoral contest. The Socialist share fell from 36·4 to 20·8 per cent, the Communists and extreme left from 18·2 to 15·6, and the CDS from 12·4 to 9·7. These figures gave the Social Democrats 88 seats, the Socialists 57, the PRD 45, Communists 38 and CDS 22. Once again, therefore, there was no outright winner. Eanes called upon Silva to form a Government. Silva chose a team of 14 PSD members, including himself, and two independents, and presented his programme to the Assembly on 15 November. It promised austerity, a further liberalization of the economy and a start in the adjustment of Portugal to the requirements of its membership of the EEC. The new Government and its programme were approved by the 110 votes of PSD and CDS and opposed by the 95 Socialist and Communist members. The 45 PRD members abstained.

The new party thus showed its power in the Assembly, but outside it suffered an early reverse. It polled only 13 per cent of the votes at the local elections in December, the Social Democrats picking up what they lost, and it displayed disunity when it chose its candidate for the January 1986 presidential election. Its national council divided on whether to support the candidature of the former Premier, Maria de Lourdes Pintasilgo. She was of the left, but a practising Catholic. They compromised in favour of a one-time member of the Socialist Party, Francisco Salgado Zenha, not a particularly popular figure.

GIBRALTAR

The determining event of the year, which set the scene for the ensuing twelve months, was the unrestricted opening of the frontier with Spain. On 10 and 11 January British and Spanish officials met in Madrid, La Linea and Gibraltar to clarify the text of the Anglo-Spanish Agreement of November 1984 (see AR 1984, pp. 169–70 and 173). On the eve of the opening Sir Geoffrey Howe, British Foreign Secretary, with Sir Joshua Hassan, Prime Minister of Gibraltar, met Sr Fernando Morán, Spain's Foreign Minister, in Geneva. The final obstacles were surmounted, and at midnight on 4/5 February Sr Mariano Baquedano, the civil governor of Cadíz, unlocked the gates which had been closed on General Franco's orders in June 1969.

Immediate reactions in Gibraltar were muted, not because of the effect on trade and tourism—there followed a mini sales-boom during the year as Spanish and British visitors crowded into the Colony—but because of the possible long-term consequences. During the eight-year transition period following Spain's entry into the EEC, Spanish workers would not have the right to apply for jobs in Gibraltar, but what was likely to happen thereafter if there were still $2\frac{1}{2}$ million Spanish unemployed?

Mr Joe Bassano of the Gibraltar Socialist Labour Party talked now of the need for a special status for Gibraltar within the EEC. Sr Morán preferred to talk of 'lease-back', or a condominium, or self-governing status for Gibraltarians within the Spanish Republic. A local opinion poll showed the mixed reactions: 76 per cent wanted the gates open, 18 per cent wanted them closed: but 94 per cent rejected any suggestion of Spanish sovereignty. The opening ceremony was marred by the burning, by Spanish right-wing protesters, of five British-Gibraltar cars parked on the Spanish side of the frontier and, more modestly, by the pelting with eggs and vegetables of the first Spanish visitors.

A flurry of visits followed the opening. On 18 April Sir Joshua crossed into Spain for the first time in more than twenty years to talk with officials over lunch at the farm-house which had belonged to Sr José Maria Ruiz Mateos and his expropriated Rumasa company (see AR 1983, p. 159). In May, the British Minister for Overseas Development, Mr Timothy Raison arrived and during the week 2–9 June Sir Geoffrey Howe became the first Secretary of State for Foreign Affairs to visit the Rock for 14 years. Then on 18 June discussions were revealed in Madrid concerning a possible joint use of the isthmus airport along the lines of the Franco-Swiss agreement for transit passengers at Basle airport. The subject surfaced again on 8 December when Sir Geoffrey Howe journeyed to Madrid for talks with Sr Francisco Fernandez Ordoñez.

In the background of all these visits, talks and announcements lay not only the consequences of Spain's entry into the EEC but also the planned visit of King Juan Carlos and Queen Sofia to London in April 1986 and the forthcoming referendum in Spain on Nato membership (see p. 161).

On a different front, but also indicative of future trends, plans were announced, supported by Sir Joshua Hassan and opposed by Joe Bassano, for the reclamation of some 40 acres of land from the sea on the east side of the Rock facing Marbella. The £120 million scheme was the subject of a feasibility study by Wimpey-Trocon and envisaged a new luxury yacht-marina, shops, arcades and a casino (Gibraltar's third).

MALTA

The most dramatic event of the year came on 23 November, when a hijacked Boeing 737 of Egyptian Airlines landed at Luqa airport (see also p. 183). The flight had begun in Athens but was interrupted after leaving Cairo when terrorists from a PLO splinter group forced the aircraft to change course for Malta. The authorities refused permission to land and blacked out the airport, but the hijackers ordered the captain to use the lights of a parked Singapore Airlines plane. Fighting had already broken out in flight between the hijackers and Egyptian guards: one terrorist was killed; a guard was wounded and thrown off the plane at Luqa. Two

Israeli passengers were also shot by the hijackers. Once they had landed, the Government insisted that all the passengers be released before refuelling. Then, at 9.20 am on Sunday 24 November, Prime Minister Dr Bonnici authorized the storming of the plane by a special task force of 25 Egyptian commandos flown in from Cairo. No Maltese forces were used in the assault.

The result was horrendous. Of the 90 passengers, 60 died, most in the storming of the plane. Dinar Marzouki—the leader of the hijackers and their only survivor—was struck on the head with an axe by the Egypt-Air captain, Hani Galal. He was placed in intensive care in St Luke's hospital, Valletta. Dr Noel Cuschieri opened a formal inquiry on 26 November but the immediate concern was the large number of fatalities. The United Kingdom and United States gave full support to Dr Bonnici's decision to allow the attack, but Mr Paul Mifsud, Director of Information, voiced a general unease when he was reported as saying: 'At the time we thought the action justified; now we are disappointed by the number of people dead'.

The main domestic issue was the settlement of the dispute between the Government and the Catholic hierarchy over church schools. It was an unhappy legacy of the Mintoff years, culminating in mass rallies against the Government and bomb explosions at the end of 1984. On 8 March, Dr Bonnici and Dr Fenech Adami (the Leader of the Opposition) met to try and settle the problem; further talks were then held with church leaders and Vatican representatives, and on 27 April a joint communique was signed by Dr Joseph Cassar, Senior Deputy Prime Minister, Mgr Mercieca, Archbishop of Malta, and Mgr Achille Silvestrini, Vatican Secretary of Public Affairs. It provided for the gradual introduction of free education in church schools over a three-year period. There would be a common secondary-school entry examination, but no government interference in the teaching. A joint commission would be established to discuss church-state issues, including the troubled question of church property.

Other events during the year bore witness to the moderate tone of Dr Bonnici's control as Prime Minister. In May he announced to parliament that Malta would mend its fences with the EEC, renewing its lapsed membership of a number of Community institutions. A new financial protocol promised aid of 29·5 million European currency units (Mecus), about £16½ million, in the period up to 31 October 1988—10·5 Mecus in grants, 3 Mecus in soft loans and the balance at market rates through the European Investment Bank.

On 3 June, the International Court of Justice issued a ruling on the maritime boundary dispute between Malta and Libya. The Court set a median line 18 nautical miles north of the line equidistant between Libya and Malta, the contention being that Libya's coastline had a length of 192 miles as against Malta's 24 miles in the area under dispute.

GREECE

Three events of major importance during the year were the constitutional crisis of March, the general election of June and the tough austerity package announced by the re-elected Pasok Government in October. Despite the manifest personal antagonism between the Prime Minister and the leader of the opposition New Democracy party (ND), Konstantinos Mitsotakis, it appeared early in 1985 that there was some kind of tacit understanding between the two leaders. In return for ND's support for the new electoral law, which was far removed from the simple proportional representation to which Pasok was committed, Pasok, it was widely assumed, would support the re-election of Konstantinos Karamanlis for a second term as President on the expiry of his first five-year term in the spring.

The appearance of detente, however, was to be rudely shattered when on 9 March Mr Papandreou announced that Pasok's candidate in the presidential election would be not Mr Karamanlis but Mr Christos Sartzetakis, a judge of the Supreme Court who had played a major part in bringing to justice, in the early 1960s, the assassins of the left-wing deputy Grigorios Lambrakis. This decision came as a clear surprise to most of the party but, taken with Mr Papandreou's concurrent proposals to curb the considerable residual powers vested in the presidency under the 1975 constitution, it clearly delighted the rank and file. President Karamanlis resigned shortly before the expiry of his term of office and the country was forthwith plunged into its most severe political crisis, apart from the establishment of the Colonels' dictatorship in 1967, since the great crisis of July 1965 which had brought the downfall of the Centre Union Government of George Papandreou, Andreas' father.

Mr Papandreou's move was puzzling; for Pasok had no hope of mustering the 200 votes in parliament necessary to secure Mr Sartzetakis' election in the first two of three ballots and, indeed, was clearly going to be hard pressed to secure the 180 votes (three-fifths of the seats) required in the third ballot, failing which parliament would have to be dissolved. It soon became apparent that the contest was likely to hinge on the casting vote of Mr Yannis Alevras, a Pasok deputy and 'Speaker' of parliament, who had assumed the role of acting President. ND questioned the validity of Mr Alevras' exercising his vote in the presidential election and declared that it would not recognise the new President if he were thereby elected.

ND was bitterly critical of the use of coloured ballot papers and other measures designed to ensure that Pasok deputies did not break ranks and vote against Mr Sartzetakis. In the event, after abstaining in the first two round, Mr Alevras' vote in the third round was instrumental in securing Mr Sartzetakis' election with the constitutional minimum of 180 votes.

ND duly withheld recognition from the new President and reiterated its call for new elections as the only way out of the impasse. Once a new President had been elected Pasok was able to introduce its constitutional amendments.

After President Sartzetakis had acceded to Mr Papandreou's request for early elections, a general election was held on 2 June. The tone of the election, one of the most polarized in the post-war period, was soon set by the declaration of a senior Pasok Minister that what was at issue was not 'tomatoes and oranges but a confrontation between two worlds'. Mr Mitsotakis echoed this sentiment with his insistence that the election represented the last chance of preserving pluralist political institutions and preventing the country's inexorable slide towards a one-party authoritarian dictatorship.

It suited both main parties to cast the election in the form of a duel. Pasok argued that a further four-year term was indispensable to its commitment to socialist transformation and painted a picture of a vengeful right determined to wreak its revenge on the progressive forces. ND, in its turn, espoused a platform of economic and political liberalism, promising to unleash the entrepreneurial spirit of the Greeks by trimming an overblown state sector. The polarized nature of the election was indicated by the fact that 87 per cent of the votes were cast for the two main parties, the highest percentage since the downfall of the military dictatorship in 1974.

Some observers had predicted that the constitutional crisis would frighten centre voters who had voted Pasok in 1981 into voting for ND in 1985. There was little evidence for this, however, and Pasok's share of the vote, at 46 per cent, was only two per cent down on its 1981 share and produced a comfortable working majority of 161 seats in the 300-seat parliament. ND's share of the vote at 41 per cent (126 seats) was up 5 per cent in comparison with 1981. The Communist Party (KKE), with a 10 per cent share of the vote and 12 seats, lost one percentage point and one seat in comparison with the previous general election. The new electoral system enabled the broadly 'Eurocommunist' KKE of the Interior (KKE-es) to secure one seat with a 1·8 per cent share of the vote.

In the wake of his electoral defeat, Mr Mitsotakis stood for re-election as leader of ND, securing the support of 82 of the party's deputies. Konstantinos Stephanopoulos, the deputy leader, subsequently resigned from the party and, with nine other ND deputies, formed a separate party, Democratic Renewal. This was the most serious internal split in ND since its foundation in 1974.

The country's mounting economic problems, including a foreign debt of over £11,000 million and an inflation rate approaching 24 per cent, had been largely ignored in the election. In October, however, the new Pasok Government was forced to introduce a tough austerity programme. This was aimed at reducing the country's massive external and internal deficits by discouraging imports, cutting public expenditure and increasing government revenue. The measures included a 15 per cent devaluation of the drachma, compulsion on importers to deposit with the Bank of Greece, for six months without interest, between 40 to 80 per cent of the value of some goods, the abolition of certain tax exemptions, more rigorous collection of existing taxes, increased prices for public utilities and a two-year wage and salary freeze.

At the same time Greece obtained an emergency loan of £1,050 million from the European Community to back up the austerity programme. Agreement was also reached to delay the introduction of VAT and to continue exchange controls and certain export subsidies after December 1985, the end of the five-year post-entry transitional period. The austerity measures provoked widespread industrial unrest and the expulsion from Pasok of eight union leaders who had supported strike action.

Towards the end of the year some improvement was noted in relations with the United States in the wake of widespread resentment at the imposition by the US State Department of a 'travel advisory' notice, warning US citizens against travelling to Greece after the June hijacking of a TWA aircraft on a flight from Athens (see p. 167 and p. 183). This had caused widespread losses to the country's tourist industry. In October, the British Government formally rejected Greece's claim for the return of the Elgin marbles; the Ministry of Culture responded that Greece would continue to press its case through Unesco and other channels.

TURKEY

In the second year of Mr Turgut Özal's Government, the Turkish economy grew (by an estimated five per cent), the political scene became lively, and the country continued its recovery from the crisis of the late 1970s, which had culminated in the military takeover of 12 September 1980. Internally, rising prices and Kurdish separatist terrorism in the south-east constituted the main problems. In foreign affairs, the maintenance of profitable relations with the West required much effort, while the persecution of ethnic Turks in Bulgaria caused distress.

The regrouping of the opposition, on the left and on the right, did not pose an immediate threat to Mr Özal's right-of-centre Motherland Party, which continued to command an absolute majority in Parliament. The parliamentary left, represented by the Populist Party (the official left-wing party allowed to contest the 1983 general elections), acquired a new leader in the person of Professor Aydin Güven Gürkan, and, after losing a few dissidents, merged with the extra-parliamentary left, represented by the Social Democracy Party (SODEP). The latter had not been allowed to fight the 1983 parliamentary elections, but it contested the local government elections in March 1984, when it outdistanced the Populists. Any hopes that the Social Democratic Populist Party (SPP), which emerged from the fusion, would speak for the whole left were, however, disappointed when the Party of the Democratic Left (PDL) was formed on 14 November and proceeded to elect to its leadership Mrs Rahşan Ecevit, wife of the banned former Prime Minister Mr Bülent Ecevit who had led the left-of-centre Republican People's Party before its dissolution by the military. The PDL recruited some of the dissident ex-Populists, who gave it a small voice in Parliament. At the end of the year, the SPP had not yet completed its unified organization, while the PDL was just starting to organize itself. Both set their sights on the by-elections due in 1986, rather than on the parliamentary elections which need not be held until the autumn of 1988.

On the right, the Nationalist Democracy Party (NDP), which had been groomed for power by the military but had failed to achieve it in 1983 (see AR 1983, p. 173), deposed its founder, retired General Turgut Sunlap, and elected to the leadership Mr Ümit Söylemezoglu, who sought an understanding with the supporters of another banned politician, Mr Süleyman Demirel, former Prime Minister and former leader of the dissolved Justice Party. While Mr Demirel's supporters had formed the Party of the Right Path (led by Mr Hüsamettin Cindoruk), two other right-wing leaders, Mr Necmettin Erbakan and Colonel Alpaslan Türkeş, who were released from custody after being acquitted by the courts, found new names for their old parties. Mr Erbakan's Islamic fundamentalists reformed their dissolved National Salvation Party as the Welfare Party, while Colonel Türkeş's Nationalist Action Party reappeared as the Nationalist Labour Party. No action was taken to restrict political tours and speeches by the banned politicians, none of whom, however, could hold office in the successor parties.

The emergence of a more relaxed political atmosphere was helped by the gradual lifting of martial law which, at the end of the year, remained in force in only nine of the country's 67 provinces, while in 16 others civil governors retained emergency powers. The administrative capital, Ankara, the commercial capital, Istanbul, where the national press was concentrated, and the important port city of Izmir, all reverted to civilian rule. Martial law was retained in the south-east, where security forces sought to suppress the campaign of violence launched in August 1984 by the outlawed Kurdish Workers Party (PKK), from bases in neighbouring Muslim countries. By the end of 1985, some 60 members of the security forces had been killed by PKK terrorists, whose campaign had caused some 250 deaths in all. Although arrests of PKK militants (as well as those of non-Kurdish political outlaws throughout the country) were regularly reported, the authorities were clearly preparing for prolonged operations.

In the meantime Turkey remained under pressure from human rights supporters in the West. Amnesty International called on the Turkish Government to put an end to torture. The same demand was made by the SPP, whose spokesman stated in Parliament on 16 December that 113 persons had died under torture. Mr Özal denied repeatedly that systematic torture had been practised during his term of office, and his assurances led five member-countries of the Council of Europe to drop their case against Turkey for violation of human rights. However, two controversial trials awaited conclusion, those of the leaders of the dissolved, marxist Confederation of Revolutionary Trade Unions (DISK), and of the similarly dissolved Turkish Peace Association. In the latter case, the Military Court of Appeal ordered on 19 December yet another retrial of 23 of the accused, some of whom were in detention.

On 23 November the European Parliament accepted a report critical of the human rights situation in Turkey, and voted that relations with it should remain suspended. However, relations with individual European countries developed. Prime Minister Turgut Özal paid private visits to West Germany and to France, and the Federal German Chancellor Helmut Kohl visited Turkey in July, when military cooperation was one of the subjects discussed. He was preceded in February by the British Foreign Secretary, Sir Geoffrey Howe, who sought Turkish support for the efforts of UN Secretary-General Perez de Cuellar to solve the Cyprus problem. Turkey had expressed regret at the failure of the talks which the latter had organized in New York in January between President Spyros Kyprianou of Cyprus and the Turkish Cypriot leader Mr Rauf Denktash (see pp. 174–5). Thereafter Turkey continued to help in consolidating of the Turkish Cypriot administration, which Turkey alone recognized as the Turkish Republic of Northern Cyprus.

Relations with Greece continued to be strained. Whenever Turkish forces held manoeuvres in the Aegean, Greece complained of violations of its air space. Visits to the two countries in November by Nato Secretary-General Lord Carrington and US Assistant Secretary of State for Political Affairs Michael Armacost did little to heal the breach between the two Nato allies. In the meantime, Turkey and the US continued to renegotiate their Defence and Economic Cooperation Agreement, which was due to expire at the end of the year but was continued in force pending agreement on a new text. The two countries did, however, sign an agreement guaranteeing American investments, which Turkey wished to attract. The visits which Mr Turgut Özal made to the USA in April and the Far East in July centred on economic subjects: the promotion of Turkish exports and the encouragement of foreign investments. In May a Japanese-Italian-Turkish consortium began building a second bridge across the Bosphorus. The first bridge had been built by a British-German group and the United Kingdom Government expressed its disappointment that the bid made for the second bridge by a British-led consortium had been turned down.

The efforts of the Turkish Government to bring succour to its oppressed kinsmen in Bulgaria proved fruitless. A Turkish offer to take them in was turned down, as were numerous Turkish notes of protest to Bulgaria. The Ankara Government then took the problem to international forums, trying, in particular, to mobilize the support of Muslim states. However, relations with the USSR seemed unaffected, and the chief of the general staff, General Necdet Ürug, visited Moscow in November.

According to provisional results of the five-year census held in October, the net annual population growth had increased from 21 to 28 per thousand, and Turkey now had 51·4 million inhabitants.

CYPRUS

The year started amid the highest hopes felt in Cyprus for ten years that a major new movement towards reunification of the divided island was on the cards. Cyprus had been inching towards permanent partition since Turkey invaded and occupied the northern 37 per cent of its land and 28 per cent of its population in 1974 after a coup engineered in Nicosia by the military junta then ruling Greece. The Turkish army enforced an exchange of populations, some 200,000 Greek Cypriot refugees being expelled from the north.

After nine years of fruitless negotiations between the two sides, refereed and guided by the United Nations, Turkish Cypriot leader Rauf Denktash's unilateral declaration of independence for the 'Turkish Republic of Northern Cyprus' in December 1983 spurred renewed efforts by the UN Secretary-General to get a sense of urgency into solving the Cyprus problem. Their culmination was a promising draft accord, outlining the structure of a new federal republic, which was to be put to Mr Denktash and President Spyros Kyprianou at a summit meeting in New York in January 1985. The accord had been so carefully drafted in consultation with both sides that the meeting itself seemed to be a mere formality so that the two leaders could shake hands over the birth of a new Cyprus. That indeed was how Mr Denktash saw it. But for close watchers of the Cyprus scene the signs were ominous; Mr Kyprianou made it clear that he had many aspects of the document still to negotiate.

The key points of the plan were that a federation be established in which both communities would have a great measure of autonomy to run their own affairs. The central government would have a two-chamber parliament with 50–50 representation in the upper House and 30–70 in favour of Greek Cypriots in the lower. Mr Denktash dropped a demand for a rotating presidency in favour of a Turkish Cypriot Vice-President, and got in exchange the promise of the Foreign Ministry for Turkish Cypriots. There were to be elaborate deadlock-breaking procedures on issues affecting the welfare of either community. On the ground, Turkish Cypriots would retain some 29 per cent of the land of Cyprus and return the deserted city of Famagusta-Varosha to Greek Cypriots.

On paper there appeared to be little separating the two sides beyond technical details. Yet the summit talks collapsed in disaster on a procedural issue: Mr Denktash said the draft accord was for signing and the details would be farmed out to joint working groups; Mr Kyprianou said it was for negotiation by the leaders *in toto*. In the post mortem, some of the blame was attached to the Secretary-General, Javier Perez de Cuellar, who in his eagerness to chalk up a major negotiated success story for the UN's 40th year had apparently raised the hopes of both Cypriot communities that their separate views would prevail.

But it was Mr Kyprianou who suffered most internationally and politically. His approach to the meeting was the one which appeared to diplomats and the media as plodding, unimaginative and nit-picking, when it seemed that a grand gesture of 'sign and be damned' was the order of the day. Mr Kyprianou's very sincere reservations were lost in a wave of disappointment and astringent editorials. He returned to Nicosia to find the knives were out in his own community; in a rare show of unanimity, the right-wing Rally party and the communist AKEL party jointly blamed him for the failure of the talks and called on him to resign.

The ebullient Mr Denktash, who seemed not at all perturbed by the federal failure while relishing the acute embarrassment of his counterpart in the squabbling south, set about organizing a three-fold lesson in democracy for his neighbours. He called a referendum on a new constitution for May, followed by parliamentary and presidential elections in June. The constitution which he sponsored won 70 per cent support. Mr Denktash then surprised even himself by winning a 70 per cent landslide victory in a six-cornered presidential race. In the northern assembly election the party he founded, the National Unity Party, won 24 seats and made an alliance with the 10-seat Communal Liberation Party (TKP). The left-wing Turkish Republican Party (CTP) won 12 seats and a party of mainland settlers, New Dawn, won four.

In the south, having censured Mr Kyprianou in parliament in February by 23 votes to his supporters' 12, the two main opposition parties proceeded to block Council of Ministers legislation when Mr Kyprianou refused to resign. As an executive President he was not bound by a House censure. After almost a year of continuous wrangling and political insults, the House decided in October that the deadlock had lasted long enough and unanimously dissolved itself, calling elections for 8 December.

In the old 35-seat house, AKEL had 12 seats, Rally 11, Mr Kyprianou's Democrats nine and the socialist EDEK three. The elections brought some surprises in a country where voting patterns had been traditional and mostly unchanging. Cypriot voters learned to swing and almost every party claimed a victory except AKEL. The communist party's ageing leadership had badly misjudged the mood of the time and its formerly faithful followers left in droves. Mr Kyprianou won a moral victory, the Rally became the biggest party in the new 56-seat expanded House, and EDEK was also pleased to increase its support. Rally won 19 seats, the Democrats 16, AKEL 15 and EDEK 6.

The first three parliamentary sessions ended in wrangles over voting procedures as the House failed to elect a parliamentary president—the second most powerful job in Cyprus since the House leader was the state President's deputy. The Democrats eventually deprived Rally leader Glafkos Clerides of the job by throwing their votes behind EDEK leader Vassos Lyssarides. The choice drew alarmed condemnation from north Cyprus where the leaders claimed that, with a friend of Greek Premier Papandreou in the presidency and an even closer friend in the House leader's job, the Greek Cypriots were completely 'in the pocket of Pasok', Papandreou's party in Greece.

Cyprus suffered from an upsurge of Arab-based terrorism throughout the year; some incident was recorded almost every month and several hijacks passed through Larnaca airport. Island-wide security was tightened to unprecedented levels. The worst incident came in September, when three Palestinian sympathisers brutally murdered three Israelis—two men and woman—on their yacht in Larnaca marina. A Jordanian, a Syrian and a Briton were subsequently gaoled for life, and, in a reprisal raid on PLO headquarters in Tunis, Israel killed over 60 Palestinians and Tunisians.

Economically, Cyprus had a slightly less successful year than 1984, chiefly due to bad weather hitting agriculture early in the year. Real growth in GDP was estimated at 3 per cent for the year. Inflation remained low at around 5 per cent, as did unemployment at 3·6 per cent. Tourism boomed: some 800,000 tourists brought in about $700 million in foreign exchange, an amount equivalent to 98 per cent of that earned by exports. A 1986 budget with a deficit of $238·6 million on revenues of $700·5 million and expenditure of $939·1 million was tabled in December. Major problems to be tackled included a soaring current account deficit, which was estimated to have reached $170 million by the end of 1985, falling export earnings and rising public expenditure. In the north the year remained economically gloomy. The few figures available showed inflation running at around 60 per cent, salary levels at about one quarter the $6,000 per capita income in the south, and stagnating tourist, export and manufacturing industries.

V THE MIDDLE EAST AND NORTH AFRICA

Chapter 1

ISRAEL

ISRAEL may remember 1985 as the year of the Government with nine lives. The Government of national unity, formed in September 1984 (see AR 1984, p. 183) as a result of electoral stalemate rather than budding fraternity across the Labour–Likud divide, had just resolved its first major coalition row as it entered the new year, and passed through its ninth crisis in November 1985.

So marked was the terminal tendency of this last episode, in which Trade and Industry Minister Ariel Sharon challenged the leadership of Prime Minister Shimon Peres, that several newspapers under banner headlines announced the fall of the Government. When Sharon issued a torrent of public insults to Peres on the grounds that the Prime Minister's peace diplomacy infringed the unity agreement, Peres appeared ready to go to the country on the issue. He changed his mind when the small religious parties whose votes he needed to form a Labour Government withheld the support for this move they had initially led him to expect.

Although in November he drew back from the brink Peres undoubtedly weighed the advantages of ditching the Likud partnership. Time was running out for Labour to take this gamble. Journalists predicted with near unanimity that the extraordinary agreement between Labour and the Likud which obliged the Prime Minister to hand over his office to Likud's Yitzhak Shamir in October 1986 would never be honoured.

Sharon, for his part, had managed to crawl back from the edge of the political wilderness to which he had been consigned by his role in the disastrous war in Lebanon (see AR 1983, p. 176). This he accomplished with the help of *Time* magazine, over which he won a technical victory in his libel suit in a New York court in February. Showing signs of renewed ascendancy towards the end of the year, Sharon wanted to bring down the Government of which he was a member, the better to launch his bid for the leadership of Herut and Likud from a platform of radical opposition to the 'land for peace' formula favoured by Peres and many of his followers.

While the Government merely survived the pressures of party strife and the constant jostling for future electoral advantage, the Prime Minister himself positively blossomed in public esteem. Peres gained in stature and dispelled many of the doubts that had cast a shadow over his political career for a full decade. He was personally credited with drawing the economy back from the brink of collapse, pulling the army out of Lebanon and pushing the 'peace process' to its rhetorical limits.

The unity Government was again and again torn apart on the issue of relations with the Arabs but was with equal regularity pinned together again by the cause in which it originated: the need to fend off economic collapse as the bills rolled in for the Lebanon war and occupation, as well as for the electioneering profligacy and maladministration of the previous Government (see AR 1984, p. 184).

The package deal between government, employers and the Histadrut to freeze prices and wages until February as a stop-gap measure was successfully extended to July, and thereafter, with adjustments and relatively few strikes, to the end of 1985 and beyond. The secretary-general of the Histadrut, Israel Kessar, showed qualities of leadership which advanced him to the front rank of Labour politicians and brought him a convincing victory in the Histadrut polls in May. Labour chafed a good deal but cooperated in a policy which forced real wages down to about 1980 levels, as well as causing an extension of poverty and an increase in unemployment to 8 per cent, a level reached only once before in Israel, in the recession of 1965–66 (see AR 1966, p. 298).

If the economy was not exactly on a convincing course for recovery by the year's end, at least the annual rate of inflation, officially measured as 445 per cent for 1984, was brought down to an estimated rate of about 185 per cent for 1985, with some prospect that control could be sustained into 1986. Foreign currency reserves were raised above the danger-level to which they had sunk, and on 31 December the new shekel knocked three zeros off the old, which it replaced, to enable computers and bank clerks to cope with their paperwork in 1986.

American aid, the constant safety-net of Israel's militarized economy, was enhanced by supplementary grants and reductions of interest on past loans. In late April the two countries signed an agreement, the first of its kind in American history, providing for the phased elimination of all trade barriers between them within ten years.

Of all the economic targets set by the Government the most difficult to achieve was the cutting of its own expenditure. Health, education and defence proved to be the most resistant to cuts. The Minister of Finance was experiencing great frustration at the end of the year in his efforts to obtain additional cuts of $600 million for his next draft budget.

A considerable saving was effected in early June as the Israeli occupation forces were almost completely withdrawn from Lebanon after three years of war. Peres, with the close cooperation of his erstwhile antagonist Defence Minister Yitzhak Rabin, ignored initial Likud criticisms of the main withdrawal, but succumbed to the temptation to leave behind a contingent of Israeli soldiers on Lebanese soil to assist Israel's local clients to maintain security in the south of the country. Whether because of the continued Israeli presence in Lebanon or in spite of it, the security of Israel's northern border was certainly much improved during the second half of 1985.

The same could not be said for the security of Israeli citizens and others travelling abroad. In May Israel itself possibly contributed to making 1985 a worse than average year on the terror front by yielding to the demands of Ahmed Jibril, leader of the Popular Front for the Liberation of Palestine general command, based in Damascus, to release 1,150 prisoners, including 160 who were serving life sentences for murder, and no more than 130 of whom were followers of Jibril, in exchange for three Israeli soldiers captured in Lebanon in 1982.

What the Prime Minister and Defence Minister did not anticipate in sponsoring the deal was that some Likud members of the Government who voted for it would exploit the exchange to argue for clemency for convicted Jewish terrorists and for the summary release of 15 suspects still undergoing trial. Peres withstood the pressure for political intervention in the judicial process, although he was unable to contain public agitation on the issue for the rest of the year. All 15 were convicted and sentenced at the end of July, three to life imprisonment for murder and the rest to lenient terms for acts of violence against Arab civilians. The judiciary retained its reputation for independence, but the options of a political amnesty or the exercise of presidential pardon in the future still remained.

It may be that the exposure of the Jewish underground, involving some highly-respected religious nationalists, undermined the appeal of their movement for Jewish settlement in the occupied West Bank. Jewish vigilantes and followers of Rabbi Meir Kahane, the self-avowed racist fanatic, continued to provoke the Arab villagers at every opportunity, but the settlement drive ran out of steam. A land-sales fraud involving top officials saw the year out on a note of high scandal. Also, although the Government had promised the United States that no Falashas from Ethiopia (see p. 202) would be settled on the West Bank, in December the first nine families to leave the absorption centre were placed for permanent residence in Ma'aleh Adumim.

When it withdrew its army from Lebanon Israel took with it some 700 Shia prisoners whom it had held for interrogation. This enabled Shia militants, in hijacking a TWA plane at Beirut in June, to claim that the repatriation of the prisoners, which Israel had in any case already decided to effect, was achieved by their trade in hostages. Israel found it hard to counter the view that hijacking and terror could pay off in dealing with it.

If Israel's actions played a part in bringing this about, similarly the actions of the PLO assisted Israel to score heavily in its campaign to persuade the rest of the world that the organization was no more than a gang of terrorists whose leaders could never be credible interlocutors for peace. Responding to the murder of three Israelis in Cyprus in September, Israel used a surgical air strike to obliterate the PLO headquarters near Tunis, killing some 65 Palestinians and Tunisians. The PLO or its associates, in hijacking the Italian cruise liner *Achille Lauro* and murdering an innocent American passenger in a wheelchair, lost Yassir Arafat credit, whether he was regarded as personally responsible or as unable to control his own organization. By the end of the year, when murderous outrages were directed at the El Al terminals at Rome and Vienna airports (see pp. 139 and 159), all eyes were raised skyward, awaiting an Israeli retaliation for the atrocity.

The diplomacy of peacemaking seemed to offer Peres his best prospect of restoring Labour to monopoly power. This he played for all its worth with a war-weary public. Just after the conclusion of the Amman pact between King Husain and Arafat in February (see below) Peres launched his own diplomacy by calling on the President of Romania, who had facilitated President Sadat's peace initiative in 1977. Peres stuck doggedly all year, through countless verbal convolutions, to the pursuit of talks about talks in spite of all the adverse vicissitudes in the Husain–Arafat camp and the undisguised American scepticism about the timeliness of the whole effort.

He also tried unsuccessfully to persuade his Likud partners to accept arbitration on Taba as the Egyptians wished, but he hesitated to risk the Government on an issue so narrow. Although he managed to reopen talks with Cairo he was unable to infuse new warmth into the relations between the two countries. The year ended with Peres preparing to visit Europe in the hope of breathing new life into his peace campaign.

Chapter 2

THE ARAB WORLD—EGYPT—JORDAN—SYRIA—LEBANON—IRAQ

THE ARAB WORLD

By December any optimism about peace in the Middle East seemed hardly justifiable. Lebanon's Government failed to control or disarm the rival militias. In the Gulf war stalemate did not bring Iran to the conference table. Extreme factions committed atrocities which shocked the world and made the US Government reluctant to press concessions on Israel. The three conflicts reacted on each other; militancy in Teheran inspired Shia fanaticism in Lebanon, which was intensified by Israel's insensitive occupation, and the hatreds thus aroused bred terrorism and hindered negotiation on the Palestine issue.

This was tragic because an Arab consensus had been developing towards a settlement whereby Israel would surrender, to a Jordanian-Palestinian confederation, territory in exchange for peace and Arab recognition. In Amman on 11 February King Husain of Jordan signed an agreement with the PLO chairman, Yassir Arafat, whereby Israel's withdrawal from the occupied lands, including Jerusalem, would be negotiated at a peace conference. References to 'UN Resolutions' (unspecified) and to the Fez decisions (see AR 1982, p. 189) implied, but did not constitute, recognition of Israel in its 1967 frontiers. The agreement also fudged the relations between Jordan and the Palestinians, speaking only of the 'proposed confederation of the Arab states of Jordan and Palestine'. The conference was to comprehend the five permanent members of the Security Council and the parties to the conflict, including the PLO represented in a joint Jordanian-Palestinian delegation. The PLO's executive accepted the agreement on 20 February but added that UN Resolution 242 'did not constitute a sound basis for a just settlement'. Five days later President Mubarak of Egypt suggested that the US should arrange a meeting between Israel and the joint delegation. The PLO's acceptance had been neither unanimous nor, as already noted, complete. Some of Arafat's own supporters criticised it and positively disliked Mubarak's proposals. Israeli reaction was mixed, between hawks and doves. Conflicting Palestinian statements later cast further doubt on the Amman agreement's meaning. In late December Mubarak called openly on the PLO to announce their acceptance of Resolutions 242 and 338; he was immediately rebuffed by Abu Jihad, Arafat's senior commander.

Discussion of Mubarak's plan had meanwhile centred on the composition of the Jordanian-Palestinian delegation. The difficulty was to find Palestinians acceptable to West Bank opinion without being too closely connected with the PLO, whose participation Israel persistently rejected.

After King Husain's visit to President Reagan on 29 May Jordanian spokesmen advocated negotiation by stages, in which, successively, the US would meet a Jordanian-Palestinian (but not PLO) delegation; Arafat would declare himself ready to recognize Israel; the US would publicly accept self-determination for the occupied territories in confederation with Jordan; the US–Jordan–Palestinian meeting would reconvene with PLO representatives and plan the international conference, to include Israel—which promptly redrafted this scenario without the PLO. Nevertheless some slate of Palestinians acceptable to the Americans and Israelis was emerging and the US seemed less opposed than before to the international conference. On 21 October the Israeli Prime Minister called on the UN to help convene talks between Israel and the Arabs.

Meanwhile the British Prime Minister visited Cairo and Amman in late September and invited to London a Jordanian delegation to include two West Bank Palestinians on condition that they publicly recognized Israel's existence and condemned violence. This plan collapsed on 14 October when one of the two rejected the formula for this declaration which, he claimed, had been reached without him (see pp. 38–39).

This rather sluggish current towards negotiation was worse obstructed by recurrent Arab terrorism, including the TWA hijack (see pp. 163 and 191); the massacre of three Israeli yachtsmen in Cyprus on 25 September, followed by Israel's retaliatory raid on Tunis, killing 65 Arabs; the seizure of the *Achille Lauro* and the Malta hijack (see pp. 167 and 183); and the 27 December murders in Rome and Vienna (see pp. 139 and 159). Such grisly episodes inevitably prejudiced the peace process and one could only conclude that they, and especially the murders of Israelis, which would infallibly raise Israeli clamours for revenge, were meant to wreck it; unfortunately for Arafat, wreckers could be found, or suspected, not only on the rejectionist fringe but even in his own entourage.

On 7 November Arafat had been induced by Mubarak to distance himself from the wreckers by condemning all terrorism against unarmed civilians outside the occupied territories; he had spoken differently two days before. Doubts about this pledge, or Arafat's ability to enforce it, revived after the concerted Rome and Vienna attacks on 27 December. These were, however, immediately condemned by the PLO and suspicion fell on Abu Nidal (see AR 1978, p. 185). If so, his objective—to discredit Arafat and the mainstream PLO—was one he shared with the Israeli Government.

Jordan's reconciliation with Syria (see p. 185) was a step towards internationalizing Middle East peace talks by bringing in Syria's Soviet allies. It was unlikely, however, to narrow the ideological chasm in the Arab world, highlighted when the rejectionist states boycotted the August summit in Morocco. There reconciliation committees were set up under the Saudi Crown Prince to tackle Syrian quarrels with Jordan and Iraq.

The year was more favourable to Soviet than US influence. The US Government, excessively responsive to domestic pressures and opinion, did themselves harm when Congress refused to authorize arms for Jordan, when American fighters intercepted an Egyptian aircraft and when Mr Reagan approved, off the cuff, Israel's raid on Tunis. The USSR had a nasty shock when Soviet representatives were kidnapped in Beirut, but established diplomatic relations with Oman and the UAE.

The continuing slump in oil began seriously to affect Arab oil producers and those who depended on them for loans, subsidies or employment—i.e., most Arab states.

EGYPT

President Husni Mubarak welcomed the Jordan-PLO agreement at Amman (see pp. 180–1) but his supporting initiative failed and he was embarrassed by Palestinian terrorism. Islamic fundamentalism grew and economic difficulties multiplied.

Mubarak had long sought a moderate Arab consensus. On 25

February, following the Amman agreement, he proposed that the US Government should arrange talks between the Israelis and a joint Jordanian-Palestinian delegation. He belittled the difficulty of finding suitable Palestinians, interpreted the Amman agreement as accepting UN Resolution 242, and thus Israel's existence, and suggested that the proposed international conference should simply endorse a previously-reached agreement. In Washington on 11 March he found President Reagan wary of involvement; some progress was made, however, towards finding Palestinians qualified to represent their countrymen but also acceptable to the Americans and Israelis. The peace process then wilted under Palestinian terrorism, which sometimes involved Egypt, and Israeli reprisals.

In the *Achille Lauro* affair four Palestinians boarded an Italian cruise liner at Genoa on 7 October. On the crew's discovering their weapons, they first forced the ship towards Syria (when, it later transpired, they murdered a crippled American Jew, Mr Leon Klinghoffer) and being turned away there sailed for Egypt, whose Government, helped by Abu Abbas, head of a PLO sub-group, persuaded the Palestinians to disembark and surrender.

Indignant at Mr Klinghoffer's death and still smarting from the TWA hijack (see p. 63) the US Government saw red when Egypt simply packed the terrorists off to Tunis. American aircraft intercepted the Egyptian plane carrying them with their Palestinian and Egyptian escorts and forced it to land in Sicily, where tension developed over US extradition demands (see p. 138). The sole American *locus standi* was Klinghoffer's death; the ship was Italian, had started from Italy and put into Alexandria where Egyptian action saved the passengers from further danger. America's high-handed intervention angered the Egyptian Government and people. As intended by the terrorists, the possibility of peace talks even indirectly involving the PLO had been reduced. Mubarak's initiative had been further prejudiced when, on 23 November, an Egyptian aircraft flying from Athens to Rome was seized by unidentified Arabs. After a mid-air fight which killed an Egyptian security guard and one hijacker, the pilot landed in Malta. The hijackers demanded more fuel and began shooting at the passengers, having first segregated the Israelis, Americans and other Nato nationals, but killed only one of them, an Israeli. Next day the Egyptians flew in a commando unit, which after nightfall stormed the aircraft but gave the hijackers time to shoot and throw grenades. About 60 people died in the melée; one hijacker survived (see also p. 167).

The Egyptian Government initially claimed success, concealed the facts from their public and accused Libya of complicity; tension on the Libyan–Egyptian frontier followed. All this, with Egypt's humiliation in the *Achille Lauro* affair, weakened Mubarak's prestige, as did the poor US and Palestinian response to his peace initiative; when in late

December he begged the PLO for an explicit acceptance of Resolution 242 he was immediately snubbed.

In April the overthrow of President Nimairi while in Cairo (see p. 203) clouded the future of Egyptian-Sudanese cooperation, left Egypt with yet another embarrassing guest and rejoiced its *bête noire* Libya, which also expelled many foreign workers including Egyptians and on 2 November tried again to murder or kidnap Libyan exiles in Cairo (see AR 1984, p. 188, and p. 206).

Relations with Israel remained uneasy, Israel still demanding that Egypt return its ambassador to Tel Aviv but rejecting Egypt's stated conditions, namely, complete evacuation of Lebanon and the return of Taba or reference of its status to arbitration under the peace treaty. The murders of an Israeli diplomat in Cairo on 20 August and in October of several Israeli tourists in Sinai by a deranged Egyptian NCO were grave embarrassments.

Economic difficulties aggravated Egypt's reverses abroad. Persistent drought around the headwaters of the Nile had reduced the High Dam to 30 per cent of its capacity. Foreign exchange earnings fell. Increasing domestic consumption cut oil exports; falling prices made them less profitable; and depression in the Gulf reduced emigrants' remittances and Suez Canal traffic. Imports grew and servicing of foreign debts (now over $30,000 million) took 24 per cent of foreign exchange receipts. Exchange shortage also fed on itself, as merchants at home and suppliers abroad took forestalling action; the UK's Export Credits Guarantee Department (ECGD) put Egypt in its 'worst risk' category.

The Prime Minister's January request for $915 million more in US aid for the next fiscal year could extract only a cash grant, approved in June, of $500 million. Egypt also asked the IMF for a standby credit of $1,500 million but as before (see AR 1978, p. 182) the Fund demanded politically explosive cuts in subsidies and a unified exchange rate, both sure to raise prices. No agreement was reached but the Government moved in the desired direction, setting exchange rates for imports closer to the black market rate, raising petrol prices by 30 per cent and reducing the bread subsidy.

These difficulties produced ministerial changes. In March the Economics Minister was succeeded by a Harvard-trained technocrat and on 4 September the Prime Minister, General Kamal Hasan Ali, was replaced by Ali Lutfi, once Finance Minister. He and the President demanded radical reform, with less foreign borrowing and subsidies only for those in need.

Economic hardship strengthened the fundamentalist opposition, whose leaders denounced the reinstatement of the Coptic patriarch (see AR 1981, p. 192) and in June proclaimed a march to demand the introduction of Sharia law. Government forbade the march and detained 500 agitators. On 26 June a prominent cleric, Shaikh Hafiz Salama, was arrested. There was talk of Parliament's banning alcohol, and observers noted more women in strict Islamic dress, with only faces and hands exposed. A law protecting women's rights in divorce, inspired by Sadat's wife Jihan, was annulled by the courts.

JORDAN

The agreement reached in February between King Husain and Yassir Arafat, chairman of the PLO (see p. 180) did not explicitly recognize Israel or renounce violence and was thus inadequate to persuade the US Government to admit the PLO to the peace process. Husain and President Mubarak of Egypt tried thereafter to bring the Palestinians and Americans together, but neither would make the one concession necessary to set the machine in motion; Arafat dodged unequivocal acceptance of UN Resolution 242 and the US persistently rejected negotiation with the PLO. The deadlock was aggravated by spectacular outrages by anti-Arafat Palestinians and by US refusal of arms to Jordan and was followed by a reconcilliation between Jordan and Syria, Arafat's bitter enemy.

Before and after the agreement, Husain often received Arafat in Amman and also saw President Reagan's Middle East adviser and his Secretary of State before calling on Reagan on 29 May. The meeting produced little; the Americans still wanted to see the colour of Husain's money—i.e., an explicit PLO acceptance of Resolution 242. On 4 June Congress refused to sanction arms sales to Jordan unless it negotiated direct with Israel. This made Jordan seek arms elsewhere. Much was expected from the USSR, negotiations continued with France, and on 10 September Jordan contracted with Britain for military material worth $350 million.

Jordan now sought reconciliation with Syria. This had loomed ever since 4 April when Zaid al Rifai, known for his Syrian connections, replaced Ahmad Obaidat as Prime Minister. Saudi Arabia, whose money both governments needed, promoted the reconciliation, and the two Prime Ministers met twice, in September and October, on Saudi soil. The Amman–Damascus railway reopened and Jordanian electric power flowed again to Syria. On 12 November Rifai reached Damascus, bearing a letter from Husain deploring the past activity of those who, unbeknown to him and on the pretext of religion, had carried out from Jordan destructive activities in Syria which he promised would not recur. Rifai returned with Asad's invitation to Husain, who reached Damascus on 30 December. No published communique followed, but Husain had long been in agreement with Asad that peace negotiations must involve all the parties concerned and be in an international forum; and he had clearly undertaken to continue resisting Israeli pressures for bilateral talks, despite persistent rumours of his clandestine meetings with the Israeli Prime Minister.

This reconciliation could hardly please Israel, the US or above all Arafat, now anathema to Asad. It was noted that though Arafat visited Amman on 28 October and spoke blandly to the press, Husain's throne speech on 13 November hardly mentioned the PLO. For Husain, however, the reconciliation had also secondary advantages; the reopening of the Syrian market to Jordanian exports, which had fallen 70 per cent from 1980 to 1984, and a possible reduction in terrorist attacks. In March such attacks abroad on the Jordanian airline Alia had been closely followed—*post* but not necessarily *propter hoc*—by similar attacks on Syrian property.

The Foreign Minister was in Moscow on 27 May; he was reported to have found the Soviets unwilling to receive a Jordanian–Palestinian delegation on tour to explain their joint position to permanent members of the Security Council.

As usual the King was a nimble traveller, being seen in Algeria, Austria, Spain and Britain besides the USA and his several visits to Iraq and the Gulf. These latter probably had a financial character; Jordan was suffering, as in 1984, from foreign exchange shortage and most of the oil states were behindhand with their payments under the 1979 agreement. Imports were growing and in August the Government took steps to discourage them; emigrants' remittances were falling.

Jordan gained its first woman pilot, who won her wings with Alia, and lost its first woman Minister. She had apparently opposed the Government's disciplining the press for criticizing the regime's alleged partiality to the bedouin and their traditions—an incident which revealed Husain's sensitivity on this important subject.

Abdul Moneim al Rifai, a former Prime Minister and kinsman of Zaid, died on 17 October.

SYRIA

President Hafiz al Asad, though secure at home and now without rival in Lebanon, could hardly impose order there, let alone extricate his forces. But he was in constant touch with the Lebanese Government and the militia leaders, and much Lebanese business was transacted in Damascus, where in December the militias met to sign an ambitious agreement guaranteed by Syria. Although his wider Arab policy was still based on Arab rejection of a limited Middle East peace and on his hostility to Yassir Arafat, he accepted a rapprochement with King Husain of Jordan, whom he doubtless hoped to separate from Arafat and to dissuade from any bilateral settlement with Israel. He maintained Syria's links with Khomeini's Iran.

In March the Maronite militia's revolt against President Gemayel challenged Asad, who immediately promised Gemayel his support. No sooner was this crisis defeated than another erupted, as Syria's Shia friends flung themselves first on the Sunni militia and then on the pro-Arafat Palestinians in the Beirut camps. The latter operation, which Syria was accused of encouraging and certainly did not condemn, united pro- and anti-Arafat elements against Syria. Syria's weakness was also demonstrated by Israeli encroachments into Lebanese airspace, two Syrian aircraft being shot down on 19 November while intercepting Israeli planes. Syria then installed new anti-aircraft missiles whose withdrawal Israel and the US demanded. Though Syria helped release the hijacked TWA passengers (see p. 63) it could not liberate Western residents of Beirut seized by pro-Khomeni gangs or save the life of a kidnapped Soviet national.

Indeed Syria's links with Iran—emphasized by periodic high-level Iranian visits to Damascus and the Syrian Prime Minister's to Teheran in December—brought Syria as much embarrassment, especially in Lebanon, as advantage. They were unpopular in Kuwait, where parliament tried to withhold Syria's subsidies under the 1979 agreement. However, Iran continued supplying oil on concessionary terms to replace Iraqi crude for Syrian refineries. The latest agreement, signed on 17 March, allocated Syria six million tons, one million being free of charge. This was less than before and supply was threatened, perhaps even interrupted, by Syrian delays in payment. Another consequence of Syria's Iranian connection was Saudi efforts, backed probably with funds, to persuade Damascus to influence Teheran towards ending the Gulf war; in January and February two Saudi princes visited Damascus with this purpose. Similar Saudi tactics, it was suspected, assisted the Syrian-Jordanian reconciliation (see pp. 180–1), culminating in King Husain's December visit to Damascus.

Relations with the superpowers underwent little change. The US acknowledged Syria's help in securing the release of the TWA hostages but with little grace. US aid to Syria did not resume, though Congress rescinded its ban on Syria's receiving US money through international organizations. Asad visited Moscow from 19 to 22 June and a five-year agreement for economic and technical cooperation was signed on 15 May. In the same month Asad received a delegation from the government party in Afghanistan.

With most Arab governments relations continued much as before, being close only within the 'Steadfastness Front' (Libya, Algeria and South Yemen, all of which, like Syria, boycotted the Arab summit at Casablanca); but even they were inclined to censure the attack on the Palestinian camps in Beirut.

In a referendum on 10 February Asad was re-elected President—his third term—by 99·97 per cent. This followed the eighth Ba'ath party congress, their first for five years. Changes were made in the Regional Command Council appointed by Asad himself and in the Central Committee. Asad's brother, Rifa'at, despite his eclipse in 1984, belonged to both, besides retaining his vice-presidency. Discussions centred on economic subjects and especially on how to revivify the private sector and curb the public sector's inefficiency. On 8 April a new but not radically changed Cabinet was announced.

In April to June there were attacks on Syrian offices abroad and on 21 August explosions—the first since 1982—in Damascus. Six Syrians were executed for spying for Israel. Eight holders of Syrian official passports were expelled from London on suspicion of plotting attacks on PLO representatives. Bombings of Jordanian offices abroad were possibly Syrian-inspired.

The main internal preoccupations were financial. Defence, especially the Lebanese commitment, was still costing 50 per cent of current expenditure, only a little less than in 1984. There was a severe drought. Cotton and oil exports fell. The new oilfield discovered by an American company near Deir al Zor seemed unlikely to yield more than 40,000 barrels per day, but these being light oils, unlike other Syrian crudes, would be usable in Syria's refineries. The Arab states, except Kuwait and Saudi Arabia, were not paying all the subsidies promised in 1979. It was thus an achievement to balance the budget but this was at the cost of austerity; petrol prices rose 38 per cent in September. Inflation was estimated at 10 per cent. No progress was made towards a unified exchange rate but new regulations simplified the issue of exchange for imports.

LEBANON

The Government of President Amin Gemayel and Prime Minister Rashid Karami disappointed expectations, being impotent *vis-à-vis* the militias. Israel's ruthless tactics in defending a buffer zone provoked the Shia inhabitants. Syria failed to impose discipline and compromise on those it supported; the result of its last, impressive effort would not be known till 1986. The ailing economy seemed in terminal decline.

As 1985 opened Israel occupied most of Lebanon south of Beirut. In January, when the Lebanese Government refused any role in Lebanon to Israel's surrogate, the South Lebanon Army (SLA), and rejected its proposal to move Unifil further north, Israel left the UN-sponsored talks and decided unilaterally to evacuate in stages. Withdrawal from the Awali to the Zahrani river was completed by 16 February; in April Israeli forces left Nabatiya, Tyre, part of the Beqa'a and its observation posts on Mount Baruk. The incomplete evacuation ended in June.

This dawdling retreat, during which Israeli forces, attacked by suicide squads, made punitive raids into Lebanese villages, together with the

illegal transfer to Israeli territory of many Lebanese and the retention of a
'security zone' along the frontier, prevented the evacuation from
soothing Lebanese feelings and intensified militancy among the once
apathetic Shia now populating south Beirut as well as south Lebanon.
Throughout the year Israeli aircraft attacked, and caused casualties in,
villages which allegedly harboured Lebanese or Palestinian terrorists.

Evacuation was not, as feared, followed by intercommunal massacres
but there was constant bloodshed. The Lebanese army was unceremoni-
ously pushed aside by various squabbling militias, and the dominant Shia
Amal (led by the relatively moderate Nabih Berri) confronted extremists
who replaced Lebanese flags with Khomeini's.

Equally intractable were the problems, which neither the Geneva
conference (see AR 1983, p. 188) nor the subsequent coalition nor Syrian
intervention had tackled, of a) replacing the obsolete Christian ascendancy by something reflecting the Muslim and especially Shia numerical
predominance, and b) disarming the militias and strengthening the Government. Whenever Maronites moved towards concession, other Maronites called it betrayal. The Muslims showed a similar though less
marked tendency, with the added complication that those readiest for
compromise, the Sunni townsmen, were less numerous, warlike and
geographically concentrated than the Shia and the Druze and had no
significant militia. The ever-cautious Syrians were inhibited by their
obsession with destroying Yassir Arafat and their ties to Khomeini's Iran.

Gemayel's Government could not maintain peace even in Beirut. Its
forces were divided and weak and Gemayel had lost the support of the
Forces Libanaises (FL), the Maronite militia, who now regarded him as a
Syrian creature. In mid-March a puritanical FL leader, Samir Geagea,
rebelled and started an offensive against Muslims around the recently
evacuated Sidon. Syria promised to defend Gemayel by force. A solution
was reached on 9 May when Elie Hobaika took over the FL from Geagea.
On 18 May Hobaika announced a unilateral ceasefire in Beirut and closed
the FL's Jerusalem office, odious to Muslims.

Meanwhile the Cabinet was dissolving. Berri and the Druze leader
Walid Jumblatt, though nominally members, had long boycotted its
meetings when, on 17 April, Karami, the Sunni Prime Minister, resigned.
President Asad persuaded him to stay, but clearly any settlement must
now involve the holders of real power, the militias. Muslim-Christian
hostilities, sometimes using time-bombs, continued between east and
west Beirut. Elsewhere, too, partition had set in, the hills and coast north
of Beirut being firmly Maronite, the far north being controlled by
ex-President Franjieh and his Syrian friends, the Chouf by the Druze
(now with an access to the coast) and the Beqa'a by the Syrians themselves. From south of Beirut many Christians had fled and the area was
now predominantly Shia with Sunni and Christian enclaves.

Violence was also frequent between Muslims. In April the Shia militia took on and defeated the Sunni Murabitun in west Beirut and then turned on the Palestinian camps. Although some PLO fighters had returned since 1982, most inmates were civilians, supporters of Arafat. The attack ignited Palestinian fellow-feeling and Arafat's people were joined by their opponents. In mid-June Damascus negotiated a ceasefire, by which time UNRWA calculated that 15,000 of the 40,000 Palestinians had fled the camps and 500 had died.

In Tripoli the endemic inter-Muslim feuds (see AR 1984, p. 194) intensified in September. The Sunni fundamentalist militia of Shaikh Sha'aban, supported paradoxically by the Iranians, fought the secular, pro-Syrian Alawites of the Arab Democratic Party (ADP) until Syrian forces intervened and on 6 October imposed a ceasefire in the ADP's favour. Over 580 were reported killed and a third of Tripoli's population had fled the city. On 30 October elements in Beirut released three of the Soviet officials they had kidnapped a month earlier to put pressure on the Syrians; the fourth had been killed.

In Beirut's battles Shia and Druze did not always combine, the Druze not sharing the Shias' anti-Palestinian animus. Even the Druze–Shia conference at Shtura on 6 August, which produced a nine-point plan for Lebanon's future, could not end conflict between them. But out of it came a major Syrian search for a settlement more lasting than the usual ephemeral ceasefire. From September on there were negotiations in Damascus between the Muslim and the Christian militias; and after hitches due to grass-roots Maronite recalcitrance and renewed Shia-Druze fighting an impressive document was formally signed on 28 December.

This provided for an abandonment of hostilities under Syrian guarantee, the dissolution of the militias and collection of their armaments, the lifting of 'barriers to circulation' (i.e., the innumerable checkpoints) and the gradual return of refugees to their homes, together with a detailed plan for the political reforms to follow, namely, a transitional phase when the confessional balance in parliament and government would tilt towards the Muslims and finally the deconfessionalization of Lebanese politics, which might take fifteen years to reach.

The signature was a ceremonial affair but without representatives of other Lebanese groups; no Sunnis, Islamic fundamentalists, Falangists or Lebanese Government. These absences were a bad omen, confirmed on 31 December by the attempted assassination in east Beirut of a key FL leader. The veterans of the Maronite community, Camille Chamoun and Sulaiman Franjieh, were reported to be cooperating to reject or modify the Damascus agreement, and Gemayel, who had had no part in it, was alleged to be saying 'It's fine but . . .'. This was despite the fact that important changes had been made to the first draft to meet Maronite objections by leaving more powers to the President and by lengthening the transition to deconfessionalization.

Before this slight parting of the clouds, continual fighting had cost many lives—about 3,000 to judge from government figures. But what struck the Western media was hijackings and kidnappings of Westerners. The most sensational came on 14 June when Shias, encouraged perhaps by Israel's having exchanged, on 20 May, 394 Arabs for three Israelis, seized a TWA aircraft flying from Athens to Rome, demanded the release of 1,200 of their co-religionists held in Israel, killed an American passenger and forced the pilot to shuttle between Beirut and Algiers. Eventually the passengers were disembarked and disappeared into the slums of south Beirut. President Reagan rejected a rescue by force as risking a massacre. Tortuous negotiations ensued, mainly through Syria, to release both hostages in Beirut and detainees in Israel but without publicly admitting any deal. On 30 June the hostages were moved to Damascus and released. Israel's detainees were gradually freed. This fresh humiliation influenced America's tough tactics in the *Achille Lauro* affair (see pp. 64 and 183), rather as previous anti-US outrages must have prompted the CIA (so the *Washington Post* alleged) to arrange the 8 March attempt on the life of a Shia leader in which 80 were killed.

There were recurrent seizures of US, French and British subjects in Beirut by extremist Shias aiming to bargain them against Shias arrested in Kuwait (see AR 1983, p. 199). The Archbishop of Canterbury's envoy, Mr Terry Waite, strove for the release of those kidnapped.

The fanatical intransigence and violence were accompanied by accelerating economic decline, as gross domestic product fell and the balance of payments worsened. The Lebanese pound fell from 8·8 to the $ in January to 17·8 in December. Government finances were in large deficit. Expenditure on defence and salaries grew and revenues dwindled as imports through private ports run by the militias (now again controlling Beirut harbour) escaped customs, normally the Government's chief revenue. The deficit was met by borrowing from the banks, with consequent hyper-inflation; one index showed 100 per cent from January to March. Public debt rose 30 per cent from January to July.

Former President Elias Sarkis died in Paris on 27 June (see OBITUARY).

IRAQ

Despite Iran's costly offensives and Iraq's efforts to reduce Iran's oil income and impair civilian morale, stalemate continued. Iraq, short of men and money, would stop its air attacks only in return for total peace. Iran clung to its refusal of any such peace with President Saddam Husain and the Ba'ath regime but, being weak in the air, wanted the fighting limited to ground operations. Attempts to argue the belligerents into negotiation failed, Iran being the more obdurate. (See also Pt. VIII, Ch. 1.)

Reliable information about hostilities and casualties was still unobtainable; Iran was reported to hold 55,000 Iraqi prisoners. On land an Iranian offensive from 11 to 23 March in the marshes opposite Basra briefly crossed the Tigris, threatening Basra and its links to Baghdad, but it was contained. Casualties were believed to be very heavy. There was a series of local Iranian attacks in June. Against the March offensive Iraq appeared again to have used chemical weapons. A UN report published in February accused both belligerents of maltreating prisoners.

The reciprocal abstention from air attacks on civilian targets (see AR 1984, p. 196) broke down. In March the Iraqis bombed the steel works at Ahwaz; the Iranians retaliated by shelling Basra and possibly launching missiles at Baghdad. Further Iraqi raids followed on Teheran, Isfahan and elsewhere, though the UN Secretary-General appealed to both sides to spare civilians. On 15 June Iraq declared a ceasefire on such targets but Iran rejected it and shelled Iraqi cities. In November Iraq again attacked Ahwaz after Iran had raided Iraqi power stations. Although war weariness was reported from Iran, government policy was unaltered despite occasional Iranian hints at more flexibility.

Iraq's more important and successful air campaign aimed to diminish Iran's oil income by attacking tankers, thus raising insurance costs and reducing Iran's receipts, and later to reduce Iranian exports by bombing the loading quays at Kharg; they were damaged several times but not permanently. Iran later attempted to retaliate by searching foreign vessels for goods bound for Iraq.

Appeals for peace and attempts at mediation abounded as before. The UN Secretary-General visited Teheran and Baghdad but admitted having found the positions of the two Governments far apart. Both sides sent envoys to Tokyo, the Japanese gaining the impression that Iran was now readier for a ceasefire, but nothing came of it, nor of Indian efforts, nor yet of visits exchanged between Iran and Saudi Arabia.

The US Government now had an embassy in Baghdad but would not supply either belligerent with arms, though Iraq did obtain some US helicopters. The USSR and France remained Iraq's chief arms suppliers.

Iraq's internal stability, the strength of actual or potential opposition, was hard to assess. The regime suffered a setback with the Kurds. It had previously exploited their tribal divisions, especially between the Barzanis of the Kurdish Democratic Party (KDP) and Jallal Talabani of the Patriotic Union of Kurdistan (PUK). On 15 January talks with the PUK collapsed and hostilities followed. There was now talk of a united opposition, embracing both Kurdish factions, the remaining Communists and Shias of the Iran-supported Da'wa party. Although an amnesty for political opponents was proclaimed on 11 February, seven KDP and ten Shias, kinsmen of the exiled leader Muhammad Baqir Hakim (see AR 1983, p. 201), were executed within a month. There were further clashes with the PUK in June, and in September the KDP leader said that his forces would continue helping Iran till the Ba'ath regime fell. The Da'wa were accused of causing explosions in Baghdad but these were probably Iranian missiles.

Reports put the cost of the war at $15 million a day. Iraq's $35,000 million reserves had almost gone and its foreign debts had risen to an estimated $40,000 million, including about $25,000 million owed to the Gulf states, probably irrecoverable. As development projects, though reduced, continued, commercial debts accumulated. Several countries had to accept deferred repayments or partial payment in oil. Foreign expenditure grew as imports replaced production lost by war, e.g. from farms flooded for defence, and foreign labour replaced Iraqis under arms.

Oil income was well below its prewar level. Hope of reopening the Syrian pipeline was abandoned, Iraq seeming certain to lose against Syria at the Organization of Arab Petroleum Exporting Countries (Oapec); but over a million barrels per day (b/d) went through Turkey and in October the Red Sea pipeline opened and was carrying an estimated 200,000 b/d—40 per cent of its capacity. Saudi Arabia and Kuwait were still selling between them 2–300,000 b/d for Iraq's benefit. Iraq was already over its Opec quota of 1·2 million b/d and no action followed its request to raise it to 2 million b/d but Opec's increasing impotence made this unimportant. Contracts were signed during the year for additional pipeline capacity through Turkey and Saudi Arabia, and negotiations for a line to Aqaba dragged on.

Chapter 3

SAUDI ARABIA—YEMEN ARAB REPUBLIC—PEOPLE'S DEMOCRATIC REPUBLIC OF YEMEN—THE ARAB STATES OF THE GULF

SAUDI ARABIA

MANY of the problems which had faced Saudi Arabia in 1984 continued unabated and some were exacerbated during 1985. The violent turmoil in Lebanon, the destructive war of attrition between Iran and Iraq, the spread of terrorism and the depressed state of the international petroleum market were all matters of great concern to the Government.

In the early months of the year Saudi Arabia continued to support the avowed policy of Opec, namely, restricting production voluntarily in the hope of sustaining price levels. It became increasingly clear, however, that some other member states were exceeding their agreed production quotas and were discounting their prices too. As a result, Saudi Arabian production fell to around 2 million barrels per day (b/d). After repeated attempts to persuade the other members to adhere to the professed policy, Riyadh announced that it would be prepared to reduce the price of its oil in order to restore higher levels of production. This was done by means of a series of 'netback' agreements with American and French oil companies which were signed in September and October. Under the terms of those contracts the price of Saudi Arabian crude oil was linked to the prevailing market price of its refined derivatives. It was estimated that the result was equivalent to a discount of approximately $2 per barrel. The new approach proved to be effective and by the end of the year it was estimated that Saudi production had increased to around 4 million b/d.

This was welcome news for the Government, which had been obliged to continue to make further withdrawals from the country's large foreign exchange reserves. Renewed attempts were made to limit government expenditure and some developmental plans were reconsidered. It was announced that gradual reductions would be made in the level of subsidies for foodstuffs, petrol, electricity and water supplies and that the price of those items would therefore increase. It was also decided to cut the amount of subsidy paid to those farmers who grew wheat, as the country now had an embarrassingly large surplus of that commodity. The new price was still several times the prevailing world market price, but the reduction was a sign that unlimited government subsidies were no longer possible.

During the year the big petrochemical plants at Jubail and Yanbu began large-scale production and export markets were actively sought. This gave rise to some tension between Saudi Arabia and the EEC, which imposed import duties on several key products.

Plans were announced for the building of an additional crude-oil pipeline from the oilfields to the Red Sea port of Yanbu, but otherwise the construction industry remained in a depressed state. Several local companies went bankrupt and others had to reschedule their debt payments. In Jeddah and Riyadh some commercial buildings remained without tenants and the number of expatriate workers in the country fell considerably—a change not unwelcome to the Government.

Defence expenditures were still a major element in the state's spending programme, but even here some changes were noticeable. In an agreement to purchase additional air-defence equipment from Boeing, the American company undertook to invest funds in Saudi Arabian industrial ventures, while the purchase of aircraft from France was, in part, paid for with supplies of crude oil.

The Government continued, unsuccessfully, to seek ways of bringing an end to the strife in Lebanon and to the war between Iran and Iraq. In pursuit of the latter objective the Foreign Minister, Prince Saud al Faisal, paid a visit to Teheran in May. This was the first visit of a Saudi Minister to Iran since the fall of the Shah. While that visit was taking place two bombs exploded in Riyadh on 18 May, killing one person and injuring several others. The Islamic Jihad movement claimed responsibility for those attacks, but the Iranian Government insisted that they were the work of Iraqi agents. Apprehensions about security matters were increased with the attempted assassination of the ruler of Kuwait on 25 May (see p. 198). These events prompted renewed consultations on security and defence procedures between the members of the Gulf Cooperation Council, and those issues were discussed at the annual meeting of the GCC in Muscat in November. The annual pilgrimage to Mecca and Medina in August was again seen as a possible opportunity for political protests by visiting Iranian Muslims, but the security arrangements worked well and there were no reports of any serious disturbances.

The turmoil in Sudan (see p. 203) was also a cause of concern to the Government, which offered additional financial assistance to help restore that country's economy. King Fahd visited the United States in February and met President Reagan in Washington; Riyadh was one of the destinations on Mrs Thatcher's foreign tour in April.

In the midst of so many difficult and worrying circumstances there was one great occasion for celebration and congratulation. In June a nephew of the King, Prince Sultan bin Salman bin Abd al Aziz, joined the team of an American space-shuttle flight and was in charge of the launching of a communications satellite to be used by the Arab states. This event caught the imagination of the population and was seen as a tribute to the Government's sustained attempts to provide modern education for its citizens.

YEMEN ARAB REPUBLIC

In political terms, the year was a relatively uneventful one for the Yemen Arab Republic, as the Government continued to give considerable attention to economic affairs. In October the President, Mr Ali Abdullah Saleh, stated that the oilfield which had been discovered near Marib in July 1984 had been found to have reserves of some 300 million barrels. Plans were announced for the construction, by a consortium of South Korean companies, of a refinery to serve the needs of the domestic market. It was recognized by officials, however, that the remote location of the oil wells, and the current depressed state of the international petroleum market, meant that the potential for crude oil exports might be less than had been expected. Nevertheless it was said that oil sales would reach 200,000 b/d by 1988. Such an additional source of income was eagerly anticipated by the Government, which saw little evidence of any significant increase in the value of remittances from citizens working in the oil-producing states of the peninsula.

Policies of economic austerity were therefore maintained. Renewed, but largely unsuccessful, efforts were made to restrict the importation of luxury goods, and the country remained in the unhappy position of exporting less than one per cent of the value of its imports. Under those circumstances dependence on external economic assistance, particularly from Saudi Arabia, continued to be high. Some of those funds were again devoted to reconstruction work following the very serious earthquake of 1982 (see AR 1982, p. 203). There were no major changes in international affairs, but it was announced in January that diplomatic relations had been established with Niger and Comoro State.

THE PEOPLE'S DEMOCRATIC REPUBLIC OF YEMEN

The political situation in 1985 was marked by the re-emergence of former rivalries, but the course of events and their precise significance remained obscure. In February the President, Mr Ali Nasser Muhammad, resigned as Chairman of the Council of Ministers but he retained the posts of head of state, secretary-general of the ruling Yemeni Socialist Party and Chairman of the Presidium of the Supreme People's Council. The new head of the Cabinet was Mr Haidar Abu Bakr al Attas, who had previously been Minister of Construction. Several other ministerial changes were made at the same time.

The most surprising political event of the year took place in March with the return from exile in Moscow of Mr Abdul Fattah Ismail, who had been replaced as President by Ali Nasser Muhammad in April 1980 (see AR 1980, p. 202). There was much speculation about the reasons for the reappearance of that hard-line orthodox marxist politician in Aden. Several observers suggested that it was an indication of the Kremlin's displeasure with Ali Nasser Muhammad's established policy of fostering good relations with, and seeking financial aid from, the conservative oil-producing states of the peninsula.

During the summer there were several reports that supporters of Mr Abdul Fattah Ismail had been placed under house arrest. At the congress of the Yemeni Socialist Party held in October, Ali Nasser Muhammad was re-elected as secretary-general but the size of the Politbureau of the Party was expanded from 13 to 16 and one of the new members was Abdul Fattah Ismail. This was seen as further evidence of a weakening in the position of the President and as an indication that a new struggle was under way for control of the party and its policies.

In international affairs the PDRY remained a vocal member of the 'Steadfastness Front' of radical Arab states, but it was careful not to take any action which would seriously antagonize any of its three neighbours, the Yemen Arab Republic, Saudi Arabia and Oman. Relations with Teheran remained quite good, and the refinery at Aden continued to process Iranian oil, some of the products then being returned to that country. The trial began of 11 men who were charged with espionage and with plotting, on behalf of Iraq, to destroy that refinery.

THE ARAB STATES OF THE GULF

As in 1984, for the Arab states of the Gulf the year 1985 was dominated by the twin issues of the Gulf war and the continuing crisis inside the world oil market. Behind these dominant concerns, two other vital regional problems affected the Gulf—the ramifications of the Arab-Israel conflict, particularly its implications for US Middle Eastern policy, and the linked consideration of the renewed Soviet drive for formal relations with moderate Middle Eastern states. There were purely local concerns, too, such as the issue of migrant labour, the growing restrictions on foreign banking and commercial activities, particularly in the UAE, and anxieties over domestic order, which were sharpened by an assassination attempt on the Emir of Kuwait.

Anxieties over the Gulf war were concentrated, as in the past, through the Gulf Cooperation Council (GCC). The GCC organized a Foreign Ministers' meeting in Riyadh in March at which member states called for a negotiated end to the war. There was little evident result—as might have been anticipated—except that Iraqi attacks on shipping in the Gulf intensified and concentrated on the area east of Qatar, where 18 ships were attacked during the early months of the year.

Gulf states' anxieties over the war were not aroused only by the continuing political instability in the region, but also reflected their economic concerns. Qatar, for example, feared that rises in shipping rates would damage its export potential, while shipping bound for Kuwait was subjected to peremptory search by the Iranian navy at various times during the year in consequence of Iranian claims that Kuwait was serving as a port of entry for war materials destined for Iraq. The ships involved were not only those under Kuwaiti flags; European and US shipping was also affected, with the result that, at the end of the year, the US warned that it might take action if Iran continued to claim a right to search neutral ships on the high seas.

At the same time, it was evident that Iran was anxious to restore relations with Arab Gulf states. In January, the Iranian deputy Minister for Foreign Affairs, Muhammad Arab, visited Bahrein, in a move to quieten Bahreini fears after the tensions of recent years, when Iran had threatened to renew its claim to the island. The Saudi Foreign Minister, Prince Saud al-Faisal, visited Teheran in May—the first visit by a Saudi Minister since the Gulf war began. Nevertheless, Iranian hostility towards Kuwait intensified, fired by the emirate's relations with Iraq, the hijack of a Kuwaiti airliner to Teheran in December 1984 and Kuwaiti plans to fortify Bubiyan island.

One major issue between Iran and Kuwait was the latter's imprisonment of the 25 persons convicted of involvement in the suicide bombings of US and French diplomatic installations in Kuwait in December 1983. The December 1984 hijack (see AR 1984, p. 203) was one attempt by the clandestine Iraqi Shi'a resistance movement to force their release, and other such attempts followed during 1985. In May, the Emir of Kuwait, Shaikh Jabar al-Ahmad al-Sabah, narrowly escaped a car bomb attack during a motorcade through the city, and in July the bombings of cafes in Kuwait took a heavy toll. Kuwait responded by tightening security regulations further and by expelling persons of Iranian origin illegally present in the emirate.

The GCC states responded to this general situation by expanding and improving their military capacity. In addition to major defence programmes undertaken by Saudi Arabia in a 'Peace Shield' project, other states improved their armaments capacity. Bahrein purchased six F-5 fighters from the USA and ordered a further six, at a cost of $92 million. It was also constructing a new airbase at a cost of $100 million. Oman almost completed its military expansion programme; the US Army Corps of Engineers let its last contract and plans were revealed at the end of 1985 to purchase either eight Tornado aircraft or 16 F-16 fighters at a cost of between $220 million and $300 million.

The GCC also tried to put more teeth into its own concerns over the situation on the Gulf. Joint GCC military exercises were held in northeastern Saudi Arabia in August, shortly after Omani forces had engaged in their largest-ever operations, involving 10,000 men and 3,000 vehicles. In November, the annual GCC heads of state meeting took place in Oman, shortly after the lavish celebrations marking the fifteenth anniversary of Sultan Qaboos's rule. The meeting again condemned the Gulf war and deputed several of its members to visit the capitals of Iran and Iraq in an attempt to put negotiations in train. Oman itself, as host state, was put in charge of this initiative—which, like so many before it, failed against the continuing weight of Iranian intransigence.

Oman also took the lead in another major Gulf political initiative. To universal surprise, Oman, which had always been most resolute in its anti-Soviet attitudes, announced that it had decided to open formal diplomatic relations with the USSR. The move appeared to result from Oman's improved relations with South Yemen, with which, once an outstanding border dispute had been resolved, Oman was ready to exchange ambassadors. The issue had apparently been under discussion for two years, an indication of the change in Moscow's policy that began under the Andropov regime in the shape of a renewed effort to establish good relations with moderate Middle Eastern states.

The Omani example was followed towards the end of the year by the UAE, which had also opened diplomatic relations with China in 1984. The UAE had been noted for its non-aligned but conservative attitudes in foreign affairs. Bahrein had also been expected to follow the Omani example but, at the end of 1985, confirmed that it did not consider the time appropriate for such a move—echoing in this respect the attitude of Saudi Arabia. Nonetheless, three states in the Gulf now had good relations with Moscow, and one of them—Kuwait—had also turned to the USSR for weapons supplies.

The diplomatic opening towards the USSR took on particular significance in regard to the Palestinian issue, since it meant that the Arab states of the Gulf would increasingly consider that the USSR should become a legitimate partner in any resolution of the Arab-Israeli dispute. Qatar initiated two moves over the Palestinian issue during 1985. During the fighting between Christian and Muslim militias in southern Lebanon in the wake of the Israeli withdrawal, Qatar attempted to mediate. Throughout the year the Qatari Government attempted to persuade the Reagan Administration to take the joint Palestinian-Jordanian initiative seriously. Qatar had a large expatriate Palestinian community, as did Kuwait.

In domestic terms, 1985 was notable for two constitutional developments. In February, there were elections for a new National Assembly in Kuwait, and, towards the end of the year, the much-delayed meeting of the Rulers' Council took place, against the background of the belated publication of the federal budget which appeared only on 31 October, thus maintaining the tradition of late publication, the 1983 budget having been published in August and the 1984 budget in July. In fact the rulers' meeting achieved little, since no major decisions were taken. Instead it merely reconfirmed the continued existence of the federation, despite its recent vicissitudes, Dubai and Abu Dhabi being increasingly at odds over economic and political issues.

Kuwait's elections, however, were a far more exciting affair. The returns in February produced a much more radical Assembly in which the fundamentalist presence had dropped. The Government and the Assembly came into conflict on several occasions, particularly over the aftermath of the Souk al-Manakh unofficial stock market crash in 1982 (see AR 1982, p. 206; 1983, p. 197; 1984, p. 207). The Government was anxious to clear up the economic outfall from the collapse, while the Assembly pushed for punishment of those considered responsible, even though the consequent spate of bankruptcies would have a serious effect on economic confidence in the emirate. Another area of conflict was the Assembly's opposition to any attempt by the Government to reduce its subsidy bill by passing on costs to consumers. However, the effect of the terrorist attacks on the Emir and on cafes in mid-year damped down the tensions.

All Arab Gulf states, except Oman, which was not a member of Opec, confronted major problems over oil-related revenues during 1985. Unlike the other states, Oman constantly increased its crude production—from 468,000 b/d in the first quarter to perhaps as much as 500,000 b/d by the end of the year. Japan took 73 per cent of all Oman oil exports during the year, largely because Oman lies outside the Gulf and its oil supply was thus not subject to the vagaries of the war. Omani oil revenues during the year were expected to total at least OR.1,292 million, according to the 1985 budget, which would have reduced the budget deficit to OR.198 million—three per cent lower than in 1984. Total budgetary revenue was expected to be OR.1,719 million (a 10 per cent rise), including a 25 per cent contribution from non-oil export revenues, and expenditure to be OR.1,918 million (8·6 per cent above 1984). However, the steadily growing level of oil production was expected to convert this deficit into a surplus of the order of OR.216 million.

Oman also benefited from a 31 per cent increase in gas production and from revenues from copper exports as the Sohar copper complex moved into profit. The increases in revenue enabled Oman to purchase a 125,000 b/d refinery from Arco for $420 million, enabling the country to follow Kuwait into developing a vertically-integrated oil company with foreign outlets. Oman also prepared its third five-year plan during the year. Preliminary reports made it clear that non-oil sectors were to receive the bulk of investment, while the increased level of oil exports allowed the aim of a relatively high growth rate, as much as 5 per cent per year. Problems were encountered in other directions, however, particularly over the Government's desire to complete its Omanization programme for banks. By the end of 1985, the banking sector should have been under 90 per cent Omani control, but it proved difficult to provide sufficient trained Omani staff or to retain them in the sector.

The situation elsewhere was far more gloomy. Kuwait suffered a prolonged recession which left its economy at the end of 1985 more stagnant than at any time since the 1950s. The Government called in a team from the International Finance Corporation, the World Bank and the IMF to advise it on future economic strategy. In the wake of the Souk al-Manakh crisis, many firms had been unable to recover and the private sector was in deep depression. Government expenditure was saddled with massive social costs which the National Assembly would not allow it to recover through a more realistic pricing policy. Nonetheless, the Government showed that it was determined to alter this situation through the five-year plan announced in March, which provided for very low growth rates and a reduction in government expenditure.

Despite the adverse domestic economic scene, Kuwait's external accounts stood up well to the continued restraint in oil revenues imposed by Opec quotas (see pp. 193–4). The balance of payments for 1985 was still in surplus and foreign currency reserves continued to grow. This was largely the consequence of past policies of heavy investment abroad and of the vertical integration of Kuwait's oil industry.

For the UAE, the crucial consideration was the enforced decline in oil revenues as a result of the more stringent Opec quotas. Abu Dhabi, for instance, anticipated revenues falling by 12 per cent to $8,000 million. Further problems arose because of Dubai's attempt to maximize its own oil liftings at the expense of Abu Dhabi. The general problems faced by the federation were underlined by the delayed federal budget. Although it foresaw an increase in expenditure of 10 per cent over the 1984 level to Dh.16,600 million, federal ministries had been forced to limit their expenditure to monthly figures based on the overall 1984 expenditure levels.

One consequence of the decline in oil revenues was that major projects were increasingly postponed. Adco shelved two major enhanced-recovery programmes in May, and other projects, including a pipeline, a petroleum coking plant and a hydrocracker extension, would go ahead only if suitable financing packages also emerged. Projects which did proceed included the Taweelah power station and part of the road-building programme, also, in the smaller emirates, petroleum and petrochemical-based developments, providing them with their first opportunity of accelerated development.

The development that most exercised federal minds throughout the year, however, was the proposed privatization of Gulf Air through public sale of 49 per cent of its shares, the remainder being held by the four Gulf states that founded the airline. The privatization was threatened by the unexpected announcement from Dubai that it was forming a separate, competing airline, Emirates Air. The new group, with two airplanes leased from Pakistan, had permission to serve only destinations in India and Pakistan, but it could eventually provide worrying competition to Gulf Air.

The economic situation was little different in Qatar. The 280,000 b/d Opec quota was insufficient to sustain operations at Qapco, where petrochemical production during the year was expected to run at a record loss of more than $40 million. Another source of worry for Qapco was the EEC's readiness to impose quotas on Qatari petrochemical exports to Europe, which led to acrimonious discussions with the EEC. The financing problem was also underlined by the Qatari budget, published in April, which anticipated revenues at below QR.10,000 million for the first time since 1978, while expenditure was set at QR.17,048 million.

The result was that, although the North Gas Field project would go ahead, with a $100 million first phase designed to produce 22·6 million cu.metres per day from reserves estimated to total 4,300 billion cu.m., otherwise only medium-scale projects were accepted. The Wusail power station went ahead, together with a new air base as part of Qatar's expanded defence provisions. Japan took a 7·5 per cent stake in Qaligas, leaving a further 7·5 per cent share still available for foreign participation. In the hope of discovering more oil reserves, Qatar also offered concessions, one of which was taken up by Sohio in mid-year.

Despite the adverse circumstances, Bahrein saw its oil revenues from crude and refined products—82 per cent of its overall revenues—rise by 5 per cent over the year. Oil production rose slightly to 41,892 b/d. The 1985 budget and its successors for 1986 and 1987 anticipated restrained growth of 2 to 3 per cent per year. Some major projects were to go ahead, including the 20,000-unit housing development at Fasht al-Adham. The opening of the causeway with Saudi Arabia, due in December 1985, was postponed for a year, while a similar causeway to Qatar was mooted. The $35 million aluminium rolling complex was completed. The financial sector, however, experienced a decline, as foreign banks cut back on staff and benefits from offshore banking shrank. Overall, the economic outlook for the Gulf states at the end of 1985 was sombre.

Chapter 4

SUDAN—LIBYA—TUNISIA—WESTERN SAHARA—ALGERIA—MOROCCO

SUDAN

THE year began with the disclosure of Operation Moses, masterminded by Israel with help from the United States and Sudan. A Belgian charter company airlifted most of the 25,000 Falashas (Ethiopian Jews) to Israel via refugee camps in eastern Sudan, where they congregated with other Ethiopians fleeing the drought and famine. This operation enraged the Sudanese people and Arab countries in general, and President Nimairi was accused of accepting financial inducements for his collaboration. After Nimairi's overthrow the Government ordered the expulsion of three refugee agencies implicated in the smuggling of the Falashas from Sudan, and former Vice-President Omer Al-Tayib was charged with high treason as a result of his involvement in the airlift.

Devastating drought and famine in Ethiopia caused an influx of about one million refugees in addition to those already present from Chad, Uganda and Eritrea. A severe drought, kept secret by Nimairi, hit western and eastern parts of Sudan and affected about four million Sudanese. The Government appealed for international help. Despite considerable amounts of aid reaching Port Sudan, distribution was hampered by lack of petrol and poor transport facilities. However, West German, Belgian, British and American planes transported food and aid to the drought-stricken areas. The British Government, the EEC, the Red Cross, Oxfam, the Save the Children Fund and others contributed over $100 million towards relieving the famine and aiding the refugees. The US pledged $800 million for famine relief in Ethiopia and Sudan. Live Aid, organised by Mr Bob Geldof, raised £60 million for famine relief in Ethiopia, Sudan and other African countries affected by drought. Nevertheless, Oxfam and the FAO forecast that Sudan would require exceptional food aid in the coming year.

The Sudan People's Liberation Army (SPLA) continued their armed struggle against Nimairi's policy of decentralization and the application of Sharia laws in the south. Juba, Wau, Malakal, military garrisons and installations were under siege, and the Government accused Libya and Ethiopia of arming and supporting the SPLA. Many expatriate and relief workers were airlifted from southern Sudan. The SPLA released six foreign hostages who had been working on the Jonglei Canal. Nimairi offered to make Colonel John Garang, leader of the SPLA, a Vice-President and coordinator of economic development in the south, and he proposed the formation of an independent council for the south. But the SPLA rejected these offers. Colonel Garang stipulated that the re-structuring of Sudan's political and economic institutions was a pre-requisite for peace.

Widespread discontent was expressed in strikes, organized by professional associations, and in street protests. A further cause was the excesses of the Sharia law, particularly the hanging of Mahmood Muhammed Taha, the leader of the Republican Brothers Party. Despite a visit of support by the US Vice-President and the removal of the Muslim Brothers from their positions of power, the political situation continued to deteriorate. Riots followed a 33 per cent increase in the price of bread and many people were arrested, including leading lawyers, academics, doctors and students.

While Nimairi was on a visit to America, General Abd Al-Rahman Muhammed Al-Hasan Suwar Al-Dhahab (commander of the army and Minister of Defence) assumed power on 6 April in order to avoid mutiny in his own army. Thus Nimairi was overthrown and went into exile in Egypt. A 15-member Transitional Military Council (TMC) was formed to rule the country in association with a civilian Cabinet, representing various political factions (including three southerners), under the premiership of Dr Dafalla Al-Jizouli. The new regime abolished the National Security, the Sudan Socialist Union, the National and Regional assemblies, and regional ministries. Sharia economic laws were repealed, but criminal laws remained, though amputation and flogging were stopped. The TMC signed a temporary constitution which provided a legal framework for the country until general elections could be held in April 1986. Close associates of Nimairi were arrested. Nimairi's adviser, Baha Al-Din Idris, was sentenced to ten years' imprisonment and a fine of Sud.£5 million.

The new Government improved diplomatic relations with the USSR, Syria, Ethiopia, Iran and Libya, causing concern to Egypt and the US. Despite Egypt's refusal to extradite ex-President Nimairi, the Government emphasized the continuity of Sudan's special relations with Egypt and America. Libya announced that it had ceased to support the SPLA and it agreed to provide Sudan with military equipment.

John Garang rejected any agreement with the TMC, and the SPLA continued attacks on military garrisons and civilian settlements. The SPLA and its Nuba sympathizers were blamed by the Government for the attempted coup in September. Shooting broke out at barracks in Omdurman and Khartoum North between government troops and army mutineers led by Corporal Samuel Bol Jok; four people were killed and 162 soldiers and civilians were arrested. To encourage the SPLA to negotiate a peaceful settlement, the Government established a 27-member committee, chaired by Professor Muhammed Omer Beshir, who met Garang in Addis Ababa, and it was agreed to hold a peace conference in December. Meanwhile the SPLA had been welcomed as a member of the national grouping of political parties, professional associations and trade unions.

The change of government left the economic situation still serious. The Government tried to reschedule the $9,000 million international debt. Subsidies on certain commodities were cut and the Sudanese pound was devalued. These measures did not help in curbing the high rate of inflation, estimated by the Government to be about 40 per cent. The chronic shortage of petrol was met temporarily by Saudi Arabia (2·2 million barrels), Libya (300,000 tonnes), America (a $40 million loan) and $4·2 million from the Netherlands for an oil-import facility. The EEC, the US, Britain and the World Bank contributed $56 million towards modernizing the railway network, whose defects had hindered relief operations. Credits and loans amounting to $168 million from America and the IDA were earmarked for agricultural development, electricity supplies and other projects. The Netherlands loaned $56·4 million for balance-of-payments support, and Arab funds provided a $300 million lending programme.

LIBYA

The 'Lone Falcon', as his press took to calling Colonel Qadafi, appeared to have fewer friends than ever before. There were the usual reports of attempts on his life, one followed by the execution of 60 officers, and there were rumours that the troops refused to march when ordered into Tunisia. Economic stringency meant that the army lost many of its privileges, and it resented the prospect of 'gradually disappearing', according to Qadafi's theory, 'into the people to form the people in arms'. The police were antagonized by the creation, after new security laws, of parallel forces to deal with 'crimes and conspiracies against the Revolution'. At the end of the year, amidst tales of murders, quarrels and defections, Qadafi encouraged attacks on government officials and technocrats—'the past masters in the art of anaesthetizing the masses'. His sole support seemed to be based on the Revolutionary Committees.

Economic difficulties added to the general air of unease. Oil revenues were less than half those of the record year 1980, while reserves, already regarded as being at danger-level, continued to fall despite efforts to husband them by the simple expedient of not paying bills. Development and administrative budgets were both about 20 per cent less than in the previous year, and in March Libya summarily terminated 400 building contracts and even prestige projects suffered postponement. Prices rose by 15 per cent in less than six months and there was a black market in hard currency and imported goods: Qadafi urged the eating of camel meat rather than beef and mutton bought from abroad.

Libya's lack of money meant that foreign countries were less concerned to seek its friendship. The Swiss indicated that Qadafi would not be welcome in Geneva at the time of the superpower summit. With Britain connections were minimal. The prisoners held virtually as hostages (see AR 1984, p. 211–2) were released in February through the efforts of the Archbishop of Canterbury's emissary, Mr Terry Waite, helped by the discrete advocacy of mutual friends such as King Hassan of Morocco. The Libyans hoped for political concessions in return, but the British were not prepared to grant more than talks at diplomatic level in Rome, which led to some relaxation on the issue of visas. Libyan 'students' in Britain arrested for terrorist offences in 1984 were brought to trial, one receiving a prison sentence of 15 years. Qadafi continued to support the IRA, but, as an apparent gesture of goodwill, allowed Britain to be restored to the weather map of the world published by Tripoli Television.

No such forgiveness was accorded to the USA. Qadafi urged North American Indians to revolt and offered arms to the Black Muslims. He announced that he would attend the UN with a picked bodyguard of international revolutionaries but finally decided that even so his life would be in danger. In November an American newspaper leaked news of a secret plan to lure Qadafi into an adventure which would provide his internal or external enemies with an opportunity to topple him. In December the Americans claimed that recent Libyan purchases of rockets would endanger legitimate traffic and later seemed to be indicating that they would not discourage Israel from seeking revenge on Libya for acts of terrorism, laid at its door upon rather scanty evidence. Qadafi promised that he would retaliate by starting a world war. American calls for a European boycott of Libya went largely unregarded although European countries did reduce still further their own extremely limited trade with Tripoli.

Libya also threatened Italy with war if compensation were not paid for the pre-war occupation, and France if troops were sent to Tunisia. Libyan agents pursued their quarrels with weapons in the streets of Italy,

Austria, Malta, West Germany, Cyprus, Greece, Turkey, Spain and Switzerland. A Libyan agent was expelled from Bangladesh, Zaïre claimed to have dismantled a spy-ring and Uganda to have intercepted an aircraft taking weapons to supporters of Idi Amin. The Australians warned of Libyan intrigues in the Pacific, particularly in New Caledonia.

Qadafi visited black Africa twice. In the spring he embarrassed his hosts in Burundi by calling for the murder of President Mobutu and in Rwanda by fiercely denouncing the Catholic Church. Despite the fact that he had expelled many of their nationals, a December tour to Senegal, Benin, Ghana, Mali and Burkina Faso caused few problems and Qadafi may have even have played a helpful part in mediating in the brief war between Mali and Burkina Faso. Although he once declared that he would annex all Chad, he appeared to take no very positive action there in 1985.

After the overthrow of his enemy President Nimairi, Qadafi went uninvited to the Sudan, startling his hosts with a cash offer of $3,000 million in return for immediate union and joint action to overthrow President Mubarak. Some agreements were made, particularly in the military sphere, and Qadafi promised to end aid to the Southern guerrillas, but the new rulers in Khartoum were unwilling to antagonize Egypt and the USA by too close contact with Libya.

Relations with Egypt were consistently bad, with regular arrests there of Libyan agents. Incredibly, despite the farcical bungle of the previous year (see AR 1984, p. 212), Libyan agents again carried out an attempt on the life of the former Prime Minister Abd al-Hamid Bakkoush. This failed even more spectacularly with the Egyptian police filming the plotters at work, to provide the best television drama of the year. In July Libya accused Egypt of preparing for war but this never seemed probable, even though Mubarak denounced 'the inhuman action of the international adventurer' in expelling 100,000 Egyptian workers who had refused to take Libyan nationality. In November, after the bloody hijacking of an Egyptian aircraft (see p. 183) Qadafi complained to the UN of a military build-up on his frontier.

The expulsion of 32,000 Tunisian workers and the violent press criticism that this evoked seemed to make war on that frontier slightly more likely, but strong support for Tunisia by Algeria showed that this would have been a rash undertaking. Libya was on consistently bad terms with Algeria and stated that it did not recognize the boundary between them.

In January the Libyans made an attempt to mediate in the Gulf war but when this failed were reported to have supplied Teheran with rockets capable of hitting Baghdad. This led to a formal breach of diplomatic relations by Iraq in June, and increased support for the exiled National Front for the Salvation of Libya.

Qadafi's waywardness worried the other Arabs. He denounced the

Arab League as useless and called for unity by force and 'revolution by day and night', to promote which he formed the National Command of the Revolutionary Forces of the Arab World, of which nothing more was heard. He went uninvited to Saudi Arabia and broke all protocol by making a controversial speech in Mecca.

Qadafi's only Arab friends were Morocco, which could only regard their alliance as one of convenience rather than conviction, and Syria, which he urged to annex Lebanon but could not forbear from lecturing on its policy towards the Palestinians.

His supply of Russian rockets to Iran was one of the causes of difficulties which arose during Qadafi's visit to Moscow in October. Other grounds for dispute were Libya's failure to pay its debts, Russia's cautious attitude towards Israel and the USA, and the Kremlin's unwillingness to buy unwanted Libyan oil, supply submarines and a nuclear reactor that could be used for warlike purposes or sign a friendship treaty binding itself to defend an unpredictable ally.

An observer commented that 1985 saw the completion of the decline of Qadafi from being a Caliph on a white horse to one on a little Libyan donkey with the gilding wearing off its hoofs. There was an impression that he was tottering towards a fall from which he could perhaps be saved only by ill-advised external pressure applied to accelerate it.

TUNISIA

At the beginning of the year the mayor of Rome came to sign a document which put a formal end to a state of war with Carthage that had apparently continued unnoticed since its instigation by M. Porcius Cato in 148 BC. If there were hopes that this would be a good augury for a period of tranquillity, they were soon to be disappointed.

The Government appeared to be paralysed as President Bourguiba, too old and ill to govern in person, showed unwillingness that anyone else should take the task. The struggle over the succession continued despite his endorsement of the Prime Minister, Muhammed Mzali, in March; for Bourguiba's influential wife, his son and the hard-liner Muhammed Sayah remained dissatisfied.

Another man believed to harbour presidential ambitions was the 72-year-old Habib Achour, for many years leader of the 350,000-strong trade union movement (UGTT). The UGTT, the oldest and most independent-minded Arab union organization, was split internally, but Achour moved the majority of its members to the left. Negotiations with the Government over wages, which had been frozen for two years, limped along for months. In April, for the first time, the UGTT refused to support the Government party (PSD) in the forthcoming local elections. It then started a campaign of strikes which the Government regarded as a deliberate challenge. Its newspaper was suspended for six months and its local offices, except in the labour strongholds of Gafsa and Gabès, were seized by PSD militants or closed by the police. In October a Government reshuffle was centred on an attempt to control the UGTT; Nur al-Din Hached, son of the 'martyr of Tunisian labour', was appointed Minister of Labour. In November Achour, accused of inciting rebellion and collaboration with Libya, was placed under house arrest and an interim secretary-general of the UGTT appointed. All the opposition parties pledged support for the UGTT. In December Mzali introduced an austerity budget which, with its cutbacks in every sphere, was bound still further to antagonize the unions. Earlier strikes by young magistrates and by airline staff showed that the middle classes were also having difficulties.

There were further worries about the Islamic fundamentalists; they were gaining ground amongst the students, who took violent action in the university, and amongst young officers whose expertise was said to be used in clandestine training camps.

Political opposition groups appeared ineffective. All decided to boycott the local elections but nevertheless the Government claimed a turn-out of 92 per cent. Two-thirds of those elected were newcomers, mostly under 40 years of age and including many women and graduates.

Despite a bumper harvest, the economic position was hardly encouraging. Unemployment increased rapidly to over 20 per cent, the service of the foreign debt absorbed 23 per cent of export earnings and the search for further oil deposits failed, leading to estimates that the country would have a shortage by 1990. Overall loomed the fear that agriculture would receive a fatal blow from the EEC entry of Spain and Portugal, which took 60 per cent of Tunisia's exports. Schemes to reclaim the great lagoon of Carthage at an estimated cost of $2,000 million and of irrigating the chotts (salt depressions) of the south seemed purely visionary.

If at times the Government seemed threatened by internal forces, those abroad were even more dangerous. Relations with Libya were rarely good after the incidents of the previous year (see AR 1984, p. 215) and the two countries' media exchanged insults—particularly the Libyan-based Radio of Vengeance and Sacred Hate, which criticized the Tunisians for not massacring their indigenous Jews. In August the Libyans started to expel Tunisian workers, and within a fortnight about 28,000 of the 80,000 had been put across the frontier, often with complaints of robbery and brutality. The causes of Qadafi's move were variously interpreted as economic stringency, or desire to embarrass the Tunisians by adding to the already large numbers of unemployed, or to put pressure on Bourguiba to abandon his pro-Western stance, symbolised by his recent visits to Paris and Washington. Tunisia expelled 253 Libyans, including some diplomats, and the press war intensified. Soon Tunis complained of Libyan over-flights and of troops massing on the border as Qadafi threatened 'recourse to arms' to stem the criticism. The remaining Libyan diplomats were accused of posting letter-bombs to Tunisian journalists and were also expelled when diplomatic relations were broken. Mzali recalled the remaining Tunisian workers to prevent their being used as hostages and closed the border until 'Libya behaved in a civilized manner'. Qadafi responded by offering union. He ignored attempts at mediation by Morocco, the Arab peninsular states and some Africans. Algeria made it very clear that it would accord Tunisia armed support if necessary, and the point was underlined by President Chadli in an unscheduled visit.

During this crisis Hamman-Chatt, a small town near Tunis housing the offices of the PLO, was bombed with the loss of 45 Palestinian and 20 Tunisian lives and a further 100 wounded. At first it was assumed that Libya was responsible but then it was learned that the Israelis were carrying out a 'reprisal' for the murder of three of their citizens in Cyprus.

During the crisis with their foe Qadafi, the Americans spoke of guaranteeing Tunisian territory but they soon made it very clear that this did not apply against their ally Israel and indeed they assisted the raid. Tunisia was further involved in a problem not of its seeking when the Americans hijacked an Egyptian aircraft bound for Tunis with alleged terrorists on board. Relations with Washington were patched up superficially but deep resentment remained.

Again Algeria stood firmly with Tunisia and this association became the keystone of Tunisia's foreign policy. Early in the year it abandoned a much-desired Maghreb summit rather than annoy the Algerians by the omission of the Sahrawis. Tunisia made several attempts to reconcile Algeria and Morocco. Following the Algerian lead, the Tunisians resumed contact with the Egyptians for the first time since Camp David in 1977.

Relations with the EEC countries, particularly Italy and France, continued to be very good and Mzali also went to Madrid. Closer relations with the Eastern bloc were marked by various agreements with Czechoslovakia and Poland, whose leader was received, and in December there were some unprecedented military conversations with a visiting Russian admiral.

WESTERN SAHARA

The military situation was confused, all observers entertained by the rival forces giving reports satisfactory to their hosts. In March, for example, one group of journalists stated that Polisario was increasing its strength in tanks and anti-aircraft weapons while another party regarded the war as virtually over with the Moroccans completely victorious. The situation was still further confused by unverifiable claims by the Sahrawis of the enormous casualties that they had continued to inflict—311 killed in early January, 113 in May, 141 in June, 210 in July for example, with a total of 5,673 in three years.

There was, however, independent evidence that Polisario forces were still active, for in February they shot down both a British and a West German light aircraft and in August they sank a German boat, capturing its crew of two. In September they took a Spanish fishing-boat with a crew of six, killed another fisherman and a petty officer of a Spanish warship sent to investigate.

Despite a series of ground attacks to prevent them, the Moroccans continued their strategy of building walls to enclose ever more territory. In January, the fourth wall, 400 miles long, was completed to seal off the Algerian frontier, and work started immediately upon a fifth in the extreme south. By the end of the year it appeared that about 85,000 of an estimated total of 100,000 square miles was embraced within ramparts protected by electronic devices which, it was claimed, could detect a jackal over 20 miles away.

Polisario could boast some diplomatic successes. India became the 63rd state to recognize the Saharan Arab Democratic Republic (SADR), and its President, Muhammed Abd al-Aziz, was nominated a vice-president of the OAU. There were also losses: the new Mauritanian Government which had taken power in December 1984 (see AR 1984, p. 240) restored diplomatic relations with Morocco after four years, and Spain, incensed by the attacks on its ships, expelled Polisario representatives and subsequently refused political asylum to 21 Sahrawis who had crossed into Ceuta. Libya proved loyal to its alliance with Morocco, refusing to host a meeting of Afro-Arab states if SADR representatives attended, and its Foreign Minister argued strongly against an independent Sahara at the UN. Even African states regarded as friendly allowed their diplomats to accept Moroccan hospitality in Al Ayoun.

The one constant friend of the SADR remained Algeria, but even its support was tempered by a general indifference on the part of its people and an unwillingness on the part of its Government to inflict upon Morocco a humiliation so great as to incur a risk that the monarchy might be overthrown and replaced by an Islamic republic. Nevertheless Algeria frustrated Tunisian hopes of a Maghreb summit, maintaining that one was 'inconceivable' without the official representation of the Sahrawis. President Chadli did admit to 'secret exchanges of views' with a personal representative of the King.

The old question of a referendum, accepted at the Nairobi summit (see AR 1981, p. 218), made spasmodic appearances, Hassan continuing to express his willingness for one organized by the UN, saying he had lost confidence in the OAU. At the UN his Prime Minister offered to hold one in January 1986, coupled with an immediate unilateral ceasefire, but the Polisario rejected both as 'old merchandise in new wrappings' and made preconditions of an immediate evacuation of the Moroccan army, civil administration and 100,000 settlers and direct talks. The UN urged direct talks, which the Moroccans had always refused although earlier in the year there were reports of secret meetings which were officially denied.

The King announced his intention of celebrating his Accession Day in Al Ayoun in the Sahara in early March but did not do so, perhaps as a conciliatory gesture to Algeria on American advice. He did, however, go there later in the month, with a large party which included his sons and the former King of Bulgaria. He received an enthusiastic welcome, appointed a local man as Minister of Saharan Affairs and announced that he would never abandon the Sahara and was prepared to spend $1,000 million to consolidate Moroccan rule. New plans to modernize agriculture and develop phosphates and other industries were outlined, a grand new airport was opened and the installation of a Club Mediterranée promised. Accompanying journalists noted that Al Ayoun had grown from an obscure village populated by a few hundreds into a flourishing city of over 100,000 in its ten years under the Moroccan flag.

ALGERIA

In the two decades since independence was won, the Algerian state scarcely ever had occasion to use arms in matters of internal security, but in 1985 this became necessary more than once. In April there was trouble over housing in the Algiers Casbah, while in June there were violent incidents in the Saharan town of Ghardaïa which left two dead and 56 wounded. More troublesome, however, were the Islamic fundamentalists, who denounced the Government as 'a band of atheists'. Some were sentenced to life imprisonment in April but one, Mustafa Bouiali, condemned *in absentia*, formed an armed band leading a 'Robin Hood' existence. In August they attacked a police college, killed a guard and captured weapons. In October, ambushed by the police with helicopters, they shot their way out, killing five gendarmes. There were two further battles in November.

The readiness to resort to violence was symptomatic of a political malaise. The ruling party (FLN) was split, with widespread allegations of corruption and reservation of all favours for veterans of the war of liberation. Followers of the late President Boumédienne continued to demand socialism *à l'outrance*, which President Chadli, despite his desire for pragmatic politics, did not feel strong enough publicly to disavow. He argued that the public sector would not be replaced by private enterprise but complemented by it. Throughout the year he campaigned for an 'enrichment' of the National Charter of 1976 which in fact meant dilution of many of its principles. At the end of December the FLN, behind closed doors, held its first congress for two years and decided to submit a revised Charter to a referendum in January 1986.

Despite its internal divisions, the FLN was quick to pounce upon anyone attempting to form any other political organization. Berber leaders campaigning for more equality with Arabs were soon in gaol. A Human Rights League, similar to those in Morocco and Tunisia, was at once declared illegal and twenty of its leaders imprisoned. Non-violent supporters of the exiled former President Ben Bella received up to 13 years' imprisonment in December.

The main crisis, however, lay in the future. In 1963 Algeria produced 93 per cent of its own food but in 1984 the proportion had shrunk to 40 per cent, with 75 per cent of some items such as eggs having to be imported. The arrival of over 40,000 starving refugees from the Sahel countries added to the difficulties, but the real problem was that Algeria had almost the highest birth-rate in the world, leading to estimates of a population of 120 million by the year 2100. Any suggestion of family planning fuelled the anger of Muslim fundamentalists.

Long-term planning was anyway rendered difficult by the lack of certainty about the future price of oil and gas, upon which the country relied for 98 per cent of its export earnings. A five-year plan announced in June anticipated a fall in revenue and decreed that 40 per cent of investment should be in agriculture. Algeria's advocacy of a policy of low production and high prices led to frequent disputes within Opec, particularly with Saudi Arabia. Hopefully the Algerians experimented running buses on liquified gas and using olive oil as a lubricant.

In the early days of his rule it was noticed that President Chadli took little interest in foreign policy, but in 1985, despite his domestic difficulties, it seemed his main preoccupation. Unlike its neighbours, Algeria did not fear the accession of Spain and Portugal to the EEC and felt no need to court its members. Relations with France were cool, with suspicions that Paris had had a hand in the overthrow of the pro-Algerian Government of Mauritania, and it was constantly alleged that North Africans in France were the victims of racist persecution. Algeria also showed pique at the decision of the new French Prime Minister to go first to Rabat. Instead Chadli turned to the USA, making in April the first visit by an Algerian President. Profiting by American displeasure at the Moroccan–Libyan alliance he concluded the first official arms deal between the two states, and he took particular interest in agriculture and high-technology institutions. He went on to Mexico, Cuba and Venezuela, where he called for South-South cooperation against the North.

Relations with Spain greatly improved after the settlement of a dispute over the 1975 agreement by which Madrid had committed itself to importing more gas than the subsequent recession made it possible to use. Señor Moran in Algiers stressed the importance of the country in Spain's foreign policy 'for geopolitical and strategic reasons', and an agreement was signed for arms sales and military and naval cooperation. In July Chadli visited Madrid.

Amidst gibes from Qadafi that Chadli was a second Sadat, Algeria turned its back on the old Steadfastness Front and took a moderate line in Middle Eastern politics. He welcomed King Husain and Yassir Arafat after their February agreement and no longer regarded Egypt as a pariah, high-level representatives going to and fro. In North Africa, Algeria stood firmly with Tunisia, giving a promise of complete support if it were attacked by Libya, and presenting surly, some thought rather pointless, hostility to Morocco. Algerian diplomacy in Africa was extremely active, mainly concerned with rallying support for the Polisario. Relations with the Eastern bloc were good but lost the air of intimacy that had existed in the days of Boumédienne.

MOROCCO

It was expected that the elections of September 1984 (see AR 1984, p. 219) would rapidly be followed by a Cabinet reshuffle, and the general uncertainty was shown by difficulties over the budget, of which only the defence allocations received unanimous support. Changes were in fact delayed until April and produced only nine newcomers in the Ministry of 30. The Istiqlal was unrepresented for the first time since 1977 and the 'social democratic' USFP refused a post because of its opposition to the financial policies of the Prime Minister, Karim Lamrani. He announced a bold and controversial programme of 'denationalization, returning to private enterprise everything that naturally belongs to it'. Some public utilities and large tracts of land taken from French settlers at independence were to be sold. Opening a new parliamentary session the King called for further participation by the private sector, a reduction in bureaucracy and an increase in foreign investment. At the same time educational reforms, consisting of nine years' compulsory schooling, followed by three more with stress on technical training, were announced.

The respect in which international financiers held the realistic policies of Prime Minister Lamrani was shown immediately after his raising the prices of essential commodities for the first time since 1983. The IMF granted a stand-by loan of $318 million and agreed to a rescheduling of debts on favourable terms. This led to a *de facto* devaluation of the dinar, with beneficial results.

The economic position was further improved by the best harvest for ten years, 50 per cent above that of the previous year, and the opening of a large new dam near Agadir. Hassan proclaimed his hope that Morocco would be 'the workshop of the North serving the South, of the East serving the West' and this was encouraged by the opening of new textile factories with British and Italian participation.

There was no major political or industrial unrest during the year but the authorities were clearly alarmed by the activities of Muslim fundamentalists, particularly those of the Jeunesse Islamique, led by the exiled Abd al-Krim Mottei who had thrice already been sentenced to death. In September a tribunal decreed 14 death sentences (nine *in absentia*) for plotting the overthrow of the monarchy, and 26 others received prison terms of from five years up to life. They were said to have received money, arms and training from Algeria, which denounced the allegation of its involvement as 'a deliberate falsehood'.

This was merely one symptom of the bad relations between the neighbours despite secret talks early in the year. Algeria continued to press the claims of the Polisario in every available forum to the detriment of Moroccan interests. In January, after a Moroccan aircraft had been shot down from Algerian territory, there were suspicions that Algeria was trying to goad Morocco into reprisals, but the King stated that 'war with Algeria would not only be a crime but the worst of stupidities'.

Algerian hostility was not mitigated by the surprising endurance of the friendship of King Hassan with the notoriously volatile Colonel Qadafi, with whom he spoke frequently on the telephone. The Colonel cancelled a conference of Arab and African Ministers in deference to a Moroccan refusal to attend if Polisario were represented, and, while foreign workers of many nationalities were expelled from Libya, the number of Moroccans actually increased. In July a joint Assembly of 60 Moroccan and 60 Libyan parliamentarians, held to work out procedure for closer cooperation, resulted in a secretariat with committees to coordinate political, economic, cultural and technological policies. To some extent the King managed to persuade most of his Western friends that he could exercise a restraining influence over his partner.

Relations were very good with France, which gave more aid to Morocco than it did to any other country, including grain which the Americans had refused to supply, and awarded many new contracts. The French Prime Minister and his Foreign Minister both made very successful visits to Rabat. They and the Italian Foreign Minister Andreotti managed to assuage most of Morocco's apprehensions about the possible difficulties ensuing from the adherence of Spain and Portugal to the EEC.

America was more difficult to convince that Hassan had not deserted the West and appeared to lean more towards Algeria. Moroccan faith in American friendship was strained by the realization, engendered by the Israeli attack on Tunis (see p. 209), that Arab allies were of secondary importance. The King immediately cancelled a visit to New York.

With Spain relations varied. There was trouble over the Praesidios, which Morocco feared might become a Nato base, while Spain was apprehensive that its large Muslim community might be 'a fifth column',

but the King said vaguely 'there will always be problems but no difficulties'. After a visit by the Spanish Deputy Defence Minister an agreement was signed providing for military cooperation, naval manoeuvres
and arms deals. Desultory discussions were held on whether the two
countries should be linked by a bridge or a tunnel.

Early in the year the King remarked that he felt closer to the EEC
than to the OAU, in which Morocco was practically isolated. In
February, however, he appointed a new Foreign Minister, Abd al-Latif
Filali, a former ambassador and a connection by marriage, to lead a new
drive for friends. Filali proved extremely successful, both in black Africa
and in Latin America. Morocco restored relations with Mauritania,
remitting its debts, tried to settle the problem of Chad, and won back
many African friends, particularly at the francophone summit in Paris at
which the King was a central figure.

Morocco continued to take a lead in Arab affairs. The King called for
a special summit to discuss the plight of the Palestinians after the Shia
attacks on the refugee camps in Beirut. However, the meeting which
eventually assembled at Casablanca in August was poorly attended and
could not be regarded as a success for Moroccan diplomacy. Much more
successful, taking place simultaneously in Casablanca, were the Pan-
Arab Games in which 2,200 athletes (including 700 women) from every
Arab country except Egypt participated. Morocco emerged as easily the
largest winner of gold medals. It was said that its long-distance runner
Aouïta was the best-known man in the country after the King (see Pt.
XVII, sport).

Another success in August was the visit of the Pope, who received a
welcome more enthusiastic than he had had in several Catholic countries.
There was success, too, for Moroccan women, two of whom qualified as
airline pilots on large jets.

VI EQUATORIAL AFRICA

Chapter 1

ETHIOPIA—SOMALIA—DJIBOUTI—KENYA—TANZANIA—UGANDA

ETHIOPIA

DROUGHT and famine continued to dominate the scene, while the massive international relief operation was maintained. In his report to the Central Committee of the Workers' Party of Ethiopia (WPE) in September, General Secretary Mengistu Haile-Maryam estimated that 900,000 metric tons of food and over Eth.birr 1,000 million (about US$500 million) of other emergency aid had been received since the previous October, and distributed to nearly 7,500,000 Ethiopians. Despite severe distribution problems, the situation generally improved over the year, and numbers in relief camps fell. The main summer rains were mostly good, except in parts of Wollo and Hararge regions. Crop production, some 20 per cent up on the disastrous 1984 harvest, was still, however, some 15 per cent below normal levels, and the government Relief and Rehabilitation Commission estimated that nearly six million people would still need help in 1986. The British Royal Air Force contingent, which pioneered dropping emergency supplies in inaccessible areas, left in December.

Relations between Western aid agencies and the Government were sometimes strained. The burning of a relief camp housing 58,000 people by government troops at Ibnat near Gondar in April aroused widespread condemnation, and the Government promised to rebuild the camp and discipline the local official primarily responsible. Other disputes concerned excessive port charges for grain imports, and restrictions on relief supplies to rebel-held areas. The main area of contention, however, was the Government's resettlement programme, under which about half a million families were moved from the famine zones to lowland areas in the south and west of the country. Claims by the French agency Médecins sans Frontières, which was expelled in November, that 50–100,000 people died in the move were probably exaggerated, but substantial casualties certainly resulted both from the famine victims' physical inability to withstand the journey and from their lack of immunity to lowland diseases such as malaria. Persistent reports of cholera were vehemently denied by the Government. Simultaneously, the Government embarked on a villagization campaign to group scattered farming homesteads into compact settlements. This started in the Hararge highlands, following local disturbances early in the year, and was later extended to Shoa, Arsi and Welega regions. While justified by government spokesmen as a means to improve social services, it also presaged closer control over agricultural production and marketing.

The economy as a whole had a poor year. Ethiopia failed to meet its international coffee export quota, despite high international prices and rigorous controls on domestic consumption. Total exports of Eth.birr 800 million (US$392 million) in the 1984–85 financial year, the lowest since 1978, indicated a further deterioration in the already weak balance of payments. Economy measures announced by Mengistu Haile-Maryam on 9 February included a special famine relief tax, petrol rationing, a ban on car and textile imports and restrictions on house-building. The last of these exacerbated an already chronic urban housing shortage, while the textile ban was implemented by requiring employees earning over 500 birr per month to wear uniforms made from local cloth. No new Western investment was reported, but projects for a cement factory, a textile mill, mineral exploration, hydroelectricity and various irrigation schemes were implemented in collaboration with socialist states, including East Germany, Bulgaria, Czechoslovakia and North Korea.

Politically, it was a year of consolidation following the establishment of the WPE in 1984. Regular Central Committee plenums were held in April and September, and the first annual meetings of the Party primary organizations in August. In September, Mengistu announced that a constitutional commission would shortly be established to prepare the framework for the projected People's Democratic Republic of Ethiopia, but this had yet to be formed by the end of the year. Flight Lieut. Jerry Rawlings of Ghana was the guest of honour at the annual Revolution Day celebrations in September. Following the introduction of national military service in 1984, thousands of youths were conscripted in January, and after completing six months' basic training some of these were posted to Eritrea, where the Eritrean People's Liberation Front (EPLF) reported capturing a number of them in August. A further round of conscription took place in late December.

The three smaller Eritrean resistance groups, the Revolutionary Council, the Popular Liberation Forces-United Organizations and the PLF-Revolutionary Committee, announced a new umbrella organization called the Eritrea Unified National Council in Khartoum in January, but did not appear to be active in the field. The EPLF, on the other hand, captured the government stronghold of Barentu in western Eritrea in July, but was forced to abandon it after heavy fighting on 25 August. Ethiopian troops then reoccupied Tessenei on the Sudanese border and much of the surrounding territory. A fresh offensive against Nacfa, the EPLF redoubt in northern Eritrea, started in October, but after initial successes got bogged down like its predecessors. Government forces had a better year in the Tigré region, capturing two small towns, Sekota in the south and Sheraro in the north-west, which had been held by the Tigré

People's Liberation Front (TPLF) for several years. Guerrilla activity was also reported in parts of Gondar and Wollo regions, but an appalling rail crash near Awash in eastern Ethiopia in January, in which 392 people were reported killed and a further 370 injured, was evidently accidental.

The Ethiopian Government protested vigorously against the airlifting of most of the 25,000 Ethiopian Falashas from Sudan to Israel in late 1984 and early January 1985, and welcomed the overthrow of President Nimairi (see p. 203). An improvement in Ethio-Sudanese relations seemed likely after a visit to Addis Ababa by the new Sudanese Foreign Minister in June, when each side pledged to respect the other's territorial integrity and refrain from interfering in its internal affairs—a formula tacitly referring to Sudanese support for Eritrean secessionists on the one hand, and Ethiopian support for Southern Sudanese resistance on the other. While this accord may have aided the later Ethiopian victories in western Eritrea, it soon came under strain, and in November a senior Sudanese officer accused Ethiopia of training 12,000 Southern Sudanese guerrillas with Cuban assistance, while the Sudanese border was still open to the EPLF.

Ethiopia's relations with the West remained cool, and despite its heavy reliance on Western grain for relief assistance the Government made it clear that its basic socialist policies would be unaffected. US Assistant Secretary of State Chester Crocker complained in November that overtures for a better relationship had been rebuffed. Mengistu visited Moscow in November, although he was unable to announce any increase in Soviet economic or military aid, and North Korea. His visit to India in December was his first to any non-communist and non-African state.

SOMALIA

The general elections held on 31 December 1984 produced a turn-out of 99.8 per cent of the registered electorate of 4,220,466 voters, all but 0.05 per cent of whom opted for the single slate of candidates presented by President Siyad's ruling Somali Revolutionary Socialist Party (SRSP). Forty-six of the 171 candidates were new. A new 23-member Council of Ministers was named on 22 February, though the leading members of the previous Government retained their portfolios, and appointments to the SRSP secretariat were announced two days later. The economy was in dire straits, with inflation up to 90 per cent in 1984, while 1983 exports of US$82 million had covered less than 22 per cent of the $378 million import bill. Following government moves to balance the budget, dismantle price controls and liberalize the foreign exchange market (including a substantial devaluation), a group of Western donors pledged further balance-of-payments support in January, and the IMF announced assistance of $54.7 million in February. Foreign Minister Abdurahman Jama Barreh appealed for drought relief aid on 30 April, claiming that more than three million people were affected, and Italy pledged $500 million for development projects in the arid regions following a visit by Prime Minister Craxi in September.

The security situation evoked conflicting claims by the Government and the two opposition movements, the Somali National Movement (SNM) and the Democratic Front for the Salvation of Somalia (DFSS), both of which broadcast on Radio Halgan from Ethiopia. Both sides noted an increased level of fighting in September, DFSS claiming to have killed nearly a thousand government troops, while the Government accused Ethiopia of attacks across the frontier. In moves designed to undermine the Government's diplomatic position, Radio Halgan also alleged that Somalia had received military aid from South Africa and Israel, and had agreed to act as a dumping-ground for American toxic nuclear waste.

DJIBOUTI

No significant political developments were reported, but the economy remained depressed, following a progressive shift of Ethiopian trade to the port of Assab. Two giant cranes, designed to win back some of this trade, came into operation in February, and a meeting of the Djibouti-Ethiopian joint ministerial council in July agreed to increase cooperation in agriculture, livestock and fisheries. An agreement to extend the airport, with aid from Saudi Arabia, Kuwait and Abu Dhabi, was signed in October.

KENYA

At the beginning of July, the Kenya African National Union (KANU), Kenya's ruling party, held its first national election since October 1978. Returned unopposed were President Daniel Arap Moi as party president, Mr Mwai Kibaki, the Vice-President and Minister of Home Affairs, as party vice-president, and Mr Laban Kitele, an assistant Minister, as national organizing secretary. Mr Justice Ole Tipis, a Minister of State in the President's Office, was re-elected national treasurer, but Mr Robert Matano, Minister of Information and Broadcasting, was defeated in the election for secretary-general by Mr Burudi Nabwera, a former ambassador to the USA. Mr Omolo Okero stepped down as party chairman in favour of Mr David Okiki Amayo, formerly MP for Karachuonyo. These elections followed a very successful recruitment drive which, it was claimed, brought the party strength to 5 million out of a population of 19 million.

President Moi reshuffled his Cabinet early in August, partly to reflect changes in the party hierarchy—Robert Matano was dropped and replaced by Mr Noah Ngala, a former assistant Minister in the President's Office—and partly to strengthen the Government's economic planning capability. The Ministry of Planning, which had been incorporated into the Ministry of Finance since October 1983, was re-established and combined with National Development; Dr Robert Ouko, a former Minister of Labour and Foreign Minister, was appointed Minister.

Students at Nairobi University boycotted classes from 5 February after three of their leaders had been expelled and five others had lost their scholarships; possibly they were affected by the increase in political tension in Nairobi resulting from the pardoning of Mr Charles Njonjo, a former Minister who had been accused of trying to overthrow the Government (see AR 1983, p. 214). A well-attended outdoor meeting on 10 February was dispersed by police, using tear gas. Thirty students required hospital treatment, of whom one later died; a postgraduate student leader, who was among those arrested, was subsequently charged and imprisoned for twelve months. The boycott continued and on 12 February the Government closed the main university campus and sent home over 2,500 students; the latter were readmitted on 23 April, when the University reopened, but only after each of them had signed a pledge of future good conduct before a magistrate. President Moi blamed foreigners and disgruntled Kenyan politicians for fomenting student unrest.

Following two years' discussion and planning, a new educational system was launched in January. It provided for eight years in primary school, four in secondary school and four more at university, and was accompanied by new syllabuses designed to promote vocational and trades training.

Diplomatic sources in Nairobi reported the secret execution in the Kamiti prison, Nairobi, in July of the 12 airmen who had led the 1982 coup attempt (see AR 1982, pp. 224–6), after they had lost their appeal to the High Court against the death sentences imposed on them for treason. In the North-Eastern Province, the surrender to the administration of a top *shifta* leader and six others, with a large arsenal of weapons, led the Government to declare a general amnesty throughout the province on 23 July; bandits who did not give themselves up by 10 August were to be flushed out and prosecuted. An agreement with Uganda to maintain peace and stability along their common border, signed at Eldoret in late January, was difficult to maintain because of the unsettled political situation and fighting within Uganda.

TANZANIA

The most important event during 1985 was the voluntary stepping-down from office of Julius Nyerere, President since mainland Tanzania became a republic in 1962; now aged 63, he had given his country over 20 years of political stability and had greatly improved its social services and international standing. As chairman of the constitutionally supreme Chama cha Mapinduzi (CCM), the ruling party, until 1987, Mr Nyerere would continue to guide general policy. He himself predicted that, with his going, the style of government would change but not the policies. In the short term, the latter were likely to reflect his strong commitment to non-doctrinaire socialism, rural development, the liberation of Southern Africa and reform of the existing international economic order.

Possible successors to President Nyerere were the Pemba-born Mr Salim Ahmed Salim, Prime Minister, former Foreign Minister and Tanzania's chief representative at the United Nations in the 1970s, whose name was widely associated with measures of economic liberalization, and Mr Rashidi Kawawa, the secretary-general of the party and a trade union leader in the pre-independence period who had become Prime Minister in January 1962 and Vice-President in November 1962. The introduction in July of a new currency which curtailed the activities of private traders was seen by some observers as a victory for the old guard of the party and an indication that Mr Kawawa was the favoured candidate. He had the backing of senior and middle-level public servants because of his known opposition to the Government's plan to shed 27,000 state employees; this figure was reduced to 12,000 and those declared redundant were offered jobs in new cooperative undertakings.

In the event, neither Mr Salim nor Mr Kawawa was chosen. In mid-August President Nyerere, with whom the choice effectively lay, announced that Mr Ali Hassan Mwinyi, national Vice-President and President of Zanzibar, would be the sole presidential candidate in the October elections. This nomination was subsequently confirmed at a CCM special national conference, and Mr Mwinyi, having won 92 per cent of the vote in the ensuing popular election on 27 October, was sworn in as Tanzania's second President early in November. President Mwinyi, aged 60, a former teacher, had wide experience as a United Republic Minister; a devout Muslim and committed socialist, he had a reputation for flexibility and honesty. As President of Zanzibar from early 1984 he displayed skill and tact in defusing an explosive situation. He conciliated islanders who urged that Zanzibar should secede from the United Republic and introduced economic reforms, such as liberalizing trade laws and allowing citizens to operate foreign bank accounts.

It was on the economic front that, as President of Tanzania, he faced immediate challenges: agricultural output was dropping, partly because of poor government planning and excessive state intervention, while most industries, without spare parts and essential inputs, were operating at only a third of their capacity. Foreign exchange was desperately short and there was a heavy foreign debt, yet the five-year old negotiations with the IMF, resumed in February in Dar es Salaam, remained deadlocked. There was a need to relax the present rigid and stultifying state control of the economy, but in making such a move President Mwinyi would have to reckon with entrenched political and bureaucratic interests.

President Nyerere served as chairman of the Organization of African Unity (OAU) in the first half of the year and was instrumental in securing recognition of the Saharan Arab Democratic Republic (SADR), thus firmly closing this contentious issue (see Pt. XI, Ch. 5). He played a vital part in negotiations for the release of four British hostages in Libya and in March made a four-day official visit to Britain, where he spent much of his time discussing problems of economic development and food production. In May he announced the privatization of sisal plantations poorly managed by the state-owned Tanzania Sisal Authority, admitting, with typical frankness, that nationalizing them in 1967 had been a mistake. Mr Neil Kinnock, leader of the British Labour Party, visited Tanzania and Kenya in July.

Under the terms of Zanzibar's 1984 constitution, a new judicial system restored the right (abolished in 1970) of an accused person to be represented by defence counsel in the Zanzibar High Court; a defendant was again presumed innocent until proved guilty by the prosecution.

UGANDA

There was no evidence to support the statement made in Nairobi by Mr Elijah Mwangale, the Kenyan Foreign Minister, on 26 July that Milton Obote was 'the only leader who can unite Uganda'. The President lost support even within his own Government as a result of the brutal suppression of university disturbances earlier in the year, the split between warring Langi and Acholi factions within his ill-disciplined army, and a bungled attempt on 6 July to arrest Mr Paulo Muwanga, Vice-President and Minister of Defence, for plotting against him. According to Amnesty International and other sources, the army continued to perpetrate atrocities against rural villagers, especially Baganda living in the Luwero triangle to the north of Kampala, the capital. Luwero was an important stronghold of the National Resistance Army (NRA), the largest, best organized and disciplined of the country's guerrilla forces, led by Mr Yoweri Museveni, a former Minister of Defence. The NRA's main base was now in the south-west, where it controlled several towns and districts and the movement of traffic and food to and from that part of the country; headquarters were established at Fort Portal, following its capture on 25 July. Despite the help of 1,000

North Korean 'advisers', the Ugandan army was unable to prevent the NRA from rendering a substantial part of the west and centre of Uganda virtually ungovernable.

On 27 July a contingent of the Tenth Brigade under Brigadier Basilio Ilara Okello advanced on Kampala from the north and captured the city; the President, with several of his Ministers, fled to Kenya. Lieut.-General Tito Okello, the 71-year-old chief of defence forces (no relation of the coup leader, but, like him, an Acholi), who had been Obote's chief of staff in 1970 and head of the newly-reconstituted army since 1979, was sworn in as head of a new Acholi-dominated, ten-member Military Council; he promised to restore 'peace, stability and full reconciliation' and to hold democratic elections within a year. Talks between the military and political leaders opposed to the former regime were extended to Cabinet Ministers in the Obote Administration and resulted, unexpectedly, in the appointment of Mr Paulo Muwanga as Prime Minister and of Mr Abraham Waligo, Minister of Housing under President Obote, as Finance Minister. Mr Paul Ssemogerere, the leader of the largely Roman Catholic Democratic Party and (like Mr Muwanga) a Muganda, became Internal Affairs Minister; Mr Wilson Toko, a retired air force colonel and chief executive of Uganda Airways, from West Nile, became Minister of Defence, and Mr Olara Utunno, a former diplomat, was named Foreign Minister. Basilio Okello was made army commander with the rank of Lieut.-General, and in mid-August Mr Peter Allen, a British-born High Court judge, was appointed the new Chief Justice.

The NRA's cooperation was essential for both political stability and economic recovery, yet the guerrilla army and the National Resistance Movement (NRM), its political wing, complained that it was not being properly consulted by the military Government. Mr Museveni was holding out for more seats in the Cabinet and an expanded Military Council than the Government was yet willing to concede and was, in any case, reluctant to join a regime which in many respects resembled that of ex-President Obote. The sacking of Paulo Muwanga as Prime Minister in late August, after less than a month in office, removed one stumbling-block to agreement, though his successor, Abraham Waligo, was also an ex-Obote Minister. The NRA joined the Government in peace talks, held at periodic intervals between August and December, mostly in Nairobi under the chairmanship of Kenya's President, Daniel Arap Moi.

As sporadic fighting continued, the NRA consolidated its military strength and raised its conditions for a peace agreement; it stipulated that the NRA itself should provide the nucleus of a newly-structured national army. A despairing military regime sought to stiffen its own lethargic forces by bringing in some 500 former soldiers of ex-President Idi Amin who had operated as a guerrilla force—the Uganda National Rescue Force (UNRF)—in the West Nile district; they were part of the estimated 10,000 soldiers from Amin's army who had fled to Sudan and Zaïre in

1979. The regime also imported a large amount of military equipment from Egypt.

The lawless behaviour of these soldiers from the Muslim north, whose leaders secured representation on the Military Council, was in sharp contrast to the orderly conduct of the members of the NRA, whose respect for the civilian population gained them political credibility. The NRA, which was drawn predominantly from the Buganda, Ankole and Toro peoples in central and western Uganda, was led by well-educated and ideologically-motivated commanders, many of whom, including Mr Museveni himself, were reputed to be puritanically-minded. By November the NRA had grown to an estimated 16,000 men and was equipped with heavy weapons imported through Zaïre and Burundi; it had established an effective administration in the 'liberated' areas of south-western Uganda.

An internally-divided military Government made further concessions to the NRA and on 17 December, when hopes of a settlement had virtually disappeared, the Government and the NRA signed a power-sharing agreement, which provided for parity of representation between them on the Military Council (to be chaired by General Tito Okello, who was to remain head of state) and near parity for their respective forces in the new national army; the smaller guerrilla groups were to be given reduced representation. Kampala was to be demilitarized, the NRA administration in south-western Uganda was to be disbanded, and a national conference was to be organized to prepare for an interim Government and national elections. Upon the NRA's insistence, there was to be no immunity for those accused of violating human rights. (A large number of members of the disbanded National Security Agency, Obote's secret police, were in prison awaiting trial.) More than 1,200 political detainees were released in August and in December the British-born Mr Bob Astles, who had been head of Amin's anti-corruption squad and had been acquitted of murder in 1981, was allowed to travel to Britain after renouncing his Uganda citizenship.

The agreement assumed, without justification as far as Britain and Canada were concerned, that they, with Kenya and Tanzania, would provide a monitoring force to oversee the ceasefire and the formation of the new army. Britain, for its part, would only pledge itself to contribute towards rehabilitating Uganda's devastated economy and to resume a military-assistance programme, including the training of a new army, once order had been fully restored: the nucleus of a 20-man British military training team had remained in Uganda, though inactive, throughout the recent unrest.

As fighting and violent outbursts continued in this unhappy, wartorn country, it was clear that only a multinational peacekeeping force could secure the observance of the terms of the peace agreement. Since such a force was not forthcoming, there was scant prospect that the agreement would be implemented. As the year ended, General Tito Okello retained a precarious hold on power and the NRA was poised to march on Kampala.

Chapter 2

GHANA—NIGERIA—SIERRA LEONE—THE GAMBIA—LIBERIA

GHANA

FLIGHT Lieut. Rawlings continued to govern the republic under military rule but admitted civilian advisers in growing number to his Provisional National Defence Council (PNDC). Conditions improved slowly: the drought ended, the bush fires died out, the IMF granted new loans enabling a resumption of imports, food began to reappear in the markets although at high prices, the universities reopened. The road to recovery was still hazardous. There were further attempts (so it was reported) at a coup in January, renewed expulsions of Ghanaians from Nigeria and difficulties with the country's western neighbour, the Ivory Coast. But nothing in 1985 was quite as bad as during the first years of Rawlings's rule.

The PNDC was reconstituted over a period of months. At the end of July the Council consisted of Flight Lieut. Rawlings, Mrs Dana Enin, Mr Ebo Tawiah, Mr Justice J. S. Annan, Mrs Suzanna Alhassan and Alhaji Mahamad Idrisu. In addition, civilians were appointed as secretaries for Ministries: they included Dr Kwesi Botchwey (Finance and Economic Planning), Dr Obed Y. Asamoah (Foreign Affairs), Mr G. E. K. Aikins (Attorney-General), Dr Adjei Marfo (Agriculture), Mr B. W. K. Caiquo (Trade), Miss Joyce Aryee (Education) and Dr Emmanuel Hansen (secretary to the PNDC). The National Economic Commission continued under Mr Justice Annan; local defence councils were reconstituted as Committees for the Defence of the Revolution—a Libyan formula but without Libyan oil.

On 19 April the cedi was again devalued (by 5.6 per cent) and on 12 August (by 7 per cent), bringing the official rate to Cedi 54 to $1. In his 1985–86 budget, Dr Botchwey drew a more optimistic picture of the economy than had been possible for some years past. The rate of inflation was said to be down from 130 per cent to 40 per cent. There were increases in the production of food crops, including maize, although the rains had come too late to augment the cocoa harvest. At the beginning of the year the daily minimum wage for urban workers was raised to Cedi 35, but many Ghanaians still went hungry in the main towns of Ashanti and the south, while rural poverty in the three northern regions was alleviated rather than ended by the increased rainfall.

At the end of January a plot to assassinate Rawlings was unearthed in Kumasi. On 2 February the alleged conspirators were put on trial. On 1 April they were sentenced to death: executions followed, on 25 May, of Major John Ocran, Sgt. Francis Anku, Sgt. Joseph Issaka, Major Akwasi-Anto and Mr Sheibu Ibrahim. Also on 25 May civil servants found guilty of 'economic sabotage' at the Bank of Ghana were executed or given long terms of imprisonment.

An unusual development later in the year involved a 'swap arrangement' between Accra and Washington. Mr Michael Soussoudis, said to be a cousin of Rawlings, was sent back to Ghana in September in exchange for the release to other African countries of eight Ghanaians allegedly working for the CIA in Ghana. Soussoudis was arrested in the United States on 10 July along with Sharon Scranage (a CIA employee); they were charged with passing secrets, including the disclosure of agents' names, to a foreign power. The agents had been arrested in Ghana, but were then released against the return of Soussoudis.

On 16 April some 300,000 Ghanaians were expelled once more from Nigeria. The Government did what it could to ease their plight, but levied a resettlement charge on the grounds that they had acted contrary to official advice by returning to Nigeria after the expulsions of 1983 (see AR 1983, p. 220). The Government also accused the Nigerian police of shooting 25 Ghanaians at the border crossing on 13 May, a charge subsequently rebutted by Lagos.

On 1 September a football match in Kumasi, in which the Ivory Coast eliminated Ghana from the Africa Cup of Nations competition, led to fighting among spectators in which a number of Ivoirians were injured. Reprisals were swift and massive. By the middle of September an estimated 10,000 Ghanaians in the Ivory Coast had asked the Ghana Government for help: they were frightened, many had been beaten and had their property stolen by angry mobs. Both the Accra and Abidjan Governments deplored the violence and by the end of the month tempers had cooled, particularly after several hundred Ghanaians had been helped to leave the Ivory Coast under embassy supervision.

In September, Flight Lieut. Rawlings attended the eleventh anniversary celebrations of the Ethiopian revolution, on his way to China for a first official visit.

NIGERIA

For the first nine months of 1985 the Buhari Government, under the triple leadership of General Buhari himself, General Idiagbon, the chief of staff headquarters, and Mr Rafindadi, the head of the national security organization (NSO), continued to run a particularly harsh 'corrective' military regime. More journalists were imprisoned under decree No. 4.

The two doctors' unions, the NMA and NARD, were declared illegal after their strike, and all the doctors involved were dismissed and told to reapply for their jobs. The National Union of Nigerian Students was outlawed and harassed by the NSO. The death penalty, which had already been extended by decree to offences of dealing in drugs and illegal dealing in petroleum products, was applied to three convicted drug-smugglers who were shot in public. The shock produced by this public execution, which was denounced as an outrage by Wole Soyinka, the poet, and others, was further exacerbated by the death sentence passed on two women for concealing drugs on their persons at Lagos airport. Chike Offodile, the Attorney-General, made the situation worse by saying that if there was a sentence worse than death the Supreme Council would be prepared to impose it.

Discussion of Nigeria's political future was declared to be illegal under the preventive detention decree No. 2, and a most distinguished Northerner, Alhaji Sule Katagum, was detained together with a distinguished Northern journalist for taking part in a radio programme discussing the political prospect. Detentions under decree No. 2 rose to an unprecedented level as the NSO became a law unto itself, responsible neither to the Supreme Military Council nor to the people.

The regime sealed its own fate by alienating the army command under General Ibrahim Babangida, the chief of army staff. Criticism of the regime by retired senior soldiers, such as General Obasanjo, a previous head of state, General Oluleye and General Hassan, demonstrated that the Buhari Government was no longer respecting the consensus of the armed forces. It was no surprise therefore when the regime was overthrown in a bloodless coup on 26 August and replaced by a new 'Armed Forces Ruling Council' (AFRC) headed by General Babangida. Buhari and Idiagbon were placed under house arrest and Rafindadi was imprisoned after the press had been shown the cells and their inmates at NSO headquarters. The hundred inmates were released, together with eighty other Ministers and senior figures of the Shagari regime who had been held in prison awaiting trial since January 1984. These included Professor Ishaya Audu, the former Minister for External Affairs, and Sola Saraki, the former leader of the Senate. Muhammed Gambo, the deputy inspector-general of police, declared that the policy of the new regime would be to give priority to respect for human rights. The coup was very popular, since it implemented the deep Nigerian sense that even under military rule Nigerians must retain the rights of free speech and freedom from arbitrary imprisonment typical of their open society.

The new regime at once set in motion a broad national debate on whether or not to accept the IMF loan of $2,500 million on conditional terms of revaluing the naira, taxing internally-consumed oil and liberalizing imports (see AR 1984 p. 233). After three months, opinion had hardened against the perceived humiliation of these terms and the AFRC announced that they were terminating the four-year-long negotiations with the IMF, and were putting a ceiling of 30 per cent of foreign exchange earnings on their rate of repayment of debts totalling $18,000 million. This percentage represented, as Professor Akinyemi the new Foreign Minister put it, a careful balance between the duty of honour to repay genuine debts and the limit of what the Nigerian economy could bear without collapsing. It was well below the 44 per cent of foreign exchange earnings paid for debt servicing by the Buhari Government in 1984. Nigeria met with an understanding response from creditor countries.

The Babangida Government backed this firm stand by a policy of sacrifice by all sections of the people. A 30 per cent additional import tax and an extra tax on company profits were imposed. Army pay was cut on a sliding scale from 20 per cent for the top ranks down to 2½ per cent for private soldiers. Pay of all civilian government employees was similarly cut, but, to relieve the burden on the poorest sections of society, primary school fees were abolished.

Nigeria's oil revenue improved slightly to $11,000 million, through higher sales and production of nearly 1.6 million barrels per day, well in excess of the Opec quota of 1.4 million b/d. A contract was signed with Japanese, Italian and Nigerian companies for a fourth oil refinery at Port Harcourt. The Government plan to produce liquid natural gas on a large scale by 1990 was implemented by the signing of a preliminary contract.

The Babangida Government retained many members of the old Supreme Military Council and six members of the old Federal Executive Council, including Professor Tam David-West, the Minister for Oil, on the new AFRC. Six of the 19 former governors were also retained. Alhaji Adebola, the President of the Bar Association, which had often been at odds with the harsh policies of the Buhari Government, was made Attorney-General.

Commodore Ebitu Ukiwe, an Ibo, was brought into the second most senior role in the AFRC, that of chief of staff at headquarters (in charge of political affairs), though the independence of the army command was made clear in the emphasis on the position of General Sani Abacha as chief of army staff. Babangida was very keen to avoid jealousies between the senior officers involved in political roles and those still occupied in ordinary military command.

Nigeria's relations with Britain began gradually to improve with an exchange of visits at Foreign Minister level and the release of Mr Covey-Duck, a British citizen detained under the Buhari Government. The problems created by the Umaru Dikko affair, however (see AR 1984, p. 41), remained. The four kidnappers involved, including Major Mohammed Yusuf of Nigeria's NSO, received long prison sentences from a British court (see p. 40). A Nigerian court imprisoned two British engineers, Kenneth Clark and Angus Patterson, to fourteen years each for 'conspiring to steal an aeroplane'. Diplomatic relations at high commissioner level had not been restored by the end of 1985.

In December, the residue of army supporters of Buhari, combined with some ambitious military officers who felt themselves left out of the highest command, planned a coup based on Markurdi air-force base and the airborne division. The plot was discovered before action was taken and fourteen fairly senior officers headed by Major-General Momman Vatsa were arrested.

Commissions were appointed to review the cases of the former President, Shehu Shagari, and Vice-President, Alex Ekueme, to see whether they could be released, and those of senior politicians convicted by military tribunals under the Buhari regime. Decree No. 4 against the press was repealed immediately. The Babangida regime made it clear that it did not envisage staying in power beyond 1990 and in December appointed a political commission to take evidence as to the best method of military disengagement and establishment of a representative government.

Law and order was on the whole successfully maintained, but the Maitatsine religious movement (see AR 1980, p. 231) caused a further riot in Gombe. The Government continued to be frightened of the potential of fundamentalist preachers in both Muslim and Christian communities to cause religious strife. A tribal struggle over land on the Tiv-Ogoja border caused loss of life.

Nigeria remained conscious of its role as a champion of Africa and the Third World. The Nassau Commonwealth agreement on South Africa (see Pt. XI, Ch. 2, and DOCUMENTS) was not welcomed by the Foreign Minister, Professor Akinyemi, and at first Nigeria refused to associate itself with the Commonwealth group of 'wise men', but later relented and appointed General Obasanjo, the former head of state, who was made its co-chairman.

Appointments made in 1985 included Justice Ayo Irikefe as Chief Justice on the retirement of Chief Justice Sowemimo, and Professor Mrs Alele-Williams as vice-chancellor of Benin University, the first woman ever to be appointed to such a position in Nigeria. In the field of sport Nigerians were delighted by the victory of the under-17 football team, the 'Baby Eagles', in the junior world football competition for the Kodak Cup.

SIERRA LEONE

There was little change or cheer on the economic front during the year but significant and encouraging political changes took place. After eighteen years in office and endless speculation about his political retirement the octogenarian head-of-state, President Siaka Probyn Stevens, finally handed over power to his successor, Force Commander Major-General Joseph Saidu Momoh, on 15 November. Momoh was the sole presidential candidate chosen at the special delegate conference of the ruling All People's Congress (APC) in August, despite strenuous attempts by the First Vice-President, S. I. Koroma, to obtain the nomination. Stevens also relinquished the post of secretary-general of the APC to Momoh but remained party chairman.

In the national presidential election held on 1 October Momoh obtained 2,784,591 votes out of 2,975,065. Sceptics questioned the remarkably high turn-out and vote but Momoh was undoubtedly a popular choice. His appointment ensured the loyalty of the armed forces and avoided the possibility of open conflict among rival civilian contenders. Momoh's mixed ethnic and regional background, his reputation as an honest and efficient soldier and his lengthy political experience as a nominated MP and Cabinet Minister also stood in his favour. Following his appointment, command of the armed forces passed to Brigadier Shehu Tarawali.

The new President immediately addressed himself to the daunting range of political, administrative and economic problems facing the country. A number of the APC 'old guard', including S. I. Koroma, were dropped and the over-large Cabinet reduced in numbers. Reform of the selection process for parliamentary candidates was implemented and new and fairer general elections promised. A war against indiscipline and corruption in the public service was launched and several corrupt businessmen were prosecuted. A new government Gold and Diamond Office was established to handle the purchase and export of these important minerals. A programme for economic recovery was outlined in which agriculture was given priority, together with income-generating activities. Severe problems of indebtedness and trade imbalance remained, but the new Administration hoped to attract back foreign investors and restore relations with the IMF.

THE GAMBIA

It was another year of economic hardship for the Gambian Government and people. President Jawara frankly admitted that there was no speedy resolution of the worsening trade imbalance and foreign exchange deficit. Groundnuts, the major foreign-currency earner, halved in volume, as did food crops, because of drought. At the same time external debt repayments became increasingly burdensome; food and fuel imports further eroded the dwindling foreign-exchange reserves; and there were frequent shortages of basic goods. In addition to the austerity measures adopted in the July budget the Government was obliged to introduce further cuts in August. It also announced the setting-up of a 'task force' to spearhead its programme of 'stabilization and growth'. Some relief was provided by a partial rescheduling of external debts, another record tourist season and adequate summer rainfall.

Relations with Senegal continued to show signs of strain, at both the official and popular levels. Another year passed without agreement on an economic and monetary union, despite Senegalese insistence on their completion. Gambian officials also expressed dissatisfaction with some of the hurriedly-signed earlier confederal protocols, while popular animosity towards the Senegalese occurred during a football match in Banjul and caused a diplomatic incident. Even so, given The Gambia's economic predicament and military dependence on Senegal, there was no immediate prospect of the Confederation's breaking-up.

LIBERIA

The year witnessed the further consolidation of General Samuel Doe's power. Though nearly killed in a bungled assassination attempt by Colonel Moses Flanzamaton in April, he went on to claim victory in the much-disputed presidential and parliamentary elections in October and narrowly survived another coup attempt the following month. Combining the positions of civilian President and army chief, with his opponents crushed or cowed and his special relationship with Washington still intact, Doe's remaining problems were economic rather than political. The mining industry continued to contract as external debts piled up and foreign investors kept away because of the political situation.

Given the harassment of opposition parties by the Government, the partisan behaviour of the special commission responsible for the impartial supervision of the elections and the unwillingness of the American Administration to do more than protest at the irregularities, there was little prospect of defeat for Doe or his National Democratic Party of Liberia. Two popular opposition parties—the Liberian People's Party led by Dr Amos Sawyer and Bacchus Matthews's United People's Party— were banned because of their radical leanings. The remaining oppositon parties—the Liberian Action Party headed by Jackson Doe (no relation of the General), Gabriel Kpolleh's Liberian Unification Party and the Unity Party of Edward Kesselly—failed to unite and faced constant intimidation and widespread vote-rigging. Despite a high turn-out and unexpectedly peaceful voting, few impartial observers accepted the results. Doe claimed 50.9 per cent of the vote in the presidential election and the NDPL obtained 21 of the 26 seats in the Senate and 51 of the 64 seats in the House of Representatives. Many felt that Jackson Doe was the real winner but the American Administration accepted the result, praising it as a step toward the restoration of parliamentary rule in Liberia. Unsatisfactory as they were, the elections were probably less manipulated than those held during the ascendancy of the disbanded True Whig Party.

Opposition parties challenged the election results and threatened to boycott the new parliament. More seriously, the disputed polls led to another coup attempt on 12 November. Thomas Quiwonkpa, one of the architects of the 1980 military coup and a senior figure in the Doe Adminstration until forced to flee in late 1983, narrowly failed in his bid to overthrow his former colleague, and he and hundreds of his supporters died in the fighting and the wave of repression that followed. Jackson Doe and other opposition leaders were detained but a number of these were released in December as part of a reconciliatory move by General Doe. Diplomatic relations with Moscow were broken off in the summer, and those with Freetown became strained when it was claimed that Quiwonkpa had entered Liberia from Sierra Leone with official backing.

Chapter 3

SENEGAL—GUINEA—MALI—MAURITANIA—IVORY COAST—BURKINA FASO—
NIGER—TOGO AND BENIN—CAMEROON—CHAD—CENTRAL AFRICAN REPUBLIC—
GABON AND PEOPLE'S REPUBLIC OF THE CONGO—EQUATORIAL GUINEA

SENEGAL

ALTHOUGH Senegal was one of the few countries left in West Africa to have kept the military out of government, its democracy could scarcely be said to be in a healthy state. On the one hand, the ruling Parti Socialiste (PS) continued to be described, not least by its own members, as having lost effectiveness and no longer relating to the people, while on the other the multitude of opposition parties (the total number of parties increased to 16 during the year) remained fragmented and demoralized.

The main opposition leader, Maître Abdoulaye Wade of the Parti Démocratique Sénégalais (PDS), returned from a long unexplained absence in Paris in January and launched a critique of Government economic policy, especially the influence of the IMF, to which President Abdou Diouf responded that policy was 'made in Senegal'. In April the PDS called for a campaign of prayers every Tuesday, which led to an incident at the Dakar mosque in which several prayer-campaigners were arrested. In June the PDS joined with four other opposition parties to form the Alliance Démocratique Sénégalaise (ADS), an informal grouping which also ran into trouble at the end of August when it tried to organize an anti-apartheid march. The march was banned at short notice and in the ensuing confusion both Maître Wade and the ADS President Dr Abdoulaye Bathily were arrested and detained for a week, though the case against them was eventually dismissed. The ADS itself was subsequently told by the Ministry of the Interior that it counted as a coalition and was therefore illegal under the constitution.

President Diouf in the meantime had been selected as chairman of the OAU in July (see Pt. XI, Ch. 5) and clearly took the post very seriously. This led to some domestic reproaches that he was not spending enough time dealing with Senegal's continued problems, but there were many Senegalese who felt that the chairmanship was an honour to Senegal. Although the rains of 1985 were plentiful, the consequences of the drought of 1983–84 were still being felt, and the 'new agricultural policy' announced in April, completing the abolition of the costly and ineffective state produce-marketing organizations, nonetheless seemed to be having teething troubles. The flourishing of 'parallel markets' still caused particular concern.

GUINEA

The central political event of the year was the abortive coup attempt of the night of 4–5 July by the Education Minister, Colonel Diarra Traoré. It took place while the head of state, Colonel Lansana Conté, was away at the West African summit in Togo, although there was some indication that he had had foreknowledge of a coup plot, and had made dispositions to crush it before his (delayed) departure. At all events, the radio station captured at 10 pm on 4 July was back in the hands of the loyalist troops by 5 am on 5 July, and it appeared the rebels had failed to capture any other key installation. Colonel Traoré had been one of the main figures in the coup of April 1984, and as Prime Minister had appeared to be the most powerful figure in the regime until his demotion in December 1984 (see AR 1984, p. 239).

The coup attempt and its failure were thus a shake-down of power in the still fairly new military Government, but they could also be seen as a product of the prevailing atmosphere of drift. In the recriminations after the failure, scores were settled against members of the Malinke tribe, from which came both Traoré and the former President Sekou Touré (who died just before the 1984 coup), and there were persistent reports that leading members of the former regime, as well as some of the coup plotters, had been murdered. Inflammatory statements by Colonel Conté and his Foreign Minister Facine Touré were later tempered, especially by playing down the potentially dangerous ethnic aspect to the affair, but the impression remained of yet another unsavoury episode in Guinea's often bloody history since independence.

In the latter part of the year the focus was increasingly on the economy, which had been ravaged by the fruitless attempts of the Sekou Touré regime to achieve a spurious economic independence. It appeared that under guidance from Western advisers (especially from France, the US, the IMF and the World Bank) the nettle of Guinea's almost valueless currency was finally being grasped, with a weighty devaluation in October and the promise of more to come. Most experts reckoned, even so, that the target of rejoining the franc zone was still a long way off.

MALI

Although, like other areas of the Sahel, Mali benefited from the good rainy season, which eased some of the worst effects of the drought, the economic and social side-effects of the drought years remained. The slow advance of the Sahara was, after all, still continuing, and the structural development problems remained unsolved. Towards the end of the year the donors' conference tried to maximize the considerable foreign aid input Mali was receiving, and the IMF accorded a new stand-by credit, Mali being one of the countries applying their conditions (liberalization, privatization and food self-sufficiency among others).

In spite of his July re-election as President the 17-year-old regime of President Moussa Traoré seemed to be hitting a new spell of political difficulties, from the direction both of trade unions and of students. Indeed it was these discontents that were said to have caused the President not to go to the Franco–African summit in Paris in December, shortly after which Mali became embroiled in an end-of-the-year war with neighbouring Burkina Faso (see page 236).

MAURITANIA

The new 'strong man', Colonel Maaouya Sid' Ahmed Ould Taya, who took power in a bloodless coup in December 1984, spent the following year in consolidating his position. Internally he did this by ensuring that he controlled the main levers of power: as well as President of the Republic he was Prime Minister and Minister of Defence. He also engaged in five Government reshuffles in the course of the year, not only to maintain his own power position, but also to balance the main groups—the Moors and the Blacks—and the country's external interests, not least because Mauritania was in the front line of the Polisario war. It was suggested after the 1984 coup that Taya might pursue a less overtly pro-Polisario line than his predecessor, and some saw this borne out when diplomatic relations were resumed with Morocco in April, and with Morocco's ally Libya in July. There was still, however, some distrust of Libya's inclination to dabble in Mauritania's internal politics, and relations with the other major neighbour to the north, Algeria, remained cordial. The pro-Polisario faction continued to have an important voice in government circles, a voice maintained in successive reshuffles. The drought-wracked economy remained the main problem of government. Cautious attempts at reform of administration were also embarked on during the year.

IVORY COAST

The long-drawn-out dramas of the succession to President Félix Houphouet-Boigny (who passed 80 during the year) took another few twists, but still showed no sign of being resolved. After a congress of the ruling Parti Démocratique de la Côte d'Ivoire (PDCI) in October, he announced that he was abandoning the idea of appointing a Vice-President and thus naming a successor, and was reverting to the former constitutional provision that the provisional succession goes to the President of the National Assembly pending an election. He then stood as a candidate in the presidential elections at the end of October, obtaining a 99·9 per cent vote (later officially amended to 100 per cent), thus giving a clear indication of intention to continue running the country as long as he lived.

Meanwhile one of the main candidates for the succession, Emmanuel Dioulo, mayor of Abidjan, was obliged to leave the country following implication in a bank scandal, which he claimed was a frame-up. Attempts to effect a reconciliation failed, but Dioulo's threat to reveal some of the secrets of the regime also failed to materialize. The constitutional amendment also greatly reinforced the chances of the Assembly President, Henri Konan Bédie, but most speculation still seemed to leave the question open.

The high abstentions in the other elections—parliamentary and local—caused renewed comment on fears for the general political situation: fears that the ruling party was not in good shape, that the younger generation was frustrated and waiting for change, and that continuing economic problems, despite an upturn during the year, might lead to social disturbances when the political change did come. Meanwhile, friction with Burkina Faso and Ghana increased, in the latter case aggravated by riots following a football match. At the end of the year, Ivory Coast resumed diplomatic relations with Israel, broken since 1973.

BURKINA FASO

The revolution of Captain Thomas Sankara, which celebrated its second anniversary on 4 August, continued its often turbulent career. If at home Sankara seemed to be treading a path between left and right— between conflict with trade unions and left-wing groups on the one hand

and on the other the continued investigation of crimes of preceding regimes—the regime seemed to be becoming more controversial in West Africa. Antipathy to the Sankara revolution seemed particularly strong in Ivory Coast, and was displayed within two regional organizations to which both belonged—the Ivory Coast-dominated Council of the Entente and the Communauté Economique de l'Afrique de l'Ouest (CEAO), an embryonic customs union of most francophone states in West Africa.

Early in the year tension was aggravated by a bomb in Sankara's hotel suite in Ivory Coast hours before he arrived, but the summit at which friction came out into the open took place in September, when an organization (grouping Ivory Coast, Burkina, Togo, Benin and Niger) which normally discussed economic issues tried to concentrate on security problems following bomb explosions in Lomé and a Touareg attack in Niger. Sankara refused to sign a communique expressing sympathy for the two countries, saying that the Entente had never expressed sympathy for Burkina, despite 'aggressions' in which people had died. He also claimed that the Ivory Coast had been funding a virulent international press campaign against Burkina for two years.

The CEAO battleground was more tempestuous, because the organization had its headquarters in the Burkina capital, Ouagadougou. Following a scandal in which $14 million of the Community's Solidarity Fund (FOSIDEC) disappeared, the Senegalese secretary-general Moussa Ngom and an Ivoirian businessman Mohamed Diawara were arrested (the latter was extradited from Mali, and the arrests were approved by the leaders of both Mali and Niger). Later in the year, however, relations with Mali deteriorated after Ngom's successor, a Malian, Driss Keita, gave an interview which was seen as insulting to the Burkina leader. Keita was declared persona non grata, and at the end of the year had still not returned to his headquarters. Nor had a summit scheduled for October been held.

At the end of the year a war started with Mali, when an old border dispute, which had already caused fighting in 1974, flared up again. The immediate cause was an attempt by Burkina census officials to count villages which the Malians reckoned as theirs, but serious fighting broke out on Christmas day, and it was only after serious skirmishes and bombing raids by both sides, and mediation by almost every West African country as well as Libya and Algeria, that a ceasefire was agreed and the disputed frontier referred back to the International Court of Justice, where it had been since 1983.

NIGER

Despite good rains, the great 1984 drought continued to have its impact in both social and economic difficulties. President Kountché continued his difficult balancing act between Libya and Nigeria.

Although diplomatic relations with Libya were resumed, relations remained cool, and were exacerbated by a commando attack at the end of May by a group of Touaregs in north-east Niger, allegedly sponsored by Libya. The group was also reported to be linked to Abdoulaye Diori, son of former President Hamani Diori, overthrown in 1974. The latter returned to house arrest.

In June President Kountché launched a massive campaign against corruption, involving the death penalty for certain offences, and in August, on the 25th anniversary of independence, he inaugurated a massive reafforestation campaign, of which he said 'we may have found the beginnings of a solution to all action in the rural world'.

TOGO AND BENIN

As the two mini-states sandwiched between the larger countries of Ghana and Nigeria continued to suffer from border restrictions, especially the closure of Nigeria's border throughout the year, their own political climates began to deteriorate. In Togo a wave of bombs (which mostly either did not go off or caused little damage) created a climate of insecurity, and was followed by arrests of suspected opponents, although they had not been brought to trial by the end of the year. The opposition in exile made new charges of torture and killing of detainees, centring on the death of Colonel Koffi Kongo, officially from a heart attack, after his detention in March.

In Benin there was student unrest in May which led to two deaths and the closure of the National University. Although the immediate cause was the Government's ending of guaranteed employment for graduates in the civil service, it was undoubtedly encouraged by economic recession and charges of government corruption. In June there was a major re-shuffle in which one of President Kérékou's oldest colleagues, Colonel Michel Alladaye, Minister of Education, and the top officials of the university were all dismissed.

CAMEROON

After the storms of 1984, it was a quieter year for President Paul Biya. A congress of the ruling single party was held in Bamenda in March, at which it changed its name from the Cameroon National Union (CNU) to the Cameroon People's Democratic Movement (CPDM). This was done in the spirit of 'rigour and moralization' which Biya had made his watch-word, and was followed by a large-scale renewal of party officials, and, later, of government and administration. Some of the government changes were surprising in that they included some of Biya's closest associates, but it was said this was designed to show that nobody should take him for granted, and to consolidate his power. There were continued rumblings during the year among the minority English-speaking community of the former West Cameroon, and at the end of the year there were reports of arrests in circles connected with the banned opposition party, the Cameroon People's Union (UPC).

CHAD

After several years of dramatic events, 1985 was a period of uneasy stalemate, in which the country experienced a *de facto* partition. On the one hand the forces of the GUNT (the former Transitional Government of National Union) held the northern one-third of the country, with backing from a Libyan military presence, which the Libyans ceased to deny. On the other hand President Hissène Habré remained in power in Ndjamena, internationally recognised as President of Chad, protected by French guarantees that any disruption of the stalemate would bring in their troops from the nearby Central African Republic, but restrained from launching any attack to recover rebel-held territory for fear of triggering a Franco-Libyan confrontation.

Habré consolidated his position by visiting the south of the country, in the past a major centre of opposition. Attacks by codos (*commandos rouges*) continued, but opposition to Habré was weakened by the serious fragmentation which developed in various opposition groups, not least the GUNT itself. Sundry peace meetings and conferences were held, including one in Cotonou to reconcile factions of the GUNT, and the OAU mediation by President Sassou Nguesso of the Congo continued fruitlessly. At the end of the year, an important splinter movement led by southerner General Negue Djogo became reconciled with the Habré Government. In December Colonel Qadafi, the main GUNT supporter, visited West Africa to propose a new African force for Chad, as a solution 'without the French', but his proposal met a very unenthusiastic response.

CENTRAL AFRICAN REPUBLIC

At the end of an unstable year, dominated by the problems coming from the unresolved situation in Chad, President André Kolingba hinted after the Franco-African summit in Paris that he would be prepared to accept an increase in the French military presence there. Early in 1985 a joint Chad-CAR offensive was mounted against the 'codos' who were operating from CAR into Chad, but the problem continued through the year. A former Minister, François Gueret, was gaoled in July for threatening state security: in September, for the first time, civilians were permitted to be Ministers.

GABON AND PEOPLE'S REPUBLIC OF THE CONGO

Rich oil-producers with small populations, both countries were obliged to continue to tighten their belts as world oil prices continued to drop, although Gabon had more revenue from other sources to cushion the effects. In August a Gabonese air force captain, Alexandre Ngokouta, was shot for plotting a coup, and May saw one of President Bongo's periodic campaigns against foreigners. In the Congo there were signs of student unrest towards the end of the year, although President Sassou Nguesso, like President Bongo, showed no sign of losing his domination of the political scene.

EQUATORIAL GUINEA

In a quiet year politically, there was a methodic progress in moving the country's ravaged economy slowly towards recovery. The 'grand lines' had been set at the beginning of the year with the formal entry of Equatorial Guinea into the franc zone, meaning in practice the use of the CFA franc as currency, and its adherence to the Central African Central Bank. Relations with France, thus consolidated, continued to improve, with a flow of financial aid and in January a military aid agreement. In July, at a meeting of the Club of Paris, a 10-year rescheduling of 246 million French francs of external debt was approved by France, Spain and Italy. This was accompanied by the opening of an IMF credit of 9·2 million Special Drawing Rights, and led to an increase in optimism in business circles and a series of visiting missions from banks and the private sector.

VII CENTRAL AND SOUTHERN AFRICA

Chapter 1

ZAÏRE—RWANDA AND BURUNDI—GUINEA-BISSAU AND CAPE VERDE—SÃO TOMÉ
AND PRINCIPE—MOZAMBIQUE—ANGOLA

ZAÏRE

PRESIDENT Mobutu Sese Seko gained a measure of international approval by resolutely sticking to the tough policy of economic austerity and reform demanded by the country's external creditors led by the IMF in return for an agreement to reschedule interest payments on the $4,000 million debt. At the same time the President continued to display the political adroitness that had enabled him to hold power for twenty years, making substantial changes in the country's administrative structure to prevent any potential challenge from building up an effective power-base.

Without rescheduling, Zaïre's repayments during 1985 would have reached nearly $1,000 million, equivalent to 60 per cent of export earnings. In May the IMF agreed to provide a 12-month standby loan of $195 million, while Western creditor nations, members of the 'Paris Club', rescheduled $305 million. But creditor countries were coming to realize that debt relief was not enough. Zaïre was in urgent need of aid and investment. An Israeli industrial group, Tamman, announced plans to invest $400 million in Zaïre in 1985–86, but other potential investors, mindful of obvious difficulties, showed greater hesitation. Aid was particularly urgently needed to rebuild the country's once extensive road system, much of which was reported to have reverted to bush.

Ordinary Zaïreans bore the brunt of the austerity measures. The situation of the urban poor was succinctly described by a nun working in one of the poorer parts of Lubumbashi, the former Elisabethville and the country's second largest city: 'Before 1965 people had three meals a day; two-and-a-half meals between 1965 and 1970; two meals from 1970 to 1975; one-and-a-half meals from 1975 to 1980, one meal a day until 1984. Now there are a great many people who cannot afford to have even one meal a day.' Popular reactions to the austerity measures struck foreign observers as 'muted': 'the public mood', wrote an American correspondent, 'is one of sullen acquiescence'. Early in the year there were reports of student unrest and the closing of some provincial universities. 'Every time we make a protest', one student commented, 'the university is closed down and conditions get worse.'

In his speech of 5 December 1984 at the ceremony marking the commencement of his third term of office President Mobutu proclaimed his intention of 'getting some order where it is needed'. He set about the task in January by announcing a 'restructuring of the territorial administration' and declaring that he would 'wage war' against senior officials who had managed to accumulate a number of lucrative posts for themselves. Shortly afterwards the central committee of the Popular Revolutionary Movement (MPR), the country's only political party, was reduced from 125 to 80 members and a number of senior officers were dismissed from the armed services. In August the President announced the creation of a Civil Guard of 20,000 men to be trained by a team from West Germany. Other units in the 60,000-strong Zaïrean army were being trained by military advisers from France, Belgium, Israel and China. But there were frequent reports of lack of discipline in the armed services; soldiers were said to be establishing road blocks and extorting goods or money from passing travellers in order to supplement their meagre pay.

In June the President's most prominent political opponent, Nguza Karl-i-Bond, returned to Zaïre after four years of voluntary exile in Belgium (see AR 1982, p. 244). At the same time the President, who had always shown a subtle capacity to disarm his opponents, announced the removal of all restrictions on the thirteen parliamentarians who had formed the Democratic Union for Social Progress in 1983, the only visible internal opposition group (see AR 1983, p. 234, and 1984, p. 247). Towards the end of the year, however, two of the parliamentarians were again arrested. In June there was a repetition, though on a smaller scale, of the November 1984 attack on the small town of Moba on the shores of Lake Tanganyika (see AR 1984, pp. 247–48). The assailants who came in boats were repulsed: they were reported to be members of a group known as the People's Party.

On June 30 Zaïre celebrated the twenty-fifth anniversary of its achievement of independence. Among those attending the grandiose ceremony held in Kinshasa was King Baudouin of the Belgians. President Mobutu made a point of stressing the close relations that now existed between his country and its former colonial power, and the cordial reception accorded to the Belgian King by the people of Kinshasa served to confirm his words.

In August Pope John Paul II paid his second visit to Zaïre (see AR 1980, p. 245). In Kinshasa he conducted a service for the beatification of Sister Anuarie Nengapeta, a nun killed by rebel soldiers in 1964 and the first African woman martyr in the modern history of the Roman Catholic Church.

In February the Angolan President José dos Santos paid his first visit to Zaïre, a visit that led to the signing of an agreement for 'security and defence'. The terms of the agreement were not published, but it was clear that both countries had an interest in ensuring that their Governments' political opponents—Unita in the case of Angola, the Katangese who mounted invasions of Shaba in 1977 and 1978 in the case of Zaïre—did not establish bases in neighbouring territory. Given the practical difficulties that both Governments faced in maintaining control over outlying provinces, it was not clear how effective such an agreement would be. No incidents were reported on the previously troubled frontier with Zambia (see AR 1984, pp. 248 and 255).

RWANDA AND BURUNDI

In May both countries received a visit from Colonel Qadafi of Libya. The Governments of both Rwanda and Burundi signified their approval of a Libyan proposal to establish a 'Front of Progressive States' to oppose 'the interventionist tactics employed by the forces of imperialism, neo-colonialism and racism'. In speeches in Kigali and Bujumbura the Libyan leader denounced President Mobutu as an 'agent of zionism' and even advocated his assassination. He also spoke vigorously in favour of the expansion of Islam in Africa.

Signs of internal tension in Burundi came with reports of increasing strains between church and state. Ever since President Bagaza took power in 1976 and consolidated the dominant position of the Tutsi minority, there had been periodic official accusations that Roman Catholic priests, half of whom were missionaries from overseas, were attempting to 'export the revolution', a reference to the revolution in the last years of Belgian rule in Rwanda that had brought the majority Hutu to power. Thus while in Burundi there were reports of missionaries being expelled and of arbitrary arrests, in Rwanda the relationship between the Roman Catholic hierarchy and the Government of President Juvenal Habyalimana was exceptionally cordial.

Upon the downfall of President Milton Obote of Uganda most of the refugees who had fled to Rwanda in 1982 after being expelled from Uganda returned to their original homes (see AR 1982, p. 246, and 1984, p. 248).

GUINEA-BISSAU AND CAPE VERDE

Cape Verde continued to maintain its reputation as one of the best governed and most stable members of the Organization of African Unity. In 1985 there was not a single political prisoner in the archipelago and the Government was singularly free of allegations of corruption. With foreign aid running at $139 per capita, Cape Verde was one of the most generously supported countries in the Third World. The planting by voluntary labour of ten million trees since independence was one indication of the country's commitment to development.

In Guinea-Bissau the Vice-President, Paulo Correira, was arrested on 5 November together with more than twenty other citizens, including senior army and police officers: they were accused of organizing a coup to overthrow the President, João Bernardo Vieira. A range of motives was suggested for the attempted coup: ethnic rivalry (most of those arrested were members of the country's largest ethnic group, the Balante); disquiet over corruption; and growing discontent at the Government's insistence on trying to run the economy on rigidly marxist lines.

SÃO TOMÉ AND PRINCIPE

In February the annual summit meeting of ex-Portuguese African countries was held in São Tomé, whose President, Manuel Pinto da Costa, used the occasion to stress his country's policy of non-alignment. Among the signs of a clear shift from its formerly pro-Soviet line were the reduction from 2,500 to 400 of the number of Angolan soldiers who had provided the islands' main security force, the signing of an agreement with the United States to provide American training for a small detachment of locally-recruited soldiers, the dismissal or demotion of pro-Soviet Ministers and the removal of controls on the economy based on Soviet models. Between 1975 and 1984 the production of cocoa, the country's main foreign-exchange earner, dropped from 10,000 to 4,450 tons; 90 per cent of the population's food now had to be imported; and the Government became increasingly anxious to attract foreign investment.

MOZAMBIQUE

The high hopes raised by the Nkomati Accord, the treaty of 'non-aggression and good neighbourliness' signed by Mozambique and South Africa in March 1984 (see AR 1984, p. 249), were completely dashed in the course of 1985. The Accord had no effect in diminishing the activities of Mozambique National Resistance (MNR), the anti-Frelimo guerrilla movement. Under the impact of war the economy declined still further, so that by the end of the year Mozambique presented the bleakest picture of any country in Southern Africa.

'Partial asphyxiation' was the vivid phrase used by President Samora Machel to describe the impact of MNR on the life of the country. 'Our generation', the President declared in a speech to mark the tenth anniversary of independence, 'still must bear sacrifices, face war and endure hunger and wretchedness. . . . The international conspiracy using bandit-ry as an instrument of destabilization continues to keep Mozambique under economic aggression and terrorism.'

'Eye-witness reports over the past year', Reuter's correspondent in Maputo reported in June, 'tell of increasingly brutal attacks on villages, farms and buses. Their activities have made many roads impassable and peasants cannot grow their crops in peace. Power lines are sabotaged and factories are barely operating.' The Government's description of MNR guerrillas as 'armed bandits' seemed to many Western observers amply justified as they noted the rebels' 'terrorist tactics' in regularly attacking 'soft' targets. Observers commented too on the 'fecklessness' of the rebel movement, its lack of obvious leaders and its unwillingness to present a clear political programme. The MNR point of view was expressed by one of the movement's spokesmen on a visit to London in October; 'We are operating in every province of the country with popular support for our fight against a repressive marxist regime.'

The rebels' most substantial achievement during the year was to carry the war to the suburbs of Maputo, rendering travel out of the city increasingly dangerous, disrupting food supplies and bringing off a spec-tacular symbolic coup by sabotaging a munitions depot on 25 September, a public holiday celebrated as National Army Day. Outside the capital, power lines, rail links and roads proved particularly vulnerable.

Hopes raised after the Nkomati Accord that Mozambique would be able to resume supplying South Africa with electricity from the hydro-electric works at Cabora Bassa were dashed by the constant sabotaging of pylons. The presence of 10,000 Zimbabwean troops did not suffice to protect the railway from Beira to Tete from regular attacks. Insecurity on the roads seriously disrupted the distribution of food aid to the estimated 2·5 million people living in drought-affected areas. Between 1983 and 1984 the country's exports dropped by 22 per cent: this was due in part to the difficulty of transporting timber, cashew nuts and cotton, all valuable foreign-exchange earners. In the climate of mounting insecurity South African entrepreneurs, enthusiastic after the Nkomati Accord to revive Mozambique's once-flourishing tourist trade, found their plans aborted.

On 5 January President Machel, for the first time, publicly accused the South African Government of violating the Nkomati Accord by permitting the flow of aid to the MNR. But the Pretoria Government continued to affirm its commitment to the Accord: 'Our priority now', the South African Deputy Foreign Minister declared at the end of March, 'is to get rid of the MNR.' After the South African police had discovered in Johannesburg a cache of forged US dollar and South African rand notes allegedly destined for MNR, the South African Foreign Minister, Mr R. F. ('Pik') Botha, spoke of a 'web of international bankers, finan-ciers and businessmen with MNR connections intent on turning Mozambique into their own private economic preserve'. Independent analysts reckoned that MNR was receiving support from a wide range of backers: Portuguese now resident in South Africa or Portugal, who had had to abandon property in Mozambique, right-wing foundations in West Germany and an unnamed Arab potentate allegedly planning to establish an Islamic state among the Muslims of northern Mozambique. There were reports that rebels in the north of the country were receiving arms airlifted from the Middle East by way of the Comoros.

The only substantial success achieved against the rebels came in August when the Mozambique army, aided by powerful Zimbabwean support, captured a major MNR stronghold in the Gorongoxa National Park. The rebels made what they described as a 'strategic withdrawal', leaving behind a mass of documentary material, extracts from which were later published by the Mozambique Government. They provided clear evidence of the continuing support accorded to MNR by the South African military in glaring violation of the Nkomati Accord.

Mozambique continued to receive aid from a wide range of donors. The Soviet Union supplied equipment and military training for the army and provided most of the country's oil. The United States sent 110,000 tons of maize, and substantial quantities of aid were received from other Western countries. The chief executive of Lonrho, Mr 'Tiny' Rowland, established a cordial relationship with President Machel as a preliminary to possible investment. International oil companies, including Shell and BP, undertook exploration for oil and gas. In the field of foreign policy the most significant development was the increasingly cordial relationship with the United States. President Machel paid his first visit to Washington in September, had a notably amicable meeting with President Reagan and spoke of having established 'a solid basis for long-term cooperation in all fields'. The unusual spectacle of President Reagan entertaining a marxist head of state aroused the fury of right-wing groups in the US: some Republican Congressmen urged the President to give aid to MNR. Another significant link with the West was established by President Machel's decision to accept a British offer to take middle-ranking Mozambique officers for training by the British military mission in Zimbabwe.

ANGOLA

11 November 1985 marked the tenth anniversary of Angola's independence, but there was no sign of any end to the war that had racked the country for the past decade. Unita continued to wage its guerrilla struggle, backed by vigorous support from South Africa. The MPLA Government received additional aid from the Soviet Union, Cuba and other socialist countries. And by the end of the year there were signs that the United States was moving away from its position as 'honest broker'—

trying to bring about a complex settlement involving a South African withdrawal from Namibia, a Cuban withdrawal from Angola and some sort of negotiated settlement between MPLA and Unita—to the one-sided position of giving military aid to Unita.

In April the last South African troops were formally withdrawn from Angola under the terms of the Lusaka Agreement of February 1984 (see AR 1984, p. 253). But only a few weeks later the Angolan Government announced that two South African commandos had been killed and a third captured close to a major oil installation in the northern enclave of Cabinda. Statements made by the captured South African indicated that the group was engaged on a mission of sabotage. In early July and again in September South African forces crossed into Angola on the pretext of 'hot pursuit' operations against Swapo guerrillas. The position was further confused by reports that some Swapo forces, whose total number was put at 8,000, were engaged in assisting the MPLA in its war with Unita. In September the South African Defence Minister, General Magnus Malan, admitted that South Africa had been giving Unita 'humanitarian, material and moral support', adding that 'military intervention cannot be excluded'.

During the year there were reports of very substantial quantities of military aid reaching Angola from the Soviet Union, and some observers put the number of Cuban troops in the country as high as 35,000, 5,000 higher than any previous estimate. Among the aid received was the equipment (radar and ground-to-air missiles) for a sophisticated air-defence system. FAPLA, the MPLA Government's armed forces, was reported to have improved greatly in training and morale. As a result the Government was able to launch its most powerful offensive of the ten years' war against Unita. In August a substantial amount of lost territory in eastern Angola was reoccupied. But at the end of September FAPLA suffered a decisive check in a hard-fought battle near Mavinga in south-eastern Angola, a battle in which the South African air force was reported to have played a decisive role. In December there were further reports of South African incursions into southern Angola.

In July the US Congress repealed the Clark Amendment, passed in January 1976, restraining the Administration from giving aid to rebel groups in Angola. This congressional act led to a temporary breakdown in the negotiations between Washington and Luanda, in which Dr Chester Crocker, the Under-Secretary of State for African Affairs, had been prominently involved for the last four years. But discussions were resumed at the end of November, when Dr Crocker and senior Angolan Ministers met in Lusaka.

By this time, however, there were signs of a possible major shift in US policy. Right-wing Republicans introduced a Bill into Congress for the supply of $27 million of 'non-lethal' aid to Unita, to be followed by a similar amount of military equipment. The situation was further confused when President Reagan stated at a press conference on 22 November that he preferred to see 'covert' as opposed to 'overt' aid being given to Unita, whose adherents right-wing Americans were now describing as 'freedom-fighters'. There was clear division within the US Administration, the State Department being in favour of using diplomacy to reach a negoti-ated settlement and the Pentagon and the CIA being strongly in favour of aiding Unita. Critics of the policy of helping Unita pointed out that the United States would then be seen to have established a *de facto* alliance with South Africa.

The MPLA Government's relations with Portugal deteriorated dur-ing the year as a result of the unchecked activities of Unita supporters in Lisbon. But Portugal continued to provide military assistance in the form of a training team of specialists in counter-insurgency operations. Close relations were established with Spain, which signed an agreement to provide Angola with 37 fishing boats, and with Brazil, whose trade with Angola had increased from $4 million in 1973 to $230 million in 1984, making the country Angola's third largest trading partner. During the year President José dos Santos visited three notably pro-Western African states—Zaïre, Gabon and Ivory Coast—and normalized relations with Morocco.

In December the MPLA held its second national congress, the first having been held in 1980 (see AR 1980, p. 250). The congress brought about substantial changes in the party's Politburo, most of the old mili-tants who had fought in the independence struggle against Portugal being replaced by younger men.

Chapter 2

ZAMBIA—MALAWI—ZIMBABWE—NAMIBIA—BOTSWANA—LESOTHO—SWAZILAND

ZAMBIA

THERE was no significant change in Zambia's acutely depressed economic position. The price of copper remained low and the decline in produc-tion, from 600,000 tons in 1981 to just over 500,000 tons expected in 1985, continued; yet copper still provided 90 per cent of the country's foreign-exchange earnings. In these circumstances President Kenneth Kaunda had no alternative but to accept the programme for economic reform urged on his Government by the IMF—a programme regarded as one of the most severe ever to be required of a Third World country. Central to the reform programme was a massive devaluation: the introduction of a system of regular foreign-exchange auctions had the effect of reducing the value of the kwacha from 50 US cents to 20. All consumers were affected by a doubling of the price of petrol and the consequent escalation of transport costs, while the price of mealie meal, the country's staple food, rose by 50 per cent when the last government subsidy was removed. Even before these changes, the President had described the cost of living for ordinary people as being 'unbearably high'. Since reserves of copper were thought likely to be exhausted by the end of the century, the need for a fundamental restructuring of the economy was widely recognized, a restructuring that would make better use of the large amount of potentially productive agricultural land. But the Government, still dominated, in spite of substantial Cabinet changes during the year, by a visibly aging elite, seemed incapable of making the dynamic response the situation demanded.

Popular discontent remained at a surprisingly low level. Early in the year a series of strikes by hospital workers, bank employees and others were checked by a presidential decree banning all strikes in essential services and threatening strikers with dismissal. Despite reports of a great deal of private grumbling there was no evidence of any significant opposition to the President, either in or outside parliament.

In November a long-maturing scandal came into the open when thirty individuals, some of them one-time associates of the President, were alleged to be involved in the smuggling of mandrax. The drug, an hallucinogenic sleeping pill, could be easily and cheaply bought in India by Zambian middlemen who passed it on to dealers in South Africa, where it sold for a very high price. The undisguised affluence of the smugglers had for some time been a subject of popular comment and resentment, so there was widespread satisfaction when President Kuanda announced the establishment of a tribunal to investigate the ramifications of the smuggling 'mafia'.

MALAWI

Malawi continued to demonstrate its capacity to cope with daunting economic problems better than most African countries. In 1984 it had been the only country in Southern Africa to produce an exportable surplus of maize, an achievement due in part to good rains which spared the country the worst effects of the drought that afflicted its neighbours. In April the Minister of Finance was able to report a growth in real GDP of 7·6 per cent over the past twelve months, a result mainly attributable to a 6·3 per cent growth in agricultural production. Particularly significant was the improved productivity of peasant smallholders as opposed to large estates. Encouraged by the introduction of more generous producer prices, part of the reform programme urged on the Government by the IMF, Malawian smallholders increased their output by 7·8 per cent, an achievement which very few other African countries could rival.

Apart from the major long-term task of debt servicing and a 3·1 per cent population growth rate the most serious economic problem facing Malawi in 1985 derived from the closure, as a result of rebel (MNR) activity in Mozambique, of the land-locked country's shortest routes to the sea at the ports of Beira and Nacala. Consequently most of Malawi's trade had to pass along lengthy and circuitous routes southwards to Durban or northwards to the notoriously inefficient port of Dar es Salaam. Higher freight charges were estimated to be costing the country Kwacha100 million (£55 million) a year. The profits earned from the export of tea and tobacco, the source of 70 per cent of the country's foreign-exchange earnings, were substantially reduced. Agriculture suffered from the higher cost of fertilizers and the delays and uncertainties over deliveries, and there were occasional serious shortages of petrol and diesel oil.

The political scene was even quieter than in previous years. For the Life President, Dr Hastings Kamuzu Banda, whose age was thought to be at least 85, the most memorable event of the year was his four-day state visit to Britain in April, a visit that served to confirm the cordial relations between the two countries. In July Malawi broke new ground in its foreign policy by establishing diplomatic relations for the first time with two East European countries, Romania and Albania. Relations with another notably independent communist state, North Korea, had been established in 1982. But Dr Banda still refused to establish diplomatic ties with Moscow or Beijing and still maintained Malawi's close relationship with Taiwan.

ZIMBABWE

For Zimbabwe 1985 was a year of sustained economic recovery. After three successive years of drought, the summer of 1984–85 brought an excellent rainy season, launching a boom year for agricultural production. Included in the Z$2,100 million agricultural total was the country's biggest-ever maize harvest. In May the Foreign Minister, Mr Witness Mangwende, announced a donation of one million dollars and 25,000 tons of maize for famine relief in Ethiopia. Zimbabwe thus became a giver of aid, as well as a recipient of it, the first non-oil-producing African state to achieve that status.

Agriculture represented the country's most profitable sector, contributing Z$900 million to foreign earnings, or two-thirds of total exports. In addition to maize, the tobacco and cotton crops had a record year, the key improvement in cotton coming from the communal 'peasant' farms. In mining the value of non-gold mineral production approached Z$600 million for the year, an increase of 10 per cent, with higher outputs recorded for asbestos, nickel, coal, copper and chrome. The Zimbabwe Mining Development Corporation, established in 1984, undertook further mineral exploration and promoted the efficient exploitation of small mining ventures.

Improvement in the mining and agricultural sectors, along with a 6 per cent increase in manufacturing output, resulted in an overall GDP growth-rate of 5 per cent for the year. The production of food for export pushed the balance of payments into surplus for the second year running. This led to a relaxation of the exchange controls imposed on remittances of profits and dividends in 1984 (see AR 1984, p. 259) and a useful 30 per cent increase in foreign exchange allocations for importers. South Africa remained the major source of Zimbabwe's imports, though for the first time Britain became the largest customer for the country's exports, taking over Z$200 million worth of goods.

Domestically the Budget of 30 July, and an earlier financial statement of 30 January, maintained high levels of spending and hence of government borrowing. Education, at 16·7 per cent of total spending, remained the Government's main priority. The Minister of Finance, Economic Planning and Development, Dr Bernard Chidzero, defended the budget deficit on the grounds of the need to alleviate growing unemployment. Inflation, however, remained below 10 per cent.

The most important political event of the year was the general election, the first since independence in 1980. Originally scheduled for February, the election was postponed until June to enable the electoral commission to continue its registration of eligible voters among Zimbabwe's 8·4 million population, and the delimitation committee to complete the work of drawing up constituency boundaries based on the new rolls. During the extended period of electioneering that followed, opposition parties accused the Government of mounting a campaign of political intimidation. Fighting between supporters of the two main parties, a frequent occurrence in the previous year (see AR 1984, pp. 257–8) flared again early in the new year.

Pitched battles between followers of the ruling Zimbabwe African National Union, or Zanu (PF) party, and the locally powerful Zimbabwe African People's Union (Zapu), led by Mr Joshua Nkomo, caused three deaths in Bulawayo in late February. On 2–3 March, security forces sealed off the city in an operation to search for arms, ammunition and anti-government dissidents. There were reports of abductions, by soldiers of the army's Fifth Brigade and members of Zanu's youth league, of Zapu supporters throughout Matabeleland. Later that month the Catholic Commission for Justice and Peace sent evidence to the Prime Minister, Mr Robert Mugabe, of several hundred such incidents. Mr Nkomo, launching the Zapu election campaign on 10 March, declared there was no possibility of a free and fair election. The ruling Zanu (PF) party announced that its slogan for the forthcoming poll was 'unity'.

In the first round of polling on 27 June, 34,000 white voters elected 20 representatives to seats in the House of Assembly reserved for them by the terms of the Lancaster House agreement (see AR 1979, p. 513). Against expectation the confrontationist Conservative Alliance of Zimbabwe (CAZ), led by the former Prime Minister, Mr Ian Smith, won 15 seats; in the previous parliament it held only 7. The moderate Independent Zimbabwe Group, advocating racial reconciliation, took four seats and Mr Christoper Anderson, an independent Minister of State in the Prime Minister's Office, the remaining one. The result denied Zanu (PF) the cooperative block of white MPs it needed to support amendments to the independence constitution (see AR 1979, p. 513) and Mr Mugabe angrily threatened white voters who had spurned 'the hand of friendship'. Alarmed whites began to talk of voluntary abolition of the entrenched white seats and, in November, more than 19,000 demonstrated their commitment to the country by renouncing dual nationality in favour of Zimbabwean citizenship.

On 1 and 2 January the common-roll elections were held: 2·9 million black voters chose 80 MPs from 258 candidates representing six political parties. Zanu (PF), with 57 seats in the previous parliament, took 64 seats, while Zapu, with 20, won only 15. Significantly Zapu won all the 15 seats in Matabeleland and none elsewhere. A breakaway section of Zanu, led by Rev Ndabaningi Sithole, won a single surprise victory in the eastern Chipenge constituency. The United African National Council of the former Prime Minister of Zimbabwe-Rhodesia, Bishop Abel Muzorewa (see AR 1979, p. 255), lost the three seats it had won in 1980: in November Bishop Muzorewa announced his retirement from politics.

The composition of the new 26-member Cabinet, announced on 15 July, reflected Zanu (PF)'s major victory and signalled the end of inter-party reconciliation. With the dismissal of Mr Dennis Norman, the particularly successful CAZ Minister of Agriculture, and two deputy Ministers, Mr Anderson remained the only non-Zanu member of the Government. The appointment of Mr Enos Nkala, a noted enemy of Mr Nkomo, to the Home Affairs portfolio presaged tough measures against Zapu. Amidst accusations that his party was continuing to foment dissident activity in Matabeleland, security officers visited Mr Nkomo's homes in Harare and Bulawayo on 23 July, removing weapons and detaining 11 guards. Further raids on Zapu offices occurred at the beginning of August; one MP and several Zapu councillors were taken into custody. Mr Nkomo's passport was confiscated and, on 16 September, he himself was briefly detained for questioning. Simultaneously five senior army officers with Zapu affiliations were removed from their posts.

While the Home Affairs Minister spoke publicly of 'wiping out' Zapu, Mr Mugabe announced on 23 August the appointment of a three-member committee to reopen, for the first time in two years, unity talks with Zapu (see AR 1982, p. 255). After preliminary meetings between the two sides, the opening session on 2 October being attended by the Prime Minister and Mr Nkomo, a document of general agreement in principle was drafted. At the end of the year the issue remained delicately unresolved.

Following a landmine explosion in the northern Transvaal at the end of November the South African Government warned that it would strike beyond its borders if Zimbabwe continued to provide bases for ANC guerrillas. Elsewhere Zimbabwe's relations with its neighbours remained good; it cooperated with security forces in Mozambique to combat continuing banditry on their joint border. In September Zimbabwe was nominated to host the conference of Non-Aligned nations in 1986 and Mr Mugabe was elected the Movement's chairman for the following three years.

Within the country instances of fraud, theft and financial mismanagement in the police force, the civil service and the railways attracted widespread publicity and severe punishment. For the second year the report of the Comptroller and Auditor-General, Mr John Hilligan, pointed to careless accounting, bribery and corruption in the administration of several ministries (see AR 1984, p. 259). More positively, the year saw the commissioning of the Mazowe earth satellite station, a facility providing Zimbabwe with direct telephone, television and telex links with Europe, Africa and North America, reducing the previous dependence on South Africa.

NAMIBIA

By proclamation of the State President of South Africa, published on 17 June, a pre-independence 'transitional government' was instituted for Namibia, to hold office for two years. The South West African Peoples' Organization (Swapo), which had long operated an Angola-based guerrilla insurgency against the South African administration of Namibia, was invited by the Multiparty Conference (MPC), the forerunner of the transitional government, to join in but declined. Swapo argued that the regime would be a South African puppet and an obstacle to an internationally acceptable settlement. The MPC, a grouping of several internal parties, was estimated to enjoy the support of between 20 and 40 per cent of the population, mainly outside Ovamboland, a Swapo stronghold. The Administrator-General, answerable to Pretoria, continued to enjoy vast constitutional powers and Pretoria retained full control over defence and foreign affairs.

The Swapo insurgency continued throughout the year. Territorial Force (SWATF) and South African Defence Force (SADF) units claimed a kill rate of 10 guerrillas a week, totalling nearly 600 by the end of the year. In April South Africa announced the withdrawal of the joint monitoring commission (JMC) but warned that the SADF would cross into Southern Angola again if Swapo moved into the areas vacated by the

JMC (see AR 1984, p. 260). In July SWATF and SADF units launched a major incursion across the border into Angola which was described as a 'hot pursuit' operation. In September the South African Air Force made an air strike into the Kuando-Kubango province of Angola, apparently to rescue Dr Jonas Savimbi's rebel Unita movement from a major offensive by the ruling MPLA. There was also a SWATF raid into Angola, which SWATF said was to disrupt Swapo's rainy-season offensive. In December Angola was claiming that South African forces were again established in the south of Angola.

Throughout the year the American-led diplomatic effort to achieve internationally-approved independence for Namibia continued, apparently without significant headway.

BOTSWANA

There was an international outcry against South Africa when commandos of the South African Defence Force (SADF) crossed the Botswana border on 14 June and killed 12 people in attacks on a number of houses and offices. Botswana denounced this action as a 'terror raid' and demanded reparation. The chief of the SADF, General Constand Viljoen, said the purpose had been to disrupt the 'nerve centre' of the African National Congress (ANC) in Botswana. Since the Nkomati Accord between South Africa and Mozambique (see AR 1984, pp. 243–250 and 263), General Viljoen said, the majority of ANC guerrillas coming into South Africa had entered from Botswana. He remarked that it was unfortunate that some people—one woman and two children—had been 'caught in the crossfire' during the raid. South Africa's Foreign Minister, Mr R. F. Botha, said that the SADF would raid Botswana again if it became necessary to do so. Following the raid the United States recalled its ambassador in Pretoria, Mr Herman Nickel, for consultations, indicating its strong displeasure. The member states of the European Economic Community joined in condemnation of the raid and described it as a serious violation of Botswana's sovereignty.

On 7 October President Quett Masire, in a public speech, accused South Africa of increasing military pressure on neighbouring black states to force them into submission. He described the South African campaign against ANC refugees as 'state terrorism' and contrary to international law.

LESOTHO

Relations between Lesotho and South Africa continued to be strained, Pretoria again accusing Lesotho of harbouring guerrillas of the

African National Congress (ANC). On 21 December Lesotho blamed the South African Defence Force for a commando raid on two private homes in Maseru in the small hours of the morning in which nine people were killed, six of them refugees or members of the ANC and three of them Lesotho nationals. In one of the attacks a South African woman and her husband were shot dead in their apartment in a middle-class neighbourhood. The claim of South African culpability for the raid was denied by the South African Minister of Foreign Affairs, Mr. R. F. Botha, but was widely believed.

It was subsequently reported from Pretoria that the Department of Foreign Affairs had sent a diplomatic note to Maseru a few days earlier saying that Pretoria had learnt of a planned Maseru-based incursion by the ANC into South Africa which was to take place at Christmas-time. Lesotho had replied to the note, asking for further particulars. Hours later, however, the commando raid into Lesotho took place, according to a Lesotho spokesman, who said his Government believed that it was not the Foreign Minister who was in control of South Africa's foreign relations, but the military. The Lesotho Government considered that the raid was a reprisal for casualties caused in the Northern Transvaal in December by explosions of landmines planted by the ANC. As the year ended, relations between Pretoria and Maseru were at their lowest ebb for some time.

SWAZILAND

Swaziland, which had signed a non-aggression pact with South Africa, kept on reasonably good terms with its powerful neighbour in 1985, arresting members of the African National Congress (ANC) found on Swaziland soil and prosecuting them for illegal entry into the country. In October, however, Swaziland complained in the UN General Assembly that South African 'destabilization' of Mozambique was spilling over into Swaziland. Repeated derailments on the Maputo line and an uncontrollable influx of refugees were eroding Swaziland's own resources. At the end of the year 28 detained members of the ANC were deported from Swaziland and flown to countries of their choice.

In November it was reported that the ruling group in Swaziland had been ousted in a quiet palace coup. The two men who had led Swaziland since the death of King Sobhuza II in 1982, Prince Mfanasibili and Dr George Msibi, were removed from the ruling council of state, the Liqoqo, by order of Queen Regent Ntombi. It was said that the two men had lost the favour of Crown Prince Makhosetive, who would succeed to the throne. It appeared that the inner circle of the royal family had taken back control of the government. The commissioner of police, Mr Majija Simelane, was removed from office by order of the Queen Regent.

Chapter 3

THE REPUBLIC OF SOUTH AFRICA

IN 1985 the chronic South African unrest became acute. Amid widespread violence in the black areas, which continued throughout the year, a state of emergency was declared, the rand currency collapsed and some people concluded that the country was on the verge of revolution. By the year's end, in spite of a dreadful toll of casualties, it was plain that this conclusion was premature.

Yet the South African state had been shaken to its foundations. In response to the violence, the Afrikaner Nationalist Government of President P. W. Botha abandoned the rhetoric of apartheid, conceding that black South Africans were entitled to rights of citizenship. It was by no means clear, however, whether this indicated an intention to concede real political power to blacks. It seemed more likely that President Botha would seek to co-opt some non-militant blacks in a supportive role, rather as some coloured (mixed race) and Indian politicians had already been co-opted into a system in which white political power remained firmly in control (see AR 1983, pp. 482–94, and 1984, p. 263).

The township violence which started in the Vaal triangle in September 1984 dragged on into 1985 and flared up again with renewed vigour, disclosing intense anger among blacks at their exclusion from rights in Parliament under the new constitution. As this came into force, a ruthlessly effective campaign of assassination of blacks seen as 'collaborators' with the apartheid system was set in train. There were frequent clashes between police and rioting and/or protesting crowds in the townships. Consumer boycotts of white-owned shops were launched by activists, with considerable success, particularly in the Eastern Cape, where many small undertakings went out of business.

As the year advanced, South Africa found itself in the spotlight of critical world attention. On 21 March, the anniversary of the Sharpeville shootings in 1966, 21 people died when police in armoured vehicles, using automatic weapons, fired into a procession of unarmed blacks at Langa township outside Uitenhage. Soon two or three blacks were dying by assassination or by police gunfire almost every day. Violence had become endemic, invoking tougher-than-ever police action, assisted by units of the South African Defence Force.

Figures published in *The Times* (London) of 20 December 1985, based on statistics compiled by the South African Institute of Race Relations, supplemented by *The Times's* own records, showed that 965 people had died in the last four months of 1984 and in 1985 up to 10 December. All but a handful were blacks, coloured people or Indians. Almost all the violence had been contained in the segregated black townships which are situated outside the towns and cities. According to

The Times, about half of the deaths were caused by police action. Feuding between rival black factions and the assassination of 'collaborators' accounted for the balance. The worst single month was August, when 163 people died. There was widespread arson. Statistics released by the Minister of Law and Order, Mr Louis Le Grange, showed that 920 schools had been either destroyed or extensively damaged, as well as 33 churches, 17 clinics, 639 shops, 286 liquor stores, 2,528 private houses, 5,054 buses and 5,338 cars. Damage to property totalled R100 million.

Apart from township riots and clashes with the police, there was also a dramatic surge in guerrilla insurgency. Pretoria University's Institute of Strategic Studies cited 398 cases of guerrilla violence since 1976, of which 136 took place in 1985. These included hand-grenade, limpet-mine and rocket attacks, car bombings, sabotage, murder or attempted murder, landmine explosions and skirmishes with the security forces. In the closing weeks of the year, at which stage whites were still relatively unscathed, six whites died in landmine explosions in the Northern Transvaal border region. On 23 December a bomb placed in a shopping centre at Amanzimtoti, a Natal seaside resort, killed five whites.

The South African security forces were again active in counter-insurgency operations beyond South Africa's borders, attracting criticism in the international community for violating national boundaries. The South African Defence Force raided the town of Gaborone, Botswana, in June, killing 15 alleged or suspected activists of the African National Congress (ANC), which was operating a campaign of sabotage and urban guerrilla insurgency, infiltrating South Africa from neighbouring territories.

In May two South African commandos were killed and one captured in a raid into the Cabinda oil enclave of Angola which was said to be aimed at the ANC but which, to foreign observers, seemed designed to relieve the pressure on Dr Jonas Savimbi's Unita rebels in Angola by sabotaging the oil installations and striking a blow at the economic lifeline of the MPLA regime. In September, the South African Defence Force launched an incursion into southern Angola, describing this as a pre-emptive strike against guerrillas of the South West African People's Organization (Swapo), which was operating from bases in Angola. Later in the month Pretoria made its first public admission that South Africa was providing direct aid to the Unita movement. By the end of the year it seemed that the South African Defence Force was again established in southern Angola.

In December, a clandestine commando raid into Lesotho, for which Pretoria denied responsibility, resulted in the death of nine people, including a number of ANC activists. As the year ended, it seemed plain that South Africa had resumed an aggressive posture in the region, acting to pre-empt guerrilla actions mounted from neighbouring territories. The regional peace-making diplomacy of Nkomati and Lusaka (see AR 1984,

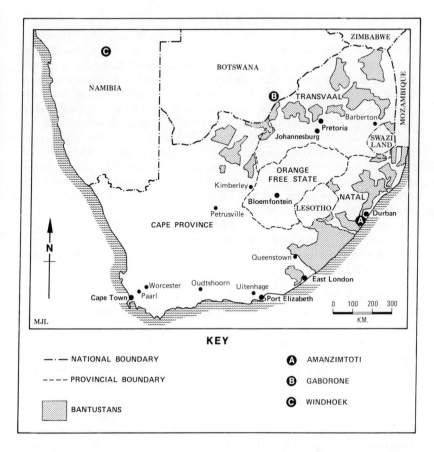

KEY

— · — NATIONAL BOUNDARY   **Ⓐ** AMANZIMTOTI

— — — PROVINCIAL BOUNDARY   **Ⓑ** GABORONE

          Ⓒ WINDHOEK

[▒] BANTUSTANS

p. 263) was visibly falling apart. Pretoria's hawks were seizing the initiative.

As unrest rumbled on in many parts of the country, a state of emergency was declared in July in 36 districts, giving the security forces sweeping powers to abrogate civil liberties. In August, the unrest flared up strongly in the Cape peninsula, mainly in black and coloured townships, following an attempted march on Pollsmoor prison, where ANC leader Nelson Mandela was imprisoned. The march was broken up by police wielding whips. By this time, the sight of policemen whipping protesters in South African streets had become familiar to millions of television viewers throughout the world. In the US and Britain public opinion became strongly anti-South African. The ailing South African rand currency came tumbling down with a vengeance when a keenly-awaited 'reformist' speech by President Botha on 15 August turned out to be a public relations disaster, giving the world the impression of truculent defiance. American bankers called in short-term loans to South Africa and President Reagan imposed symbolic political sanctions. Business confidence ebbed away.

By now, unrest was going on intermittently in many parts of the country, much of it involving black youths who were staying away from schools in their thousands. There was acute anxiety in the business community, which regretted its enthusiastic support of the new Botha constitution and began casting around for alternatives. Business leaders, including Mr Gavin Relly and Dr Zac de Beer of the Anglo-American Corporation, flew to Lusaka to meet Mr Oliver Tambo of the ANC for discussions, incurring the publicly-expressed wrath of President Botha and straining the alliance between big business and government. In October the Cape peninsula was included in the state of emergency and detentions without trial and police crack-downs were intensified. Then in November the Government used emergency powers to curb news coverage of the unrest, arguing that the media acted as a catalyst which kept the violence going. Pictorial coverage of the unrest ceased, and reports of what was happening became sketchy and inadequate. Yet the death rate increased. In Queenstown, in the Eastern Cape, and in Mamelodi, outside Pretoria, police shootings again took a heavy toll in casualties, attracting as much attention around the world as had the shooting at Uitenhage.

It seemed that the country was in the throes of a black insurrection against white political control. By December, it was plain that the use of force was proving counter-productive, serving to prolong the violence. The Government insisted that it was in favour of negotiation and President Botha said plans were in the pipeline to grant citizenship to all blacks. However, the possibility of a negotiated compromise between warring Afrikaner and African nationalism seemed remote. The Botha Government insisted that it would not negotiate with the ANC as long as that organization continued its policy of violence. The ANC, on the other hand, said it could not consider abandoning the 'armed struggle' as long as it continued to be a banned organization, with its leaders restricted or in detention and wholly excluded from the legitimate political process. To break the stalemate, the leader of the Progressive Federal Party opposition, Dr F. van Zyl Slabbert, proposed that the ban on the ANC should be lifted and the organization encouraged to take part in the political process.

A critical problem facing the South African Government as 1985 ended was the crisis of international confidence in the future of the country. During the year, from peak to valley the rand lost nearly 35 per cent of its value against the dollar, nearly half of its value against the British pound, the Deutschmark, the Japanese yen and the Swiss franc. In the twelve months ended in September, 1985, the outflow of foreign capital had amounted to the unprecedented figure of R7,700 million. In the previous twelve months, South Africa had a net inflow of private capital of R32 million. After the American banks had called in their short-term credits in July, South Africa was obliged to impose a moratorium on repayments. An international banker, Dr Fritz Leutwiler, agreed to act as mediator between South Africa and its foreign creditors. After meeting members of the South African Government in December, Dr Leutwiler said he was hopeful that an agreed solution could be reached with the 300 banks concerned. Most observers agreed, however, that it would take a really significant improvement in the political climate to convince the investor community that the country's racial problems were being properly addressed.

On the labour relations front, 1985, in spite of the recession, was marked by record levels of strike activity, but most strikes were of short duration. Significant developments during the year were the emergence of the black National Union of Mineworkers as an important force and the formation of a new, radical labour federation, the Congress of South African Trade Unions (COSATU) with a membership of more than half a million workers, promising to overshadow the politically centrist federation, the Trade Union Council of South Africa (TUCSA).

VIII SOUTH ASIA AND INDIAN OCEAN

Chapter 1

IRAN—AFGHANISTAN

IRAN

THE year 1985 was unmitigatedly poor for Iran. The Gulf war entered its fifth year but brought the conflict no nearer to a peaceful resolution. Iran ended the year significantly weaker in the military field than it had begun it. The claims of war affected the national economy almost invariably in an adverse way. Oil exports were made difficult by Iraqi bombardment of Kharg Island terminals, while the weakening of oil prices on the international market exacerbated Iranian problems.

The major difficulty besetting the state remained involvement in the Gulf war, in which Iraq appeared to be growing stronger in fire-power, armour and aircraft as Iran itself grew weaker. Iran was the object of an international arms embargo that denied it access to anything but a small-scale flow of arms from a few friendly countries in the shape of Syria and Libya. By year-end it was reported that Iran had so few serviceable fighter aircraft that it could no longer maintain even a basic defence against Iraqi air attacks. Negotiations for purchase of Chinese-origin tanks and aircraft were begun during the year.

One of the few weapons at the disposal of the Iranian high command was the dedication to the war of the volunteer battalions and the revolutionary guards. It was on the strength of this one advantage that Iran returned to the offensive in March after a sustained period of Iraqi harassment which included air strikes against shipping using Iranian ports, bombardment of Iranian economic targets and air raids on civilian settlements. Iranian amphibious troops were pushed rapidly forward into the Hawizah marshlands on 11 March, catching the Iraqi defenders by surprise and eventually breaking through to the west bank of the river Tigris. There were reports at that time that the Iranians were close to severing Iraq's main north–south arterial links. In the event, the Iranian forward positions were not held in the face of a heavy armoured assault by the Iraqis, supported by close air cover. The Iranians had neither the arms nor the logistical strength to sustain their drive. By 21 March they had been altogether eliminated from Iraqi soil in the area of the attack.

The pace of the war increased markedly as a result of the intensification of the land war. Iraqi attacks were launched in March against major Iranian towns such as Teheran, Tabriz, Esfahan and Shiraz. Sustained bombing of Teheran in particular caused major problems for the Iranian

Government, which in retaliation stepped up its artillery barrage against Basra and other eastern Iraqi cities and bombed Baghdad and Kirkuk. The war of the cities, as it became known, went on into April with tit-for-tat exchanges and flared again in June and July. While Iran suffered badly from indiscriminate air attacks against civilian populations it was able to achieve a number of missile attacks, all but the first directed against Baghdad. The missiles, thought to be of Libyan origin, were small but adequate to persuade the Iraqis that they could not strike at Iran with total impunity. The war of the cities came to an eventual halt in July, though only after the Iranian regime had been severely discomfited.

Iraq turned to new tactics in the war in July. Iran's main oil export terminals at Kharg Island became the focus for air attack from 15 July, in parallel with strikes against oil tankers serving it. Whereas previous assaults against Kharg had been half-hearted, the raid of 15 July was at low level and was pressed home. Real damage was done to the storage tanks and loading facilities. A steady aerial bombardment of the island throughout the rest of the year effectively led to the terminal's losing capacity, so that by December Iran's shuttle of crude oil from Kharg to the safer terminal at Sirri, further south in the Gulf, gave partial way to exports from temporary loading-points elsewhere along the Gulf coast-line. Iranian plans for a pipeline to carry oil to export terminals beyond the range of Iraqi air attacks were advanced as a further measure to offset the problems of exporting through Kharg.

Setbacks on the field of battle did not deter the Government from establishing a new strategy in the war in which attrition was formally adopted as the main means of pursuing the conflict. It was announced that Iranian forces would put their efforts into a series of land attacks along the length of the front with Iraq, so that the Iraqis would be kept constantly in a high state of readiness. Following the Iraqis' success in the battles of March, their demonstration of superiority in the air through the bombardment of Iranian cities and Kharg Island and the clear evidence that Iran would not win an early victory in the war, optimism flared that peace talks could be started. In fact, the attitudes of the Iranian leadership towards the war had changed scarcely at all. Peace initiatives from the Arab states, the UN, Japan and others went unwelcomed in Teheran. Ayatollah Khomeini in particular seemed to hold as fast as ever to the view that the rulers of Iraq must be removed from power before peace could be achieved.

Two important internal political changes came about in the year. First, Mr Mir Moussavi was reappointed as Prime Minister on 17 October and was able to get most of his ministerial nominations accepted by the Islamic Assembly. Second, there was a growth in the influence of the Freedom Movement, a mixed group of secular and clerical interests led by the former Prime Minister Dr Bazargan, which called for open democracy, a return of Islamic leaders to the mosque and an end to war.

In the international arena Iran performed slightly better than in the recent past. Some attempt was made to come to terms with the USSR despite increasing Russian criticism of Iran's involvement in the war. The USA remained the principal target of Iranian venom, a posture reinforced by the restoration of formal diplomatic relations between the USA and Iraq. A concerted effort was launched to improve relations with other states, including the Arabs of the Gulf area. In general, however, the threat of exported Islamic revolution, together with association of the country—rightly or wrongly—with international terrorism, left Iran isolated. Only Syria and Libya maintained pro-Iranian stances, the former with decreasing commitment.

Economic trends were almost wholly adverse. Oil suffered from falling exports and declining unit values of crude on the international market. Average production was estimated for the year at some 2·5 million b/d and oil income at $16,000 million, much below budget forecast. Overall, the economy stagnated or drifted into slight decline as a result of the fall in oil revenues. High inflation continued to affect the economy. Stringent controls on imports helped to restrain the worsening of the balance of payments, and the steady drain on limited foreign-exchange reserves. Iranian payments to suppliers were delayed but the country stayed unencumbered by foreign debt.

The domestic economy was held back by the low rate of state expenditures on all but the war. The development programme was effectively abandoned except where human resources could be deployed. Heavy industry fared badly as a result of low capital investment and difficult access to foreign supplies of spares or raw materials. Small-scale industry did better, with a rising level of output. In agriculture a good grain harvest was achieved.

AFGHANISTAN

In 1985, as in 1984, Soviet and Afghan government forces continued to face strong opposition and sporadic harrying attacks throughout Afghanistan from the mujaheddin (holy warriors). The guerrilla fighting undoubtedly had a serious effect upon the Afghan economy, and some reports alleged that large parts of the country might be on the verge of famine.

Repeatedly during the year there was speculation by outside experts that Soviet forces in Afghanistan, hitherto estimated to number about 105,000 troops, had been increased to as many as 140,000. Be that as it may, the official Afghan army continued to be weak and demoralized. Kabul radio announced on 23 October that all Afghan male nationals up to 40 years of age had been ordered to enlist for three years' military service, regardless of whether they had already completed a tour of duty.

The Panjshir valley, a major rebel stronghold to the north of Kabul and a salient for mujaheddin operations against the main highway linking Kabul with the Soviet Union, continued to experience throughout the first half of 1985, as it had done in 1984, some of the fiercest fighting to have taken place since the Soviet intervention in 1979–80. Major Soviet-led offensives aimed at cutting the supply routes of the mujaheddin from Pakistan were sustained in the eastern and south-eastern parts of the country. Soviet troops were also reported to have been deployed in large numbers in the extreme south-west and around the city of Herat in the west. There were reports, too, of almost continuous fighting in and around the city of Kandahar in southern Afghanistan, where a large-scale and prolonged bombing campaign resulted in the destruction of crops in the nearby countryside, while the city was reported to be without electricity for long periods, as well as suffering severe petrol shortages. Mujaheddin operating in and around Kabul mounted intermittent attacks throughout the year, resulting in heavy loss of life.

At the same time there appeared to be some evidence of continuing factional conflict within the Afghan government leadership, suggesting that the waves of assassinations of government officers were not exclusively the work of the mujaheddin but that some of them stemmed from the bitter rivalries between the Parcham (Flag) and Khalq (People) factions of the ruling party, the PDPA (see AR 1978, p. 261, and 1981, p. 270).

The desire to acquire at least a patina of legitimacy and some semblance of popular acceptability was undoubtedly a continuing, but mostly frustrated, ambition of the Government in Kabul. On 6 April the Afghan Revolutionary Council announced that a Loya Jirga (grand assembly or supreme council—a nationwide traditional gathering of tribal leaders) would be held during the current Afghan year. A government statement over Kabul radio stressed that such an assembly had traditionally been called at 'sensitive historic moments', adding that this forthcoming Loya Jirga would discuss ways of 'maintaining reliable peace and security, halting intervention by imperialist and reactionary forces, preventing Afghan blood being shed by Afghans, and implementing the revolution'. A special commission to be chaired by President Babrak Karmal was appointed to organize elections to the assembly and to set a date for its convocation. The Loya Jirga took place on 23–25 April. On its last day the 1,796 delegates 'unanimously' adopted a resolution approving the continuing Soviet military presence in Afghanistan. The resolution also called upon Afghans who had fled the country to return and the opposition groups of mujaheddin to lay down their arms.

Towards the end of the year there were a number of signs of a drastic overhaul of policy by the Kremlin and its accomplices in Kabul. On the sixth anniversary of its formation on 27 December 1979 the Babrak Karmal regime appointed eight non-communists to senior government posts, in what was widely interpreted as an attempt to demonstrate that the regime was broadly-based and merited wide international recognition. The Politbureau of the ruling communist party, in effect acknowledging the persisting chasm between their regime and the masses, had ostensibly directed Karmal to draft prominent people from outside the party into the existing 27-member Cabinet and to other key positions. The new appointees included a Hindu, a Hazara, a Nuristani, an Uzbek and representatives of the majority Pashtuns and Tajiks. These appointments, together with the removal of General Abdul Qadir, the former Defence Minister, and General Najibullah, the head of Khad (the secret police), from their positions of power, were part of a general shake-up in the top echelons of government. Government media accorded much prominence to the return to Afghanistan of Mr Noor Ahmed Noor and to the doings of Mr Sultan Ali Kishtmund, giving rise to speculation that either or both of these might be beneficiaries if there were to be a change in the presidency or in the control of the party.

Overall it seemed as if the power of the old guard leadership of the armed forces was on the wane. General Abdul Qadir was the air force commander who had led the coup d'état that brought the communists to power in the so-called Soviet Revolution of 1978 (see AR 1978, pp. 261–2). In fact the Afghan army played a minor role in the fighting during 1985, almost the entire brunt of the summer offensives being borne by Soviet troops.

Chapter 2

INDIA—PAKISTAN—BANGLADESH—SRI LANKA—NEPAL

INDIA

INTENSE electioneering at the state level, an active but businesslike foreign policy directed especially at relations with the two superpowers and with regional neighbours, and reappraisal of the country's economic and fiscal policies—these were the three main motifs of 1985 for India.

Prime Minister Rajiv Gandhi began the year flushed with the success of a huge electoral victory (see AR 1984, p. 272). Winning a parliamentary majority of over three to one and more than half the votes polled, his party, Congress (I), had reduced the national opposition parties to a few scattered remnants and had secured the electoral defeat of all but a handful of the opposition leaders. Only a few regional parties (notably in Karnataka, Sikkim, Jammu and Kashmir, and Andhra Pradesh) managed to resist this electoral tide (which had undoubtedly had contained a considerable sympathy vote for Mr Gandhi) and were readily prepared to fight again—as was demonstrated in state elections within the year.

Indeed, only ten weeks after the general election, to consolidate his national gains Mr Gandhi called for assembly elections in eleven states and the Union territory of Pondicherry (where one seat was contested and Congress was returned to power after 16 years). Mr Gandhi campaigned vigorously, mostly in Southern India where the major states of Andhra Pradesh and Karnataka were ruled by the Telugu Desam and Janata parties respectively. In the event (Pondicherry apart) Congress won eight of the eleven states which went to the polls. Its major gains were only in the so-called Hindi belt states of Madhya Pradesh and Himachal Pradesh, where it won almost a 75 per cent majority, and the two peripheral states of Orissa and Gujerat, where it had a majority of over two-thirds. In its traditional power-base of Uttar Pradesh, the most populous Indian state, and Bihar, the second most populous, it gained only simple majorities.

These results seemed to support the thesis that the Indian electorate was mature enough to distinguish between national and local issues: that the electorate saw no contradiction between opting for a strong centre and voting into power locally a national opposition party; and that after voting in one power-bloc it was quite capable of opting for another the next time round. The state assembly elections thus served Mr Gandhi as a reminder of the transitoriness and variability of political power, especially when it rests ultimately on electoral backing. More than 25 per cent of the national electorate had not gone to the polls in state elections and Rajiv Gandhi was to encounter political troubles in those omitted—especially in Punjab and Assam.

On 3 January, less than a week after his new Government had been sworn in, Mr Gandhi appointed a Cabinet committee to examine ways to resolve the Punjab problem. Eight Sikh leaders, including Sant Longowal, Mr Barnala and Mr Jagdev Singh, were all released from prison on 11 March: they had all been imprisoned in June 1984 after the army action at the Golden Temple. Mr Gandhi made his first visit as Prime Minister to Punjab on 23 March—a few days after he had announced the appointment of Mr Arjun Singh as Governor of the state.

The Government announced on 11 April that a judicial investigation would be held into the anti-Sikh violence in Delhi which followed Mrs Gandhi's assassination on 21 October 1984, and that more Sikh detainees would soon be released. The agitation campaign called by the Akali Dal leadership was to have been resumed on 13 April but its postponement was announced the day before.

Throughout the year there was much evidence of bitter debate and disagreement within the Akali Dal leadership. On 1 May, for instance, Mr Joginder Singh (the father of the militant Sikh leader, Sant Jarnail Singh Bhindranwale, who was killed during the army's assault on the Golden Temple) announced the merger of both main groupings within the Akali Dal, led by Sant Longowal and Mr Talwandi respectively, into a unified party under his own leadership, with a new nine-member committee to oversee its affairs. Before the end of the month, however, a moderate group of district and state Akali Dal officials had reaffirmed their support for Longowal and Talwandi and had repudiated Joginder Singh's committee.

Mr Gandhi told Parliament on 24 July that he and Sant Longowal had signed a memorandum for a settlement of the Punjab problem. The 11-point accord assigned to Punjab the federal territory of Chandigarh, which hitherto had been shared as the state capital of both Punjab and Haryana. To resolve the rival territorial claims of the two states a commission was set up and requested to give its recommendations by 26 January 1986. The Indian Government agreed to consider legislation which would establish a nationwide set of rules for the management of Gurdwaras (Sikh temples). On the even more contentious issue of sharing the waters of the Sutlej, Beas and Ravi rivers among Punjab, Haryana and Rajasthan, a tribunal headed by a Supreme Court judge was required to make its recommendations within six months.

This accord was greeted with bitterness in Haryana. Opposition members of the Haryana state Assembly threatened to resign in protest against what they described as a sell-out of Haryana's interests. Militant Sikhs also dismissed the agreement as inadequate.

Following the assassination of the former party president, Sant Harchand Singh Longowal, on 20 August, Mr Surjit Singh Barnala was elected interim president of the Akali Dal on 25 August. A former Minister of Agriculture in the central Government (1977–79), he was a staunch supporter of the Longowal-Gandhi accord of 24 July.

Elections were held on 25 September, both for the Legislative Assembly of the Punjab and for the 13 Punjab seats in the Lok Sabha (Lower House of Parliament) for which there had been no polling during the December 1984 general election. In the Assembly elections Mr Barnala's moderate faction of the Akali Dal won 73 of the 115 seats, the Congress (I) won 32, the Bharatiya Janata Party (BJP) four, the Janata Party one, the Communist Party of India (CPI) one and independents four. In the contest for Lok Sabha seats the Akali Dal won seven and Congress (I) six. These results were widely interpreted as a popular endorsement of the 24 July accord—though clearly this did not end all dissent, intimidation and terrorism in the Punjab.

In Assam, elections were held concurrently on 16 December for the 126 seats in the Legislative Assembly and the 14 Assam seats in the Lok Sabha. The decisive victory of the Asom Gana Parishad (AGP), formed a mere 67 days before the elections, ushered in a new era of change in Assam, with untried young leaders at the helm. Forty-eight of the 64 Assembly seats were won by the AGP from Congress (I), which secured only 25 seats. AGP won 7 of the Lok Sabha seats and Congress (I) only 4. The new Chief Minister, Prafulla Kumar Mahanta, was only 32 years old when he took office—the youngest ever to rise to that position—and the average age of his Cabinet was less than 40. The polarization of the vote along communal lines left the future of the Assam accord between state and centre uncertain.

A tough Terrorist and Disruptive Activities (Prevention) Bill was passed on 21 May, despite some opposition protests against the broad definition of 'disruptive activities' named and castigated in the Bill.

After months of difficult negotiations India and the United States signed an agreement in mid-May described as 'the Indo-US high technology transfer accord', permitting the use of sophisticated American technology for Indian business and military ventures. Mr Malcolm Baldrige, the US Secretary of Commerce, who signed the agreement in New Delhi, said that he expected Indo-US trade to increase sharply in future years, even though the US was already India's largest trading partner, exporting about $1,500 million of goods to India in 1984–85, while India exported about $2,500 million to the US. Mr Baldrige acknowledged at a news conference, however, that joint business ventures might be adversely affected if there were no settlement in the lawsuit by India against the Union Carbide Corporation for alleged negligence as a result of the disastrous leak of toxic gas in December 1984 at Bhopal (see AR 1984, p. 276).

Mr Gandhi paid a six-day visit to Moscow in late May, his first official state visit to the Soviet Union, during an extensive foreign tour which also took him to Egypt, France, the United States, Algeria and Switzerland. In Moscow he and Mikhail Gorbachev signed a number of agreements providing for Soviet assistance to India's oil, coal, power generation and machine-building industries, and agreed on arrangements for substantial new Soviet credits for India's development projects. In October Mr Gandhi visited London, where he had discussions with Mrs Thatcher and British Ministers before attending the Commonwealth meeting in Nassau (see pp. 39–40 and Pt. XI, Ch. 2) and the 40th anniversary meetings of the UN in New York. Throughout the year there was press speculation that India was about to buy 21 Westland W30 helicopters—reports which remained doubtful because of uncertainties about the Westland company's future (see pp. 33–34).

During the year Indo-Pakistan relations overall moved on to a cautiously constructive plane of agreement, despite the Indian Government's public charges that some Pakistanis were aiding terrorism in the Punjab and despite some skirmishes between Indian and Pakistani troops in the icy wastes of north-west Kashmir near the Siachen glacier. When President Zia-ul-Haq stopped in New Delhi to talk to Mr Gandhi in mid-December on his way home from the Dhaka summit (see p. 270) this was their sixth meeting within 14 months. A six-point agreement they issued then included an understanding not to attack each other's nuclear installations and measures aimed at curbing cross-border terrorism.

Otherwise, Indian diplomacy towards regional neighbours concentrated on low-key constructive measures, both through SAARC (see p. 272) and bilaterally. India sought assiduously to promote talks and mutually acceptable agreements between Tamils and the Sri Lankan Government. Principally because of Indian urging, two rounds of talks were held in Thimpu, the capital of Bhutan—but with no marked success. India continued to be chairman of the Non-Aligned Movement and until the end of the year was also a non-permanent member of the UN Security Council.

The budget for 1985–86 was presented to Parliament on 16 March by the Finance Minister, Vishwanath Pratap Singh. It outlined the financial aspects of Rajiv Gandhi's promised policies for improved productivity, absorption of modern know-how and the greater use of technology. A number of industries were specifically earmarked for expansion and stress was placed on releasing the energies of private enterprise and reducing dependence on publicly-owned financial institutions by creating an environment for savings, reducing the cost-structure of industry and channelling investment into key areas. A number of far-reaching changes were proposed in the system of personal taxation.

The budget also incorporated a variety of measures to assist the weaker sections of society. Insurance was proposed for selected crops, for instance, and small farmers and landless farm labourers would henceforth get social security benefits. Workers in all categories were promised accident insurance cover. Lower prices for electronic goods, home appliances and cotton textiles were intended to benefit the consumer. But a 15 per cent rise in prices of petroleum products would make road transport and cooking gas costlier. An increase of Rs14,000 million in levies on petroleum products would have a serious impact on industrial costs, of cement and paper, for example. Mr Gandhi's many critical remarks about the performance of public-sector enterprises had aroused much speculation that some of them would be privatized, but his statements during the budget debate and at other times suggested that his aim was greater efficiency in the public sector, rather than its contraction. The budget did not spell out any measures to improve the performance of the public sector, mostly because this was a managerial rather than a fiscal problem.

In November India's Planning Commission, having considered several alternative development scenarios for the seventh five-year-plan, 1985–90, announced that it was planning for 5 per cent annual growth over the next 15 years, in line, it said, with the achievements of the sixth plan, which had attained the target of a 5·2 per cent annual growth rate. The seventh plan was based on a 15-year perspective, aiming to make India, by the year 2000, a modern, technologically progressive economy, capable of growth without large infusions of external financial or technical aid, and meeting the basic needs of the people. The plan envisaged a direct attack on poverty, unemployment and regional imbalances. It sought to emphasise programmes and policies that would increase food-grain production, generate productive employment and step up productivity, and to bring down the fraction of the population living below the poverty line from 36·9 per cent (273 million) in 1984–85 to 25·8 per cent (211 million) by 1989–90, the bulk of the improvement being in the rural areas.

In a speech at the end of the year, to mark the 100th anniversary of the Congress Party, the Prime Minister was scathing in his criticism of opposition politicians, bureaucrats and many others. 'We have civil servants who do not serve the people, policemen who do not maintain law and order, and tax collectors who connive with evaders', he said. Opposition parties were 'shielding the corrupt'.

PAKISTAN

Pakistan's uneasy relations with India and the stepped-up ground and air offensive of the occupying Soviet forces against the Afghan freedom-fighters along the western frontier continued to be sources of anxiety for the Pakistani people throughout 1985. At home the Government of General Zia-ul-Haq was faced at times with active opposition from various political parties demanding the abolition of martial law and the restoration of an elected parliamentary government.

President Zia, in a message addressed to Mr Rajiv Gandhi, Prime Minister of India, on the National Day of India on 26 January, said: 'Friendly and good neighbourly relations between Pakistan and India serve the best interests of our two peoples and also of peace and stability in the region.' When the India-Pakistan joint ministerial commission met in July in New Delhi and concluded agreements in the fields of agriculture, research development and exchange of scientists, technologists and scientific equipment, Mr Romesh Bhandari, India's Foreign Secretary, said: 'Seen in the context of the history of the past 38 years of suspicion, hostilities, mistrust and distrust the outcome of the joint talks was really noteworthy.' Three months earlier, in April, the annual report of the Indian Defence Ministry had described Pakistan as India's principal security concern.

During his visit to the United States in June, Mr Rajiv Gandhi, in a television interview, accused Pakistan of developing a nuclear bomb; and again in October, in an interview with *Newsweek* magazine, he said that India had circumstantial evidence to prove that Pakistan was making an atom bomb. Pakistan repeatedly denied these accusations and insisted that its nuclear programme was for peaceful purposes only. In his address to the UN General Assembly in October, President Zia-ul-Haq reiterated Pakistan's policy of developing nuclear energy for peaceful purposes and declared that Pakistan had neither the capability nor the desire to develop nuclear weapons. An allegation made by the Indian chief of the army staff, General A. S. Vaidya, that Pakistan was planning to carry out its first nuclear test in China's northern Sinkiang, at Lop Nor, was categorically denied by China as well as Pakistan.

During the later half of the year, the Indian Government reported clashes in the Siachen glacier region north of the terminus of the line of control in Kashmir. Indian claims to the Siachen glacier area had been denied by Pakistan. Pakistan also repudiated Indian attempts to implicate it in India's Sikh problem and reiterated its full adherence to the principle of strict non-interference in the affairs of all countries including India.

In December, President Zia and Mr Rajiv Gandhi agreed at a meeting in New Delhi not to attack each other's nuclear installations and to improve relations generally. In what was described by a section of the Western press as the most cordial of their six meetings since Mr Gandhi became Prime Minister, the two leaders also agreed to reopen talks early in 1986 on a peace treaty, to negotiate a pact on economic cooperation and cultural exchanges and to go step by step towards normalizing relations between the two countries. Furthermore, the Indian Prime Minister accepted an invitation to visit Pakistan, the first Indian leader to do so in 25 years. Other issues, some of them contentious, were left to be tackled at future meetings. Among them was the question of Kashmir. During 1985 troops from both sides died in skirmishes on Kashmir's 18,000-ft-high Siachen glacier.

Referring to his talks with Mr Gandhi President Zia said: 'We have agreed to go step by step in a systematic manner' to resolve the issues between the two countries. The most difficult issues dividing the two countries—the dispute over Kashmir and the details of Pakistan's nuclear policy—would not be discussed to begin with. 'We are starting out with areas of agreement rather than the disagreements,' said the President.

Earlier, President Zia had attended the first-ever heads-of-state meeting of the South Asian Association for Regional Cooperation (SAARC) held on 7–8 December at Dhaka in Bangladesh. His visit to the Maldives on 15–17 December was the first by a Pakistani head of state. From the Maldives, he went on to visit New Delhi on 17 December.

On 30 December, in a nationally televised speech before a joint session of parliament, General Zia-ul-Haq announced the ending of eight years of martial law and the restoration of Pakistan's constitution. He also announced the disbandment of military courts, the appointment of civilian provincial governors and the closing-down of martial law offices in the country. He warned legislators to avoid personal differences and work in the national interest in order to avoid future intervention by the armed forces, which, he said, had restored Pakistan's political and economic health and turned over a revived and progressive state to civilian government. Defending the establishment of martial law on 5 July 1977, he said that the armed forces deserved homage for their efforts to save the nation from internal discord. Today, he declared, the people of Pakistan lived in an atmosphere of peace and tranquillity under Islam and were proud of Pakistan. With the lifting of martial law, 260 political dissidents held in gaols were freed in Punjab.

The annual report of the State Bank of Pakistan for 1985 warned that the country was living beyond its means, and that failure to increase export earnings was a matter for serious concern. However, the economy as a whole showed an improvement over its performance in 1984. Agriculture, in particular, showed a growth of 9·9 per cent after a 6·1 per cent decline in the previous year. The improved performance was due mainly to a bumper cotton crop, more than double the 1984 figure. Wheat yield was up by 8·3 per cent, while industrial production rose by 8·1 per cent. But the State Bank drew attention to the large deficit on the balance of payments, due mainly to reduced exports and smaller remittances from Pakistani workers abroad, many having returned home from the Middle East. Foreign-exchange reserves declined, largely for the same reasons.

The Rs.25,000 million Pakistan Steel Mill, the nation's largest industrial venture, was inaugurated on 15 January. It had been set up with the Soviet Union's help. It was expected to contribute Rs.20,000 million annually to the national income when in full production and save Rs.21,000 million in foreign exchange every year.

BANGLADESH

On 1 March President Lieut.-General H. M. Ershad banned political activities and strikes, cancelled his earlier announced plans for parliamentary elections to be held on 6 April, and said that instead a referendum would be held on 21 March to seek support for his continued rule, pending future general elections. At the same time Ershad, who also held the post of chief martial-law administrator, revived the offices of martial-law administrators at all levels of government, and for the conduct of summary and special military courts, while ordering the firm application of all martial-law provisions. Ershad said: 'Relaxation or withdrawal of martial law will depend on the creation of the necessary atmosphere and situation.'

These moves came after more than a year of bitter wrangling between the President and the main opposition parties over how best to return the country to civilian rule. This had been Ershad's avowed aim ever since he seized power in a bloodless coup on 24 March 1982 (see AR 1982, p. 276).

There was much sporadic political unrest and protest from within the universities, especially in Dhaka, against the government. In late July, for instance, hundreds of students demonstrated at Dhaka University, demanding free political activity, the release of detained politicians and autonomy for Bangladesh's six universities. In the early hours of 12 September, in an effort to rid the campus of illegal weapons held by members of various student bodies, 2,500 policemen, accompanied by a group of university teachers, undertook a five-hour-long search of three of the eleven large student dormitories, which each accommodated about 500–600 men. In mid-August more than 15,000 lawyers boycotted courts in protest against bomb blasts which had injured 25 people attending a murder trial.

It was a year of considerable foreign travel for President Ershad. He paid state visits to South Korea and Japan (14–23 June) and to China (4–9 July). The latter visit, which had been scheduled to begin on 29 May, had been postponed after cyclonic storms and serious tidal flooding had devastated large coastal areas of Bangladesh. In September and October the President travelled extensively, visiting Jeddah, attending the Commonwealth heads of government meeting in Nassau and addressing the UN General Assembly in New York during its 40th anniversary celebrations. During his stay in Jeddah, President Ershad had bilateral discussions, *inter alia*, with the Malaysian Prime Minister, Dr Mahathir Mohamad (who, he proposed, should head a peace mission to Iran and Iraq on behalf of the Organization of the Islamic Conference), with President Zia-ul-Haq of Pakistan and with Yassir Arafat, chairman of the PLO.

In undoubtedly the highlight of Bangladesh's foreign relations in 1985, the new regional grouping of seven countries—India, Pakistan, Bangladesh, Nepal, Sri Lanka, Bhutan and the Maldives—the South Asian Association for Regional Cooperation (SAARC), was endowed with a Charter of ten articles at its first summit meeting of heads of state and government, held in Dhaka on 7–8 December. They also adopted what they dubbed as the 'Dhaka Declaration'. The idea of the grouping was first mooted by President Ziaur Rahman of Bangladesh in 1980 (see AR 1980, p. 282) and it had taken five years of careful and cautious negotiations, including a drafting session for the Charter at Thimpu in Bhutan in July 1985, to prepare for this Dhaka summit. The heads of state or government agreed that SAARC's standing committee should set up a study group to examine the problem of terrorism and to make practical recommendations. They also directed that a similar exercise be carried out with regard to the problem of drug trafficking and abuse. They agreed that they should concert their views on the 'new international economic order' and the improvement of the world trading system through GATT, paying particular heed to the interests of the least developed among the developing countries. They also decided that SAARC should have a secretariat, and directed their Foreign Ministers to consider details regarding its location, structure, functions and financing, and submit proposals for consideration at its next annual summit meeting, to be held in India in November 1986.

Bangladesh and Burma formally agreed on 12 August to a map of their common 123-mile border, prepared jointly by their respective survey departments. This completed the demarcation work on their common boundary—stretching from the southern end of the Naaf river to the junction of the Bangladesh–Burma–India boundaries—started under an agreement signed in May 1979.

On several occasions President Ershad gave public warnings of the impending danger of a population explosion in the country. In a speech in mid-June he said that if the present trend of growth continued unabated the country's population would be 150 million by the end of the present century.

SRI LANKA

The affairs of Sri Lanka continued to be dominated by the armed struggle of Tamil separatists and by the attempts of the Indian Government to resolve the situation. While some progress was made, emergency regulations lasted throughout the year and there was a considerable exodus of Tamils, mainly to South India. These came largely from the 'prohibited zone' in the north (see AR 1984, p. 282) where the fishing industry had been virtually destroyed. By April 20,000 refugees had gone to India and this increased to an estimated 50,000 by the end of the year.

In January the Catholic bishops of Chilaw and Mannar protested against the killing of the parish priest of Vankalai, Father Mary Bastian, although the Government claimed that he had not been killed during an army attack on his church and his body was never produced. On 19 January a train from Kilinochchi to Colombo was blown up with the loss of 38 lives, mainly soldiers. Serious rioting between Tamils and Muslims broke out in the Eastern Province and in Mannar on 16 April. Violence escalated with the deaths of 75 at the hands of the military at Valvettithurai, for which the Sri Lanka Government denied knowledge or responsibility. Most deaths recorded were of Tamil civilians but on 14 May nearly one hundred Sinhalese, including Buddhist monks, were massacred at the bus station in the holy Buddhist city of Anuradhapura. This action, which could have sparked off massive Sinhalese reaction, was repudiated by all the major Tamil separatist groups.

The deteriorating situation caused India once more to attempt a reconciliation. The Indian Foreign Secretary, Romesh Bhandari, visited Sri Lanka on 7 April and again on 8 August to discuss the problem with leaders of the Government and Opposition. On 23 April the Chief Minister of Tamil Nadu, M. G. Ramachandran, led an all-party delegation to Prime Minister Rajiv Gandhi which urged him to 'take all steps' to secure Tamil rights in Sri Lanka. Meanwhile negotiations with the separatists had been made easier by the agreement of four major groups on 10

April to form a united Eelam National Liberation Front (ENLF). One major group, the People's Liberation Organization of Thamileelam (PLOT), did not join, but the fragmentation which had made the terrorists so elusive and unpredictable was diminished. After a meeting between President J. R. Jayawardene and Mr Rajiv Gandhi on 1 June, a ceasefire was arranged between the Sri Lanka Government and the Tamil groups and a conference arranged at Thimpu in Bhutan which began on 8 July and was reconvened on 12 August. This was attended by the main parliamentary group, the Tamil United Liberation Front (TULF), the newly-united ENLF and PLOT.

As at the conferences arranged at Indian insistence in 1984 (see AR 1984, p. 281), these conferences broke down upon the refusal of the Government to accept the possibility of secession, and of the separatists to abandon their claim for recognition of the Tamils as a distinct nation with the right to self-determination. The immediate cause of the collapse was news that two hundred Tamils had been killed at Vavuniya on 16 August, confirming fears that the Sri Lanka armed forces were not effectively under control and were continuing to persecute civilians. The main opposition party, the Sri Lanka Freedom Party (SLFP) of Sirimavo Bandaranaike, was also exerting pressure against talks and recruiting support among the Buddhist clergy. Indian annoyance at the collapse of its initiative was evident from the deportation orders against ENLF leaders, though there was some hesitation about this and some of those deported were allowed to return to India in October.

Despite the collapse of the talks Indian pressure continued to be exerted, and on the initiative of Bhandari a ceasefire monitoring committee was set up on 10 October, consisting of six Sinhalese, three Tamils and two Muslims. Its duties were to inspect breaches of the ceasefire and the conditions of those in detention. By October an estimated 41,000 people were living in refugee camps in the Northern and Eastern Provinces, but their fate was not a responsibility of the new committee. Continued fragmentation among the separatists and the intrusion of criminal elements into the disordered situation were held responsible for the murder of two former TULF parliamentarians, V. Dharmalingam and A. M. Alalasunderam, in Jaffna on 3 September.

President Jayawardene and his party continued secure in the Sinhalese south, winning a by-election at Mulkirigala on 12 September. The President attended the Commonwealth heads of government meeting at Nassau in October and the inaugural conference of the South Asian Association for Regional Cooperation at Dhaka on 7 December. Mrs Margaret Thatcher visited Sri Lanka in April to open the Victoria project of the Mahaweli irrigation scheme.

NEPAL

There was intermittent evidence of much feverishness in the conduct of Nepal's political and economic affairs during the year. The Government, with Mr Lokendra Bahadur Chand as Prime Minister, which had been formed in July 1983 (see AR 1983, p. 270), had been subject to major reshuffles in September 1984 and minor ones in late 1983 and again in April 1984. During 1985 it underwent another major reshuffle in mid-May and a smaller one in July.

In spite of the official ban on political parties (introduced in January 1961, when the panchayat system of government was formally launched, and reaffirmed in the May 1980 referendum when the reintroduction of a multiparty system was narrowly rejected), the Nepali Congress held a national convention in Kathmandu from 11 to 13 March which was attended by about 1,200 party workers and delegates—the first such plenary meeting since December 1982. In his opening address the President, Mr Krishna Prasad Bhattarai, stressed support for the monarchy, describing it as an essential political institution in maintaining 'national integrity and unity'.

Most shops were closed in the capital, Kathmandu, and other parts of the country on 19 May during a general strike called by the left-wing All Nepal Free Students' Association in support of teachers who were demanding an increase in pay and official recognition of their trade union.

The Nepali Congress launched a civil disobedience movement, a satyagraha, on 23 May in order to press demands for the revival of a multiparty system of government, the release of all political prisoners and more effective economic management. This campaign was called off, however, on 21 June after a series of explosions, strongly condemned by the Nepali Congress, in Kathmandu and other parts of the country. The Prime Minister announced on 8 July that 1,400 people had been arrested in connection with the explosions. A letter from Mr Rajiv Gandhi, India's Prime Minister, was delivered by his special envoy to King Birendra on 5 July assuring him that India was committed to cooperating with all countries in curbing 'the growing menace of terrorism'. This followed reports that those suspected of being responsible for the series of explosions in Nepal in June were based in India.

A meeting of the Indo-Nepal Inter-Governmental Committee in Kathmandu on 15 January agreed to set up a joint inspection team to patrol their 1,000 km common border in order to control unauthorized trade. The head official of India's Ministry of External Affairs, Mr Romesh Bhandari, had talks with his Nepalese counterpart, Mr Bishwa Pradhan, in Kathmandu on 1 April, especially on setting up a joint commission for economic relations and on ways to increase cooperation in banking, commerce, trade and the development of water resources. In the financial year 1984-85 India's aid to Nepal was 180 million Indian rupees and was used for 21 development projects.

Mr Bill Hayden, Australia's Foreign Minister, said in Kathmandu on 12 May, at the end of a three-day visit, that Australia endorsed King Birendra's proposal for a zone of peace in the region.

The Government invited foreign oil companies to bid for exploration tracts in the southern lowland sub-tropical region of the country. Bidding for ten exploration leases, of about 5000 sq. km. each, began on 9 April and closed on 15 October.

King Birendra Bikram Shah attended the first two-day summit of the South Asian Association for Regional Cooperation (SAARC) in Dhaka in mid December (see p. 272) and offered Kathmandu as the site for the permanent secretariat, Dhaka being the chief alternative base.

Chapter 3

SEYCHELLES—MAURITIUS—MALAGASY—COMORO STATE

SEYCHELLES

FOR much of 1985 the René Government focused on the needs of the economy and the requirements of internal security. It was not until the end of the year that Seychelles briefly regained its former prominent international profile.

Early in the year Western reports indicated growing opposition to the left-wing Government. This issue had already been raised by Bishop Felix Paul of the Seychelles when he argued that President René had the support of not more than 30 per cent of the people. In February a report in the London *Sunday Times* gave a colourful account of the internal and exiled opposition and the President's security and intelligence service, designed to foil potential coup-makers.

The release of Colonel 'Mad Mike' Hoare from a South African gaol provided a momentary reminder of the coup attempt against President René in 1981 (see AR 1981, pp. 282-3). Likewise the mystery surrounding the murder of the Seychelles resistance leader, Gerard Hoareau, on 29 November in London rekindled international interest in the Seychelles political scene and generated much speculation about the overseas intelligence activities of the René Government.

The security-consciousness of the Government remained much in evidence. North Korean troops, imported to protect the President, continued to provide essential security assistance (see AR 1984, p. 285), as did the Soviet advisers reported to be supervising the installation of ground-to-air missiles at the international airport. The Seychelles' strategically sensitive location ensured that the domestic fortunes of the René

Government attracted the attention of the superpowers and their allies and clients, and helped explain the presence of members of various foreign intelligence services in the islands.

The wider strategic and ideological contest being conducted in the Indian Ocean was also reflected in the sources of aid to the Seychelles Government. For the fourth consecutive year Seychelles received aid from the United States, including $2 million to buy fuel for electricity production. Two agreements were signed with France for loans to finance agricultural development and phosphate exploitation, in addition to credit provided by the French Central Fund for Economic Cooperation to the Seychelles Development Bank. Victoria was already in receipt of an Arab loan for a fisheries project (see AR 1984, p. 285).

The economy proved to be the Government's second major preoccupation. It was reported in February that the 1985–89 five-year plan envisaged a total investment of $380·5 million. The plan aimed to create 11,000 jobs, improve the balance of payments, re-establish the 7 per cent annual growth in GDP recorded in the late 1970s and increase exports. The emphasis on the productive sector, which took 40 per cent of the total investment, was regarded as the main innovation.

The Government looked to tourism (its main source of foreign currency), fishing and cash crops to boost its foreign exchange revenue. In particular, an anticipated rise of more than 50 per cent in the number of tourists, from 64,000 in 1984 to 100,000 in 1989, required spending some $46·5 million on tourism projects, including accommodation and the national airline's long- and short-haul fleets. In line with the projected expansion, Air Seychelles inaugurated its second link with Europe in July and indicated a future link with the Far East, to reach the Japanese market. The importance of Africa for the Seychelles tourist industry was highlighted in September when the Seychelles tourist office opened a regional office in Nairobi.

This surge in support for tourism underlined the difficulties faced by the Government in its attempt to diversify the economy. Tourism, like Western aid, was seen to be necessary, but it was also increasingly lucrative. In its review for the final quarter of 1984 the Seychelles Central Bank reported a rise of 21 per cent over the previous year in earnings from tourism.

Fishing, accounting for 3 per cent of GNP, received an investment of $29·3 million in the hope that production would more than treble by 1989 and rise still further once the Victoria port and fisheries project was completed. The five-year plan also allocated $30 million for agriculture. However, it was clear that the Government would be heavily dependent on foreign aid to finance its five-year plan: hence the one-party socialist state's need to attract foreign investment.

President René referred specifically to the problems of the economy when he opened the sixteenth annual congress of the Progressive Front of the Seychelles People (SPPF) in Victoria on 27 September. He called for self-sufficiency in food, a reduction in unemployment, more professional training and housing. The President acknowledged the improvement in the living standard of Seychellois since his Government came to power, but insisted there was a need for greater mobilization among the people, and argued that 'the rights of the majority came before the rights of the individual'.

MAURITIUS

Political stability and signs of an up-turn in the economy allowed Mauritius to widen its international horizons during 1985 as the Government of Prime Minister Aneerood Jugnauth continued to consolidate its position.

In his review of the economy prior to the June Budget, Finance Minister Vishnu Lutchmeenaraidoo warned that the problem of debt servicing and the balance of payments deficit would continue to constrain the economic recovery. This had begun in 1984 with a real growth rate of 4·2 per cent in GDP (compared with 0·3 per cent in 1983), which reflected considerable expansion in the export and tourism sectors. The Budget on 28 June reinforced the Government's free-market approach to the economy and underlined the commitment to adhere to IMF guidelines determining conditions for a $49 million loan to Mauritius. Although the Budget was generally well-received, it was not thought likely to counter the high rate of youth unemployment.

Efforts to diversify the vulnerable and largely monocrop economy raised problems for the agricultural sector. The 1984–86 development plan published in March contained proposals for financial and other incentives for industry, whereas agriculture faced heavy taxation. However, in an attempt to prevent further decline in agriculture the Government produced in March a Sugar Action Plan designed to restructure and modernize the sugar industry, improving its productivity and profitability and encouraging diversification into other crops as the sugar acreage was gradually reduced. There were also plans to use the residue of sugar cane (bagasse) to generate electricity. The Government also found an opportunity to dispose of the 1984 bumper tea harvest on the world market at the highest prices since the 1970s.

The agricultural diversification programme was matched by similar programmes in manufacturing (notably textiles) and tourism, respectively the second and third largest foreign exchange earners after sugar.

The operation of direct flights by the national airline, Air Maurice, between Mauritius and Paris in July, to accommodate the projected increase in the tourist trade, followed hard on the heels of the announcement in April of plans for a new five-star hotel complex financed by the

Government and the Sun Resorts Company. As the potential 'Hong Kong of the Indian Ocean', Mauritius sought to promote itself as the African gateway to the Middle East, Europe and the Far East, in addition to offering tax incentives to attract international capital. In an attempt to shake off its dependence on sugar the Government embarked on a major investment drive involving bilateral agreements with European governments and a more aggressive marketing effort to reduce its trade deficit with South Africa, while simultaneously attracting South African businessmen and tourists.

The Government pursued a pragmatic and generally pro-Western foreign policy. Within this framework it sought to diversify its foreign relationships. It accepted economic aid from India, China and France while exploiting commercial links with Pretoria. Although it remained sensitive to superpower machinations in the Indian Ocean, particularly activities on Diego Garcia, this was no longer a priority. Instead, the Jugnauth Government concentrated on actively promoting and consolidating its regional relationships, while using outside powers, notably France, as a bulwark.

In January, the Indian Ocean Commission, which had been established in 1982 to promote regional cooperation between Malagasy, Mauritius and Seychelles, admitted the Comoro Islands as its fourth member. Subsequently, diplomatic relations were established between Mauritius and the Comoros. The growing political and economic enmeshment of the Indian Ocean island states was accelerated in October when the Deputy Prime Minister, Sir Gaetan Duval, in the wake of a preferential tariff agreement between Mauritius and Malagasy, led an important economic and commercial delegation to Antananarivo. The mission encouraged Mauritian Government hopes of a 500 per cent increase in trade with Malagasy and raised the possibility of that country's eventually replacing South Africa as a major trading partner.

The announcement in May of the removal, for an experimental six-month period, of the visa requirement for Mauritians travelling to Réunion, together with a declaration of French support for Mauritian development programmes, underlined the growing importance of the French connection for the Government in Port Louis.

The death in December of Sir Seewoosagur Ramgoolam, the island's Governor-General who was regarded as the 'father' of independent Mauritius, marked the end of an era in Mauritian politics (see OBITUARY).

MALAGASY

The political life of the 'great island' was increasingly disturbed by the bizarre phenomenon of 'kung-fu' clubs, which had become a focal point for opposition among young people. More than 100 members of an unpopular youth movement Tanora Tonga, linked to the ruling party, were killed in a confrontation in December 1984, and the subsequent rapid growth of the kung-fu clubs led to an army assault on a 6,500 strong kung-fu headquarters at the end of July, destroying the building and leaving a heavy death toll. The row led to an increase in the unpopularity of the regime of President Ratsiraka in the capital Antananarivo, and heightened tension with teachers, students, the trade unions and the church. These problems came on top of a difficult economic situation, with austerity still prevalent, although the IMF was said to regard Malagasy as one of its African success stories.

COMORO STATE

Evidence mounted during the year that the political situation of President Ahmed Abdallah, in power since a coup d'état organized by mercenaries in 1978, was growing more and more troubled. In March a reported army mutiny appeared to have led to a political ascendancy of the mercenaries who were still said to keep the President in power. Described by President Abdallah as 'a well-planned operation intended to transform the country through revolution and abolish religion', it led to a major trial of 68 people, of whom 17 were sentenced to forced labour for life in November. Amnesty International charged that arrested members of the presidential guard had been tortured, some of them to death. An opposition group in Paris described the trial as a 'masquerade' and there were frequent stories of rivalry between different mercenary groups, notably between Colonal Bob Denard, who engineered the 1978 coup, and Commandant 'Charles', field commander of the mercenaries, who was reported to be really Roger Ghys, an insurance clerk from Liège. In this atmosphere President Abdallah extensively restructured his Government in August, but he was reported to be more and more isolated.

IX SOUTH-EAST AND EAST ASIA

Chapter 1

BURMA—THAILAND—MALAYSIA—BRUNEI—SINGAPORE—INDONESIA—
PHILIPPINES—VIETNAM—KAMPUCHEA—LAOS

BURMA

In August the fifth congress of the Burma Socialist Programme Party (BSPP) re-elected Ne Win as chairman, Aye Ko as general secretary and Sein Lwin as joint general secretary. San Yu, Ne Win's chosen successor, was elected to the new post of vice-chairman. All four were former generals and there was no sign that the disciplined regime run by Ne Win since 1962 would relax its grip on power or its austere economic policies. Elections to new national and local assemblies were held on 6 October with candidates only from the BSPP, and in November the national People's Assembly re-elected San Yu as President and elected Aye Ko to the new post of Vice-President.

The Chinese President paid a state visit to Burma in March. In May Ne Win visited China as BSPP chairman, having always previously done so in a state capacity. This suggested that the Communist Party of China recognised the BSPP as a fraternal party, reflecting the improved relations between the two countries and the withdrawal of Chinese aid to the Burmese Communist Party (BCP). Both China and Bangladesh engaged with Burma in demarcation work on their common boundaries. Loss of Chinese support diverted BCP activity from insurgency to securing income and supplies from opium trading and possibly from Vietnam. This enabled the Burmese army to concentrate on a sustained offensive against the Karen guerrillas along the eastern border and led to severe fighting, army attacks on Karen villages behind their lines and retaliatory Karen attacks on the railways, while obstructing the flow of smuggled necessities to the domestic market.

The fifth four-year plan proposed an annual growth rate of 6 per cent, which seemed optimistic in the light of declining rice export earnings, slender foreign reserves, rising foreign debt and a very high debt-service ratio. The economic impetus provided since 1977 by improved rice strains having diminished, continued efforts were made to extend the range and yields of other crops, using similar breeding and cultivation methods. These efforts were, however, restricted by limited supplies of fertilizer, pesticides, machinery and fuel and by transport and storage difficulties. Development proposals concentrated on fertilizer production and power and port facilities; and, where the techniques or capital required were beyond Burmese resources, joint ventures were permitted with foreign concerns to develop natural resources, such as the Gulf of Martaban natural gas discoveries.

THAILAND

Incursions by Vietnamese troops fighting the Khmer resistance increased, causing casualties among both Thai civilians and troops and a renewed influx of Khmer refugees. Thai defensive action against these incursions involved at times use of heavy weapons and aircraft.

China reaffirmed support for Thailand, and the Chinese President and deputy chief of general staff visited Bangkok in March and the Chinese Foreign Minister in December. The Prime Minister, Prem Tinsulanond, visited Indonesia, the USA and Western Europe in September and was visited by the Singapore Prime Minister in June. There were visits and approaches by USSR Ministers and officials seeking a greater Soviet presence in Thailand, but no response to a Thai request that the USSR should reduce military aid to Vietnam. In December the Thais avoided a visit to Bangkok by a Soviet Deputy Premier. The US Secretary of State visited Bangkok in July and spoke of building up the Thai capacity to deter attack, US annual military aid to Thailand having already trebled over the previous four years. The US permitted the sale to Thailand of advanced jet fighters, helped up-grade existing Thai air force fighters and in October agreed on cooperation to permit rapid arms supply in an emergency.

The USA briefly banned Thai textile imports in October because quotas had been exceeded, causing especial concern because markets and prices for more traditional Thai exports such as rice, tapioca and maize were so weak that tourism had displaced rice as the largest foreign exchange earner, with remittances from Thais working abroad in third place. Thailand nevertheless achieved increased export volume, an improving trend in export earnings and a further reduction in the visible trade deficit, helped by rising local production of natural gas and oil. In December the baht was slightly devalued to stimulate exports and reduce capital outflows. GDP real growth fell to 4.4 per cent from 6 per cent in 1984. Price indices, which barely moved in 1984, rose by 3 per cent. The Government proposed to reduce heavy deficits arising from uncoordinated investment by state-run corporations, some of which were to be privatized, while strengthening control of private banking and making pyramid funds illegal.

The budget for the fiscal year starting in October provided for a rise in nominal expenditure of around 4 per cent over 1984-85. Reduced investment in the state sector increased high unemployment amongst people with tertiary education, most of whom worked in state institutions. The Cabinet did allow the eastern seaboard development of gas-based heavy industries and related industrial and commercial seaports to proceed, although private financing was not assured, but abandoned the Asean joint project to make soda ash from rock salt and did not sanction heavy investment to improve the Bangkok bus service. A scheme to support farm prices for rice came under sharp criticism.

Economic malaise was the excuse given for another attempted military coup in September. The middle-rank leaders of the coup expected support from senior officers which was not forthcoming and the attempt rapidly collapsed with some loss of life. The government reaction was unexpectedly severe and 40 people of standing, both civilian and military, were subsequently charged. This failure, and cases of senior officers taking early retirement to enter politics, suggested that support for electoral democracy was becoming more firmly established. In a May by-election the successful Democrat Party candidate was a retired admiral and his leading opponent a retired general. In a December by-election the leading contenders were both retired generals, the Democrat candidate again winning; in this two-member constituency and in two earlier by-elections civilian Democrat candidates also won seats. Democrats won 35 of the 54 seats in the Bangkok city council elections, but an independent, who resigned from the army to stand for election two days after being promoted major-general, won the governorship of Bangkok.

MALAYSIA

In January, the report of an inquiry into the affairs of Bank Bumiputera's Hong Kong subsidiary Bumiputera Malaysia Finance provided a detailed account of the biggest financial scandal in Malaysia's history. It charged six former executives with corruption. In December, Lorraine Osman, former Bumiputera Malaysia Finance chairman, and Mohammed Shamusdin, a former director, were arrested in London on Hong Kong extradition warrants, charged with conspiring to defraud the bank between 1979 and 1983.

On 19 November, police were ambushed while seeking to arrest an Islamic teacher in Kampung Memali near Baling in the state of Kedah. Ibrahim Mohammed had been an official and parliamentary candidate of Parti Islam and had refused to surrender to an arrest warrant under the Internal Security Act issued in September 1984. In an armed confrontation which went on for five hours 18 people were killed, including Ibrahim Mohammed and four policemen. Prime Minister Dr Mahathir Mohamad claimed that 37 wanted men had concentrated in Ibrahim Mohammad's house at the time of the incident. A ban on political gatherings in six states was lifted one month later.

After a political struggle lasting nearly two years, the leadership of the Malayan Chinese Association was decided on 24 November. Delegates to a special conference voted overwhelmingly to remove acting-President Neo Yee Pan in favour of the self-made millionaire Tan Koon Swan. Tan's political standing was diminished in early December when Malaysia's stock exchange closed temporarily in response to the closure of its Singapore counterpart. The Singapore closure had been precipitated by the failure of Pan-Electric Industries in which companies controlled by Tan Koon Swan had major holdings. When Malaysia's stock exchange reopened, three companies controlled by Tan were suspended from trading.

In December, two Australians convicted in July of trafficking in heroin in Penang and sentenced in August to death had their appeals rejected. They were the first caucasians to be tried under an amended Act which made the death penalty mandatory on conviction of possession of 15 grammes or more of heroin or morphine.

In April, state assembly elections in Sabah were won by Parti Bersatu Sabah (PBS) which had been established only some seven weeks previously. It secured 25 out of 48 seats, while the ruling Parti Berjaya won only 6 seats, three of which were lost almost immediately by defection. The leader of PBS, Datuk Joseph Pairin Kitingan, had to wait for twelve hours to be sworn in as chief minister, because a previous incumbent, Tun Mustapha Harun, whose United Sabah National Organization won 16 seats, had persuaded the head of state that the constitution permitted him to nominate sufficient members of the state assembly to command a majority. Datuk Kitingan was sworn in after the Federal Government had indicated that the decision of the electorate should stand.

In September, a daring robbery by some twenty armed Filipinos was committed on a branch of the Standard Chartered Bank in Lahad Datu in Sabah. In early October, a Philippine marine general alleged that four Malaysian gunboats and three helicopter gunships had raided the island of Maddanas in the southern Philippines in an act of reprisal.

In April, Mrs Thatcher paid the first official visit to Malaysia by a British Prime Minister. She reached agreement with Dr Mahathir on a long-running dispute over a demand by Malaysia's national airline to operate a fifth weekly flight between Kuala Lumpur and London. An air services agreement was signed in August.

BRUNEI

In January, the Sultan of Brunei bought the Dorchester Hotel in London's Park Lane. The successful takeover bid for House of Fraser, the Harrod's stores group, in March by Alfayed Investment and Trust SA was linked in the British press with financing from the Sultan of Brunei.

On 30 May, the Brunei National Democratic Party was registered in Bandar Seri Begawan. It was the first political party to be formed since an abortive rebellion in December 1962. Its secretary-general, Abdul Latif Chuchu, described its aims as promoting democracy and constitutional monarchy. An initial membership of 1,500 was drawn mainly from the Malay business community. Undoubtedly established with royal approval, the new party gave the impression of being more directly concerned with economic than with political matters.

SINGAPORE

On 7 March President Devan Nair resigned from office after admitting that he was an alcoholic and could no longer discharge the responsibilities of head of state. Chief Justice Wee Chong Jin became Acting President. On 3 September, after a unanimous parliamentary vote, Wee Kim Wee, a former diplomat and chairman of the Singapore Broadcasting Corporation, was sworn in as the Republic's fourth President and its first ethnic-Chinese head of state. In September Devan Nair refused a state pension approved by Parliament on condition that he continued to receive and abide by medical treatment for alcoholism, because, he said, it amounted to financial coercion.

In his traditional May Day message Prime Minister Lee maintained that the city-state was not in any danger of imminent financial collapse. He indicated, however, a future marked by greater austerity. His projection that Singapore's economy could still record a growth rate of between 5 and 7 per cent was soon disproved. Official figures for the first quarter showed annual growth of only 3 per cent, the lowest increase since 1974. Revised figures for the second quarter announced by Prime Minister Lee in August showed that growth had fallen to minus 1·4 per cent through a major decline in construction and manufacturing, especially in oil refining, in shipbuilding and repair and in electronics.

By the end of the year the growth rate had sunk to minus 2 per cent, while business confidence in the Republic as a financial services centre was shaken by a three-day closure of the Singapore stock exchange at the beginning of December. The decision to close the stock exchange was taken to avoid panic selling after Pan-Electric Industries had been placed in receivership on the initiative of a consortium of banks to whom it owed some $120 million, in part as a consequence of forward share trading. When the stock exchange reopened the Monetary Authority of Singapore imposed new rules which forbade forward trading. In response to the economic downturn, the Government relaxed its tax regime and acted to restrain wage increases. Responsibility for longer-term economic reforms was entrusted to a committee chaired by the Minister of State for Trade and Industry, Lee Hsien Loong.

In March, Faber House in Singapore's main thoroughfare, Orchard Road, which housed the Israeli embassy, was badly damaged by a bomb explosion. In September, B. J. Jeyaretnam, the secretary-general of the Workers' Party and leading parliamentary critic of the Government, together with party chairman Wong Hong Toy, were sentenced to three months' imprisonment upon conviction of making false statutory declarations. They were released on bail after giving notice of appeal. They had been acquitted on the same charge in January 1984, but on appeal by the prosecution the Chief Justice had ordered a retrial. In December staff of the *Asian Wall Street Journal* were fined for contempt of court for an editorial on the conviction.

Prime Minister Lee visited China in September primarily to promote trade and business in Singapore. At the end of his two-week tour he warned against becoming too dependent on China, which despite its open-door policy was still communist. In October, he visited the United States, where he made a strong appeal to a joint session of Congress not to pass protectionist legislation.

INDONESIA

Official efforts to depoliticize Islam, to weaken the hitherto purely Muslim PPP (United Development Party) and to bring religious, professional and cultural, as well as political, organizations under control by obliging them to adopt the state ideology, Pancasila, might have achieved the second and third of these purposes, but they also aroused resentment amongst Muslims. Some mosques became centres of radical fundamentalism, and sporadic bombing and arson attacks on state property and Indonesian Chinese businesses were attributed to committed Muslims.

Several distinguished people connected with the critical Petition of 50 group, including retired Ministers and generals, were charged with offences connected with bombings and a 1984 riot in Tanjong Priok. Alleged offences included helping with publication of a White Paper which disputed the account given of the riot by the security forces and preaching inflammatory sermons. These trials enabled defendants and witnesses publicly to criticise the security forces for their actions in the Tanjong Priok riot and the regime for discarding its original principles. Several defendants, including two Muslim preachers, received gaol sentences of 14 to 20 years and similar sentences seemed likely for other defendants. In May and July four men, sentenced to death ten years earlier for trying to revive the the Communist Party, were executed, and the Security Command subsequently required the dismissal, by oil and other concerns, of several thousand employees said to have former connections with communist trade unions.

The fortieth anniversary of the armed forces and the retirement of almost all the officers of the founding generation were celebrated during the year, while structural changes were introduced to strengthen central control and coordination of the armed forces and to reduce the number of commands. An even more sweeping reform dealt decisively with the damagingly corrupt and inefficient ports and customs services. All Indonesian international ports were thrown open to foreign shipping, port fees were rationalized and most customs inspections were to be done in foreign ports of origin or destination by a Swiss private contractor, while over 6,000 customs officials were sent on indefinite paid leave on 1 May. Increased port efficiency was subsequently reported.

Customs reform supported efforts to lessen dependence on oil and import-substitute industries by stimulating non-oil exports and to improve the balance of regional development. Development expenditure was devoted primarily to education, agriculture, energy and communications, including modernizing ports to improve productivity. Economic growth in 1984 had risen slightly to 4·5 per cent, but was well below average growth in the 15 years before 1982. It slipped back in 1985 to 3·5 per cent or less, with a prospect of further decline as world demand for crude oil and other mining and agricultural export products weakened. The annual inflation rate dropped late in 1984 to below 5 per cent, from almost 10 per cent for the previous three years, and this was maintained. Improvements in the current account balance and the level of international reserves were helped by a rise of one-third in natural-gas export earnings and the success of agricultural improvement schemes; over the previous few years these had turned food deficits requiring heavy rice imports into surpluses which by 1985 had become embarrassing. The current account deficit halved in 1984–85, but subsequently rose again as export earnings fell back.

In April Indonesia celebrated the thirtieth anniversary of the 'Asia-Africa Conference' with a two-day meeting in Bandung attended by 80 delegations. The declaration concentrated more on economic development and less on new political ideas than the original Bandung declaration, but, as in 1955, the presence of a Chinese delegation attracted major attention, partly because of speculation that it might lead to resumption of diplomatic relations between Indonesia and China which had been suspended in the aftermath of the 1965 coup attempt. The debate on this issue within the Government persisted, but in May permission was given for a visit, in July, to China by businessmen organized by Kadin, the Indonesian Chamber of Commerce and Industry; it had been preceded by an agreement, signed in Singapore, between Kadin and its Chinese counterpart for a resumption of direct trade. On the governmental level relations with Papua New Guinea, Malaysia, Australia and the United Kingdom were improved, and a Soviet Deputy Premier visited Jakarta in October. Indonesia also pursued a dialogue with Vietnam on behalf of Asean, taking a rather stiffer line than in 1984.

PHILIPPINES

The murder of Benigno Aquino in 1983 and the popular reaction to it greatly weakened the ability of President Marcos to deter or suppress opposition. The press and radio, in which criticism had been stifled since 1972, recovered its nerve, despite frequent murders of critical journalists. Businessmen became openly resentful of the damaging effects of mono-polistic 'crony capitalism', while army officers expressed support for reform.

The conclusion of the board of inquiry headed by Mrs Corazon Agrava that Aquino had been the victim of an armed forces conspiracy achieved general acceptance, which was not shaken by the acquittal, by a special court appointed by Marcos, of General Ver, 24 other soldiers and a civilian and the immediate reinstatement of Ver as chief of staff. A petition, whose signatories included former Supreme Court judges, spoke of 'serious irregularities in the proceedings and the manifest bias and partiality' of the three judges. The acquittal was also sharply criti-cised by Cardinal Sin, while a US State Department spokesman said that 'it is very difficult to reconcile the exemplary, thorough work of the Agrava board and the conclusions it reached after a year of hard work with the outcome of the trial' or to see how the reinstatement of Ver 'squares with Marcos' professed desire to initiate serious reforms'. There was talk of Ver's becoming chairman of the board to reorganize the army, but Marcos evidently wanted him in command until after the elections.

Marcos came under increasingly open pressure from the US Admin-istration and Congress to make real, and not merely cosmetic, reforms in the army, the economy and the field of human rights. A stream of American officials and members of Congress urged Marcos to correct 'economic, social and political conditions which fuel insurgency' and a visit by Senator Laxalt, a close friend of President Reagan, indicated to both Marcos and the opposition that the US President, as well as his officials, thought changes essential. The USA also supported IMF efforts to secure compliance with the terms of a 1984 standby loan agreement, while the Church became increasingly critical, Cardinal Sin speaking of 'a well-orchestrated pattern of repression'. In August the opposition tabled an Assembly resolution to impeach Marcos for offences including trans-fer abroad by his family and supporters of huge sums of money—one American report spoke of US$650 million. The resolution was hastily dismissed by the Assembly's majority of Marcos' KBL supporters in order to avoid public debate, but the issue resurfaced in US courts and in a congressional sub-committee concerned with US aid.

In November Marcos called a snap presidential election to strengthen his position in the expectation of a divided and unprepared opposition.

On 11 December he announced his own candidacy, with Arturo Tolentino as a critical and independent vice-presidential candidate. The rival opposition candidates immediately united, Mrs Corazon Aquino standing for President and Mr Salvador Laurel for Vice-President. It subsequently seemed that, although Marcos controlled the state and electoral machinery and most of the media, and could rely on bribery and intimidation of voters and falsification of electoral registration, votes and returns, Mrs Aquino aroused sufficiently widespread popular support to present a formidable challenge.

GNP fell by 5·5 per cent in 1984 and about 4 per cent in 1985. Mining and agricultural exports suffered from low demand and prices, inefficient organization and earlier over-expansion. Ill-considered capital-intensive investments in heavy industry, tourist hotels and other developments over the previous decade proved uneconomic and weakened the banking system; over 40 per cent of the combined assets of the two largest government-owned banks were said to be 'non-performing'. The largest recent sources of foreign exchange, electronics assembly and remittances from 500,000 contract workers abroad, were affected respectively by over-supply and weak Middle Eastern oil income.

Inflation was over 50 per cent in 1984, due partly to the Assembly elections, and interest rates remained very high. During 1985 technocrat Ministers, on IMF advice, imposed a degree of austerity. Some of the large foreign debt was rescheduled. The balance of payments improved, with import expenditure dropping faster than export earnings, and the inflation rate halved. The budget concentrated on reducing the deficit, but there were large increases in provision for defence, because of growing insurgency, and for public works, a customary source of electoral funds. Little was done effectively to reform the coconut and sugar monopolies, and productive activity remained depressed. In consequence unemployment rose, the real incomes of most workers continued steadily to decline and there was an increase in strikes.

VIETNAM

Concern was aroused in Hanoi, following a successful visit to Beijing by a Soviet Vice-Premier, lest a Sino-Soviet rapprochement should intensify the isolation into which Vietnam had fallen as a result of the invasion of Kampuchea. This anxiety was heightened by the more amiable Chinese view of the USSR suggested by a statement by Deng Xiaoping in April and the cooler attitude towards Vietnam displayed by the Soviet leadership during a visit by Le Duan. A joint declaration on 30 June required Le Duan to approve normalization of Chinese relations with the USSR, a view that the Vietnamese party's press did not share. The USSR agreed to provide soft loans for a further five years and to reschedule

Hanoi's rouble debt, but this seemed minimal support and Vietnam had to undertake to 'make the greatest possible efforts to successfully fulfil its commitments for the delivery of goods to the USSR'. The Chinese, meanwhile, exerted continued pressure on Vietnam, through sporadic limited engagements along the northern border, reports of reinforcement of Chinese forces in the area and, in November, a refusal to resume trade with Vietnam. China did not, however, embark on a second major assault on Vietnam and each was a little less intransigent towards the other.

Faced with this situation and the acute need for Western assistance, Hanoi softened its approach to the USA, starting, in tune with an Indonesian suggestion, by becoming more forthcoming towards the American wish for a full accounting for Americans missing in action in the Indo-China war.

A slightly more realistic exchange rate of Dong 100 to US$1 was announced; the former official rate was 11·7 and the black market rate 350 to 400 to US$1. Internally the currency was redenominated at one new to 10 old Dong. For the first time since payment on some US$5,000 million of foreign debt was suspended in 1982 a debt-rescheduling agreement was concluded; this covered US$160 million of Japanese trade credits. It was reported that foreign firms were to be allowed to participate in the development of Vietnamese oil resources. After a visit by the Indian Prime Minister in November it was announced that three offshore blocks had been offered for exploration to the Indian Oil and Natural Gas Commission, while a Belgian oil company signed a joint-venture agreement for offshore exploration near Danang.

Poor management and, in 1985, an unusually severe typhoon kept food output below target levels and malnutrition remained a serious problem. The success of more liberal economic methods in Vietnam itself and the progress made by neighbouring countries pursuing more market-oriented policies, including China, persuaded a majority of the Communist Party at its plenum in June to extend economic reform. Bureaucratic centralism and planning by administrative order were to be replaced by 'socialist economic accounting and business', with economic return on capital as the guiding principle. Subsidies for loss-making enterprises and on food for state employees were to be ended and 'financial autonomy' was to be promoted, government concerns becoming individually responsible for profit and loss. Wages were to be linked to productivity and 'heavy egalitarianism' in wage-scales was to be abolished. In September Le Duan insisted that they 'must resolutely renovate economic management, get rid of red tape and the subsidy regime, changing completely to cost accounting and socialist business.' There were, however, leaders of the Party and the army who disapproved strongly of these departures from former ideological dogma.

KAMPUCHEA

After its embarrassing failure at Amphil in 1984 (see AR 1984, p. 299) the Vietnamese army committed much larger resources, including massed artillery, to a much earlier 1984-85 dry-season offensive than in previous years. It concentrated first on over-running the border camps run by the KPNLF, then those of Prince Sihanouk's ANS and finally Khmer Rouge camps and, when that was done, setting out, using conscripted Khmer civilian workers, to fortify and mine a defensive cordon along parts of the western frontier. Some 230,000 civilians from these border camps took refuge inside Thailand, while resistance forces were deployed elsewhere. There was stiff fighting, but guerrilla losses were not heavy. Resistance activity in the interior of Kampuchea, which the Vietnamese regarded as the crucial front, was maintained, especially by the Khmer Rouge and the ANS. The chief purpose of the offensive was to destroy the credibility of the resistance with Asean and the United Nations; the UN General Assembly, however, again increased the large majority supporting the resistance coalition.

The Foreign Minister, Hun Sen, succeeded Chan Sy as Prime Minister of the Heng Samrin regime in January and later there was a party reshuffle with an enlarged Central Committee. Heng Samrin himself was re-elected leader of the Party and expressed dissatisfaction with internal security and the performance of his regime's armed forces.

The Khmer Rouge tried to soften its image. It accepted in July that it might not be able to participate in a new national government and that the Heng Samrin regime was a legitimate partner in such a government. In September it announced that Pol Pot would retire, ostensibly on grounds of age, as commander of the Khmer Rouge and would be succeeded by the Defence Minister, Son Sen; this announcement was widely thought purely presentational. The ANS continued to build up guerrilla activity within Kampuchea, but the KPNLF was split by an internal dispute which prevented it from concentrating on more widespread guerrilla activity and also restricted the coordination of KPNLF and ANS activity.

LAOS

In a speech on 2 December the Party First Secretary and Prime Minister, Kaysone Phomvihane, stressed that unity between Laos, Vietnam, the Heng Samrin regime in Kampuchea and the USSR was the cornerstone of Lao foreign policy. He was, however, conciliatory towards China and Thailand, although a dispute over frontier demarcation between Laos and Thailand smouldered on, fanned it seemed by

Vietnam in order to prevent relations between the two countries becoming too friendly. The Laotians were also cooperative towards the American wish to search for US servicemen missing in action during the Indo-China war. The Laotian Foreign Minister and Vice-Foreign Minister both talked with State Department officials while in the USA. There seemed a prospect that the Americans might resume economic aid to Laos, and committees of both Houses of Congress recommended Bills permitting this.

There was renewed pressure for private producers to join in state-run cooperatives, but the economic structure remained only marginally socialist, less than a fifth of agricultural production being under state control; state farms were acknowledged to be a financial failure and there were denials that collectivization, having failed once, would be relaunched. The peasants produced enough rice to cover consumption, although distribution problems remained. Much the largest official export remained electricity to Thailand from the Nam Ngum hydro-electric plant, whose output was in the process of being increased from 120 to 150 megawatts.

Chapter 2

CHINA—TAIWAN—HONG KONG—JAPAN—SOUTH KOREA—NORTH KOREA

PEOPLE'S REPUBLIC OF CHINA

THE most significant events of the year occurred at three meetings held in September: the fourth plenary session (Plenum) of the 12th Central Committee of the Communist Party of China (CPC), the National Conference of CPC delegates and the fifth Plenum of the 12th Central Committee of the CPC. At the first, on 16 September, the agenda included the question of succession in leading CPC organizations and draft recommendations for the seventh five-year plan (FYP) 1986–70. It was reported that 131 veteran leaders had written to the Plenum requesting they be permitted to resign. As a result, 64 members of the CPC Central Committee, 37 members of the Central Advisory Commission and 30 members of the Central Commission for Discipline Inspection, including such eminences as Ye Jianying, Deng Yingchao, Xu Xiangqian, Nie Rongzhen, Ulanhu, Wang Zhen, Wei Guoqing, Li Desheng, Song Renqiong and Zhang Tingfa, departed at a stroke, widely interpreted as marking a success for Deng Xiaoping in his quest for reform of the system (since many doubting voices were removed) and rejuvenation of the leadership (since the successors were younger and better qualified).

The Plenum was followed on 18 September by the National Delegate Conference, whose agenda comprised the 7th FYP and the succession of a new generation of leaders for the organizations of the CPC. It was attended by more than 900 delegates from the provinces, military areas and central departments of the CPC, the government and the armed forces (PLA). The outcome was that 56 full and 35 alternate new members were elected to the Central Committee of the CPC (the average age of 64 of whom was 50 years and of whom 71 per cent had higher education), 56 new members were elected to the Central Advisory Commission and 31 to the Central Commission for Discipline Inspection. It was noted that most successors had been promoted through the ranks since the 12th National Party Congress in 1982.

The other main agendum at each of these three meetings, the 7th FYP, focused on recommendations (to the State Council charged with formulating the plan) on providing an appropriate economic and social environment for the new economic system, accelerating the construction of key projects, upgrading technology, developing intellectual resources and raising living standards. Closing speeches on 23 September revealed the issues confronted. Deng Xiaoping admitted that certain negative phenomena had arisen in the course of reforms but insisted that current policies served China's socialist development; he upheld the need to study marxism (as a guide to action rather than as a dogma), noting that some argued in favour of studying professional skills. Chen Yun's speech, described by foreign commentators as 'chilling', contained critical comments on economic policy, particularly the increasing reliance on market forces to regulate the economy. He insisted that planning was necessary for macro-economic control and for stimulating the micro-economic forces in an orderly rather than chaotic way, while warning of the adverse consequences of excessive rates of growth.

The 5th Plenum of the CPC 12th Central Committee elected Wu Xueqian, Hu Qili, Yao Yilin, Tian Jiyun, Qiao Shi and Li Peng to the 22-person Political Bureau, and Li Peng, Hao Jianxiu and Wang Zhaoguo to the 11-person Secretariat of the CPC. It was also reported that Deng Liqun had been removed as head of the CPC Propaganda Department.

To a large extent, those three historic meetings marked yet another stage in the ongoing process of political and economic reform launched in December 1978. The second stage of the CPC 'rectification' got under way at the end of 1984, involving some 13·5 million members, compared to 960,000 in the first stage (see AR 1983, p. 291, and 1984, p. 307), in two phases. The first extended to the winter of 1985, when organs at county and prefectural levels were involved, together with educational and research enterprises having similar status, the second from the winter of 1985 into 1986, involving the rectification of units below these levels. The significance of the second stage was its effect on units linking higher authorities with the grass-roots organizations, which had close relations with the public and implemented CPC policy. The specific aims were to raise ideological consciousness (synonymous with negating the cultural revolution), to restructure leading bodies and combat evil practices, and to integrate rectification with the implementation of reform. It was stressed there was no contradiction between *adherence to* and *development of* marxism, since marxism develops on the basis of practice: to ossify doctrine would be to produce dogmatists unable to cope with the challenge of modernization. Thus it was the role of the CPC to distinguish between what was applicable and what was not.

In this context, it is noteworthy that Volume V of the *Selected Works of Mao Zedong* was withdrawn from circulation because, so it was reported, it contained material giving expression to errors of judgment in the theory of class contradictions. However, the historiography of the 50th anniversary of the Zunyi conference praised Mao Zedong, comparing its role to that of the 3rd Plenum of the 11th CPC Committee in 1978.

Since restructuring started in 1982, of the 22 million CPC cadres 900,000 had retired to the second and third lines, and over 80,000 young and middle-aged cadres had been promoted to posts at and above county level. However, lack of educated personnel and deficiencies in attitude remained problems to be resolved. Evil practices included money worship and corruption, both the results of spiritual pollution and neglect of ideology.

In the third quarter details emerged of a most serious economic crime. Committed between January 1984 and March 1985, it centred on Hainan Island and involved officials who had illegally imported 89,000 motor vehicles, 2·86 million TV sets, 252 video recorders and 122,000 motor bicycles from Japan, entangling others in central departments and even military transport units in a widespread web of corruption. Despite frequent references to negative factors in 'commodity economic relations', undermining morality and encouraging the tendency to pit rectification against economic reform and construction, the latter were promoted relentlessly during the year.

The theme in economic policy continued to be reducing the scope of mandatory planning while expanding that of guidance planning and market regulation. In agriculture, with the abolition of most procurement quotas the 30-year-old state agricultural purchasing system disappeared, prices being linked to market demand and a predominantly market-orientated rural economy being established. The state would buy 75–80 million tons of grain (30 per cent at a basic procurement price, 70 per cent at a preferential price), while the remaining four-fifths of production would sell at market prices. Elsewhere, commercial departments entered into contracts with peasants based on negotiated targets. In future the agricultural tax would not be paid in grain alone, but would include a cash element to match the development of a commodity economy. It was announced that restructuring of the communes had been completed, their administrative and economic functions having been separated. The urgent need for price reform, to eliminate irrational pricing which reflected neither value nor the relationship between supply and demand, was recognized in a state directive envisaging a five-year period of structural reform (during which some prices would rise and some would fall) allowing incomes to rise following increased productivity.

The main economic indicators were impressive: expressed in constant prices, national income in 1984 was 12 per cent above that in 1983, and combined agricultural and industrial gross value output (GVO) increased by 12 per cent. Production of grain was up 9·2 per cent at 407 million tons, of cotton up 31·05 per cent at 6·08 million tons, of coal up 8·0 per cent at 772 million tons, of crude oil up 8 per cent at 114·5 million tons, of electricity up 6·6 per cent at 374·6 million kwh, of rolled steel up 9·7 per cent at 33·7 million tons, of cement up 11·8 per cent at 121 million tons, of washing machines up 58·1 per cent at 5·78 million units and of TV sets up 45·7 per cent at 9·96 million. Exports increased by 14·6 per cent to 58,060 million yuan and imports by 24·7 per cent to 62,000 million yuan. Manufactured goods constituted 54·4 per cent of all exports and 81 per cent of imports. In 1984, the PRC attracted foreign funds exceeding US$ 2,600 million, including loans of $1,320 million and direct investment $1,340 million. Japan was China's main trading partner: in 1984 imports from Japan amounted to $7,210 million and exports to Japan $5,950 million.

The evidence of sustained stable economic growth with better balance between agricultural and industrial sectors and between heavy and light industry, and a more rational relationship between consumption and accumulation, all had to be viewed alongside inadequate energy supplies, a strained transportation network, excessive funding of fixed investment and consumption, and inflation. Surveys showed the average cash wage of workers and staff to be 961 yuan (up 13·2 per cent in real terms) and the wage of a worker in a state-owned or urban collective enterprise to be 1,143 yuan (up 26 per cent in real terms since 1980). Reported price rises in 1984 included food grains 19·5 per cent, edible oils 18·1 per cent, eggs 16·1 per cent, TV sets 53·3 per cent, refrigerators 130 per cent. A review of the 6th FYP to 1984 urged the need for more macro-economic control to curb excessive money supply, improvements to the taxation system (the shortfall in state revenue in 1984 amounted to 5,000 million yuan), greater emphasis on quality rather than volume of output and sustained efforts to maintain standards.

Other foci of reform included education, where the ministry concerned, regarded as having failed to give adequate leadership, was replaced by a State Education Committee under Li Peng. A national conference preceded a CPC Central Committee decision on reform, seeking gradually to introduce a 9-year compulsory system, the restructuring of secondary education and the promotion of professional and technical training. Similarly the development of an *armée de métier* proceeded with decisions to reduce the size of the armed forces by one million, to issue new uniforms distinguishing between officers and other ranks, to reintroduce ranks in two years' time, to establish an institute for strategic studies, to reduce the average age of teaching personnel and to emphasise that the development of the People's Liberation Army (PLA) was subordinate to economic growth. The development of the legal system was apparent in the adoption of laws on accountancy, economic contracts involving foreign firms, state-owned enterprises and inheritance.

The impact of the reforms and the debate within the hierarchy as to their optimum extent appeared to reach to the public arena with the organization of various demonstrations. Most noteworthy were a number of student demonstrations against Japan, using the 50th anniversary of the patriotic students' movement (anti-Japanese) and the 40th anniversary of the Japanese surrender, together with Mr Nakasone's visit to a war-shrine, to draw attention to the economic dominance of contemporary Japan and to political, social and economic problems arising in China's increasingly market-orientated economy. The demonstrations were never out of hand, but taken with protests by rusticated youth seeking to return to the cities whence they had been banished in the cultural revolution, and with demands by Xinjiang Uygur minorities for an end to nuclear testing and penal labour camps and for greater autonomy in their region, not to mention a serious outbreak of soccer hooliganism in Beijing following Hong Kong's victory over China in a World Cup match, they constituted a new and unpredictable trend in social attitudes.

External affairs continued to reflect the requirements of the modernization programme. Towards the end of the year Sino-US relations, depressed by American protectionist sentiment, were boosted by the lifting of remaining US restrictions on the export of high technology. Sino-Japanese relations were clouded by the problem of the huge imbalance in trade, perceived in China as economic imperialism. Sino-Soviet relations improved marginally through increased trade, but the talks being conducted at deputy ministerial level were not upgraded. Some misgivings were expressed about the achievements of the special economic zones, but the open-door policy was reaffirmed; while priority support would be given to Shanghai, Tianjin, Dalian and Guangzhou, the indications were that more coastal and riverine cities would be opened to foreign investment and trade. Sino-British relations continued to improve with the ratification of the Joint Declaration on Hong Kong and the announcement that the Queen would visit China in 1986.

The contracts for China's first commercial nuclear power plant at Daya Bay, Shenzhen, involving Framatome, Electricité de France and the (British) General Electric Company were signed at the end of the year after prolonged negotiations. The first of the two 900 megawatt units would be commissioned in 1992, the second a year later; Hong Kong would purchase 70 per cent of the power generated.

Incidents involving a mutiny on a torpedo boat and the defection of an aircraft gave evidence of improved Sino-South Korean relations, reinforced by China's decision to participate in the Seoul Olympics in 1988. Relations were established with Bolivia, Grenada and Nicaragua and there were signs that China sought to resume links with Indonesia. The level of international diplomacy by Chinese leaders was maintained with visits to Australia, New Zealand and the South Pacific by Hu Yaobang, to West Europe by Zhao Ziyang and to Canada and the USA by Li Xiannian, matched by many incoming visits. (For text of Zhao Ziyang's speech in London on China's foreign policy, see DOCUMENTS.)

TAIWAN

Judged by standards achieved in the recent past, 1985 was a less successful year for Taiwan. Having coped reasonably well with the challenge of an internationally-determined lower growth rate, Taiwan was beset by two major scandals, one political, the other economic, which together appeared to tarnish its image and undermine relations with its main ally, the USA. The ruling Kuomintang (KMT) Government dealt with the sources of these scandals, limiting their damage by bringing most of those involved before the courts, where swift justice was meted out.

The major political scandal erupted when the Ministry of National Defence admitted on 15 January that military intelligence officials had been involved in the murder of Henry Liu at Daly City in the USA (see AR 1984, p. 308). Not only did the incident recall for Americans the mysterious death in Taiwan in 1981 of Carnegie Mellon University Professor Cheng Wen-cheng (see AR 1981, p. 304), but the murder of a US citizen on US soil threatened the annual US$780 million arms sales to Taiwan. Under intense pressure from Washington the authorities arrested the director of the intelligence bureau, Vice-Admiral Wong Hsi-ling, and a deputy director of a bureau department, Colonel Chen Hu-men. On 9 April, after a civil court trial in Taipei, Chen Chi-li and Wu Tun, leaders of the Bamboo Union Gang said to have been ordered by the intelligence officials to 'teach Liu a lesson for betraying his country', were sentenced to life imprisonment, the third defendant, Tung Kuei-sen, remaining at large. Security personnel Wong Hsi-ling, Hu Yi-min and Chen Hu-men were sentenced on 19 April, after trial in a military court, respectively to life for ordering the murder, two years' and six months' imprisonment as accessories. The swiftness with which the cases were dealt with satisfied the immediate calls for justice and enabled the US President to refrain from weakening the strategic relationship with Taiwan, but left some questions unanswered, since doubts were not entirely dispelled about the overt motives and covert links of those involved.

The major economic scandal concerned the collapse of the financial conglomerate the Cathay Plastics Group. Controlled by the Tsai family, the group, the second largest in Taiwan, had assets of US$2,500 million in some 100 companies spread over the property, insurance, construction, plastics and banking sectors of the economy. It focused on parts of the group, involving Tsai Chen-chou, a relatively recent member of the KMT and of the Legislative Yuan. There had been massive financial fraud, exposing weaknesses in the financial system, and negligence at high levels in the Government and KMT, engendering suspicions of corruption. The Government declined to go to the aid of the group. The crisis appeared to have contributed to the decision of the Secretary-General of the KMT, Tsiang Yien-si, to resign shortly before the collapse. Subsequently it led to the resignations of the Minister of the Economy, Hsu Li-teh, in March, and the Minister of Finance, Lo Jen-kong, in August and damaged the professional reputation of the Premier, Yu Kuo-hwa.

After a period largely dominated by political and financial scandal, elections were held on 16 November to elect 21 mayors or county magistrates, 77 members of the provincial assembly, 51 Taipei city and 42 Kaohsiung city councillors. The KMT, which had 157 candidates compared to the main opposition Tangwai's 47, won 146 of the 191 posts contested, on a 72 per cent poll, confounding predictions that public disapproval of earlier events would be expressed in a low poll. Retaining 70 per cent of the popular vote, the KMT won 59 of the assembly seats, 17 of the posts of mayor or county magistrate, 38 of the Taipei and 32 of the Kaohsiung city council seats.

US demands for greater import liberalization of the economy achieved significant success, and indications were that in common with other newly-industrialized countries (NICs) Taiwan's export performance had not kept up with the rate of growth in world trade, despite progress in upgrading its industry. On the basis of total foreign trade of US$42,150 million for the first ten months (down 4 per cent) comprising exports of $25,460 million (down marginally) and imports of $16,680 million (down 8·6 per cent), growth was expected to reach US$10,000 million, while reduced imports of producer goods cut the deficit with Japan over the first ten months to US$1,810 million. Domestic investment to September totalled US$8,250 million, down 5·7 per cent, but foreign (mostly US and Japanese) and overseas Chinese investment increased to reach US$508 million. Unemployment was estimated at 4 per cent. Price stability was maintained. Foreign exchange reserves, at some US$1,000 million, gave import cover for 12 months. The new Labour Standards Law, formulated in a better economic climate, continued to encounter opposition from the business sector who saw it as a cause of reduced domestic investment.

There was no major change in Taiwan's international position but the severing of diplomatic relations with Bolivia and Nicaragua followed the trend towards diplomatic isolation. The People's Republic of China (PRC) maintained pressure explicitly through seemingly generous proposals for the autonomy of Taiwan following a reunification, and an improvement in its informal relations with South Korea, and implicitly through its own enhanced international standing under reformist leaders. The outcome of the Hong Kong agreement remained an important criterion for the international community. Meanwhile there was speculation about the succession to the presidency, and Chiang Ching-kuo confirmed that it would be determined at the time by the National Assembly and that his successor would not be a member of his family.

Despite adverse publicity from the Liu case, security personnel were not deterred from prosecuting a number of sedition cases during the year. These incidents, which appeared to be efforts by the authorities to contain both PRC united front and Taiwan independence movement activities among the overseas Chinese, contributed to tension in relations with the USA. The National Day celebrations were designed to restore morale with impressive demonstrations of military capability and the appearance of Chinese defectors Hsiao Tien-jun, who crash-landed a bomber in South Korea (killing his crewman and a South Korean farmer), and two others, Shih Hsiao-ning a militiaman and Cheng Mu-chu a doctor, who commandeered a fishing vessel to flee to Matsu island.

HONG KONG

Opinion continued to be affected by doubts about the real intentions of Beijing officials towards the future of Hong Kong after 1997 and the undertakings in the Sino-British Joint Declaration (for text, see AR 1984, pp. 515–24), including the provisions that 'The legislature of the Hong Kong Special Administrative Region (SAR) shall be constituted by elections' and that 'The executive authorities shall abide by the law and shall be accountable to the legislature'. The Hong Kong Government was criticised within Hong Kong for the extreme caution of the first steps to introduce an element of election into the Legislative Council, while there was further severe complaint at the failure of Britain to offer local people an effective emigration option, in the form of 'somewhere to live under British dominion', if the arrangements for their future likely to be provided by Beijing appeared insupportable.

Chinese officials directly concerned with Hong Kong expressed their disapproval of the very limited advances towards partial direct elections suggested in a government consultative document aimed at providing 'a system of government the authority of which is firmly rooted in Hong Kong', and it was made clear that, in the Chinese view, sovereignty would be transferred to China and not to the people of Hong Kong, who would get only such elements of self-government as Beijing thought fit to provide in the SAR Basic Law. It seemed also that Chinese officials had in mind an SAR administration in which power should be concentrated in the hands of a chief executive with an advisory legislature whose members would be appointed by 'democratic consultation' rather than direct election.

The Sino-British Joint Liaison Group made what was described as a 'friendly and cooperative' start to its work of devising ways of dealing with such problems as maintaining Hong Kong's particular economic relationships and its place in such arrangements as GATT and the man-made fibres quota system and the form of travel documentation for Hong Kong residents after 1997. The elections to district boards in March, with just under 500,000 votes cast, were followed in September by the first, indirect, elections to 24 of the 56 seats in the Legislative Council, 12 from the district boards and 12 from occupational constituencies. Concern that Beijing should be so alarmed at the prospect of an independent-minded Hong Kong elected legislature, together with the insensitive way in which Chinese officials selected the Hong Kong members of the Basic Law Drafting Committee and the Basic Law Consultative Committee and conducted the proceedings of these bodies, undermined confidence and sustained the continued large outflow of local capital and the search for havens abroad in which to invest and, if necessary, to live. This in turn contributed to the sluggish (by local standards) response to trade recession.

After the exceptionally high growth of domestic exports and re-exports in 1984, overall orders in hand in manufacturing industries fell steadily for most of the year, the export decline being especially noticeable in electronics while clothing exports did relatively well. Towards the end of the year the trend in domestic exports and in imports of raw materials and semi-manufactures began to improve, while re-exports fell back, thanks partly to greater caution over foreign exchange spending in China. In the short term the sharp growth in trade with China had been of great value in offsetting recession in other markets, but might have contributed to reducing the flexibility and swiftness of reaction to the state of Western markets where Hong Kong's greatest trading strength had usually lain. This slack trading performance nevertheless produced a considerable visible trade surplus.

Unemployment was kept down to under 3·5 per cent, although with less overtime than in 1984, and average wages in manufacturing improved further. Private building revived, but plant and machinery and public-sector capital investment fell. The Mass Transit Railway (MTR) Island line was completed and the decision was taken to build a joint road and MTR tunnel across the eastern end of the harbour. Overall economic growth was expected to be no more than 1 per cent in 1985–86, but with prospects of improved performance in the coming year.

JAPAN

Japan in 1985 stood on the threshold of an 'age of maturity'. Living standards had so risen that its people 'enjoyed the richest life they had ever experienced. Health, security and education had reached the highest-ever levels.' So declared the Economic Planning Agency in its annual report, which added that 81·8 per cent of Japanese now felt themselves 'part of the middle class'.

Certainly they were citizens of no mean country. Japan had displaced West Germany as the world's largest exporter of industrial products. Overseas trade was $46,141 million in surplus on a customs-cleared basis, Direct investment abroad stood at $71,141 million, more than $10,000 million of it invested in the latest year alone. Only Britain and Canada had larger stakes in the USA.

Japan was the world's leading creditor nation. Its net outstanding overseas assets had doubled in a year to $74,346 million. Japanese banks' international lending exceeded that of their USA counterparts. A Tokyo-London-New York financial axis seemed assured in the fairly near future. Japan was second only to the USA in official development assistance to the poorer countries. And, as became one of the principal technological exponents, it topped the list of USA patents granted to foreigners.

On the domestic scene, consumer prices rose by only 2·1 per cent and the wholesale index declined by 1·1 per cent, to 99·5 against the 1980 base of 100. Life-expectation of Japanese women, at 80·18 years, was the longest in the world and their menfolk could expect 74·54 years. Four decades ago Japanese had been old in their middle 50s; now the problem was that 10 per cent of the 121,047,196 Japanese were over 65—1,740 of them centenarians, including the world's oldest person at 120. How best to live with an aging society?

Unemployment ended the year at 2·6 per cent, worrying in Japanese terms, and for the first time more women had jobs than were keeping the home fires burning for the male workaholics. The nation of savers was reckoned to possess an average $32,000 per household, and there had been a heavy outflow of funds to cream-off high American interest. The sensible Japanese workers in major enterprises settled for a 5·1 per cent wage rise in their unions' ritual 'Spring Offensive', unprepared to rock the boat even when much of industry was benefiting from the world economic recovery. They knew the bell was tolling for some of the older sectors of industry.

Not everything in the Japanese garden was lovely, however. Japan's trading partners, already huffed by the 1984 $33,610 million surplus, were in a mood to block prospects of an even bigger surplus in 1985. Yet how could they stop their people from acquiring at least one or two of the many attractive Japanese consumer products set before them? Their own manufacturers had been tardy in meeting the expectations of the affluent 1980s, quite unlike the Japanese, who seemed to be born salesmen. But was Japan as interested as it should be in other nations' wares, particularly the import of manufactured products, which it sometimes appeared to regard as inferior to its own?

For the third year in succession Prime Minister Yasuhiro Nakasone donned the mantle of Horatius, keeping open the bridge of free trade between Japan and its partners. He called on all hands to boost imports under the kind of catchphrase loved by Japanese: 'Reach out to the countries of the world through imports.' The Premier went on television with blackboard and ruler to point the way; he was pictured shopping in department stores for imported foreign products, though his act seemed to lack a Pied Piper touch.

The Minister of International Trade and Industry cajoled a promise from top executives of Japan's 60 major businesses—automobiles, electrical appliances, electronics, machinery, leading traders, large department stores and supermarket chains—to step-up their imports. 'Japan must import more' became a litany in commercial and business circles but it hardly set the tills ringing in the shops with their sometimes-hard-to-find foreign displays.

Goaded by the USA (chief contributor to Japan's surplus), the EEC, OECD and many individual countries, who engaged in a 'Fire's Burning' part-song of complaints, Japanese bureaucrats worked far into the night over June and July to give birth, on 30 July, to an 'Action Programme', designed to meet many of the criticisms on tariffs and non-tariff barriers. The snip of scissors cutting red tape echoed throughout Kasumigaseki, the Tokyo seat of government ministries. Anguished civil servants made the sacrifices of a lifetime, obliterating cherished rules and regulations.

Hardly had a precis of the Action Programme reached foreign parts before the 'Too little, too late' brigade reassembled, though people with patience enough to digest the lengthy document found that the new Japanese package contained quite a few goodies and much future if not instant promise. After their mountains of discontent about non-tariff barriers, in particular, had become molehills in face of Japan's suggested solutions, the complainants proceeded to ask Tokyo to set import targets—a ploy they might have found difficult to exercise if put to themselves. Tokyo wasn't having any.

The protectionist bogey was paraded against Japan at every turn. Any American Senator or Congressman worth his salt and knowledgeable about public relations deemed it necessary to draft a Bill—they numbered 82 at one time, many apparently aimed at Japan—and US Senate majority leader Robert Dole told the Japanese in Tokyo 'the protectionist pot is boiling over'. President Reagan got investigations started 'to identify any unfair trade practices by foreign countries'. Which? Japan?

Japan stood by its 'foreigners can do very well in the Japanese market but are inclined to be lazy' stance, but just then relief came from an unexpected quarter. With the American dollar threatening to outdo Halley's Comet, Japan's Finance Minister joined his counterparts from USA, Britain, France and West Germany on 22 September in a summit decision to intervene in the foreign exchange markets and drive down the dollar (see Pt. XVIII, Ch. 1). For Japan, frequently accused of contriving a weak yen, this meant driving its currency upwards. Between 22 September and 31 December the dollar rate slid from 242 to 202, showing a yen appreciation of 16·5 per cent.

This would probably produce a much more marked effect, at no great distance in time, on Japan's trade surplus, particularly with the USA, than any Action Programme or other Government initiative could hope to achieve. It all depended on whether the Americans, Japan's best customers, and the Europeans were prepared to pay more for Japanese goods. Profit-squeezed products like cars, cameras, electronic appliances, steel and construction machinery would have to cost more, and 200 yen to the dollar was regarded by many sectors of industry as the last notch of export profitability. Thereafter some of the weaker brethren among exporters might go to the wall. Of course, taking the Japanese economy across the board, there were beneficiaries of the yen's rise and dollar's fall, such as electric power and gas companies and oil refiners.

OECD experts foresaw that Tokyo's agreement to the yen's appreciation might reduce the threat of protectionist measures by Japan's trading partners. The yen's sharp rise should give imports a strong boost and slow down exports, it forecast.

Mr Nakasone, coiner of apt phrases (or recipient of good advice on the subject) won headlines abroad when he told the National Press Club in Tokyo, in relation to Japan's trade surpluses: 'We must try to change our industrial structure so it will not be harmful to others. Otherwise Japan might face the chance of disappearing from earth overnight, like Carthage. Can we go on living with surpluses of $30,000 to $40,000 million a year? It's like playing mah-jong—if you keep winning nobody wants to play with you any more.'

But he added that a moderate surplus was always necessary for Japan's survival. He was not to know that by 31 December there would be a surplus of $46,000 million to live with, or that the year's import total would in fact be five per cent down.

However, Mr Nakasone had more than trade on his mind. This most memorable Japanese Prime Minister of recent times had to make sure he did not suffer a Carthage himself. He did well in regular opinion polls; President Reagan was more than willing to sustain the 'Ron-Yasu' relationship that had marked his premiership; he was popular with fellow-summiteers (to whom he would be host in Tokyo in 1986); he was the most identifiable Japanese around the world; he articulated Japanese policies and problems. He had surely earned the accolade of 'the best Prime Minister we've got'.

But Japanese politics did not work that way. It was a 'You move over, I take over' art. Two years was the most anybody was expected to occupy the premiership—which went with the presidency of the Liberal Democratic Party (LDP), the nation's rulers for long years now—be he brilliant or pedestrian. Nakasone, first elected in 1982, got a second term in 1984 and looked for a third in 1986 (though he would have been the last of Japan's 121,047,196 citizens to lay claim for himself).

As he changed his Cabinet in the dying days of 1985—no 'night of the long knives' but a mere ritual departure of 17 out of 21 Ministers of whom it may be said 'sufficient unto the day . . . your turn may come again'—it was noteworthy that Mr Shintaro Abe remained as Foreign Minister and Mr Noboru Takeshita as Finance Minister. Two men of political calibre, both aspiring Premiers, better perhaps within the Cabinet gainfully employed than outside gamefully employed. Mr Abe looked set for another 'handshaker of the year' title as he added further countries to the 34 visited in three years.

Both Mr Abe and Mr Takeshita would rally around the Premier until the summit, certainly, but thereafter Japanese politics were sure to have a severe 'touch of the factions' as candidates for the LDP presidency (plus premiership) sought to win friends outside their own factions. For the first time in a decade, Mr Kakuei Tanaka, leader of the biggest faction, would not have the last word as 'kingmaker'; he had been felled by a stroke shortly before his appeal against sentence and conviction in the Lockheed scandal had begun. Mr Nakasone, whom he had supported, was now his own man. Would he be strong enough to win again?

No account of Japan in 1985 would be complete without a reference to the Japan Air Lines' jumbo jet crash in August. The aircraft took off from Tokyo for Osaka with 524 aboard, a bulkhead soon ruptured, putting the plane outside the desperate pilot's control, and it smashed into a mountain. Astonishingly, four survivors were found hours later among the 520 dead. It would be a long time before Japan forgot the day that put it into the record books with history's worst single-plane accident.

SOUTH KOREA

North–South relations were punctuated by contradictory events, some indicating improvement, others the contrary. The reuniting of long-lost relatives on the 38th Parallel proved to be an exception in a fairly gloomy year. On 20 September a hundred northerners filed across the demarcation line at Panmunjom to meet relatives on the other side. It was their first encounter since the Korean war of 1950-53. There were estimated to be ten million divided families in Korea. Although primarily a propaganda exercise the exchange was emotionally charged and added a little impetus towards building better cross-border relations. Otherwise North–South contacts, such as economic and parliamentary talks, tailed off disappointingly.

Progress had inched forward since Seoul agreed to accept disaster relief from the North following severe flooding in September 1984. Following this, Pyongyang had agreed to begin economic talks with the South and to resume Red Cross negotiations, broken off in 1973. By the year's end the economic talks had achieved little, nor had agreement been reached on approval of Seoul's staging of the 1988 Olympics, a cause dear to the South's heart. The leader of the southern delegation, Dr Kim Ki-Hwan, had hoped to secure some practical results such as beginning commodity trading and reconnecting the North–South railway. The North, however, wanted to set up a joint economic committee before considering such practicalities.

Nevertheless, the year ended with strong hints that progress had been made towards setting up a summit between the leaders of North and South Korea. In September Mr H. Dam, an influential member of the ruling North Korean Workers' Party, visited the South—a visit returned the following month by Mr Chang Se Dong, head of the South's National Security Planning Agency.

President Chun had stated his willingness to meet President Kim at any time or place. Yet even if such a summit were staged the North would be unlikely to make any significant concession without at least securing a non-aggression pact, which would raise the issue of the removal of US forces from the South.

Internally, the opposition New Korea Democratic Party (NKDP), formed on 18 January 1985 by various opposition figures whose political rights had been restored on 29 November 1984, emerged as a major opposition force. It won 29.2 per cent of the vote in the National Assembly elections of 12 February 1985—elections won by the ruling Democratic Justice Party with 35.3 per cent. The main policy commitments of the NKDP were to freedom of the press, an independent judiciary and direct presidential elections.

At the year's end the NKDP felt confident enough to launch a national petition campaign aimed at replacing the electoral college system with direct presidential elections. The NKPD planned both regional and local campaigns to back its petition. Despite the presence of such active anti-government centres scattered around the country the Government showed its self-confidence by lifting the ban on 6 March on the remaining 14 opposition politicians originally banned from political activity in 1980. Among them were Kim Dae Jung, former presidential candidate, Kim Young Sam, former head of the New Democratic Party, and Kim Chong Pil, former head of the Democratic Republican Party.

NORTH KOREA

The wish to attract foreign investment, to modernize the economy and to emulate the South's success in achieving international prominence persuaded the North's leaders to continue a more conciliatory approach to the outside world. Despite the opening of dialogue with the South, however, there remained grounds for believing that the North had little interest in making real progress on trade and humanitarian issues: its aims were primarily political. President Kim had vowed to reunify Korea in his lifetime and much of the inter-Korean diplomacy seemed designed to undermine the Seoul Government's internal authority rather than to build bridges. Even the only solid inter-Korean achievement of the year—a brief reunion of divided families—was coloured by the North's insistence that it could go ahead only on condition that the southerners would not go beyond the showpiece capital, Pyongyang, rather than visit their relatives' more run-down home towns.

An uncertain factor in the detente with Seoul was the North's continuing search for equipoise between the Chinese and the Russians. In recent years China had urged Pyongyang to negotiate with the South and to encourage foreign investment. While doing this the North Koreans had also reactivated links with the Soviet Union, notably through Kim Il Sung's extended tour of the USSR and Eastern Europe in 1984. In August 1985 Soviet warships visited a North Korean port for the first time. The USSR had also supplied the North with about 40 MiG-23s and now enjoyed overflying rights for its aircraft going to Da Nang in Vietnam.

At home there were signs that the succession issue was not yet settled: there still appear to be complications in the handover of power to Kim Il Sung's son, Kim Jong-il.

X AUSTRALASIA AND SOUTH PACIFIC

Chapter 1

AUSTRALIA—PAPUA NEW GUINEA

AUSTRALIA

THE structure of government and politics remained substantially the same as in the previous year (see AR 1984, p. 316). In Victoria, a general election for the state parliament on 2 March registered a small swing against the Australian Labor Party (ALP) government, reducing its Assembly majority from 17 to 6 and leaving it in a minority of one in the Upper House. However, a South Australian state general election on 4 May returned the ALP government, previously kept in power by two independents, with a clear Assembly majority of 9, and for the first time ever with an Upper House majority (of one) over the Liberal opposition, a Labor-inclined Australian Democrat holding the balance of power. Those two states also adopted four-year (instead of triennial) parliaments, with fixed terms of three years subject to dissolution in emergency circumstances, and with dissolution at discretion of Ministers in the fourth year.

The ALP federal Government of Mr Bob Hawke retained its substantial public support and the Prime Minister his extraordinary personal rating in opinion polls, notwithstanding factional disputes in his party and claims by its left wing that Hawke's 'consensus' policy involved too many concessions to the capitalists and failure to pursue socialist ends. A specific issue was the effort by the federal, Victorian and New South Wales ALP governments to bring about the deregistration of the militant Builders Labourers' Federation, which pursued strike tactics and deals with employer groups in breach of the 'Accord' between the governments and the Australian Council of Trade Unions, designed to stabilize wage levels (see AR 1983, p. 303). The Accord was renewed for a further two years, and although there was some increase in disputes and in wage levels the rates of increase remained much below those of pre-Accord years. The moderate policies of the ALP governments made it natural for the Liberal oppositions to move right, in order to present a clear alternative. This included the advocacy of de-regulation of business, 'privatization' of publicly-owned enterprises and cuts in spending on social services. The most striking outcome of the consequent disputes between Liberal 'wets' and 'dries' was the removal of Mr Andrew Peacock, regarded as somewhat 'wet', from the federal Liberal parliamentary leadership and his replacement by Mr John Howard, more of a 'dry'.

The Hawke Government abandoned its previous commitments to constitutional reform and wound up the Australian Constitutional Convention, replacing it with a nominated Commission and committees of experts and public figures. However, a technically profound constitutional change was set on foot. The federal and the six state governments agreed with the UK Government to enact a series of statutes with the joint effect of severing the remaining legal links between Britain and Australia, and by December the Australian state and federal parliaments had enacted their contributions to the process. The most important applications of the statutes would be to end the vestigial authority of the UK Parliament over state law-making and the need for state governments to approach the Queen through a UK Minister, which had been abolished for Australian Commonwealth affairs by the Statute of Westminster 1931; and to extend to cases on state matters in state Supreme Courts the 1975 abolition of appeals to the Judicial Committee of the Privy Council on federal matters, while preserving the force of state Constitution Acts. The provision regarding direct access to the Monarch was especially important in relation to the appointment and dismissal of state governors. In October, a possible embarrassment to the Queen over the threatened dismissal of the governor of Victoria under the still-applicable 'old law', for accepting free transport from an international airline, was avoided by his resignation.

The national economic fortunes were mixed. Good rains ensured bumper crops and herds, but world prices for the produce remained low except for some recovery of fine wool prices. Important mineral discoveries continued, notably gold strikes in South and Western Australia, and the world's greatest diamond mine—the Argyle in Western Australia—commenced operations, but international metal prices remained low. Unemployment fell from 8·5 per cent of the work-force in January to 7·8 per cent in December, but GNP growth fell from 5 to 4·5 per cent. Financial and distributive organizations, and some manufacturers, achieved high profits, but manufacturing industry in general, particularly motor car manufacture, continued to experience poor financial results and structural weakness.

The most specific economic problem, entailing the most difficult policy decisions for Mr Hawke and his Treasurer, Mr Paul Keating, was the depreciation of the Australian dollar by more than 10 per cent against the US dollar, and by lesser but significant ratios against other major currencies. Following its flotation in 1983, the Australian dollar had settled at a rate of about 82 cents US, but in February 1985 it began to slide to a rate at times below 60 cents, recovering to the 70s in September, and settling in the high 60s from November on. The main immediate causes were a preponderantly unfavourable balance of payments, a high rate of external government borrowing and the increased rate of inflation (7·6 per cent in November).

The devaluation did not immediately have the classic consequences of increasing exports and decreasing imports. Under Treasurer Keating's direction the Commonwealth Reserve Bank maintained a tight-money policy which forced prime bank rates up from 14 per cent in January to 21 per cent in December, so adding to the difficulties of business and threatening the economic recovery on which the popularity of the Hawke Government and its relations with the labour movement depended. In December, Mr Keating stated that he would not allow his tight-money policy to endanger his Government's broader welfare policies, but he continued to hope that the external payments problems would respond to the measures so far adopted within the ensuing six months; the December figures did not indicate a lessening of the trade deficit.

The federal Budget, opened on 20 August, adhered to the principles to which the Government committed itself at the 1984 election (see AR 1984, p. 318). Expenditure for 1984–85 was a little below estimate and the 1985–86 estimate was a little higher; the tax burden was slightly decreased, and the deficit slightly reduced. This was achieved by detailed cuts in expenditure, many in the 'social wage' area, resented by the Labor left wing.

The Treasurer had suffered a defeat on tax policy at a 'tax summit' conference held in July, pursuant to an election promise. The Treasurer put forward three possible general reforms. His favoured option was a substantial shift from the long-established federal reliance on direct and in particular income taxation to a much increased reliance on indirect taxes, in particular a broad-based retail sales tax on both goods and services; he rejected the European VAT system which some Australian tax experts advocated. This policy would have enabled him to reduce substantially the rate of income taxation, in particular the component collected from wage and salary earners at source (PAYE), which as a result of inflation and increased wage rates had begun to be experienced and resented by a large body of ALP voters. However, this option was strongly opposed by most of the trade union and employer representatives at the summit conference, for different reasons, and the Hawke Cabinet accepted the verdict.

Hence the Budget continued substantially the same basic mix of direct and indirect taxation, with detailed amendments, mainly to combat tax evasion. These included a specific tax on capital gains, previously untaxed, and likewise on many of the 'perks' connected with employment previously treated as deductible expenses, such as the 'business lunch'. The Australian Democrats used their balance of power in the federal Senate to compel some amendments to the Budget, in particular concessions to farmers and small businesses in connection with the capital gains tax, but leaving the main thrust of the Budget intact.

In foreign affairs, the Hawke Government and its world-roaming Foreign Minister, Mr Bill Hayden, had to pick a careful way between the conflicting claims of national security, the idealistic world vision of the labour movement and the stringent anti-Americanism of both the Labor left and many of the Australian Democrats. The dilemmas arose particularly in the context of New Zealand's anti-nuclear stand and its consequent refusal to admit US warships and planes on US terms as required for the practical working of the 1951 Anzus defence pact. The Australian Government made no attempt at influencing New Zealand policy, nor did it act as honest broker in the matter, an attitude which mollified the Australian Labor left and the anti-nuclear organizations who supported the New Zealand policy. On the other hand, Mr Hayden resisted demands that Australia should follow New Zealand's example and proclaimed Australia's continued adherence to the Anzus pact and to reliance on US defence and intelligence aid. He accepted the US requirement that Australia should not transmit to New Zealand any defence intelligence acquired from the USA, but also stated that Australia would otherwise regard itself as bound to New Zealand by the Anzus pact, would share with New Zealand its intelligence resources not derived from the US, and would continue joint defence exercises with the New Zealanders.

In February Mr Hawke was embarrassed by the disclosure that when visiting President Reagan he had confirmed an earlier undertaking to allow US military planes to use Australian bases when testing the MX missile programme, which otherwise his Government declined to support. After outcries from the anti-Americans, the US tactfully let Mr Hawke off the hook by moving the location of the tests from Australia. In August, Australia helped negotiate, and itself joined, the treaty declaring the South Pacific a nuclear-free zone (see DOCUMENTS), but ensured that the treaty did not prevent the use of the high seas for the transit of nuclear-powered or nuclear-armed vessels or their porting with consent of a relevant government.

In August, Mr Hawke confirmed Australian recognition of Indonesian sovereignty in East Timor, contrary to the vociferous views of the Labor left and of most Australian journalists, who still remembered the murder of five of their colleagues in the course of Indonesia's conquest. Messrs Hawke and Hayden were also much criticized in such quarters for endorsing the appointment of former Liberal Prime Minister Malcolm Fraser as joint chairman of the Commonwealth committee to monitor South Africa's progress towards the dismantling of apartheid (see DOCUMENTS), especially since this occurred during the tenth anniversary wake recalling the dismissal of the Whitlam ALP Government by the Governor-General, attributed to the actions of Mr Fraser, then Opposition leader.

Policy with respect to the claims of the Australian Aborigines caused sharp divisions in public opinion and between the federal Government, inclined to make extensive land grants giving the Aborigines inalienable freeholds including mineral rights, and state governments (including ALP ones) either rejecting that policy or wishing to modify it in various ways. A notable gesture towards the Aborigines was the vesting of freehold title to the celebrated Ayers Rock monolith in central Australia in an Aboriginal tribal group, pursuant to federal legislation, with a ceremonial handing-over by the Governor-General, Sir Ninian Stephen. This was opposed by the National Party government of the Northern Territory, even though the Aborigines immediately, as previously agreed, leased the Rock and its surrounds back to the government for joint administration to encourage the large non-Aboriginal tourist traffic.

Aboriginal claims also formed an important feature of the controversial McLelland Royal Commission Inquiry into the British nuclear tests carried out in the 1950s and '60s in South and West Australia, with the approval of the Menzies Liberal-Country Party Government and the cooperation of Australian scientists. The Commission recommended that the British Government should pay the costs of rendering safe for Aboriginal occupation the considerable area of land affected by radiation, and was in general scathing about the supervision, safety controls and public accountability of the enterprise.

Following allegations in the Melbourne *Age*, and a federal Senate inquiry, the federal Director of Public Prosecutions began a prosecution before New South Wales courts (exercising federal jurisdiction) against Mr Justice Lionel Murphy of the High Court of Australia on two charges of attempting to pervert the course of justice. The charges arose from claims by a New South Wales chief magistrate and a district court judge that Justice Murphy, in conversations with them, had sought favours for a solicitor of his acquaintance who was facing charges in connection with immigration matters. Justice Murphy denied the charges and was vigorously defended. After a protracted trial accompanied by much publicity, a Supreme Court jury brought in a verdict of guilty on one of the charges. On appeal to the Court of Criminal Appeal of New South Wales, the verdict was set aside on a number of technical grounds and a new trial directed. The Director of Public Prosecutions decided in December to continue the prosecution in 1986. This was the first indictment of a superior judge in Australian history.

PAPUA NEW GUINEA

In 1985, Papua New Guinea celebrated the tenth anniversary of its independence. The ceremonies, clustered around 16 September, were chaotic and cheerful and the year as a whole gave evidence of the accomplishments and the challenges of the past decade.

Politically, Papua New Guinea proved once again that its parliamentary institutions were flexible and resilient. The Prime Minister at the opening of the year was Michael Somare, the leader who had brought the country into independence in 1975. On 21 November, after a vote of lack of confidence, he was replaced by a coalition led by a Highlander, Mr Paias Wingti, who until March had been Somare's Deputy Prime Minister. Mr Wingti formed the People's Democratic Movement from defectors from Somare's Pangu Pati and elements from other political factions. Somare had been ousted before (in 1980) and took the new defeat with aplomb. If the best test of the hardiness of a new state structure is its ability to arrange for orderly successions in power, Papua New Guinea had so far passed handily.

Rapid social change, highly visible inequalities and the growth of squatter settlements with few amenities and ragged social frameworks combined to produce severe problems of robbery and violence in the capital city of Port Moresby. In June, the national Government declared a curfew in Port Moresby, which was prolonged until after the independence celebrations. Although crime rates declined sharply and at year's end a low incidence of robbery, theft, rape and assault was being maintained, there was concern that few successful charges had been laid against those who underpinned the crime of the city—the receivers of stolen goods and the political protectors of the 'rascal' gangs.

PNG's economy continued to weather the trying 1980s with better-than-average success. The 1985 inflation level was low; difficult negotiations with an influential transnational corporation, the Ok Tedi Mining Company, were completed successfully; and at the end of the year rising coffee prices brought encouragement to a sector of the economy where indigenous entrepreneurship had been most active. An independent review of the economy, made at the request of the PNG Government, nevertheless struck a sombre note. It pointed out that growth rates were slow; new jobs were too few to keep up with new job-seekers; inter-regional and rural-urban inequalities were widening; and servicing the external debt had become a heavier burden.

Papua New Guinea's porous border with the Indonesian province of Irian Jaya continued to plague international relations. The 10,000 refugees in PNG were a mixture of customary border-crossers from local ethnic groups, guerrilla fighters from the OPM (West Papuan Liberation Movement) and a large proportion of terror-stricken people. A solution seemed to lie in some combination of resettlement and return under guarantees. By year's end little progress had been made in finding new homes for refugees in PNG or abroad; resistance to return to Irian Jaya remained strong and there was still tension between PNG and Indonesia.

All told, Papua New Guinea remained one of the few areas in the developing world where optimism reigned and seemed amply justified by the record.

Chapter 2

NEW ZEALAND

THE country experienced easily its most decisive year in recent memory. In January, the ruling Labour Party's parliamentary caucus insisted that the Government hold firm to its 1984 election pledge to ban nuclear-powered or nuclear-armed ships from entering New Zealand ports and harbours. A proposed visit of USS *Buchanan*, it was held, did not meet such criteria; to Washington's embarrassment, this call was then refused. The State Department announced that such a cancellation could not go 'cost free' and that, henceforth, planned military exercises involving New Zealand under the Anzus arrangement were cancelled, processed American intelligence relayed to New Zealand was suspended, and a proposed July Anzus Ministerial Council in Canberra 'postponed'.

As the dispute intensified, the Americans warned New Zealand that, should it proceed with its planned legislation to block nuclear ship access to its ports, then the United States would no longer regard itself as bound to provide a security guarantee under Anzus, notwithstanding the relevant treaty's lack of commitment to do so. At the heart of the dispute, which attracted widespread international as well as domestic debate and attention, was the Lange Government's claim that New Zealand neither wanted, needed, nor was obliged to be defended with nuclear weapons. For the United States, such ship visits were warranted as a normal component of alliance responsibilities, and were a contribution to total deterrence by the West. Any presence of nuclear weapons aboard visiting platforms, the US continued to insist to New Zealand, remained a secret that could be neither disclosed nor denied.

An attempt made through a September visit to Washington by Deputy Prime Minister Palmer to convince the Americans that proposed anti-nuclear legislation remained compatible with Anzus failed to bridge differences. A Bill brought before Parliament in December, and scheduled for study in committee in 1986, placed the onus for deciding whether any visiting naval vessel was nuclear-capable on the New Zealand Prime Minister. For the United States, however, Anzus remained inoperative. Within New Zealand, public surveys indicated majority support for a retention of Anzus, but also majority support for a ban on nuclear weapons entering the country in any form.

Such opposition was doubtless influenced by the bizarre *Rainbow Warrior* affair. In July, agents of the military arm of the French secret and intelligence services mined and sank the *Rainbow Warrior*, docked in Auckland harbour, the flagship of the international environmental organization Greenpeace. The bombing, which caused the death of a crewman, was shortly followed by the police arrest of two of the terrorists involved, Marfat and Prieur, who were charged with murder, arson and conspiracy. Three other French agents faced similar warrants for arrest, but escaped by yacht to New Caledonia and thence to France, where the Government refused to assist the New Zealand police in either their location or their return to face charges. In August, the hastily-prepared Tricot report (see p. 130), exonerating the French Government and secret services from complicity in the outrage, was greeted with widespread incredulity in New Zealand, where it was dismissed by Mr Lange as being so transparent as not even to constitute a whitewash.

Subsequent press revelations in France that indeed the bombing was officially authorized led to the resignation of Defence Minister Hernu, the demand for substantial material reparation by New Zealand and the deterioration of relations between the two countries to an all-time low. In a brief November court appearance, Marfat and Prieur pleaded guilty to reduced charges of manslaughter and were sentenced to ten-year terms of imprisonment. Claims by French officials that the pair would be repatriated to France as part of a reparations deal were refuted by the New Zealand Government. The year finished with the reparations issue unsettled, though the New Zealand Government still held out the possibility of conducting a full inquiry into the sinking, where evidence, much of it damaging to France, would emerge in public for the first time.

Elsewhere in its foreign relations, the Government was relieved of unwanted international attention in July when the NZ Rugby Football Union made a late cancellation of its controversial plans to tour a side to South Africa in 1985. In a case brought by two rugby-playing Auckland lawyers, Justice Casey awarded an interim injunction against the tour's proceeding on the grounds that to do so was contrary to the Union's stated aims of fostering and promoting this sport, and that leave for it to go ahead would vitiate the necessity for a full hearing. Following an April tour of Commonwealth states in Africa, Prime Minister Lange chose Harare, Zimbabwe, as the site for New Zealand's first full diplomatic presence in Africa, to commence in 1986.

In its handling of the economy, the Government continued its deregulation of the financial sector, removal of import restrictions and phasing out of subsidies and incentives to farmers and exporters. These measures were combined with a tight rein on monetary conditions, even though interest rates peaked in the third quarter to between 25 and 30 per cent for 90-day commercial bills. The currency was floated in March, a move which, while relieving the Government of having to borrow external capital, saw the New Zealand dollar appreciate sharply in the third quarter through high interest rates. Although these movements dampened inflationary pressures, which increased in the first two quarters through buoyant trading, exports and investment, demands intensified for the Government to intervene to lower the value of the currency. It did not do so, claiming that the real enemy remained inflation, its concern being heightened by a round of wage settlements that averaged between

15 and 20 per cent; the rises were undoubtedly influenced by a decision of the independent Higher Salaries Commission to approve delayed remuneration packages with typically 35 to 40 per cent increases to top civil servants, academics and the judiciary.

Although the internal deficit before borrowing was approaching NZ$2,000 million by the final quarter (when interest rates and the value of the New Zealand dollar both fell), it was reduced as a percentage of GDP, this more through increased revenue than through restraint on public spending, where outlays for health, education, the social services and defence were all expanded. Balance-of-payments difficulties continued; the deficit on overseas exchange transactions in the year to October stood at NZ$2,000 million, which, at 6·4 per cent of GDP, was a four-year high. Despite increases in gross sales of exports such as fish, manufactures and horticultural products, the terms of trade remained adverse.

A major budgetary decision was the announcement of a comprehensive goods and services tax for inception in October 1986 at an initial rate of 10 per cent. This was allied to planned lowering and simplification of personal tax margins, greater incentives for small savers and attempts to encourage enterprises to operate for income advantage rather than capital gain.

In addition to the extensive legislation required for the new tax regime, other enactments included a wide range of measures affecting commerce, land transfer, family law, conditions of employment in the state services, marketing, transport and state-run corporations. The legislature itself underwent reform through strengthened committees and a revision of standing orders, while a major governmental reorganization saw the emergence of a new Ministry for Conservation, involving a shift in functions from Forestry, Works and Land Use agencies. A major White Paper directing public attention to a proposed Bill of Rights, following Canadian precedent, was published, as were Green Papers on industrial relations and defence and security, all documents regarded as a means of furthering interest-group participation in the formulation of planned policy.

The most acrimoniously debated domestic public issue was a private member's Bill brought before Parliament by a Labour backbencher, Francis Wilde. This sought to decriminalize homosexual acts between consenting adults over the age of sixteen. Although a parliamentary majority was discernible for reform, decision on the age of consent and enactment of the proposal remained incomplete when Parliament completed its longest session on record in December.

The National opposition remained unable to dent the substantial level of public support that the Government maintained through the public opinion polls, notwithstanding its recapture of a seat from Labour in the June by-election in Timaru. During the final quarter, bickering within

National's ranks reached a level where its leader, Mr McLay, found it necessary to banish Sir Robert Muldoon, the former Prime Minister, to the most remote corner reserved for the lowest-ranking opposition member in Parliament. This followed public calls by Sir Robert for the removal of Mr McLay, disquiet within the party about its finances and management, consistently poor poll showings by the leader and doctrinal disagreements over economic policy, The smaller parties saw the ebullient Mr Robert Jones attempting to disband the New Zealand Party he had created in 1983, resigning from it, but then threatening to re-enter public life if Sir Robert Muldoon staged a comeback. To little public effect, Social Credit renamed itself the Democratic Party.

The year also saw the appointment and installation of New Zealand's first Maori Governor-General, Paul Reeves; the award of the Booker prize for fiction to Keri Hulme for her novel *The Bone People*; and the final completion of the synthetic petrol plant in Taranaki province.

Chapter 3

THE SOUTH PACIFIC

DEVELOPMENTS in NEW CALEDONIA overshadowed all else in the region (see also p. 130). In January Edgard Pisani, President Mitterrand's special high commissioner to New Caledonia, recommended that the territory accelerate its self-determination under a scheme whereby it would elect four regional assemblies with devolved powers on the important land question, these to form a constituency for election to a territory-wide Congress. Shortly afterwards, a key pro-independence Melanesian leader, Eloi Machoro, and his deputy, Marcel Nanaro, were killed in a mêlée. Further violence continued, resulting in the sabotage of critical nickel-mining facilities, causing that industry and tourism heavy financial losses. Later in January, President Mitterrand visited the island and indicated that France would strengthen its military presence in New Caledonia.

In April, French Prime Minister Fabius approved the Pisani plan, indicating that the Congress chosen by the four regional assemblies would be responsible for implementing a referendum on independence for the colony before the end of 1987, with the distinct possibility of some form of continuing security and military association with France. However, those aspects of the plan granting a heavier weighting to indigenous, largely rural, Melanesian representation—given the European demographic concentration in just one region, the capital Noumea—caused widespread resentment among local settlers and their direct enlistment of metropolitan French conservative political support. This was brought to bear through modifications of the plan by the French

Assembly, following objections by the Constitutional Court, but more particularly through active campaigning for the September territorial elections by figures such as MM Chirac and Le Pen. Clearly with an eye to the March 1986 French elections, these figures raised the political temperature in New Caledonia by stating their unequivocal support for the local Rassemblement pour la Calédonie (RPCR) and National Front in their determination to stay with France. Although these anti-independence groups won a 61 per cent share of the total vote, and a clear majority in the planned 46-member Congress, within three of the four regional assemblies the pro-independence Front de Libération Nationale Kanak et Socialiste (FNLKS) won local majorities. This meant further polarization of already bitterly divided positions. The final months saw sporadic bombings against postal, land authorizing and judicial facilities.

In late August, President Iremai Tabai of KIRIBATI survived a parliamentary motion of no-confidence in his Government, precipitated by a fishing deal recently concluded with the Soviet Union. Under the agreement, a Soviet fishing company was granted rights to operate 16 vessels within the Kiribati 200-mile extended economic zone for an annual fee of US$1·5 million. Such vessels were not permitted entry within the 12-mile territorial limit. Denying that this presence threatened Western interests in the region, President Tabai maintained that he had signed the deal because the American Tunaboat Association had refused to negotiate an agreement.

In FIJI the formation of a Labour Party in July was precipitated by worsening disarray in the main opposition National Federation Party and a freeze on wages which continued throughout the year. With the backing of white-collar workers in the Trade Union Congress, the new party won seats in the Suva municipal elections, but narrowly missed parliamentary representation in a December Indian communal by-election. Fiji suffered loss of life and extensive material damage from two January hurricanes, won increased aid from Japan and China following visits by Prime Minister Nakasone and General Secretary Hu Yaobang respectively, and concluded new sugar export deals with New Zealand, China and the EEC.

In WESTERN SAMOA, a February poll saw the sitting government grouping, the Human Rights Protection Party, win 31 of the 47 seats in the Legislative Assembly. A month later, Tofilau Eti was re-elected unopposed as the country's Prime Minister. However in July, and again in December, challenges were mounted to his authority, including lack of support for 1986 budgetary initiatives. In the last week of the year he failed in an attempt to have fresh elections called, and was replaced as Prime Minister by Vaai Kolone.

In the COOK ISLANDS, Premier Dr Tom Davis sacked his Deputy, Geoffrey Henry, leader of the Cook Islands Party (CIP). This was a further episode in continuing difficulties between two dominant figures that embarrassed the Government on the eve of the South Pacific Forum meeting in Rarotonga. A month later, those CIP politicians who had accepted portfolios in the Davis Government were expelled from the party.

The SOLOMON ISLANDS saw Prime Minister Sir Peter Kenilorea survive a no-confidence motion in September, after a suspension of parliamentary sittings caused by a boycott of five Government members. At a time unsettled by public service strikes, opposition leader Mamaloni attacked the Government for poor leadership, financial mismanagement and bad planning.

The year also saw the assassination in PALAU, in July, of President Haruro Remelik, replaced in office by Alfonso Oiterong; the evacuation by Greenpeace of 250 islanders from former atomic bomb test-site Rongelap to Majuto, Kwajelein lagoon, the MARSHALL ISLANDS; and an attempt to boost tourism through the extension of the WEST SAMOAN airport to take wide-bodied jet aircraft.

XI INTERNATIONAL ORGANIZATIONS

Chapter 1

THE UNITED NATIONS AND ITS AGENCIES

A report on the United Nations at forty by its Social Commission pointed to 'the stiffening resistance of an inflated body to reshaping itself' and the erosion of member states' early enthusiasm for cooperation in important fields such as development and peacekeeping. And at the General Assembly's opening session on 17 September its President, Sr de Pinies of Spain, repeated the well-worn message that the organization had not lived up to its founders' hopes because 'it could do no more than its members wanted it to do'.

Eleven former Presidents, meeting in June, suggested that the Assembly's work could be improved if the following year's President and committee chairmen could be elected or nominated at the end of the previous session in order to negotiate all possible consensus resolutions in advance; and that the opening general debate, which invariably took about a month, should be restricted to a few current issues. They did not agree on a ten-minute limit on the 159 members' speeches, which would cut debate by three weeks, but they did agree to meet again.

The anniversaries of the signing and ratification of the Charter were marked in San Francisco on 26 June and for several days around 24 October when representatives of the five permanent Security Council members spoke. They were less concerned with the organization's past efforts than with current preoccupations—President Reagan with the Strategic Defense Initiative, the Soviet Foreign Minister with a comprehensive test ban treaty and his country's offer to consider additional on-site inspections; the French with superpower arms reductions in which they would join 'when the time came'; the British Prime Minister with 'an all-out war on terrorism'; and the Chinese with the right of people to choose their own social systems.

Bulgaria, Congo, Ghana, the United Arab Emirates and Venezuela were elected as non-permanent members of the Security Council to serve for two years from January 1986, joining Australia, Denmark, Malagasy, Thailand and Trinidad & Tobago which had a second year to serve.

SECRETARIAT. One of the Secretariat's exceptional 'first men', Brian Urquhart, was to retire in January 1986, forty years after he became its second recruit as Trygve Lie's personal assistant. Urquhart had had unparalleled experience of all five peacekeeping forces and most of the ten observer missions, becoming under-secretary-general in charge of peacekeeping in 1974. His successor was to be Marrack Goulding, an Arabist and lately British ambassador to Angola. Goulding did not have his predecessor's first-hand knowledge as a soldier-turned-peacekeeper; but the experience of contingents from 40 countries numbering over a quarter of a million men would be available to him as a senior Secretariat member, though the Secretariat was fairly strictly controlled by the 39th floor. Even in the late 1970s some new contingents complained that they had had too little briefing for a different kind of job.

The Secretary-General informed the Security Council's fortieth anniversary meeting that he was setting up an 'early warning' system of incipient disputes. The UN Association of the USA had described the lack of information available to the Secretariat as 'an international scandal', and had recommended that it should have more access to national satellite data and a computerized data bank. Certain Secretariat staff—Afghans, Cubans, Iranians, Libyans, Russians and Vietnamese—were banned from travelling more than 25 miles outside New York on US security grounds.

BUDGET. The 1986–87 budget (that is, excluding the much larger voluntary fund contributions) was approved at $1,600 million. A revised scale of assessments was approved by 109–15 with 27 abstentions. The US (25 per cent) would still pay over $2 million more than the next two contributors, the USSR and Japan, put together. The Assembly was expected to meet early in 1986 to discuss a US cut to 20 per cent under the Kassebaum amendment unless other members agreed to weighted voting according to their contributions.

The Assembly adjourned on 18 December, leaving several issues unconsidered.

POLITICAL

TERRORISM. The Assembly passed resolutions on 9 and 11 December by consensus. The first denounced 'acts of international terrorism . . . which endanger or take innocent lives and jeopardize fundamental freedoms' and called on states not to instigate or take part in them. The second called on states to prosecute and extradite perpetrators of violence against diplomatic missions and their officers, and approved continued work on a convention banning the use of mercenaries.

On 18 December the Security Council, without debate, condemned hostage-taking and abductions and demanded the release of all victims currently held. The US and USSR had consulted on this draft, which had apparently resulted from the death of an American Jew during the hijacking of the cruise ship *Achille Lauro* and the abduction of four

Russians by Arabs in Lebanon who killed one of them. The Assembly suggested further action by UN civil aviation and shipping bodies.

MIDDLE EAST. In the spring the Secretary-General reported to the Security Council that the position of the UN Interim Force in Lebanon (Unifil) was being made increasingly difficult by Israel's slow withdrawal south and the tough measures it used against resistance groups. The ten countries with contingents in Unifil expressed fears for their troops' safety. The force had been mandated to operate freely throughout the border area down to the international boundary.

Since there was no proposal from the Secretary-General, Security Council or Assembly to strengthen Unifil as Lebanon asked, Israel established itself in half of the area where Unifil had been intended to keep the peace. While the other half remained quiet, Israel and its allied Christian militia issued identity cards and set up check-points between the border and Tyre, making freedom of movement impossible for the inhabitants, even when accompanied by UN personnel. Finnish soldiers who tried to help defectors from the Israeli-controlled militia were taken hostage, but were released after higher UN intervention. After the US refused to bring pressure to bear on Israel to withdraw behind its boundaries, the Dutch withdrew their contingent in October, declaring the UN's mandate 'senseless'.

The director-general of the UN Relief and Works Agency (UNRWA) for Palestine refugees, Olof Rydbeck, was succeeded on 1 November after over six years of dedicated work by Giorgio Giancannelli of Italy. In his last annual report Sr Giancannelli had asked for additional aid. Families had houses, their men were in work, they no longer needed food aid, but their numbers had doubled to two million since 1950. The aid was needed for welfare and educational services, which were better than the Middle East norm, and for rebuilding houses destroyed around Beirut. Most of UNRWA's local staff were Palestinians, but the small international staff were in danger from terrorists, and some were still unaccounted for at the end of the year. Assembly resolutions deplored the situation of Arab refugees on the Israeli-occupied West Bank, which continued to be tightly restricted, particularly economically. Large majorities demanded that Israel should halt the removal of refugees from both the West Bank and the Gaza Strip. It seemed unlikely that UNRWA-assisted refugees would move to the West Bank under any proposed 'peace initiative' unless their subsidies were withdrawn.

The Security Council renewed the mandate of the UN disengagement force on the Golan Heights. The Truce Supervisory Organization (UNTSO) continued to monitor the Beirut situation, and UNTSO observers also worked in Egypt in accordance with Council decisions.

DISARMAMENT. Over 70 Assembly motions included an appeal to nuclear-weapon countries to agree to a freeze 'on a global scale and with appropriate verification'. The estimated 17 non-supporters were mostly Western countries which argued that a freeze should be balanced and accompanied by negotiations about deep cuts in nuclear arsenals. Other resolutions called on all countries to 'prevent actively' the militarization of outer space; asked the Conference on Disarmament to study 'verifiable prohibition of fissionable material production', to negotiate the ending of neutron weapons production and to 'elaborate' a comprehensive test ban treaty. A draft advocating a convention against further development of chemical weapons received an inconclusive vote.

ATOMIC ENERGY AGENCY. On 21 February the Soviet Union agreed to inspection of some of its civilian nuclear facilities, suggesting that the terms might provide a model for on-site verification of arms control pacts. The US and UK already allowed selective inspection. China joined the International Atomic Energy Authority in 1984 and was building its first plant. It was reported in January that an expert group testing the reliability of sophisticated verification had detected two Soviet tests which Moscow had not reported to international monitors. A medium-sized H-bomb detonated by the US in December brought protests from the USSR, which had announced a temporary moratorium on tests. Eighty-six of the 131 states parties to the Nuclear Non-proliferation Treaty took part in the third review conference in August.

SOUTH AFRICA AND NAMIBIA. The Security Council tried to obtain reparations for damage and loss of life caused by increasing South African raids into Angola, Botswana and Lesotho. As unrest and unemployment in the Republic's black townships grew and police methods hardened the Security Council expressed its concern at the repression of 'defenceless opponents of apartheid'. After Pretoria declared a partial state of emergency in July the Council urged the imposition of sanctions 'against apartheid' in general terms. Voting was 13 in favour, with the US and UK abstaining. The Assembly later requested the International Monetary Fund not to grant new loans to South Africa, and an international conference of maritime unions in London discussed methods of stopping oil supplies.

A more specific Council draft of 15 November involved Namibia and sought to impose mandatory selective sanctions. This was vetoed by the US and UK; France abstained, and the other 12 members voted in favour. The text had demanded that the 'so-called interim government in Namibia', set up in June, should be dismantled. Oil, arms and new investments would have been embargoed. Although there had been Congressional moves towards sanctions, the US Administration felt that the resolution would have 'utterly negated' its search for a negotiated solution for Namibia.

SEA-BED CONVENTION. On 10 December the Assembly called on all states to become parties to the Law of the Sea Convention on exploitation of the sea-bed and to desist from undermining its purpose in national legislation. It called for an early adoption of the rules for registration of pioneer investors. The resolution noted an earlier statement by the Sea-bed Authority that claims or actions incompatible with the Convention were illegal. Voting was 140 to 2 (Turkey, US) with 5 abstentions (West Germany, Israel, Peru, UK, Venezuela).

The resolution arose from an increasing realization, particularly by developing countries, that deep sea-bed mining was further away than originally thought and that while detailed rules were being defined decisions were being made in national capitals. In particular the eight countries making up the four multinational consortia designated as 'Pioneers' had received exploration licences from two of the non-signatories (US and UK) under their domestic legislation and were preparing to mine inside or outside Convention rules. The 'get-rich-slow' aspect of the Preparatory Commission's work was the least complicated, and the Secretary-General, amongst others, hoped that more progress would be made in developing a stable Law of the Sea.

OTHER POLITICAL ISSUES. Among the items deferred until the 40th Assembly resumed in 1986 were the situations in Central America, Cyprus and the Gulf war. The Assembly had recommended that the trade embargo imposed on Nicaragua should be lifted. (See also under Human Rights, p. 328.) Sr Perez de Cuellar had persisted with attempts to persuade the Cypriot factions to agree, but there were still four major issues to be decided; and the UN force in Cyprus, voluntarily funded, was $128·7 million in arrears. The Secretary-General also continued to mediate between Iran and Iraq, visiting both capitals. A UN team visited prison camps and reported that both countries mistreated prisoners in violation of the Geneva conventions. In spite of recommendations by the Security Council and Sr Perez de Cuellar only small groups of disabled prisoners were released during the summer.

A record 122 Assembly members called for the withdrawal of all 'foreign' troops from Afghanistan and the safe voluntary return of refugees, and reaffirmed the Afghan people's right to their own form of government. The so-called proximity talks between Pakistan and the Soviet-backed Afghan Government continued with the aid of the Secretary-General's special representative, Diego Cordovez. The Assembly requested the UK and Argentina to negotiate on 'all aspects of the future of the Falkland Islands (Malvinas)' by 107–4 with 41 abstentions, and a smaller majority rejected a British amendment reaffirming the islanders' right to self-determination before any change of sovereignty. The European Community was split, some having become impatient with Britain's refusal to accept the Secretariat's good offices. A large majority (114 to 21, with 16 abstentions) called for the withdrawal of foreign troops from Kampuchea and asked Sr Perez to continue his discussions with the committee of the 1981 international conference. Opponents included Laos, USSR and Vietnam. Prince Norodom Sihanouk said that if Vietnam would implement UN resolutions there would be no reprisals against collaborators, but there was great fear of forcible Vietnamization by the importation of hundreds of thousands of settlers.

Large Assembly majorities favoured changes in the Antarctic Treaty and UN control of the continent's minerals. They demanded the removal of South Africa from the 18-nation Consultative Parties (including Britain) which had adhered to the treaty in 1959. The treaty was open to review in 1991 if one of the parties requested it. The UK and the US urged that it had kept the polar region demilitarized, encouraged scientific research and frozen territorial disputes, and that the resolution was *ultra vires*.

ECONOMIC AND FINANCIAL

The Assembly's economic and financial committee agreed to complete its business before the spring session of the Economic and Social Council. Its agenda items were concerned with the effect of the world economic crisis on the developing countries, and the Secretary-General's report on them expressed concern as to whether the US recovery could be sustained long enough to make any difference to them. The acting director of the UN Conference on Trade and Development, Mr McIntyre, was replaced at the end of the year before he could make headway on a short-term plan to tide some producing countries over until more rational cooperation with consumers could be worked out. A new round of negotiations through the General Agreement on Tariffs and Trade (GATT) was unlikely, since France would not discuss trade separately from money and the Third World feared the extension of GATT rules permitting Western take-over of their insurance, banking and other services.

Overall aid levels to developing countries had increased by about 4·4 per cent in 1984, and most major debtors continued their efforts to repay loans, while the IMF, banks and large developed countries continued to reschedule them. The IMF's austerity measures did, however, reduce production and increase unemployment and inflation. Average per capita incomes in most of Africa went back to 1970 levels and in Latin America to those of 1975. The Group of Ten major industrialized countries continued to reject any return to fixed-rate policies or the issue of additional Special Drawing Rights.

Loans by the World Bank (IBRD) to developing countries for the year ending June dropped, for the first time since 1967, by 4·9 per cent, although its net income doubled during the year to over $1 million. It was not set up to be a profit-making institution, but its President, Mr Clausen, explained that there had been problems with the credit-worthiness of borrowers and relations with the IMF. The joint IBRD-IMF Governors intended that lending should rise again, and a multilateral investment guarantee agency was planned to encourage non-commercial projects such as the exploitation of small oilfields. The US agreed late in the year to resume help with long-term credits for the poorest countries through the International Development Association provided they gave evidence of economic improvements.

The forthcoming US Treasury's 'global initiative', intended to defuse the debt crisis, was unsettling. It apparently proposed to downgrade the unpopular IMF, but by making the Bank police the prompt repayment of loans which it was intended to encourage. Mr Clausen was due to retire in mid-1986. In an unusual intervention, Japan and West European countries impressed on the US that his successor would need exceptional experience, both national and international, to carry out a difficult and sometimes conflicting mandate, while remaining independent of the US Treasury and retaining the respect and goodwill of other countries.

ENERGY AND ENVIRONMENT. The decline in oil prices reduced funds and enthusiasm for earlier plans to develop alternative fuels for the Third World, though the Assembly urged the transfer of more technological know-how in this field. The UN Environment Programme, though painfully short of funding for work on problems of soil erosion and deforestation, co-sponsored a conference on Africa's environmental crisis. It also produced a register of potentially toxic chemicals, including consumer and industrial chemicals, pesticides and drugs, whose sale or use had been banned or restricted in any country. This was to be updated annually. The US was the only country to oppose it, as an undesirable restraint on free trade. A Convention for the Protection of the Ozone Layer was completed, but was unlikely to come into effect until good substitutes for chlorofluocarbons were available.

ECONOMIC RELATIONS. The Commission on International Trade Law continued attempts to codify or harmonize some practices in this wide area. It adopted a model law on international commercial arbitration in June, and continued work on draft conventions on international bills of exchange and international cheques. Guidelines on the electronic transfer of funds were nearing completion; and a study was under way on the problem of cross-border automatic data-processing and the need for better legal security to replace paper-based means of documenting activities.

SOCIAL AND HUMANITARIAN

FOOD AND AGRICULTURE. About 4·5 million tonnes of food grain were shipped to Africa during the year by UN governments and voluntary aid organizations—not as much as was said to be needed, but the harvest was good in most parts of the continent. A small New York-based Office for Emergency Operations (OEOA) speeded up deliveries and harmonized the activities of too many competing bodies. A serious disaster was averted in Chad; Kenya, Zimbabwe, Lesotho and other eastern and southern states of Africa no longer needed free food; only some parts of Ethiopia and Sudan still suffered starvation. Ethiopia had diverted up to 30,000 tonnes of grain to feed its soldiers and civil servants. Some voluntary organizations supplied Eritrea, Wollo and Tigré direct. The head of Ethiopia's relief commission, Mr Dawit, disappeared, apparently to the US, fearing that he would be made a scapegoat for the Government's shortcomings as the drought moved south during the autumn.

OEOA warned in November that continued food aid to most areas would only deepen their dependence on outside help. Peasant farmers now needed money to revive their fragile agricultural economy. For this the World Bank, the UN Development Programme and the small International Fund for Agricultural Development (Ifad) were vital. Ifad, originally funded jointly by OECD and Opec, had lent small sums for better seeds and new ploughs to 40 million of the world's poorest farmers, not only in Africa. But when Libya, Iran and Saudi Arabia ceased to contribute to Opec the US also opted out; and Ifad had largely kept going with funds from three Scandinavian countries and Italy. In September the US appeared to be thinking again. Although it was disenchanted with the UN and aid agencies as a whole, it had no complaints about Ifad's value-for-money aid and small running-costs.

REFUGEES. Jean-Pierre Hocké, Swiss director of operations of the International Red Cross, succeeded Poul Hartling as High Commissioner for Refugees (UNHCR) at the end of the year. There had been some support for an Egyptian diplomat, Butros Ghali, but the post was traditionally considered non-political. In June Mr Hartling had reduced his annual budget for UNHCR's 10 million refugees to $319 million to bolster his special appeal for Africa which reached over $102 million by December. Seven European countries asked for greater efforts to stem the increasing flow of refugees to Western Europe. These, mainly Tamils from Sri Lanka and Iranians, were expected to number 105,000 in 1985.

HEALTH. The World Health Organization (WHO) opened a research centre for the Acquired Immune Deficiency Syndrome (AIDS), of which 28,000 cases had been notified by October. Only 5 to 20 per cent of carriers developed the lethal virus. No black African or East European country except Czechoslovakia had reported cases, but a WHO conference of nine Central African states (where AIDS was rife) provided more information (see Pt. XIV, Ch. 1). Health care experts and representatives of pharmaceutical firms discussed how to prevent the dumping of dangerous or unwanted drugs on Third World countries.

POPULATION. The UN Children's Fund (Unicef) expected to save the lives of an additional $3\frac{1}{2}$ million children a year by 1990 through its immunization and oral rehydration programmes. This would produce a secondary population explosion which could be stemmed only if more money was devoted to family planning. Infant mortality rates had halved and life expectancy had risen by 41 per cent since the 1950s.

The United States withheld $4·7 million from the UN Fund for Population Activities (UNFPA) in 1985 because of China's abortion practices, although UNFPA kept a separate account for American funds which it did not spend on China. Congress stated its intention to withdraw its full $47 million contribution (one-third) from the fund in 1986. Unicef was popular with many Americans, but the 'right to life' lobby was powerful.

WOMEN. The conference to review the Decade for Women was held in Nairobi in July. Both Russia and the US had opposed the proliferation of large UN conferences, but President Reagan's daughter successfully headed the American delegation. Seventy-eight of the states who sent delegations were said to have ratified the Convention on the Elimination of Discrimination against women. The Decade provided useful surveys on the situation of women in developing countries, in the apartheid system and in occupied Jewish territories.

EDUCATION AND INFORMATION. The conference of the UN Educational, Scientific and Cultural Organization (Unesco), meeting in Sofia in October, approved a budget for 1985 and 1986. American staff were not to lose their jobs because of US withdrawal, but future recruitment would give preference to nationals of member states. Unesco had made some financial reforms but had turned down a Western proposal to concentrate only on programmes which had universal support. The British Prime Minister, confirming the UK's provisional notice of withdrawal (see AR 1984, p. 47), stated that it was not in Britain's interest to remain in Unesco after December. The serious debates about the so-called New World Information and Communication Order (NWICO), which had been a major reason for the UK decision, had moved, however, from

Unesco to the UN Committee on Information. NWICO had been a badly-handled attempt by Third World countries to get more sympathetic media treatment for their problems and less emphasis on their failures. Some Western journalists believed that NWICO could lead to censorship and distortion.

HUMAN RIGHTS. The Assembly expressed deep concern at various reports on human rights violations. Felix Ermacora of Austria alleged mass killings in Afghanistan and widespread removal of Afghan people into towns and destruction of agricultural land and irrigation systems in order to starve out insurgents. Iran's summary executions, torture and denial of freedom of thought and religion continued. Chile's new constitution reduced democratic and human rights. 'Involuntary disappearances' were still as common as before in Guatemala; and government and insurgents alike in El Salvador consistently violated the Geneva Conventions on treatment of prisoners. Syria failed to persuade members that no action should be taken on the first two reports, and the US abstained on resolutions on the last two.

OTHER ISSUES. Rules for the administration of juvenile justice were adopted by the Congress on the Treatment of Offenders in Milan. The Food and Agricultural Organization (FAO) approved an international code for the distribution and use of pesticides.

Chapter 2

THE COMMONWEALTH

ONE subject dominated the politics of the Commonwealth throughout 1985 and the Commonwealth heads of government meeting (CHOGM) held in Nassau in October—South Africa. As the violence persisted in the republic and international calls for sanctions multiplied, it became clear early in the year that the major issue for Nassau would be the need for Commonwealth action to help dismantle apartheid and win political participation for the blacks. The Commonwealth had long been committed to equal political rights in South Africa; the 1983 New Delhi communique had gone so far as to declare that a just solution could be achieved only by 'majority rule on the basis of a free and fair exercise of universal adult suffrage by all the people in a united and non-fragmented South Africa'.

In the months before Nassau increasing pressure from Commonwealth countries for economic sanctions produced repeated statements by the British Government that it did not believe sanctions either workable or desirable. The Prime Minister, Mrs Margaret Thatcher, argued that they would damage South Africa's infrastructure and bring more hardships on blacks than on whites. On 23 July, in a major policy speech to the Royal Commonwealth Society in London, Sir Geoffrey Howe, Foreign and Commonwealth Secretary, put down the British marker for Nassau. He said, unequivocally: 'We remain firmly opposed to economic sanctions of any kind.' In this view the British stood alone in the Commonwealth. Australia and New Zealand were firmly pro-sanctions and even the Conservative Canadian Government of Mr Brian Mulroney gave Mrs Thatcher little comfort.

Right up to Nassau Britain stood firm. At the formal opening on 16 October, India's Rajiv Gandhi called for comprehensive mandatory sanctions and all the other speakers opposed the British line. For the two days of the weekend retreat at nearby Lyford Cay the leaders wrestled with Mrs Thatcher to find common ground. The outcome was a compromise (see DOCUMENTS). Mrs Thatcher would not have the word 'sanctions', but she did agree to certain 'measures' and the sending of 'signals' to Pretoria.

In the negotiations at Lyford, largely carried on by Mr Mulroney and Mr Gandhi, Mrs Thatcher insisted on a call for suspension of violence on all sides, and that any economic action should be accompanied by an attempt to achieve a dialogue between all communities in South Africa. This dialogue, it was agreed, should be initiated by a group of eminent Commonwealth persons (an Australian proposal). Commonwealth leaders insisted on a time limit; the leaders of seven countries or their deputies were to meet after six months to decide whether 'adequate' progress had been made, and, if it had not, 'some of us' would consider further sanctions.

Britain had become, albeit reluctantly, part of a Commonwealth process on South Africa. To that extent Mrs Thatcher had been moved further than she had wished to go. Her fellow Commonwealth leaders had not taken her as far as they had wanted, but they had considered unity essential in dealing with South Africa.

The 'eminent persons' group was assembled in the following weeks. Its seven members were Mr Malcolm Fraser (Australia), General Olusegun Obasanjo (Nigeria), Lord Barber of Wentbridge (Britain), Dame Nita Barrow (Barbados), Mr John Malecela (Tanzania), Sardar Swaran Singh (India) and Archbishop Edward W. Scott (Canada). Mr Fraser and General Obasanjo were to be co-chairmen. The seven met in London in December and agreed on a plan of action. Their needs were transmitted to Pretoria, whose immediate response was muted, and a reply was received on Christmas Eve.

Besides the Accord on Southern Africa, the Nassau summit issued a Declaration on World Order, which arose from anxieties over the drift from multilateralism that had been a feature of Western policy in recent years. The Declaration was seen as a 40th birthday message of support to the UN. Commonwealth leaders later took some satisfaction from the fact that whereas the UN failed to agree on a birthday declaration, the Commmonwealth—nearly one-third of the UN membership—was able to do so with ease. In making their Declaration the leaders had particularly in mind the pending British withdrawal from Unesco—another issue on which Britain found itself almost isolated in the Commonwealth. The British rejected pleas by most Commonwealth countries, including Australia and Canada, to rescind the notice of withdrawal given a year earlier, and they quit the organization on 31 December.

In mid-year the Commonwealth Secretariat celebrated its 20th birthday and the Secretary-General, Mr Shridath Ramphal, began his third five-year term of office. Diplomat Mr 'Inoke Faletau of Tonga took over as director of the Commonwealth Foundation on 1 January. The Commonwealth Fund for Technical Cooperation (CFTC) continued to win support for its widely-admired aid programme. Its annual expenditure in 1985–86 was expected to reach £27 million, compared with a final figure of £20.5 million in 1984–85. Canada continued to be the major donor. Almost every developing country was making a financial contribution, and 70 per cent of the experts provided by the CFTC were from developing countries.

The Commonwealth continued in 1985 to put emphasis on small states. The Bahamas was the smallest country so far to host a Commonwealth summit, while the annual Finance Ministers' meeting was held in the even smaller state of the Maldives, which had just transferred from the category of Special Member to full membership of the Commonwealth. After South Africa, small states' security was the most important topic at Nassau. The leaders had before them the report of the 14-member study group set up a year earlier, entitled *Vulnerability: Small States in the Global Society*. Officials, it was agreed, should meet and begin implementing its 79 recommendations.

Other major Commonwealth meetings during the year included: in February a Canada–Caribbean meeting of Prime Ministers in Kingston, Jamaica; in March the first-ever meeting of prison officials in Hong Kong; in April a meeting of consular officials in London; in May a workshop, also in London, to discuss how to counter South African propaganda; in June a youth conference in Ottawa to mark International Youth Year; in July the first meeting of Ministers responsible for women's affairs in Nairobi; and in September a meeting of foresters in Victoria, British Columbia.

The Queen visited the Bahamas at the time of the Nassau summit and made a major Caribbean tour of nine other countries, including Grenada, from which American troops had by then been withdrawn.

A cloud over prospects for the 1986 Commonwealth Games in Edinburgh lifted in July when last-minute court action led to a decision by the New Zealand Rugby Football Union to call off a tour of South Africa, after months during which the Union had defied government appeals to stop the tour and abide by the Gleneagles Agreement.

At Nassau the leaders agreed that Canada would host the 1987 summit—almost certainly to be held in Vancouver.

Chapter 3

THE EUROPEAN COMMUNITY

THE European Community entered 1985 in a mood of foreboding. The prospect of Spain's and Portugal's accession within 12 months cast a heavy shadow, since the most difficult elements of the enlargement negotiations were still to come, and the member states were still locked in argument over the development of the Community's policy-making system and their differing long-term concepts of Europe's future. There were, however, some more promising signs. A new European Commission took office, headed by M Jacques Delors, a man committed, so he said, to the end of Euro-pessimism, and the member states entered the year with few general elections due, thus anticipating a period of political calm during which progress could be achieved.

It did indeed prove to be a year of crises, but a year in which some of them were resolved. The negotiations for the enlargement were successfully completed by the end of March and the second half of the year saw major advances in achieving a broad consensus on the structure and nature of the Community. Although the problems of agriculture and the budget still haunted much EEC activity, other aspects of business were taking an increasingly prominent role. There were a further commitment to making a reality of the common market by 1992, new developments in the European research field and a further extension of external relations policy. The Community found itself a role in monetary affairs when the United States accepted the need for concerted international action to tackle the crisis of the over-valued dollar.

The year as a whole thus provided a more promising overture for the enlarged Community than many had anticipated. A number of issues fundamental to its future had been resolved and the new Community of 12 could feel somewhat more confident in its capacity to develop.

ENLARGEMENT. It was always clear that the accession of Spain and Portugal would mean spending money within the existing Community. Investment was needed to damp down political opposition to enlargement in the Mediterranean regions of France, Italy and Greece and to finance the process of adjustment that would be needed to cope with competing agricultural products from the new member states. It was not foreseen, however, how fiercely the Greek Government would block progress on enlargement unless a generous settlement was made for Greece—a situation made all the more complex because of the difficulty of settling the Community budget for 1985.

The threat of Greek Prime Minister Andreas Papandreou to use his country's veto against the enlargement pushed Greece to the centre of the negotiations and required a package of decisions which would settle the transitional arrangements for Spain and Portugal, agree money and measures for the Mediterranean regions of present member states and determine the shape of the Community budget. The process was compressed into the last week of March, culminating in the European summit of 29–30 March in Brussels.

The accession negotiations were eventually concluded at 4 o'clock in the morning of 29 March, when Italy's Foreign Minister Giulio Andreotti, as President of the Community's Council of Ministers, announced that the 10 had reached agreement with the two applicant countries on the major outstanding questions: agriculture, fisheries, social affairs, finance and the status of the Canary Islands. The announcement marked the end of more than six years of difficult negotiations and made Spanish and Portuguese accession possible for January 1986. The detailed points still unsettled were soon negotiated, to allow the Treaties of Accession to be signed in Madrid and Lisbon on 12 June 1985.

MEDITERRANEAN PROGRAMMES. The terms for resolving the Greek demand for extra finance were embodied in the Integrated Mediterranean Programmes (IMPs), proposed by the Commission in 1981 but not finally agreed until the summit of March.

The formula agreed provided for seven-year programmes designed to improve the economic structures of the Mediterranean regions of Greece, France and Italy to enable them to adjust to enlargement. A total of 4,100 MECU[1] (million European currency units) was allocated as grant aid, plus a further 2,500 MECU in loan capital. Greece would be assured of 2,000 MECU in grant finance. These sums would be channelled partly through increased regional and social funds and partly through a specific IMP fund of 1,600 MECU. Agricultural and rural problems would have a high priority in the programmes, but the improvement of communications and development of small and medium-sized businesses would also receive help.

While the deal imposed a substantial new burden on member states as a whole, Britain could accept it with equanimity. Thanks to the newly-negotiated system of rebates for the UK (see AR 1984, p. 344), Prime Minister Margaret Thatcher was able to announce that the deal would cost her government no more than £10 million extra a year.

---

[1] 1 MECU = approximately £600,000

THE COMMUNITY BUDGET. The institutional struggle for power between the European Parliament and the Council of Ministers continued to centre on budgetary affairs, one of the few areas of Community activity in which the Parliament had significant power jointly with the Council. At the beginning of the year the Parliament had already refused to endorse the 1985 budget as put forward by the Council; by its end the Council was refusing to accept a 1986 budget which had been voted and signed by the Parliament.

The 1985 budget presented the more fundamental problem. Because the Community had reached the limit of its spending powers and could not call up more finance through the EEC resources system until the beginning of 1986, the Council had effectively settled for a draft budget based on 10 months' spending. Parliament expressed the view that 'a budget which does not cover 12 months of revenue and expenditure is not acceptable' and refused to sign, so giving the budget no legal validity. This obliged the Community to operate month by month on the basis of 1984 spending, and forced Ministers to seek a solution.

The solution was simple enough: that member states would sign an inter-governmental agreement to meet the shortfall through national contributions outside the normal budget system. Almost 2,000 MECU would be required. This was not a formula which much appealed to the Parliament, but MEPs had made a telling point on the bigger issue and they finally signed a new 1985 budget on 13 June. It totalled 28,400 MECU. The special rebate of 1,000 MECU which had been agreed for Britain and the further rebate for Germany were to be settled by a reduction in their contributions.

The institutional conflict loomed again over the 1986 budget, when the Council of Ministers insisted on paring down the Commission's original proposals. In the view of both Commission and Parliament, the Council's draft provided inadequate resources to meet the costs of enlargement or the demands of food aid. Towards the end of the year agreement between Council and Parliament seemed in sight, but, when the matter came to plenary session of Parliament, members voted for substantial further increases in the budget, in the Council's view exceeding the legal limit. This version of the budget, amounting to 33,400 MECU, was duly signed by Parliament, accepted by the Commission and put into effect. The Council did not accept this decision and voted to take the European Parliament to the Court of Justice to test the legality of its action.

EUROPEAN UNION. After years of abortive effort, the Community at last succeeded in making real progress towards better decision-making and a clearer definition of the Community's ambitions. At the Luxembourg summit of 2–3 December, heads of government agreed on amendments to the Community treaties and a new Treaty of Political

Cooperation, subject to Italian and Danish reserves. The arguments concerning the future direction of the Community seemed resolved, at least for a few years.

The steps towards the December agreement were hindered by widely divergent views on many aspects of the Community's future, and it seemed to the last that the negotiations might end in stalemate and recrimination. The most far-reaching approach was that of the Italian Government, which chaired the Council of Ministers for the first half of 1985. Its position reflected the federalist views on European Union expressed by Altiero Spinelli, president of the institutional affairs committee of the European Parliament. At the other end of the spectrum were Denmark, Greece and the United Kingdom, all anxious to keep in check any moves towards political union.

A report from an ad hoc committee on institutional affairs (the Dooge Committee) was presented in March and provided the basis for much of the further negotiation. This report stressed the need for a 'qualitative leap'. The common political will must be stressed, said the report, 'by the formulation of a genuine political entity among European states: i.e., a European Union'.

This need for a qualitative leap was felt most keenly among the original six member states, but the strength of their feeling was under-estimated by others. Thus at the Milan summit of 28–29 June the British Prime Minister, who had taken advantage of a cooling atmosphere between President Mitterrand of France and Chancellor Kohl of Germany to present practical proposals for improving decision-making without modifying the existing treaties, found herself defeated when Prime Minister Craxi of Italy called for a vote on the setting-up of an inter-governmental conference to consider amendments to the Treaty of Rome. Denmark and Greece joined the UK in voting against. Another conflict seemed imminent as the three non-believers struggled to resist far-reaching changes, but they need not have worried, for the commitment of other member states was also unsure when it came to the detailed negotiations.

During the autumn the inter-governmental conference—made up of the Foreign Ministers of member states assisted by the Commission—met regularly to develop a common position. This was finalized at the Luxembourg European Council in December, but subject to reserves by the Italians, who would give their agreement only if the European Parliament agreed, and by Denmark, which faced a more threatening problem in requiring the blessing of the Danish Parliament, where there was considerable opposition and the Government had no majority.

The agreement reached at Luxembourg set limits on the scope of Community ambitions, while at the same time strengthening the decision-making procedures in the sectors where the EEC institutions already had a role. It was decided to adopt a single European Act, but with two separate titles, one establishing a Treaty for Political Cooperation and the other amending the Treaty of Rome. The foreign policy of the Community was thus kept at arm's length from other EEC activities rather than being integrated in an amended treaty of Rome as some had demanded. Against the arguments of the Commission, which had opposed setting up an alternative centre of power, a small secretariat was to be established to service political cooperation. The Commission was given a seat at the political cooperation table and the European Parliament was assured of close involvement, but neither institution was given a central role.

Under the amendments to the existing Treaty, various new elements were to be introduced, including the European Monetary System (EMS), research and technology policy and environment policy. Incorporation of these new texts was designed to provide a firmer constitutional basis for developing policies in these fields, but did little to extend the powers of the EEC institutions. Thus the EMS remained the subject of 'cooperation between member states' who would 'respect existing powers in this field'—a reference to the policy-making role of certain central banks.

On research and technology the amendments were designed to encourage Community activity, although falling short of the desire of some smaller member countries to subordinate all major research projects—including the French-inspired 'Eureka' project—to Community management. The text finally agreed called for a multinational framework programme for EEC activities in research and technology, with provisions to encourage the establishment of cooperative ventures, the possibility of Community participation in projects involving some but not all member states, and new rules for financial aid to projects.

The most far-reaching changes proposed to the Treaty of Rome concerned the elimination of the obstacles to a free internal market, described as 'an area without frontiers in which the free movement of goods, persons, services and capital is ensured'. For a long time governments had moved at a snail's pace in eliminating non-tariff barriers, such as varying industrial standards and health and safety regulations. Majority voting was to be introduced into several articles of the Treaty to speed the process, and the European Parliament was to be given new powers to amend legislation in certain circumstances—a meagre extension of the powers of the Strasbourg Assembly, but a step forward from its purely consultative role.

The amendments to the internal market articles of the Treaty named 1992 as the date by which obstacles should have been removed—subject to various exceptions on legitimate health and safety grounds and a general right for governments to take any steps they deemed necessary to deal with immigration from non-Community countries and to combat terrorism, crime and drug trafficking. Final agreement on this package of reforms was dependent on ratification by all national parliaments, a prospect reserved for 1986.

INTERNAL MARKET. The commitment of member states to achieve a genuine common market by 1992 was based on proposals put forward by the Delors Commission in a June White Paper. It was clear enough that a new approach was needed. Common Market in name was no common market in practice. Ministers had struggled over the years to reach decisions on particular technical standards which varied so widely between member states that in some sectors free trade simply did not exist. New barriers arose as quickly as the old ones were eliminated.

The Commission proposed that by 1992 a genuine common market should be created with no internal frontiers. 'The objective', said the Commission, 'is total removal of barriers, not just their reduction'. The measures proposed would cover physical control at custom posts, import restrictions such as technical standards, mutual recognition of qualifications and indirect taxation.

This programme was endorsed by Ministers, who accepted the need for a new initiative, but progress continued to be slow for the remainder of the year and the timetable for progress agreed by Ministers was already slipping by the end of 1985.

AGRICULTURE. The chronic problems of the common agricultural policy (CAP) and its mounting costs were unabated. The strength of the dollar in the early part of the year kept world commodity prices reasonably high and made it easier for the Community to sell its produce in world markets, but as the dollar began to fall so the financial burden of the policy increased, requiring substantially larger sums to subsidise the sale of EEC surplus production. Even so, stocks were not sold fast enough to keep up with rising output, so the Community ended the year with official stockpiles of farm commodities valued at 9,000 MECU. Of this, 4,000 MECU would have to be written off as the value of the stocks declined—a financial liability left for 1986 and subsequent years.

The Commission's efforts during the year to speed the process of adjustment were only partially successful. It proposed a virtual freeze on prices, but with a cut of 3·6 per cent in the guaranteed prices for grains. This proposed reduction had both practical and symbolic importance, but it proved too much for the German Minister, Herr Kiechle.

In May the Agricultural Ministers did reach an agreement on most elements of the Commission's package. The quotas on milk production were to be reduced by a further 1 per cent and most product prices were subjected to minor adjustments, but a proposal for a cut in grain prices was resisted to the last by Herr Kiechle. When Mr Frans Andriessen, Commission member responsible for agriculture, halved his demand to 1·8 per cent and tried to push the matter to a vote in the Council, the German delegation, for the first time in Community history, invoked the Luxembourg compromise of 1967 and imposed a veto. This step had special irony when the German Government was pushing so strongly for qualified majority voting in discussion about the Community's future. Grain prices were never formally fixed for the year, leaving the previous year's figures still applicable.

The Commission continued to push for change in the agricultural policy. In the summer it produced a 'Green Paper' analysing the problems facing Community agriculture and setting out various options for reform, including drastic price cuts and the general imposition of production quotas. The response of the farming organizations to these ideas was predictably hostile and by the end of the year the Commission was putting forward concrete proposals of a less draconian kind, designed to remove the open-ended guarantee system for beef and cereals under which products could always be sold to intervention agencies if there was not enough demand in the market place. Proposals were mooted earlier in the year to allow milk producers to sell their quota allocation on giving up milk production, and further ideas were put forward for providing special 'pre-pension' allowances for farmers between 55 and 65 who wished to leave farming.

The Council of Ministers did take some important decisions. In March they agreed a package of measures for improving agricultural structures and adopted long-awaited measures for curbing the production of poor-quality wines. The Community's arrangements for managing the sugar market were renewed for a further five-year period, with continuation of a quota system coupled with higher charges on producers to meet the costs of the policy.

EXTERNAL RELATIONS. Growing pressure in the US Congress for trade protection conditioned the Community's trade relations with the United States. EEC negotiators faced a dilemma. They were eager to maintain a tough stance in the two main areas of contention, steel and agriculture, yet they were conscious that the Reagan Administration was under intense pressure to take more aggressive action against imports. There seemed little choice for the Community but to ease the Administration's task in reaching agreements, albeit restrictive ones, on Community exports. The alternative was confrontation which might provoke still more protectionist sentiment on the other side of the Atlantic.

Virtually all Community steel exports to the US, amounting to about 6 million tonnes and worth $2,500 million, were brought under special arrangements during the year. The 1982 arrangement on carbon steel, which accounted for 80 per cent of Community exports to the US, were renewed until 1989. It restricted sales to a certain percentage of American consumption and included for the first time a number of products which previously had been subject only to 'consultation' procedures. Stainless steels were also brought into this arrangement, having been subject before to unilateral American measures. For pipes and tubes, an arrangement was concluded in January 1985 restricting Community exports to 7·6 per cent of American consumption, except where American industry was unable to meet domestic demand.

Agricultural trade issues continued to dog relations with the US, which announced in May the introduction of a commodity export programme known as BICEP. The purpose of this mechanism was to stimulate sales of American commodities on world markets, and after the US Government had concluded a deal to sell 500,000 tonnes of wheat to Egypt it was warned that the Community would react by cutting its own export prices. Later in the year the US filed a complaint in GATT against the Community's subsidized wheat sales programme. Despite these skirmishes, neither side had the budget resources to indulge in full-scale price war.

Other products caused problems too. Old anti-dumping complaints were revived in America against French and Italian wine. In July the Community agreed—in the face of unilateral increases in US duties—to reduce export refunds on pasta products exported to the US. President Reagan vetoed a Bill restricting footwear imports, but the threat of American restrictions on textile imports continued to worry the Community, fearful that developing-country suppliers would direct trade to Europe.

Trade relations with Japan were in stalemate, although political contacts between Japanese Government and the Commission continued to develop. The Community tried to exert pressure on the Japanese to open their markets to manufactures and processed agricultural products, to liberalize their financial markets and to internationalize the yen. At the end of July, shortly after a first visit to Brussels by the Japanese Prime Minister Yasuhiro Nakasone, the Japanese announced a programme of trade liberalization measures, but the Community refused to accept these as an adequate response to the growing trade deficit between the Community and Japan.

Relations with the United States and Japan did bear some useful fruit. It was agreed that a further round of trade talks should be held in the GATT, a decision taken at the Bonn world economic summit in May despite opposition from President Mitterrand of France. He refused to support such talks without action on the monetary front—a wish that was largely fulfilled when the Group of Five met in September to agree a programme for massaging down the value of the dollar (see Pt. XVIII, Ch. 1). This initiative was warmly welcomed by the Community.

Chapter 4

COUNCIL OF EUROPE—WESTERN EUROPEAN UNION—NORTH ATLANTIC
ASSEMBLY—EUROPEAN FREE TRADE ASSOCIATION—ORGANIZATION FOR
ECONOMIC COOPERATION AND DEVELOPMENT—NORDIC COUNCIL—COMECON

COUNCIL OF EUROPE

In 1985 the European Community agreed to its enlargement from 10 to 12 members and was seeking to strengthen its integration. These circumstances made it necessary to consolidate that European identity which is founded on commitment to human and democratic values. In this respect the 21-nation Council of Europe, with its special responsibility to pursue the ever-closer union of Europe, was of paramount importance. Those Council member states which could not, or at present did not desire, to join the European Community felt an increasing need for multilateral cooperation with all the democratic states of Europe and sought to narrow the gap between the two groups.

The intensifying of cooperation between the Council of Europe and the European Community formed the subject of Committee of Ministers' Resolution (85)5 of 24 April 1985, instructing the Council's Secretary-General to join with the competent bodies of the Community in elaborating concrete proposals for joint activities in all areas where it would be likely to secure further progress towards European unity.

The same objective was shared by the report of the Commission of Eminent European Personalities under the chairmanship of the former Italian Foreign Minister, Emilio Colombo, which had been mandated by the Parliamentary Assembly to work out perspectives for European cooperation beyond the present decade. The Colombo Commission suggested a whole series of practical measures to develop machinery of cooperation between the Community and the Council of Europe and to raise the level of cooperation among the 21.

European Music Year 1985, prepared and organized by the Council of Europe and the European Community, was an excellent example of their joint activity. This cultural project, the biggest ever jointly undertaken by the states of Europe, included thousands of projects organized in cooperation with national committees in 24 European countries, including Yugoslavia, as well as in Israel and Japan; projects under the auspices of Music Year also took place in Canada, the USA and Brazil.

In the cultural field two more European Conventions were concluded in 1985, demonstrating member governments' unremitting interest in the Council's standard-setting efforts: the Convention on offences relating to cultural property and the Convention on the protection of the architectural heritage.

The European Ministerial Conference on Human Rights (Vienna, March 1985) adopted a Declaration on Human Rights in the world at large, the first text to state the common position of member states on the global protection of human rights. In evaluating the achievements of the European Human Rights Convention, Ministers initiated the improvement of procedures before the European Commission and Court of Human Rights. Following another suggestion from the conference, the Committee of Ministers set up a new committee to study all the problems posed for law, ethics and human rights by progress in the bio-medical sciences. The Committee also adopted in May a recommendation to national governments embodying practical advice on teaching and learning about human rights in school.

The European Commission on Human Rights announced on 7 December that a friendly settlement had been reached by the parties on the applications brought in 1982 by Denmark, France, the Netherlands, Norway and Sweden against Turkey. The five countries agreed to drop their inter-state application following Turkey's promise to speed up its return to democracy.

As part of the International Youth Year, the Council of Europe organized in July 1985 a European Youth Week in Strasbourg, in which 600 young people participated, and from 17 to 19 December the first conference of European Ministers responsible for youth, dealing with youth participation in society and particularly young people's responsibility in decision-making in areas that concern them. For its part the Parliamentary Assembly had organized in September, at The Hague, a public hearing on youth and employment.

In the public health field the Committee of Ministers adopted, in September, a recommendation to member governments on screening methods for AIDS (Acquired Immune Deficiency Syndrome) with important ethical, medical and social implications for blood donors (see pp. 385–6).

Specially notable was the speed with which the Council of Europe drafted and adopted a European Convention on spectator violence and misbehaviour at sports events, particularly football matches. The Convention was drafted in June within the framework of the Conference of European Ministers responsible for sport, was adopted in July by the Committee of Ministers and came into force (after ratification by three member states) on 1 November.

Council of Europe action in the political field was characterized by increased political dialogue among the 21 under the auspices of the Committee of Ministers. In accordance with a resolution on Council of Europe action in the political field, adopted on 21 November 1984, the main international problems and questions of common concern in 1985 were East-West relations, with particular attention to the CSCE (Conference on Security and Cooperation in Europe) process, and the adoption on 24 April of a resolution on European cultural identity stressing the importance of cooperation with Eastern European countries.

WESTERN EUROPEAN UNION

The reactivation of WEU as the major engine of European coopera-tion in security policy, pronounced by the Rome Declaration of October 1984 (see AR 1984, p. 351), caused some creaking in the relations between its ministerial and parliamentary bodies. The ministerial Coun-cil, in its necessarily closed deliberations, appeared active enough, and top Ministers who addressed WEU's Assembly—Herr Genscher of West Germany in May, Sr Andreotti of Italy and M Dumas of France in December—all firmly underlined the organization's unique role as the forum for seeking European consensus on defence matters. A new Secretary-General, charged by the Council with applying the Rome Declaration, established a political division of the secretariat and reorganized its defence side in three agencies, dealing respectively with arms control issues, threat assessment and cooperation in arms require-ments and manufacture.

The Assembly, however, at its May session complained that the information the Council had given about its activities was 'incomplete and inadequate'; it was specially annoyed that the Council's report omitted reference to the US Strategic Defense Initiative (SDI). Observ-ing that 'the US invitation to the European states to take part in the research programme relating to the SDI is raising many questions in Europe,' the parliamentarians urged the Council to obtain 'a collective answer' from the several member Governments. They recommended that the Council's chairman-in-office should participate fully in Assembly debates on its annual report. At both its 1985 sessions the Assembly was also concerned about the no-growth budget available for its reinforced duties.

The May Assembly passed a further Recommendation calling on the Council to seek common European positions not only on the SDI 'in order to prevent an arms race in outer space and ensure respect for existing treaty obligations', but also on a treaty to ban chemical weapons, on a comprehensive ban on nuclear tests and on General Secretary Gorbachev's declaration of a unilateral freeze on nuclear missiles in Europe. Between the two sessions the Council replied welcoming the Reagan-Gorbachev talks on nuclear arms, stressing that the SDI was no more than a scientific research programme and that tests or deployment would have to be a matter for negotiation, and emphasising the import-ance of preventing any erosion of the ABM treaty. The Assembly, at its December session, responded by asking the Council, if it could not agree on a common front on SDI, to harmonize as far as possible the responses of the seven European member countries to the US initiative, a response which should permit European industry to participate in all areas of SDI research on terms providing a genuine exchange of technology and ensuring the development of Europe's technological capacity, particularly the Eureka programme (see pp. 393–4). The Recommendation emphasized the need for the US and its European allies to discuss the political as well as the military implications of the SDI research, instructed the new WEU agency for arms control to report annually on the impact of the SDI, and called for 'maintenance of the nuclear deterrent capability of the Atlantic Alliance as long as Europe's security is not effectively guaranteed by other means'.

The Assembly also addressed itself directly to the issue of European space policy and potential. In December it asked the Council to urge member governments, *inter alia*:

> 1. to consider the adoption of a coherent space programme composed of two main elements: participation in the American space station and further development of the European launcher system—Ariane-5 with the HM-60-engine—leading to an independent European manned transportation system;
> 2. to help the European space industry ('far more scattered and less rationalized than American industry, resulting in over-equipment and excess capacity') to reorganize itself in order to ensure its independence and competitiveness in the international market.

Other matters of concern to WEU in 1985 included the Helsinki process, the need to establish 'a genuine European defence industry' based on joint research and a high degree of standardization, agreement on a common European fighter aircraft for the 1990s and the development of relations between Europe and China.

THE NORTH ATLANTIC ASSEMBLY

The North Atlantic Assembly's activities and debates in 1985 focused on a wide range of Alliance issues, including strategic defence, arms control, economic cooperation, technology transfer, terrorism and information policies.

The Assembly's spring plenary session in Stuttgart passed a key resolution on economic cooperation urging Alliance governments and parliaments to coordinate economic policies, to work towards the orderly elimination of existing trade restrictions, and to increase intra-alliance cooperation to ensure that burdens and benefits were more equitably shared.

The Assembly's annual tour in August concentrated on Nato's northern region. The twelve-day trip to Norway, Denmark and northern

Germany was highly successful in acquainting the participating MPs with some of the complexities inherent in defending this vital but vulnerable area.

The 31st annual plenary session was held in San Francisco from 10 to 15 October. A resolution supported the US Strategic Defense Initiative (SDI), within the limits of the ABM treaty. The assembly passed a resolution condemning terrorism and agreed to establish a special working group to study the question further. The plenary session was addressed by Secretary of State George Shultz. Ambassador Paul Nitze, Lord Carrington, Secretary-General of Nato, and the director of the SDI organization, General Abrahamson.

The Assembly's six committees (political, economic, civilian, military, scientific and technical, and nuclear strategy and arms control) met regularly throughout the year and adopted reports based on their findings.

EUROPEAN FREE TRADE ASSOCIATION

Efta, like OECD, celebrated its 25th anniversary in 1985. A commemorative function in the Hofburg, Vienna, on 10 May was immediately preceded by meetings of Efta Ministers, parliamentarians and representatives of economic life; links with the EEC were emphasized by a meeting between Efta Ministers, the President of the European Commission and the External Relations Commissioner and by a joint meeting of delegations from Efta's consultative committee and the EC's economic and social committee. Again like OECD (see p. 344), Efta Ministers observed that economic recovery, actual and expected, was marred by such grave problems as massive unemployment in Europe and large budget and trade deficits in the USA. 'They felt that there was scope for economic policy action in Europe, on the demand side as well as on the supply side, to achieve greater dynamism and improved growth performance.' They expressed support for 'new comprehensive trade negotiations in GATT', believing that a new GATT round was necessary to resist the menace of protectionism—a theme to which the Efta ministerial council vigorously returned at its meeting in Geneva on 4–5 November.

There, 'Ministers recognized that, with growth in the US declining, European countries had an important contribution to make to efforts aimed at ensuring stable and balanced growth.' In this respect, the close relations between Efta and the EEC, fortified by the Luxembourg Declaration of April 1984 (see AR 1984, p. 353), were obviously of great moment. During the year joint Efta-EC expert groups tackled the priority areas of technical barriers to trade, origin rules, border controls and trade documentation, with the ultimate objective of a total European free trade system. Welcoming recent meetings between Efta and EC high officials, Efta Ministers at their December session 'reiterated their determination to expand cooperation or the exchange of information in other areas of common interest, such as research and development, anti-dumping procedures, access to public procurement, protection of the environment, economic prospects and policies and certain export restrictions'.

In March Efta signed an agreement with the two European standards institutions (general and electrotechnical) setting out guidelines for European cooperation in standardization, and in June a joint declaration of intent with the European Conference of Postal and Telecommunications Administrations on standards and acceptance of tests for telecommunications equipment.

Efta welcomed the accession to the European Community of Portugal, until then a member of Efta, and Spain, which was thus recruited into the European open trade system. During 1985 Efta's Industrial Development Fund for Portugal approved seven new loans to a total value of 1,524.5 million escudos (about $9.1 million). A meeting of the joint Efta-Yugoslavia committee, held in Dubrovnik on 7–8 October, called for fresh efforts to reduce the imbalance in Yugoslav trade, by trade promotion in European markets and otherwise.

On 4 November the Efta Council formally approved the accession of Finland, previously linked by an association agreement, as a full member of Efta from 1 January 1986.

ORGANIZATION FOR ECONOMIC COOPERATION AND DEVELOPMENT

In 1985 the OECD celebrated its 25th anniversary, fortunately in a tone of confidence. Its ministerial Council, meeting in Paris on 11–12 April, noted a marked improvement in the general economic situation in the past two years. Recovery among its member countries was proceeding broadly, and inflation had been substantially reduced. Business profits and investment had risen. A significant increase in world trade, led by strong growth in the USA, had benefited both developed and developing countries. Growth in the US was expected to slacken but to continue positive, in Japan to stay vigorous.

Nevertheless, urgent problems remained, headed by persisting high levels of unemployment, particularly in Europe. OECD's December *Economic Outlook* recorded that 'the average rate of unemployment in OECD countries rose slightly in the first half of 1985. . . . Over the next 18 months, virtually no change is expected'. In Europe, the total out of work was likely to stabilize in 1986 at around 11 per cent of the workforce, more than 19 million people, though the numbers might fall in West Germany, the UK, Denmark and the Netherlands.

The Organization addressed itself directly to the unemployment problem to the extent of urging greater flexibility and mobility in labour markets, moderate wage settlements, and 'increased dynamism and adaptability' of national economies. However, the main thrust of its recommendations was, as before, to maintain the conditions for non-inflationary growth by resisting protectionist pressures, reducing major imbalances in international trade in goods and services, easing structural rigidities, controlling government spending and where necessary reducing budget deficits.

Economic Outlook identified lower interest rates as probably the most desirable route to faster growth of demand. 'Such an easing of monetary conditions would be assisted by some further downward pressure on the dollar, and this in turn would be assisted by firm action on the US federal budget deficit.' Unless this core problem was attacked soon, attempts by monetary policies to follow up the Group of Five's September initiative (see DOCUMENTS) would risk jeopardizing low US inflation and Japanese expansion. 'Monetary policies cannot be an effective substitute for appropriate fiscal policies.'

One vital aspect of fiscal policies was addressed in an OECD report on 'Social Expenditure 1960–1990', the first of a new series of social policy studies, published in March 1985. It showed that government social expenditure, currently averaging one-quarter of GDP, had grown faster than national income throughout the OECD in the last two decades. The principal conclusions were that a further increase in social spending's share of GNP could conflict with sustained economic growth, and that, although some improvements in benefits might be possible in certain countries, 'through the end of the 1980s there will be little or no room for increasing the scope and coverage of the welfare state', whose essential features could nevertheless be preserved.

Members of the Development Assistance Committee (DAC), meeting on 2–3 December with representatives of the World Bank and IMF, reviewed 25 years of development cooperation and drew the lessons of experience for future aid policies. Despite recent severe setbacks, especially in sub-Saharan Africa and Latin America, over the period as a whole development progress had been impressive. Average per-capita incomes of developing countries (high-income oil exporters omitted) had almost doubled, and health, education and life-expectancy standards had been much improved. While financial and technical assistance had played a part, 'development achievements have been mainly attributable to the efforts of developing countries themselves'. The DAC listed ten major tasks for development cooperation in the next 10 years, including reversal of economic decline in sub-Saharan Africa; comprehensive economic reform in heavily indebted countries; stimulating the creative energies of small farmers, private entrepreneurs and investors; aiding a 'green revolution' in staple food crops; improving public administration, education, training and health services; enlarging the opportunity to regulate human fertility; and protecting the natural resource bases of development from ecological degradation. These tasks required more and better development resources, including international aid.

The OECD Environment Committee, meeting at ministerial level on 18–20 June, adopted a declaration embodying a number of important policy points, including control of air pollution from fossil fuel combustion, environmentally favourable energy options, noise abatement and international cooperation concerning trans-frontier movements of hazardous wastes—a subject on which OECD Environment Ministers, meeting in Basle on 26–27 March with representatives of other institutions concerned, made constructive recommendations to member governments. The ministerial Governing Board of the International Energy Agency, on 9 July, adopted, *inter alia*, important conclusions on energy and the environment. The main points agreed were that energy efficiency and conservation remained highly important; that coal production, the most abundant OECD energy resource, should be expanded in substitution for oil; that further action was needed to realize the potential of nuclear power without harm to safety or the environment; that international cooperation was essential in regard to the prospective increased supply of natural gas from outside the OECD area; and that 'stronger and more effective research and development efforts', internationally coordinated, were 'an essential part of achieving long-term energy security'.

OECD also concerned itself with the impact of the communications revolution. Meeting on 11 April, Ministers adopted a Declaration on issues arising from transborder data flows, such as commercial information, intracorporate flows, computerized information services and scientific and technological exchanges. The Declaration was described as 'the first international effort to address economic issues raised by the information revolution'. And on 18–20 November a conference of experts from government, telecommunications, industry and trade unions was held to review recent developments in telecommunications and highlight the main international policy issues they aroused.

NORDIC COUNCIL

The 33rd session of the Nordic Council was held in Reykjavik from 4 to 8 March 1985. In terms of the number of important measures approved it was one of the most productive sessions in recent years.

The Council adopted 25 recommendations for action by the Council

of Ministers. Most important was the revised plan for economic development and full employment, resubmitted by the Council of Ministers
following the 32nd session's unanimous rejection of the original plan (see
AR 1984, p. 356). The revised plan was generally considered a good basis
for a major step forward in Nordic cooperation. It contained a large
number of clearly specified and financially supported measures designed
to promote the two aims in the plan's title. Emphasis was laid on
measures to develop further the Nordic area's internal market, including
large investments in physical infrastructure (roads and rail), the removal
of non-tariff barriers to trade, liberalization of capital movements, reduction of state subsidies hindering competition and encouragement of
frontier trade. There was also financial support for measures to promote
Nordic exports and the Nordic tourist industry; encourage Nordic technical research and development, especially in data technology; and
improve labour skills and combat youth and long-term unemployment.

Regional policy, always important in the Nordic countries, was
encouraged on a transnational basis, with measures to help the North
Cape, Mid-Nordic and West Nordic regions, including in particular the
establishment of a West Nordic fund to encourage investment in that area
(Greenland, the Faeroes and Iceland). Further recommendations in the
economic field included the development of joint Nordic economic forecasting, the encouragement of a broad debate on the public sector's role
in the Nordic economies, and the adoption of two programmes proposed
by the Council of Ministers, the first a revised labour market programme
to replace the last one adopted in 1975, the second a programme for
cooperation in agriculture and forestry, the latter representing a new
departure in Nordic cooperation.

Recommendations were also passed for common action in other
areas, *inter alia* that the Council of Ministers' proposed action programme against drug abuse (see AR 1984, p. 357) be adopted subject to
some changes; that a parliamentary committee explore the possibility of a
comprehensive harmonization of Nordic environmental legislation; that
the Council of Ministers give financial support to the International
Centre for Rehabilitation and Research into Torture in Copenhagen and
explore the possibility of making the proposed Research Institute for
Human Rights in Oslo into a Nordic institution; and that the Nordic
Council help finance the Nordic Association's regional information
centres and increase the educational material on Nordic affairs available
to schools.

The Council also adopted important recommendations, based on the
High Level Committee's report of November 1983 (see AR 1983, p. 356,
and 1984, p. 357), to improve the effectiveness of the Council and the
Council of Ministers. The Presidium's role would be strengthened, its
membership doubled from five to ten, and its composition made to reflect
the strength of the various political groups in the Council. A new

14-member budget and accounts committee would be established. The Council of Ministers would have a single common budget instead of two, its two existing secretariats (the Council of Ministers' secretariat in Oslo and the cultural secretariat in Copenhagen) would be replaced by a single secretariat in Copenhagen, while a new Nordic centre for industrial research and development would be established in Oslo.

The question of an experimental Nordic television and radio satellite (Tele-X), the first stage in a long-term programme (NORDSAT), was prominent at Reykjavik following the breakdown of negotiations between the national governments the previous month. Strong pressure from the Council, which recommended a resumption of negotiations and their completion by 15 May and then maintained the pressure on national governments throughout the summer and autumn, eventually led to the signing on 10 November of an agreement between Sweden, Norway, Finland and Iceland to proceed with the experiment. The three-year experimental satellite would start broadcasting in the second half of 1987 and the estimated cost of SKr 334 million would be shared in proportion to the four countries' respective gross national products. The Danish Government did not sign the agreement but pressure on it to participate in this Nordic cultural venture was growing.

The general debate was characterized by a more optimistic assessment of the economic situation than in recent years. National economic trends were improving, although unemployment remained a serious problem. Most speakers considered that the plan for economic development and full employment would further help strengthen their economies. Finland's Prime Minister, Mr Sorsa, for example, described Nordic cooperation in general and the plan's many concrete measures in particular as more important than ever in the light of the problems threatening the world economy. A few speakers criticized the plan as insufficiently ambitious and lacking in genuinely new ideas. Norway's Prime Minister, Mr Willoch, however, stressed the noteworthy fact that the five Nordic Governments, despite differing political complexions, had been able to agree on general economic guidelines and how most effectively to increase employment.

Several speakers strongly criticized the UK for not responding positively to the joint Nordic note of December 1984 on sulphur pollution (AR 1984, p. 357). The Nordic countries would intensify their pressure on Britain, especially in the context of the negotiations in Geneva on a binding agreement to reduce sulphur emissions by 30 per cent by 1993. Mr Willoch pointed out that at Geneva Britain had already shown a readiness to compromise and that this was a hopeful sign.

COMECON

It was a measure of the problems of integrating centrally-planned economies that in two years Comecon had met four times at Party or Government summits. Such frequency had not occurred since 1969. In 1985, as in 1984, Comecon held an 'Extraordinary Session' in addition to its 'Ordinary' annual meeting. The four sessions were linked by the need to improve the production and information technology of the industrialized members, where not only did standards fall short of those in the West, but the speed of Western advance had also patently been faster. The 1984 summit meeting of Party leaders established priority for a coordinated programme of technology transfer and application (see AR 1984, p. 358) but its formulation into agreed specific measures took eighteen months. In summarizing the outcome of the XLI (Extraordinary) Session (Moscow, 17–18 December), the Chairman of the USSR Council of Ministers, Nikolai Ryzhkov, who presided, acknowledged that there had been delays in drawing up the elaborating agreements; but in an opening address the Soviet Party General Secretary, Mikhail Gorbachev, assured delegates that the programme was based on 'time-tested principles of equitable and mutually-beneficial cooperation'.

Three agreements were signed: two were for multilateral cooperation in areas where the lag behind the West was especially serious—computerized design and fibre optics for information technology. Both envisaged inter-member collaboration in designing and applying the technology, but the second also called for a single, unified fibre-optic transmission system for the USSR and Eastern Europe (Cuba, Mongolia and Vietnam hardly yet needing it). The third agreement created an international organization, Interrobot, which besides conducting research would undertake development and execute production in robotics. Speaking after the meeting, the chairman of the USSR State Committee on Science and Technology and the corresponding Comecon chairman, Gury Marchuk, observed that the programme would run to the end of the century, a period aligned with the new Soviet Party programme and the Soviet five-year plan for 1986–90, which incorporated forecasts to the year 2000. A GDR Committee member, Werner Liebig, pointed to the political contrast with the US Strategic Defense Initiative, which, he said 'is aimed at the arms race and militarization of outer space and is not at all compatible with our programme'.

These agreements and other measures to accelerate technical progress were aimed at economizing the use of two crucial inputs in the industrialized states of Comecon—manpower and materials, especially energy. The Soviet five-year plan was the first ever to forecast no increase in manpower and to anticipate that the entire increment in national income would be derived from productivity gains. The application of robots was what could be termed an 'engineering' solution, but much overmanning and maldeployment could be combated by an 'economic' solution, by reform of central and enterprise management. Such a reform would require a profound restructuring of prices and it was significant that Comecon established a standing conference of heads of price administration. Its chairman, Nikolai Glushkov, chairman of the USSR Committee on Prices, writing in the April issue of the Comecon journal, drew attention to Soviet price changes from 1 January 1985 for certain high-technology products and to the need for revision of energy and raw materials pricing. His paper was in the same vein as the document of the XLI Session, which spoke of 'sharply reducing the specific consumption of energy and raw materials per unit of national income in the CMEA countries by the year 2000'.

The cut in Soviet energy deliveries to Comecon partners in 1982 had not been restored by the time of the December 1985 Session and the fall in Soviet oil production in both 1984 and 1985 did not augur well. But the Soviet five-year plan, to the surprise of many Western observers, set a 1990 target well above the 1983 peak output (and a gas target also well above many Western expectations) and the 1986 annual plan budgeted for 31 per cent more investment in the oil industry. The Comecon Prime Ministers must, it seems, have been faced with a Soviet demand for a contribution to that energy investment. The offer had often been made before: if Comecon partners wanted more supplies of capital-intensive natural resources, they must provide some of the capital, including convertible-currency for equipment available only in the West. Romania was discontented with Soviet offers and demands, for President Ceauşescu bluntly said after the Session that adequate steps had not been taken to solve Comecon's energy and material shortage; it could be deduced that Soviet oil and iron ore had not been earmarked for Romania at the price it had been seeking.

If the new, much higher, Soviet five-year plan targets for 1990 for oil and gas were achieved, the physical quantities could be available, but the large debts of the East European states to the USSR did not permit them to pay world prices, even in transferable roubles. The issue of indebtedness in the multilateralization of the transferable rouble was said by the 113th meeting of the Executive Committee (Moscow, 14–16 January) now to have a political dimension. A commentary on recommendations of its permanent commission on currency and finance problems by Vasili Garbuzov (who was later replaced as USSR Minister of Finance, but was then commission chairman) included the need for an uninterrupted settlements procedure (doubtless there had been blockages of debtors by creditors) and for equivalence among participating currencies. His report, in the same April issue of the Comecon journal, showed that Cuba joined the transferable rouble system in 1976 and Vietnam in 1981, and noted that they, with Mongolia, should be entitled to concessionary credit.

The inadequacy of Comecon's financial system contrasted with progress on inter-enterprise agreements on specialization in specific physical terms. Commenting on the XLI Session, the Secretary-General, Vyacheslav Sychev, observed that, of 35,900 million roubles of mutual trade in engineering goods in 1984, 42·6 per cent was exchanged under Comecon specialization and cooperation agreements, against 21·7 per cent of 13,800 million roubles of trade in 1975. The 116th meeting of the Executive (Moscow, 24–26 September) recommended more direct relations between enterprises and institutes to improve technology transnationally and to engage in joint research and development. It also resolved on a new phase of standardization during 1986-90, especially in high technology (robotics and microprocessors especially) and of metrology to unify measurements practices in these new fields.

Comecon's ordinary meeting (XL Session, Warsaw, 25–27 June), attended by observers from Afghanistan, Angola, Ethiopia, Laos, Mozambique, Nicaragua, South Yemen and Yugoslavia, produced a draft programme for cooperation on economizing the use of materials to the year 2000 and examined members' investment plans for 1986-90 within the context of Comecon coordination. Most members, it noted, had signed bilateral agreements with each other on their cooperation to the end of the century. It heard progress reports on Soviet nuclear power plants which would supply electricity to Bulgaria, Czechoslovakia, Hungary, Poland and Romania, and on the pipeline from the Yamburg deposit (now under development with East European funding) to supply gas throughout East Europe.

The Session 'approved proposals for the establishment of relations between Comecon and the EEC'. A few days before, on 30 May, Gorbachev, at a banquet in Moscow for the Italian Prime Minister, Bettino Craxi, had said; 'It is time, I think, to establish between them mutually beneficial relations in economic matters', and revealed that Comecon was preparing a document. Craxi was appropriately the first bearer of the new policy, being then the Chairman of the European Council, though the 1984 Comecon summit had indicated what was in the offing (see AR 1984, p. 360). The official communication came via the ambassador of Poland (then holding the presidency of Comecon's Executive Committee) to the President of the European Commission, Jacques Delors, on 14 June, and on 19 June the European Council authorized the Commission to proceed with discussions with Comecon.

In October the latter made it clear to the Commission that it recognized the differences between the two groups and that any treaty should be 'within their respective fields of competence'. Shortly afterwards the European Commissioner for External Relations, Willi de Clerq, warned that the EEC would not accept Comecon 'as a kind of intermediary between those Comecon member countries which wish to maintain relations with us'. The formulation was disingenuous in that in the negotiations of the 1970s the Comecon Secretariat had accepted that any EEC treaty would be with each Comecon member plus the Secretariat and not with Comecon as a body, but it was doubtless inspired by Hungary's renewal of interest in a separate treaty, following the 1984 breakdown (see AR 1984, p. 360), which János Kádár expressed during his November visit to the UK, and by Romania's acceptance of an EEC study (to be undertaken in 1986) on joint ventures and similar cooperation with EEC entities. The Commissioner's statement was made in the European Parliament (23 October) and did not constitute the EEC's formal and fuller response.

The other three Executives were linked to the Council, two of them at the time of its meetings (the 115th in June and the 117th in December) and the 114th (15–18 May) preparing the agenda both for the XL Session and for a conference of Party Secretaries responsible for the economy (Moscow, 20–21 May), at which Mikhail Gorbachev's address and the reported discussion centred on promoting technological progress and economic efficiency.

Technology to reduce requirements of energy and raw materials was the principal topic at the 32nd meeting of the Comecon Committee for Scientific and Technical Cooperation (17–19 July); it was held in Belgrade, the first occasion on which a Comecon meeting had been held outside a member country, as a gesture for the twentieth anniversary of the agreement giving Yugoslavia observer status.

The Council of the International Bank for Economic Cooperation (IBEC) met in Moscow on 18-19 April (its 61st session) to approve the balance sheet for 1984 and the credit plan for 1985. For the first time the Bank for International Settlements (BIS) and the African Development Bank were represented; Comecon's other bank, the International Investment Bank (IIB), also participated, under an agreement between the two banks, and the representation of Comecon observers was widened by the inclusion of the Banco Central de Nicaragua; the non-Comecon central banks already represented, as also in 1985, were those of Afghanistan, Ethiopia, Finland, Laos, Mozambique, South Yemen and Yugoslavia.

The BIS reported a turn-round in East-West financial flows. In contrast to 1984, East Europe was a net taker of funds from Western banks. In 1984 East European deposits in the West had been increased by $2,418 million but $528 million were withdrawn in the first half of 1985; in 1984 East Europe's liabilities were cut by $3,762 million but they rose in the first half of 1985 by $3,141 million. The principal contributor was the USSR, which had borrowed as much as it had lent in 1984 (by $419 million each way), but ran deposits down by $1,809 million in the first half of 1985 while raising new credits by $2,422 million. Overall, the OECD put the USSR net debt at the start of 1985 at $15,000 million (gross $24,000 million) and that of the rest of Eastern Europe at $50,100 million (gross $59,900 million).

Chapter 5

AFRICAN CONFERENCES AND ORGANIZATIONS—SOUTH-EAST ASIAN
ORGANIZATIONS—CARIBBEAN ORGANIZATIONS—ORGANIZATION OF AMERICAN
STATES—SISTEMA ECONOMICO LATINO-AMERICANA—SOUTH PACIFIC REGIONAL
INSTITUTIONS

AFRICAN CONFERENCES AND ORGANIZATIONS

THE change that came over the Organization of African Unity at its previous summit in 1984, when the increasing pressure of Africa's economic problems seemed at last to have come home to its leaders, was maintained and consolidated in 1985. The summit held in Addis Ababa from 18 to 20 July had Africa's economy very definitely as the main item on the agenda.

The resultant Addis Ababa Economic Declaration excited a certain amount of attention, if only because the African leaders recognized in franker terms than is usual at such conferences that part of the blame for Africa's economic woes lay in the policies of the African states themselves. This recognition also led to a strong reassertion of the doctrine that 'the collective effort of the member states is the most important weapon for tackling the current economic crisis'.

The measures to be adopted began with a restatement of the Lagos Plan of Action of 1980, which President Nyerere of Tanzania, the outgoing Chairman of the OAU, told the conference had so far been a failure. Observers had noted that in the five years since the Plan was launched most of Africa's economic indicators showed increasingly negative figures, which had been worsened by the drought years of 1983–84. The Plan provided for development of both agriculture and industry, stressing infrastructure development and the need to develop regional groupings with the aim of establishing an African Common Market.

The 1985 Declaration, while saying that measures should be taken to accelerate the Plan's implementation, in fact sharpened its immediate objectives in the light of experience, and put special emphasis on agriculture and 'improvement of the food situation'. Recording that nearly half the OAU member states were now dependent on food aid, it committed them to 'the gradual increase in the share of agriculture in national total public investment of between 20 and 25 per cent by 1989'.

The most dramatic statistics to come out of the summit concerned Africa's indebtedness, which by the end of 1985 was estimated at $170,000 million, 59 per cent of the continent's Gross National Product.

In 1984 one quarter of Africa's total export earnings went to debt servicing, and for some countries it became more than 50 per cent. The Declaration appealed for assistance from creditors in easing the burden, and called for an international conference to discuss the matter. More radical proposals for a debt moratorium were buried early in the discussion, and in a key passage the heads of state said: 'We recognize that the external debts are obligations that our member states have individually contracted, and which they have to honour'.

Despite the importance of the joint Declaration, it was still the individual governments that had to implement the policies. The precedent of the Lagos Plan was not encouraging, although the five years which followed it were a period of world recession and drought, as well as the worst political crisis in the OAU's history. However, the African economic crisis had now reached such dimensions that the leaders saw their own political survival in the balance. This meant that politics were relegated to the sidelines: the Western Sahara issue did not feature at all although there were some offstage noises from Morocco, now no longer a member; and Chad, while the subject of a resolution on reconciliation, was not a matter for controversy.

The one political issue still central to the OAU's vocation was that of South Africa. As the crisis there mounted, the OAU's positions, which in the past sometimes seemed desperate rhetoric, came to have more urgency. The resolutions condemned South African aggression against Angola and Botswana, and criticized the US policy of constructive engagement. There was also a warning to the US that any interference in the internal affairs of Angola would be seen as a 'hostile act' towards the continent as a whole (a reference to possible US assistance to the rebel Unita movement).

It was impossible, however, to keep politics out of the election of the OAU Secretary-General. Although it was predicted that Niger's Foreign Minister, Ide Oumarou, would be elected unopposed, Mali's Foreign Minister, Blondin Beye, unsuccessful in two previous elections, stood again. Though he withdrew after the first round, M Oumarou could still not obtain the requisite two-thirds vote, and it was only after serious talk of a new 'third man' and dramatic appeals from a number of leaders that a consensus emerged, and Oumarou was elected on the seventh vote.

The new Chairman of the OAU, President Diouf of Senegal, took his functions very seriously, and proceeded on a tour of the front-line states to see the Southern African situation for himself, before going to the UN for its fortieth anniversary. Both there and on a subsequent visit to Washington, he pleaded not just on the Southern African issue, but also on economic issues, and secured vital US support for the holding of a special session of the UN General Assembly on Africa's problems. The proposed conference on African debt met with more objections, although at the end of the year, at the Franco-African summit in Paris, remarks made by President Mitterrand suggested that France was ready to support the proposal—the first major convert to the idea in the West. Most Western governments felt that debt was better discussed case by case.

The Franco-African summit was otherwise not notable for any new political developments, as the participants valued it largely for the informal contacts that could be made there. It was noted that the French-speaking countries reasserted their supremacy, which had been in danger of dilution. The difference between full members and observers was clearly re-stated, the invitation list was more carefully restricted, and the French-speakers were permitted a session to themselves. King Hassan of Morocco attended in person for the first time, and Morocco's status was raised from that of observer to full member. 'Morocco returns to Africa via Paris' was how one magazine put it.

It was in general a difficult year for regional organizations. The Southern African Development Coordination Conference (SADCC) continued to be frustrated in its objectives of lessening dependence on South Africa by the blocking of railways in Mozambique and Angola by South African-backed rebels. The Preferential Trade Area (PTA) in East and Central Africa continued to look embryonic, as did the Economic Community of Central African States.

In West Africa, groupings seemed to be positively ailing: the Economic Community of West African States (ECOWAS) was obliged to postpone its summit from May to July, because of tension following a new round of expulsion of 'aliens' from Nigeria (see p. 226). ECOWAS members were increasingly concerned that Nigeria, the main architect of the grouping, was losing its commitment to it because of domestic economic problems. At the summit in Lomé in July, Nigeria inherited the chairmanship of the organization. Economic and political difficulties were behind the inability to hold summits of two other groups—the CEAO (see Burkina Faso, p. 236), and the Mano River Union, which included Sierra Leone, Liberia and Guinea. All African groupings were seriously impeded in their operations simply because members found it increasingly hard to pay their subscriptions.

SOUTH-EAST ASIAN ORGANIZATIONS

An early and massive 1984-85 dry-season Vietnamese offensive compelled the Khmer resistance to abandon temporary settlements just inside Kampuchea and to evacuate 230,000 civilians across the border into Thailand. The offensive did not inflict sufficient losses on the resistance forces to persuade the Asean countries and the United Nations to abandon their cause. Instead, early in February, the Asean Foreign

Ministers for the first time called on friendly countries to sustain the Khmer resistance to the Vietnamese occupation with arms supplies.

The Indonesians again probed Vietnamese intentions in formal and informal meetings, but concluded that Vietnam was not yet ready to compromise on Kampuchea. In April Vietnam and the Khmer coalition were represented at an Indonesian celebration of the thirtieth anniversary of the Bandung Conference (see AR 1955, p. 165). The validity of the principles set out in 1955, including respect for territorial sovereignty and independence, was reaffirmed, but reference to Kampuchea and Afghanistan was avoided. In July the Asean countries proposed indirect talks between the Khmer resistance groups, Vietnam and the Heng Samrin regime, but this was rejected by Vietnam. In August, with the UN session approaching, Vietnam, Laos and the Heng Samrin regime displayed more flexibility and 'took note' of the indirect proposal. A related proposal, made originally by Prince Norodom Sihanouk, for an informal social meeting between the three coalition groups, the Heng Samrin group and the Vietnamese was still receiving attention late in the year.

The UN Secretary-General visited the region in late January, his main concerns being the Kampuchean and East Timor issues. In Bangkok he undertook to use all the resources of his office to seek a solution to the Kampuchean problem, but after talks in Hanoi he concluded that the gap between the two sides was too wide to warrant any early further visit to the area. In November the UN General Assembly again called forcibly for Vietnamese forces to be withdrawn from Kampuchea and for it to be freed from outside interference. The General Assembly vote was 114 to 21 with 16 abstentions, a further advance in the growing majority for such motions since 1979. A new Austrian president of the UN International Conference on Kampuchea proposed to visit South-East Asia early in 1986. Meanwhile the Secretary-General's Special Representative continued to coordinate the flow of official and private humanitarian aid to the Khmers within Kampuchea and in the border camps, amounting since 1980 to US$850 million, while the UN High Commissioner for Refugees tried to assist the resettlement of refugees from Vietnam, Laos and Kampuchea and to reduce the disincentives which inhibited merchant ships from picking up 'boat people' in distress. The 'boat people' coming from Vietnam at a rate of over 1,000 a month were increasingly economic rather than political refugees.

Escap (the UN's Economic and Social Commission for Asia and the Pacific) placed some emphasis on regional cooperation in environmental problems and transfer of technologies. Economic cooperation within Asean was again restricted by the competitive rather than complementary nature of the member economies. The Asean industrial project for Thailand, designed to produce soda ash from rock salt, was abandoned and the main component of trade between Asean countries, petroleum and its products, declined as member countries developed their own refining capacity. The prospects for private joint ventures seemed greater than for state joint ventures. Asean economic Ministers, however, found it useful to hold talks as a group with major economic powers or groupings, especially Japan, the USA and the EEC.

All the countries in the region were affected, in general adversely, by growing protectionism in major markets for industrial products and by the decline in demand for and prices of primary commodities, notably rice, vegetable oils, sugar, mineral oils, rubber and tin. In October the inability of the International Tin Council's buffer stock to sustain tin prices at artificial levels led to the suspension of tin trading in London and Kuala Lumpur and to the prospect of prices that would force many mines to close down. The threat of protectionism was a little eased at the end of the year by the decision to launch another GATT round and by the presidential veto in the USA of a Bill to increase protection for the American textile, footwear and copper-mining industries.

CARIBBEAN ORGANIZATIONS

The slowness of Caribbean Community (Caricom) countries in implementing the 'Nassau Understanding' (see AR 1984, p. 366), which prescribed a new common external tariff and the removal of non-tariff barriers to intra-regional trade, caused continuing concern. The heads of government conference of Caricom states, meeting in 1985 in Barbados, produced few positive outcomes. One such was an agreement on a new 'marketing regime' for free intra-regional trade and a common external tariff on a list of primary products and livestock. The member countries were encouraged to purchase their sugar requirements from regional suppliers and to channel the proceeds to meet debts owing under the now non-functioning Caribbean multilateral clearing facility.

Caricom countries expressed deep concern over declining US interest and commitment in the region. Continuous reductions in the Caricom sugar quota to the US market since the 306,500 tons of 1974 had put the 1984–85 quota at 134,420 tons, a cut of 15 per cent on the previous year. This came as another harsh blow to a failing industry so vital to several of these countries. Other protectionist measures, notably restrictions on textile products and ethanol entering the US market, also worried Caricom leaders. US aid flows to the Caribbean, as a result of moves to reduce the huge federal budget deficit, were sharply curtailed.

However, donor countries, comprising the Caribbean Group for Cooperation and Development, agreed at a meeting in Paris in May to enlarge their financial aid to the Caribbean by US$400 million. The Canadian Prime Minister, Mr Brian Mulroney, met with Caricom leaders in Jamaica and agreed to honour a commitment to double Canadian aid to the region to US$280 million between 1982 and 1987 and to open the

Canadian market further to duty-free and preferential trade with the Caribbean Community. The European Commission also proposed to provide a duty-free import quota for 1985–86 to the African, Caribbean and Pacific states. The Organization of American States announced an allocation of US$20 million over the next two years, one-third of its technical funds, to the Caribbean for technical assistance.

The war on the marijuana and cocaine trade was stepped up immensely in Caricom countries after dire warnings from the US Government that they could be deprived of access to US aid programmes. Highly successful operations were carried out in the Bahamas, Belize and Jamaica.

Queen Elizabeth visited ten Caricom states in October and November. Elected representatives from the French, Spanish, Dutch and anglophone Caribbean agreed to establish a regional parliamentary forum, and right-wing ruling parties in the Eastern Caribbean agreed to set up an Eastern Caribbean Institute for Democracy. The Organization of Eastern Caribbean states was negotiating a double-taxation treaty with the US government. Plans for a regional security service appeared to have been dropped in favour of establishing paramilitary 'special support units' within the police forces of those states without a defence force, and of some form of closer coordination on security and defence policies.

ORGANIZATION OF AMERICAN STATES

In January, Chile refused permission for the Inter-American Commission on Human Rights to visit the country, charging that in its three previous reports on Chile it had shown 'a constant lack of objectivity and impartiality'. Subsequently it tried but failed to persuade other members to support an appeal against the Commission's work to the Inter-American Juridical Committee. The report, which appeared in October, stated that 'disappearances' had again been reported since the beginning of 1984. In 1983–84, it claimed, 55 Chileans had died in consequence of 'undue use of weapons' by government forces; torture of detainees remained commonplace. The 1980 constitution, it added, 'does not fulfil the basic requirement of a constitution'.

The OAS role in Central America, too, was confined principally to the investigation of human rights violations. Costa Rica denounced Nicaragua for the arrest, on 24 December 1984, of José Manuel Urbina, a law student, when he left asylum in the Costa Rican embassy where he had been since August. It was referred to the Contadora Group. On 7 June an emergency session of the Council was summoned at Costa Rica's request, and voted unanimously to send a commission of representatives of the Contadora states under the Secretary-General, Sr João Clemente Baena Soares, to investigate the Nicaraguan border incident on 31 May, in which two Costa Rican civil guards were killed. President Daniel Ortega Saavedra of Nicaragua, where the incident was regarded as a deliberate provocation by the US-backed Contras to bring about US intervention, subsequently welcomed the Commission's findings, published on 28 June, that 'at no time' had the Sandinista army entered Costa Rican territory. A request by Costa Rica to censure Nicaragua was turned down by the Council, receiving, under the influence of Mexico and Brazil, only 17 of the necessary 21 votes. President Luis Alberto Monge subsequently maintained his position belligerently, despite extensive evidence of Nicaraguan rebel activity in his country, and denounced both the OAS and the Contadora Group when at Cartagena the latter refused a Costa Rican request for OAS observers to patrol the border region.

At the meeting of the OAS General Assembly held in Cartagena, Colombia, at the beginning of December President Belisario Betancur, backed by the representatives of Mexico, Nicaragua and Peru, urged the Foreign Ministers present to reform the OAS by accepting the principle of universality, regardless of ideological differences. Criticizing 'unilateral' US moves in Central America, he added: 'An organization that is working for peace like the OAS will find itself in crisis if it does not work with unanimity or if it serves the interests of only one of its members.' US Secretary of State Shultz, saying that the time was not yet ripe for this reform, rejected appeals from the Contadora Group to resume talks with Nicaragua, and, in line with the Baker Plan announced in October (see p. 466), which President Betancur had cautiously welcomed as 'insufficient', warned that Latin American states would get no significant relief from their creditors until they sold off state enterprises to foreign investors. 'Growth has been hindered by hostility to direct foreign investment,' he said. 'This has not only added to the dependence on debt financing, it has also shut out the potential benefits from the technology and marketing capabilities of multinational firms.' How these firms had most scope for action in the states that were most heavily in debt he did not explain.

SISTEMA ECONOMICA LATINO-AMERICANA

Following the position taken at the Quito conference of the Latin American Economic System (SELA), the Secretary-General, Sr Sebastian Alegrett, continued to defend the proposal to limit all Latin American debt repayments to a ceiling of 25 per cent of exports. Making comparisons with the German reparations issue following World War I, he argued in August for a Marshall Plan for Latin America, and, while stating that the countries of the region fully recognized their responsibility to pay their debts, stated that at the same time there was an 'inseparable link between trade and international finance'.

At the meeting of SELA held in Caracas on 17 October criticism was made that the United States initiative on the debt crisis, announced in Seoul by the US Secretary of the Treasury, James Baker (for details, see p. 466), was inadequate. Following the meeting, Sr Alegrett said that at Seoul delegates had accepted what Latin Americans had been saying for some time—that they were all in the same boat. 'The strategy of adjustments and case-by-case, short- and medium-term solutions has failed', he added. 'The only solution is growth'. The US plan to increase World Bank lending to Latin America marked the beginning of 'a negotiating process that would yield shared responsibility between creditors and debtors'.

At the meeting of the Latin American Council held in Caracas from 6–8 December, regional officials, formulating the Latin American response to the US plan, discussed common policies on the debt crisis, the GATT, the US Caribbean Basin Initiative and regional trade with Europe.

SOUTH PACIFIC REGIONAL COOPERATION

At the sixteenth South Pacific Forum heads of government meeting, held in Rarotonga in August and attended by 13 nations, a limited Nuclear-Free Zone Treaty was approved (see DOCUMENTS). Signed at the meeting by eight Forum governments, the treaty prohibited the manufacture, storage, testing or use of nuclear explosive devices in the region. Dumping of radioactive waste was also banned. The treaty did not deal with the contentious issue between Forum governments—especially dividing Australia and New Zealand—concerning the access of nuclear-armed or nuclear-powered military platforms to signatory countries; nor did it cover the export of uranium, a fact which led Vanuatu leader Lini to claim that the treaty was incomplete. Attached to the treaty and adopted with it were three draft protocols calling on metropolitan powers with colonies in the region, as well as nuclear weapons powers, to recognise the zone, adhere to its provisions, and neither use nor threaten to use nuclear weapons against the South Pacific zonal signatories.

On New Caledonia (see pp. 130–1 and 316–7), the Forum reiterated calls for self-determination and an early transition to independence, but in a manner which guaranteed the rights of all inhabitants. It also called upon France to clarify its future intentions regarding military facilities in New Caledonia, and established a watchdog group to monitor developments in the territory, but declined calls emanating from an earlier meeting of Vanuatu, Papua New Guinea and the Solomons that the pro-independence FLNKS be accorded observer status at Forum meetings. A request for similar observer status by French Polynesia was declined.

On trade, the Forum welcomed an Australian decision to allow across-the-board duty-free access to all exports from Forum island countries, other than those to which its sectoral policies applied—mainly garments, sugar and footwear. Concerning the special needs of very small countries, the meeting recommended enhanced development assistance, planning, and regional cooperation for fisheries, tourism, transport and agriculture. Throughout the year, representatives of the US and the South Pacific Forum Fisheries Agency made gradual progress towards a multilateral treaty governing commercial fishing access, especially in regard to tuna. The Americans lifted their embargo on the importation of this species from the Solomon Islands.

The South Pacific Commission's annual conference held a quiet meeting in Honiara, the Solomon Islands, in early October. Support for the South Pacific Regional Environment Programme was endorsed, renewable energy was identified as a key theme for discussion in 1986, and a recommendation that Palauni Tuisosopo of American Samoa succeed Francis Bugotu as secretary-general of the organization in 1986 for a three-year term was accepted.

Chapter 6

THE NON-ALIGNED MOVEMENT

SOUTHERN African questions were the dominant concern of the Non-Aligned Movement (NAM) in 1985. In April, timed to coincide with the twenty-fifth anniversary of the foundation of the South-West Africa People's Organization (Swapo), the Coordinating Bureau held its sixth extraordinary ministerial meeting in New Delhi on the question of Namibia. The President of Swapo, Sam Nujoma, obtained support for an extensive declaration and 'programme of action'. The broad problem for the Non-Aligned was that it was Western policy that had to change in order to affect South African policy. While the Bureau did appreciate 'the pressures being exerted by non-governmental organizations in a number of Western countries', they regarded the US Government's policy of 'constructive engagement' as 'strengthening the racist regime'. Another particular target was Israel, for 'facilitating the marketing of South African products'.

The Bureau exhorted the Non-Aligned themselves to take voluntary measures against South Africa. Of the measures proposed, sporting and cultural boycotts and the ending of diplomatic relations were already virtually totally effective. A complete oil embargo and the breaking of air and sea communications by the Non-Aligned might have had an impact, but no monitoring procedure was established to bring deviant members into line.

Pressure on the West was sustained by calling for a meeting of the

Security Council. On the day before the Delhi meeting, the South Africans announced plans for an interim government in Namibia. The President of the Security Council announced this to be 'null and void', and in June a Non-Aligned resolution to that effect was passed by the Council.

In July, when the South African state of emergency was declared, the Bureau at the level of officials in New York was slow off the mark. It did not issue its condemnation of the emergency until after the Security Council had done so at France's instigation. The Council took its first step towards economic sanctions by urging UN members to consider six financial, trade and social measures against South Africa, but a Non-Aligned amendment to the French resolution, trying to threaten the possibility of mandatory sanctions, was vetoed by Britain and the USA.

Later in the year the NAM's concern was again focused on Southern Africa by the convening of its first major meeting in black Africa for 15 years. The triennial conference of Foreign Ministers went to Luanda, Angola in September. The new features of the issue which came to the fore were the likening of apartheid to nazism, a decision to send a team of experts to assess the need of Southern African countries for assistance against South African actions, concern over repeal of the Clark Amendment (which had prohibited American interference in Angola) and welcome for the release of the Swapo leader, Toivo ya Toivo. The Foreign Ministers also endorsed the OAU's proposal for a world conference on sanctions against South Africa in June 1986 to mark the tenth anniversary of the Soweto uprisings and called for a special session of the UN General Assembly in September 1986 to mark the twentieth anniversary of the UN's termination of South Africa's mandate over Namibia. Much to the annoyance of some Western delegates the UN passed both these proposals. Continuing priority of Southern Africa for the Non-Aligned was ensured by the choice of Harare, Zimbabwe, as the site for the eighth summit in 1986.

The Non-Aligned again convened the Security Council in November after President Botha had informed the UN of plans for an election in Namibia using proportional representation. At the end of the debate the Non-Aligned resolution calling for sanctions was vetoed by Britain and the USA.

The second issue of concern to all the Non-Aligned which was given special attention at Luanda was the international financial system and the debt crisis. Despite lack of progress they were still determined to push the idea emerging from the 1983 summit (see AR 1983, p. 366) of an international conference on money and finance for development. A greater role for the IMF was sought by re-establishing the scale of its financial resources, by expanding the use of Special Drawing Rights, and by applying its surveillance to all countries, not only to debtors.

The NAM Ministers firmly rejected the Cuban idea that the debts could not and should not be honoured. However, it was also asserted that a political solution must be agreed by creditor and debtor governments with international financial institutions, so that debt service payments would not exceed a reasonable percentage of export earnings. The debt crisis was linked to Africa's food crisis, and an OAU proposal for a special session of the UN General Assembly 'to mobilize the international community to contribute to Africa's economic recovery' was endorsed first by the Non-Aligned at Luanda and then by the UN.

The Foreign Ministers again made a strong commitment to the Palestinian cause, the main focus for future action being a call for an 'international peace conference on the Middle East'. The most divisive issues were the Iran-Iraq war, which an overwhelming majority wished to see ended, and East Timor, on which 13 delegations supported a call for dialogue between Indonesia, Portugal and representatives of the East Timorians, while 25 delegations wanted the paragraphs deleted. The future of Antarctica also caused problems. Some countries affirmed the principle that the territory was the common heritage of mankind, while others defended the Antarctic Treaty system. A compromise was agreed at Luanda whereby the UN should keep the subject under review.

In April a meeting was held in Bandung to commemorate the thirtieth anniversary of the Afro-Asian Conference, but only the Indonesians and the Chinese made much of the occasion. The Non-Aligned did refer to the anniversary in their declaration at Luanda, but were careful to indicate that they did not wish to revive the Bandung idea of Afro-Asian solidarity.

The ninth annual meeting of Ministers and heads of delegations in New York took place in October, but coming less than a month after the Luanda conference it had much less significance than usual (see AR 1984, p. 370). The only substantive content of the main communique was a reaffirmation of 'deep and abiding commitment to the United Nations'. In addition a special communique condemned Israel's bombing of the PLO's headquarters in Tunisia as aggression.

XII ARMAMENTS AND DEFENCE

Chapter 1

THE GLOBAL SCENE

A series of bilateral talks on regional problems demonstrated the super-powers' growing concern with the Third World. Superpower summit fever increasingly tied regional issues to the arms control dialogue between Washington and Moscow. As Third World conflicts remained as intractable as ever, the spiralling arms trade continued to fuel local tensions, strengthen force levels and sustain the overall growth in military strength. The ambitions and intransigence of smaller powers disrupted regional dialogue, while disaffected groups perpetrated acts of terrorism which had profound implications for global security.

Washington's concern to achieve military cohesion with its North Pacific allies manifested itself in the annual US–South Korean exercise 'Team Spirit 85' in January. The arrival of US F-16 fighters in northern Japan in April was further evidence of Tokyo's increasingly assertive foreign and defence policies, and of the growing US–Japanese military enmeshment. This, together with Japan's assumption of a regional crisis-prevention role and the predicted removal of the ceiling on Japanese defence spending, provoked Soviet fears that a Nato-type alliance was developing along the Pacific rim. The appearance of a Soviet carrier battle group conducting Western-style exercises in the Pacific, and reports of a Soviet naval task force entering the Indian Ocean en route to Vladivostok, promised to intensify the naval build-up in an already volatile and highly militarized region.

The superpowers continued to vie with one another for Beijing's affections. The apparent strengthening of Sino-American ties was matched by the revival of Sino-Soviet trade links in July. The alarm caused in Hanoi by the prospect of improved relations between Beijing and Moscow warned the latter that it risked sacrificing its influence in Indochina along with its expanding military facilities at Cam Ranh Bay. Mindful of the build-up of Soviet military strength in the region and of the continuing confrontation between Vietnamese and Thai forces on the Kampuchean border, members of the Five-Power Defence Arrangement (FPDA) proceeded with their annual 'Starfish' exercise in May.

In contrast to its strengthening ties in the north-west Pacific, the US' bilateral alliance with the Philippines and its collective defence pact with Australia and New Zealand both threatened to become unravelled. Washington was initially inclined to cajole Manila with military and economic aid, but by October US fears for the future of its military bases if President Marcos were overthrown prompted stern warnings from Washington to its ally to mend its ways.

The Anzus alliance, the cornerstone of US defence strategy in the South Pacific, was in disarray. New Zealand's refusal to bow to US pressure to modify its anti-nuclear stance (see p. 313) generated an unprecedented crisis within the alliance. Washington's re-examination of its military relationship with Wellington resulted in New Zealand's exclusion from joint military exercises and US intelligence sharing. The postponement of the Anzus Council meeting in July suggested that the defence agreement had come to exist in name only. The declaration of a nuclear-free zone by the South Pacific Forum (see p. 360 and DOCU-MENTS) and Premier Lange's proposal for a regional security plan further antagonized Washington. In September the New Zealand Government's rejection of the US nuclear umbrella, along with the strategy of deterrence, appeared to sound the death-knell of the 34-year-old alliance. After a year of brinkmanship Washington announced its intention to end its defence obligations to New Zealand, while preserving the Anzus defence pact, if the Lange Government passed a law banning nuclear vessels and weapons from its territory.

Although tensions between India and Pakistan snapped into open conflict on the Himalayan frontier on several occasions, international concern focused on the apparently growing nuclear ambitions of New Delhi and Islamabad.

The normalization of relations between the US and Iraq confirmed Washington's tilt in favour of Baghdad in the Gulf war (see AR 1984, p. 375). The conflict escalated in March when both sides switched their attacks to civilian targets (see pp. 192 and 261). Reports that Iran was using modified versions of Soviet-made missiles and Teheran's campaign to intercept vessels en route to Iraq added new dimensions to the war. Iran's threat to close the Strait of Hormuz failed to provoke any notable international reaction as the war continued into its sixth year.

Soviet diplomatic gains in the Gulf states challenged Western predominance in the region and caused disquiet in Washington. Riyadh's disenchantment with President Reagan's Middle East policies was seen to be a major factor in the secret Saudi-Soviet talks reported in March. Likewise, Kuwait's purchase of Soviet surface-to-air missiles reflected a more even-handed approach towards the superpowers by Gulf states. This trend was confirmed in September when Oman agreed to establish formal relations with the Soviet Union, and again in November when the United Arab Emirates followed suit.

Whereas Moscow quietly continued to re-establish a regional role for itself, the United States demonstrated uncharacteristic caution in its dealings with the Middle East. Washington remained on the sidelines licking its wounds, and prepared to re-engage only if and when the moderate Arabs agreed to a common front. By the end of the year a significant shift in local alignments appeared to be under way.

Initially the Jordan-Palestinian Amman accord was received in a muted fashion by Washington. The accord, however, provoked differences between Washington and Israel, raised the possibility of Soviet participation in an international conference for a Middle East peace settlement and widened existing rifts in the PLO. While US support for King Husain faltered over the role of the PLO, the 'peace process' ground to a halt with the onset of Palestinian terrorist activity.

Israel's hazardous withdrawal from southern Lebanon concluded a humiliating and costly episode for America's ally. In contrast, President Asad, Moscow's independently-minded regional ally, emerged as the strong man of the Arab world and arbiter of Lebanon's warring factions (see p. 186). Reports in November that Syria had consolidated its air defence system were followed by confirmation that Soviet air defence troops had transferred control of SAM 5 missiles to Syrian forces. The war of nerves between Syria and Israel escalated in December when Damascus deployed SAM 6 and SAM 8 anti-aircraft missiles in Lebanon's Beka'a valley. On the diplomatic front President Asad began to repair relations with his neighbours, Jordan and Iraq, a move which promised a radical reshaping of regional alignments.

The overthrow of President Nimairi in Sudan on 6 April unsettled the power balance in North Africa. Egyptian fears of encirclement by a hostile, assertive Libya seemed to materialize when the new military government in Sudan signed a military protocol with Colonel Qadafi. Khartoum's reversion to a policy of non-alignment led it to ban joint military exercises with the US Rapid Deployment Force (RDF) in August. Subsequently the RDF's Operation 'Bright Star' involved joint exercises with Egypt, Somalia and Jordan. Tension heightened between Egypt and Libya in November when the hijack of an Egyptair plane caused President Mubarak to mobilize Egyptian forces in the Western Desert (see p. 183).

The United States continued to flex its military muscle in Central America as part of its strategy to prop up its regional allies and counter left-wing guerrilla groups and the Nicaraguan Sandinista Government. In the spring a four-month-long series of manoeuvres, Big Pine III, began in Honduras involving several thousand troops and a major naval presence. Similarly Washington's concern to discourage destabilizing influences in the Caribbean inspired the joint exercise 'Exotic Palm' with the east Caribbean states in September.

Conciliatory moves by Managua failed to persuade Washington to soften its anti-Sandinista campaign. Subsequently, the blossoming of Soviet-Nicaraguan relations encouraged President Reagan to threaten to wage economic war against the Sandinista regime. In November the US claimed that an SR 71 Blackbird reconnaissance flight over Cuba had monitored a significant increase in Soviet arms shipments to Managua.

Throughout the year fears grew that improved superpower relations would become hostage to uncontrollable forces in the Third World. Washington and Moscow continued to demonstrate their 'geopolitical paranoia' and contributed to global militarization in the process.

Chapter 2

NATO AND THE WARSAW PACT

THE NORTH ATLANTIC TREATY ORGANIZATION. The North Atlantic Alliance faced a variety of challenges in 1985. The impact of the US Strategic Defense Initiative (SDI) on arms control and on future conventional defence expenditure joined with perennial problems to threaten allied solidarity and generate new uncertainty over future Nato strategy. 1985 also saw Nato military targets coming under terrorist attack.

Harmonization, coordination and improved efficiency were among the key themes of Nato assemblies as the allies focused on the need to strengthen conventional forces. While the commitment to an annual real growth in defence expenditure appeared to lapse, it was reported in March that Nato Defence Ministers had agreed to raise the alliance infrastructure fund to $7,850 million for the period 1985-90.

At the Luxembourg meeting of the Nuclear Planning Group (NPG) on 26-27 March, Nato Defence Ministers considered SACEUR's proposals to reduce the European stockpile of tactical nuclear weapons from 6,000 to 4,600 by the end of 1988. The issue re-emerged in November when General Rogers confirmed that he was prepared to make additional reductions to those already agreed upon if more efficient nuclear and advanced conventional weapons systems were acquired under the modernization programme.

A meeting of the 14 allied Defence Ministers in Brussels on 22 May endorsed the Military Committee's planning document—the Conceptual Military Framework—concerned to improve the efficiency of Nato's conventional defence capability in order to counter the Warsaw Pact's capacity to launch a full attack on Western Europe without necessarily risking nuclear retaliation. The plan also sought a fresh political effort to coordinate European arms procurement, as with the E 3A Advanced Warning and Communications Systems (Awacs) aircraft, and a military framework which would enable Nato to plan its priorities. The document was an addition to the improvement programme already under way. During the meeting the US Defense Secretary failed to obtain Nato's political endorsement of a plan to produce a new generation of nerve-gas weapons in the United States.

In June the allied commanders announced new tactics involving the Northern Army Group which it was hoped would make Nato less dependent on the early use of battlefield nuclear weapons.

European cooperation in weapons and technology proved problematical, as divisions in the Independent European Programme Group (IEPG) over development of the European fighter aircraft, and financial and organizational differences arising in the Eureka project (see pp. 393–4), testified.

The military activities of the alliance began in January with the first winter reinforcement manoeuvres in five years, 'Reforger', and exercise 'Hardfall' in Norway. From 28 May to 6 June Allied Forces Northern Europe conducted the first of a new type of air exercise, the 'Tactical Fighter Meet 1985'. Nato's largest naval exercise in the biennial 'Ocean Safari' series, comprising allied maritime, surface and air forces, was held between 28 August and 20 September. Involving over 150 vessels, including French naval forces, 'Ocean Safari 85' was designed to test the alliance's ability to reinforce Europe from the US in time of tension or war.

Washington's Nato partners fully endorsed the outcome of the Shultz-Gromyko talks in January (see p. 373). At the same time the US reinforced its pledge to keep the allies fully informed on future superpower arms negotiations. However, signs of a thaw in East-West relations did not prevent the Soviet Union from continuing its campaign to disrupt Nato's nuclear modernization programme by attempting to dissuade Belgium and the Netherlands from fulfilling their commitment to deploy Cruise missiles. Early in the year Belgium came under strong pressure from its allies to maintain the Cruise deployment timetable. After an attempt to make deployment conditional on progress at the Geneva arms negotiations the Belgian Government agreed in March to proceed with deployment. Later in the year allied relief at the Dutch Government's acceptance of its quota of Cruise missiles was immediately replaced by concern about a reduction in the number of nuclear tasks carried out by the Dutch armed forces for Nato.

The controversial SDI research programme increasingly preoccupied alliance assemblies. Although during the March meeting of the Nuclear Planning Group (NPG) Nato Defence Ministers formally welcomed the American invitation to join the programme, serious misgivings had already begun to surface. The veneer of Nato unity on space weapons began to crack almost as soon as the Geneva negotiations got under way. Amid warnings that SDI could cause serious divisions in the Western alliance President Reagan proceeded with his controversial European tour in May. Although intended as a bridge-building exercise the tour was seen by many in Europe as emphasising the transatlantic gulf.

At the Nato Council meeting at Estoril on 6–7 June Foreign Ministers, fearing the imminent abrogation of SALT II by the US and its consequences for the Geneva arms talks, urged Washington to abide by the Treaty. On SDI, the Netherlands expressed its reservations about proceeding with research and France voiced its fear that space weapons developments would destabilize the strategic balance. Allied fears that a defensive shield in space could decouple the US from Europe were partly assuaged by Washington's redefinition of the 'Star Wars' programme, its reinstatement of mutual assured destruction (MAD) as the cornerstone of Nato defence policy and its emphasis on the central importance of the French and British strategic nuclear arsenals. The refusal of Denmark, France, Norway and Canada to join in SDI research testified to the growing strains within an alliance already challenged by tensions and uncertainties on its southern flank.

The call by Greece and its non-aligned colleagues (see AR 1984, p. 378) for a moratorium on space weapons, and the adoption by Athens of a new defence policy focusing on the threat from Turkey, emphasised Greek discomfort within the alliance and confirmed the rift between Washington and the Greek Government. This was worsened by the announcement in March that a $3,000 million modernization plan for the Greek armed forces was linked to the new defence doctrine. Greek dissent resurfaced when the Papandreou Government boycotted all Nato exercises in protest at the allocation of defence tasks in the Aegean.

The issues of continued Spanish membership and the American military presence in Spain dominated alliance concerns in the Western Mediterranean. Urged by President Reagan and the allies to remain within the alliance, while facing strong domestic pressure to withdraw, Premier González stated he would not necessarily consider as binding the results of the promised referendum on Spain's continued membership. Talks in October and December on the future of US bases on Spanish soil resulted in agreement to negotiate withdrawals early in 1986.

Allied disarray appeared again in October in the run-up to the Geneva summit. France refused to attend a pre-summit meeting of Western leaders in Washington from which the Belgians and Dutch complained they had been excluded. At a Foreign Ministers' meeting in Brussels on 15 October, hastily arranged to placate the aggrieved countries, the US tried to mollify these European allies who were particularly dismayed by Washington's response to new Soviet proposals for nuclear arms reductions (see p. 374), and decidedly uneasy about the SDI. Washington's failure to inform its Nato partners of its intention to table revised arms control proposals at Geneva caused further irritation. In contrast the outcome of the 'fireside summit' between President Reagan and Mr Gorbachev brought welcome, if momentary, accord to the alliance.

Defence Ministers, meeting in Brussels on 2–4 December, having urged rapid progress at the Geneva arms talks, discussed plans to improve conventional defences, armaments cooperation and various aspects of SDI, including a West German plan for a European SDI-type defence system.

Although, meanwhile, Britain's participation in the SDI research programme had been announced, at the Nato Council meeting on 12–13 December Secretary of State Shultz faced widespread concern at the possibility that SDI would ignore allied security interests and that the US failure to reaffirm its commitment to SALT II would threaten the new momentum in superpower relations achieved by the Geneva summit. Although the final communique stressed Nato's cohesion, the meeting was marked by considerable unease about prospects for progress in East-West relations and anxiety about the potential for future disruption within the alliance, not least as a result of the proposed cuts in the US defence budget.

THE WARSAW TREATY ORGANIZATION. The build-up of military power within the Warsaw Pact continued, as the alliance gained a new sense of purpose and direction under rejuvenated Soviet leadership during 1985.

Early in the year, as the Warsaw Treaty was about to expire, TASS reported Moscow's concern to improve the cohesion and unity of the alliance. The allies took a major step in this direction in March when, despite speculation that Hungary and East Germany had joined Romania in pressing for the treaty's extension period to be shortened and some of its commitments redefined, it was reported that all the Eastern bloc countries had reached consensus on the renewal of the Pact for a further 30 years. The death of President Chernenko in March and his replacement by Mikhail Gorbachev ended an uneasy period for Eastern Europe, during which Moscow's frequently indecisive and confusing policies had caused its allies concern.

The Warsaw summit on 26 April formally extended the defensive military alliance for a further 30 years in order to 'guarantee the reliable security of the members and ensure their close cooperation in international affairs'. The resulting communique stressed the desire for dialogue and claimed that the Pact was not striving for military superiority. However, it made it clear that the Soviet bloc would continue to build up its military strength. The communique also sought to reassure the southern members of the Pact that it had not become a two-tier alliance, by declaring that cooperation between the allies would be on the basis of equality. Mr Gorbachev took the opportunity to warn the West that the Soviet Union would respond with a nuclear build-up if the United States persisted with its plans to develop a space defence system.

The mystery surrounding the crash of a rogue Soviet tactical missile in Finland at the end of December 1984 (see also p. 100) exercised Western political and defence analysts into the new year. It was subsequently confirmed that the missile had originated in the Barents Sea, where the Soviet Northern Fleet was exercising. The incident raised questions about the efficiency of Soviet missile technology and the reliability standards of the Soviet armed forces. Although it brought an unprecedented Soviet apology to the Governments of Norway and Finland and drew only a low-key response from the Western alliance, this dramatic and apparently unscheduled demonstration of Soviet military power emphasised the danger that a military mishap might provoke an international crisis.

The Warsaw Pact's regular land manoeuvres were overshadowed by 'Summerex 86', the largest exercise in Soviet naval history, which brought over 100 combat and auxiliary vessels into the North Atlantic and the Norwegian Sea in June and July.

Soviet military power continued to preoccupy Western defence analysts. In January it was reported that Moscow had opened a new SS-20 missile base, bringing the total force of launchers to 396. In addition the Soviet Union was reported to be continuing a major SS-20 base construction programme in both Eastern and Western Russia. In December Nato sources disclosed that the Soviet Union had not increased the number of SS-20s deployed from the 441 launchers which had been estimated to exist in October. The deployment of new Soviet missile systems, including the SS-25, and a new radar system became the focus of Western debate over the extent of Moscow's violation of SALT II.

Continuing debate within the US intelligence community again produced conflicting estimates of Soviet defence expenditure (see AR 1984, p. 380). The CIA reported that Soviet defence spending had been growing at about two per cent a year since 1976. The slow-down in Soviet military growth, attributed to reduced spending on procurement, contrasted sharply with the Pentagon's view of an unrelenting Soviet military build-up.

Although Poland continued to be an embarrassment to the Soviet bloc the East Europeans appeared to assume a more quiescent role within the alliance. President Ceauşescu of Romania, constrained by economic problems at home and potential threats to his leadership, adopted an uncharacteristically low profile in Pact affairs. Reports in December of fundamental shifts in Romania's foreign policy, coupled with a substantial revision of its defence strategy, suggested the possibility of closer relations with Moscow and greater support for, and collaboration with, the Warsaw Pact.

Warsaw Pact leaders assembled in Sofia for a meeting of the Political Consultative Committee on 22 October to coordinate Eastern bloc policy towards the West before the superpower summit. The Pact members endorsed Moscow's latest nuclear arms reduction proposal (see p. 374), stressed their resolve to stand united in the face of Western imperialism and urged Nato to respond positively to Soviet peace initiatives.

On 21 November Mr Gorbachev crowned his successful meeting with President Reagan by presiding over a post-summit briefing for his East European allies in Prague. Besides offering his colleagues a new perspective on superpower relations he confirmed the emergence of the kind of positive Soviet leadership which the Warsaw Pact had experienced only briefly during the previous decade.

Chapter 3

ARMS CONTROL

MUTUAL AND BALANCED FORCE REDUCTIONS. The Vienna talks on reduction of conventional forces in Central Europe entered their twelfth year when the 35th round of negotiations between Nato and the Warsaw Pact opened on 31 January.

The Eastern bloc tabled a draft proposal on 14 February to remove, within twelve months, 20,000 Soviet and 13,000 American troops, as a step towards bringing final force levels to 900,000 troops on each side. The proposal was aimed chiefly at overcoming the main obstacle to progress at the 19-nation talks, namely, Nato's refusal to accept Warsaw Pact figures for the number of troops deployed by the Eastern bloc in central Europe. These figures underestimated the number by 160,000, according to Nato sources. Despite the inclusion of provisions for monitoring these initial reductions and a slight change in the Warsaw Pact's position, Western spokesmen argued that the problem of verification remained unresolved. The West spent the rest of the session seeking clarification of the new provisions. When the 36th round opened in mid-May to the familiar deadlock, Nato was still seeking internal agreement on its response. There were few positive signs of progress other than reports that Britain, the United States and West Germany were working on new ideas. When the talks resumed on 26 September there were rumours of disarray within the Western alliance. However, on 5 December Nato states formally tabled their own proposal for initial cuts, calling for reductions of 5,000 and 11,000 men by the US and the Soviet Union respectively within the first year of a three-year interim agreement. During this time it was hoped to generate greater mutual confidence which would produce a second agreement bringing the ground forces of both alliances to a common ceiling. Despite Western claims to have opened new areas of agreement between the two sides, Soviet opposition to the verification measures accompanying the package gave little cause for optimism that the least glamorous, if most predictable, East–West arms control forum would witness a sudden breakthrough.

ARMS CONTROL NEGOTIATIONS. Superpower arms control negotiations returned to the centre of the East-West stage in 1985. The impasse was broken at the Geneva meeting between the US Secretary of State, George Shultz, and the Soviet Foreign Minister, Andrei Gromyko, on 7–8 January when it was agreed to resume negotiations on offensive strategic and intermediate nuclear forces and to include defensive and space systems. However, the path to renewed US-Soviet dialogue was far from smooth. Mutual accusations of violation of existing arms control agreements were a particular source of tension. While Moscow stepped up its campaign against the US 'Star Wars' project (SDI), President Reagan sought to treble the American budget for new strategic offensive weapons.

The talks on nuclear and space arms opened in Geneva on 12 March amid mutual promises of goodwill. Three groups were set up to discuss intermediate nuclear forces (INF), strategic nuclear forces (START) and space weapons. Some indication of the gulf to be bridged came when the two sides established their negotiating positions. The Soviet Union insisted that progress in limiting nuclear weapons depended on halting an arms race in space, while the US stressed the separateness of the three sets of negotiations.

The INF talks, opening on 28 March, were preceded by the publication of Moscow's long-standing proposal for a mutual freeze on the deployment of missiles in Europe. On 7 April Moscow again took the initiative when Mr Gorbachev announced a unilateral moratorium on further deployment of its intermediate-range missiles and called on the US to reciprocate. During the opening session the US tabled its proposal for an equal number of warheads on each side in Europe.

Soviet reaction to the proposed construction of an additional 21 MX ICBMs by the US threatened early deadlock in the START negotiations, where Moscow attempted to take the initiative by calling for a freeze on nuclear arsenals. Moscow's propaganda offensive on disarmament was further heightened with the announcement that it had proposed mutual cuts of 25 per cent in strategic weapons and was willing to consider even deeper mutual cuts. In response, the United States, concerned that the Soviet Union had begun to deploy mobile inter-continental missiles, indicated that it would consider a mutual reduction of 5,000 warheads. The first round of talks adjourned in deadlock, not least over space weapons, where the positions of both sides were diametrically opposed: the US refusing to table its SDI or to accept limitations on its research programme, and the Soviet Union proposing a moratorium on the development of space weapons and the removal of existing anti-satellite (ASAT) systems.

As mutual recriminations cooled hopes of a superpower summit, President Reagan came under pressure to abandon the SALT II agreement. Hopes that a meeting between Mr Shultz and Mr Gromyko would break the deadlock at Geneva and set the date for a summit proved illusory, although Washington's concern to maintain the negotiating process was reflected in its decision to ensure that space weapons research remained within the terms of the 1972 ABM Treaty.

A general air of pessimism haunted the negotiations when they resumed on 30 May. President Reagan instructed his negotiators to remain inflexible until the Soviet Union produced some new proposals, while Mr Gorbachev warned that SDI could wreck the talks. Nevertheless, the Soviet Union extended its offer on INF to include a freeze on SS-20 missiles deployed in eastern USSR, and the elimination of missiles removed from Europe (see AR 1983, p. 337).

The START negotiations remained stymied and were more notable for developments beyond Geneva than for those at the negotiating table, where Moscow formally submitted its offer to cut strategic launchers by 25 per cent but without mentioning the limit on warheads which for the United States was a prerequisite for progress.

The fate of SALT II was partially decided in Washington on 10 June when President Reagan announced that the US would continue to adhere to the agreement, but reserved the right to respond to Soviet violations. As a result, accelerated spending on America's Midgetman, MX, SDI and Poseidon programmes was predicted and the Kremlin's condemnation was assured.

Prospects for progress at Geneva remained bleak. The deadlock seemed to threaten the entire future of the talks when, on 27 June, Mr Gorbachev warned that Moscow would revise its attitude unless US policy on space weapons changed. The Soviet Union's unilateral decision to halt nuclear testing did little to improve the East-West climate. In response Washington issued an ultimatum to Moscow to halt its alleged violations of SALT II and the ABM Treaty. Consequently the announcement of a superpower summit to take place in November came as something as a surprise, as did the Soviet suggestion in Geneva that Moscow would no longer insist on banning US 'Star Wars' research. Signs of greater flexibility evaporated almost immediately as the Soviet Union threatened to lift its moratorium on ASAT launchers if the United States proceeded with its programme for testing its own ASAT weapons.

The third round of talks, which began in Geneva on 19 September, saw the first comprehensive proposal from the Soviet Union and a counter-proposal from the United States. Having promoted Moscow's 'Star Peace' plan at the United Nations, Foreign Minister Shevardnadze initiated an intense period of manoeuvring between the superpowers by apprising President Reagan of the forthcoming Soviet arms initiative at Geneva. The proposals, tabled on 30 September, included a 50 per cent cut in strategic nuclear delivery vehicles (SNDVs) and the banning of all air-, sea- and ground-launched Cruise missiles (ALCMs, SLCMs,

GLCMs) with a range of over 600 km, together with new weapons yet to be tested or deployed.

Subsequently the Soviet leader unveiled his initiative for closer relations with Western Europe. He called for separate talks with France and Britain on medium-range missiles and raised the possibility of a European agreement separate from strategic and space weapons. Details of the Soviet proposals were formally presented at the INF negotiations later in October. In the first phase each side would freeze its deployment of missiles in Europe from 1 December 1985. Over the following 18 months the US would be required to remove all its Pershing II missiles, while the Soviet Union would cut its SS-20s until the warhead total equalled US GLCMs together with those on British and French missiles. Initially the US responded with a major propaganda offensive in support of SDI. Then, on 1 November, in the wake of President Reagan's offer to share space technology with Moscow, the American negotiating team in Geneva tabled its counter-proposal. The offer, encouraged by America's Nato allies, provided for a mutual reduction of warheads on intercontinental ballistic missiles (ICBMs) and submarine-launched ballistic missiles (SLBMs) to 4,500, with a limit of 3,000 on land-based systems. Limits would be placed on ALCMs, deployment of heavy missiles would be forbidden, and mobile missiles such as the SS-24, SS-25 and the US Midgetman would be banned. Each side would reduce its intermediate-range missile launchers to 140.

Agreement to extend the talks raised hopes that the gulf between the two sides was narrowing, but the main stumbling-block to progress on nuclear weapons remained the Soviet effort to abort America's SDI. The US counter-proposal continued Washington's commitment to space weapons research. It called for a dialogue on the transition from offensive to defensive systems and an exchange of information.

Overall, the frantic and sometimes confusing pre-summit diplomacy suggested that the superpowers remained poles apart on arms control. But, once under way, the summit generated considerable optimism that evident goodwill on both sides could be translated into real progress at the Geneva negotiations. In the event, the 'fireside summit' (19–20 November) produced no substantive agreement. The leaders confined themselves to calling for early progress on the principle of a 50 per cent reduction in nuclear arms and the exploration of an interim INF agreement. They reaffirmed their commitment to the Non-Proliferation Treaty (NPT) and their support for the elimination of chemical weapons; emphasised the importance of the MBFR talks and pledged themselves to seek early and successful completion of the Stockholm Conference on Disarmament in Europe (CDE). (For text of the joint statement, see DOCUMENTS). The euphoria surrounding the summit dissipated somewhat as Moscow renewed its uncompromising stand against the militarization of space, and Washington rejected a Soviet offer of a nuclear freeze and proceeded with its underground and anti-satellite testing programmes. By the end of the year progress on arms control seemed marginally less remote than it had appeared in recent years.

The third Review Conference of the Nuclear Non-Proliferation Treaty (NPT) was held in Geneva from 27 August to 21 September. While the outcome disappointed the non-nuclear-weapons states by failing to bring disarmament among the nuclear powers any closer, the conference did endorse the concepts, objectives and efficacy of the NPT in preventing nuclear proliferation.

THE CONFERENCE ON DISARMAMENT IN EUROPE. The slow thaw in US-Soviet relations generated by the Shultz-Gromyko meeting in early January (see p. 373) raised hopes that the limited achievements of the fourth session of the Stockholm Conference (see AR 1984, p. 386) could provide the basis for real progress in 1985. The Conference resumed on 29 January, when the Soviet Union tabled proposals for a treaty on 'mutual non-use of force and relations of peace'. The Western response confirmed Nato's earlier objections to such a treaty, particularly since the alliance had reserved the right to first use of nuclear weapons in the event of a Soviet bloc attack.

During February the West tabled details of its six-point proposal (see AR 1984, p. 385), including a plan for a 35-nation 'hotline' communications network linking the participants of the Conference with the intention of limiting misunderstandings about military activities. The Conference concluded its fifth session on 22 March amid optimism among Nato delegates that an agreement on measures to reduce the risk of conventional war could materialize.

When the talks resumed in May the delegates continued to establish and elaborate upon their formal positions. The Eastern bloc countries introduced three military confidence- and security-building measures (CSBMs) calling for 30 days' notice of military exercises which involved more than 20,000 troops, 200 aircraft or 30 warships. Although Western countries welcomed these detailed proposals they opposed the notification requirement for naval and air exercises which did not affect European security. Nato objected to notifying manoeuvres far out at sea or those merely moving through European waters or airspace en route elsewhere.

When a familiar impasse ensued, Western officials looked to the neutral and non-aligned group (NNA) to produce a compromise draft proposal which would enable real bargaining to begin. The NNA duly submitted their proposal when the eighth session began on 5 November, mindful that the CDE had just twelve months to present a draft agreement on CSBMs to the CSCE Review Conference in Vienna beginning in November 1986. Western commentators speculated that with this deadline looming a compromise draft would eventually emerge which would accommodate all parties to some extent. The talks adjourned on 20 December amid optimism among US and Soviet negotiators that an agreement incorporating measures to prevent accidental conflict, as well as a non-aggression declaration, would be forthcoming by the autumn of 1986.

Parallel developments within the CSCE framework did not augur well for the Helsinki process. The six-week 35-nation Ottawa Conference to review compliance with the human rights provisions of the Helsinki Final Act ended in June without a concluding declaration, as a result of fundamental differences between Nato and the Soviet bloc on the issue of a follow-up conference.

The tenth anniversary meeting of the Helsinki Declaration on Security and Cooperation at the end of July was held amid charges and counter-charges of human rights violations by Nato and the Warsaw Pact, and rival attempts by the superpowers to gain public support for their commitment to halt the nuclear arms race. Mr Shultz took the opportunity to launch an attack on Moscow's human rights record. In contrast, the new Soviet Foreign Minister, Mr Shevardnadze, avoided the anti-American polemics of his predecessor, Mr Gromyko, and instead introduced a surprisingly conciliatory tone to the proceedings. The meeting failed to produce a joint statement from the 35 participating countries, but there was a general conviction that the Helsinki process should be sustained.

However, even the post-summit 'spirit of Geneva' failed to induce consensus among the participating nations at the Budapest meeting on European culture at the end of November when, true to the Helsinki tradition, the problems of producing a concluding joint declaration appeared insurmountable.

XIII RELIGION

THE POPE'S DIVISIONS. On 8 May the writings of the Brazilian Franciscan, Fr Leonardo Boff, on 'liberation theology' (see AR 1984, pp. 390 and 512–5) were said by the Doctrinal Office of the Vatican to endanger 'the sound doctrine of the faith'; it imposed a one-year period of silence, forbidding him to preach, attend conferences, teach or write for publication. Fr Boff accepted, preferring 'to walk with the Church rather than walk alone with my theology', declaring he was not a marxist but a Christian with a commitment to liberty, justice and the poor. In January Fr Fernando Cardenal and three other Jesuits were barred from exercising priestly functions because of their work with the Nicaraguan Government.

Visiting the Netherlands in May, Pope John Paul II came under strong criticism from clergy and laity; meetings were poorly attended and protest rallies were organized. Liberal reforms in the Dutch church since the Second Vatican Council, and many defections from the priesthood, had led to the papal appointment of conservative bishops, but disputes continued on the role of women, married clergy, mixed marriages and contraception. The Pope insisted that his opposition to 'promiscuity', homosexuality, birth control and abortion would remain 'the standard for all time'. He spoke at Utrecht of 'fundamental doubts' about relations with other churches and this brought protest from English Jesuits in a letter to *The Times* stating that the decrees of Vatican II left no room for such doubts, though this pontificate had encouraged 'ecumenical recession', and that the papal visit to Canterbury cathedral in 1982 had implied acknowledgement of 'the Christian reality of the Church of England'.

In January the Pope called an 'extraordinary' Synod of bishops for two weeks at the end of the year to celebrate the twentieth anniversary of Vatican II. A *Report on the Faith* by Cardinal Joseph Ratzinger outlined the purpose and aims of the Vatican for the Synod, which were criticised in two long articles on 'Fear of Freedom' in the *Toronto Globe and Mail* by visiting Professor Hans Küng (see AR 1979, p. 377). He said that 'because I am constantly made to feel how many men and women—especially fellow priests—suffer under the Vatican's present course, I can no longer keep silent'. Cardinal Ratzinger's first chapter defended the necessity of excommunication, clearly threatening, said Küng, 'critical Catholic theologians with a censure that had never been pronounced against notorious "Catholic" criminals like Adolf Hitler or Latin American dictators'. The Vatican had criticized church broadcasts in Austria, dismissed the dean of Le Saulchoir theological faculty in Paris, reproved American episcopates and summoned Dutch and Swiss bishops to Rome for closed sessions.

Ratzinger's *Report* had warned against 'protestantization' as the beginning of 'modernization' and 'decadence'. Ecumenism meant return to Rome, which appropriated the Bible, since 'the Bible is Catholic' and to accept it 'means to join the Catholic church'. It held that Vatican II had produced 'misleading' and 'disastrous' elements, leading to 'progressive decay'. Declining numbers of priests and nuns, in some countries by nearly half in twenty years, were attributed to political theology and feminism, and the cure was 'Mary, the Virgin, enemy of all heresies'. A demand for an 'integral Catholicism' meant 'recentralization' on Rome and discipline consolidated by curial power.

In the second article Professor Küng criticized the Pope for 'empty words, lost chances'. Despite his charm and untiring travel, the 'real intentions' of the Pope were increasingly clear: halt the conciliar movement, stop church reform, block ecumenism with Orthodox, Anglicans and Protestants, and supersede dialogue with the modern world by unilateral preaching. Even as a member of Vatican II's commission on birth control the future Pope had been conspicuous by 'politically well-calculated absence', and he was leading 'an almost unbelievable battle' against modernization of women's orders and female ordination. His social appeals were ambivalent, with degrading treatment of Latin American bishops and priests, and, while paying lip-service to the Africanization of the church, he spoke relentlessly against 'African theology'. His opposition to birth control allowed commentators to hold the Pope partly responsible for the population explosion.

Further criticism came from former priest Professor Adrian Hastings (see AR 1979, p. 377), who argued that the legalized, centralized, authoritarian church should have been changed by the Council into an open conciliar body, but in fact the leadership had set itself to re-establish uniformity and 'world-wide papal monarchy'. Fr Michael Winter, Dean of St Edmund's House, Cambridge, argued that the Church was ignoring the reformist legacy of the Council. On contraception, although the deliberations of the experts of the Council commission had been secret, 'it leaked out eventually that all but four of them agreed that the ban on artificial birth control could not be sustained from Scripture or theology. In spite of that the Pope acted on his own responsibility and declared that the use of contraceptives was morally wrong.' That decision had created chaos, with many laity disobeying official teaching and priests leaving the Church. Despite the principle of collegiality, which should make the bishops responsible for the whole Church, the Pope had sole competence in appointing bishops, a new phenomenon in Church history.

The Extraordinary Synod opened on 24 November with much publicity but, according to a writer in the *Catholic Herald*, it was 'hastily prepared and too brief' and 'seemed unlikely to produce anything but an anodyne result', so that 'the deep wound of division refuses to heal'. There were assurances that the spirit of Vatican II would be preserved, but also complaint of 'superficial interpretation of the Second Vatican Council's doctrine in one sense or another'. Plans to centralize the Pope's powers were referred to committees, and there was indirect criticism of 'certain tendencies' in liberation theology and of the 'base communities' of lay people which had formed 150,000 centres in Brazil and spread elsewhere. A 13-page report, chiefly the work of Cardinal Ratzinger, stressed the 'mystery of the Church' and urged the framing of a 'universal catechism' for the world's 790 million Roman Catholics in order to avoid deviations from orthodoxy.

In Britain the Law Lords in October quashed an appeal by Mrs Victoria Gillick in an action to prevent doctors from providing contraceptive advice and treatment for girls under age without their parents' knowledge or consent (see p. 407). Mrs Gillick asserted that Roman Catholic bishops gave 'comfort to the enemies of the family', but Cardinal Basil Hume of Westminster questioned the wisdom of 'choosing the courts' as a place for this campaign, and stated that 'on the issue of parental responsibility Catholic moral teaching holds no clear line between parental rights and the growing responsibility of young people'.

In Ireland new legislation allowed the sale of contraceptives without prescription or proof of married status. At Ballinspittle in County Cork a statue of the Virgin Mary which was said to move back and forth attracted great crowds, but on 31 October the head and hands of the statue were badly damaged by a 'Christian preacher' who with two youths was charged with malicious damage.

Compulsory eating of fish on Fridays was finally abolished for Roman Catholics in Britain, and the laity were allowed to take consecrated wine at Mass, which had been an issue at the Reformation. In April the Prince and Princess of Wales had an audience with the Pope but the Queen vetoed their attendance at a private Mass.

FAITH AND POLITICS. *Faith in the City*, a 400-page report by the Archbishop of Canterbury's commission on 'urban priority areas' in Britain, which appeared in December, was critical of both government and church and was duly attacked (see pp. 20–21). Mr Kenneth Baker, Secretary of State for the Environment, declared that it was 'negative and out of date'. The report claimed that present policies gave 'too much emphasis to individualism' and had the danger of 'letting economics suffocate morality', while the great growth of unemployment made them 'unacceptable.' For its part the church had 'a single highly intellectual style of doctrinal formulation', its priests were mostly middle-class, and ordinary people were confused by a new prayer book with over a thousand pages. Although the report was Anglican it was defended by the Roman Catholic Archbishop of Liverpool, Mgr Derek Worlock, as a 'conscientious debate on issues of major concern'. Other churches in

Britain were also active, and, while some were declining, black-led churches were increasing by five per cent a year.

The General Synod of the Church of England approved by large majorities the ordination of women as deacons and clergy but not as priests. There was strong disapproval of government plans for unrestricted Sunday shopping (see p. 27). Proposals for the remarriage of divorced persons in church, twice approved by Synod, were rejected by 31 of the 44 Anglican dioceses (see AR 1984, p. 388). The Methodist Conference in July voted against its members becoming Freemasons and banned Masonic meetings on its premises.

In the US the 'moral majority' movement, founded by Rev Jerry Falwell in 1981, went to further extremes with the fundamentalist preacher Pat Robertson and his television show 'The 700 Club' and he was named as a possible Republican presidential candidate. On the other wing, twelve members of the National Sanctuary Defense Fund went on trial in Tucson, Arizona, charged with harbouring aliens by aiding Central American refugees to enter the US secretly and using churches as their bases. The Episcopal (Anglican) church of the US still debated women's ordination, though only nine of its 102 dioceses refused to accept female priests.

In January the Coptic Pope Shenouda III was released from banishment in monasteries at Wadi Natroun and preached to large congregations in St Mark's cathedral, Cairo, on reconciliation with Muslims as their 'flesh, blood and bones' (see AR 1981, p. 379). Mr Terry Waite, the Archbishop of Canterbury's special envoy, arranged the release of four British hostages in Libya in January, and in November began discussions with the kidnappers of four Americans in Lebanon.

Mgr Denis Hurley, Roman Catholic Archbishop of Durban, charged with making untrue allegations of South African police brutality in Namibia, was cleared on the evidence of tapes in February. Dr Allan Boesak, president of the World Alliance of Reformed Churches, was arrested with others during a demonstration in Cape Town in March and released on bail. The Anglican Bishop of Johannesburg, Rt Rev Desmond Tutu, declared in August that he would defy a ban on attending funerals in restricted areas, and in October said that he was 'very close' to seeing the violent overthrow of white minority rule in South Africa as the lesser of two evils.

On 3 July Ignatius Kung (Gong Pinmei), former Roman Catholic bishop of Shanghai, was released after 30 years in prison for 'serious crimes of high treason'; it was said he had 'admitted his crime and shown repentance'. At Christmas Beijing's Beitang Roman Catholic church was crowded for its reopening, restored from being a warehouse five months earlier. In Taiwan the Pope praised the 'lofty moral values' of the Chinese, and in China *The People's Daily* declared that religion was an aid to national unity.

In August Rev Sun Myung Moon of the Unification Church was released after 13 months in gaol in the US and was hailed as a martyr (see AR 1982, p. 382). He found surprising allies in other church leaders, including Rev Jerry Falwell, who claimed that the tax money for non-payment of which he had been imprisoned belonged to his church, and that he was victim of religious persecution.

PROBLEMS FOR JUDAISM. The completion of Operation Moses, an airlift to Israel of Falashas ('strangers'), black Jews of Ethiopia, was revealed in January; 15,000 Falashas had been settled in Israel, leaving some 10,000 in Ethiopia to face famine and persecution. Their absorption in Israel, however, proved difficult, since both Sephardi and Ashkenazi Chief Rabbis maintained that there had been intermarriage between Jews and non-Jews in Ethiopia, and that divorce laws were not strictly observed, as the Falashas did not know Hebrew or use the Talmud. Their Jewishness being uncertain, demands were made of them to undergo symbolic circumcision and ritual immersion (*tevila*). After protests the former requirement was dropped, but *tevila* was insisted upon until demonstrations by Falashas forced a compromise under which dubious cases would be referred to special courts.

In Britain the Farm Animal Welfare Council recommended manda-tory stunning of livestock before slaughter, instead of the ritual killing (*shechita*) practised by both Jews and Muslims. Most sections of British Jewry approved a protest stating that they were not allowed to eat blood and stunning was no more humane than *shechita*.

In Israel liberal Jews were worried over orthodox revival and fanati-cism. More men were allowed by orthodox rabbis to practise bigamy. After a devastating Israeli air raid on Tunisia in October Louisa Weizmann, great-grand-daughter of a founder of Israel, protested against the slaughter, saying 'I am a Zionist with a guilty conscience'.

Pope John Paul II in October referred to 'the Jews' having killed Jesus, and a member of the Vatican hierarchy was reported to have apologised to the Chief Rabbi of Rome. The Church of England, per-suaded by the racially Jewish Bishop Montefiore of Birmingham, agreed to delete anti-semitic Reproaches from the liturgy of Good Friday. In the US, the 1·3 million Reform Jews numbered more than Orthodox or Conservatives, but a traditional Jewish-Black alliance was broken by a bitterly anti-semitic speech from Black Muslim leader Louis Farrakhan.

ISLAMIC AND ASIAN MILITANCY. Harsher penalties were imposed in Iran for breaking Islamic laws: mutilation for theft, stoning for adultery, and beating for women dressed to show more than hands and face. Revival of veiling increased in Malaysia and in Lebanon Shias smashed liquor stores. In Sudan the leader of a liberal Republican Brothers movement was executed in January for criticizing *sharia* law, but four others were reprieved after recanting.

In India Sikh extremists bitterly criticised the hierarchy of the Golden Temple of Amritsar for coming to terms with Mr Rajiv Gandhi's Government. In January the custodian of the temple, and in November its head priest, were wounded by bullets. After fighting at the temple when Sant Longowal addressed a meeting he was shot and killed at the village of Sherpur in August.

Communal violence in Sri Lanka brought a massacre of pilgrims at the ancient Buddhist centre at Anuradhapura and the burning of a Hindu temple in revenge (see p. 273). Buddhist leaders at the Temple of the Tooth in Kandy urged peace negotiations but held that the state should still be dominated by the majority Sinhalese Buddhism. In Japan Prime Minister Nakasone visited the Yasukuni shrine in Tokyo, memorial to the dead of wars and revolutions but regarded by Buddhists and Christians as a focus of Shinto nationalism. In London a pagoda of Universal Peace was opened in Battersea Park through the efforts of Japanese Buddhist monks and nuns.

On 15 October leaders of the commune of Shree Bhagwan Rajneesh (see AR 1981, p. 378) left Oregon amid accusations of theft and attempted murder. The Bhagwan himself fled by private jet but was intercepted and returned to Portland, where in court he admitted arranging sham marriages to enable his foreign disciples to remain in the US illegally. He agreed to leave the country immediately and on his arrival in India the Government refused to admit his foreign devotees.

BOOKS

Jaroslav Pelikan in *Jesus through the Centuries* claimed him as the dominant figure in Western culture, and Pinchas Lapide in *The Resurrection of Jesus* gave a Jewish but unorthodox acceptance of the risen faith. Keith Ward's *Battle for the Soul* discussed a neglected subject. Edward Schillebeeckx in *The Church with a Human Face* outlined a pastoral theology, Michael Winter's *Whatever Happened to Vatican II?* found its results meagre, and Anthony Kenny in *A Path from Rome* sketched his journey from priesthood to Oxford philosophy. In *God in America* Furio Colombo argued that religion there took the place of the ideologies of Europe. *If Only My People* by Sir Immanuel Jakobovits expressed support for Zionism but doubts of present Israeli policies. *The Jews of Islam* by Bernard Lewis provided historical and modern material, but in *The Bible Came from Arabia* Kamal Salibi tried unconvincingly to suggest new locations for ancient Israel. *Radical Islam* by Emmanuel Sivan discussed medieval theology and modern politics, and Islamic militancy was considered in *Iran under the Ayatollahs* by Dilip Hiro and *The Reign of the Ayatollahs* by Shaul Bakhash. *The Baha'i Faith* by W. S. Hatcher and J. D. Martin expounded the religion of its three million followers in 200 countries. Oliver Statler's *Japanese Pilgrimage* described visits to 88 Buddhist shrines in Shikoku island. *The Paranormal* by Brian Inglis and *The Other World* by Janet Oppenheim discussed psychic phenomena and research.

XIV THE SCIENCES

Chapter 1

MEDICAL PROBLEMS AND PROGRESS

THE death, on 2 October, of the famous American film star Rock Hudson did as much as the ever-more-alarming statistics to make 1985 the year in which, as Dr James Curran, head of the AIDS (Acquired Immune Deficiency Syndrome) unit at the American Centre for Disease Control, said, people became aware of the magnitude of the AIDS problem. During the year real progress was made towards effective treatments for and a vaccine to protect against AIDS and tests to identify the virus came into use. Much was also discovered about the way in which the HTLV III virus (Human T-Cell Lymphotrophic III Virus) which caused AIDS was spread, and about how it affected the immune system.

The numbers of cases of AIDS reported in the USA nearly doubled during the year, from 8,000 to over 14,000. The British Royal College of Nursing produced a report forecasting that there could be one million cases of clinical AIDS in the USA by mid-1988 and a million in the UK by 1991. This forecast came from a conservative extrapolation of the exponentially-increasing numbers of cases in 1985. During the year it also became apparent that cities in Central Africa, where the condition was believed to have originated, were experiencing an AIDS epidemic on the scale of those in American cities.

In Kinshasa, a city of 3·4 million people in Zaïre, the number of serious cases approached 2,000 in comparison with the total European figure of 600. In Rwanda and Zambia one in ten of those sampled at random were carriers of the AIDS virus. Unlike the USA, where the majority of cases were still among homosexuals, in Africa they were mainly heterosexual, while the incidence of AIDS showed a strong link with promiscuity in both sexes. Prostitutes were clearly a main route for spreading the disease; 80 per cent of a group of prostitutes studied in Rwanda had either serious AIDS symptoms or conditions known to be related.

Several factors were thought to be responsible for the rapid spread of AIDS in Africa, among them non-sterilization of hypodermics, poor nutrition and the high incidence of endemic parasitic and other diseases which could render tropical Africans more vulnerable to attack by HTLV III. The first African cases of AIDS had been reported in the late 1970s. Scientists speculated that the virus might have entered the human population from animals. High levels had been found in African green monkeys in Zaïre. Macaques were another suspected source.

The detailed effects of the HTLV III virus on the cells it infected were reported in July, in the *New England Journal of Medicine*, by Dr Clifford Lane of the US National Institute of Health. He had shown that the class of white blood cells called T-Cells (Thymus-Derived Lymphocytes) were invaded by the HTLV III virus via the receptors on their surfaces through which the T-Cells would normally recognize foreign organisms in the body. This rendered the infected T-Cells unable to perform their normal immunity function, that of recognizing and attacking foreign organisms, and was therefore responsible for the defective immune response in AIDS.

A hopeful development came from leukaemia researcher Professor William Jarrett of Glasgow University, who successfully tested a vaccine able to protect cats against a form of leukaemia caused by a virus very similar to the AIDS virus. The feline virus also caused symptoms very similar to those of AIDS in some infected cats. By the end of the year Jarrett's team were developing the same technique to try to make a vaccine against human AIDS.

An experimental French treatment for AIDS using Cyclosporin A, an immunosuppressive drug normally used to prevent the rejection of transplanted organs, had some beneficial effects in a small number of patients, but their improvement was not maintained. Immunovir, an anti-viral drug produced by the Wellcome group originally to treat herpes infections, gave more solidly-based ground for hope that it might have some real value against AIDS, and full-scale clinical trials were being organized at the end of the year. The suggestion, by a Harley Street specialist in sexually-transmitted diseases, that HTLV III might be a variant of other viruses, deliberately altered genetically by Soviet scientists for use in germ warfare, was dismissed as nonsensical by AIDS experts.

The most depressing AIDS revelation came at the end of the year from American doctors who showed that the AIDS virus could infect the brains and spinal cords of victims, thus evading both the host's immune response and most drugs, which could not pass the blood–brain barrier to attack infective organisms in central nervous tissue. The findings suggested that people with no overt AIDS symptoms, or those who had apparently been cured of the condition, might suddenly be afflicted, years later, with severe and progressive symptoms of dementia, paralysis and incontinence, which were already appearing in some patients infected with AIDS virus.

Cloning continued to make rapid progress. This was the technique, still only ten years old, whereby human genes for potent compounds made naturally in the human body were isolated, transplanted into bacteria and multiplied millions of times over by growing the cultures so that the bacteria would then produce large quantities of the human-type compounds. Such compounds were coming into use as drugs more potent and specific in their effects than conventional synthetic pharmaceuticals. Among the numerous such compounds cloned and tested during the year were angiogenin, a natural stimulator of blood-vessel growth to be used to treat coronary heart disease; renin, a hormone which naturally controlled blood pressure; and cartilage induction factor, which naturally stimulated the early stages of bone formation and might accordingly be valuable for treating fractures.

Genetic engineering was also used to produce an experimental vaccine using the vaccinia virus used for many years as an inoculation to protect against smallpox until that disease had been eliminated. Vaccinia was now being used as the basis of a vaccine able to protect against several infectious diseases simultaneously. This was made possible by implanting genetic material taken from each of several disease organisms into the vaccinia viral DNA. Genes from influenza, herpes and hepatitis B viruses were inserted into vaccinia in this way. Tests showed that rabbits into which the altered virus was injected made antibodies against all three viruses.

A vaccine able to protect against Epstein-Barr virus, a cause of Burkitt's tumour in Africa and nose and throat cancer in China, was produced by Professor Tony Epstein (after whom the virus was named) at Bristol University, and was successfully tested in monkeys. Cloning techniques were being developed to make the vaccine widely available. Two of the human body's natural modifiers of immunity, Tumour Necrosis Factor (TNF) and Interleukin 2, were cloned and tested, TNF in mice, Interleukin 2 in humans, as possible additional forms of anti-cancer chemotherapy. Monoclonal antibodies (very pure and specific natural reagents) were also used in experimental cancer treatments to direct radioactive isotopes specifically to liver tumours. The treatment proved more successful for forms of liver cancer than any conventional treatment, though it did not provide a cure.

An astonishing finding reported at the end of the year was that leukaemia patients given chemotherapy in the morning were more than four times as likely to suffer relapses years later than patients given the same therapy in the evening. Circadian rhythms had been shown to affect the efficacy of drug treatments for other conditions, but this was the most extreme example of such effects to date. More research was evidently required to enable doctors to take account of such effects in planning treatment regimes.

Techniques for pinpointing defective DNA in tissue samples from foetuses made rapid progress, thus making possible earlier and more reliable prenatal diagnosis of genetic diseases and earlier therapeutic abortion if requested. A genetic marker which diagnosed cystic fibrosis sufficiently reliably for it to be used clinically was the most widely-applicable such advance to become available in 1985. Other tests were developed and used for polycystic kidney, haemophilia A and haemophilia B (the two commonest forms of the condition), and for abnormal genes which predisposed towards coronary heart disease. This last genetic probe test, developed at St Mary's Hospital in London, allowed people at special risk of heart disease to be identified and warned to adopt an appropriate lifestyle.

Leicester University scientists developed a test which enabled the individuals responsible for blood or body fluid stains to be reliably identified by DNA analysis. The test was used to prove the identity of an immigrant to the UK and was coming into use to identify rapists. It was found that the bacterium responsible for Legionnaires' disease spent part of its lifestyle inside amoebae, which explained how the bacteria were able to survive disinfecting of the cooling towers in which they thrived and suggested new means of controlling them. Difluoromethylornithine (DFMO), a drug first used against sleeping sickness where it achieved remarkable results in trials in the Sudan, also showed promise against bowel cancer, malaria and some human virus diseases, because of its unique ability to block the transcription of DNA into protein in infective organisms and cancer cells without affecting normal cells. Trials of the leprosy vaccine produced in armadillos began in Malawi.

A new type of artificial heart for use as a stopgap while awaiting a suitable human heart donor was successfully used in Pennsylvania. The precise 3-D structures of viruses responsible for polio and the common cold were worked out by computer, revealing in the case of the cold virus how it was able to avoid elimination by the immune system. In the cold virus, the receptors by which it fastened itself to the cells it infected were buried at the bottoms of pits on the surfaces of virus particles, pits too narrow-necked for antibodies to enter and recognize and destroy the virus.

Biotechnology made strides in agriculture as well as medicine. Plant Genetic Systems, of Ghent in Belgium, transferred into tobacco plants genes taken from a bacterium which produced a natural pesticide, thus providing the tobacco crop with its own built-in insect repellant. A Monsanto team inserted the same gene into another bacterium, Pseudomonas fluorescens, which lived naturally on the stems and roots of crop plants, as another natural, on-the-spot specific and non-polluting means of protection. In mid-November a third group, Advanced Genetic Sciences of California, obtained the first-ever permit from the American Environmental Protection Agency (EPA) to release a genetically-altered organism into the environment. This again was P. fluorescens, but this time with a gene deleted in order to prevent the bacterium acting as a natural nucleus for ice crystal formation and to convert it instead into a protective against the effects of frost on the crops on which, or around which, the bacterium grew. Tests showed leaves treated with this so-called 'Ice-Minus' form of P. fluorescens could resist temperatures down to minus five degrees C without freezing.

Dr Chris Pickett of the UK Unit of Nitrogen Fixation at Sussex University demonstrated a system which imitated natural bacterial nitro-gen-fixing systems with a tungsten-based catalyst able to fix atmospheric nitrogen into ammonia at room temperatures and atmospheric pressure. The break-through opened the way towards small-scale, solar-powered plants making nitrogen fertilizer in remote areas in tropical countries where conventional large-scale expensive plants using the Haber process to fix nitrogen at high temperatures and pressures would be impossibly expensive. The Nobel prize for medicine went to Drs Michael Brown and Joseph Goldstein of Texas University for their discovery of the genetic mechanisms responsible for abnormal vulnerability to stroke and heart disease.

Chapter 2

THE UNIVERSE, SPACE AND EARTH

On 8 May an editorial in *Nature* opened with the words 'We had best learn to live with the idea that there is a black hole in the centre of our galaxy.' The clinching evidence for what had long been suspected came from the most detailed radio map of the galaxy ever made. This used six American radio telescopes detecting very short radio waves which between them made it possible to put a size limit of 20 astronomical units (the size of the solar system out to the orbit of Saturn) on the immensely powerful radio source at the centre of the Milky Way. The interpretation offered was that a black hole was swallowing stars and producing radio energy as they accelerate inwards towards it. A black hole would accelerate stars and dust to enormous speeds before they disappeared for ever into its unknowable interior. In June measurements of the movements of clouds of gas in the galactic centre showed they are indeed moving at speeds of up to 600,000 km per hour. This further evidence of a black hole power-ing the centre of our own galaxy was paralleled by more evidence that other galaxies too had black holes in their centres. The spectra of radi-ation from 75 nearby galaxies were analysed by computer and the wave-lengths produced by stars eliminated electronically. This procedure, in about 18 of the 75 galaxies examined, left the faint but unmistakable spectral signals of quasars.

Quasars were the very distant, very compact and powerful energy sources believed to represent early stages in galactic evolution, with black holes actively swallowing stars in their centres. These new discoveries added weight to the belief that black holes were still common and active in quite nearby galaxies, where they could be observed in much more recent epochs of their history than quasars seen earlier. Increasingly, it appeared probable that the gravitational forces exerted by black holes were the most important source of energy in the universe.

A super-cluster of galaxies, 10,000 times the size of the Milky Way and much the largest 'structure' yet to have been found in the universe, was located during the year. The significance of this irregularity on such a vast scale was two-fold. On the one hand it demonstrated that some asymmetry must have entered the universe at a very early stage of its formation, to account for the fact that its matter was not perfectly evenly distributed in space. On the other hand the supercluster's existence supported the theory that the universe was full of invisible, 'dark' matter, in the form of neutrinos, black holes, clouds of cool gas, small planet-like objects, or perhaps all four, on the premise that only the additional mutual gravitational attraction of such 'dark' matter could account for the phenomena observed.

Evidence for asymmetry in the universe at the level of sub-atomic particles as well as galaxies emerged during the year. If the sub-atomic universe were perfectly symmetrical, evidence was needed of the existence of so-far undiscovered particles to balance the properties of known particles; 'squarks' to balance quarks and photinos to balance photons, for example. The search for such particles, intensified during the year, failed to come up with any. This omission was so marked that it was leading some physicists to speculate that, at the sub-atomic as at the galactic level, the universe was not completely symmetrical.

Physicists in Rome examining photographs of experiments at the European CERN particle physics centre were the first, in April, to see the tracks of so-called 'Beauty' quarks. Quarks, the smallest sub-atomic particles yet discovered, had been found to fall into several classes, arranged in pairs with opposite properties; the up-and-down, charmed and strange, and truth and beauty quarks. Previously, there had been only indirect evidence of the existence of the beauty quark.

On 1 October the Spallation Neutron Source at the UK's Rutherford Appleton Laboratory, a machine ten times more powerful than any other of its kind in the world, was formally inaugurated by the Prime Minister. It had already been in partial use for some months, providing several beams of neutrons simultaneously to probe the structures of things ranging from virus particles to silicon chips. In April the UK Science and Engineering Research Council announced its launching of a massive coordinated research effort into Low Dimensional Structures, LDS for short, a programme involving fifteen universities. The behaviour of electrons in sheets of material so thin that the electrons behaved as if they were effectively confined in two dimensions was of paramount importance for the development of solid-state lasers, optical computers and other new technology.

The USA, Britain, the USSR and Japan all launched space probes which would rendezvous with Halley's comet in March 1986. In

September another space probe, the *International Cometary Explorer* (ICE), successfully intercepted another comet, Giacobini-Zinner, and for the first time ever sent data about the nucleus of a comet seen from close up.

Space shuttle launches had become routine. But there were three specially significant missions, in May, July and November, which were the second, third and fourth occasions on which shuttles—four of which were now operational—had carried the elaborate European Spacelab into orbit. This signalled the real start of true science in space. Any one of the Spacelab missions did more research work than all the previous manned space flights by the USA and USSR together.

Investigations in the aftermath of the disastrous eruption of the Nevado del Ruiz volcano which killed 25,000 people in Colombia on 13 November showed that the warnings of nature and of scientists had been ignored. Earthquakes starting in November 1984 had been followed by emissions of gases and explosions and minor eruptions of ash in September, followed again by mudflows. In September geologists had rushed to the volcano and positioned five seismometers around it, which recorded tremors due to the underground movements of molten rock. A UN geologist had advised the Colombian Government on 25 September to take measures to protect the population and another geologist had actually prepared plans for evacuation.

An official comparison of research spending in five different countries, produced by the UK Cabinet Office, showed that Britain was bottom of the league in the proportion of national wealth devoted to non-defence research purposes—1·6 per cent of GDP in the UK compared to 1·7 per cent in France, 2·5 per cent in Western Germany and Japan and 2·0 per cent in the US. A committee chaired by Nobel prize winner Sir John Kendrew recommended in June that the UK could not afford to continue to pay ever-growing sums to support increasingly expensive international particle physics research at CERN.

The Nobel prize for physics was awarded to West German Professor Klaus von Klitzing for his work on the quantized Hall effect, an aspect of the behaviour of electrons in low-dimensional structures of importance to quantum theory as well as to future microelectronic component design. The prize for chemistry was awarded jointly to Professors Herbert Hauptman of the Medical Foundation of Buffalo, New York, and Jerome Karle of the US Naval Research Laboratory in Washington for their development of the direct method of X-ray crystallography used in determining the structures of organic and inorganic molecules and crystals.

Chapter 3

TECHNOLOGY

On 6 December 1985, Britain became the first country to join the US in its project to develop a defensive system against strategic nuclear weapons. The research programme of the Strategic Defense Initiative (SDI)—popularly called 'Star Wars' after a science-fiction film—was due to spend $33,000 million by the year 1990 on technologies to detect, track and destroy nuclear weapons during their trajectories. While many of the technologies involved, beam weapons for example, were still at early stages of development, the very size of the SDI promised to have a profound impact on the development of new technologies around the world.

Research that stood to gain from large injections of funds included work on sensors to detect missiles, beam weapons and intelligent projectiles to destroy them, and most importantly, the telecommunications and computing systems to control a planet-wide defence. The SDI also looked set to give a new impetus to space technology. Planners were working on the idea of putting weapons in space to detect and destroy missiles at their most vulnerable stage, soon after they emerged from their siloes.

Much of the technology involved in the SDI was highly controversial. In 1985, many prominent researchers argued that the job of managing a fail-safe defensive network would be beyond the ability of any computer programme produced by existing or foreseen methods. In particular, such a programme would be impossible to test for the purpose of 'debugging'—removing the errors that inevitably creep in. Other computer scientists disagreed. Their argument was that recent advances in the storage and handling of data as optical rather than electronic signals, in artificial intelligence and in writing computer code automatically would make the necessary computing power a reality.

Despite arguments, American private industry took up the challenge with enthusiasm. By the end of the year the top 10 contractors accounted for almost $500 million of the programme's $1,400 million budget for the year. British firms were anxious to receive their share. Before the memorandum of understanding which brought the UK into the project, the British Government had identified 18 areas in which British scientists and engineers could contribute. The details remained secret, but, despite the continuing 'brain drain' to the US, Britain retained a lead in some areas of high technology, particularly in designing software for computers.

Perhaps as a result of interest in the SDI, the international transfer of high technology became an important political issue during the year. In the US, concern mounted about the leakage of advanced products to the Eastern bloc. By 1985, the Soviet Union and its Comecon allies were lagging badly behind the West in the revolution that had transformed technologies such as computing and communications over the previous ten years. According to experts in the US, even the Soviet armed forces depended on Western technology for complex electronics systems, such as the guidance circuits in missiles. The Soviet Union's strategy was to obtain products such as computers and manufacturing machinery in the West, usually through third countries, and to 'reverse engineer' them to make copies. The Soviet Union's skill in this area became obvious when it began selling copies of Western computers at highly competitive prices. For example, in 1985 the USSR produced a 32-bit computer comparable to the highly successful VAX machines that the Digital Equipment Corporation of the US had been selling since 1980.

The United States, the country most concerned about the trade, announced two strategies for stemming the flow of technology to the Soviet Union. The first was to strengthen the committee that had been charged since 1950 with the job of regulating exports, the Coordinating Committee for Multilateral Export Controls, or COCOM, based in Paris. The US lobbied hard for tighter controls, particularly on the re-export of American equipment by Europe. European governments, however, argued that tighter rules would place European industry at a disadvantage compared with the Americans, who would be able to obtain export licences more easily.

In November, a proposed visit by American officials to Britain illustrated the tension that the tighter export regulations were causing. The US Office of Export Administration wanted to inspect six of the 600 firms in Britain that had licences to import sensitive technologies from the US. The firms opposed the visit, and Britain's Department of Trade and Industry refused to help the Americans. In the end, the Americans cancelled the proposed inspection.

The US Government had more success with the other part of its campaign—enforcing its domestic criminal laws against unauthorized exports. In May, an engineer received a record sentence of five years in prison for illegally exporting equipment for the manufacture of silicon chips and a system for testing bubble memories (an important component of information-processing equipment 'hardened' against nuclear radiation). By mid-year, the Pentagon was able to estimate that the tightened restrictions on exports had cost the Soviet Union $13,300 million over the previous two years.

Despite the efforts of the Americans, most Europeans saw the US and Japan as their main technological rivals. European governments spent much of the year discussing ways in which the continent could recover some initiatives. One much-talked-about scheme, which originated in France, was to set up a European-wide initiative called Eureka. The idea was to stimulate certain key technologies by injecting funds on a similar scale to those of the SDI, which it was feared would otherwise eclipse

European efforts. Among the projects under discussion were a plan to develop internal-combustion engines made from ceramics rather than metals, for higher efficiency; the development of stabilized plant embryos, created by genetic engineering, to be sold as seeds; and work on 'third generation' robots, capable of making their own decisions in response to changes around them. However, by the end of the year, although 18 European countries had joined Eureka, including all in the EEC, the programme had yet to take shape, and no money had been made available for participating schemes.

In September, a conference on robotics in Tokyo illustrated the advances that the Japanese were making in that area, and the widening gap between Japan and Britain. British researchers presented only four of the 200 papers at the conference, and by the end of the year Japan had 218 robot makers to Britain's 15. In Japan, robots were steadily moving into new industries, such as the microelectronics sector, where they were increasingly replacing human beings at tasks that needed great precision.

Another reason for gloom in Britain was the poor performance of its home-computing industry, which had been one of the country's few technological bright spots in previous years. Two of Britain's pioneering companies, Acorn and Sinclair, ran into financial difficulties when the demand for home computers fell off. It was a particularly bad year for Sir Clive Sinclair, the engineering entrepreneur who had largely created the British microcomputer industry. His company's main product, the remarkable QL 32-bit microcomputer, failed to sell well. Meanwhile, Sinclair lost much of his reputation for technological wizardry in another spectacular failure. He introduced an electrically-powered tricycle, with a plastic body, designed to take advantage of a clause of the law that exempted such vehicles from many traffic regulations. However, the vehicle, known as C5, which was slow, open to the elements and difficult to see from other vehicles, failed to catch on.

But British firms were not the only ones to have problems. A similar recession swept through Silicon Valley, the region south of San Francisco that had given birth to the microelectronics industry. One victim was Apple, a company founded in a garage that had started the home-computer boom. The company's founder, Steven Jobs, resigned in September after a year of poor results. Even IBM, the giant of the industry, had to reduce the price of its personal computers by one-third to maintain sales. The feeling in the industry was that almost everyone who needed a personal computer had already bought one.

It was reckoned that only a dramatic technological break-through— such as the development of a true hand-held computer with a full display screen—would bring back the boom times.

Chapter 4

ENVIRONMENT

THE African crisis continued to dominate environmental news through 1985, as growing numbers of commentators and scientists pointed out that the famines which killed perhaps one million people owed as much to long-term environmental degradation as to the failure of rains.

Vast areas of sub-Saharan Africa were facing 'environmental bankruptcy' resulting from the intensified activity of growing populations of people and their animals in a relentless search for food and firewood, according to Maurice Strong, executive coordinator of the UN's Office for Emergency Operations in Africa. 'The inevitable result', he added, 'has been a drastic reduction in vegetal cover, both trees and grasses, and the degradation of vast tracks of land which have become, or are on the way to becoming, deserts.' Some 6·9 million sq. km. of Africa, an area more than twice the size of India, were under direct threat of desertification in 1985, according to UN estimates.

As the year closed it was certain that Ethiopia, Sudan, Mozambique, Angola (all countries also suffering civil war), Botswana and Cape Verde would continue to need massive food imports to prevent further deaths by starvation. Africa would also need money, about $1,000 million in 1986 alone, for agricultural tools, medicine, seed and soil and water conservation work. Yet, since most donors perceived the emergency as over, UN and relief agency officials were not hopeful that these funds would be forthcoming.

The year also witnessed several natural disasters and industrial accidents which raised environmental issues. In 1984, millions in Bangladesh had been stricken by flood-waters from the deforested Himalayas of India and Nepal; in May 1985 some 10,000 people died when a cyclone struck the coast of Bangladesh. Many of the victims lived on the rapidly-growing islands formed by silt brought by rivers all the way from those same bare mountains. Farmers cut mangroves to clear farmland, destroying the buffer to cyclones' storm surges.

The series of earthquakes which levelled the centre of Mexico City in September, taking over 7,000 lives, pointed up once again the vulnerability of burgeoning Third World cities, growing far faster than planners and building inspectors could organize. Though office buildings and fashionable hotels fell, so too did high-rise tenements housing the poor, many of whom had been driven to the world's most populous city by a deteriorating agricultural environment in the countryside, as well as being lured by the prospect of jobs. In Colombia, the Nevado del Ruiz volcano erupted in mid-November, killing an estimated 25,000 people when avalanches and mudslides covered the farming town of Armero and eight nearby villages. The victims had been warned to evacuate the area, but few did, as they had nowhere else to go where they could find food and lodging. As some of the world's richest soil is found near volcanoes, they had acted as magnets to poor farmers throughout the Earth's volcano belts. Such disasters were bound to take more lives as rural populations grew.

In August, chemicals leaking from a Union Carbide plant at Institute, West Virginia (US), sent 135 people to hospital. The incident carried echoes of the disastrous leak from a Union Carbide plant at Bhopal, India, in late 1984 (see AR 1984, p. 276), and raised further questions concerning the ability of companies using hazardous chemicals to keep them out of the local environment. Both accidents happened during work on storage tanks, both occurred at weekends, when supervision was lax, and both brought complaints from local emergency officials that they were unprepared and insufficiently informed.

In one of the strangest incidents in the history of the environment movement, French government agents planted a bomb aboard and sank a ship belonging to the environmental protest group, Greenpeace (see pp. 130 and 313–4). Despite an international furore, the French Government, the opposition and the majority of the French people rallied behind the nuclear weapons tests against which Greenpeace was protesting.

Both the science and the international politics of acid pollution continued to dominate environmental issues in the northern industrial nations, along with stark new findings on the effects of any 'nuclear winter' following a nuclear war.

Earlier in the 1980s, acid pollution and its apparent devastation of forests and lakes were thought to be a fairly straightforward process by which sulphur dioxide emissions, mainly from coal and oil-fired power stations, turned to sulphuric acid, which was deposited on trees and open water. During 1985, various studies and meetings confirmed some researchers' suspicions that the chemicals implicated were more numerous and the chemical pathways more complex. Nitrous oxides and ozone, largely derived from car exhausts, and ammonia, mainly from fertilizers, seemed to play a bigger role than thought previously. The 'buffering' effects of soils—the ability of a soil to neutralize acid—were also now seen to add to scientific uncertainties. Furthermore, reports of acid pollution were coming in from Third World countries such as Zambia, Malaysia, China, Venezuela and Brazil. There were fears that the more fragile tropical soils might not be as effective as northern soils at buffering the effects of such pollution.

In July, the third meeting of the executive body of the Convention on Long-Range Transboundary Air Pollution (signed by 35 countries in 1979), meeting in Helsinki, gave slightly more substance to that weak Convention. A protocol binding signatories to a 30 per cent reduction in sulphur dioxide emissions (or in transboundary flows) by 1993, from a 1980 baseline, was opened for signature and immediately signed by 21 nations—enough to bring it into force in October 1985. Britain, the United States and Poland were among the main polluters which did not sign. The nations represented at Helsinki were unanimous that work should begin on a nitrous oxides protocol to the Convention.

In September, the Scientific Committee on Problems of the Environment (SCOPE), established by the International Council of Scientific Unions, released the main findings of its study on 'nuclear winter'—the period of cold and dark expected to follow any major nuclear exchange. They confirmed the essentials of the nuclear winter theory, and quantified some of the effects. The study showed how the crops of the major northern Third World nations—especially the populous rice-growing countries such as China, Thailand, the Philippines and Bangladesh— would be wiped out. The SCOPE study, *Environmental Consequences of Nuclear War*, scheduled to be formally published in early 1986, found that many of the effects of nuclear winter would be so severe that most scientific uncertainties—such as degrees and durations of cold and darkness—became largely irrelevant in terms of human, plant and animal survival. Death would be widespread whether or not the scientists were a few degrees, or a few months, off in their reckonings. The Steering Committee of the SCOPE report concluded: 'Any disposition to minimize or ignore these effects and the possibility of a tragedy of unprecedented dimensions would be a disservice to the human race.'

In June, the EEC Committee of Environmental Ministers finally adopted a Community Directive calling for prior assessments of the environmental impacts of public and private development projects. The proposed Directive, which had been subjected to five years of wrangling, made prior assessment obligatory for certain types of projects, optional for others. While it would not take effect until July 1988, it was already forcing the redrafting of legislation around Europe, and the British Government set up a working party to begin this task.

In July, the European Commission published a 'Green Paper' on the future of the Common Agricultural Policy (CAP). Given the controversial nature of its suggestions on prices and subsidies, the sweeping recommendations for protecting the agricultural environment went almost unnoticed. The paper tentatively proposed extending the EEC's role in regulating the use of fertilizers and pesticides, and in evaluating livestock's environmental impact before permits for livestock units were issued. It also called for the promotion of more 'environmentally friendly' farming practices: zones of restriction on the use of fertilizers and pesticides, rules of pasture use and the cessation of drainage and irrigation. Perhaps its most radical suggestion was that up to 10 per cent of the EEC's agricultural land should be set aside to create a network of large protected zones connected by ecological corridors.

In a coincidentally related move, the World Wildlife Fund began in September a global campaign to conserve 'wetlands': swamps, bogs, fens, mires, estuaries, mangrove forests and the like. The Fund's feeling was that, while the value of these wetlands in terms of pollution control, wildlife habitat, tourist and recreation amenities and water supplies was now at last being recognized by Northern scientists, at the same time they were being drained and filled throughout the tropics in the name of 'development', and that in the North farmers were still being encouraged by tradition and subsidies provided by governments (and under CAP) to turn wetlands into farmland.

In what might prove to be the opening bell of a very long-lasting environmental controversy, the US Department of the Environment approved in November the release of a 'man-made' bacterium into the environment, actually in a California strawberry field (see p. 388). Critics of such open-air experiments argued that scientists simply did not know the long-term environmental and evolutionary effects of man-made creatures. Crop strains were being designed which resisted herbicides, thus encouraging heavier spraying and the release of more herbicides into the environment. Researchers were working to produce hardier crops resistant to drought and salt damage, raising fears that these plants might spread across the landscape, overpowering natural vegetation. Environmentalists in the United States blocked through legal action some tests of genetically-engineered bacteria.

Two incidents in Britain cast doubt on the effectiveness of the nation's established planning system. The Government planned to go ahead with drilling for oil on Furzey Island in Poole Harbour, Dorset, without a planning inquiry, and also to build, along with France, a fixed link across the Channel, again without inquiry. Environmentalists protested against both decisions.

XV THE LAW

Chapter 1

INTERNATIONAL LAW

THE International Court of Justice had another busy year. The most significant developments, and the most ominous for the future of the Court, were those to do with the case of *Military and Paramilitary Activities in and against Nicaragua.* In 1984 the Court had decided that it had jurisdiction to decide this case on the merits (see AR 1984, p. 409), but the United States refused to accept this decision. In January the US withdrew from the case; it alleged that the judgment of the Court was manifestly erroneous as to both fact and law and said it remained firmly of the view that the Court was without jurisdiction to entertain the dispute and that the Nicaraguan application was inadmissible. The US repeated its argument that the conflict in Central America was an inherently political problem that was not appropriate for judicial resolution. It also made certain serious allegations about the long-term implications for the Court of its decision, which it described as a departure from the Court's tradition of judicial restraint and as a risky venture into treacherous political waters that brought with it the danger of politicization of the Court against the interests of the Western democracies.

In response to the United States' withdrawal Nicaragua invoked Article 53 of the Statute of the Court, which allows the Court to decide a case even in the event of the non-appearance or failure to defend its case by one of the parties. The Court went ahead with the case and hearings were completed in September. In October the US went a step further and gave six months' notice (in accordance with its 1946 Declaration) of the termination of its acceptance of the Court's jurisdiction under the Optional Clause. However, it said it would be willing to accept the jurisdiction of the Court on the basis of special agreements. These US decisions must tend to undermine the authority of the Court and harm the reputation of the United States for respect for international law.

Another case in which the commitment of the parties to pacific settlement seemed less than wholehearted was that submitted in April to a five-man Chamber of the Court by Burkina Faso and Mali. This was only the second instance of resort to a Chamber of the Court and it followed the precedent set by the *Delimitation of the Maritime Boundary in the Gulf of Maine Area* (see AR 1984, p. 409). The parties requested the delimitation of part of their land boundary. But on 25 December fighting broke out in the disputed area (see p. 236).

In June the Court gave judgment in the *Case concerning the Continental Shelf (Libya/Malta)*. By 14 votes to 3 it adopted a modified median line as the boundary of the continental shelf between the two states. The Court limited the scope of its decision to those areas in which only the parties before the Court had claims. Thus, although the Court had earlier rejected Italy's application to intervene (see AR 1984, p. 408), the Court now ensured to Italy the protection it had sought to obtain by intervening. This result was criticized as unduly restricting the area of delimitation out of excessive deference to the claims of Italy.

The Court's decision on the delimitation of the continental shelf reflected recent developments both in the 1982 Convention on the Law of the Sea and in customary international law. In particular the evolution of the 200-mile exclusive economic zone had an impact on the continental shelf regime. Although the Court had been requested to delimit only the continental shelf boundary, it said it could not leave out of consideration principles and rules underlying the exclusive economic zone, and that in any delimitation of the continental shelf greater importance would be attributed to factors common to both concepts, such as distance from the coast. On the basis of state practice and the 1982 Convention a state could now claim up to 200 miles continental shelf whatever the geological or geomorphological features of the seabed within that distance. The trend in earlier Court decisions on continental shelf delimitation, namely, to play down geophysical factors, had clearly been continued and strengthened.

The Court also followed its earlier practice in rejecting Malta's argument that equidistance should be regarded as the primary rule in continental shelf delimitation, and reaffirmed that there was no single obligatory method. Its decision would be made on the basis of equitable principles applied in the light of relevant circumstances in order to achieve an equitable result. However, as in earlier cases, the significance of the Court's rejection of the primacy of the equidistance method of delimitation was reduced by the actual choice of boundary line. For the Court, in its provisional delimitation, upheld the equitable nature of the equidistance method in cases of delimitation between opposite states. The Court then went on to test the equitable nature of the result that would be produced by this provisional method of delimitation; it rejected Libya's argument that the size of the land mass was a relevant consideration but accepted that the large disparity in the length of the parties' coastlines should *inter alia* be taken into account, and adjusted the median line to allow for this by moving the line nearer to Malta. Here, as in earlier cases, the problem for those seeking general guidance from the decision was the lack of any clear objective link between the Court's discussion of equitable principles and of relevant circumstances and the actual determination of the boundary line.

This was a problem also in the 1982 *Continental Shelf (Tunisia/Libya)* case (see AR 1982, p. 398). In December the Court gave its unanimous decision on *The Application for Revision and Interpretation* of this judgment. On the claim for revision, the first such claim ever decided by the Court, the Court accepted that Tunisia had produced a new fact relevant to the dispute, a fact concerning the grant of oil concessions in the disputed area. The Court nevertheless rejected Tunisia's claim for revision since it had not shown that its earlier ignorance of the fact was not due to negligence, nor had it shown that the new fact would, if known at the time of the Court's original decision, have produced a different decision. The Court accepted that the new fact would have affected the language of its decision but said that the substance of that decision would not have been altered. The Court also rejected Tunisia's alternative claims, nominally for interpretation of its earlier judgment but essentially a disguised claim for revision.

Judge Nagendra Singh was elected President of the Court, and Judge Ladreit de Lacharrière Vice-President. Judge Morozov resigned because of ill-health, and Mme Bastid, ad hoc judge in the Tunisia/Libya revision case, was the first woman to be appointed to the Court.

In February there was another decision on the delimitation of maritime boundaries, an arbitral award by a tribunal independent of the Court but consisting of three of the Court's judges. Guinea and Guinea-Bissau requested the determination of a single maritime boundary delimiting their territorial waters, exclusive economic zones and continental shelves. Here again the tribunal relied on the 1982 Convention on the Law of the Sea for guidance even though it was not yet in force; it held that the aim of any delimitation process was to achieve an equitable solution having regard to relevant circumstances. Because the coastline of the two states was concave the equidistance method would not produce an equitable result. The tribunal therefore decided to focus upon the entire West African region; an equitable delimitation would be achieved by following a direction which took account of the convex shape overall of the West African coastline and would be adaptable to the pattern of present or future delimitation in the region.

In March the Council of Europe opened for signature Protocol No. 8 to the European Convention on Human Rights. This was designed to improve and expedite the procedure of the European Commission of Human Rights because the number of individuals bringing petitions had continued to increase and the delays in dealing with these had been causing concern. The most important innovation made in the Protocol was the grant of competence to the Commission to set up Chambers to handle those petitions which could be dealt with on the basis of established case law or which did not raise any serious question under the Convention. Sixteen of the twenty-one member states of the Council of Europe signed the Protocol immediately but because of its procedural nature it would not enter into force until all parties to the European Convention on Human Rights had expressed their consent to be bound.

EUROPEAN COMMUNITY LAW

Legal developments during the year took place against a background of triple constitutional change. The accession of Spain and Portugal was confirmed by treaty and came into operation as the year went out, to the accompaniment of a flood of amending legislation. The discussions on a new treaty of European Union were brought to a head in the autumn, whereupon they slowed and dwindled in the face of detailed negotiation between the member states but culminated in a successful agreement at the Luxembourg summit in December. The agreement, which was to be incorporated in a treaty in 1986, fell short of the earlier ambitions for a thorough remodelling of the Community's constitition and in particular made only minor amendments to the unanimity rule for legislation. Even so it caused an incipient crisis when the Danish Parliament refused to allow the Danish Minister to take part in a formal signing ceremony, which was then postponed.

The third facet was of greater direct impact on lawyers. Of the new European Commission under M Jacques Delors which came into office at the beginning of the year, both Mr Peter Sutherland (Competition) and Lord Cockfield (Internal Market) revealed themselves as powerful legislators, with a will to tackle difficult issues with quiet firmness and imagination. This was shown particularly in the latter's presentation in the spring of a White Paper on 'completing the internal market', a detailed programme for removing the multitude of obstacles still operating against the free movement of goods between member states. Lord Cockfield made clear that this was his overriding goal; and in order to avoid the head-battering of earlier attempts to harmonize the detailed rules governing each separate product he announced a radical change of approach. No longer would he seek to unify manufacturing standards to a Community norm. The complex systems of type and pattern approval, so prominent in the motor vehicle industry and others, would in principle not be extended. Instead, following the European Court's hint in *Cassis de Dijon*, the member states themselves would set the standards (as they did already) but within the overall context of a Community framework directive and without the power to reject the import, sale or use of products lawfully made in other member states. Such a legislative technique would avoid the detailed argument over standards and hopefully remove the most serious form of non-tariff barrier.

No sooner had this new initiative been announced than the same principle was extended to services, particularly the professions. The Commission had become impatient of the slow progress in agreeing directives on the right of establishment, faced as they were with tenacious adherence by practitioners to their ancient ways (alike in training, conduct and monopoly rights). Although an architect's directive was finally adopted—after many years—it was perhaps the failure of the lawyers to agree a text on establishment and the apparent impasse into which their discussions had sunk which stimulated the Commission to cut the Gordian knot with a bold proposal.

A draft directive on the equivalence of higher education diplomas was presented. In spite of its name, this was not concerned with university education as such but with the recognition of qualifications in the regulated professions. The problem was that professionals qualified in one member state could not be refused permission to practise in another member state on grounds of their foreign nationality but could be on grounds of lack of local qualifications. The new framework directive would remove that restriction. Qualification in one member state would in principle qualify to practise in any other member state as well. This immediately raised the indignation of lawyers who pointed out that a qualification in German law would not suffice for practice in the English courts. The Commission remained adamant but said that if the European legal (or any other) profession would agree internally on a replacement directive for itself, and could guarantee its acceptance by the member state Governments in the Council, then that could take the place of the framework directive for that profession. Such a clever technique of putting the burden of negotiating legislation on the interested parties, the 'penalty' for failure being the operation of a more rough-hewn and perhaps inappropriate equivalence rule, had never been used before but seemed likely to succeed and to have great potential.

The year was remarkable for the quantity and importance of its legislation. Four long-standing directives were finally passed. Of these the most controversial was the Products Liability Directive, which imposed direct liability on manufacturers for harm caused by defects in their products. It would introduce substantial changes in the English law of tortious liability and was fiercely opposed. The Environmental Impact Assessment Directive was potentially of equally fundamental importance since it required new industrial projects to have an assessment made of their likely effect on the environment before being permitted to proceed. The Doorstep Sales Directive introduced protective procedures (cooling-off period, information in writing) for consumer sales which take place away from shops or equivalent premises. Its original text made it apparent that the draftsmen had completely ignored mail order as a major selling technique in the UK; this was only partly remedied in the final draft. In addition, special provision had to be made for home delivery of milk and other groceries and small-value goods. Even so, the directive covered far more than foot-in-the-door salesmen of encyclopaedias and insurance.

The fourth directive, on the European Economic Interest Grouping, was somewhat exotic for British lawyers. Based on the French *groupement d'intérêt économique*, it provided a legal form for collaborative ventures between existing enterprises. Of importance in those formalistic member states which deny recognition to the acts of entities having no proper legal form, it was likely to be less useful in the UK and Ireland, which are more flexible in their attitudes to legal status.

The series of group exemption regulations under the anti-trust rules of Article 85(3) EEC, begun the previous year, continued with regulations on specialization agreements and agreements for joint research and development. It was rumoured that these would conclude the present series and that the position of joint ventures and of franchising would be dealt with by guidelines (which were being prepared in the Commission) rather than by binding legislation. The procedural regulation on the notification of agreements in order to obtain individual exemption or negative clearance by use of Form A/B was thoroughly redrafted and issued as a new regulation. In addition, the new Commission policy of speeding disposal of cases by using 'comfort letters' rather than formal decisions to approve agreements was implemented.

Other important legislation during the year included the farming regulation which introduced radical changes in the Common Agricultural Policy rules on agricultural structures; and the presentation of draft directives on mortgage credit and on counterfeiting trade marks and the get-up of goods. The great cliff-hanger of recent years—the coming into force in Britain of the EEC Judgments Convention—continued unresolved since Belgium (the last of the old member states still to ratify) failed to make the expected progress with its ratifying Bill. By the year's end there was still no firm prediction of when that process might be completed.

Making information about Community law better available to professionals and the public continued to cause concern. In an attempt to speed translation (one of the delaying factors) the President of the European Court reformed the drafting style of its judgments, but translations continued to take an inordinate length of time. The Court's own reports of its cases were now taking 18 to 20 months before publication. Unfortunately, a major commercial source of information about the court's case law, the computerized database EUROLEX, was closed down suddenly after it was sold off to its rival.

The Court's case law increased steadily in quantity and importance. The highlight was perhaps the action by the European Parliament against the Council complaining that no legislation had been passed to implement the common transport policy. In May the Court held[1] that, while the Treaty obligation to introduce such a policy could not be judicially

---

[1] [1986] 1 CMLR 138.

enforced, nevertheless the Council was culpable in not implementing the freedom to supply transport services.

An unusual case was unsuccessfully brought by Italy against the EC Commission[2] to annul the latter's decision directed against British Telecom for abuse of a dominant position. The British Government itself supported the Commission. Such harmony did not apply in the successful action by the Commission against the UK[3] to have new UK legislation requiring imported goods to indicate their country of origin declared contrary to Article 30 EEC. And Stanley Adams, an executive of Hoffmann-La Roche in Switzerland who betrayed his company to the EC Commission under Article 86 EEC and was penalized under the Swiss law on business secrets, at last obtained redress when the European Court held that the Commission had revealed his identity to his employers although they owed him a duty to keep it secret, and ordered them to pay him damages.

Chapter 2

LAW IN THE UNITED KINGDOM

THE Government continued its reform of local government by abolishing (as from 1 April 1986) the Greater London and metropolitan county councils and transferring their functions to other existing local authorities and to certain newly-created authorities: *Local Government Act*. In the *Local Government (Access to Information) Act* provision was made for greater public access to local authority proceedings. The *Representation of the People Act* (relating to both local and parliamentary elections) facilitated voting by both 'overseas' and 'absent' electors and increased to £500 the deposit at parliamentary elections while reducing the forfeiture threshold from one-eighth to one-twentieth of votes cast. The *Transport Act* provided for the privatization of the National Bus Company and amended significantly the duties of local authorities and Passenger Transport Executives with regard to the provision of public passenger transport in their areas.

The *Prosecution of Offences Act* established for England and Wales a Crown Prosecution Service whose chief function was to take over the conduct of criminal proceedings instituted by the police. A number of statutes created new criminal offences. Under the *Interception of Communications Act* it became an offence to intercept postal or other communications without either one party's consent or a government warrant

[2] [1985] 2 CMLR 368.
[3] [1985] 2 CMLR 259

issued for security, crime prevention or like reasons. Following unprecedented levels of football crowd violence in 1985 the *Sporting Events
(Control of Alcohol etc.) Act* created new offences relating to the possession and consumption of alcohol on coaches and trains and at sports
grounds. The mounting scourge of drug abuse was addressed in the
Controlled Drugs (Penalties) Act which increased to life imprisonment
the maximum penalty for unlawful supply of certain drugs; and under the
Intoxicating Substances (Supply) Act it became an offence to supply to
minors solvents for inhalation. 'Kerb crawling' and persistent soliciting of
women for the purpose of prostitution became an offence under the
Sexual Offences Act, which also increased to life imprisonment the maximum penalty for attempted rape. Following the Warnock Report (1984)
and the much publicized case of 'Baby Cotton'[1] the *Surrogacy Arrangements Act* made it a criminal offence for an agency to promote surrogate
maternity arrangements on a commercial basis.

Included in the *Administration of Justice Act* were new powers for the
Law Society in the field of solicitors' discipline and provisions for the
creation of a new profession of Licensed Conveyancers following the
Farrand Committee report[2]. The *Charities Act* authorized trustees of
certain local or small charities to modify the trust objects or transfer the
trust property to another charity or (in the case of very small charities) to
wind them up. Under the *Enduring Powers of Attorney Act* an individual
was enabled to appoint an attorney to manage his affairs even after the
individual had become mentally incapable. In a major reform of corporate and personal insolvency law the *Insolvency Act*[3] made provision for
the licensing of legal practitioners in the field, for the disqualification and
unlimited personal liability of company directors in certain circumstances, and for reform of the law on receivership, liquidation and
individual bankruptcy. The *Rent (Amendment) Act* improved the position of a landlord who wished to recover possession of property for his
own or his family's occupation, but who had not been in occupation of the
property when it was let. Strenuous opposition notwithstanding, the
Water (Fluoridation) Act empowered water authorities to increase to a
prescribed maximum the level of fluoride in water supplies if requested to
do so by the area health authority.

Finally on statute law, certain provisions of the *Data Protection Act
1984* and of the *Children Act 1975* came into force in 1985. The former
Act obliged persons holding computerized 'personal data' relating to
others to disclose the holding on an official register and to permit a 'data
subject' to have access to the details relating to him. The register opened
on 11 November. Under the custodianship provisions of the *Children Act*

---

[1] *Re a Baby* [1985] New. Law Jo. 106.
[2] AR 1984, p. 420
[3] See also Bankruptcy (Scotland) Act 1985.

(which came into force on 1 December) persons who had been looking after a child for certain periods were permitted to apply to a court for 'custodianship', a status carrying substantially the rights and obligations of a parent or guardian.

Turning to case law, perhaps the *cause célèbre* of 1985 was *Gillick* v *West Norfolk Area Health Authority*[4]. By a majority of 3 to 2 the House of Lords (overturning a unanimous Court of Appeal[5]) ruled that it was not necessarily unlawful for a doctor to give contraceptive advice and treatment to a girl under 16 years of age without the knowledge and consent of her parents. The majority, while holding that it was a question of fact whether a particular under-age girl had the capacity to consent to medical treatment, emphasised that a doctor should proceed without parents' knowledge only in exceptional circumstances. In particular, he should not proceed unless satisfied both of his inability to persuade the girl to involve her parents or to desist from intercourse, and that, in all the circumstances, the girl's best interests required him to proceed. In another case[6] raising issues of consent to medical treatment, the House of Lords confirmed that English law did not require a doctor to disclose to a patient all possible risks in proposed treatment. But, although the question of disclosure remained primarily a matter of clinical judgment, there were certain risks which no reasonably prudent doctor could fail to disclose. Furthermore, specific questions from patients should be answered both accurately and fully.[7]

Of general relevance in personal injuries litigation was the commencement[8] of the procedure[9] by which a court may make a provisional damages award and, later, a further award if an anticipated deterioration in the victim's condition occurs. Still on personal injury damages, a convicted rapist obtained damages against a car driver for negligent infliction of brain damage which caused the plaintiff to develop his proclivity to rape;[10] but after the rapist's victims had obtained a damages award against him[11] his claim that the car driver's insurer should indemnify him in respect of the award failed, since that damage was too remote in law from the driver's negligence.[12] In another case,[13] the first of

---

[4] [1985] 3 All E.R. 402.

[5] AR 1984, p. 419.

[6] *Sidaway* v. *Bethlem Royal Hospital Governors* [1985] 1 All E.R. 643 (see also A.R. 1984 p. 419).

[7] See also *Lee* v. *S.W. Thames Regional Health Authority* [1985] 2 All E.R. 385 (disclosure of treatment given).

[8] Statutory Instruments 1985 Nos. 846, 858.

[9] Provided for in Supreme Court Act 1981 s. 32A (inserted by Administration of Justice Act 1982 s. 6).

[10] *Meah* v. *McCreamer* [1985] 1 All E.R. 367.

[11] *The Times* 11 December 1985, p. 1 refers.

[12] *Meah* v. *McCreamer (No. 2)*, *The Times* 12 December 1985.

[13] *Condon* v. *Basi* [1985] 2 All E.R. 453.

its kind in English law, the Court of Appeal upheld an award of damages in negligence against one football player who had broken the leg of another by foul play.

In criminal law, the House of Lords held[14] that a person who had received goods mistakenly believing them to be stolen was not guilty of dishonestly attempting to handle them, since the accused could not be said to have done, as the Act required, any 'act which was more than merely preparatory to the commission of the [substantive] offence'[15]: indeed, she had acted entirely lawfully. In two cases under the Theft Act 1968 the House of Lords held[16] that where a person left a hotel without paying his bill, and was charged with dishonestly making off with intent to avoid payment, the prosecution must show an intention to avoid payment permanently, not merely to delay or defer payment; and the Court of Appeal held[17] that where a cinema projectionist secretly removed films for 'pirate' copying and resale, but returned the films undamaged and in time for scheduled performances, he was not guilty of theft: in the circumstances the borrowing was not 'equivalent to an outright taking or disposal'.[18]

The meaning of 'malice aforethought' in the law of murder remained obscure. In a case[19] where the drunken accused had killed his father with a shotgun the House of Lords replaced the murder conviction with one of manslaughter on the ground that mere foresight of the probability of death or serious injury was insufficient: what had to be shown was intention—which could be inferred if the accused foresaw the result as a 'natural consequence' of his act. But in a case[20] arising from the miners' strike of 1984-85 the Court of Appeal reduced from murder to manslaughter the conviction of two striking miners who had killed a taxi driver by dropping a concrete block on his car from a bridge. The Court observed that the phrase 'natural consequence' was ambiguous and that the jury should be directed that it referred to a high likelihood of death or serious injury.[21]

The legal repercussions of the miners' strike continued in 1985. In November the National Union of Mineworkers (NUM) purged its contempt[22] and the sequestration order was discharged.[23] Despite the

[14] *Anderton* v. *Ryan* [1985] 2 All E.R. 355.
[15] Criminal Attempts Act 1981 s. 1 (1).
[16] *R* v. *Allen* [1985] 2 All E.R. 641.
[17] *R* v. *Lloyd* [1985] 2 All E.R. 661.
[18] Theft Act 1968 s. 6 (1).
[19] *R* v. *Moloney* [1985] 1 All E.R. 1025.
[20] *R* v. *Hancock, R* v *Shankland, The Times* 1 November 1985.
[21] The House of Lords dismissed the Crown's appeal and promised reasons later: *The Times* 13 December 1985, p. 2 refers.
[22] See AR 1984, p. 416.
[23] *Taylor* v. *N.U.M., The Times* 20 November 1985.

appointment of new trustees, however, the receivership[24] was continued because of the unwillingness of NUM leaders to cooperate in the matter.[25] Striking miners failed to obtain judicial review of supplementary-benefit authorities' deduction from benefit payments of an amount for notional strike pay: the court held that the statutory appeals procedure should be followed.[26] On the other hand, a miner who refused to participate in the strike, but who was subsequently made redundant, was held[27] to be disqualified thereafter from unemployment benefit because he was 'directly interested'[28] in the dispute. But working miners did obtain injunctions restraining their branch union from organizing intimidatory picketing, which, the court held, constituted an actionable tort as being an unreasonable interference with the plaintiffs' right to use the highway for the purpose of entering and leaving their place of work.[29]

During 1985 the Government suffered a number of reverses in the courts. The Secretary of State for Transport was held to have exceeded his power to intervene in the affairs of the Greater London Council when he purported to prohibit a proposed night-time and weekend ban on heavy lorries in Greater London.[30] The same Minister's 150 per cent increase of Severn Bridge tolls was held null and void because of a failure by his department to consider all the points made by objectors.[31] And although the Minister suffered a third defeat[32] over the amount of grant to be paid by the Greater London Council to the London Transport Executive when he took control of the latter, the matter was ultimately resolved by statute.[33]

The Social Services Secretary failed in his attempt to encourage young people to move from place to place in search of work when regulations permitting him to reduce their supplementary benefit payments if they stayed in one place were held *ultra vires*.[34] The same Minister was held to have abused his powers to adjust future NHS payments to opticians when he purported to use them to recover from opticians what he considered to be past 'unintended profits'.[35] Likewise, his attempt to reduce Government payments to pharmacists in respect of drugs upon which the

---

[24] See AR 1984, p. 417
[25] *The Times* 23 October 1985, p. 1 refers.
[26] *R* v. *Chief Adjudication Officer ex p. Bland*, *The Times* 6 February 1985.
[27] *Cartlidge* v. *Chief Adjudication Officer*, *The Times* 3 December 1985.
[28] Social Security Act 1975 s. 19(1).
[29] *Thomas* v. *NUM and others* [1985] 2 All E.R. 1.
[30] *R* v. *Secretary of State for Transport ex p. GLC*, *The Times* 31 October 1985.
[31] *The Times*, 13 December 1985 p. 1 refers.
[32] *R* v. *Secretary of State for Transport ex p. GLC* [1985] 3 All E.R. 300.
[33] London Regional Transport (Amendment) Act 1985.
[34] *R* v. *Secretary of State for Social Services ex p. Cotton*, *The Times* 14 December 1985.
[35] *R* v. *Secretary of State for Social Services ex p. Westhead*, *The Times* 17 October 1985.

pharmacists had obtained a high discount was held to be unlawful since it contravened EEC legislation applicable to the UK.[36]

However, the Government preserved a crucial plank in its rate-capping strategy when the House of Lords[37] (reversing the Court of Appeal[38]) held that in fixing rate support grant levels the Environment Secretary might discriminate in favour of low-spending authorities. And two rate-capped authorities failed in their attempts to challenge the lawfulness of the action on largely technical grounds.[39]

In two cases which attracted much public attention, prosecutions under the Official Secrets Act 1911 failed. In February, Clive Ponting, a senior civil servant, was acquitted by an Old Bailey jury of one of the 2,324 offences chargeable under the notorious 'catch-all' section 2.[40] And in October seven British servicemen serving in Cyprus were acquitted of espionage charges under section 1 in 'the longest, largest and most secret espionage trial in British legal history'.[41] As on several recent occasions,[42] a number of Northern Ireland terrorist prosecutions based on 'super-grass' evidence failed;[43] but in December Carswell J. convicted 26 men of terrorist offences on the evidence of Henry Kirkpatrick whom the judge found 'a credible witness'.[44]

In his annual review[45] the Master of the Rolls reported that although the Court of Appeal had disposed of more appeals in 1984-85 than in previous years, the number of appeals set down had increased so that the backlog of appeals remained substantially undiminished. Some 76 per cent of all appeals (and some 89 per cent from the Divisional Court) were dismissed. Lord Diplock, one of the chief architects of the current renaissance of judicial review of official action, died on 14 October (see OBITUARY).

[36] *R* v. *Secretary of State for Social Services ex p. Bomore Ltd.*, *The Times* 16 December 1985.
[37] *R* v. *Secretary of State for the Environment ex p. Nottinghamshire C.C.*, *The Times* 13 December 1985.
[38] *The Times*, 4 October 1985.
[39] *R* v. *Secretary of State for the Environment ex p. Leicester City Council*, *The Times* 1 February 1985; *R* v. *same ex p. Greenwich L.B.C.*, *The Times* 19 December 1985.
[40] *The Times*, 11 February 1985, pp. 1, 2 refer.
[41] *The Times*, 29 October, p. 2.
[42] See AR, 1983, p. 396, and 1984, pp. 53, 419.
[43] *The Times*, 25 February and 1 April 1985 refer.
[44] *The Times*, 19 December 1985, p. 2 refers.
[45] *The Times*, 3 October 1985.

XVI THE ARTS

Chapter 1

OPERA—MUSIC—DANCE/BALLET—THEATRE—CINEMA—TELEVISION AND RADIO

OPERA

OPERATICALLY speaking, the centenary year of the births of Handel and J. S. Bach was naturally dominated by the former, though full stagings of both the *St Matthew* and the *St John Passions* (Milan and Venice respectively) struck a blow for the latter: both were mounted with due seriousness and well received, as was Handel's *Messiah*, produced as a modern mystery play at the Deutsche Oper, Berlin. Most opera companies, whether major or minor, staged at least one Handel opera during the year, and many were sensibly toured to more than one venue. The better-known works enjoyed up to six or more new productions each: amongst the more notable were a stylish and witty *Serse* at the English National Opera (winner of a SWETM Olivier award) and *Giulio Cesare* at Purchase, N.Y., in a modern-dress version directed by Peter Sellars that skimped nothing on musical values despite being set in a Cairo hotel bombed by terrorists. The latter was played in repertory with a staging of *Tamerlano* directed by the critic Andrew Porter in authentic 18th-century style—a juxtaposition that confirmed Handel's continuing dramatic vitality regardless of time and place. *Agrippina*, *Alcina*, *Orlando*, *Rinaldo* and *Ariodante* received many stagings world-wide.

But the most valuable aspect of the centenary year was the revival of Handel's lesser-known operas, many of them scarcely heard since the 18th century: *Floridante* (Halle); the anti-heroic *Flavio* (Batignano and London); *Giustino*, in a flippant production by Harry Kupfer (Halle, Berlin and elsewhere); *Alessandro* (Halle and Göttingen); *Amadigi di Gaula* and *Almira* (composed 1705), his earliest surviving opera (Halle); *Teseo* (London, Athens, Versailles, Purchase and Manchester); *Berenice* (Keele); *Poro* (Birmingham); and most interestingly his first Italian opera, *Rodrigo*, parts of which had only recently been unearthed, staged complete in London for the first time since 1708. All such enterprises confirmed that incalculable riches remained to be discovered in Handel's 40 or more operas, and all faced in diverse and varyingly successful ways the problems of performing them to modern audiences.

There was, nevertheless, no shortage of new operas in Handel year, many of them in America. One of the most ambitious was John Eaton's *The Tempest* (Santa Fe, 27 July), imaginatively staged and judged to be one of the most successful post-war American operas; the same was said of Thea Musgrave's *Harriet: the Woman called Moses* (Norfolk, Virginia,

1 March), a heartfelt study of the heroic ex-slave Harriet Tubman and the exodus she led during the American Civil War. There were two new operas at St Louis, Stephen Paulus's *The Woodlanders*, based on Hardy's novel (13 June), and Minoru Miki's *Joruri* (30 May) on a Japanese subject. By strange coincidence two new works based on the same Schnitzler novella were premiered within a week of each other on opposite sides of the Atlantic—Dominick Argento's *Casanova's Home-coming* (Minnesota, 12 April), a comedy full of musical parody, and Girolamo Arrigo's *Il ritorno di Casanova* (Geneva, 18 April), a less sharply-etched treatment; and to compound the coincidence Lortzing's forgotten *Casanova* (1841) was revived in Oberhausen.

New European operas included Alexander Goehr's *Behold the Sun*, a thoughtful account of the Anabaptist uprising in Münster whose success was somewhat compromised by the management's cavalier massacre of the score during rehearsal (Duisburg, 19 April); Franco Donati's *Atem* (Milan, 14 February), a collage of existing music strung together in vaguely dramatic form; Marco Tutino's *Pinocchio* (Turin, 23 May), mysteriously forbidden to audiences under 18; and Sutermeister's *Le Roi Bérenger*, based on Ionesco, a notable success at the Munich Festival on 22 July. Konrad Boehmer's *Docteur Faustus*, winner of the Liebermann prize, was coolly received at the Paris Opéra on 20 February, but Marcel Landowski's *Montségur*, set amongst the Cathars, was a success both at its premiere (Toulouse, 1 February) and later in Paris. A new Australian opera, Brian Howard's Kafka-based *Metamorphosis*, was spectacularly staged in Sydney (3 January), but neither Edward Harper's *Hedda Gabler* (Glasgow, 5 June) nor Iain Hamilton's *Lancelot* (Arundel, 24 August) caused much of a stir. Oliver Knussen's *Higglety Pigglety Pop!* was finally staged, more or less complete, at Glyndebourne on 5 August.

Sir Michael Tippet's 80th birthday was celebrated with an outstandingly successful production of *The Midsummer Marriage* by Opera North (Leeds, 30 September), and with a fine revival of *King Priam* at Covent Garden, later taken to the Athens Festival. The Berg centenary was marked by countless revivals of his two operas and the completion of George Perle's magisterial two-volume study of his music.

The Semper Opera House in Dresden was reopened on 13 February, 40 years to the day after its destruction by bombing. *Ring* cycles were completed to much acclaim in San Francisco (June), Berlin (October) and Cardiff (September). The popular success of the year at the Paris Opéra was an extravagant revival of Meyerbeer's *Robert le diable*, and in New York the Met scored with a sell-out new production of *Porgy and Bess*. In London, Lord Harewood retired after 13 years as managing director of the English National Opera, during a year that saw successful ENO productions of *Tristan und Isolde*, *Faust* and Philip Glass's *Akhnaten*. The highlight at the Royal Opera was a spectacular staging of Stockhausen's *Donnerstag aus Licht*.

Among the year's scandals were, predictably, Ken Russell's *Faust* in Vienna (more than one member of the cast defected) and the introduction of a lavatory into *Don Giovanni* in Glasgow. It was also a year of slaps. The Bonn music director, Gustav Kuhn, slapped his general administrator in public and was dismissed for his pains; in Salzburg the producer Piero Faggioni slapped the festival administrator when told he would not be allowed naked witches in *Macbeth*. Faggioni stayed, but the witches went.

The year's obituary list included the legendary soprano Viorica Ursuleac at the age of 91, the great Czech tenor Beno Blachut, the baritones Karl Schmitt-Walter and George London, the conductors Lovro von Matacic and Wilhelm Brückner-Rüggeberg, the composers Roger Sessions and William Alwyn, the much-respected British voice teacher Frederic Cox, and Mosco Carner, doyen of critics and biographer of Puccini.

MUSIC

1985 was designated 'European Music Year', and 21 June 'Music Day', the aims being as general as they could be: to make music of all kinds and all eras universally accessible. Yet, apart from providing a field-day for the bureaucrats in Strasbourg, whose organizing committee comprised representatives from 24 countries, little of consequence was achieved that would not have happened in the normal course of events. Three tercentenaries were celebrated, those of J. S. Bach, Handel and Giuseppe Domenico Scarlatti. Apart from performances too numerous to specify, the most important result was the discovery in a library at Yale University of 33 chorale preludes for organ by Bach. Christoph Wolff, a Bach authority at Harvard, intended to announce the existence of this exciting manuscript in Leipzig on Bach's birthday, 21 March, but pressure of the 'Music Year' caused the news to leak out, and the rush to be first thereupon led to the issue of two recordings, neither satisfactory—one by an American, Joseph Payne, the other by a German, Werner Jacob.

Ironically, in spite of the hopeful European title the year seemed weighted in favour of American music. American composers certainly played a dominant role in London. *A Bite of the Big Apple* at the Bloomsbury Theatre in May was built round the New Music Consort of New York; also in May the Merce Cunningham Dance Company had a two-week season at Sadler's Wells; June saw a festival at the Almeida Theatre in Islington, organized by the pianist Yvar Mikhashoff, as well as the performance of Philip Glass's *Akhnaten* at the Coliseum. Much of the music proved undisguisedly weak; Glass's static, repetitive idiom, and Claude Vivier's immaturity in structuring ideas, underlined the falsity of much of the advance publicity; but there could be no denying the assertive vitality of the American *avant garde*. It was, as they say, here to stay.

The founding fathers (if that is the correct term) of minimalism—
Terry Riley, Steve Reich and Philip Glass—also had a good year for
recordings; Glass in particular saw his opera *Satyagraha* (see AR 1981,
p. 423) appear in the CBS Masterworks series, performed by the New
York City Opera, with the prospect of their taking it into their repertory
for 1986. The essence of the repetitive, minimalist style is the steady,
unruffled unfolding of the music, with a glowing calm totally devoid of
nervous intensity. Tension, climax, the ebb and flow of musical dialectic
associated with the symphonic schools of the past are foreign to it. This
objective was not always achieved in the recording, probably because of
the insensitivity of the conductor, Christopher Keene. Nevertheless
Satyagraha was a highspot of the records of 1985.

The New York City Opera, under the effective direction of Miss
Beverly Sills, gave further evidence of shrewd artistic judgment in presenting another contemporary opera, though one very different in mood
and idiom from *Akhnaten*: *Casanova* by Dominick Argento. Argento's
style, which is tonal with a difference, and traditionally based, proved a
successful recipe for a comedy about the events following Casanova's
return to Venice, a favour granted to him on the unfulfillable condition of
his good behaviour. The opera had been heard earlier in the year in
Minnesota, where Argento was Professor at the University, and much of
that production was used for the New York performances (see also
p. 412).

The achievement of the New York City Opera in successfully promoting two much-contrasted contemporary operas by living American composers was one not to be under-estimated, breaking as it did the barrier
between the ghetto-like world inhabited by most contemporary composers and the large audience that attends traditional concerts and opera
performances. It might even be said that two irreconcilable approaches to
music were represented by this barrier; that of the *avant garde* on one
side, that of publicly accessible music on the other. Certainly 1985
showed yet again that all-too-many London promoters went about their
business on this principle, which led to monotonous repetition of the
well-worn repertory, motivated chiefly by box-office profit. Conversely,
on those occasions when flair and initiative were shown in giving contemporary performances, two ingredients for success were lacking—an audience and an informed press. The BBC Symphony drew only 400 people to
an (admittedly curious) twentieth-century programme in the 3,000-seat
Festival Hall; the London Sinfonietta drew the same number (many,
indeed, the same people) to hear Berio conduct his own works; none of
the audiences for the four concerts in the Redcliffe Concerts 'Tippett
Generation' series topped the figure of 200. The conclusion was inescap-
able; London had a great deal to offer the living composer, except what
was needed most: a public.

No doubt this was not unrelated to the paucity of space allowed to

English musical journalists and their limited range. There was no equivalent in London to the space allowed weekly to music in the *New York Times*; London had no Donal Henahan or John Rockwell, whose articles contained not merely reportage, but deeper discussion of aesthetic issues.

Two of the most successful events of 1985 in London took place at the Barbican. The first was a week-long retrospective of work by Stockhausen in January, *Music and Machines*, organized by the BBC; the second was a series of six concerts under the title 'Mahler, Vienna and the Twentieth Century', directed by Claudio Abbado with the London Symphony Orchestra. Ancillary events included two operas by Zemlinsky at Covent Garden and various lectures, exhibitions and television programmes. Among the latter were two programmes on Mahler contributed by Leonard Bernstein, which went a long way to earning the latter the title of composer/conductor of the year. His great insight into Mahler's symphonic idiom, and essential Jewishness, were clothed in words of great geniality and wit.

Even more immediate, certainly more popular, was the television showing of the recording sessions of *West Side Story*, in which Bernstein the conductor was seen to be the ideal interpreter of Bernstein the composer. *West Side Story* was the best-selling record even in the by-no-means-inconsiderable catalogue of Deutsche Grammophon; so much so that composer and record company signed in December a new long-term contract that covered not only a new Mahler series but also some works by living American composers (something unthinkable in England). It also allowed for the possibility of taping live performances, thus not only capturing a more immediate sense of performance than in a studio but, perhaps more important, making recording cheaper.

Several anniversaries divisible by five helped their owners to obtain more performances in 1985 than otherwise would have been the case; Aaron Copland was 85, Tippett was 80, Berio was 60; but for those less fortunate, those many composers whose works still awaited performance, few outlets were apparent. In London, mainstream concerts ignored British composers, and the most prominent festivals, such as the Proms or Cheltenham, remained hidebound by tradition. One needed to look off the beaten track for interesting new developments. One such major event of the year was the publication and performance of the oratorio *Confitebor* by the 18th-century composer Samuel Wesley, which was performed by a choir in Wimbledon in May (see AR 1982, p. 423). In New York notable premieres made possible through the American Composers' Orchestra included William McKinley's *Clarinet Concerto* and Lou Harrison's *Piano Concerto*. Also, the Kronos Quartet specialized in new music, through the 'Composers' Forum' concerts; and the Symphony Space opened its 8th season in 1985 with 'Composers in Red Sneakers', a group from Boston disenchanted with the outlook adopted all-too-frequently by performers towards their work. Any member of the public in red sneakers was admitted free.

But it was non-Western music that achieved most exposure in America; no doubt this reflected the multiracial nature of American, particularly New York, society, containing as it does a cross-section of the ethnic variety of the entire world, many people with distinctive musical and folk forms of expression, many trying to rediscover cultural roots. So New Yorkers were overwhelmed with art music from the Middle East, Indonesia, Japan, China, and folk and popular music from Africa, Latin America and the Caribbean. Peter Grilli, the Director of Performing Arts at the Japan Society, aptly summed it up: 'People want something new and different.' Nationalism was always one of the strongest driving-forces in music; ethnic concerts provided the outlet. In London, and other British cities, such events also occurred, though not necessarily in the form of concerts. The Notting Hill Carnival was an important demonstration of West Indian folk music. But frequently in London such 'ethnic concerts' were politically-motivated protests, in support of this or that cause.

The record industry in 1985 seemed to have only one priority, the issue of as many compact discs (CDs) as possible. In the spring they numbered some 3,000; by December the figure was 8,000 and rising. The main companies gave much thought to the reclamation of older classical recordings, and most of the CD releases in the pop and jazz section of the market were reissues. Nevertheless the total of LPs on the market was still about 40,000; and tucked away in the far corner (many indeed not available through the retail trade at all) could be detected just a few recordings issued not for reasons of commercial gain, nor for the furtherance of a particular artist's career, but for artistic and archive purposes: partly the discovery and preservation of a cultural heritage, partly the performance of new or experimental music that might not otherwise be heard. New World Records were doing just such invaluable service for American composers; and most European countries supported their nationals in this way—but not, need it be said, Great Britain.

As for the world of pop music, just one event dominated 1985—Live Aid; and just one name—Bob Geldof. Following on the experience of Band Aid the previous year (see AR 1984, p. 435), this thrusting, unstoppable Irishman organized an even bigger and brasher pop concert at Wembley in July 1985—a 10-hour spectacular, featuring the A-Z of pop history, all of whose artists gave their services. It was the biggest rock event ever; it was repeated at the John F. Kennedy Center in Philadelphia; it was relayed live by satellite to all countries, reaching an estimated audience of a thousand million (thus outstripping the Royal Wedding); it was a global juke-box; and it was all done for the purpose of raising money for famine relief in Ethiopia and northern Africa. By the end of the year the worldwide total of pledges was £60 million. Bob

Geldof became an international celebrity, even an embarrassment to some governments. Pop music, too, had adopted a new image, one of responsibility and caring.

Of the English-language books published in 1985, two of the most informative, and most likely to remain of value for a long time, were *Mademoiselle: Conversations with Nadia Boulanger* by Bruno Monsaingeon, translated by Robyn Marsack (Carcanet), and *Tchaikovsky's Ballets* by Roland John Wiley (Oxford).

Among those who died in 1985 were the composers William Alwyn and Roger Sessions, the pianists Stefan Askenase and Emil Gilels, the conductor Eugene Ormandy and the Russian violinist Efrem Zimbalist (for Ormandy and Zimbalist see OBITUARY).

DANCE/BALLET

The year was not a good one for Britain's Royal Ballet, although towards its close there were signs that Anthony Dowell, appointed associate director of the Company for 1985-86 and destined to succeed Norman Morrice as director in 1986-87, would take steps to bring the troupe back to its former international eminence. The troubles came from slackness of execution in overall standards, a disastrous revival of Balanchine's *Ballet Imperial* and growing unrest in the audience about unadventurous programme-building. There was much criticism about the choice of artists to design ballets; in the previous year the distinguished painter Victor Passmore had provided admirable designs for David Bintley's *Young Apollo*, but in 1985 those produced by Christopher Le Brun for *Ballet Imperial* were almost universally condemned, while by the time of the first performance of Michael Corder's *Number Three* (Covent Garden, 9 March) the choreographer had disassociated himself entirely from the costumes provided by the American painter Helen Frankenthaler—her backcloths, however, were greatly admired.

By the end of the 1984-85 season criticisms were rife—about slackness in teaching, coaching, casting—and although Morrice was not held wholly responsible the acceleration of decline was described by a critic as 'the most serious charge against his regime'.

There were bright moments. Antoinette Sibley returned to the company, albeit briefly and as a guest, to set the ballerina example, and both Mikhail Baryshnikov and Fernando Bujones came (at the express invitation of Anthony Dowell) from American Ballet Theatre to show male dancing of breathtaking quality. Elisabeth Platel came, too, from the Paris Opéra Ballet to dance classic roles, sometimes with her Paris partner Charles Jude. There was plenty of talent in the young generation of Royal Ballet dancers, but all of them needed more coaching, more hard work in the classroom.

Two choreographers made their Covent Garden debuts. Jennifer Jackson contributed a fairly abstract dance ballet, *Half the House*, to Bartok's 1939 *Divertimento for Strings*, and Wayne Eagling had a big, popular, Béjart-style success with *Frankenstein, the Modern Prometheus*, danced to a score by Vangelis with costumes by the Emanuels and an audacious abundance of stage effects.

The beginning of the 1985-86 season brought a vastly-improved staging of *The Sleeping Beauty* (supervised by Dowell with Dame Ninette de Valois' cooperation), a fine new production by Peter Wright of *Giselle* (28 November) in imaginative designs by John F. Macfarlane, and a Christmas revival of last year's *Nutcracker* (also by Peter Wright), with Gennady Rozhdestvensky of the Bolshoi Ballet winning from the orchestra a magical account of Tchaikovsky's score. Mark Ermler, also of the Bolshoi, conducted some *Sleeping Beauty* performances. Irina Yakobson and Galina Samsova were brought in to teach and coach. No fewer than three dancers made more than promising debuts in *Giselle*, namely Maria Almeida, Fiona Chadwick and Ravenna Tucker. David Bintley made his third ballet for Covent Garden, *The Sons of Horus*, to a commissioned score from Peter McGowan with designs by Terry Bartlett, an agreeable translation of Egyptian myths into dance.

Sadler's Wells Royal Ballet (SWRB), under the direction of Peter Wright, had a good year. Their Covent Garden season in April/May brought Wright's 1984 spectacular staging of *The Sleeping Beauty* to London, and Evelyn Hart of the Royal Winnipeg Ballet returned as a welcome guest. Young choreography continued to be commissioned and good work was done by Jennifer Jackson, Michael Corder, Susan Crow, Graham Lustig and, especially, David Bintley, resident choreographer of SWRB, who made two delightful Scottish ballets, *Flowers of the Forest*, using music respectively by Malcolm Arnold and Benjamin Britten. An important tour of New Zealand, Korea and India was undertaken; seasons were given in the company's 'second home' at the Birmingham Hippodrome, and the company also danced in the 'Big Top' circus tent at popular prices. Standards of dancing were very sound, and exceptional talent was shown by some of the lesser-known dancers in addition to the established stars.

London Festival Ballet, under the artistic direction of the Danish dancer Peter Schaufuss, sought to widen their repertory with works by Ashton (*Romeo and Juliet*), Roland Petit, Maurice Béjart and Paul Taylor and a staging of the Kingdom of Shades scene from *La Bayadère* by Natalia Makarova. A new production of *Coppélia* by Ronald Hynd (now successful director of the Munich State Opera Ballet) proved good box office. Very young dancers such as the American Katherine Healy and the Spanish Trinidad Sevillano were given opportunities (and much publicity) and Festival played open house to innumerable guests from abroad. Patrick Armand, formerly of the Ballet Théâtre Contemporain of Nancy, France, was a notable acquisition to company ranks. Natalia Makarova gave guest performances as Tatiana in Cranko's *Onegin* which were among the sensations of the year.

Ballet Rambert, under the direction of Robert North and with Richard Alston as resident choreographer, did excellent work and staged new ballets by Alston (*Java*, to songs by the Ink Spots, was outstanding), Christopher Bruce and North himself. London Contemporary Dance Theatre sustained its high standard of performances and in addition to new works by company members acquired Jerome Robbins's ballet-in-silence *Moves*. The granting of the first honours degrees in contemporary dance by the University of Kent was celebrated by a performance in Canterbury Cathedral; three company members, Anca Frankenhaeuser, Charlotte Kirkpatrick and Patrick Harding-Irmer, were then capped and gowned. The London School of Contemporary Dance, which feeds this company, was now also feeding not only the smaller contemporary companies in Britain but many in the USA too—the Martha Graham company among them.

Scottish Ballet staged a full-length *Carmen* ballet by its director Peter Darrell at the Edinburgh Festival. Northern Ballet Theatre had a London season which contained a good revival of Cullberg's *Miss Julie* with Nureyev as guest artist.

There was another Dance Umbrella (see AR 1984, p. 425) of very varied quality, the best offerings coming (as usual) from America—namely, David Gordon and his Pick Up Co., Mark Morris and Karole Armitage.

Visiting companies included the highly proficient Matsuyama Ballet from Japan, who danced *Swan Lake* and *Giselle* with Nureyev as guest; Yoko Morishita had a personal triumph. Merce Cunningham brought his company back to Sadler's Wells with a fantastic new repertory and won enormous acclaim—also the coveted Olivier Award for outstanding achievement in dance.

In the United States, the New York City Ballet (NYCB) sustained its great Balanchine repertory and its superb standard of dancing, the company fed by the School of American Ballet. Peter Martins continued to choreograph and Jerome Robbins made *Eight Lines* to music by Steve Reich and *In Memory of . . .* to Berg's *Violin Concerto*, with a central role for Suzanne Farrell. Helgi Tomassen retired from dancing but, as always with this great company, young talent emerged consistently from the ranks. A minor rebellion against Lincoln Kirstein within the School of American Ballet was quickly quashed and Kirstein, a founder-director of NYCB and its School, remained more firmly in command than ever.

American Ballet Theatre (ABT) had a difficult year. Director Mikhail Baryshnikov spent too much time away from the company making guest appearances. Kenneth MacMillan was appointed as associate artistic director and staged his full-length *Romeo and Juliet* and a one-act version of *Anastasia*. The older ballets in the repertory, including the Tudor works, fell below their proper standard and some people bemoaned the loss of star personalities who had always contributed to ABT's popular image. Alessandra Ferri of the Royal Ballet joined ABT in August 1985 at the invitation of Baryshnikov and had the anticipated success in MacMillan's *Romeo and Juliet*, which she had danced in London (and on television in both the UK and the USA).

A curiosity, and a great success, was the staging of an old Bournonville ballet, *Abdallah*, on 20 February in Salt Lake City by Ballet West. The revival was done by Toni Lander (already terminally ill) and Bruce Marks, helped by Flemming Ryberg from Copenhagen.

The Joffrey Ballet, about to celebrate its 30th anniversary, continued its policy of staging new ballets, by Gerald Arpino among others, and careful revivals from other repertories.

Dance Theatre of Harlem had an unexpected and very successful season at the Metropolitan Opera House, New York. The Cunningham and Paul Taylor companies had major New York seasons. Meredith Monk revived her multi-media work, *Quarry*. Trisha Brown and her company packed the City Center. The Brooklyn Academy of Music presented John Neumeier's Hamburg Ballet and hosted Next Wave festivals of contemporary dance. The Berlin Ballet was also seen at the Met in Roland Petit's *The Blue Angel*, in which the choreographer and his star Natalia Makarova had personal successes, although the ballet was not much liked. A projected visit by the Paris Opéra Ballet was aborted by lack of funds.

In Paris, Nureyev continued his direction of the Opéra Ballet, staged his versions of the classics, introduced an all-Tudor evening and endeavoured to enliven the repertory. In this he was only partially successful— his version of *Washington Square* was as much of a laughing-stock as was Franco Zeffirelli's new staging of *Swan Lake* at the Scala, Milan—but the reputation of the Paris Opéra dancers never stood higher. Critics of all nationalities sang the praises of *étoiles*: of Pontois, Piollet, Clerc, Legrée, de Vulpian, Loudières, Platel and young Sylvie Guillem among the women; Denard, Guizerix, Dupond, Jude, Lormeau, Hilaire and Legris among the men.

At the very end of 1985 the Ballets de l'Opéra de Monte Carlo, a new company under the direction of Ghislaine Thesmar and Pierre Lacotte, re-established classical ballet in its traditional home in Monaco.

The Bolshoi Ballet, still directed by Yuri Grigorovich, made a tour of West Germany in the spring of 1985 and brought to the West for the first time the new version of *The Golden Age* which had been made by Grigorovich using the original Shostakovich score, with some additions, and in brilliantly versatile designs by Simon Virsaladse. The ballet proved to be enormously enjoyable, putting across with sincerity but no sentimentality its moral tale of a corrupt bourgeoisie overcome by honest fisherfolk. Natalia Bessmertnova was undisputed ballerina of the troupe but a whole new generation had sprung up since the Bolshoi was last seen in Western Europe. The male dancers, dominated by Irek Muchamedov and Gediminas Taranda, were sensational.

The Russians, of course, still tended to take most of the honours in international competitions but in 1985 the Chinese suddenly came into their own in very elegant classical schooling. Julio Bocca of Argentina won the men's gold medal in Moscow; the Japanese Yoko Morimoto won all hearts there; and Edward Stierle, aged 16, of the USA won the 1985 student competition, the Prix de Lausanne.

In Scandinavia, Beryl Grey mounted in November a new production of *The Sleeping Beauty* for the Royal Swedish Ballet in designs by David Walker. The Royal Danish Ballet, after two years of nomad existence, moved back into their rebuilt and restored Royal Theatre on 2 November and, under the new directorship of young Frank Andersen, presented the premiere of John Neumeier's *Amleth, Prince of Jutland* (the Hamlet legend), which gave a good start to what everyone hoped would be a brave new era.

The *Dancing Times*, the world's oldest dance magazine, celebrated 75 years of uninterrupted publication in London with its October 1985 issue. During the year 75th birthdays were also celebrated by Galina Ulanova, Dame Peggy van Praagh, Vakhtang Chaboukiani and Dame Alicia Markova.

Important publications of the year were: *Tchaikovsky's Ballets* by Roland John Wiley, *The Life and Works of John Weaver* by Richard Ralph—both definitive studies—and *Balanchine's Tchaikovsky*, interviews with Balanchine about Tchaikovsky's music, by Solomon Volkov.

The dance world lost a number of distinguished people. Lisa Ullman, a disciple of Rudolf von Laban, died on 25 January; in April the shoemaker Ben Sommers of Capezio died, as did the designer Barry Kay; May saw the deaths of Phyllis Bedells, the first English ballerina, the Danish ballerina and teacher Toni Lander and the doyen of American dance critics, John Martin; Karel Shook, a co-founder of Dance Theatre of Harlem, died on 25 July; and James Monahan, writer and critic of the dance and a former BBC administrator, died on 23 November.

THEATRE

Peter Brook staged his dramatization of the Indian epic poem *The Mahabharata*—an enthralling narrative, performed by a multinational company—at the Avignon Festival in July. It subsequently played in Paris, which had displaced London as showcase for world theatre. The irony was that Brook remained a director of the Royal Shakespeare Company (RSC) but rarely nowadays worked with the company: his

Carmen and *The Conference of the Birds* had still not been seen in the UK. It was in Paris that major productions by leading ensembles and directors such as Strehler, Mnouchkine, Chéreau, Bergman, Stein, Berghaus and Vitez were likely to be found.

When the RSC was evolving in the 1960s, its most significant productions—by Peter Hall, Peter Brook, John Barton, Trevor Nunn—were mounted alongside, and almost in comparison with, Peter Daubeney's World Theatre seasons at the Company's then London base, the Aldwych Theatre. The indigenous RSC productions were enhanced by their participants' exposure to the best new work from elsewhere. The best 'foreign' play the RSC could find to put on in 1985 was an anglicized version of the leaden French musical *Les Misérables*, derived from Victor Hugo's mammoth novel. Whether or not the RSC staged *Les Misérables* cynically, it was co-produced with a commercial impresario, Cameron Mackintosh, and, after a few months at the Barbican, was destined to slip into the Palace Theatre. Directed by the RSC's joint artistic director, Trevor Nunn, and John Caird and lavishly designed by John Napier, its cast included only two RSC actors. They happened to give the strongest performances. One, Alun Armstrong, had to leave the Stratford-upon-Avon production of *Troilus and Cressida* before the season's end to bolster up *Les Misérables*. Pragmatism or opportunism?

A report on London, even British, theatre in 1985 must be, depressingly, more to do with finance—or, rather, lack of it—than, with few exceptions, artistic success. A committed Minister for the Arts, Lord Gowrie, resigned and was replaced by Richard Luce, whose first subsequent published remark was that he was looking forward to seeing Donald Sinden in Chichester's most successful production of the year (it transferred to Her Majesty's, and was, admittedly, great fun), *The Scarlet Pimpernel*. Gowrie had a seat in the Cabinet, not so Luce, some indication of the Prime Minister's lack of concern for the arts. The Government seemed unprepared to acknowledge that, for the last 20 years, theatre had been one of Britain's finest achievements. Without adequate subsidy, artistic excellence cannot be achieved.

Sir Peter Hall, director of the National Theatre (NT) and the profession's primary public spokesman, was said to have enraged the Prime Minister by continually asking for more, not only for his own three-theatre complex on the South Bank but for the theatre as a whole. The Arts Council being kept on a slim diet of funds by central government, and the Greater London Council and other metropolitan councils being on the point of extinction, theatres with artistic ambition had a tough year.

Neither RSC nor NT took kindly to adverse comments by reviewers: hurt or cross directors dispatched letters to critics thought to have stepped out of line. For press critics there was a dilemma here: should a misconceived production of, say, Gogol's *The Government Inspector*

(NT) be praised when, perhaps, if it is damned audiences may stay away, and the financial and thus artistic position of the theatre may be further depressed? This particular production, ingeniously designed—provincial Russia as a sea of paper, legal documents and ink—by John Gunter, starred a fashionable young television comic, Rik Mayall. Mayall (whose presence was presumably intended to wean the television generation to the live theatre), used to the intimacy of television cameras, could not command the vastness of the Olivier auditorium. On the play's 1966 outing at the RSC, Khlestakov had been played by Paul Scofield, with Paul Rogers as the mayor. Need more be said?

Sir Peter Hall set up four separate companies of actors under different directors, each company to do one production in each of the three NT theatres. He himself was in charge of one of the groups, and directed lovingly John Fowles's translation of Jean-Jacques Bernard's *Martine*, about love and class in the France of 1922. He also directed what was arguably the year's most specious piece, Peter Shaffer's *Yonadab*, derived from Dan Jacobson's astringent novel, *The Rape of Tamar*, and the Old Testament. Alan Bates gave a panicky, camp performance as the eponymous stirrer-up-of-trouble at the Court of King David. *Yonadab* was but one of innumerable plays which brought gratuitous nudity, male and female, back to the London stage with tedious monotony. Well, there was little enough money for costumes.

In *Pravda*, Richard Eyre's and David Hare's NT group had a hit and a half. In Hare's and Howard Brenton's Jonsonian satire on Fleet Street, capitalism and manipulation, Anthony Hopkins gave the biggest bravura performance by an actor in a new play since Olivier as Archie Rice. It was not a great play but a theatre play for the times, expertly directed by Hare and owing little to the thin dramatic gruel of television. The latest Alan Ayckbourn, *A Chorus of Disapproval*, was also a joy. Directed with brio by the author, it was an investigation of love and knifing-in-the-back by amateur dramatic enthusiasts presenting *The Beggars' Opera*. Bob Peck and Michael Gambon gave gloriously rich, contrasted performances. It was—as always—a year of remarkable acting: Antony Sher's savage water-boatman-like Richard III came to London from Stratford, and tickets on the black market were said to be going for £400.

Peter Wood's group opened with a lacklustre reproduction of his own twenty-year-old production of Congreve's *Love for Love*—same ravishing sets by Lila de Nobili, different and duller actors, a production that had ceased to have a point of view. The most prolific group was that led by Ian McKellen and Edward Petherbridge, who came up with a stylish but foully-spoken *Duchess of Malfi*, directed and designed by Philip Prowse; and a manic double bill of Sheridan's *The Critic* and Stoppard's *The Real Inspector Hound* (the former directed by Sheila Hancock, the first woman to direct a main house production at the National, the latter by the author). And they found theatrical gold in Mike Alfred's exquisite production of *The Cherry Orchard* in the Cottesloe, McKellen excelling as the least boorish of Lopakhins. At last at the National it felt as if a group of actors had met before they went on stage that evening. There was not a single weak characterization.

Peter Gill directed the NT Studio, and to celebrate in the autumn the reopening of the Cottesloe (it had been closed because of lack of funding) he mounted a series of five new plays, or rather five evenings of new plays. More memorable was Bill Bryden's production, at the start of the year, of *The Mysteries*, three plays drawn from various cycles of medieval Mystery plays and rendered into thrilling, sensuous, alliterative verse by Tony Harrison. On certain days all three plays—*The Nativity, The Passion* and *Doomsday*—could be experienced morning, afternoon and evening. The audience promenaded in the smoky atmosphere of the Cottesloe as the infinitely-varied celebrations of story-telling and of English life were presented by a heavenly cast, including Brian Glover as God, Karl Johnson as Jesus, Robert Stephens as Herod and Pilate and Jack Shepherd as Judas and Satan.

The NT appointed Thelma Holt, previously associated with Ray Cooney's Theatre of Comedy (which had a bad year, with Cooney himself departing), to coordinate tours abroad and negotiate for foreign companies to appear on the South Bank. Her initial plans included a projected, if modest, world theatre season for 1987, which was good news.

The RSC had found it ever more difficult to persuade leading actors to give up two years of their lives to performing at Stratford in the first year, in Newcastle-upon-Tyne and London in the second. This year *Othello* was the final Shakespeare production to enter the repertoire by the Avon, and was to play at the Barbican from January 1986. Could this be because the Moor (and he played him as a Moor) was essayed by Ben Kingsley, and the star of *Gandhi* had only a few months to loan to the RSC? Only four Shakespeare productions were staged, to enable a recreation of Trevor Nunn's and John Caird's production of David Edgar's dramatization of *Nicholas Nickleby* to run at Stratford from December, then spend time in America during 1986 gathering dollars.

Kingsley's Iago was the similarly-built David Suchet. Otherwise the casting was the weakest of the season, and the set and direction (by Terry Hands) unsympathetic. *Troilus and Cressida*, also designed, but brilliantly, by Ralph Koltai, was magnificent. Howard Davies's production wrestled with a notoriously intractable text to produce an impassioned political debate about the spoils of war. It is a mystery why some productions at Stratford have the verse spoken both for meaning and for sound, while others—by the same directors, same actors, same voice coaches— are spoken neither for sound nor for sense.

Adrian Noble directed what most critics thought a perverse *As You Like It*, where court and Forest of Arden were one and the same place, the latter a figment of the characters' imaginations, without a tree to be discovered. Fiona Shaw placed Celia at the centre of the play, but when Juliet Stevenson's intelligent Rosalind fell out of love with her cousin and into love with Hilton McRae's sullen Orlando the production lost credibility. Bill Alexander's *The Merry Wives of Windsor* was set in the 1950s, with Peter Jeffrey's Falstaff presiding as a blazered ex-RAF officer canoodling in the Garter's snug. Mistress Ford (Lindsay Duncan) and Mistress Page (Janet Dale) conspired under hairdriers.

At Stratford's Other Place, John Caird offered a superbly detailed production of Gorki's first play, *Philistines*, and Howard Davies a triumphant dramatization by Christopher Hampton of Laclos's epistolary novel, *Les Liasions Dangéreuses*. The lack of original plays that were not in essence ostensibly television pieces was balanced by the number of stage adaptations of novels: Shared Experience, with a tiny cast and much doubling, wittily presented Richardson's *Pamela*.

Apart from Stratford transfers, the RSC at the Barbican presented Peter Barnes's comedy about the Black Death, *Red Noses*, in a frenetic production by Terry Hands. Antony Sher starred (as he did upon leaving the RSC) in the interminable *Torch Song Trilogy*, more special pleading than adult entertainment. At the Pit there were seasons of plays by Edward Bond and Howard Barker. Bond's apocalyptic concerns and drab writing bored as usual, but the Barker plays had a corruscating, brutal poetry and dramatic energy which were a pleasure to experience after the arid, unambitious texts of most other contemporary British playwrights. Ian McDiarmid led the company vehemently in both writers' works.

The commercial theatre was beleaguered and only the occasional production was worth much—notably *The Seagull* with Vanessa Redgrave and Jonathan Pryce, but it started life in Oxford. Musicals were dire, the Royal Court undernourished. The Almeida excitingly staged Lyubimov's *The Possessed* in English with British actors. Christopher Fettes directed with vision and commitment two plays by Freud's contemporary and fellow-countryman, Schnitzler, revealing him as a playwright for our times: at the Old Vic (which otherwise had a disappointing year, artistically), *The Lonely Road*, with a mesmerizing Anthony Hopkins; and at Greenwich, *Intermezzo*, with Sheila Gish radiant. Otherwise, the smaller the theatre (the Bush invariably gratifying), the more rewarding the evening.

If London theatre seemed intellectually and dramatically unenterprising, New York was infinitely worse. There were few new plays by American writers, and Shepard and Mamet continued to do better in London than New York. Most of the plays and productions that received more than a modicum of critical approval started life in London. (See *New York Theatre* below.)

1985 was the centenary of Victor Hugo's death, and in Paris there were at least three productions of his grandiloquent, absurd plays: Jean-Louis Barrault's *Angelo, Tyran de Padoue* visited the Edinburgh Festival and was admired; Antoine Vitez staged a memorable *Hernani* at the Théâtre National de Chaillot; and at the end of the year, in the same auditorium, Vitez mounted a stunning *Lucrèce Borgia*.

The year saw the death, in March, of Sir Michael Redgrave (see OBITUARY); and the publication of two remarkable books by actors: in *The Year of the King*, Antony Sher published an edited version, illustrated with his own drawings, of the months spent preparing for his role as the most renowned Richard III since Olivier; and in *Being an Actor* Simon Callow wrote about precisely that. He described with precision and energy how an actor prepares for a role and how, as often or not, that work is sabotaged by a schematic director. Playwright Simon Gray, in *An Unnatural Pursuit and other pieces*, presented an account of the fate of his play, *An Unnatural Pursuit*, from his completing the script to the reception of Harold Pinter's production at the Lyric, Hammersmith, in 1984. Apart from everything else, its detailed portrait of Pinter at work was illuminating. Michael Meyer's weighty, essential biography of *Strindberg* had the audacity to argue that much, even most, of the Swedish genius's output was rubbish but that his major achievements were among the most remarkable works of dramatic art. Sir Alec Guinness's *Blessings in Disguise* was more about his stage contemporaries than the personal memoir it purported to be.

The New York Theatre

Despite the fact that at season's end (31 May) fewer shows had opened than in any year in this century, and theatre attendance was the lowest since mid-1970s, the year offered a series of stellar performances: the eternally radiant Rosemary Harris in a stylish production of Noël Coward's *Hay Fever*; too infrequently seen, Uta Hagen, whiskey-voiced and authoritative as the brothel-owner in Shaw's *Mrs Warren's Profession*; and Glenda Jackson remarkably vulnerable 'even vapid' in O'Neill's *Strange Interlude*, imported from London with its fine cast nearly intact. Jason Robards recreated with greater depth and maturity his 1956 triumph in O'Neill's *The Iceman Cometh*, directed by O'Neill's chief interpreter, José Quintero; Athol Fugard performed in and directed a revival of his 1961 play *Blood Knot*, Zakes Mokai, the only other cast member, giving the definitive performance of his role. The play was still gripping in face of the continued anguish of South Africa's turmoil. Not all the best acting was in revivals. Lily Tomlin gave a *tour de force* solo performance, creating numerous characters with lightning speed and precision without change of costume, make-up or props, in Jane Wagner's *The Search for Signs of Intelligent Life in the Universe*. This portrayed a period in the life of one feminist with bitter, comic insight.

Two respected playwrights reached a masterful maturity: Sam

Shepard, in *A Lie of the Mind*, drew a relatively realistic portrait of two families, their warring inter-relationships between both siblings and generations, the author himself directing a superior cast which included Geraldine Page; and in Wallace Shawn's *Aunt Dan and Lemon*, which originated in London's Royal Court Theatre, nazism was given a voice to prove how desensitizing a fascination with repeated violence can be to a civilization. In Neil Simon's annual play, he returned to his most honest, direct and dramatic period of roughly fifteen years ago, continuing his autobiographic account of growing into a writer in *Biloxi Blues*.

It seemed inevitable that there would be a play about the dread Acquired Immune Deficiency Syndrome, AIDS. Two outstanding such plays arrived, Larry Kramer's *The Normal Heart*, and William Hoffman's *As Is*. The latter, originating at Circle Repertory Company, was the more successful, having more compassion, more fully developed characters and less polemic. Lanford Wilson reworked the third play of his trilogy about the Talley family since its 1981 premiere, *Talley and Son*, but it failed to strike the affectionate and compassionate tone of his best work of this series.

Centres away from New York continued to provide theatrical nourishment. A group of Vietnam veterans in Los Angeles, through improvizations on their war experiences, wrote a documentary montage of a play, *Tracers*, which, though somewhat formless, exerted an unforgettable emotional impact about the bond between them. Chicago's Steppenwolf Theatre provided Lyle Kessler's *Orphans*, an intensely feral study of two young brothers who kidnap a mobster, and are themselves incorporated into his sinister and opulent life.

Because of the paucity and manifest inferiority of musicals which opened during the season, the committee for the theatre's most distinguished award, the Antoinette Perry ('Tony'), for the first time in its history eliminated three whole categories—best actor and best actress in a musical, and best choreographer. Nevertheless, the calendar year offered a musical treatment of Dickens's unfinished novel, *The Mystery of Edwin Drood*, a jolly gallimaufry in which the audience voted for the ending, thus retaining the communal fun which characterized the original open-air performance in summer in Central Park. Drood himself was performed *en travestie* by Betty Buckley, who shared the stage with such gifted players as Cleo Laine and George Rose. The best-musical 'Tony' award went, *faute de mieux*, to *Big River*, a crude adaptation of Mark Twain's *The Adventures of Huckleberry Finn*, notable chiefly for some engaging tunes by the 'country' music composer, Roger Miller, and some admirable directing by the gifted young Des McAnuff. An anomalous, emotionally-rich musical was fashioned by Peggy Harmon from Christina Rossetti's poem, *Goblin Market*, with music by Polly Pen as well as Brahms and John Gay.

As usual a stimulating covey of plays arrived from London, including

Hugh Whitemore's *Pack of Lies*, weakly constructed but notable for the performances, chiefly that of Rosemary Harris; David Hare's *Map of the World*, well-intentioned but confusing, even fatuous in its excessively intricate plotting and political posture; and Michael Frayn's *Benefactors*, which fared best, thanks principally to a cast who found emotional depths in an essentially conventional theme—artistic integrity forced to compromise.

During the 1960s and 1970s the creative originality of theatre artists which proved to be too great a financial risk for Broadway had moved off Broadway principally to downtown lofts and churches, but now the movement had settled further afield, chiefly in Brooklyn's Academy of Music theatres. This centre was home, in its Next Wave Festival, to numerous international as well as local dance companies, but also to such visionaries as Robert Wilson (*Einstein on the Beach*, *The Civil Wars*), in whose mode the director's concept not the play's the thing.

THE CINEMA

Although cinema box-offices in America were reported in September to be suffering a recession, the industry was nevertheless supporting some 19,000 screens, in comparison with Britain's 1,200. Britain's attendance figure dropped below 50 million in the year. Jack Valenti, redoubtable president of America's Motion Picture Association, had challenged in May the cinema's growing rival, VCR (with films on video rentable as low as one dollar each) as a 'parasitical instrument' and maintained his faith that the future lay with 'theatrical film', threatened though that 'embattled industry' was by piracy of its product through unlicensed video recording as well as by over-inflated production costs ($10 to $15 million a picture, never recovered by six out of ten) and by the invasion of new technology. Producers began to learn that the pattern of movie-distribution must change. In America PPV (pay-per-view) served through cable, which enabled viewers to see certain new films simultaneously with their initial theatrical release, was likely to reach a public of some 20 million by 1990. Nevertheless, new entrepreneurs were entering the industry at a high price: Mr Rupert Murdoch became the sole private owner of 20th-Century-Fox for $487 million in September, and Mr Ted Turner, a cable-TV pioneer, acquired MGM/UA for $1,500 million, with all its great wealth of past films available for Turner's television interests.

Producers in America continued to make films outside California in those US states offering inducements in finance and facilities—notably Texas where thirty major films were shot in 1983, including *Terms of Endearment*, *Tender Mercies* and *Silkwood*. Other states attracting producers included Colorado, Arizona, Tennessee, Oklahoma and

Louisiana. British studios also gained increased production from America when the pound declined against the dollar, and the abandoned Ardmore studios in Ireland were acquired by MGM Enterprises for around $1·3 million.

In Britain the Eady levy was finally withdrawn in May, and the privatized Film Finance Corporation became the British Screen Finance Consortium, headed by producer Simon Relph, with an annual fund of £3 million (half initially from government). In France the Government initiated tax relief for film sponsorship and set up a fund of Fr.10 million for script development, as well as up to Fr.1·4 million in aid for producers to assist project development, along with reduced interest on loans. In New Zealand the Government gave marked support for film production, allotting £1·29 million to its Film Commission; five notable films from New Zealand appeared in Britain, including *Utu* and *Came a Hot Friday*. In Australia, however, reduced tax incentives for film production resulted in some contraction in output. Japan, another country experiencing a decline in cinema attendance, staged its first international film festival in Tokyo, emphasizing films by young film-makers and films by and about women. Reports emanating from the Soviet Union indicated that the new Gorbachev regime had initiated a somewhat more liberal policy towards film-makers.

In spite of many Oscar nominations for Roland Jaffe's brilliant film, *The Killing Fields* (dramatizing the war in Cambodia, and shot in Thailand), and David Lean's fine adaptation of *A Passage to India*, they won comparatively few Oscars for Britain, Milos Forman's stylish American adaptation of Peter Shaffer's play *Amadeus* sweeping the board. Indeed, 1985 proved more an American than a British year in terms of notable production, with phenomenal box-office success for Martin Brest's *Beverly Hills Cop* and above all for Stallone's star vehicle *Rambo: First Blood, Part II*, which refurbished America's lost pride in the Vietnam veteran in the dangerous form of bloody violence that can earn this muscular, macho, human fighting-machine $12 million for a single film. 'I want to stay uncivilized,' he has said.

American films of distinction dominated by their leading players included Mark Rydell's *The River* (a farming disaster film much like *Country*, with Sissy Spacek), Australian director Gillian Armstrong's *Mrs Stoffel* (Diana Keaton), and British director Karel Reisz's *Sweet Dreams* (Jessica Lange). Among unclassifiable American films of considerable note were Paul Shrader's *Mishima*, performed in Japanese, a remarkable, multi-layered film that merged episodes from Mishima's enclosed childhood, his later obsession with traditional military ambitions and his self-projection as a writer, leading in 1970 to his ritual suicide-of-protest against Japan's decadence. There were also the Argentinian director Hector Babenco's American film, *Kiss of the Spiderwoman*, a brilliantly-acted study of two prisoners (one political, one homosexual) housed in a single cell in a Latin American gaol, and John Huston's admirable film, *Prizzi's Honour*, a spare, ruthless study of a Mafia 'family' in marked contrast to the romantic flamboyance of *The Godfather* tradition, with an outstanding performance by Jack Nicolson.

British Film Year was initiated by Sir Richard Attenborough, chairman of the British Film Institute, which also celebrated the 50th anniversary of the establishment of Britain's national film archive, preserving films of artistic, historical and scientific importance from all countries. In a happy parallel, 1985 was also the 50th year of the department of film in New York's Museum of Modern Art. British films showed variety and originality on a modest scale, reflecting the economic condition of the industry. Political playwright David Hare's first film, *Wetherby*, with Vanessa Redgrave, was a tragic study of sexual repression in a stolidly English middle-class setting, while Hare's play, *Plenty* (adapted as an American film, directed by Fred Schepisi), offered a fascinating study of a woman's self-induced political and erotic frustration in post-war Britain, played with impressive intensity by Meryl Streep. Another film with a political thrust, *Defence of the Realm* (David Drury, with Gabriel Byrne), challenged what it maintained to be the right-wing politicization of the British press. *My Beautiful Laundrette* (Stephen Frears directing a notable script by Asian screenwriter Hanif Kureishi) confronted the multiracial aspects of contemporary British society; this film, originally conceived for Channel 4 television, underlined the gradually developing closeness between television and cinema production, exemplified also in Channel 4's *Every Picture Tells a Story* (James Scott) and *Parker*, a film thriller made by the accomplished television director, Jim Goddard.

Brazil (Terry Gilliam, with Jonathan Pryce, Robert De Niro) had a burlesque but sadistic quality derived from the darker aspect of the Monty Python cycle of films. Mike Newell's *Dance with a Stranger* (with Miranda Richardson, Rupert Everett) told the real-life story of Ruth Ellis, the last woman to suffer capital punishment in England for shooting her obsessive, upper-class lover; Miranda Richardson's tense, low-key performance in this haunting film was outstanding. In a class of its own was Nicolas Roeg's *Insignificance*, ironically encapsulating the contrariness of twentieth-century celebrity by making Einstein sort out cosmic values with Marilyn Monroe, interrupted by her sportsman husband Dimaggio and Senator Joseph McCarthy.

Jim Goddard directed *Hitler's SS: Portrait in Evil*—Britain's contribution to the current revival of interest in the Third Reich—a large-scale production made in England initially for American television and covering more than a decade of Nazi history in terms of fictional characters associated with historical figures such as Roehm, Heydrich and Himmler. More remarkable were extraordinary works from other national sources, the 16-hour West German *Heimat* (*Homeland*; Edgar Reitz), an eleven-part film spanning German history from 1919 to 1982 seen through the experiences and relationships of a cross-section of German citizens, and *Shoah* (Hebrew for 'annihilation'; Claud Lanzmann), a 9½-hour French film. Over a span of ten years Lanzmann had shot some 350 hours of material for editing; he searched Germany, Poland, Czechoslovakia, Israel and America for survivors of the holocaust, along with such former Nazi administrators as were prepared to testify. Lanzmann's documentary searched every stick and stone of the camp sites and kept his interviewees in prolonged close-shot. Despite its length, *Shoah* was a riveting document of lasting historical importance.

Outstanding foreign-language films included Resnais' *L'Amour à Mort*, the vision of death granted to one of a pair of lovers and its consequence; Marianne Rosenbaum's *Peppermint Freedom* (West Germany), a haunting child's-eye view of Germany's post-war complications during Allied occupation, and Margarethe von Trotta's feminist *Sheer Madness*, a study of the relationship of two women, with Hanna Schygulla. Godard's *Hail, Mary*, an entirely modern version of the Virgin Mary and the Annunciation, led to stormy protests from the Catholic Church in both Europe and America, and to the picketing of theatres by demonstrators for and against the film's exhibition. Above all came Kurosawa's deeply impressive second venture into creating a fully cinematic version of Shakespeare, *Ran*, a transmutation of *King Lear* into a 16th-century Japanese setting.

Among the personalities of cinema who died in 1985 were the British producer John Sutro, the director-producer John Boulting, the American writer-producers Harold Hecht and Sam Spiegel, two survivors of the 'Hollywood Ten', the screenwriters Lester Cole and Albert Maltz, the veteran Soviet director, Sergei Gerasimov, the American directors Sam Peckinpah and Henry Hathaway, the noted actor-director of *Citizen Kane*, Orson Welles, the screenwriter and actress Ruth Gordon, and the stars Michael Redgrave, Yul Brynner, Rock Hudson, Lloyd Nolan, Edmond O'Brien, Peter Lawford, Phil Silvers, Louise Brooks, Simone Signoret, Margaret Hamilton, Gale Sondergaard, Ann Baxter and the black American comedian, Stepin Fetchit, as well as Clarence Nash who was the voice of Donald Duck for half a century. (For Spiegel, Welles, Redgrave and Brynner, see OBITUARY.)

CINEMA BOOKS OF THE YEAR, *Cinema and State: the Film Industry and British Government 1927–84*, by Margaret Dickenson and Sarah Street (London, British Film Institute); *Chaplin: his life and art*, by David Robinson (London, Collins); *Film-making in 1930s Britain*, by Rachael Low (London, Allen and Unwin); *International Film Guide* (22nd Edition) by Peter Cowie (London, Tantivy Press; New York, Zoetrope); *Classical Hollywood Cinema to 1960*, by D. Bordwell and others (New York, Columbia University Press); *Images of Madness: the Portrayal of*

Insanity in the Feature Film, by Michael Fleming and Roger Manvell (Cranbury, Associated University Presses).

RADIO AND TELEVISION

The Live Aid television programme on 13 July was not only one of the longest but one of the most remarkable ever shown. The pop singer Bob Geldof almost single-handedly put together a trans-Atlantic pop concert watched by an estimated 1,000 million people in more than one hundred countries—the largest audience ever for a single programme—and in the process raised about £50 million for the famine-stricken people of Africa. A medium often criticised for its presentation of trivia, violence or obscenity first played a key role in drawing the attention of the world to people starving in remote places. It then harnessed its modern technology of satellite picture distribution to carry the songs of Bob Dylan, Paul McCartney, David Bowie and Mick Jagger to the world. Television was the medium and the message was 'Donate to Live Aid now!'

The events of that summer evening were a welcome moment of hope and achievement for traditional broadcasters facing increasing uncertainty in their relationships with governments over how to respond to the threat of competition from private television and the new media of cable and satellite television. In many parts of the world the role of public-service broadcasters was being questioned as never before, as governments in an era of financial stringency showed increasing reluctance to support the licence-fee increases the broadcasters believed they needed and encouraged the trend to more commercial television based on advertising.

In New Zealand and Canada wide-ranging inquiries into the future of broadcasting got under way and a similar review was being planned for Japan.

On 27 March the British Home Secretary, Mr Leon Brittan, at the same time as awarding the BBC a three-year colour-television licence fee of £58 instead of the £65 asked for, also announced the setting-up of a committee under the chairmanship of Professor Alan Peacock, an economics professor at Edinburgh's Heriot Watt University, to investigate the advantages and disadvantages of alternative means of funding the BBC, in particular advertising, subscription and sponsorship.

Amassing evidence for the committee was the main preoccupation of Britain's broadcasters throughout the year, in an effort to fight off the threat they saw to the UK's unique broadcasting duopoly. This system had given the BBC a monopoly of the licence fee and the independent television companies a monopoly of television advertising revenue, so that neither competed for the same source of revenue. The advertising industry and large advertisers argued that a phased introduction of advertising on BBC was possible without damaging ITV because of the natural growth in the advertising market. Most of the evidence to Peacock, however, warned of the dangers of forcing the BBC to take advertising. The ITV companies' association, supported by academic research, argued that even limited amounts of advertising could drive the price down and force some of the smaller ITV companies out of business. This argument received partial support from research commissioned by the Peacock committee itself. National Economic Research Associates found that advertising on the BBC would lead to a fall in total television advertising compared to what it would otherwise have been and that spending on other media would also be significantly reduced.

The BBC argued that the licence fee was still the best way to finance the Corporation and concentrated on ways of making it easier to pay or to spread the burden more widely by supplementing a lower TV licence with new charges for car radios and video recorders.

As the Peacock committee began its work a much sharper dispute broke out at the end of July between broadcasters and government over a documentary about extremism in Northern Ireland in the *Real Lives* documentary series, *At the Edge of the Union*. The programme, which included interviews with Martin McGuinness, alleged to be chief of staff of the Provisional IRA, and Gregory Campbell, a loyalist extremist, led to one of the most serious constitutional crises in the BBC's history. The Home Secretary, without having seen the programme, wrote to Mr Stuart Young, chairman of the BBC governors, making it clear he thought the programme should not be shown. 'The BBC would be giving an immensely valuable platform to those who have evinced an ability, readiness and intention to murder indiscriminately', Mr Brittan wrote.

The BBC governors rejected the unanimous advice of its board of management and decided that the programme should not be transmitted 'in its present form' but denied that this was because of Government pressure. Mr Young asked it to be recorded in the minutes that he thought the decision was unwise. The affair, which was widely seen as calling into question the editorial independence of the BBC, led to a 24-hour strike by BBC journalists, supported by those from ITN. After serious splits between the BBC and its management the governors reversed their decision and the programme was shown in October with minor changes. Little public notice was taken.

Almost before the dust had settled from the *Real Lives* dispute the BBC was forced to admit, following allegations in *The Observer* newspaper, that large numbers of its staff were subject to MI5 vetting. After a rapid internal inquiry the practice was drastically scaled down. In future only those who would be involved in special broadcasting services in the event of a nuclear emergency would be liable to vetting.

To add to a troubled year for the BBC the licence-fee shortfall led to a reassessment of all the Corporation's priorities. The outcome was £33 million more to spend on programmes, including the launch of daytime television in 1986, at the cost of a potential loss of up to 4,000 jobs through buying more services and equipment from outside the Corporation.

The ITV companies had problems of their own. For reasons which were never fully explained advertising revenue fell seriously in the early part of the year, and although there was a recovery in the autumn costs had to be cut and there were a number of job losses. By the date of its third anniversary Channel 4 had consolidated its reputation for original programming but its target of 10 per cent of the audience had not been met.

The sense of rapid change was emphasised by the government decision to license 21 experimental community radio stations, despite the fact that up to a dozen of the existing 48 local commercial radio stations were losing money or making only tiny profits. More fundamental was the announcement by the Department of Trade and Industry in May that individuals would in future, for a once-and-for-all payment of £10, be free to erect their own satellite receiving dishes in their gardens to receive the 18 or so new channels of television already available. And the first dish aerials started to go up.

A year in which the world of global television continued to take shape was best symbolised by the announcement in November that Mr Robert Maxwell, publisher of the *Daily Mirror*, had been awarded a channel on TDF 1, the French direct broadcasting satellite (DBS), a channel designed to rival Mr Rupert Murdoch's Sky Channel. Sky, a general entertainment channel for cable, was available in 5,300,000 homes by the end of 1985. In an even more controversial decision the French Government also announced that it was giving the licence for the first French commercial television network to a Franco-Italian grouping dominated by M Jerome Seydoux, one of France's richest men, and Sr Silvio Berlusconi, the entrepreneur who had built up a private television empire in Italy. In West Germany a new private entertainment channel for cable, Sat 1, was launched on the first day of 1985. If financial terms could be agreed it would probably transfer to the German DBS satellite scheduled for launch in August 1986.

In June, months of talking and planning for a British DBS project offering three new channels from space came to nothing. The '21 Club', made up of the BBC, three ITV companies and five non-broadcasting organizations led by Thorn EMI, decided the risk was too great.

The ITV companies did, however, take a decision in principle to go ahead with SuperChannel, a 'best of British' channel including BBC programmes for the cable networks of Europe. The Government also asked the Independent Broadcasting Authority to see if anyone else was interested in DBS. At least three groups came forward and the Home Office indicated informally its intention to ask the IBA to advertise a DBS franchise for the UK.

As doubt continued over DBS, cable television in the UK made slow progress. Seven out of 11 pilot franchises originally awarded in 1983 finally got going in 1985—most on a modest scale. By 1 December 976,671 households in Britain were passed by cable, an increase of more than 40 per cent in 12 months. But the number of homes connected, 126,262, was actually 3 per cent down and the proportion of homes passed that were actually connected to cable was only 12·9 per cent. Three unrelated events towards the end of the year indicated cable's tenuous hold so far. Mr Maxwell said he was ending active selling in 24 of his 40 existing cable networks in order to concentrate on the best prospects. Thorn EMI, one of the few large companies to invest in cable, indicated that it was selling virtually all its cable interests because they no longer fitted its corporate strategy. The Cable Authority itself had to suspend the advertising of new franchises because companies were finding great difficulty in raising finance.

In the US cable television was enjoying more optimistic times. By the end of the year an estimated 36 million homes were connected to cable— one-third of the capable total. At the same time the deregulation of cable prices increased the profits that cable operators were able to earn.

For the US television networks it was a year of extreme stress, in which all three major networks faced takeover bids and two actually changed ownership. In March the American Broadcasting Company (ABC) agreed to be acquired by Capital Cities Communications, and in December General Electric paid $6,280 million for RCA, the parent of NBC. The third network, CBS, spent most of the year avoiding an unwelcome takeover attempt by Ted Turner, proprietor of CNN, the 24-hours-a-day cable news channel. CBS bought back more than 20 per cent of its own stock to keep Turner at bay.

But in what was seen as the start of an attempt to create a fourth US television network Mr Rupert Murdoch, the Australian newspaper publisher, took out US citizenship in order to be able to take over six television stations from Metromedia, adding them to his purchase of the studios of 20th Century-Fox earlier in the year. Mr Murdoch further emphasised his international broadcasting ambitions when he set up a joint venture to explore the future of satellite television with Group Brussels Lambert—the main shareholder in Radio Tele-Luxembourg.

In a year of remarkable change one thing nevertheless stayed the same. British MPs voted yet again to exclude television cameras from the House of Commons, despite a successful experiment in the House of Lords, which their Lordships voted to continue.

Chapter 2

ART—ARCHITECTURE—FASHION

ART

In America, when the rich and the powerful get together with art, the result is Ascot, Covent Garden, the Royal Academy and Glyndebourne rolled in one. As much, it seemed, was written about the 'Charles and Di show', the visit of the Prince and Princess of Wales as patrons of the *Treasure Houses of Britain*—500 years of private patronage and art collecting—at the National Gallery of Washington (November 1985 to March 1986), as about the exhibition itself.

The show was a spectacular success, praised as much for its installations, which imaginatively suggested picture galleries, rotundas, long galleries, libraries, Dutch cabinets, as for the over 700 items on display, the great majority far more viewable than when at home in situ. While optimists crowed over the potential results for the British tourist trade, and Ford, the sponsors, said their involvement enabled them to reach circles in Washington with greater ease, cynics thought the long-term effect of the exhibition might be just to act as a vast department store of goods for sale from aristocratic houses. The catalogue—nearly 700 pages—was selling at the rate of over 400 copies a day.

Heritage was in vogue in Britain too. The National Gallery had a remarkable year. Three Sainsbury brothers (Sir John, head of the family firm, Tim, MP, and Simon, philanthropist and collector) announced a joint gift of £25 million to enable the Gallery to build its new extension without any commercial involvement. John Paul Getty, Jr, announced his gift of £50 million as a totally unrestricted grant: the Gallery said it would be used for acquisitions. And two weeks before the end of the year the Gallery announced that it had had more visitors than ever before: 3,067,769, to be exact.

Paris continued its energetic bid to reclaim an art supremacy that it had long lost to New York and London. At least fifteen specially-commissioned sculptures for particular sites were installed during the course of 1985, including Arman's huge heap of clock faces and another of suitcases, wittily outside the Gare St Lazare, while the controversial American sculptor Richard Serra had several pieces on view, including *Slat* sited at La Défense. All Paris stopped to admire the temporary wrapping of the Pont Neuf by the environmental artist Christo in September: in the artist's most ambitious city project, the bridge from the river up was totally encased in glistening golden material, and praise was almost unanimous. At the same time, the Picasso Museum opened in Paris, again to almost universal acclaim for the sensitive way in which the 17th-century Maison Sale had been restored to its authentic grandeur, and the narrative account of Picasso's life and art installed. The controversial Museum of Modern Art at the Beaubourg was also totally reinstalled with new internal walls: the Beaubourg, or Pompidou Centre, is Paris's most popular attraction, but its architecture by the Anglo-Italian firm of Piano and Rogers (1977) had long been thought inimical to the exhibition of contemporary art, and what amounts to an old-fashioned museum of small white-walled spaces has been placed within the structure to accommodate the national collection of 20th-century art.

The most interesting art controversy of the year centred on the public piece, *Tilted Arc*, by Richard Serra, located (in 1981) on the plaza of a government building complex in downtown New York, commissioned and paid for by the Federal Government's Art-in-Architecture programme. The Serra piece, a curving wall of rusted Cor-ten steel, 12 feet high and 120 feet long, had been intensely disliked by people who worked in the vicinity. The sculptor refused to countenance its relocation, on the grounds that *Tilted Arc* was site-specific. A public inquiry recommended the removal of *Tilted Arc*, and alternative sites were being considered. In St Louis, Missouri, *Quadrilateral*, another massive piece by Serra, was also the focus of public discontent. Serra is much admired in Paris, where a major piece, *Clara Clara*, was installed in the Tuileries in 1983 for several months, and his first major retrospective museum show in New York seemed likely to open up a major debate in America about public art.

Meanwhile, in Barcelona, a remarkable project neared fruition: the rebuilding of the 1929 German Pavilion designed by Mies van der Rohe for the International Exposition. Mies, who died in 1969, had given his permission for the rebuilding. Barcelona itself was in the throes of an architectural revival, with new open spaces designed by leading architects and artists—including a sculpture by the ubiquitous Richard Serra. The city, its art and culture, were the subject of a dazzling Hayward Gallery exhibition in London in the winter.

Christie's and Sotheby's had chequered seasons. The world's most expensive painting became Mantegna's *The Adoration of the Magi*, sold to the Getty for £8·1 million at Christie's in April; Timothy Clifford of Scotland's National Gallery mounted an unsuccessful campaign to 'save' the painting for the nation. Christie's suffered the resignation of their new chairman, David Bathurst, after it was revealed that they had publicly given erroneous information as to the success of sales of Impressionist paintings in New York in the early 1980s. Sotheby's indignantly denied a charge in America of selling a collection of Judaica to which the vendor had no legal title.

Major art thefts made dispiriting news. In October, the Marmottan Museum in Paris was victimized, with a daylight raid valued at £12 million, which included the priceless small oil sketch by Monet, *Impression, Sun Rising*, of the harbour at Le Havre, which gave Impressionism its name. Over Christmas, 140 jade and gold art objects—Mayan, Aztec, Zapotec and Mixtec cultures—were stolen from the National Museum of Anthropology in Mexico City.

Exhibitions, however, and exhibition attendances and new museums made good news. Perhaps most unusual was the opening of the first showing of the Saatchi Collection in a magnificently well-converted former paint factory in St John's Wood, London. Charles Saatchi of the global advertising agency Saatchi and Saatchi and his wife Doris had made the most impressive—in terms of both quality and size—collection of contemporary art to be assembled anywhere in Europe or America in recent years. A first instalment, including work by Andy Warhol and the minimalist Dan Flavin, not to mention Richard Serra, opened in March, and another—with Frank Stella and minimalist Sol Le Witt among the half-dozen or so artists—in October. It became Britain's first major private gallery, open to the public, exclusively devoted to contemporary work. Most commentators agreed that whether the actual work was outstanding or not—and several of the minimalist artists were controversial—the viewing conditions were exemplary, and the Saatchi collection had already become almost a place of pilgrimage for students.

Internationally the most popular exhibitions were those devoted to that most popular of periods, late 19th-century French art. There were very long lines at the autumn exhibition at the Museum of Modern Art, New York, devoted to the prints of Toulouse-Lautrec; and the Renoir exhibition at London's Hayward Gallery, and subsequently at Boston's Museum of Fine Art, broke attendance records, Boston hotels, indeed, advertised nationally their 'Renoir weekends'. An American firm, Norm Thompson of Portland, Oregon, offered a 'once-in-a-lifetime opportunity to own an original Monet' at only $19·95. The package consisted of 150 varieties of flowers based on the plants chosen by Monet for his world-famous garden at Giverny, the subject of many of his last best paintings. 'Now', prospective purchasers were told, 'you can experience the same kind of haven in your own backyard', and the seeds came from Thompson and Morgan, evidently the same company that supplied Monet with seeds for Giverny.

Earth-works of a different sort were taking place in Arizona, where the American artist James Turrell, known for his light-rooms, was literally reshaping Roden Crater, an extinct volcano. The artist's Skystone Foundation was financing the project by the sale of other kinds of work, and, with luck, the vast and isolated sculpture, a human intervention with a natural artefact on a gigantic scale, would be finished sometime in the 1990s. In autumn 1985 the Los Angeles Museum of Contemporary Art, host to a James Turrell exhibition, acquired for the museum another earth-work, Michael Heizer's *Double Negative*, two huge trenches cut into the Nevada desert.

While such enterprises seem suited to the gigantic scale of the USA, in

Britain much controversy was generated by the Victoria and Albert's decision to ask visitors to make a voluntary contribution (£2 was suggested as appropriate): staff of the museum mounted in their turn a voluntary picket. The painter Howard Hodgkin was awarded the second annual Turner Prize (£10,000) at the Tate Gallery in November. In the same month the ninth annual Mitchell prizes for art history were awarded to the authors Professor Otto Demus for the monumental four-volume *The Mosaics of San Marco*, and Dr Jennifer Montagu for her two-volume study of the Italian baroque sculptor Alessandro Algardi. The second International Contemporary Art Fair, held in January in London, at Olympia, was such a success that a third was announced in June 1986. The Contemporary Art Society mounted its second art market in London's Covent Garden, in October, and sold over £80,000 worth of work from young artists or more established artists within a very tight pricing policy (from £50 to £500) to a whole new group of incipient collectors.

Twentieth-Century German Art 1905–1985, concentrating on painting and sculpture almost exclusively (no prints, no drawings and just a handful of collages), at the Royal Academy in the autumn of 1985, proved a controversial exhibition. Most of the reviews were ecstatic at the opportunity to see so much Expressionist work, and the rooms which concentrated on the first three-and-a-half decades of the period were universally praised. But the organizers were criticised for not showing the art of the Nazi era, and for concentrating on Expressionism in order, it was said, to validate current trends in Western painting.

One of the most esteemed artists now working, the German Anselm Kiefer, won one of the two top prizes (the other prize-winner was—you guessed it—Richard Serra), at the 1985 Carnegie International, held in Pittsburgh, a revitalized international exhibition organized for the first time with the help of an international advisory council including Rudi Fuchs, curator the Eindhoven Museum in Holland and a new contemporary museum in Turin, Nicholas Serota of the Whitechapel Gallery, London, and Kasper Koenig of West Germany. The Whitechapel reopened in the autumn with a fine show of Howard Hodgkin's paintings, and with much-needed additional space.

As usual the world was in the grip of the blockbuster exhibition and museum fever. Undoubtedly the most spectacular—and controversial—exhibition anywhere was Vienna's own staging of *Dream and Reality—Vienna 1880–1930*, which attempted to examine nothing less than a whole culture—political, social, economic, artistic. From Freud to housing estates, art nouveau/Jugendstil to the fevered painting of Klimt and Schiele, the show was devised as a theatrical spectacular, designed by the architect Hans Hollein: a spectacular with an intellectual core. Hollein was commissioned to design the new museum of modern art in Frankfurt, where already there were new museums of architecture and arts and crafts; West Berlin opened a brand-new museum of arts and crafts, too, the first major building in the museum site around the new national gallery. Michael Graves's proposed extension for the Metropolitan Museum in New York aroused controversy; Los Angeles' new museum of contemporary art was scheduled to open in December 1986; the Tate's new Turner Museum was scheduled to open in the spring of 1986. Everywhere new collections and new museums were emerging into the light of day. Major exhibitions of the year included *Contrasts of Form 1910–1980*, international constructivist art (Museum of Modern Art, New York); the devastating and extraordinary Francis Bacon retrospective (Tate Gallery, London; National Gallery, West Berlin); *Degas as Printmaker* (Boston Museum of Fine Arts, Hayward Gallery, London); Kurt Schwitters (MOMA, New York; Tate, London).

ART BOOKS OF THE YEAR. *Alessandro Algardi*, by Jennifer Montagu (Yale); *Treasure Houses of Britain*, by Gervase Jackson-Stops *et al.* (Yale); *Art Out of the Gallery*, by Richard Cork (Yale); *Vincent by Himself*, by Bruce Bernard (Orbis); *The Sculpture of Moissac*, by Meyer Shapiro (Thames and Hudson); *Benvenuto Cellini*, by John Pope-Hennessy (Macmillan); *Edward Burra*, by Andrew Causey (Phaidon); *Kurt Schwitters*, by John Elderfield (Thames and Hudson); *The Bayeux Tapestry*, by David Wilson (Thames and Hudson).

ARCHITECTURE

In 1985 the Prince of Wales's attack on modern architecture appeared to hit home. The leading established British architects—barring the blue-chipped Richard Rogers—all suffered some great disappointment in the year and it seemed as if the Prince's influence was considerable.

The first blow to be struck was Environment Secretary Patrick Jenkin's ruling that the controversial Mies van der Rohe-designed office block proposed for a new Mansion House Square in the City of London by property developer Peter Palumbo would not be given the green light. This ended a remarkable 17-year campaign by Palumbo to build his dream project specially designed for him by the German architect in 1959 not long before his death. However, Palumbo and his apparently powerful team of supporters, including architects James Stirling and Richard Rogers as well as the distinguished Classical historian Sir John Summerson, were battled down by fierce opposition from conservation groups as well as the City of London itself. Beaten, but not defeated, Palumbo retired into his Walbrook corner only to announce a new scheme by James Stirling, whose Neue Staatsgalerie, Stuttgart, had opened to critical acclaim in the previous year. As 1985 drew to a close, Stirling's design had yet to be unveiled.

Stirling himself was having no easy time in 1985. His notorious

History Library at Cambridge University—vastly influential as a design among architects—was under serious threat of demolition. The University Senate was tired of paying for the maintenance of this great waterfall of glazing. Its future was more or less assured, but the Library was only one of a large number of experimental buildings put up in the 1960s and '70s that was proving troublesome.

Considerable defects were uncovered in Britain's two much-vaunted modern cathedrals, Coventry by Sir Basil Spence and Liverpool by Sir Frederick Gibberd. The Dean and Chapter of Coventry were forced to launch an appeal for restoration, asking the public for £500,000 to cover urgent repairs. At Liverpool a drawn-out law suit led to the architects' being faced with damages of £1,300,000. The question of liability and professional indemnity insurance plagued the British profession throughout the year. Damages were now so high that architects could and had been pursued to early graves, as had their families. When, properly, do defects become considered a natural part of the ageing of a building? When does the architect's responsibility end? These questions dominated the proceedings of the Royal Institute of British Architects (RIBA) during 1985.

Norman Foster, High Tech hero and the RIBA's 1983 gold medallist, had a mixed year, bringing both triumph and disappointment. After painstaking work on the proposed new BBC headquarters in Langham Place on the site of the Victorian Langham Hotel, the Corporation suddenly dropped the whole project and said it was now planning a new building on a site near its television studios in White City. Foster could content himself, however, with two considerable achievements. First was the completion of the dazzling headquarters for the Hong Kong and Shanghai Bank, the architectural jewel in the old colony's crown. Second, Foster won the competition for the building of a Médiathèque building facing the 2,000-year-old Maison Carrée in Nimes against fierce and chauvinistic French opposition.

The Hong Kong building is a formidable achievement: a tall building on the waterfront that represents the High Tech dream. The most expensive building ever built, as far as records go, it is an immensely sophisticated design and a revolutionary break from the conventional office type that has so disfigured our cities in Europe since the 1950s. Foster's Bank is already celebrated on a new issue of Hong Kong banknotes and the Chinese will undoubtedly prize it when the colony returns to their domain in 1997.

Winning the Médiathèque competition was also excellent news for Foster and British architecture. The French had rarely let such prestigious commissions go to outsiders and had to swallow a small, bitter pill. But they would gain a fascinating building, the first that Foster had been asked to face in stone—the antique site being particularly precious and sensitive.

I. M. Pei, the American architect, had less success in importing his brand of Slick Tech architecture to France. His building of a mock-up of the large glass pyramid that he was planning for the main courtyard of the Louvre provoked a near riot and police had to be called to restore architectural order. Rarely has a building proved to be such a political bombshell.

Real riots in London at the absurdly-named Broadwater Farm Estate in north-east London (see p. 35) brought fresh scrutiny of housing blocks designed in the 1960s. Elevated concrete gangways linking the separate blocks at Broadwater Farm not only allowed rioters—armed with guns and petrol bombs—easy escape (as they do for muggers), but also proved to be vantage-points for rioters to launch missiles at the police force in the courtyards below. These unsightly gangways seem likely to be demolished at all such access-deck estates throughout the country if and when local government finance allows.

In London, the National Gallery extension fiasco entered a new phase. Prince Charles had already dismissed Ahrend Burton & Koralek's scheme as a monstrous carbuncle on the face of an old and much-loved friend. The ABK scheme was quietly dropped by the Gallery's Trustees. The Sainsbury family then stepped in, offering to finance a new extension which would be given over wholly to art. The earlier competition had assumed that the gallery would have to be supported, literally, by lettable commercial office space. A limited competition was announced to find the right architect. The choice finally fell on the Philadelphia-based architect Robert Venturi, whose seminal book *Complexity and Contradiction in Architecture* (1966) inspired the flowering of Post-Modern architecture. It was a popular choice and was the 60-year-old Venturi's great chance to put theory into practice and to build a dignified and popular building on an historic site—Trafalgar Square.

The year did mark the completion of a number of excellent buildings which helped to redeem architecture from the controversy and failures that had been dogging it since the Prince of Wales's onslaught in 1984. Richard Rogers completed his Patscenter research building in Princeton, New Jersey. Although likened by one critic to a mechanical harvester or oversized grasshopper, this elaborate High Tech building helped to win Rogers the Royal Gold Medal for 1985. The year also marked the completion of Rogers's Lloyd's headquarters in the City of London. Along with the Pompidou Centre in Paris (designed with Italian architect Renzo Piano) this was Rogers's major testament. A vast, polished oil-refinery of a building arranged around a towering central atrium, the Lloyd's headquarters was as controversial as it was remarkable. Whatever one's personal feelings, this was the first important piece of architecture built in the City since World War II.

Three museum buildings completed during the year stood out for critical attention. These were Rafael Moneo's Roman museum in

Merida, Spain, Richard Meier's Museum für Kunsthandwerk in Frankfurt and the extension of the Whitechapel Art Gallery in East London by Colquhoun & Miller. Moneo's building is a magnificent and vast interpretation of the Roman basilica. Built of shallow Roman brick, it is a moving shrine to the Roman Empire's Iberian rule. Meier's building is a crystal-clear, white concrete construction that develops the theme of the purely rational modern building, turning it into an object of suave, understated beauty. Colquhoun & Miller's building is a sensitive and intelligent remodelling of a much-loved Art Nouveau gallery that has much improved the original building, proving that modern architecture can be enjoyable and friendly. Cramped into a tiny site, it is a good example of how architects must look to ways of stitching back the torn fabric of our cities.

Henning Larsen's sandcastle-like Ministry of Foreign Affairs in Riyadh was a significant newcomer in 1985. It showed the way ahead for a modern architecture in the Middle East that pays proper attention to indigenous cultures and climates. Previously, buildings imported into the Middle East had been banal affairs designed on the drawing-board with little or no thought for the great civilizations of the Arab region.

Perhaps the most delightful new buildings of 1985 were Glenn Murcutt's house at Glenorie, near Sydney, NSW—a beautiful and sophisticated development of the primitive Outback corrugated iron hut—and Adolfo Natalini's offices at Alzate Brianza, between Como and Bergamo, and the same architect's computer centre in Zola Predosa near Bologna. Both distinctly modern, full of colour and zest, both achieve a kind of timelessness enviable in the work of any architect, a quality that makes most historic Italian architecture so rich, humane and loved. Italian office buildings of recent years have been pretty hideous; Natalini's restored faith in a despised building type.

Finally, the RIBA launched an unprecedented attack on the British Government for failing in its duties towards housing, construction and the plight of Britain's inner cities. The inventive Austrian architect Hans Hollein walked off with the $100,000 Pritzker prize for architecture (the architectural equivalent, along with the RIBA gold medal, of a Nobel prize). Death removed a few familiar faces from the architectural scene in 1985, the planner architects Hugh Wilson and Dan Lacey and, saddest of all, the immigré architect Walter Segal, who had done more than any post-war architect in Britain to make housing humane. His famous self-build housing projects were brave attempts to bring architecture down from Olympian heights for the benefit and enjoyment of everyman.

FASHION

Following the trend set in 1984 for more shape in clothes, women continued to wear the short, straight skirt and softly-tailored jacket. The mini-skirt reappeared for summer, but on all social levels the alternative to the short look was a mid-calf, slim skirt, sometimes tightly wrapped like a sarong.

Textile designers led the strongest fabric trend for spring and summer with prints of all kinds, from small flower motifs to daring splashes of geometrics and abstract patterns in strong colour. Liberty of London stayed out in front with its own particular expertise in this field of fabric design. Added to this colourful fabric scene was chintz, the pretty traditional material used in home furnishing. Used for skirts, jackets and trousers it became a coveted 'separate' for the fashionable woman.

During the winter, the classic British look of tweeds and tailoring was up-dated with a slightly sharper shape that leaned towards the cut of traditional riding clothes. Tweeds, Fair Isle sweaters, Aran knits, pleated skirts and generously-cut overcoats combined to stand up to the cold of a hard winter.

On 17 September Laura Ashley, one of the greatest and most respected names of the century in British fashion, died after being seriously injured in an accident (see OBITUARY). She was known all over the world for the nostalgic appeal of her soft, becoming clothes, internationally popular for their rural stylishness. Through clothes and soft furnishing her major influence was in lifestyle, based on the pretty English look of the traditional small country house which produced a romantic, pastoral look that was charming and gentle. She was called 'the champion of the natural, an innate conservationist'. The Laura Ashley company embodying her 'English Dream' was 32 years old. Its profits were counted in millions and it was floated on the London Stock Exchange on 5 December 1985.

Laura Ashley was born in 1925 into a working-class family in Dowlais, a village on the edge of Brecon Beacon in South Wales. Soon after World War II she married Bernard Ashley and in 1953 they began printing textiles in a small workshop in Pimlico. Bernard Ashley designed the furnishing prints and Laura designed small items such as table mats, linen napkins and other home accessories. Early customers were Heal's and Liberty. In 1954 a limited company was formed.

After several years of consolidation and growth, by 1963 it had bought premises in mid Wales, with the space to equip the business with the larger machinery it needed. The first garments were produced by 1966 and included shirts, shirt dresses and long dresses in fine cotton for casual evenings.

The company's expansion went on: shops opened in London, Edinburgh, and other cities all over the British Isles. Licensees in Australia, Canada and Japan were set up. Furnishing fabrics and matching wallpapers, all in the pretty Ashley prints, followed in 1972, and in 1974 the homespun product went to Paris, the world's most sophisticated city for fashion. Düsseldorf followed in the same year and by the end of 1985 there were over forty shops around the world. It is company policy to site all factories in rural areas, thus promoting the continuance of village life.

Chapter 3

LITERATURE

THIS was a year when more books were published in the United Kingdom than ever before, and a year in which economic necessity caused more publishers to be grouped together in larger units. In all, a total of 52,984 new titles and new editions were published, an increase of almost 1,500 over the previous year. The number of new titles rose by $2\frac{1}{2}$ per cent, while that of new editions (almost all of them paperback, as more and more publishers discovered that there was profit to be made from reprinting classic works in their own backlists rather than leasing them to paperback publishers) rose by 3·8 per cent.

The publishing world saw the integration of the well-known firms Hamish Hamilton and Michael Joseph with Penguin Books; the passage of the Heinemann group into the possession of Paul Hamlyn, the publisher of Octopus Books; and the purchase of Hutchinson and its associate companies by the rising firm of Century. There were no immediate signs of any changes in editorial control, but it was thought that the takeovers would make the competition for paperback rights less cutthroat (since fewer firms were involved) and lessen the power of literary agents to demand uneconomic advances for their more popular authors. This was not regarded as necessarily a bad thing.

The year produced no one book that stood out from the others. It did, however, yield a number of surprises—the award, for instance, of the Nobel prize for literature to the 72-year-old French practitioner of the *nouveau roman*, Claude Simon, at a time when it was widely agreed that this particular form of fiction had proved to be a blind alley. The award of the Booker McConnell prize for fiction to the New Zealand writer Keri Hulme for her impressionistic and sometimes violent novel of life in one of the more backward parts of her homeland, *The Bone People*, also caused some astonishment. It had been a great success in New Zealand but had been little considered before it was placed on the Booker McConnell short list. It was clear that the judges were considerably divided and that the final result left a minority of them unhappy.

Indeed, the whole structure of this most-publicized prize came under increasing attack from critics. It was impossible to say how much of this stemmed from jealousy arising from the publicity success of the prize, rather than a feeling that almost every time the wrong book had been chosen. The controversy showed signs of dying down by the end of 1985 when it was discovered that the award had had less effect on the sales of the novel concerned than in previous years. This put paid to the complaint that the award of the Booker was an automatic passport to bestsellerdom. There was certainly much less controversy about the award in the US of the 1985 Pulitzer prize for fiction to Alison Lurie for her wry study of the different reactions of Americans to an extensive exposure to British life, *Foreign Affairs*.

Certainly, most critics believed that other novels, some on the Booker short list, some omitted from it, were of greater merit than *The Bone People*. Among these was Peter Ackroyd's *Hawksmoor*, a clever welding-together of early 18th-century London (parts of the novel are written in a pastiche of the prose of the period) and modern London by means of a bizarre series of murders taking place in or near churches built by the central character in the historical sections of the book. This novel was the one chosen by a preliminary panel to be considered for the Whitbread Book of the Year award. In a change of policy by its sponsors, the announcement of the winner of this prize was delayed until 1986. A selected first novel, a biography, a children's book and a volume of poetry were to be *Hawksmoor*'s rivals in a final judgment by a large jury consisting both of members of the book world and of general readers.

Another novel making use of a combined contemporary and historical setting was Barry Unsworth's *Stone Virgin*, in which the relationship between a modern craftsman working on the restoration of a renaissance statue in Venice and those originally involved in the statue's creation was explored. This was, indeed, a year of fine historical novels, another being Brian Moore's *Black Robe*, examining the relationship between Canadian Indians and the Jesuit sent to convert them. A novel on the Booker short list could also be classed as historical—*Illywacker*, by the Australian writer, Peter Carey. This was a sardonic epic based on the life of a centenarian who had lived through much of Australia's history. This is not to say that all the major novels of 1985 had historical themes. One of the best was Doris Lessing's *The Good Terrorist* (a Booker runner-up) which dealt with the plight of a middle-class girl hopelessly enmeshed in urban terrorism. Others much praised were John Mortimer's satirical *Paradise Postponed* and Jonathan Raban's amused study of an expatriate Englishman's surprised rediscovery of his native land, *Foreign Country*. Among the realistic pictures of contemporary British life were Anita Brookner's *Family and Friends* (universally regarded as superior to her Booker winner of the previous year), Alice Thomas Ellis's *Unexplained Laughter* and A. S. Byatt's *Still Life*.

There were disappointments of course: the final volume of Lawrence Durrell's pentalogy, *Quinx*, seemed almost a parody of former work; Iris Murdoch's *The Good Apprentice* was thought well below her normal accomplishment and John Fowles's *A Maggot* too self-indulgent. These were balanced by the emergence of some fine new talent, including Bob Shacochis, who won an American Book award for his debut collection of short stories, *Easy in the Islands*. There were also promising first novels from Jane Ellison (*A Fine Excess*), Grace Ingoldby (*Across the Water*) and Paul Pickering (*Wild about Harry*).

Interest in American writing was divided between Kurt Vonnegut's futuristic *Galapagos*, John Irving's robust *Cider House Rules*, Philip Roth's continuation of his account of the travails of being a bestselling author very much like himself in *The Prague Orgy* and the much-praised winner of the American Book award for fiction, Don DeLillo's *White Noise*. An outstanding collection of American short stories was Grace Paley's *Later the Same Day*.

Two seemingly lost works appeared during the year. The first of these was Graham Greene's *The Tenth Man*, a novel written as a scenario for a never-made film, which was discovered in the archives of a Hollywood studio, having been forgotten even by its author. While not comparable with Greene's best, it certainly stood comparison with some of his earlier 'entertainments'. The other 'discovery' was Barbara Pym's *Crampton Hodnett*, written by her in the early 1940s and set aside later as dated. It proved to be an interesting period piece.

The one novel that was too great to be considered with any of the others, Tolstoyan in scope and scale, more a historical document than a work of fiction, was Vassily Grossman's *Life and Fate*. This account of one man's involvement in the Russian army during World War II and in civilian life thereafter was submitted by its author for publication during the Krushchev 'thaw', but was turned down by the authorities. After the author's death it was smuggled out of the country and had now been published in translation. No comparable picture of Russia at war had been published. Indeed by its size and intensity it overshadowed all the historical fiction and, for that matter, non-fiction published during the year.

The period immediately following World War II received close examination by both historians and biographers. A work of some distinction was Ben Pimlott's life of the Labour politician, *Hugh Dalton*, the work nominated in the biography section for the Whitbread Book of the Year. The background to the immediate post-war period was dealt with thoroughly by Alec Cairncross in *Years of Recovery: British Economic Policy, 1945–51*. A broader survey of the scene was given by Robert Blake in *The Conservative Party from Peel to Thatcher*. Among the books dealing with events during World War II, Herbert B. Lottman's *Pétain: Hero or Traitor?* was of some importance, presenting as it did a rational explanation of why the revered figure of Verdun should have become the head of the Vichy Government. In many ways information derived from secret sources played a more important part in the period 1939–45 than in any earlier war. Britain's part in this was explained skilfully by Christopher Andrew in *Secret Service: The Making of the British Intelligence Community*. The more conventional business of the war in the air, and in particular the preparations that led up to actual combat in 1939, were explained from both sides by Wilkinson Murray in *Luftwaffe* and by John Terraine in *The Right of the Line: the Royal Air Force in the European War*.

The tense situation in South Africa, which dominated so much of the news during 1985, gave rise to one exceptional book by an American academic, Vincent Crepanzano, which underlined the plight of the Europeans in South Africa as well as the blacks, *Waiting: Whites in South Africa*. An earlier generation of South African whites whose buccaneering activities led to the exploitation of the country's mineral riches was chronicled by Geoffrey Wheatcroft in *The Randlords*.

The biographies of major figures included a magisterial single-volume life of the wartime leader and last Viceroy of India, *Mountbatten*, by Philip Ziegler. An earlier military leader who entered the field of politics, Lord Kitchener, was explained by Philip Warner in *Kitchener: the Man and the Legend*. The major political figures who were the subjects of multi-volume studies were Robert Peel and Lloyd George. Norman Gash began what seemed likely to be a most important work with *Mr Secretary Peel: the Life of Sir Robert Peel till 1830*, and John Grigg continued with his leisurely voyage through the life of Lloyd George, this time covering the vital period between his controversial budget of 1910 and his assumption of the office of Prime Minister in 1916 in *Lloyd George from Peace to War*. Life in the Prime Minister's office during World War II was described in the fully-reprinted diaries of Sir John Colville, then Winston Churchill's private secretary, as *The Fringes of Power*, a subtle combination of political gossip with keen observation of the management of the war.

The literary and critical biographies included two important works on 18th-century writers: Maynard Mack's monumental biography of *Alexander Pope*, which had all the hallmarks of a career devoted to a single end, the production of this book, and David Nokes's innovative *Jonathan Swift, a Hypocrite Reversed*. The other major literary biographies were Michael Scammell's vast account of the exiled Russian writer, *Solzhenitsyn*, and what was clearly likely to be a definitive work, Michael Meyer's *Strindberg*. There was also a life of *Dorothy Wordsworth*, the sister of the poet, by Robert Gittings and Jo Manton.

Somewhat surprisingly, the centenary of the birth of D. H. Lawrence, though it produced a sizeable number of minor works, failed to provide a major one. The most readable of those published contained a shrewd assessment of the writer by one of his admirers, Anthony Burgess, and was titled *Flame into Being: the Life and Work of D. H. Lawrence*. More recent writers' lives were also discussed. In *Memory Babe: a Critical Biography of Jack Kerouac*, Gerald Nicosia produced a thorough but over-stuffed account of the 'beat' novelist. Selina Hastings, in her biography of *Nancy Mitford*, showed that it was possible to produce new information even about this author's over-exposed family. Nancy herself proved to be a more vulnerable and sadder person than she had previously been shown to be.

There were biographies of two major figures in the art and design world of the 1930s and 1940s: Hugo Vickers offered *Cecil Beaton: the Authorized Biography* and Laurence Whistler tried valiantly to explain the charm of his brother, killed in action in 1944, in *The Laughter and the Urn: the Life of Rex Whistler*. This milieu, where art meets society, was reflected in other books. *The Letters of Ann Fleming* were well edited by Mark Amory, showing the active life of a society hostess, who, after marriage to Lord Rothermere, became the wife of the novelist Ian Fleming. The world of architecture and country houses was described in minute detail by James Lees-Milne in a further selection from his diaries, *Midway on the Waves*. A more Bohemian environment was brought vividly to life in *Well, Dearie! the Letters of Edward Burra*, well edited by William Chappell. The perils of life with a man with a touch of genius were amply illustrated in *Living with Koestler: Mamaine Koestler's Letters*. This collection of letters from the author's second wife was edited by Celia Goodman.

Among the new collections of writers' correspondence were *The Letters of Sydney Smith*, edited by Nowell C. Smith, *Bernard Shaw: Collected Letters, 1911–1925*, edited by Dan H. Laurence, *More Letters of Oscar Wilde*, edited by Rupert Hart-Davis, and *The Collected Letters of Dylan Thomas*, edited by Paul Ferris.

In a year that saw the death of three major poets, Robert Graves, Philip Larkin and Basil Bunting, and of one minor one, better known as an anthologist and acerbic critic, Geoffrey Grigson (for Graves and Larkin see OBITUARY), it is perhaps appropriate that the most accomplished volume of poetry (nominated for the Whitbread Book of the Year) should be entitled *Elegies*. Donald Davie was not, in fact, writing a 'Lament for the Makars' but presenting a series of moving poems that he wrote after the death of his wife. It was not a great year for poetry, nor one that produced any startling original new voices. Among those established writers who published work during 1985 were the father and son, Roy and John Fuller, the first with a *Collected* and the second with a *Selected* volume. Christopher Reid produced an interesting sequence based on an imaginary series of translations, *Katarina Brac*, and the increasingly-praised playwright and poet, Tony Harrison, published his *Collected Dramatic Verse*. The last survivor of the 1930s group of poets that gathered round W. H. Auden, Sir Stephen Spender, published not only his *Collected Poems* but also a distillation, made by John Goldsmith, from his *Journals, 1939–83*, an introspective work that gave much insight into the public and creative life of a poet.

Certain books which do not readily fall into categories nevertheless aroused considerable interest. There was, for instance, the Fifth Edition of *The Oxford Companion to English Literature*, the first total revision of the work since it was published in 1932. Margaret Drabble, the editor of this edition, started again with a team of helpers using knowledge that had become available since the 1930s, though still leaving some of the characteristic essays from the pen of the original editor, Sir Paul Harvey, who wrote so much of the original volume himself. The tradition of largely single-handed compilation of a work of literary reference was kept alive by Martin Seymour-Smith, who wrote the whole of *The Macmillan Guide to Modern World Literature*.

The outstanding travel book of the year (rightly awarded the Thomas Cook award) was Patrick Marnham's *So Far from God*, an account of his journey largely by bus through Central America in order to be able to study closely the various problems of the peoples in such different countries as Mexico, Guatemala and Nicaragua. The most popular autobiography was *Blessings in Disguise*, an odd work by the actor Alec Guinness. Unlike so many books of memoirs by actors, this was far less concerned with his time on stage or in the film studio as with his spiritual development and his friendships with the more eccentric members of his profession. Perhaps it was Sir Alec's reputation as a 'difficult' actor that led his publisher to edit the book less than he might have done with a more seemingly obliging author, thus rendering it somewhat muddled.

In addition to the sad loss of poets mentioned above, 1985 saw the death of the German Nobel prizewinning novelist, Heinrich Böll, and the Italian poet and novelist (who, had he not died in the early autumn, it was widely rumoured, was the favoured candidate for the 1985 Nobel prize), Italo Calvino. Literary and historical scholarship lost Gordon S. Haight, the biographer of George Eliot, and Sir Arthur Bryant, who in addition to his studies of Pepys and his historical works also contributed a column to every issue of the *Illustrated London News* from 1936 until shortly before his death, and the anthropologist, Geoffrey Gorer. (For Böll, Calvino and Bryant, see OBITUARY). Popular fiction lost one of its most prolific producers, Denise Robbins, and thriller-writer James Hadley Chase, who outlived by nearly 50 years the outrage at its violence that was caused by his mock-American crime story, *No Orchids for Miss Blandish*.

Among the interesting new books published during the year were:

FICTION: *Hawksmoor* by Peter Ackroyd (Hamish Hamilton); *The House of the Spirits* by Isabel Allende (Cape); *Hiroshima Joe* by Martin Booth (Hodder); *Family and Friends* by Anita Brookner (Cape); *The Kingdom of the World* by Anthony Burgess (Hutchinson); *Still Life* by A. S. Byatt (Chatto); *Mr Palomar* by Italo Calvino (Secker); *Illywacker* by Peter Carey (Faber); *The Battles of Pollocks Crossing* by J. L. Carr (Viking); *Black Venus* by Angela Carter (Chatto); *White Noise* by Dan DeLillo (Picador); *Quinx* by Lawrence Durrell (Faber); *Unexplained Laughter* by Alice Thomas Ellis (Duckworth); *A Fine Excess* by Jane Ellison (Secker); *A Maggot* by John Fowles (Cape); *Crusoe's Daughter* by Jane Gardam (Hamish Hamilton); *Light Years* by Maggie Gee (Faber); *Men and Angels* by Mary Gordon (Cape); *The Tenth Man* by Graham Greene (Blond/Bodley Head); *La Forme d'une*

Ville by Julien Grief (Corte); *Life and Fate* by Vassily Grossman (Collins/Harvill); *Coup d'Etat* by John Harvey (Collins); *The Bone People* by Keri Hulme (Hodder); *Across the Water* by Grace Ingoldby (Michael Joseph); *Cider House Rules* by John Irving (Cape); *A Family Madness* by Thomas Keneally (Hodder); *The Good Terrorist* by Doris Lessing (Cape); *Le grande empéreur* by Jean Levi (Albin Michele); *Foreign Affairs* by Alison Lurie (Michael Joseph); *Merle and Other Stories* by Paule Marshall (Virago): *Black Robe* by Brian Moore (Cape); *Last Letters from Hav* by Jan Morris (Viking); *Paradise Postponed* by John Mortimer (Viking); *The Good Apprentice* by Iris Murdoch (Chatto); *Later the Same Day* by Grace Paley (Virago); *Foreign Land* by Jonathan Raban (Collins); *The Prague Orgy* by Philip Roth (Cape); *Easy in the Islands* by Bob Shacochis (Picador); *Engineer of Human Souls* by Josef Shyroki (Chatto); *The Accidental Tourist* by Anne Tyler (Chatto); *The Stone Virgin* by Barry Unsworth (Hamish Hamilton); *Lincoln* by Gore Vidal (Granada); *Galapagos* by Kurt Vonnegut (Cape); *Mrs Henderson and Other Stories* by Francis Wyndham (Cape).

POETRY: *While You Will Hear Thunder* by Anna Akhmatova (Secker); *All Where Each Was* by Andrew Crozier (Allardyce Barnett); *Elegies* by Douglas Dunn (Faber); *Selected Poems* by John Fuller (Secker); *Collected Poems* by Roy Fuller (Salamander); *Collected Dramatic Verse* by Tony Harrison (Bloodaxe); *Collected Poems* by Geoffrey Hill (Penguin); *Extending the Territory* by Elizabeth Jennings (Carcanet); *Gifts from My Grandmother* by Meiling Jin (Sheba); *The Oxford Book of Short Poems* edited by P. J. Kavanagh and James Michie (Oxford); *Complete Poems* by Hugh McDiarmid (Penguin); *Everything Must Go* by Jonathan Price (Secker); *Katerina Brac* by Christopher Reid (Faber); *Skeffington's Daughter* by Oliver Reynolds (Faber); *People Lived Here: Selected Poems, 1949–1983* by Louis Simpson (Secker); *Collected Poems* by Stephen Spender (Faber); *Writing Home* by Hugo Williams (Oxford).

LITERARY CRITICISM: *Images of Man and Death* by Philip Ariès (Harvard); *The English Language* by Robert Burchfield (Oxford); *Flame into Being: the Life and Work of D. H. Lawrence* by Anthony Burgess (Heinemann); *Secret Gardens: the Golden Age of Children's Literature* by Humphrey Carpenter (Allen & Unwin); *The Common Writer* by Nigel Cross (Cambridge); *The Oxford Companion to English Literature. 5th Edition* edited by Margaret Drabble (Oxford); *Fair of Speech: the Uses of Euphemism* by D. J. Enright (Oxford); *The Inner I: Literary Autobiography in the 20th Century* by Brian Finney (Faber); *Poetry of the Carolingian Renaissance* edited by Peter Godman (Duckworth); *The Bodley Head G. K. Chesterton* edited by P. J. Kavanagh (Bodley Head); *Granville Barker and the Dream of Theatre* by Dennis Kennedy (Cambridge); *Alexander Pope* by Maynard Mack (Yale); *Pro and Contra Wagner* by Thomas Mann (Faber); *The Craft of Literary Biography* edited by Jeffrey Myers (MacMillan); *Jonathan Swift: a Hypocrite Reversed* by David Nokes (Oxford); *The Singing Game* by Iona and Peter Opie (Oxford); *A Man of Letters* by V. S. Pritchett (Chatto); *A Comprehensive Grammar* by Randolph Quirk (Longman); *Guide to Modern World Literature* by Martin Seymour-Smith (Macmillan); *Monuments and Maidens* by Marina Warner (Weidenfeld).

BIOGRAPHY: *Busoni, the Composer* by Anthony Beaumont (Faber); *James Boswell: the Later Years* by Frank Brady (Heinemann); *Now to My Mother: a Very Personal Memoir of Antonia White* by Susan Chitty (Weidenfeld); *C. R. Ashbee* by Alan Crawford (Yale); *Alfred Gilbert* by Richard Dorment (Yale); *Charlotte Mew and Her Friends* by Penelope Fitzgerald (Collins); *The Man Who Was Greenmantle* by Margaret FitzHerbert (Oxford); *Dorothy Wordsworth* by Robert Gittings and Jo Manton (Oxford); *Cardinal Manning* by Robert Gray (Weidenfeld); *Nancy Mitford* by Selina Hastings (Hamish Hamilton); *Brett: from Bloomsbury to New Mexico* by Sean Hignett (Hodder); *Ruskin: the Early Years* by Tim Hilton (Yale); *Shackleton* by Roland Huntford (Hodder); *Cousin Randolph* by Anita Leslie (Hutchinson); *With Friends Possessed: a Life of Edward Fitzgerald* by Robert Bernard Martin (Faber); *Strindberg* by Michael Myer (Secker); *Mahler* by Donald Mitchell

(Faber); *The Captain's Lady* by Ronald Morris (Chatto); *Memory Babe: a Critical Biography of Jack Kerouac* by Gerald Nicosia (Viking); *Queen Marie The Last Romantic: a Biography of Queen Marie of Roumania* by Hannah Pakula (Weidenfeld); *Hugh Dalton* by Ben Pimlott (Cape); *Chaplin: His Life and Art* by David Robinson (Collins); *Solzhenitsyn* by Michael Scammell (Hutchinson); *Cecil Beaton: the Authorized Biography* by Hugo Vickers (Weidenfeld); *The Laughter and the Urn: the Life of Rex Whistler* by Laurence Whistler (Weidenfeld); *Mountbatten: the Official Biography* by Philip Ziegler (Collins).

AUTOBIOGRAPHY AND LETTERS: *Gather Together in My Name* by Maya Angelogou (Virago); *The Letters of Ann Fleming* edited by Mark Amory (Collins); *Money into Light* by John Boorman (Faber); *The Adding Machine* by William Burroughs (Calder); *The Art of Captaincy* by Mike Brearley (Hodder); *My Last Breath* by Louis Buñuel (Flamingo); *Well, Dearie! the Letters of Edward Burra* edited by William Chappell (Gordon Fraser); *Home Before Dark: a Personal Memoir of John Cheever* by Susan Cheever (Weidenfeld); *A Classical Education* by Richard Cobb (Chatto); *The Collected Letters of Dylan Thomas* edited by Paul Ferris (Dent); *Envoy from a Minor City* by Janet Frame (Women's Press); *Living with Koestler: Mamaine Koestler's Letters* edited by Celia Goodman (Weidenfeld); *Blessings in Disguise* by Alec Guinness (Hamish Hamilton); *More Letters of Oscar Wilde* edited by Rupert Hart-Davis (Murray); *Siegfried Sassoon's Diaries, 1923–25* edited by Rupert Hart-Davis (Faber); *Footsteps* by Richard Holmes (Hodder); *Falling towards England* by Clive James (Cape); *Selected Letters of E. M. Forster* edited by Mary Lago and P. N. Furbank (Collins); *Wisdom, Madness and Folly* by R. D. Laing (Macmillan); *Bernard Shaw: Collected Letters, 1911–25* edited by Dan H. Laurence (Reinhardt); *Midway on the Waves* by James Lees-Milne (Chatto); *The Periodic Table* by Primo Levi (Michael Joseph); *Jackdaw Cake: 'an Autobiography'* by Norman Lewis (Hamish Hamilton); *The Diary of Beatrice Webb. Vol IV: the Wheel of Life, 1924–43* edited by Norman and Jeanne MacKenzie (Virago); *So Far from God* by Patrick Marnham (Cape); *The Diaries of Sofia Tolstoy* edited by Cathy Porter (Cape); *The Letters of Edwin Lutyens* edited by Clayre Percy and Jane Ridley (Collins); *The Man Who Mistook his Wife for a Hat* by Oliver Sachs (Duckworth); *The Letters of Sydney Smith* edited by Nowell C. Smith (Oxford); *Journals, 1939–83* by Stephen Spender, edited by John Goldsmith (Faber); *Mr Speaker: the Memoirs of Viscount Tonypandy* (Century); *Paths from a White Horse* by Peter Vansittart (Quartet); *The Berlin Diaries, 1940–45* by Marie Vassiltchikov (Chatto); *Confessions of an Optimist* by Woodrow Wyatt (Collins).

HISTORY: *Secret Service: the Making of the British Intelligence Community* by Christopher Andrew (Heinemann); *Longman's History of the United States of America* by Hugh Brogan (Longman); *The Conservative Party from Peel to Thatcher* by Robert Blake (Methuen); *Years of Recovery: British Economic Policy, 1945–51* by Alec Cairncross (Methuen); *The Lost Empire* by Philip Caraman (Sidgwick); *The Fringes of Power* by John Colville (Hodder); *Waiting: Whites in South Africa* by Vincent Crapanzano (Granada); *Easing the Passing* by Patrick Devlin (Bodley Head); *Frederick the Great* by Christopher Duffy (Routledge); *Mr Secretary Peel: The Life of Sir Robert Peel till 1830* by Norman Gash (Longman); *Lloyd George from Peace to War* by John Grigg (Methuen); *The Destruction of European Jews* by Raul Hillery (Holmes & Meir); *New Mercenaries* by C. Farrer Hockley (Sidgwick); *Firing Line* by Richard Holmes (Cape); *Pandaemonium* by Humphrey Jennings (Deutsch); *Pétain: Hero or Traitor?* by Herbert B. Lottman (Viking); *Cavour* by Dennis Mack-Smith (Weidenfeld); *Thomas More* by Richard Marius (Dent); *Luftwaffe* by Wilkinson Murray (Allen & Unwin); *The Memory Palace of Matteo Ricci* by Jonathan Spence (Faber); *The Right of the Line: The Royal Air Force in the European War* by John Terraine (Hodder); *Africa: People and Politics* by Sanford Ungar (Simon & Schuster); *The Randlords* by Geoffrey Wheatcroft (Weidenfeld); *Kitchener: the Man Behind the Legend* by Philip Warner (Hamish Hamilton); *Diocletian* by Stephen Williams (Batsford); *Roman Political Life* by T. P. Wiseman (Exeter).

XVII SPORT

TENNIS. This was the year in which Wimbledon provided the full range of emotion and entertainment for the spectators. They were drenched by violent storms flooding the courts and rooting up trees and tents, then drained by the excitement of watching a 17-year-old win the title. Germany's Boris Becker became the first unseeded player to win Wimbledon in more than a century of tournaments there. He won many hearts, too, by his youthful zest and his obvious enjoyment of his tennis. The dour and impassive Czech, Ivan Lendl, dominated men's tennis for most of the major tournaments, but there was no question that the player of the year was Becker.

Wimbledon had been an unhappy place for Becker in 1984 when he won through to the third round only to be carried from the court with an ankle injury which threatened his career. This year, too, there were moments when his hyper-active style appeared likely to overstrain his ankle again; but when at one time that did threaten to let him down his spirit was still strong enough to pull him through. Becker came to Wimbledon ranked only 29th in the world, but he had won the Young Masters championship and he went to the tournament full of confidence after beating Hans Kriek in the final of the Queen's grass-court championship—his first grand-slam win.

At Wimbledon it was a battle all the way. He lost his opening set to American Hank Pfister, but as always his answer was a powerful counter-attack which won him the next three. The power of his play, especially his fierce service, which earned him the nickname 'Boom-boom' Becker, destroyed his next opponent in his only easy match. Then it was a hard struggle against the 7th seed, Sweden's Nystrom, who led 5–4 and 6–5 in the final set only for Becker to break his service each time, and go on to win. The brilliant but erratic Henri Leconte, who had disposed of Ivan Lendl, was Becker's next victim in four sets. The Swede Anders Jarryd was similarly overwhelmed in the semi-final. The impossible dream became reality as Becker's soaring confidence proved too powerful for Kevin Curren, the strong favourite after he had destroyed the out-of-sorts John McEnroe. Oddly it was the experienced Curren who suffered from nerves, to lose the first set of the final. He won the next on a tie-break, and the decisive game came as Curren led 4–3 in the third set with his service to come. Becker at once broke back and went on to win that set and the next, becoming the youngest player ever to win a grand slam tournament.

That was Becker's peak for the year, but his impressive play was good enough to take Germany to the final of the Davis Cup. Against the holders, Sweden, Becker won both his singles, against Stefan Edberg and

Mats Wilander. But his supporting cast was not good enough, and
Sweden won again, 3–2. The drama of Becker's rise to worldwide fame
and millionaire status overshadowed the many triumphs of Ivan Lendl,
who at last began to dominate the tennis circuit, since McEnroe pro-
gressively lost his touch as well as his temper. It was Lendl who won the
US Open and Lendl who gained the prize that summed up the osten-
tatious wealth of professional tennis, a diamond-studded racquet that
became his when he beat McEnroe in one of their closer contests to win
the World Masters Championship for the third time in succession.

Martina Navratilova and Chris Lloyd again dominated women's tennis. After a series of defeats in recent seasons Chris beat Martina at last in
a three-set final at the French championships. In the 65 times they had
met, Martina was ahead by 33 to 32. But their present relative abilities fell
into true perspective in the Wimbledon final, when although Lloyd
played well the stronger Navratilova became singles champion for the
fifth successive year. In the US Open, however, Hanna Mandlikova at
last played to her full potential, surprising and defeating Navratilova.

GOLF. The balance of power in top-class golf shifted away from
America towards Europe in general, and Britain in particular. There was
a first indication of this when Sandy Lyle won the 114th British Open at
Royal St George's in Sandwich. It was 16 years after Tony Jacklin's
previous victory, thirty-four since any other Briton won this championship. For Sandy Lyle, the quiet man whose great potential had not always
been realised, this was a climactic achievement on a difficult course swept
by the sea winds.

Lyle ended the first round two under par and up with the leaders. But
the sensation of that opening day was the 64 by Christie O'Connor junior,
a six-under-par score which matched the record for a first round of the
Open. In the next, O'Connor slipped back with a 76, while Lyle maintained his form to share the lead. With the weather at its worst Bernhard
Langer played perhaps the best round of the championship, his 69 a
remarkable achievement in vile conditions which effectively eliminated
other outstanding golfers such as Severiano Ballesteros and Jack
Nicklaus. Langer followed that with a 68 to share the lead with the
consistent David Graham, as Lyle fell back.

On the final round it was Tom Kite who forged to the front until
disaster overtook him at the 10th. Lyle was still sound, rather than
brilliant, looking set to finish close behind the leaders. Then he holed a
long putt for a birdie at the 14th and had two more birdies in the final
holes. There was a slip at the last as he fluffed a chip from the clinging
rough at the edge of the 18th green to lose a stroke. Happily for Lyle both
Graham and Langer were below their best on this round, each taking 75
to finish equal third, behind Payne Stewart.

If Lyle's was an unusual British victory, Europe's win in the Ryder

Cup was unique, the first since their combined team took over from Great Britain and Ireland in 1979. Indeed the United States had not lost in the Ryder Cup since 1957, though the match was tied in 1969. Despite the care with which Tony Jacklin prepared his team for the event the start was not encouraging, as the Americans took a first-day lead. But on the second day Europe began to take charge, aided by Craig Stadler's missing the shortest and most crucial of putts. So the final singles began with Europe leading 9–7. The lead was steadily extended until Sam Torrance sank the putt that confirmed Europe's victory.

For Torrance his most memorable putt was soon followed by his most forgettable one, which cost Scotland a place in the final of the Dunhill Nations Cup. Because Torrance missed first from a few feet, and then from a few inches, the US went through instead, only to be beaten by Australia. For Sandy Lyle there was no such mixed fortune. As usual he often finished second or third, but he also won the Benson & Hedges international at Fulford and ended far ahead of Bernhard Langer and Severiano Ballesteros in the Epson order of merit for the European PGA tour.

Langer and Ballesteros, however, remained Europe's two most highly-regarded golfers; Langer earned the most money, but Ballesteros defeated him in a couple of personal duels—in the final of the Suntory World Match-play championship and in the play-off for the Carrolls Irish Open. But it was Langer who won the American Masters tournament with Ballesteros two strokes behind, thus confirming Europe's mastery. Langer finished 13th in the USPGA money list, with Ballesteros 26th through having withdrawn from some of the fifteen matches for which he had booked, a misdemeanour for which the American Board ruled he could play no more than four matches in the US in 1986.

Of the Americans the most successful was Curtis Strange, who won a record $542,321, to head their money list, closely followed by Lanny Wadkins. The US Open was won by Andy North, but there was nearly another major upset there, as Taiwan's Tze-Chung Chen was comfortably in the lead until he took an eight at the fifth hole.

ASSOCIATION FOOTBALL The experience of the City of Liverpool epitomised a year of English football in which tragedy overshadowed triumph. It will be remembered mainly for the shame of soccer hooliganism and its disastrous repercussions, as Liverpool's success in reaching its fifth European Cup final dissolved in bitter shambles at Brussels' Heysel stadium. It was a year for mourning the dead and the lost reputation of English sportsmanship rather than celebrating such remarkable feats as Everton's winning the European Cup Winners Cup, taking the League title with a record number of points, and so nearly winning the FA Cup as well.

There was a frightening acceleration of violence and disaster. The first

warning came on 4 March as Chelsea's unruly spectators ran riot when
Sunderland won at Stamford Bridge to reach the final of the Milk Cup.
The FA disciplinary committee reacted only with a warning about future
conduct. The Chelsea chairman, Ken Bates, took more positive action,
surrounding the pitch with an electrified fence with 12-volt current. The
Greater London Council, however, took out an injunction against its use.

On 13 March there were even more disgraceful scenes as Millwall
went out of the quarter-final of the FA Cup at Luton's ground. Their
supporters created havoc in the stands, then rampaged over the pitch and
through the streets, sweeping aside the 200 police on duty. The damage at
the ground alone was estimated at £15,000, yet the penalties imposed by
the FA disciplinary committee amounted only to a £7,500 fine on Millwall
and a requirement for Luton to fence off the pitch. That was hardly the
firm action which had been demanded by the Prime Minister after a
ministerial meeting to discuss the growing soccer violence, so now the
Government itself began to intervene. The Sports Minister, Neil
McFarlane, banned the holding of the England v. Scotland match at
Wembley, because of past Scottish hooliganism on similar occasions. On
1 April the English football authorities had to send representatives to
discuss with members of the Government the growing menace to society
of spectators' behaviour. Mrs Thatcher again called for firmer measures,
though still refraining from legislation in order to give the authorities a
last chance to act themselves.

On 11 May came a double disaster. At Birmingham City's ground
Leeds fans ran amok, leaving 96 police injured and a boy killed as a wall
collapsed on him. Even that was overshadowed by an horrific accident at
Bradford City. The stand was packed for the game against Lincoln City as
Bradford celebrated promotion to the Second Division. Shortly before
the interval a small fire in a corner of the wooden stand spread with such
terrifying rapidity that 52 people died and over a hundred were injured.

Then on 29 May, with some hundred million television viewers watching the European Cup Final, came the final unforgivable act, which had
all the inevitability of a Greek tragedy. Others had their share of
responsibility. Italy's Juventus supporters had a provocative element
among them, some of whom were to be seen throwing crumbling
masonry at the ineffective Belgium police, while TV focused on one with
a pointed pistol. Belgium's crowd-control measures were so inadequate,
the police and first-aid action too inept, that a Minister's resignation was
demanded and a police colonel, major and captain involved were transferred later to other duties. UEFA belatedly acknowledged its responsibility for staging the match in an unsafe stadium by banning Belgium from
holding such an event for the next ten years. But the main rioting, and the
charge which collapsed the barrier, causing so many of the 38 deaths and
the hundreds of injuries, was an English responsibility.

That responsibility was immediately acknowledged by Mrs Thatcher, while the FA voluntarily banned English clubs from playing in Europe for a year. UEFA imposed an indefinite ban on all English clubs playing in Europe, relaxing it only at the year's end for friendly matches. The Government responded with legislation banning alcohol sale on English grounds and special football trains and coaches. Despite the football authorities' ignoring the request for an identity card system for supporters, the measures taken began to have a calming influence when coupled with more effective equipment to monitor crowds, tougher action by police and stiffer sentences for hooliganism.

There were other problems making policy at least as important as the play. Failure to complete a negotiation with the BBC and ITV took regular soccer off the screens for the early months of the new season, causing great loss of revenue and considerable upset to sponsors and public. Only late in December was a package finally agreed to restore televised soccer in the new year. To that loss, and the loss of European soccer, was added huge expense for many clubs when the inquiry under Mr Justice Popplewell, following the Bradford City fire, laid down much stricter safety standards. Under all these financial pressures the League itself came close to splitting apart, as a group of leading clubs pressed for a restructuring which might have disposed of the Third and Fourth Divisions. Compromise eventually postponed any decision of importance.

Juventus beat Liverpool in that infamous European Cup Final, with Europe's best player, Michel Platini, scoring the decisive penalty. Juventus then won the world club championship in Tokyo, beating Argentinos Juniors on penalties after a 2–2 draw. Everton were at their most impressive in the final of the European Cup Winners Cup. They held Bayern Munich to a draw in Germany, then won decisively at Goodison Park. Everton also dominated the First Division, totting up a record 90 points and having a run of 28 matches without defeat. Liverpool, at one stage as low as twentieth, finished strongly to end as runners-up. In the spirit of the year Manchester United became the first team to have a player sent off in the FA Cup final, yet battled so bravely with ten men that Norman Whiteside's extra-time goal defeated invincible Everton.

The Milk Cup final was won by Norwich City; the poor quality of the match was not surprising, since both the teams were later relegated to the Second Division along with Stoke City. The rise of Oxford United under Robert Maxwell's chairmanship continued with their reaching the First Division. Aberdeen again dominated Scottish football, winning the Premier Division for the second successive year. Celtic had the consolation of winning the Scottish FA Cup with two late goals against Dundee United.

Scotland beat England, to win the new Sir Stanley Rous Cup. They also qualified for the World Cup final in Mexico by beating Australia in a two-leg play-off. That they had this chance by coming second to Spain in their group was due to their defeating Wales at Cardiff on a night when joy turned to sadness. For soon after the decisive penalty had been shot home Scotland's outstanding manager, Jock Stein, died at the ground. That defeat eliminated Wales, whose players' requests for the match to be staged on their favoured Wrexham pitch were ignored for financial reasons.

England headed their group, unbeaten in their eight matches. Northern Ireland also battled through to qualify in second place with a fighting finish that brought them victory in Romania then a draw at Wembley. In a preparatory tour England lost to Mexico, and to Italy in a very friendly match so soon after the Heysel disaster. But they beat West Germany 3–0 in a match in which old hand Peter Shilton and new cap Kerry Dixon were outstanding.

RUGBY UNION. In a surprise reversal of form, Ireland, coached by the adventurous Mick Doyle, won the five-nations championship, while Scotland followed their grand slam of the previous year by failing to win a point. The two met in the first match of the season, when Ireland's narrow win signalled the change. The Irish commitment to all-out attack brought them two tries by Trevor Ringland, the second snatching victory at Murrayfield in the final minutes. England drew with France at Twickenham, where Rob Andrew matched Jean-Paul Lescarboura's ability to drop goals or kick penalties.

The Scottish slide continued when France beat them easily at Parc des Princes, Wales narrowly in a high-scoring match at Murrayfield. At Lansdowne Road Michael Kiernan's five penalties enabled Ireland to draw with France. Ireland went on to overwhelm Wales 21–9 in Cardiff, their first win there since 1967, then beat England 13–10 at Lansdowne Road, where Michael Kiernan's final dropped goal clinched the championship. France were also unbeaten, finishing as runners-up with an easy 14–3 win over Wales in Paris. At the bottom end, Wales pulled ahead of England with a comfortable victory over them at Cardiff. England, however, won the Calcutta Cup with a 10–7 victory at Twickenham, leaving Scotland pointless. Simon Smith's try was the first England had scored in a championship match there for three seasons.

England had started the season well, beating by a wide margin the Romanian team which had previously defeated both Wales and Scotland. Later, on tour in New Zealand, they lost narrowly in the first Test, but were humiliated in the second as the powerful and aggressive New Zealanders overwhelmed them 42–15, the heaviest defeat in England's history.

The South African issue bedevilled rugby again. A New Zealand judge ordered the cancellation of a proposed tour there, and the South Africans themselves called off a proposed visit by the British Lions.

CRICKET. An exceptionally wet English summer caused much interference with play, but it was a good year for England's Test cricketers. They had just ended the worst losing sequence in England's history when they squared the series with India by winning at Delhi. The confidence this inspired, coupled with the inclusion of Neil Foster, now gave them an overwhelming win at Madras.

Foster's lively pace brought him six first-innings wickets as India struggled to 272. Another patient innings by Tim Robinson, and a second-wicket partnership of 241 between Graeme Fowler and Mike Gatting, both of whom scored double centuries, took England to 652 for 7 declared. India made a brave reply, with the exciting young batsman, Azharuddin scoring a century. But as Foster was again in devastating form, taking 5 for 59, England cruised to a nine-wicket win. The elegant Azharuddin scored yet another century in the fifth and final Test, his three centuries in three matches and an average of 106 recording the best start ever in Test cricket. But more solid batting enabled England to draw and so win the series. Captain David Gower had been sadly out of form, but his 78 was an important contribution to avoiding the follow-on after India had declared at 553 for 8.

At home, Gower's batting lapses continued as England lost the first two one-day internationals against an Australian side weakened by the defection of a number of players to tour South Africa under Kim Hughes's captaincy. Much media pressure for his replacement as captain never upset his relaxed approach to the game, and he answered with a century that won the last international, then followed it with the highest total of runs by an Englishman in any Test series.

The winning pattern was set in the first Test, when England's fast scoring against a weak attack gave them a five-wicket victory. Andrew Hilditch's opening 119 for Australia was eclipsed by Tim Robinson's 175 as England raced ahead. Ian Botham then signalled his return to Test cricket with three wickets in four balls, and with Graham Gooch and John Emburey back after their three-year suspensions for South African involvement the England team looked a strong combination.

Yet the balance shifted briefly Australia's way when they won at Lord's. Craig McDermott, one of their few successes, took 6 for 70 in England's first innings, spinner Bob Holland 5 for 68 in the second. But the match-winner was Allan Border. The Australian captain scored 196 after surviving when Gatting failed to complete a catch by trying to throw the ball up in celebration. As Australia's second innings faltered to 65 for 5 his solid batting then saw them home by four wickets.

The next two Tests were drawn, though Gower's 166 in the third, and Gatting's 160 in the fourth, were symptomatic of England's batting supremacy. After much experiment they found their match-winning bowler in Richard Ellison, who played a major part in beating Australia by an innings in both the final Tests. Ellison took 10 for 97 at Edgbaston and seven wickets at the Oval. Gower finished with a captain's flourish, scoring 215 and 157, and sharing at the Oval a stand of 351 with Graham Gooch, whose 196 was his maiden Test hundred against Australia.

For Australia there was only disappointment in a year which started brightly as they ended the West Indies' winning run in Sydney. Bob Holland spun them to victory there to give Border his first win as captain. Yet that series had already been lost as decisively as the following one was to be in England. New Zealand then further injured Australian pride by winning a series in Australia for the first time. Richard Hadlee overwhelmed Australia in the opening Test as they plunged to a third successive innings defeat. They fought back to square the series on the spinner's pitch at Sydney, but Hadlee was again too good for them in the deciding Test.

New Zealand had earlier been no match for the West Indies. After two drawn Tests, the second enlivened by Ritchie Richardson's 185 and Martin Crowe's answering 188, New Zealand were routed by a pace attack in which Malcolm Marshall was outstanding with 27 wickets at 18 runs apiece. Jeremy Coney battled hard in a vain effort to save the third Test after New Zealand had been rushed out for 94 in their first innings. After his brave 83 Coney suffered a broken arm in the next Test. Without him New Zealand again collapsed to defeat. After waiting through thirteen Tests for a victory against New Zealand the West Indies had won twice in style—but not in a style the departing captain appreciated, for Geoff Howarth made bitter charges that their fast bowlers attacked the body, not the stumps.

At home New Zealand beat Pakistan 2–0 in a three-Test series, and won all three one-day internationals as well. Outstanding batsmen in the Tests were John Reid and Jeremy Coney, with averages of 83 and 75, while Hadlee took 16 wickets at 19 runs apiece and came fourth in the batting. The decisive final Test was a match of fluctuating fortune. Pakistan, 241 for 2 at one stage, collapsed to 273 all out as Hadlee found inspiration. Set 278 to win in their final innings New Zealand were 228 for 8, with Bruce Cairns retired hurt. Yet Jeremy Coney, with an unbeaten 111, and the last man, Ewan Chatfield, fashioned a winning 50 partnership.

The happiest Test country was Sri Lanka, who not only won a Test for the first time, but the series as well. Only rain saved the Indians in the first Test. Victory came in the next, aided by Amal Silva's century and his repeat of the nine wicket-keeping victims he had also achieved in the first Test. Having beaten India by 149 runs Sri Lanka battled to a draw in the final Test, owing much to a stand of 216 between Duleep Mendis and Roy Diaz.

India had proved themselves an outstanding one-day cricket team, winning the World Cup in Australia as they had done in England the year before. In Tests, however, it was almost as bad a year for them as for

Australia, and at the year's end the two were confronting each other. Despite their home advantage, Australia had a struggle to draw the first two Tests, with rain saving them in the second.

In England there was no lack of runs for county batsmen. Somerset finished bottom of the championship table, yet Vivian Richards headed the averages with 76·50, aided by a remarkable innings of 322 against Warwickshire, and their captain, Ian Botham, was fourth. Botham also hit a record number of sixes to enliven an entertaining season. Second in the averages was the insatiable Geoffrey Boycott, still relentlessly grinding out the runs. The championship was closely fought. Hampshire led at the end of August, but Middlesex finished the strongest, to take the title. In their last match, second-place Hampshire needed a wicket off the last ball to win, but instead Roger Harper hit it for six, to give Northants an improbable victory.

There was a breathless finish to the NatWest Final as well. Nottinghamshire's Derek Randall needed only a two off the last ball, having already taken 14 off the over from Derek Pringle. Instead he was caught and it was Essex who took the trophy. With Gooch in majestic form, Essex were kings of the one-day game, winning the John Player League as well, but losing out to Gower's Leicestershire in the final of the Benson & Hedges Cup.

ATHLETICS. Steve Cram proved himself Britain's and the world's outstanding athlete as he broke three world records in nineteen days. The centrepiece was the so-called 'dream mile' in Oslo in which he beat Sebastian Coe into third place and lowered the world record by more than a second to 3 min. 46·31 sec. He also broke the 1500 m. record and finally the 2000 m. in a race in which he finished only a stride ahead of Moroccan, Said Aouita. Only Coe's 800 m. time narrowly eluded him when he just failed to add that fourth record.

Two other outstanding athletes broke world records. Said Aouita beat David Moorcroft's 5000 m. time by the almost incalculable margin of 1/100th of a second. Carl Lopes set a new marathon record of 2 hr. 7 min. 11 sec. shortly before the London Marathon, which itself set records by enrolling 11,208 runners of whom no fewer than 2,761 finished in under three hours.

English athletes performed well in the first world indoor athletics championship staged in Paris. Ade Mafe won silver in the 200 m., Todd Bennett in the 400 m., Heather Oakes in the 60 m., and Jane Finch in the 800 m. Ikem Billy won a bronze at 800 m. and Jonathan Ridgeon at 60 m.

MOTOR RACING. McLaren-Porsche were again the dominant force in the World Championship and this time it was their French driver, Alain Prost, who ended as champion. But the Manufacturer's Championship was a much closer contest than before, with Ferrari often in the lead and Williams-Honda finishing the season very strongly.

In fact the Brazilian Grand Prix in Rio de Janeiro on 7 April set the pattern for the season, with Prost winning in his McLaren followed by Michele Alboreto in a Ferrari. Prost also won the fourth race at Monte Carlo, the eighth—the British Grand Prix at Silverstone—and the Austrian and Italian Grand Prix races as well. But for the other McLaren driver, the great Nikki Lauda, it was a sad last season, brightened only by a win in the Dutch Grand Prix at Sandvoort, a fourth place in San Marino and a fifth in Germany. By Lauda's standards that was relative failure, which left McLaren fighting to win the championship, instead of racing away with it as in the previous season.

Alboreto's two wins were in Canada and Germany, but he finished second four times, compared to Prost's twice. Third in the drivers' championship was Keijo Rosberg, who also had two wins in his Williams-Honda. From September onwards, indeed, it was the Williams cars which dominated the races. In the Belgian Grand Prix their other driver, Nigel Mansell, finished second, Rosberg fourth. At Brands Hatch Mansell won the European Grand Prix, his first victory in 72 races. He celebrated immediately by winning again at the Kayalami circuit in South Africa, with Rosberg second, and in the final race on 3 November at Adelaide it was Rosberg who won. Rosberg switched to McLaren in Lauda's place for 1986, while Nelson Picquet, whose only win was in the French Grand Prix, transferred to Williams as their lead driver for the next season.

Another world championship star was the brilliant young Brazilian Ayrton Senna, who won the Portuguese and Belgian races, while the experienced Elio de Angelis was also a winner at San Marino, to give Lotus-Renault three Grand Prix victories in all. In the World Endurance Championship the champion car was the Porsche 962C-Turbo and the winning drivers Derek Bell and Hans Stuck, who won three of the ten championship races.

THE TURF. It was a year of farewells to great jockeys. Lester Piggott had become a racing legend long before his retirement at the end of a season in which he recorded his 29th Classic win. In the 2000 Guineas he rode to victory Shadeed, sired by the famous Nijinski and owned by Sheikh Maktoum-al-Maktoum, whose family had made a vast investment in bloodstock. Johnnie Francome had achieved almost equal fame in the exciting and dangerous National Hunt racing and he too retired. So did 51-year-old Joe Mercer, with 13 European Classic wins behind him.

The jockey of the year was again Steve Cauthen. The horse of the year was Pebbles; the race of the year the Grand National, in which the 50-1 outsider Last Suspect charged home to beat Mr Snugfit and those consistent National runners Corbière and Greasepaint. Last Suspect's rider, Hywel Davies, had persuaded trainer Tim Forster to enter the horse against his better judgment and he wore the black and gold colours of Anne, Duchess of Westminster, to recall the famous jumper Arkle, who was valued too highly ever to be risked in the Grand National.

In Paris, Rainbow Quest won the Arc de Triomphe in a close contest with the favoured Sagace, who passed the post first but was later disqualified. Teleprompter won the Budweiser Million in Florida. But the best combination of the year was that of Steve Cauthen and trainer Henry Cecil. They triumphed in the Derby when Cauthen confirmed his own forecast that Slip Anchor would win with ease, and then he rode home Oh So Sharp in the Oaks.

WORLD CHAMPIONS. By the end of 1985 Great Britain and Ireland had 36 individuals, 10 pairs and 11 teams entitled to call themselves World Champions. The range spanned athletes such as Zola Budd and Steve Cram to England's coarse-fishing team, which won the world freshwater championship for the first time.

The Sports Writers' Association award for outstanding achievement went to Richard Fox, who won the world single Kayak slalom title for the third successive year with a final run ten seconds faster than any rival's. But BBC TV's sports personality of the year, who most captured the public imagination, was Barry McGuigan. He won, and then retained, the World Boxing Association's featherweight title, to become a symbol of united popularity in strife-torn Northern Ireland.

The youngest champion was also one of the most consistent; for David Maw, aged 8, who had headed his age-group in the world BMX cycle championship the previous year in Japan, won again in Canada.

The first World Games for sports seeking Olympic status was staged in London in July and August, drawing 1,700 competitors from 58 nations and five continents. The sports represented ranged from roller-hockey to power-lifting, from fly and bait casting to badminton and karate. Such is the variety of sports in which so many were now striving for excellence.

XVIII ECONOMIC AND SOCIAL AFFAIRS

Chapter 1

A G5 AND US U-TURN

During 1985 a sea change occurred in international financial attitudes and actions, particularly those of the Reagan Administration. After nearly a decade and a half of floating exchange rates and several years of deliberate non-intervention by the USA, Finance Ministers and central bank governors of the major industrial countries (USA, Japan, West Germany, the UK and France) known as the Group of Five (G5) launched a new initiative aimed at restoring more stable conditions.

A key event was a meeting in New York on 21–22 September (see DOCUMENTS) when the G5 Ministers stated explicitly that 'some future orderly appreciation of the main non-dollar currencies against the dollar is desirable'. Moreover, the Finance Ministers said they stood 'ready to cooperate more closely' to bring this about. It was made clear that intervention in foreign exchange markets would have a useful role to play. There were also references to the need to resist protectionism, to reduce excessive budget deficits (a hint to the USA) and to open up markets (a warning to Japan).

The communique represented a major shift in policy from that which had prevailed since the start of the second oil-price shock in 1979. Then the emphasis in each major country had been on looking after its own affairs in an attempt both to contain large and growing public sector deficits and to reduce inflation. Although by the mid-1980s there had been considerable success in holding down inflation and in producing sustained growth, a number of problems had emerged. In particular, the current account positions of the largest countries had become exceptionally unbalanced as a result of lop-sided patterns of growth (much faster in the USA than elsewhere) and of trade. Among the reactions were the strength of the dollar and growing protectionist pressures, particularly in the US Congress, in face of the increasing problems of US exporters and a wave of imports from Japan and from low-wage Pacific Basin countries.

Under the Reagan Administration there was also a reluctance to admit that there were any difficulties about a strong dollar. Both the President and Mr Donald Regan, his first-term Treasury Secretary, regarded the strength of the dollar as a symbol of America's success and of national resurgence—and, conversely, an indication of the failures of other countries. Mr Regan was often in conflict with his opposite numbers in the other main industrial countries in denying that the large US budget deficit was contributing to high world interest rates, the over-strong dollar and the huge current account trade deficit. This attitude led to a US refusal to participate in coordinated currency intervention.

Two important changes then occurred. First, in January 1985, Mr James Baker, formerly the President's chief of staff in the White House, took over from Mr Regan as Treasury Secretary in a swap of jobs. Mr Baker proved to be more open-minded in recognising the international dimension of the problem and in accepting some of the analysis pursued by other Finance Ministers. Secondly, the threat of protectionism, together with the prospect of slower growth in the USA, made the difficulties appear more urgent.

The situation was discussed at the annual meeting of Ministers of the 24 main industrial countries of the Organization for Economic Coopera-tion and Development (OECD) in April and at the seven-nation world economic summit at Bonn in May. But the G5 announcement was the turning-point, signalling, as it did, that the participants, including the USA, recognised that exchange rates were not fully reflecting economic fundamentals and that changes in policy were desirable. The G5 state-ment was quickly backed by evidence that, for the first time in many years, the member countries were prepared to carry out significant exchange market intervention and, in the case of Japan, to put up its domestic interest rates.

Consequently, within two months some two-fifths of the appreciation of the dollar between the trough of the third quarter of 1980 and the peak of the first quarter of 1985 had been reversed. In particular, against the Japanese yen the dollar's earlier appreciation was completely cancelled out by a 17 per cent appreciation of the Japanese currency. Since Japan accounted for nearly 30 per cent of all US imports of manufactured goods, one result was to ease protectionist pressures in the US Congress.

However, the main European currencies appreciated by less than half as much as the yen against the dollar. This led to some cautious comments as to how far the initial success in reversing the rise in the dollar might be built upon, especially given the uncertainty created by the sharp fall in the price of oil towards the end of the year. Moreover, European financial leaders regarded the Japanese actions as exceptional. For instance, in November 1985, Herr Karl Otto Poehl, the president of the West Ger-man Bundesbank, said: 'Of course we have not committed ourselves to raise our interest rate level and thus reduce the gap with US rates and achieve a correction in the dollar through this means.' European govern-ments were concerned that a fall in the US dollar should be gradual—the so-called 'soft-landing'—fearing that a more rapid depreciation might trigger a sharp rise in US interest rates and thus threaten the prospects for recovery in both the US and other industrialized countries.

Indeed, at the end of 1985, the OECD concluded that there was 'a limit to how far it is possible to go towards a more internationally-compatible configuration of policies by monetary policy adjustments alone'. The argument came back to the missing item from the G5 communique, a specific commitment by the Reagan Administration to reduce its budget deficit. As the OECD argued in its December *Economic Outlook*, 'addressing in a more fundamental way the large international interest, rate differentials at the long-end in favour of dollar-dominated financial instruments would seem to require reduction of the still large budget deficit of the US. Unless this core problem is effectively attacked soon, the attempts solely by monetary policies to maintain the so far favourable outcome of the G5 initiative would indeed risk jeopardising US inflation performance and the Japanese recovery.'

Parallel to this exchange-rate initiative, US Treasury Secretary James Baker also launched a major package of proposals at the IMF/World Bank meeting in Seoul in South Korea in early October to deal with the debt and adjustment problems of less-developed countries. This also represented a major shift in US policy towards greater official involvement in international debt problems.

The Baker plan involved not only a continuing central role for the IMF but also a significant increase in lending by the World Bank and other multinational development banks in support of growth-oriented programmes of structural adjustment of their economies by debtor nations. The plan was designed to create conditions that would allow a resumption of expanded lending to these countries by commercial banks.

This initiative was welcomed both by the president of the World Bank and by the managing director of the IMF and was given general support by a number of major governments and leading commercial bankers. Dr Gerhard Stoltenberg, the West German Finance Minister, warmly welcomed the 'remarkable shift' in US thinking. Commercial bankers looked for more details, particularly about the idea of an international superbank.

By the end of the year, however, progress had been slow, nothing tangible having appeared to assist Latin American countries struggling to service their foreign debts. Admittedly, in December, US, Japanese and British banks pledged support for the Baker plan and for the call on banks to pledge new loans of $20,000 million over three years to the most heavily indebted countries. However, the West German and Swiss banks, concerned about being bulldozed by the USA without proper commercial assessments, took a more cautious approach.

The Finance Ministers of 11 Latin American nations, meeting in mid-December in Montevideo, welcomed the Baker plan as 'a positive step', but argued that it would provide insufficient funds to guarantee debt repayment and sustained growth over the 1986–88 period.

Nevertheless, by the end of the year, the two initiatives together offered the prospect of a new spirit of international cooperation and responsibility among major countries, particularly the USA, towards the future of the world economy.

Chapter 2

THE INTERNATIONAL ECONOMY

THE world economy enjoyed a third year of solid growth in 1985, extending the recovery period to twice as long as the average post-war cyclical upturn. However, there remained major problems of imbalance, both within the industrialized world and between rich and poor nations. Fresh worry about protectionism, Third World debt and currency misalignment led to two important initiatives in the autumn (see Ch. 1 above).

OUTPUT, TRADE, AND EMPLOYMENT. The continuation of overall growth in the major economies—represented by a near 3 per cent real increase in total Gross National Product in 1985—was nonetheless a slowdown from the rapid 5 per cent rate of the previous year. In part, this was due to a slackening of expansion in the USA and subdued activity in the first half of the year in France and West Germany. In many countries, private fixed investment and stockbuilding fell back. However, declining interest rates during the year helped to boost growth in most industrialized countries by the late summer and early autumn. Output increased by slightly over $3\frac{1}{2}$ per cent in the second half of the year. Generally low and falling rates of inflation also helped to sustain activity. Private consumption and investment accelerated in Japan in the autumn and there was also a pick-up in West Germany, Italy and France. Over the year as a whole, therefore, differences in economic performance between the USA and Europe narrowed.

A new factor entering calculations as the year developed was the decline in the dollar, particularly against the Japanese yen. In due time this was expected to boost US exports and check the previous rapid growth in Japanese exports to the USA. Over 1985 the growth of world trade slowed from the rapid rate of nearly 9 per cent in 1984 to only just over 4 per cent, in large part because of the slowdown in demand in the major industrialized countries in the first half of the year, coupled with the weakening demand for oil.

All this had a major impact on the position not only of the oil-producing Opec countries but also on the newly-industrialized and developing economies. The trade of the latter two groups slackened, particularly in the first half of 1985. Indeed, in October the International Monetary Fund had to revise downwards its estimate of the expected rate of economic growth in developing countries to $3\frac{1}{2}$ per cent in 1985, compared with actual growth of $4\frac{1}{2}$ per cent in the previous year.

The problems of the poorest nations in sub-Saharan Africa remained particularly acute and the communique of the seven-nation world economic summit in Bonn in May included a special section on these countries. It stressed the need for emergency food aid from both public and private sources, as well as long-term inter-governmental cooperation to improve the productivity of agricultural sectors.

The current account deficits of the non-oil developing countries worsened slightly in 1985, reflecting both a decline in demand from industrialized countries and a fall in the prices of primary commodities. Within the OECD area the surpluses of Japan and West Germany rose again, in part matching the further increase in the USA's trade deficit. A small deterioration in the position of the main European countries reflected their continued economic growth.

EMPLOYMENT. The further rise in activity in the industrialized countries generated increases in employment of around 1 per cent, which were almost sufficient to absorb the growth in the labour force. In particular, employment expanded in Europe against a slower rise in the USA and Japan. The result was that the average rate of unemployment rose only a little in the first half of 1985 to 8·4 per cent, and fell back slightly in the second six months. Consequently, over 1985 as a whole, total unemployment in the OECD area rose from an average of 30·5 million to nearly 30·8 million, the smallest increase in Europe for several years. A continuing worry was the rise in youth unemployment (in the 15–24 age-group), particularly in Western Europe.

COSTS AND PRICES. Inflation continued to be modest in many industrialized countries as a result of both government policies and continued weakness in world commodity markets. Food prices continued to fall, and by the late autumn of 1985 the real price of industrial materials was more than 12 per cent lower than a year earlier. The decline in the dollar after the spring also reduced the cost of oil (priced in dollars) and towards the end of the year the oil price itself began to fall sharply. Moreover, unit labour costs grew slowly in most major economies, partly because of the slackness of the labour markets in Europe, where unemployment remained high. In turn these factors produced very low increases in manufacturers', wholesale, or producer, prices. The result was that the annual rate of consumer price inflation fell in the late summer of 1985 to $4\frac{1}{4}$ per cent, a 16-year low. In the major industrialized economies the inflation rate was down to $3\frac{1}{2}$ per cent in the second half of the year, compared with $3\frac{3}{4}$ per cent in the first half and over 4 per cent in 1984.

GOVERNMENT POLICIES. The main Western economies maintained the anti-inflationary stance of fiscal and monetary policy, with tight controls over public spending and borrowing. In the seven largest countries policy was broadly unchanged over the year; an increase in budget deficits, as a percentage of GNP, in the USA, France and Canada was offset by reductions elsewhere, notably in West Germany and Japan. While the pattern of fiscal policy implementation had been uneven—notably between the USA and Europe—monetary policy had been more clearly responsible for the marked slowdown in inflation rates in the first half of the 1980s. The OECD pointed out in its December *Economic Outlook* that 'this is the longest-lasting disinflation in the post-war period, breaking the pattern since the early 1960s of higher average inflation in each successive business cycle.'

In addition to this macro-economic approach, the leading industrialized countries all adopted policies to enable markets to function more flexibly and efficiently. For instance, in labour markets there were moves away from centralized wage-bargaining towards local or plant-based deals (USA, Canada, Ireland the Netherlands and Sweden). These were coupled with a greater emphasis on bonus payments, profit-sharing and worker participation in the ownership of firms (USA, West Germany and Switzerland) and by increases in labour mobility, expanded training facilities and more flexible working hours. All this contributed to lower inflation by encouraging greater responsiveness of wages to market conditions.

SUMMITS. The main economic initiatives in 1985 were taken outside the normal framework of international meetings under the instigation of Mr James Baker, the US Treasury Secretary, at the Group of Five meeting in late September (see pp. 464–6). Indeed, the formal summits added little. The seven-nation summit in Bonn ended unable, because of French opposition, to agree on a date to start negotiations to eliminate barriers to free trade. Pre-summit hopes in the Reagan Administration that the Governments of Western Europe and Japan would agree to stimulate their economies were disappointed. The final declaration merely referred to continuing current anti-inflation policies 'conducive to sustained growth and higher employment'. The declaration added: 'each of our countries will exercise firm control over public spending, in order to reduce budget deficits, where excessive, and, where necessary, the share of public spending in GNP.'

In the end, the key agreement on the dollar was reached by the Group of Five and this initiative, together with Mr Baker's debt proposals, overshadowed the meeting of the International Monetary Fund and World Bank in Seoul in early October. The developing countries took a cautious initial view. Indeed, Mr Eugene Rothberg, the Treasurer of the World Bank, warned that a larger role for the institution in dealing with the debt problems of developing countries did not mean that it stood ready to bail out commercial bankers.

NOBEL PRIZE. Professor Franco Modigliani of the Massachusetts Institute of Technology in the US was awarded the 1985 Nobel prize for economics for his analyses of household saving and of financial markets. He was credited with being largely responsible for establishing corporate finance as a separate field of economic study.

Chapter 3

THE ECONOMY OF THE UNITED STATES

THE economy of the USA experienced its third year of recovery in 1985. Although the rate of expansion slowed from the rapid rate of the previous 18 months, the sharp decline in the value of the dollar during the year and important changes in fiscal policy revived the prospect of continued growth and low inflation. Consequently, Professor Martin Feldstein of Harvard University, a former chairman of the Council of Economic Advisers in the Reagan Administration, felt able to state at the year's end that 'although three years has been the average length of the post-war US business cycle expansion, the current upturn shows none of the traditional indications that a new recession is about to begin'.

OUTPUT AND EMPLOYMENT. As 1985 began, the rate of growth was slackening from its earlier hectic pace. In part, this was due to the impact of the sharp appreciation of the dollar. While domestic demand continued to rise, albeit more slowly than before, this was offset by a drop in exports and by a continuing rise in imports. At a time when a reduction in levels of stocks (inventories) was further depressing demand, the result was that industrial production levelled off from the spring until the early autumn and manufacturing employment also declined. The pressures of the strong dollar were felt in the continuing problems of the farming, petroleum and mining sectors, as well as in many branches of manufacturing, which contributed to growing protectionist pressures. Business fixed investment was also much less buoyant than in 1984, particularly spending on equipment. Overall, the pace of growth slowed from an annual rate of 4·2 per cent in the final quarter of 1984 to 0·3 per cent and 1·99 per cent in the first and second quarters of 1985 respectively.

However, the level of activity picked up in the late summer, producing growth rates of about 3·3 per cent in the third quarter and 3·6 per cent in the fourth. This was an outcome of an improvement in orders for domestic durables and firm consumer spending. The latter was in turn partly the result of a further fall in the personal savings ratio, down to a low point of 2·9 per cent in the third quarter of 1985, while consumer instalment debt grew at a rapid rate throughout the year. Consequently, while real personal disposable income rose by around $3\frac{1}{2}$ per cent during most of 1985, real consumer spending increased at an annual rate of just under 5 per cent.

The fall in personal savings could not continue indefinitely and there were favourable offsetting influences in the corporate sector. In particular, the 1982–85 recovery witnessed no over-investment in plant and equipment and no strains in the labour market or in capacity utilization. Moreover, by the end of 1985 the pressures on export orders and margins, and hence on corporate profits and liquidity, were being eased by the sharp fall in the value of the dollar.

Over 1985 as a whole, real GNP increased by just over 2·5 per cent compared with 6·8 per cent in the previous year. The slowdown in growth earlier in 1985, especially in manufacturing, meant that the total rise in employment slackened to an annual rate of just under 2 per cent. This was not sufficient to reduce the overall unemployment rate much below 7·2 per cent for much of the year, though there was a drop in late autumn. In December, the total fell by 138,000 to 8·02 million, equivalent to 6·9 per cent of the labour force. This late decline accounted for most of the 168,000 drop in the total reported over the year as a whole.

INFLATION. The rate of consumer price inflation remained low throughout 1985, thanks to a combination of the earlier appreciation of the dollar and greater domestic competition, despite the buoyancy of demand. Among the downward pressures were competition from imports, particularly in traditional manufacturing; deregulation in telecommunications, banking, airlines, trucking and railways; and the extension of non-union competition in construction. Consequently, wage increases in major private-sector collective bargaining agreements stayed under 3 per cent, and the growth of average earnings only slightly higher. But the growth of productivity slowed, so that unit labour costs rose at an increasing rate. This led to some squeeze on profit margins, since both producer and consumer prices continued to grow at only a modest rate before picking up slightly towards the end of 1985. Over the year as a whole, the consumer price index rose by 3 per cent (a 3·3 per cent rate in the fourth quarter), the lowest rate since the 1960s.

EXTERNAL TRADE. The year saw a further marked deterioration in the USA's external trade position, though by its end there were solid grounds for expecting a substantial improvement. In the first half of 1985 the trade deficit widened, in response to the earlier appreciation of the dollar, to an annual rate of $125,000 million from $108,000 million in 1984. Admittedly, the rate of growth of imports slowed from the exceptional figure of the previous year, but a drop in agricultural shipments contributed to an 8½ per cent fall in exports, at an annual rate, in the first half of 1985.

On a long-term comparison, since 1981 when the appreciation of the dollar began in earnest, the merchandise exports of the USA declined by $16,000 million up to mid-1985, of which about three-quarters reflected lower agricultural exports (also affected by a worldwide surplus of farm products). The surplus on trade in capital goods declined from $45,000 million in 1981 to $14,000 million in the first half of 1985, at an annual rate. On the same comparison, the trade deficit in automobiles rose from $11,000 million to $39,000 million over the period, and the deficit in non-auto goods increased from $22,000 million to $54,000 million. By contrast, petroleum imports fell from $78,000 million to $48,000 million.

However, the dollar began to decline from the spring onwards. After reaching a peak in March of 60 per cent above its autumn 1980 trough, the average value of the dollar against other currencies fell by 9 per cent in the six months to mid-September before dropping a further 9 per cent after the meeting of the Group of Five (see Ch. 1 and DOCUMENTS). A limited impact on trade patterns by the end of 1985 included a revival in exports and a slower expansion in imports, which was partially offset by the initial impact on prices of the depreciation of the dollar. Over 1985 as a whole the deficit on the current account of the balance of payments was $132,000 million, against $101,500 million in the previous year. Even a flattening of the previous growth in the trade deficit would be a major net plus for the US economy. After all, in 1985 the negative balance between exports and imports cut one percentage point off the rate of increase in real GNP. The absence of such a negative factor explained on its own some of the cautious optimism of the Reagan Administration and independent forecasters at the end of 1985.

FISCAL AND MONETARY POLICY. There was significant shift in the Administration's fiscal and monetary approach in 1985, as well as in its attitude towards the US dollar. The key change was a greater acceptance by both the Administration and Congress of the need to take firm action to tackle the federal budget deficit. The background was a rise in the deficit from $128,000 million in 1981–82 (fiscal year ending in September) to $222,000 million in 1984–85, equivalent to a rise from 4·1 per cent of GNP to 5·4 per cent, compared with only 0·3 per cent in 1970. The Administration proposed that its 1986 budget, starting in October 1985, should hold federal expenditure to the same nominal level as in the previous fiscal year, thus cutting the deficit by $55,000 million from previous baseline levels down to $175,000 million. However, the usual process of drift occurred as congressional committees authorized increased spending on individual programmes, and as assumptions on expected economic growth varied. By the end of 1985 (three months into the new fiscal year) the deficit was expected to be nearly $206,000 million, despite a congressional squeeze on defence spending.

The key development during the autumn was the passage by Congress, after many arguments and hiccups, of the Balanced Budget and

Emergency Deficit Control Act—the Gramm-Rudman Act, as it quickly became known after its two main authors (see p. 53). This provided for a path towards a balanced budget by 1991 with specific legislation imposing year-by-year checks upon both Congress and the Administration. Commentators argued that the Act's automatic cuts would be regarded as politically so unacceptable that the President and Congress would want to reach a compromise. In any event, Congress had already agreed resolutions calling for spending changes which would reduce the budget deficit by amounts growing from $35,000 million in 1985–86 to $100,000 million in 1987–88, with the aim of ensuring a decline in the deficit's share in GNP.

The Federal Reserve Board's monetary policy was again based in 1985 on the assumption that targets would permit a further year of expansion without renewed inflation. The range for M1 was initially narrowed to 4/7 per cent a year from 4/8 per cent previously, while the M2 target was maintained at 6/9 per cent. However, M1 grew at a seasonally adjusted annual rate of over 10 per cent in the first half of 1985. This was apparently a result of an unexpectedly sharp drop in the velocity of circulation of M1, produced by the decline in interest rates. The target was later adjusted and increasing weight was given to M2, which behaved less erratically. Despite an above-average rate of monetary growth, the Federal Reserve Board permitted a decline in interest rates, the federal funds rate falling by roughly a percentage point during the year to just over $7\frac{1}{2}$ per cent. This reflected a desire to accommodate both a further expansion in the economy and a decline in the dollar. Indeed, after the Group of Five had stressed the desirability of a lower dollar, the Federal Reserve chairman confirmed in November that there was no intention of using the monetary overshoot as a reason for tightening policy.

Chapter 4

THE ECONOMY OF THE UNITED KINGDOM

THE UK economy enjoyed its fourth successive year of recovery in 1985. This represented the longest period of sustained growth since World War II, although, admittedly, it followed the deepest recession of the period. But pressures remained on the Government's financial strategy, and major changes in the balance of both fiscal and monetary policies were announced during the year.

OUTPUT AND EMPLOYMENT. The end of the coal industry dispute in early March (see p. 7) removed a factor which had destroyed the economy over the previous year. The rebound was rapid, marked by rises in both coal production and electricity output. This happened at a time when the underlying expansion of the economy was quite strong. In the middle of 1985 total output was 5 per cent higher than a year earlier, or 4 per cent higher if the effects of the dispute were excluded. This reflected particularly strong growth in both exports and business investment, the latter resulting from an improvement in profitability together with the bringing-forward of expenditure into the first quarter before the reduction in capital allowances at the end of the 1985–86 financial year. Consumers' expenditure continued to grow in response to the increase in real incomes.

Nevertheless, by the autumn there were signs of a slow-down in the rate of expansion, caused by a smaller rise in exports and private investment. This did not mean any halt to economic growth, even though the balance was shifting towards consumer spending rather than those other components. Over 1985 as a whole, total output, as measured by real GDP, rose by about $3\frac{1}{2}$ per cent, with exports 7 per cent up, private industrial investment 13 per cent up and consumer spending $2\frac{1}{2}$ per cent up. Significantly, the surveys showed that manufacturing industry was working at fairly close to full capacity.

The continued economic growth had a further favourable impact on employment, which rose by around 300,000 during 1985, an increase of nearly $1\frac{1}{4}$ per cent. However, the labour force rose even more rapidly, an increase in the population of working age being compounded by a substantial relative increase in the number of women workers, largely because many of the new jobs were for part-time employees in the service and retailing sectors. This offered little help to the hard-core of male unemployment, and the result was a rise of roughly 75,000—half the rise of the previous year—in the number of adults out of work to just over 3·18 million, or 13·2 per cent of the labour force. The overall unadjusted total, including school-leavers, stood at 3·27 million. However, during the autumn the total had fallen, partly through the impact of the Government's various special measures, which kept nearly 500,000 people off the unemployment register. But the more favourable trend was reversed with a sharp rise in unemployment in December.

COSTS AND PRICES. There was a small, though temporary, setback in the battle to reduce inflation during 1985. The 12-month rate of increase in retail prices, which ended 1984 at 4·6 per cent, accelerated during the first half of 1985 to a peak of 7 per cent in May and June. This was the result both of a continuing strong rise in earnings and of a sharp fall in the sterling exchange rate at the end of 1984 and in January 1985, as the consequent big increase in interest rates, particularly in the mortgage rate, pushed up the cost-of-living index. However, the subsequent strong recovery in sterling, coupled with lower world commodity prices—cutting raw material costs for British industry by over 5 per cent during the course of 1985—helped to hold down manufacturers' costs. The result was a slowdown in the inflation rate in the autumn down to 5·7 per cent in December.

A worrying trend remained the level of wage settlements. Their underlying rate of increase was 7½ per cent and edging upwards for the economy as a whole, and even more in manufacturing, despite the high level of unemployment and the stabilization of inflation at around 5 per cent. Moreover, the pay rises occurred at a time when productivity growth was weakening, with the result that the rate of growth of wage costs per unit of manufacturing output accelerated to 7 per cent in the autumn, double the rate of a year earlier and much faster than in competitor countries.

EXTERNAL TRADE. Britain's trade position improved during 1985. This reflected the expansion after the end of the miners' strike, particularly in oil trade, and the strong growth in exports in the first half of the year in response to the previous decline in sterling. In the second half there were contrary trends. The appreciation of sterling, by over one-tenth on average between January and the start of a renewed period of weakness in December, helped to improve the terms of trade. Although export volume was less buoyant, the growth of imports was also less strong, following a sharp rise in purchases of manufactured goods at the end of 1984. Favourable price movements offset adverse volume trends. So, with the volume of oil exports rising in the autumn, the current account surplus rose during the year. For 1985 as a whole it was around £3,000 million, compared with a revised figure of £1,120 million for 1984.

However, by the end of 1985 there were growing worries that the fast rise in unit labour costs and the strength of the pound were damaging UK competitiveness, which was heading back to the levels of 1981. Industrial surveys revealed increasing pessimism about export prospects and order books. In December there were also increasing worries about the falling oil price and the effect this would have both on the pound and consequently interest rates, and on the balance of trade.

GOVERNMENT POLICY. The Government faced increasing problems with its monetary and fiscal policy in 1985. The miners' strike, together with higher local authority expenditure and nationalized industry deficits, led to an overshoot in public sector borrowing (PSBR) in the 1984–85 financial year—up to £10,100 million compared with a forecast of £7,200 million in the March 1984 budget. The figures would have been even worse but for the impact of higher-than-expected North Sea oil tax revenues following the decline in sterling against the dollar in late 1984.

In his March Budget, Mr Nigel Lawson, the Chancellor of the Exchequer, set a PSBR target of around £7,000 million for 1985–86, after trying to take a more realistic view of spending trends by increasing the contingency reserve for unforeseen items by £2,000 million, and after some small-scale tax changes (see p. 17). He again raised starting thresholds for graduated income tax and announced a restructuring of national insurance contributions by removing the upper limit on employers' contributions and aiming to encourage employment of the lower-paid.

However, the fall in the oil price and the appreciation of sterling meant that by the time of the autumn financial statement in November oil tax revenues for 1985–86 were expected to be £2,000 million less than had been assumed in the previous March. Moreover, public expenditure was again proving higher than planned, largely because of additions to the social security and energy budgets, with the contingency reserve fully committed. The PSBR target was raised by £1,000 million. Moreover, in the autumn discussions about public spending plans for 1986–87 the existing planning total of £134,200 million for that year was preserved only with difficulty. Spending was expected to be about £4,000 million higher than previously, but this was offset by an increase in the assumed level of sales of public sector assets from £2,250 million to £4,750 million in 1985–86, reflecting both further receipts from the sale of British Telecom and the initial proceeds of the disposal of the British Gas Corporation, and by a cut of £1,500 million in the contingency reserve. Although, unlike his custom in previous years, Mr Lawson gave no indication in November of the size of possible tax cuts in the following spring, commentators such as OECD estimated that the previous expectation of tax cuts of £3,500 million might have slipped to about £2,000 million, or even less because of the fall in the oil price.

A still more significant shift occurred in monetary policy. A sharp fall in sterling against the dollar to approaching parity had led to a reassessment of priorities, with greater emphasis than before on the exchange rate. This was reflected in the sharp increase in interest rates at the time.

Moreover, during the year increasing problems appeared over the control of the domestic money supply, particularly the main official target measure, sterling M3. Structural changes in the banking system led to diverging patterns of growth in the various monetary aggregates. The growth of sterling M3 accelerated during the late summer and early autumn to well above the top of the official target range, whereas there was no such jump in broader measures of liquidity like PLS2, while narrower measures of money like M2 and M0 showed steady or declining growth. And by the autumn sterling was strong, rising to above $1·40. Consequently, it was decided that the high rate of growth of sterling M3 could be tolerated provided other indicators remained, in the Bank of England's words, 'consistent with the ultimate objectives of declining inflation and sustained growth'.

The change of emphasis was formally recognised in Mr Lawson's Mansion House speech in October when the sterling M3 target was suspended for the rest of 1985–86. But the continuing relevance of broad money aggregates was reasserted in a context of greater emphasis upon the exchange rate as an indicator of financial conditions and a greater weight on short-term interest rates in the conduct of monetary policy. This change was matched by the announcement that sales of public sector debt would be designed to fund the PSBR outside the banking system over the year as a whole, rather than overfunding to secure monetary control on a month-by-month basis. These developments were seen as a retreat from the pure monetarism of the late 1970s and early 1980s. However, despite the urgings of many academics and, it was believed, of many Whitehall advisers, the Government stopped short of linking sterling to other EEC currencies in the exchange-rate mechanism of the European Monetary System.

Chapter 5

ECONOMIC AND SOCIAL DATA

The statistical data on the following pages record developments from 1979 to the latest year, usually 1984, for which reasonable stable figures were available at the time of going to press. Year headings 1979 to 1984 are printed only at the head of each page and are not repeated over individual tables unless the sequence is broken by the insertion of series of figures recording developments over a longer period than is shown on the remainder of the page.

Pages to which the point is relevant include a comparative price index, allowing the current-price figures to be reassessed against the background of inflation.

Unless figures are stated as indicating the position at the *end* of year, they should be taken as annual *totals* or *averages*, according to context.

Tables 2, 3, 4 and 5. Statistics which are normally reported or collected separately in the three UK home jurisdictions (England and Wales, Scotland, and Northern Ireland) have been consolidated into UK series only to show general trends. As the component returns were made at varying times of year and in accordance with differing definitions and regulatory requirements, the series thus consolidated may therefore be subject to error, may not be strictly comparable from year to year, and may be less reliable than the remainder of the data.

Symbols — = Nil or not applicable . . = not available at time of compilation.

Sources

A. THE UNITED KINGDOM
Government Sources
Annual Abstract of Statistics: Tables 1, 2, 3, 4, 5, 15, 16, 21, 22, 27.
Monthly Digest of Statistics: Tables 1, 10, 11, 12, 13, 14, 18, 19, 20, 21, 22, 23, 24, 26, 27, 28.
Financial Statistics: Tables 9, 10, 12, 13, 17, 29.
Economic Trends: 6, 7, 8, 9, 10, 29.
Social Trends: Tables 2, 3, 4, 5.
Department of Employment Gazette: Tables 23, 24, 25, 26.
Housing and Construction Statistics; Tables 5, 15.
Additional Sources
National Institute of Economic and Social Research, *National Institute Economic Review*: Tables 6, 7, 8.
Bank of England Quarterly Bulletin: Tables 11, 12.
Midland Bank: Tables 13, 14.
United Nations: *Monthly Bulletin of Statistics*: Table 1.
The Financial Times: Tables 12, 14.
British Insurance Association: Table 16.

B. THE UNITED STATES
Government and other Public Sources
Department of Commerce, *Survey of Current Business*: Tables 30, 31, 32, 33, 34, 35, 40, 41, 43.
Council of Economic Advisers, Joint Economic Committee, *Economic Indicators*: Tables 33, 39.
Federal Reserve Bulletin: Tables 36, 37, 38.
Additional Sources
A. M. Best Co.: Table 38.
Insurance Information Institute, New York: Table 38.
Bureau of Economic Statistics, *Basic Economic Statistics*: Tables 41, 42.

C. INTERNATIONAL COMPARISONS
United Nations, *Annual Abstract of Statistics*: Tables 44, 45.
UN *Monthly Bulletin of Statistics*: Tables 44, 45, 47.
IMF, *International Financial Statistics*: Tables 44, 46, 48, 49, 50, 51, 52.
OECD, *Main Economic Indicators*: Table 45.
International Institute for Strategic Studies, *The Military Balance*: Table 53.
OECD, *Labour Force Statistics,* Table 54.

ECONOMIC AND SOCIAL DATA
A. THE UNITED KINGDOM

SOCIAL

1. Population

	1980	1981	1982	1983	1984	1985
Population, mid-year est. ('000)	55,945	56,010	56,341	56,377	56,488	..
Live births registered ('000)	754	731	719	721	730	..
Crude birth rate (per 1,000 pop.)	13·5	13·0	12·8	12·8	12·9	..
Deaths registered ('000)	661·5	658	663	659	645	..
Crude death rate (per 1,000 pop.)	11·8	11·8	11·8	11·7	11·4	..

2. Health

	1980	1981	1982	1983	1984	1985
Public expenditure on National Health Service (£ million)(1)	11,859	13,374	14,549	15,431	16,301	..
Hospitals:						
staffed beds, end-year ('000)	457·9	454·9	452·6	446·4	430·9	..
ave. daily bed occupancy ('000)	369·0	365·7	359·2	354·6	347·0	..
waiting list, end-yr ('000)	763	737	871	854	828	..
Certifications of death ('000)(2) by:						
ischaemic heart disease	172·3	173·7	173·2	174.9	175·6	..
malignant neoplasm, lungs and bronchus	39·1	38·8	38·9	39·8	40·0	..
road fatality	6·6	6·3	6·1	5·8	5·7	..
accidents at work (number)	700	652	675	645	610	..

(1) Central government and local authority, capital and current. (2) Great Britain.

3. Education

	1980	1981	1982	1983	1984	1985
Public expenditure (£ million)(1)	13,289	14,491	15,562	16,392	16,989	17,620
Schools ('000)	38·2	37·9	37·5	37·1	36·4	..
Pupils enrolled ('000) in schools	10,891	10,632	10,367	10,094	9,877	..
maintained primary(2)	5,398	5,171	4,961	4,758	4,655	..
maintained and aided secondary(3)(4)	4,636	4,607	4,559	4,494	4,385	..
assisted and independent	620	619	612	606	603	..
Pupils per full-time teacher at:						
maintained primary schools	22·4	22·3	22·3	22·1	22·0	..
maintained secondary schools	16·4	16·4	16·4	16·2	16·0	..
independent schools(4)	13·0	13·2	12·5	12·2	11·9	..
Further education: institutions(5)	5,734	5,434	5,105	5,328	5,268	..
full-time students ('000)	495	510	564	603	595	..
Universities	46	46	46	46	46	..
University students ('000)	300	307	308	304	301	..
First degrees awarded (number)	68,151	70,542	72,628	74,918	..	..
Open University graduates ('000)	7·3	7·7	7·7	6·7	..	..

(1) Central government and local authority, capital and current. Figures are for financial year: 1984=year ending March 1985, etc. (2) Including nursery schools. (3) Including special schools. (4) England and Wales. (5) Great Britain.

	1980	1981	1982	1983	1984	1985
Overall price index (1980=100)	*100·0*	*110·7*	*118·3*	*124·9*	*130·4*	*138·3*

4. Law and Order

	1980	1981	1982	1983	1984	1985
Public expenditure (£ million)(1)	3,803	4,456	4,943	5,433	6,001	6,360
Police	1,768	2,139	2,365	2,562	2,846	2,943
Prisons	508	566	629	711	778	831
Administration of justice(2)	314	371	427	485	570	636
Police establishment ('000)(3)	132·1	133·2	133·5	133·7	133·9	..
Full-time strength(3)	129·1	132·6	132·6	132·7	132.2	..
Ulster, full-time strength	6·9	7·3	7·7	8·0	8·1	..
Serious offences known to police(4)	3,105	3,431	3,708	3,704	4,040	..
Persons convicted, all offences ('000)(4)	2,499	2,359	2,287	2,356	2,004	..
Burglary or robbery(5)	74	83	83	79	79	..
Handling stolen goods/receiving, theft	236	225	242	228	226	..
Violence against person	53	58	52	52	48	..
Traffic offences	1,323	1,261	1,181	1,185	1,138	..
All summary offences(4)	1,797	1,670	1,587	1,667	1,547	..
Prisons: average population ('000)	49·6	50·3	51·1	51·0	50·3	..

(1) Gross expenditure, capital and current, by central government (direct and by grant to local authorities) and by local police authorities. Figures are for financial year: 1984=year ending March 1985, etc. (2) Includes expenditure on parliament and courts. (3) Police establishment and full-time strength: Great Britain only. (4) Because of differences in juridical and penal systems in the three UK jurisdictions, totals of offences are not strictly comparable from year to year: they should be read only as indicating broad trends. (5) Specific offences: England, Wales and N. Ireland.

5. Housing

Public expenditure (£ million)(1)	5,680	4,197	3,755	4,335	4,333	3,855
Dwellings completed ('000)						
by and for public sector(2)	110	88	53	55	54	..
by private sector	130	117	124	149	158	..
Housing land, private sector,						
weighted ave. price (£/hectare)	101,991	105,765	118,924	134,933	150,942	..
Dwelling prices, average (£)(3)	24,307	24,810	25,553	28,593	30,812	33,188

(1) Capital and current, net of rents, etc., received, and adjusted to eliminate double counting of grants and subsidies paid by central government and expended by local authorities. Figures are for financial year: 1984=year ending March 1985. (2) Including government departments (police houses, military married quarters, etc.) and approved housing associations and trusts. (3) Of properties newly mortgaged by building societies.

Overall price index (1980=100)	100·0	110·7	118·3	124·9	130·4	138·3

PRICES, INCOME AND EXPENDITURE

6. National Income and Expenditure
(£ million, 1980 prices)

	1980	1981	1982	1983	1984	1985
GDP(1), expenditure basis	199,136	196,761	199,670	206,042	210,210	217,182
income basis(2)	199,384	217,089	237,716	259,513	279,359	305,076
output basis (1980=100)	100·0	98·3	100·3	103·3	106·4	110·0
average estimate (1980=100)	100·0	98·6	100·6	103·7	106·4	109·9
Components of gross domestic product:						
Consumers' expenditure	136,789	136,429	137,581	143,011	145,074	149,649
General government						
consumption	48,804	48,882	49,240	50,450	50,879	51,180
Gross fixed investment	41,609	37,959	40,470	42,010	45,361	45,932
Total final expenditure	287,591	282,670	288,875	299,450	310,116	320,288
Stockbuilding	−2,909	−2,739	−1,184	673	−142	878
Adjustment to factor cost	30,874	30,312	31,443	32,466	32,854	33,627

(1) At factor cost. (2) Current prices, £ 000 million.

7. Fixed Investment
(£ million, 1980 prices, seasonally adjusted)

	1980	1981	1982	1983	1984	1985
Total, all fixed investment	41,628	38,075	40,645	42,485	45,361	45,590
Dwellings	8,419	7,294	8,147	8,912	8,933	8,371
public	2,519	1,665	1,989	2,044	2,218	1,946
private	5,900	5,629	6,158	6,868	6,715	6,425
Private sectors	29,389	27,796	30,320	30,660	33,585	35,661
manufacturing	7,301	5,773	5,724	5,433	6,372	6,803
other	22,088	22,023	24,596	25,227	27,213	28,858
Government public corporations	12,239	10,279	10,325	11,625	11,776	9,929

8. Personal Income and Expenditure
(£ million, seasonally adjusted, current prices unless otherwise stated)

Wages and salaries	116,305	124,803	133,527	143,506	152,766	165,271
Current grants	25,468	31,137	36,375	39,519	42,795	46,077
Forces' pay	2,436	2,689	2,905	3,121	3,288	3,519
Other personal income(1)	38,717	41,622	46,522	48,844	56,495	58,221
Personal disposable income	161,364	175,897	191,283	204,708	220,829	236,210
Real personal disposable income(2)	161,364	158,078	158,718	161,597	165,438	168,840
Consumers expenditure	136,789	152,125	166,477	182,427	193,889	210,071

(1) From rent, self-employment (before depreciation of stock appreciation provisions), dividend and interest receipts and charitable receipts from companies. (2) At 1980 prices.

9. Government Finance(1)
(£ million)

Revenue(2)	80,758	95,219	112,259	121,665	128,195	138,725
taxes on income	27,023	31,847	38,056	41,843	43,536	48,297
corporation tax	4,646	4,465	4,925	5,564	6,012	8,206
taxes on expenditure	32,165	37,357	44,506	47,029	49,770	52,761
value added tax	8,186	10,968	11,860	13,815	15,218	18,534
taxes on capital(3)	1,024	1,137	1,589	1,401	1,562	1,717
National insurance surcharge	3,015	3,542	3,597	2,831	1,671	924
Expenditure(4)	79,583	96,737	110,208	121,076	130,522	141,801
social services(5)	41,980	51,589	59,758	66,232	70,971	75,910
defence	9,431	11,758	12,966	14,811	15,861	17,166
net lending(6)	2,010	2,971	−40	4,551	3,606	2,849
Deficit(−) or surplus	−6,144	−9,445	−4,924	−7,773	−12,345	−13,283

(1) Financial years ended 5 April of year indicated. (2) Total current receipts, taxes on capital and other capital receipts. (3) Capital gains, capital transfer tax, estate duty. (4) Total government expenditure, gross domestic capital formation and grants. (5) Including expenditure by public authorities other than central government. (6) To private sector, local authorities, public corporations, and overseas.

Overall price index (1980=100)	100·0	110·7	118·3	124·9	130·4	138·3

10. Prices and Costs (index 1980=100)

Total home costs per unit of output(1)	100·0	110·7	118·3	124·9	130·4	138·3
Labour costs per unit of output	100·0	109·6	113·3	117·1	120·1	..
Mfg. wages salaries/unit of output	100·0	109·3	114·7	116·2	120·1	126·3
Import unit values	100·0	107·7	116·8	129·6	139·5	145·0
Wholesale prices, manufactures	100·0	109·5	118·0	124·4	132·0	139·4
Consumer prices	100·0	111·9	121·5	127·1	133·4	141·5
Tax and prices	100·0	114·8	126·1	131·2	136·1	143·2

(1) Used as 'Overall price index' on all pages of UK statistics.

FINANCIAL

11. Banking(1)	1980	1981	1982	1983	1984	1985
(£ million, at end of period)						
Current and deposit accounts	286,328	398,333	510,858	596,164	714,282	..
Advances: to						
local authorities	7,026	10,614	9,212	7,314	6,952	..
public corporations	1,799	2,519	2,543	2,595	2,817	..
financial institutions	9,014	10,334	15,900	19,576	25,752	..
companies	36,076	41,404	45,005	48,735	53,228	..
construction	2,236	2,603	3,491	3,968	4,609	..
personal sector	17,312	25,732	35,854	44,595	49,781	..
overseas residents	150,860	225,019	285,614	339,255	406,816	..
Eligible liabilities	67,462	77,651	93,405	111,409	129,972	..

(1) Unless otherwise stated, this table covers all banks in the UK observing the common 12.5 per cent reserve ratio introduced on 16 Sept. 1971 and includes the accepting houses (merchant banks), discount houses, and, for deposits, the National Giro and the banking departments of the Bank of England. Except in the case of overseas advances, inter-bank transactions have been omitted.

12. Interest Rates and Security Yields(1)

(% per annum, end of year)

Treasury bill yield	13·45	15·39	10·20	8·88	9·15	11·17
London clearing banks base rate	14·00	14·50	10·13	9·00	9·63	11·50
2½% consols, gross flat yield(2)	11·86	13·00	11·91	10·24	10·15	10·11
10-year government securities(2)	13·91	14·88	13·09	11·27	11·27	11·06
Ordinary shares, dividend yield(2)	6·32	5·89	5·05	4·58	4·53	4·38
Interbank 3-month deposits	14·81	15·66	10·56	9·38	9·97	11·91
Clearing bank 7-day deposits	11·75	12·38	6·88	5·50	6·25	7·86

(1) Gross redemption yields, unless stated otherwise. For building societies see Table 15. (2) Revised series.

13. Companies

(£ million unless stated)

Total income	40,193	43,918	46,248	56,634	67,244	..
Gross trading profit in UK	32,392	35,504	37,960	44,931	54,744	61,658
Total overseas income	4,640	5,032	5,205	6,511	8,081	..
Dividends on ord. shares	3,260	3,225	3,587	4,458	5,408	..
Net profit	17,502	19,533	20,431	25,675	30,452	..
Companies taken over (number)	469	452	463	447	568	474
Total take-over consideration	1,475	1,144	2,206	2,343	5,475	7,090
Liquidations (number)(1)	6,891	8,596	12,067	13,406	13,721	14,895
Receiverships (number)(1)	4,038	5,151	5,700	7,032	8,229	6,772

(1) England and Wales.

14. The Stock Market

(£ million, unless otherwise stated)

Turnover (£000 mn.)	196·3	190·7	260·0	287·6	364·7	390·5
ordinary shares (£000 mn.)	30·8	32·4	37·4	56·1	73·1	105·6
New issues, less redemptions (value)	773·2	1,970	1,556	3,328	2,338	5,219
Government securities	11,245	7,488	5,909	8,183	8,953	9,232
Local authority issues(1)	−166	−157	−174	−66	−258	−566
UK companies (gross)	933	1,832	1,167	2,812	1,721	5,110
FT ordinary share index (1935=100)(2)	464·5	517·9	574·7	693·0	855·03	1,004·64
FT-Actuaries index (750 shares)(3)	271·32	307·7	341·4	434·7	516·68	631·95
Industrial, 500 shares	285·68	322·16	372·48	471·23	560·52	692·02
Financial, 100 shares	218·81	253·2	254·5	323·1	386·72	475·31

(1) Includes public corporation issues. (2) Average during year. (3) 1962=100.

Overall price index (1980=100)	*100·0*	*110·7*	*118·3*	*124·9*	*130·4*	*138·3*

15. Building Societies

	1980	1981	1982	1983	1984	1985
Interest rates (%):						
Paid on shares, ave. actual	10·34	9·19	8·77	7·26	7·74	..
BSA(1) recommended, end-year(2)	9·25	9·75	6·25	7·25	7·75	7·75
Mortages, ave. charged	14·92	14·00	13·32	11·05	11·84	..
BSA recommended, end-year(2)	14·00	15·00	10·00	11·25	12·50	12·50
Shares and deposits, net (£ min.)	3,816	3,601	6,466	6,839	8,524	7,104
Mortgage advances, net (£ min.)	5,722	6,331	8,147	10,928	14,271	14,319

(1) BSA: Building Societies Association.
(2) Predominant rates from 1984 onwards.

16. Insurance(1)
(£ million)

	1980	1981	1982	1983	1984	1985
Life assurance(1)(2), net premiums	7,593	9,343	10,656	12,910	15,770	..
investment income	4,515	5,177	6,145	6,751	7,877	..
benefits paid to policyholders	4,121	5,132	6,394	7,917	9,555	..
life funds, end-year	46,700	55,000	67,500	80,700	96,900	..
Non-life(1)(2), net premiums	7,787	9,195	11,053	11,999	14,077	..
underwriting profit +(−) loss(3)	−338·8	−610·9	−1,245·9	−1,354	−2,197	..

(1) Companies only; excludes Lloyd's. (2) World-wide business of UK companies and authorized UK affiliates of foreign companies. (3) Including net transfers of marine, aviation and transit branch revenues to/from profit and loss accounts.

17. Money and Savings
(£ million, amounts outstanding at end period, unless otherwise stated)

Money stock M_1(1)	31,230	34,301	38,190	42,680	50,620	59,780
Money stock M_3(2)	75,934	94,830	104,580	114,930	127,790	144,690
Sterling M_3	69,591	83,820	91,670	19,090	108,660	124,920
Notes and coins in circulation	10,411	11,027	11,196	12,119	12,641	12,901
Personal savings ratio (%)(3)	15·3	13·6	13·0	11·6	12·3	11·8
National savings	12,245	18,350	22,027	25,036	27,794	30,648

(1) M_1 = Notes and coins in circulation with the public plus resident private sector sterling current accounts with the banks minus 60 per cent of transit items. (2) M_3 = Notes and coins in circulation plus total deposits of the domestic sector. (3) Personal savings as a percentage of personal disposable income.

Overall price index (1980=100)	*100·0*	*110·7*	*118·3*	*124·9*	*130·4*	*138·3*

PRODUCTION

18. Industrial products and manufactures, output

Crude steel (million tonnes)	11·3	15·3	13·7	14·9	15·2	15·7
Man-made fibres (million tonnes)	0·50	0·40	0·33	0·39	0·38	0·33
Cars ('000)	924	955	888	1,045	909	1,048
Motor vehicles, cars imported ('000)(1)	858	827	898	1,020	1,006	1,076
Commercial vehicles ('000)	389	230	269	244	225	263
Merchant ships(2) completed ('000 gr.t)	431	216	453	540	411	225

(1) Including imported chassis. (2) 100 gross tons and over.

19. Industrial Production	1980	1981	1982	1983	1984	1985
(Index, average 1980=100, seasonally adjusted)						
All industries	100·0	96·5	98·6	101·9	103·2	108·1
Energy and water	100·0	103·9	110·0	115·9	110·0	120·1
Coal and coke	100·0	97·3	93·2	89·5	33·8	67·2
Manufacturing industries	100·0	93·9	94·5	96·9	100·7	103·8
Food, drink and tobacco	100·0	98·2	99·6	101·2	102·1	102·0
Chemicals	100·0	100·2	101·3	108·9	114·9	119·3
Oil processing	100·0	92·9	92·7	95·2	98·5	98·6
Metal manufacture	100·0	106·1	103·5	104·3	108·4	113·0
Engineering and allied	100·0	91·4	92·9	94·6	99·2	104·2
Textiles	100·0	92·7	91·0	94·6	97·9	101·7
Intermediate goods	100·0	99·3	102·7	107·6	106·8	112·3
Consumer goods	100·0	96·4	95·8	98·9	101·7	104·2
Paper, printing, publishing	100·0	95·0	91·6	92·0	96·3	98·7
Construction	100·0	90·0	91·7	95·3	98·6	100·0
Gas, electricity & water	100·0	99·5	98·6	100·7	95·8	106·3

20. Productivity
(Index of output per head 1980=100)

All production industries(1)	100·0	105·6	113·4	122·8	126·2	133·7
Manufacturing	100·0	103·5	109·6	118·0	124·0	128·8
Minerals	100·0	92·3	108·9	119·1	122·4	123·4
Metal manufacture	100·0	135·0	133·0	148·6	162·2	171·5
Engineering	100·0	101·3	108·5	116·0	123·3	130·3
Textiles	100·0	106·5	113·4	124·6	130·2	136·4
Chemicals	100·0	108·3	114·1	129·1	138·8	144·3

(1) Excluding extraction of mineral oil and natural gas.

21. Agriculture
(Production, '000 tonnes, unless otherwise stated)

Wheat	8,470	8,707	10,310	10,800	14,960	..
Barley	10,320	10,227	10,960	9,980	11,070	..
Sugar, refined from UK beet	1,238	1,061	1,213	1,281	1,164	1,288
Beef and veal	1,102	1,058	965	1,038	1,146	1,126
Mutton and lamb	277	263	263	286	283	290
Pork	685	710	730	762	701	731
Milk, disposals (million litres)	15,180	15,085	15,939	16,439	15,734	15,264

22. Energy	1980	1981	1982	1983	1984	1985
Coal, production (mn. tonnes)	130·1	127·4	124·7	119·2	51·2	94·1
Power station consumption (mn. tonnes)	89·5	87·3	80·2	81·6	53·4	73·9
Power stations' demand for oil						
(million tonnes coal equivalent)	11·4	8·84	10·4	7·8	36·4	18·2
Electricity generated ('000 mn. kwh.)	266·2	259·5	255·3	260·5	265·7	279·8
by nuclear plant ('000 mn. kwh.)	33·3	33·8	40·0	45·8	49·4	56·2
Natural gas sent out (mn. therms)	17,066	17,098	16,713	17,202	17,789	19,048
Crude oil output ('000 tonnes)(1)	80,472	89,388	103,080	115,200	126,000	127,200
Oil refinery output (mn. tonnes)(2)	79·2	72·0	70·8	70·9	73·2	72·9

(1) Including natural gas liquids. (2) All fuels and other petroleum products.

LABOUR

23. Employment

(millions of persons, in June each year)	1980	1981	1982	1983	1984	1985
Working population(1)	26·87	26·77	26·80	26·67	27·10	27·52
Employed labour force(2)	25·31	24·32	23·96	23·57	23·97	24·22
Employees: production industries	8·82	7·92	7·51	7·15	7·01	6·91
Manufacturing	6·84	6·09	5·79	5·51	5·42	5·38
Transport and communications(3)	1·51	1·44	1·35	1·31	1·29	1·27
Distributive trades	3·34	3·32	3·12	3·15	3·25	3·33
Professional and scientific	3·77	3·76	3·77	3·76	..	..
Insurance, banking, financial	1·71	1·74	1·75	1·80	1·86	1·93
Public service(3)	1·97	1·90	1·81	1·82	1·81	1·81
Total employees	22·97	21·87	21·47	21·03	21·15	21·28
of whom, females	9·67	9·32	9·26	9·08	9·30	9·51

(1) Including registered unemployed and members of the armed services. (2) Including employers and self-employed. (3) Excludes employees of nationalized industries but includes British Rail and Post Office.

24. Demand for Labour

	1980	1981	1982	1983	1984	1985
Average weekly hours worked, manufacturing industry, men over 21(1)	41·9	42·0	42·0	42·6	42·8	43·0
Manufacturing employees:						
Total overtime hours worked ('000)(2)	11,760	9,370	9,980	10,300	11,600	11,940
Short time, total hours lost ('000)(2)	4,006	4,352	1,769	985	619	396
Unemployed, excl. school-leavers, adult students (monthly ave. '000)(3)	1,561	2,420	2,793,	2,970	3,051	3,163
Percentage of all employees	6·4	10·0	11·7	12·4	12·7	13·1
Unfilled vacancies, end-year ('000)	98·8	107·5	117·6	146·2	153·5	162·1

(1) October. (2) Great Britain. (3) Seasonally adjusted.

25. Industrial Disputes

	1980	1981	1982	1983	1984	1985
Stoppages (number)(1)(2)	1,330	1,338	1,528	1,352	1,206	832
Workers involved ('000)(3)	830	1,499	2,101	573	1,436	598
Work days lost ('000), all inds., services	11,964	4,266	5,313	3,754	27,135	6,363

(1) Excluding protest action of a political nature, and stoppages involving fewer than 10 workers and/or lasting less than one day except where the working days lost exceeded 100. (2) Stoppages beginning in year stated. (3) Directly and indirectly, where stoppages occurred; lay-offs elsewhere in consequence are excluded.

26. Wages and Earnings

	1980	1981	1982	1983	1984	1985
Average earnings index (Jan. 1980=100)						
Whole economy	111·4	125·8	137·6	149·2	158·3	171·7
Manufacturing	109·1	123·6	137·4	149·7	162·8	177·7
Average weekly earnings(1)(2)						
Men						
Manual	111·7	121·9	133·8	143·6	152·7	163·6
Non-manual	141·3	163·1	178·9	194·9	209·0	225·0
All occupations	124·5	140·5	154·5	167·5	178·8	192·4
Women						
Manual	68·0	74·5	80·1	87·9	93·5	101·3
Non-manual	82·7	96·7	104·9	115·1	124·3	133·8
All occupations	78·8	91·4	99·0	108·8	117·2	126·4
Average hours(3)	41·1	40·3	40·2	40·1	40·3	40·4

(1) In all industries and services, full time. (2) April. (3) All industries and services, all occupations, men and women over 18 years.

	1980	1981	1982	1983	1984	1985
Overall price index (1980=100)	100·0	110·7	118·3	124·9	130·4	138·3

TRADE

27. Trade by Areas and Main Trading Partners

(£ million; exports f.o.b.; imports c.i.f.)	1980	1981	1982	1983	1984	1985
All countries: *exports*	47,339	50,698	55,538	60,386	70,511	78,416
All countries: *imports*	49,886	51,169	56,940	66,123	78,705	84,697
E.E.C.: *exports*	20,541	20,940	23,118	26,447	31,568	36,277
E.E.C.: *imports*	20,619	21,718	25,252	30,159	35,204	38,993
Other Western Europe: *exports*	6,750	6,293	6,714	7,603	8,728	9,488
Other Western Europe: *imports*	7,274	7,799	8,347	10,514	13,254	14,375
North America: *exports*	5,310	7,121	8,335	9,342	11,406	13,280
North America: *imports*	7,493	7,587	8,113	9,055	11,055	11,663
Other developed countries: *exports*	2,659	2,928	3,241	3,133	3,684	3,808
Other developed countries: *imports*	3,374	3,677	4,436	5,220	5,589	6,426
Oil exporting countries: *exports*	4,781	5,911	6,447	6,110	5,807	5,960
Oil exporting countries: *imports*	4,270	3,666	3,455	2,830	2,862	2,777
Other developing countries: *exports*	5,847	6,255	6,572	6,671	7,550	7,944
Other developing countries: *imports*	5,686	5,600	5,900	6,761	8,568	8,363
Centrally planned economies: *exports*	1,308	1,124	974	1,116	1,630	1,589
Centrally planned economies: *imports*	1,070	1,015	1,327	1,542	2,042	1,903

28. Terms of Trade

(Index 1980=100)

	1980	1981	1982	1983	1984	1985
Volume of exports(1)	100·0	99·3	101·8	102·2	112·6	119·7
manufactures	100·0	94·0	96·0	93·0	104·4	111·2
Volume of imports(1)	100·0	97·3	101·0	107·8	119·9	124·8
food	100·0	103·0	108·0	108·0	112·3	113·7
fuels	100·0	82·0	74·0	67·0	85·4	83·9
Unit value of exports(1)	100·0	108·0	116·5	126·5	136·0	143·8
manufactures	100·0	107·0	115·0	125·0	134·0	143·0
Unit value of imports(1)	100·0	107·7	116·8	127·7	137·8	142·9
food(2)	100·0	104·0	112·0	120·0	132·0	138·0
fuels(2)	100·0	128·0	146·0	153·0	167·0	171·0
Terms of trade(3)	100·0	101·0	99·7	97·8	97·5	99·2

(1) Seasonally adjusted; Overseas Trade Statistics basis. (2) c.i.f. (3) Export unit value index as percentage of import value index, expressed as an index on the same base.

29. Balance of Payments

(£ million: current transactions seasonally adjusted; remaining data unadjusted)

	1980	1981	1982	1983	1984	1985
Exports (f.o.b.)	47,415	50,997	55,565	60,776	70,367	78·072
Imports (f.o.b.)	46,182	47,325	53,181	61,611	74,758	80,140
Visible balance	+7,233	+3,652	+2,384	−835	−4,391	−2,068
Investment and other capital	−1,450	−7,420	−3,416	−5,254	−5,713	−2,860
Current balance	+2,929	+7,272	+5,551	+3,164	+879	+2,952
Official long-term capital	−91	−336	−347	−380	−327	−310
Overseas investment in						
UK public sector	+589	+188	+393	+700	+323	1,351
UK private sector	+4,654	+3,270	+3,094	+4,383	+3,271	+6,129
UK private investment overseas	−8,204	−10,670	−10,724	−11,596	−15,377	−22,247
Current surplus (+)/deficit(−)	+2,929	+7,272	+5,551	+3,164	+879	+2,952
Overall surplus (+)/deficit(−)	−835	−355	−2,880	−2,090	−4,834	+92
Official reserves, end of year	11,487	12,217	10,508	12,271	13,553	10,753
Foreign liabilities net. do.	5,010	4,381	4,865	5,638	7,362	7,868
Overall price index (1980=100)	*100·0*	*110·7*	*118·3*	*124·9*	*130·4*	*138·3*

B. THE UNITED STATES

30. Population

	1980	1981	1982	1983	1984	1985
Population, mid-year est. (mn)	227·64	229·81	232·06	234·50	236·63	..
Crude birth rate (per 1,000 pop.)	16·2	15·9	15·8	15·5	15·7	..
Crude death rate (per 1,000 pop.)	8·9	8·7	8·7	8·6	8·7	..

31. Gross National Product
('000 million current dollars)

Gross national product	2,633	2,958	3,069	3,305	3,775	3,989
Personal consumption	1,667	1,849	1,985	2,156	2,423	2,582
Gross private domestic investment	402	484	415	472	674	669
Net exports, goods and services	23·9	28·0	19·0	−8·3	−59·2	−78·4
Government purchases	538·4	595·7	650	686	737	815

32. Government Finance
('000 million dollars, seasonally adjusted)

Federal government receipts	540·8	628·2	617·4	641·1	725	785
from personal taxes(1)	257·8	298·1	304·7	295·2	311	351
Federal government expenditure	601·6	688·3	764·4	819·7	898	985
Defence purchases	132·8	153·7	179·4	200·5	237	262
Grants to state/local govts.	88·1	87·7	83·9	86·3	93·7	99·0
Federal surplus or (−) deficit	−61·2	−59·9	−147·1	−178·6	−172·9	−199·3
State and local govt. receipts	384·1	416·8	439·1	478·2	539·8	575·5
from indirect business tax(1)	171·7	192·8	210·0	228·0	254·8	271·4

(1) Includes related non-tax receipts on national income account.

33. Balance of Payments
(millions of dollars)

Merchandise trade balance	−25,544	−28,001	−36,469	−61,055	−114,109	−124,289
Balance on current account(1)	+1,897	+6,292	−9,198	−41,562	−107,361	−117,668
Change (increase) in US private assets abroad(2)	83,382	104,514	107,790	43,281	11,800	..
Change (increase) in foreign private assets in US(2)	68,448	71,333	91,863	76,383	93,895	..

(1) Includes balance on service and remittances and US government grants other than military. (2) Includes reinvested earnings of incorporated affiliates.

34. Merchandise Trade by Main Areas
(million of dollars)

All countries: *exports* (f.o.b.)	220,705	233,740	212,276	200,538	217,888	..
All countries: *imports* (f.o.b.)	241,195	260,982	254,884	258,048	325,726	..
Western Europe: *exports*	66,817	64,724	59,701	55,414	57,486	..
Western Europe: *imports*	46,352	51,430	52,908	53,476	70,626	..
Canada: *exports*	35,395	39,564	39,275	38,244	46,524	..
Canada: *imports*	41,024	45,912	48,473	52,129	66,478	..
Latin America						
exports	36,030	38,950	33,164	22,619	26,302	..
imports	29,916	32,056	38,561	35,683	42,341	..
Japan: exports	20,790	21,823	20,694	21,894	23,575	..
imports	30,866	37,655	37,685	41,183	57,135	..

Dollar purchasing power (1967=100)	*40·6*	*36·7*	*34·6*	*33·9*	*32·1*	*31·0*

35. Merchandise Trade by Main Commodity Groups

(millions of dollars)	1980	1981	1982	1983	1984	1985
Exports:						
Machinery and transport equipt.	84,553	95,717	87,128	82,524	89,973	..
Motor vehicles and parts	14,590	16,214	13,907	14,463	17,548	..
Electrical machinery	10,485	11,468	12,939	11,936	13,855	..
Food and live animals	27,744	30,291	23,952	24,168	24,463	..
Chemicals and pharmaceuticals	20,740	21,187	19,891	19,752	22,336	..
Imports:						
Machinery and transport equipt.	60,546	69,627	73,320	86,208	119,192	..
Motor vehicles and parts	24,134	26,217	29,361	35,034	45,412	..
Food and live animals	15,763	15,238	14,453	15,408	17,973	..
Petroleum and products	73,771	75,577	60,835	52,325	55,906	..
Iron and steel	7,364	7,540	7,269	6,799	11,853	..

36. Interest Rates
(per cent per annum, annual averages, unless otherwise stated)

Federal Funds rate(1)	13·36	16·38	12·26	9·09	10·22	8·10
Treasury bill rate	11·51	14·02	10·61	8·61	9·52	7·49
Government bond yields: 3–5 years	11·51	14·34	12·96	10·63	11·83	9·64
Long-term (10 years or more)	10·81	12·87	12·23	10·84	11·99	10·75
Banks' prime lending rate(2)	15·27	18·87	14·86	10·79	12·04	9·93

(1) Effective rate. (2) Predominant rate charged by commercial banks on short-term loans to large business borrowers with the highest credit rating.

37. Banking, money and credit
('000 million dollars, outstanding at end of year, seasonally adjusted)

Money supply M1 (1)	414·5	440·9	478·5	525·4	544·5	593·8
Money supply M2 (2)	1,656	1,823	1,999	2,196	2,278	2,484
Money supply M3 (3)	1,963	2,188	2,404	2,710	2,848	3,105
Currency	116·2	123·1	132·7	148·0	154·3	165·0
Deposits of commercial banks	1,239·9	1,288·4	1,409·7	1,524·8	1,605·9	..
Advances of commercial banks	915·1	975·0	1,059·4	1,149·3	1,450·8	..
Instalment credit	313·5	333·4	344·8	388·7	468·7	..
Motor vehicle contracts	116·8	125·3	130·2	141·9	173·7	..
Mortgage debt	1,419	1,583	1,654	1,826	1,983	..

(1) Currency plus demand deposits, travellers cheques, other checkable deposits. (2) M1 plus overnight repurchase agreements, eurodollars, money market mutual fund shares, savings and small time deposits. (3) M2 plus large time deposits and term repurchase agreements.

38. Insurance
($ million, unless otherwise stated)

Property-liability, net premiums written	95,600	99,276	104,000	108,400	117,100	142,000
Automobile(1)	39,153	41,143	44,221	47,816	51,285	..
Underwriting gain/(−) loss(2)	−3,334	−6,288	−10,290	−13,322	−21,000	−23,000
Net investment income(3)	11,064	13,249	14,907	15,973	17,300	19,400
Combined net income(3)	7,729	6,961	4,617	2,651	−3,817	..
Annual rate of return (%) (4)	13·1	11·8	8·8	8·3	1·8	..
Life insurance, total assets, end-year	479,210	525,803	525,803	652,904	..	..

(1) Physical damage and liability, private and commercial. (2) After stockholder and policy-holder dividends and premium rebates. (3) Property, casualty. (4) Per cent of net worth.

Dollar purchasing power (1967=100)	*40·6*	*36·7*	*34·6*	*33·9*	*32·1*	*31·0*

39. Companies(1)	*1980*	*1981*	*1982*	*1983*	*1984*	*1985*
('000 million dollars)						
Net profit after taxes	157·8	150·9	115·1	126·5	144·0	..
Cash dividends paid	58·1	65·1	68·7	73·3	78·1	..

(1) Manufacturing corporations, all industries.

40. The Stock Market
(millions of dollars, unless otherwise stated)

Turnover (sales), all exchanges	475,934	490,688	596,670	957,118	959,110	..
New York Stock Exchange	397,670	415,913	514,263	815,113	822,617	..
Securities issued, gross proceeds	154,729	156,447	162,738	206,315	238,952	..
Corporate common stock	16,858	23,552	25,449	44,842	18,510	..
Stock prices (end-year):						
Combined index (500 stocks)(1)	135·76	122·55	140·64	164·93	167·24	211·28
Industrials (30 stocks)(2)	963·99	875·00	1,046·54	1,258·64	1,211·57	1,537·73

(1) Standard and Poor Composite 1941–43=10. (2) Dow-Jones Industrial (Oct. 1928=100).

41. Employment
('000 persons)

Civilian labour force(1)	104,719	108,679	110,204	111,550	113,544	115,460
in non-agricultural industry	93,960	97,032	96,129	97,440	101,685	..
in manufacturing industry	20,363	20,174	18,850	18,677	19,412	..
in agriculture	3,310	3,368	3,692	3,381	3,321	..
unemployed	7,448	8,279	10,716	10,690	8,539	8,312
Industrial stoppages(2) (number)	187	145	96	81	62	..
Workers involved ('000)	795	729	656	909	376	..

(1) Aged 16 years and over. (2) Beginning in the year. Involving 1,000 workers or more.

42. Earnings and Prices

Average weekly earnings per workers						
(current dollars): mining	396·1	437·40	472·72	479·0	503·6	..
contract construction	367·78	395·60	423·46	441·9	456·9	..
manufactuing	288·62	317·60	330·65	354·6	373·6	..
Average weekly hours per worker						
in manufacturing	39·7	39·8	38·9	40·1	40·7	..
Farm prices received (1977=100)	134	138	133	134	142	..
Wholesale prices (1967=100)	246·9	269·9	280·6	285·2	291·2	..
Petroleum products	674·7	805·8	761·3	684·3	665·2	..
Consumer prices (1967=100)	246·8	272·4	289·1	298·3	311·1	322·2
Food	254·6	274·6	285·7	291·9	302·9	309·8
Dollar purchasing power (1967=100)(1)	*40·6*	*36·7*	*34·6*	*33·9*	*32·1*	*31·0*

(1) Based on changes in retail price indexes.

43. Production

Farm production (1977=100)	103	118	117	114	93	..
Industrial production (1967=100)	147·0	151·0	138·6	147·7	163·3	166·9
Manufacturing	146·7	150·4	137·6	148·5	164·8	169·4
Output of main products and manufactures						
Coal (million tons)	829·7	823·8	838·1	784·9	890·1	..
Oil, indigenous (000 barrels/day)	8,597	8,572	8,649	8,656	8,757	..
Oil refinery throughput (000 barrels/day)	13,481	12,470	11,774	11,672	12,055	..
Natural gas (000 barrels/day)	1,573	1,609	1,550	1,564	1,700	..
Electricity generated ('000 mn.kwh)	2,286	2,293	2,241	2,287	2,416	..
Steel, crude (million tonnes)	111·8	120·8	74·6	82·6	92·5	..
Aluminium ('000 tonnes)	5,130	4,948	3,274	3,353	4,099	..
Cotton yarn (000 running bales)	10,826	15,150	11,526	7,500	12,545	..
Man-made fibres (million lbs.)	9,493	9,743	7,892	9,299	9,433	..
Plastics/resins (million lbs.)	37,347	39,867	28,466	30,863	33,872	..
Motor cars, factory sales ('000)	6,400	6,225	5,049	6,739	7,621	..

C. INTERNATIONAL COMPARISONS

	Area '000 sq. km.	Population (millions) mid-year estimate		Gross Domestic Product (1) US $ mins (2)	
44. Population and GDP, Selected countries		1982	1983	1983	1984
Argentina	2,777	29·16	29·63	69,772	..
Australia (3)	7,695	15·17	15·38	156,467	173,510
Belgium	31	9·85	9·86	81,945	78,101
Canada	9,976	24·63	24·89	326,663	336,715
China	9,561	1,000·7	1,015·4	236,344	236,422
Denmark	34	5·12	5·11	56,427	54,634
France	552	54·48	54·73	516,736	490.096
Germany, West (incl. W. Berlin)	248	61·64	61·42	654,565	613,374
India (incl. India-admin. Kashmir)	3,268	717·76	732·26	193,821	..
Irish Republic	69	3·48	3·51	18,070	17,700
Israel (excl. occupied areas)	21	4·02	4·11	25,156	23,752
Italy	301	56·64	56·84	352,846	348,385
Japan	370	118·45	119·26	1,156,277	1,233,214
Kuwait (4)	18	1·560	1·670	21,337	21,707
Netherlands	34	14·31	14·36	132,595	123,059
New Zealand (4)	104	3·16	3·20	23,364	..
Norway	324	4·11	4·13	55,064	54,723
Portugal	92	9·93	10·01	20,668	..
Saudi Arabia	2,150	10·00	10·42	120,320	108,289
South Africa (incl S.W. Africa)	1,221	30·04	30·80	79,085	72,854
Spain	505	37·93	38·23	158,809	161,327
Sweden	450	8·33	8·33	91,998	95,161
Switzerland	41	6·48	6·48	97,137	90,735
Turkey	781	46·31	47·28	50,864	..
USSR	22,402	269·99	..	1,190,090	..
UK	244	56·34	56·38	455,995	426,747
USA	9,363	232·35	234·54	3,256,500	3,619,200

(1) Expenditure basis. (2) Converted from national currencies at average exchange rates. (3) Years beginning 1 July. (4) Years beginning 1 April.

45. World Production

(Index 1980=100)	1980	1981	1982	1983	1984	1985
Food(1)	100·0	104·0	106·0	106·4	111·8	..
Industrial production(2)	100·0	99·8	97·0	99·9	105·6	..
OECD	100·0	100·2	96·3	99·5	106·9	110·4
EEC(3)	100·0	97·8	96·2	96·9	99·9	103·4
France	100·0	99·0	97·0	98·0	99·4	100·1
Germany, West	100·0	98·5	95·6	96·3	100·0	105·0
Italy	100·0	98·4	95·4	92·3	95·4	96·5
UK	100·0	96·5	98·6	101·9	103·2	108·2
Japan	100·0	101·0	101·4	105·0	116·5	121·8
Sweden	100·0	98·0	97·0	103·0	109·0	111·0
USSR	100·0	104·0	107·2	111·3	115·7	..

(1) Excluding China. (2) Excluding China, N. Korea, Vietnam, Albania. (3) Community of Ten.

46. World Trade(1)
(millions of US dollars. Exports f.o.b.,
imports c.i.f.)

	1980	1981	1982	1983	1984	1985
World(1): exports	1,868,500	1,836,300	1,708,900	1,663,600	1,768,200	..
World(1): imports	1,923,200	1,910,600	1,779,800	1,737,700	1,842,900	..
Industrial Countries: exports	1,243·9	1,218,800	1,155,500	1,139,400	1,214,600	1,255,900
Industrial Countries: imports	1,369·1	1,297,100	1,219,900	1,200,300	1,309,200	1,360,200
USA: exports	220,706	233,739	212,276	200,538	217,890	213,144
USA: imports	252,997	273,352	254,884	269,878	341,179	361,627
Germany, West: exports	192,861	176,091	176,435	169,440	171,729	183,913
Germany, West: imports	188,002	163,912	155,370	152,940	153,007	158,490
Japan: exports	130,435	151,495	138,403	146,963	169,753	177,139
Japan: imports	141,291	142,866	131,516	126,518	136,148	130,505
France: exports	116,016	106,425	96,688	94,943	97,566	101,674
France: imports	134,874	120,953	115,708	105,416	103,726	107,768
UK: exports	110,095	103,164	96,982	91,430	93,772	..
UK: imports	115,808	101,879	99,646	100,183	104,863	..
Other Europe: exports	43,640	46,570	45,590	45,880	48,210	..
Other Europe: imports	68,790	68,360	63,920	60,190	59,360	..
Australia, NZ, S. Afr: exports	53,132	48,241	45,232	44,595	46,939	..
Australia, NZ, S. Afr: imports	47,200	54,573	50,992	42,498	48,356	..
Less Developed Areas: exports	346,640	324,230	315,170	322,110	353,230	..
Less Developed Areas: imports	377,069	429,930	386,030	371,690	384,210	..
Oil exporters: exports	293,530	271,870	216,030	175,660	170,510	..
Oil exporters: imports	133,380	160,980	154,130	141,680	128,590	..
Saudi Arabia: exports	102,503	133,328	75,838	47,816	46,857	..
Saudi Arabia: imports	30,171	35,268	40,653	39,197	33,696	..
Other W. Hemisphere: exports	85,720	89,550	86,360	82,530	79,983	..
Other W. Hemisphere: imports	107,680	109,040	83,260	67,430	63,783	..
Other Middle East(2): exports	15,980	17,840	16,040	15,130	13,417	..
Other Middle East(2): imports	29,520	39,240	35,420	35,440	37,886	..
Other Asia: exports	120,320	129,740	127,100	137,030	158,038	..
Other Asia: imports	150,420	164,080	152,330	162,010	178,448	..
Other Africa: exports	52,460	46,950	35,351	35,666	33,760	..
Other Africa: imports	54,990	58,997	50,148	45,295	44,630	..

(1) Excluding trade of centrally planned countries (see Table 47). (2) Including Egypt.
(3) Unweighted average of IMF series for US$ import and export prices in developed countries.

World trade prices (1980=100)(3)	100·0	97·2	92·6	88·6	87·2	..

47. World Trade of Centrally Planned Countries
(millions of US dollars)

European(1): exports	157,338	159,381	169,953	175,182	178,926	..
European(1): imports	154,354	155,579	154,286	158,571	162,023	..
USSR: exports	76,450	78,999	86,949	91,330	91,649	..
USSR: imports	68,523	72,960	77,793	80,267	80,624	..
China: exports	18,255	21,561	21,912	22,157	24,236	..
China: imports	19,530	21,565	18,939	21,320	25,454	..
Total: exports	176,873	182,776	193,823	199,161	205,647	..
Total: imports	176,914	180,297	177,108	183,618	191,785	..

(1) Except Yugoslavia and Albania.

48. Prices of Selected Commodities
(Index 1980=100)

	1980	1981	1982	1983	1984	1985
Aluminium (Canada)	100·0	71·1	55·9	81·0	70·5	58·6
Beef, Irish (London)	100·0	99·1	95·9	81·3	69·0	63·8
Copper, wirebars (London)	100·0	79·4	67·6	72·7	63·0	64·9
Cotton, Egyptian (L'pool)	100·0	99·0	81·4	91·2	106·7	106·8
Gold (London)	100·0	75·6	61·8	69·5	59·3	52·2
Newsprint, S. Quebec	100·0	117·2	122·1	113·6	119·6	..
Petroleum, Ras Tanura	100·0	113·4	116·8	102·2	99·3	..
Rice, Thai (Bangkok)	100·0	111·3	67·6	63·8	58·2	50·1
Rubber, Malay (Singapore)	100·0	77·6	61·6	74·2	66·7	53·3
Steel bars (W. Germany)	100·0	99·8	115·1	98·8	117·5	..
Soya beans, US (R'dam)	100·0	97·0	82·4	95·1	95·2	75·8
Sugar, f.o.b. (Caribbean)	100·0	59·1	29·4	29·5	18·1	14·1
Tin, spot (London)	100·0	84·5	76·1	77·3	72·8	..
Wheat (Canada No. 2 CW)	100·0	105·5	95·8	93·9	88·2	78·6
Wool, greasy (Sydney)	100·0	108·6	101·2	89·2	93·2	..

49. Consumer Prices, Selected Countries
(Index 1980=100)

	1980	1981	1982	1983	1984	1985
Argentina	100·0	204·5	541·4	2,403	17,462	134,842
Australia	100·0	109·7	121·9	134·2	139·6	..
France	100·0	113·3	127·1	138·9	149·3	158·0
Germany, West	100·0	105·9	111·5	115·6	118·4	121·0
India	100·0	113·0	121·9	136·5	148·1	..
Japan	100·0	104·9	107·7	109·6	112·0	114·4
South Africa	100·0	115·2	132·1	148·3	165·5	..
Sweden	100·0	112·1	121·7	132·5	143·2	153·8
UK	100·0	111·9	121·5	127·1	133·4	141·5
US	100·0	110·4	117·4	120·8	126·1	130·5
World trade prices (1980=100)	*100·0*	*97·2*	*92·6*	*88·6*	*87·2*	*..*

50. Industrial Ordinary Share Prices
(Index 1980=100)

	1980	1981	1982	1983	1984	1985
Amsterdam	100	106	107	154	197	255
Australia, all exchanges	100·0	104	79	100	117	144
Canada, all exchanges	100	97	78	110	108	..
Germany, West, all exchanges	100	101	99	132	150	200
Hong Kong (31 July 1968=100)(1)	1,580	1,406	784	867	1,200	1,752
Johannesburg	100	99	86	109	107	115
New York	100	107	99	134	135	155
Paris	100	88	75	101	136	..
Tokyo	100	116	116	136	172	..
UK	100	113	131	165	196	242

(1) Hang Seng index for Hong Kong Stock Exchange only: last trading day of year.

51. Central Bank Discount Rates
(per cent per annum, end of year)

	1980	1981	1982	1983	1984	1985
Canada	17·26	14·66	10·05	9·96	10·16	9·49
France	9·50	9·50	9·50	9·50	9·50	..
Germany, West	7·50	7·50	5·00	4·00	4·50	4·00
Italy	16·50	19·00	18·00	17·00	16·50	..
Japan	7·25	5·50	5·50	5·00	5·00	5·00
Sweden	10·00	11·00	10·00	8·50	9·50	10·50
Switzerland	3·00	6·00	4·50	4·00	4·00	4·00
UK	14·00	14·50	10·13	9·00	9·63	11·50
USA (Federal Reserve Bank of N.Y.)	13·00	12·00	8·50	8·50	8·00	7·50

52. Exchange Rates   *Currency units per US dollar*   *per £*
(Middle rates at end of year)

	1981	1982	1983	1984	1985	1985
Australia (Australian dollar)	0·8866	1·0198	1·1142	1·2115	1·4655	2·1200
Belgium-Luxembourg (franc)	38·46	46·92	56·15	63·25	50·05	72·35
Canada (Canadian dollar)	1·1859	1·2294	1·243	1·397	1·398	2·021
China (yuan)(1)	1·75	1·92	1·9889	2·7902	3·2015	4·6298
France (franc)	5·748	6·725	8·422	9·6450	7·50	10·84
Germany W. (Deutschmark)	2·255	2·419	2·753	3·144	2·445	3·535
Italy (lire)	1,200	1,370	1,670	1,935	1,670	2,415
Japan (yen)	219·90	235·0	233·7	251·6	200·2	289·5
Netherlands (guilder)	2·469	2·625	3·091	3·557	2·758	3·99
Portugal (escudo)	65·25	89·06	132·85	169·75	157·75	228
South Africa (rand)	0·9566	1·0737	1·2191	1·9880	2·5810	3·7305
Spain (peseta)	97·45	125·6	157·8	173·30	153·1	221·2
Sweden (krona)	5·571	7·295	8·051	8·980	7·580	10·957
Switzerland (franc)	1·796	1·995	2·188	2·5865	2·0600	2·9800
USSR (rouble)(1)	0·753	0·717	0·7926	0·8585	0·7642	1·0958
UK (£)(2)	1·908	1·615	1·434	1·1590	1·4455	..

(1) Official fixed or basic parity rate. (2) US dollars per £.

53. Defence Expenditure

Expenditure or budget (US $ mn.)

	1981	1982	1983	1984	$ per capita 1984	% of GNP 1984
France	23,545	21,969	21,381	20,113	365	4·1
Germany, East	6,960	8,108	8,685	7,710	459	7·7
Germany, West (incl. W. Berlin)	29,047	28,453	22,204	20,430	334	3·3
Greece	2,273	2,574	2,416	2,204	214	6·7
Iran	4,402	13,000	17,370	20,162	469	16·4
Israel	6,056	8,242	4,981	5,798	1,348	24·8
Japan	10,453	10,361	11,617	12,018	99	1·0
Saudi Arabia	24,417	27,022	21,952	22,687	2,062	20·9
South Africa	2,760	2,769	2,700	2,434	84	3·8
Sweden	3,431	2,840	2,800	2,676	321	3·0
Turkey	2,632	2,755	2,469	2,190	44	4·5
USSR(1)	17·05	17·05	17·05	17·05	..	..
UK	24,223	24,200	24,472	21,995	393	5·5
USA	176,100	215,900	245,043	265,160	1,107	7·3

(1) Official budget Roubles bn.

54. Employment and Unemployment

Civilian Employment ('000)	1980	1981	1982	1983	1984	1985
USA	99,303	100,397	99,525	100,169	105,005	..
Japan	55,360	55,810	56,380	57,294	57,660	..
W. Germany	25,745	25,548	25,066	24,592	25,947	..
France	21,127	20,959	20,984	20,839	21,361	..
UK	24,865	23,989	23,663	23,470	23,269	..
EEC, Employment by Sectors (%)						
Agriculture	7·8	7·7	7·4	7·4	7·3	..
Industry	37·2	36·2	35·4	34·6	33·8	..
Services	55·0	56·1	57·1	58·0	58·9	..
Unemployment (%)						
OECD	5·7	6·7	8·2	8·7	8·2	8·1
EEC	5·9	7·8	9·1	10·1	10·7	10·8
USA	7·0	7·5	9·5	9·4	7·4	7·1
Japan	2·0	2·2	2·4	2·6	2·7	2·6
UK	6·9	11·0	12·4	13·1	13·2	13·2

XIX DOCUMENTS AND REFERENCE

THE REAGAN-GORBACHEV SUMMIT

Text of the joint US-Soviet statement issued on 21 November 1985 after the meeting of the two leaders at Geneva.

These comprehensive discussions covered the basic questions of US-Soviet relations and the current international situation. The meetings were frank and useful. Serious differences remain on a number of critical issues.

While acknowledging the differences in their systems and approaches to international issues, some greater understanding of each side's view was achieved by the two leaders. They agreed about the need to improve US-Soviet relations and the international situation as a whole.

In this connection the two sides have confirmed the importance of an ongoing dialogue, reflecting their strong desire to seek common ground on existing problems.

They agreed to meet again in the nearest future. The General Secretary accepted an invitation by the President of the United States to visit the United States of America and the President of the United States accepted an invitation by the General Secretary of the Central Committee of the CPSU to visit the Soviet Union. Arrangements for and timing of the visits will be agreed upon through diplomatic channels.

In their meetings, agreement was reached on a number of specific issues. Areas of agreement are registered on the following pages.

Security

The sides, having discussed key security issues, and conscious of the special responsibility of the USSR and the US for maintaining peace, have agreed that a nuclear war cannot be won and must never be fought. Recognizing that any conflict between the USSR and US could have catastrophic consequences, they emphasized the importance of preventing any war between them, whether nuclear or conventional. They will not seek to achieve military superiority.

Nuclear and space talks

The President and the General Secretary discussed the negotiations on nuclear and space arms.

They agreed to accelerate the work at these negotiations, with a view to accomplishing the tasks set down in the joint US-Soviet agreement of January 8, 1985, namely to prevent an arms race in space and to terminate it on earth, to limit and reduce nuclear arms and enhance strategic stability.

Noting the proposals recently tabled by the US and the Soviet Union, they called for early progress, in particular in areas where there is common ground, including the principle of 50 per cent reductions in the nuclear arms of the US and the USSR appropriately applied, as well as the idea of an interim INF agreement.

During the negotiations of these agreements, effective measures for verification of compliance with obligations assumed will be agreed upon.

Risk reduction centres

The sides agreed to study the question at the expert level of centres to reduce nuclear risk, taking into account the issues and developments in the Geneva negotiations. They took satisfaction in such recent steps in this direction as the modernization of the Soviet-US hotline.

Nuclear non-proliferation

General Secretary Gorbachev and President Reagan reaffirmed the commitment of the USSR and the US to the Treaty on the Non-Proliferation of Nuclear Weapons and their interest in strengthening together with other countries the non-proliferation regime, and in further enhancing the effectiveness of the treaty, *inter alia* by enlarging its membership.

They note with satisfaction the overall positive results of the recent review conference of the Treaty.

The USSR and the US reaffirm their commitment, assumed by them under the Treaty on the Non-Proliferation of Nuclear Weapons, to pursue negotiations in good faith on matters of nuclear arms limitation and disarmament in accordance with Article Six of the Treaty.

The two sides plan to continue to promote the strengthening of the International Atomic Energy

Agency and to support the activities of the agency in implementing safeguards as well as in promoting the peaceful uses of nuclear energy.

They view positively the practice of regular Soviet-US consultations on non-proliferation of nuclear weapons which have been businesslike and constructive and express their intent to continue this practice in the future.

Chemical weapons

In the context of discussing security problems, the two sides reaffirmed that they are in favour of a general and complete prohibition of chemical weapons and the destruction of existing stockpiles of such weapons. They agreed to accelerate efforts to conclude an effective and verifiable international convention on this matter.

The two sides agreed to intensify bilateral discussions on the level of experts on all aspects of such a chemical weapons ban, including the question of verification. They agreed to initiate a dialogue on preventing the proliferation of chemical weapons.

MBFR

The two sides emphasized the importance they attach to the Vienna (MBFR) negotiations and expressed their willingness to work for positive results.

CDE

Attaching great importance to the Stockholm Conference on Confidence and Security Building Measures and Disarmament in Europe (CDE) and noting the progress made there, the two sides stated their intention to facilitate, together with the other participating states, an early and successful completion of the work of the conference. To this end, they reaffirmed the need for a document which would include mutually acceptable confidence and security building measures and give concrete expression and effect to the principle of non-use of force.

Process of Dialogue

President Reagan and General Secretary Gorbachev agreed on the need to place on a regular basis and intensify dialogue at various levels. Along with meetings between the leaders of the two countries, this envisages regular meetings between the USSR Minister of Foreign Affairs and the US Secretary of State, as well as between the heads of other ministries and agencies. They agree that the recent visits of the heads of ministries and departments in such fields as agriculture, housing and protection of the environment have been useful.

Recognizing that exchanges of views on regional issues on the expert level have proven useful, they agree to continue such exchanges on a regular basis.

The sides intend to expand the programme of bilateral cultural, educational and scientific-technical exchanges, and also to develop trade and economic ties. The President of the United States and the General Secretary of the Central Committee of the CPSU attended the signing of the agreement on contracts and exchanges in scientific, educational and cultural fields.

They agreed on the importance of resolving humanitarian cases in the spirit of cooperation.

They believe that there should be greater understanding among our peoples and that to this end they will encourage greater travel and people-to-people contact.

Northern Pacific air safety

The two leaders also noted with satisfaction that, in cooperation with the Government of Japan, the United States and the Soviet Union have agreed to a set of measures to promote safety on air routes in the north Pacific and have worked out steps to implement them.

Civil aviation, consulates

They acknowledged that delegations from the United States and the Soviet Union have begun negotiations aimed at resumption of air services. The two leaders expressed their desire to reach a mutually beneficial agreement at an early date. In this regard, an agreement was reached on the simultaneous opening of consulates-general in New York and Kiev.

Environmental protection

Both sides agreed to contribute to the preservation of the environment—a global task—through joint research and practical measures. In accordance with the existing US-Soviet agreement in this area, consultations will be held next year in Moscow and Washington on specific programmes of cooperation.

Exchange initiatives

The two leaders agreed on the utility of broadening exchanges and contacts including some of their new forms in a number of scientific, educational, medical and sports fields (*inter alia*, cooperation in the development of educational exchanges and software for elementary and secondary school instruction; measures to promote Russian language studies in the United States and English language studies in the USSR; the annual exchange of professors to conduct special courses in history, culture and economics at the relevant departments of Soviet and American institutions of higher education; mutual allocation of scholarships for the best students in the natural sciences, technology, social sciences, and humanities for the period of an academic year; holding regular meets in various sports and increased television coverage of sports events). The two sides agreed to resume cooperation in combating cancer diseases.

The relevant agencies in each of the countries are being instructed to develop specific programmes for these exchanges. The resulting programmes will be reviewed by the leaders at their next meeting.

Fusion research

The two leaders emphasized the potential importance of the work aimed at utilizing controlled thermonuclear fusion for peaceful purposes and, in this connection, advocated the widest practicable development of international cooperation in obtaining this source of energy, which is essentially inexhaustible, for the benefit for all mankind.

THE STRATEGIC DEFENSE INITIATIVE

1. PRESIDENT REAGAN'S ADVOCACY

Text of his foreword to an explanatory document issued by the White House on 3 January 1985

Since the advent of nuclear weapons, every President has sought to minimize the risk of nuclear destruction by maintaining effective forces to deter aggression and by pursuing complementary arms control agreements. This approach has worked. We and our allies have succeeded in preventing nuclear war while protecting Western security for nearly four decades.

Originally, we relied on balanced defensive and offensive forces to deter. But over the last 20 years, the United States has nearly abandoned efforts to develop and deploy defenses against nuclear weapons, relying instead almost exclusively on the threat of nuclear retaliation. We accepted the notion that if both we and the Soviet Union were able to retaliate with devastating power even after absorbing a first strike, that stable deterrence would endure. That rather novel concept seemed at the time to be sensible for two reasons. First, the Soviets stated that they believed that both sides should have roughly equal forces and neither side should seek to alter the balance to gain unilateral advantage. Second, there did not seem to be any alternative. The state of the art did not permit an effective defensive system.

Today both of these basic assumptions are being called into question. The pace of the Soviet offensive and defensive build-up has upset the balance in the areas of greatest importance during crises. Furthermore, new technologies are now at hand which may make possible a truly effective non-nuclear defense.

For these reasons and because of the awesome destructive potential of nuclear weapons, we must seek another means of deterring war. It is both militarily and morally necessary. Certainly, there should be a better way to strengthen peace and stability, a way to move away from a future that relies so heavily on the prospect of rapid and massive nuclear retaliation and toward greater reliance on defensive systems which threaten no one.

On 23 March 1983 I announced my decision to take an important first step towards this goal by directing the establishment of a comprehensive and intensive research program, the Strategic Defense Initiative (SDI), aimed at eventually eliminating the threat posed by nuclear-armed ballistic missiles.

The SDI is a program of vigorous research, focused on advanced defensive technologies with the aim of finding ways to provide a better basis for deterring aggression, strengthening stability, and increasing the security of the US and our allies. The SDI research program will provide to a future President and a future Congress the technical knowledge required to support a decision on whether to develop and later deploy advanced defensive systems.

At the same time, the United States is committed to the negotiation of equal and verifiable agreements which bring real reductions in the power of the nuclear arsenals of both sides. . . . Our research under the SDI complements our arms reduction efforts and helps to pave the way for creating a more stable and secure world. The research that we are undertaking is consistent with all of our treaty obligations, including the 1972 Anti-Ballistic Missile (ABM) Treaty.

In the near term, the SDI research program also responds to the on-going and extensive Soviet ABM effort, which includes actual deployments. It provides a powerful deterrent to any Soviet decision to expand its ballistic missile defense capability beyond that permitted by the ABM Treaty. And, in the long-term, we have confidence that SDI will be a crucial means by which both the US and the Soviet Union can safely agree to very deep reductions, and eventually even the elimination of ballistic missiles and the nuclear weapons they carry.

Our vital interests and those of our allies are inextricably linked. Their safety and ours are one. They, too, rely upon our nuclear forces to deter attack against them. Therefore, as we pursue the promise offered by the SDI, we will continue to work closely with our friends and allies. We will ensure that, in the event of a future decision to develop and deploy defensive systems—a decision in which consultation with our allies will play an important part—allied, as well as US, security against aggression would be enhanced.

Through the SDI research program, I have called upon the great scientific talents of our country to turn to the cause of strengthening world peace by rendering ballistic missiles impotent and obsolete. In short, I propose to channel our technological prowess towards building a more secure and stable world. And I want to emphasize that in carrying out this research program, the United States seeks neither military superiority nor political advantage. Our only purpose is to search for ways to reduce the danger of nuclear war.

2. A BRITISH VIEW

Extracts from a lecture given at the Royal United Services Institute of Defence Studies, London, on 15 March 1985 by the Rt.Hon. Sir Geoffrey Howe, QC, MP, Secretary of State for Foreign and Commonwealth Affairs. (Reproduced by courtesy of the RUSI).

Forty years ago, the nature of warfare between major powers was irrevocably altered. The extent of this revolutionary shift in international affairs has taken a long time to sink in. It was Einstein himself who said: 'After the dawn of the nuclear age, everything changed except our way of thinking.' Gradually we have learned to think differently; to realise as Bernard Brodie once put it, that: 'Thus far the chief purpose of a military establishment has been to win wars. From now on, its chief purpose must be to avert them'. Here is the core of the paradox of deterrence. . . .

President Reagan, in the historic address which launched the Strategic Defense Initiative almost two years ago, spoke of his vision that new technology might make it possible to create comprehensive defences against nuclear attack. These could render ballistic weapons 'impotent and obsolete'; they could free the people of the world once and for all from the threat of nuclear annihilation.

From the start, such a vision was always recognised as subject to uncertainty. As the President himself said in March 1983, 'It will take years, probably decades of effort on many fronts. There will be failures and setbacks just as there will successes and breakthroughs.' Nonetheless, the President's vision has already made a decisive impact in several respects. It has focused interest on military activities in space, and on new weapons systems which might theoretically be deployed or aimed there. It has also drawn to public notice the very considerable research under way in the Soviet Union on a range of potential defensive measures. To ignore or to dismiss what is happening in the Soviet Union would be not only myopic; it would be dangerous.

To use terms such as 'Star Wars' about either US or Soviet intentions is to distort the very real problems and their potential solutions. Equally, in Soviet calls for the 'demilitarisation of space' I see more propaganda than substance. Activities in space with military relevance are not by definition evil. It is neither feasible nor desirable to try to preclude all of them. At all times we must keep in mind the key question: will new developments enhance or undercut deterrence?

At present, space is used by a limited number of military systems, on both sides. First, communications and surveillance satellites, which add significantly to the effectiveness and creditability of Western defences, and thus to their deterrent effect. Second, reusable launchers. These pack-horses of the space age are equally valuable. Nor by their nature do they pose a real threat of aggression; the shuttle is too limited, too costly and too vulnerable a platform for that purpose. Third, there is the potential use of space for the delivery of nuclear warheads by ballistic missiles. We must seek to ensure that this will always remain an unrealised potential. Lastly, we face the problem of anti-satellite systems. The US intention to balance the established Soviet capability in this field is logical and prudent.

On the other hand, we must recognise the heavy Western dependence upon the existing utilisation of space technology and particularly upon satellites for intelligence purposes. The prospect, at a time of crisis, of either side being faced with the loss of its strategic eyes and ears would be gravely destabilising. It could provoke a new and even more threatening stage in any East-West confrontation. The West must therefore strive to make its satellites less vulnerable. But there may equally be good grounds for negotiating some constraints upon elements of anti-satellite activity. One other factor must be recognised: the linkage between the development of anti-satellite capabilities and the potential development of defences against ballistic missiles. . . .

In the case of anti-satellite systems, the future is now. The Soviet Union has already deployed such a system at low altitude, and the United States is in the middle of a successful testing programme. By contrast, any development beyond the research stage of defences against ballistic missiles is, in the Prime Minister's words, 'many, many years away'. If negotiations were to succeed in imposing mutual constraints on anti-satellite systems, these could have a helpful impact over a period of years. We should take that opportunity now, if it is in the Western interest. Any such ASAT Agreement could be limited if necessary to a fixed period, in order not to prejudge the future.

President Reagan's Strategic Defense Initiative, as US spokesmen have made clear, is a research programme, conducted in full conformity with the limits of the ABM Treaty. As the US Administration themselves recognise, the programme is geared to a concept which may in the end prove elusive.

Treaty obligations specifically allow for research to continue into defensive systems. Evidently, it is pointless to try to impose constraints which cannot be verified. Most activities in laboratories or research institutes come into that category. An equally important point is that a balance must always be maintained between US and Soviet capabilities, in research as in other aspects. There is a clear need for the US to match the present stage in Soviet programmes. It is for this reason that the Prime Minister has repeatedly expressed our firm conviction that US research should go ahead.

But what should happen if and when decisions are required on moving from the research to the development stage? . . . Can we afford even now simply to wait for the scientists and military experts to deliver their results? Have we a breathing-space of five, ten, 15 years before we need to address strategic concerns? I do not believe so. History shows only too clearly that research into new weapons and study of their strategic implications must go hand in hand. Otherwise, research may acquire an unstoppable momentum of its own, even though the case for stopping may strengthen with the passage of years. . . .

There would inevitably be risks in a radical alteration of the present basis for Western security. How far would these risks be offset by the attractions of adopting a more defensive posture? In other words, we must make sure we are not developing what might prove to be only a limited defence against weapons of devastating destructive force. Could the process of moving towards a greater emphasis on active defences be managed without generating dangerous uncertainty?

Let us assume that limited defences began to prove possible, and key installations began to be protected by active defences. In his 1983 address President Reagan himself acknowledged that a mix of offensive and defensive systems could be 'viewed as fostering an aggressive policy'. Uncertainty apart, would the establishment of limited defences increase the threat to civilian populations by stimulating a return to the targetting policies of the 1950s? Most fundamental of all, would the supposed technology actually work? And would it, as Mr Paul Nitze has noted, provide defences that not only worked but were survivable and cost-effective?

There would be no advantage in creating a new Maginot Line of the twenty-first century, liable to be outflanked by relatively simpler and demonstrably cheaper counter-measures. If the technology does work, what will be its psychological impact on the other side? . . .

What are the chances that there would be no outright winner in the everlasting marathon of the arms race? And if the ballistic missile indeed showed signs of becoming, in President Reagan's words, impotent and obsolete, how would protection be extended against the non-ballistic nuclear threat, the threat posed by aircraft or Cruise missiles, battlefield nuclear weapons or, in the last resort, by covert action? What other defences, in addition to space-based systems, would need to be developed, and at what cost, to meet those continuing threats? If it initially proved feasible to construct only limited defences, these would be bound to be more vulnerable than comprehensive systems to counter-measures. Would these holes in the dyke produce and even encourage a nuclear flood?

Leaving aside the threat to civilian populations, would active defences provide the only feasible way of protecting key military installations? Might we be better advised to employ other methods of protection, such as more mobile and under-sea forces? Finally, could we be certain that the new systems would permit adequate political control over both nuclear weapons and defensive systems, or might we find ourselves in a situation where the peace of the world rested solely upon computers and automatic decision-making?

Then there is the question of cost. The financial burden of developing and deploying defences goes far beyond the additional cost of providing defences against the non-ballistic missile threat. It is fair to assume that it will run into many hundreds of billions of dollars. We shall have to ask ourselves not only whether the West can afford active defences against nuclear missiles but also whether the enormous funds to be devoted to such systems might be better employed to improve our capability to oppose a potential aggressor at a time of crisis with a credible, sustainable and controllable mix of conventional and nuclear forces.

The implications for arms control must also be carefully considered. Would the prospect of new defences being deployed inexorably crank up the levels of offensive nuclear systems designed to overwhelm them? History and the present state of technology suggest that this risk cannot be ignored. Or could the same prospect—the vision of effective defences over the horizon—provide new incentive to both sides to start at once on reducing their present levels?

The ABM Treaty represents a political and military keystone in the still shaky arch of security we have constructed with the East. To go beyond research into defensive systems would be inconsistent with the terms of the ABM Treaty as it stands. It was agreed at Camp David last December that any deployment beyond those limits would have to be a matter for negotiation. We would have to be confident that that formidable task could actually be managed on a mutually acceptable basis. I attach importance to convincing the Soviet leadership that we in the West are indeed serious in our aim of maintaining strategic stability at significantly lower levels of nuclear weapons. We do not want to give them the impression that we have something else in mind.

Finally, as members of the Atlantic Alliance, we must consider the potential consequences for this unique relationship. We must be sure that the US nuclear guarantee to Europe would indeed be enhanced as a result of defensive deployments, not only at the end of the process, but from its very inception. Many years of insecurity and instability cannot be our objective. All the Allies must continue at every stage to share the same sense that the security of Nato territory is indivisible. Otherwise the twin pillars of the Alliance might begin to fall apart. Other things being equal, we welcome any cost-effective enhancement of deterrence to meet palpable weaknesses on the Western side. But we also have to consider what might be the offsetting developments on the Soviet side, if unconstrained competition in ballistic missile defences beyond the ABM Treaty limits were to be provoked. In terms of Nato's policy of forward defence and flexible response, would we lose on the swings whatever might be gained on the roundabouts?

I have posed a lengthy list of questions, to which the answers cannot be simple. Some do not admit of answers now. But that does not acquit us of the duty to pose them. They are questions so vital to our future that we cannot afford to shrug them off. It is right to ponder and debate them as research continues. In this way we stand the best chance of reaching the right policies. The attractions of moving towards a more defensive strategy for the prevention of war are as apparent as are the risks. It would be wrong to rule out the possibility on the grounds that the questions it raises are too difficult. But the fact that there are no easy answers, that the risks may outweigh the benefits, that science may not be able to provide a safer solution to the nuclear dilemma of the past 40 years than we have found already—all these points underline the importance of proceeding with the utmost deliberation.

Deterrence has worked; and it will continue to work. It may be enhanced by active defences. Or their development may set us on a road that diminishes security. We do not know the answer to that question. . . .

The Western democracies face a new challenge and an historic opportunity. The prize is a more stable peace in this trouble world. We must approach the task with due deliberation, retaining as our basic objective deterrence of aggression as the best defence against potential attack. But we must approach it too with real energy and determination. The chance is one we must take great care not to miss.

CHINA'S FOREIGN POLICY

Text of an address by Premier Zhao Ziyang to the Royal Institute of International Affairs, London, on 6 June 1985. (Authorized translation, reproduced by courtesy of the RIIA).

My current visit to Britain at the kind invitation of Prime Minister Margaret Thatcher coincides with an important juncture in the development of Sino-British relations. Not long ago, the Sino-British Joint Declaration on the Question of Hong Kong entered into force upon the exchange of instruments of ratification between the two Governments. With the satisfactory settlement of the question of Hong Kong, a source of possible friction was removed, and the prospect of Sino-British relations became brighter than ever. In order to increase our mutual understanding, I would like to take this opportunity to outline to you China's view on the current international situation and her foreign policy.

The world in which we live is fraught with complicated contradictions and international problems. But in our view, there are mainly two global and strategic issues: the East-West issue, or the issue of peace, and the North-South issue, or the issue of development.

The East-West issue arose from the establishment of the two major military-political blocs after World War II. The two blocs are in direct confrontation in Europe, but their existence affects areas beyond Europe. The key to the East-West relations is the relations between the Soviet Union and the

United States. Relying on their economic and military strength far exceeding that of other countries, the two superpowers are engaged in fierce rivalry in all spheres, causing sustained turbulence in the international situation. The all-round arms race between them is ever escalating, from conventional to nuclear weapons, from land and sea to outer space. This has posed a serious threat to world peace and the security of all nations. In our world today, the United States and the Soviet Union are the only two countries that are capable of fighting a new world war. In this sense, the global issue of peace or war is closely linked with the East-West relations.

Having suffered enough from the scourge of war, the people of all countries crave for peace. They don't want war. They are against fighting a war. On this major issue involving the future of mankind, more and more countries, big countries as well as small and medium-sized, non-aligned as well as aligned countries, are determined to take their destiny into their own hands. They are actively taking all kinds of action in an effort to maintain world peace. These countries and peoples eagerly hope that the East-West relations may be eased, and they strongly demand that the superpowers stop their arms race and carry out genuine disarmament. It can be said that although the danger of war still exists, the forces deterring war and safeguarding peace are also growing steadily. This is an important trend in the world situation today.

The essence of the North-South issue is the widening of economic gap between developing and developed countries. This is attributable to various reasons, an important one being the existence of the outdated international economic order which is unjust and inequitable. The world today has increasingly become a closely linked whole. It is impossible to expect continued economic growth of the developed countries on the basis of the continued poverty of the developing countries. Without the economic growth of those areas inhabited by three-quarters of the world's population, the developed countries will face difficulties in getting resources, markets and outlets of capital, and hence damage to their own economic interests. The logic is obvious. The relations between the developed and developing countries should be equal, mutually beneficial and complementary. The developed countries need the cooperation of the developing countries as badly as the latter need the cooperation of the former. It should be said that the North-South relationship is both an economic and a political issue. The sharpening of the North-South contradictions will not only impede the healthy development of the world economy, but also brew turbulence and confrontational elements. Quite a few developed countries in Western Europe and elsewhere can now appreciate the role of the Third World from the all-over perspective of world politics and economy and value its cooperation. This is a welcome trend in international relations.

Maintenance of world peace and economic development are interrelated and interactive. A peaceful international environment is essential for the development of any country, while expanded international cooperation and the economic prosperity and the development of most countries increase the forces maintaining world peace and stability. A lasting peace, increased friendly cooperation and co-prosperity have a vital bearing on the interests of the people of all countries, and they are becoming the goal of a world-wide effort today.

Being a developing socialist country, China is faced with the arduous task of lifting herself from poverty and backwardness and catching up with the developed countries economically. The Chinese people are determined to modernize their industry, agriculture, national defence, and science and technology through several decades of unremitting efforts so as to make their country affluent. To this end, we need an international environment of lasting peace and the friendship and cooperation of all nations. Proceeding from the fundamental interests of the people of China and the whole world and taking stock of the present international situation, the Chinese Government steadfastly pursues an independent foreign policy of peace.

China will maintain her independence at all times and in all circumstances. China will never attach herself to any big power or group of powers, nor will she yield to any foreign pressure. In international affairs, we decide on our attitudes according to the merits of each case. The basic criterion by which we judge the right or wrong of a case is whether it is in the interest of peace, international friendship and world economic prosperity. We definitely will not enter into alliance or strategic relationship with any big power, that is, not align ourselves with one against another. We will never seek hegemony, and are firmly opposed to all forms of hegemonism. As a big country with a population of one thousand million, China is aware of her responsibility and weight in international affairs. We believe that China's principled position of independence is in the best interest of world peace and stability.

China has sought to develop relations with all countries on the basis of the Five Principles of mutual respect for sovereignty and territorial integrity, mutual non-aggression, non-interference in each other's internal affairs, equality and mutual benefit and peaceful coexistence. Learning from experiences since the end of World War II, we will not let the state of our relationship with other countries be predetermined by the fact whether our social systems and ideologies are similar or not. State relations of different types have emerged since the end of the war, but only those based on the Five Principles of Peaceful Coexistence have a strong vitality and are most conducive to stability and healthy development of the international situation. We earnestly hope that the Five Principles of Peaceful Coexistence will be strictly observed by all countries, particularly by the superpowers. Accordingly, we seek a steady development of the Sino-US relations on the basis of observance of the mutual agreements by both sides. We hope to see the normalization of the Sino-Soviet relations through removal of the existing obstacles. We support the improvement of relations between the countries of Eastern Europe and Western Europe. We also wish to see the relations between the United States and the Soviet Union eased, for all these are in the interest of world peace.

China stands for the pacific settlement of international disputes in the spirit of the Five Principles of Peaceful Coexistence, and is against the use or threat of force. There are a number of disputes in the world today. Whether old ones left over from history, or those which have newly arisen, they face the choice of a way of settlement. The non-peaceful way, or the armed way, cannot eradicate any dispute but will leave long after effects detrimental to world stability. The peaceful way, or the way of negotiation is, in the final analysis, in the interests of the countries concerned and of world peace. We are pleased that the British side shows understanding for China's policy towards Hong Kong, which is formulated in accordance with state sovereignty and the concept of 'one country, two systems' for the settlement of this fairly complicated issue left over from history. Prime Minister Margaret Thatcher's foresight and vision have contributed positively to the success of the negotiations. The Chinese and British Governments have settled the Hong Kong question satisfactorily through negotiations on an equal footing in the spirit of mutual understanding and mutual accommodation, thus providing a new example for the pacific settlement of an international dispute. We believe it should not be difficult to settle disputes rationally through peaceful negotiations so long as the parties concerned sincerely desire a settlement and show mutual respect, mutual understanding and mutual accommodation.

China stands for equality among all countries, big or small, and is against the big bullying the small, the strong humiliating the weak. We firmly support the Kampuchean and Afghan peoples in their struggles against foreign aggression, the Arab people in their struggle against Israeli expansion, the South African people in their struggle against racial discrimination and apartheid, the Namibian people in their struggle for national independence and the Central American people in their struggle against external interference. As for international issues resulting from wilful violation of other countries' sovereignty and seizure of other countries' territories, it is our opinion that their political solution can be sought only on the premise of stopping expansion and aggression and withdrawal from the occupied territories. Failing this premise, the victim country and people can only put up determined resistance to aggression and expansion.

China stands for disarmament and is against all kinds of arms race, whether conventional or nuclear, whether on land or sea or in outer space. We strongly advocate a complete prohibition and thorough elimination of nuclear weapons. We welcome the resumption of the talks on arms control between the United States and the Soviet Union which were suspended for over a year. We sincerely hope that the United States and the Soviet Union, which under UN resolutions bear primary responsibility for nuclear disarmament, will heed the just voice of the people of the world, stop their dangerous arms race, and through serious negotiations reach agreements not prejudicial to the interests of other countries on drastically cutting their nuclear armaments, so as to create the necessary condition for general nuclear disarmament by all the nuclear powers.

China is a developing country belonging to the Third World. Strengthening our unity and cooperation with the other Third World countries is a cornerstone for our diplomatic work. For the sake of promoting world peace and prosperity, we are trying to promote the improvement of North-South relations in the hope of making some headway in breaking the present deadlock in the North-South dialogue created by the unwise attitude taken by individual big powers. We welcome and actively support the Third World countries taking the course of collective self-reliance and strengthening South-South cooperation. We believe that South-South cooperation and North-South cooperation, far from being contradictory, are mutually complementary. We firmly support a restructuring of the irrational old international economic order through global negotiations. The Third World is an important force of peace and an important economic force that is playing an increasing role in promoting international security and cooperation. China will forever stand together with the Third World.

China believes that since maintaining world peace and seeking co-prosperity are major questions concerning the future of the world and the fate of all peoples, every nation and people should have a say and can make their due contribution on them. We are convinced that so long as all peoples steadily develop their friendly cooperation and work together, peace of the world can be maintained and common economic prosperity and development achieved.

Increased all-round friendly cooperation between an independent China and a united and strong Europe has a significance that far exceeds our bilateral relations and is vital for world peace and international cooperation. To steadily strengthen this friendly cooperation, actively develop economic and technological exchanges and trade so as to promote peace and development is an important component of China's foreign policy.

The British people are a great people who have made significant contributions to world civilization and progress. Britain is a country that plays an important role in international affairs. China has always attached importance to Sino-British relations. We expect that in the new historical period of our bilateral relations in the years to come, our two sides will continue our close cooperation, earnestly implementing the Joint Declaration on Hong Kong, and take energetic steps to increase our cooperation in the economic, technological and other fields, so as to make Sino-British relations an example of peaceful coexistence between countries of different social systems, and of mutually beneficial cooperation and co-prosperity between developing and developed countries. We will work together with our British friends to bring about this prospect.

THE ANGLO-IRISH AGREEMENT

Signed by Mrs Margaret Thatcher, Prime Minister of the United Kingdom, and Dr Garret FitzGerald, Taoiseach of the Republic of Ireland, on behalf of their respective Governments, at Hillsborough, Northern Ireland, on 15 November 1985.[1]

The Government of the United Kingdom of Great Britain and Northern Ireland and the Government of the Republic of Ireland;

Wishing further to develop the unique relationship between their peoples and the close cooperation between their countries as friendly neighbours and as partners in the European Community;

Recognising the major interest of both their countries and, above all, of the people of Northern Ireland in diminishing the divisions there and achieving lasting peace and stability;

Recognising the need for continuing efforts to reconcile and to acknowledge the rights of the two major traditions that exist in Ireland, represented on the one hand by those who wish for no change in the present status of Northern Ireland and on the other hand by those who aspire to a sovereign united Ireland achieved by peaceful means and through agreement;

Reaffirming their total rejection of any attempt to promote political objectives by violence or the threat of violence and their determination to work together to ensure that those who adopt or support such methods do not succeed;

Recognising that a condition of genuine reconciliation and dialogue between unionists and nationalists is mutual recognition and acceptance of each other's rights;

Recognising and respecting the identities of the two communities in Northern Ireland, and the right of each to pursue its aspirations by peaceful and constitutional means;

Reaffirming their commitment to a society in Northern Ireland in which all may live in peace, free from discrimination and intolerance, and with the opportunity for both communities to participate fully in the structures and processes of government;

Have accordingly agreed as follows:

A. STATUS OF NORTHERN IRELAND

Article 1

The two Governments

(a) affirm that any change in the status of Northern Ireland would only come about with the consent of the majority of the people of Northern Ireland;

(b) recognise that the present wish of a majority of the people of Northern Ireland is for no change in the status of Northern Ireland;

(c) declare that, if in the future a majority of the people of Northern Ireland clearly wish for and formally consent to the establishment of a united Ireland, they will introduce and support in the respective Parliaments legislation to give effect to that wish.

B. THE INTERGOVERNMENTAL CONFERENCE

Article 2

(a) There is hereby established, within the framework of the Anglo-Irish Intergovernmental Council set up after the meeting between the two heads of Government on 6 November 1981[2], an Intergovernmental Conference (hereinafter referred to as 'the Conference'), concerned with Northern Ireland and

[1] Cmnd. 9657
[2] See AR 1981, pp. 497–500.

with relations between the two parts of the island of Ireland, to deal, as set out in this Agreement, on a regular basis with:

    (i)   political matters;

    (ii) security and related matters;

    (iii) legal matters, including the administration of justice;

    (iv) the promotion of cross-border cooperation.

(b) The United Kingdom Government accept that the Irish Government will put forward views and proposals on matters relating to Northern Ireland within the field of activity of the Conference in so far as those matters are not the responsibility of a devolved administration in Northern Ireland. In the interest of promoting peace and stability, determined efforts shall be made through the Conference to resolve any differences. The Conference will be mainly concerned with Northern Ireland; but some of the matters under consideration will involve cooperative action in both parts of the island of Ireland, and possibly also in Great Britain. Some of the proposals considered in respect of Northern Ireland may also be found to have application by the Irish Government. There is no derogation from the sovereignty of either the United Kingdom Government or the Irish Government, and each retains responsibility for the decisions and administration of government within its own jurisdiction.

Article 3

The Conference shall meet at Ministerial or official level, as required. The business of the Conference will thus receive attention at the highest level. Regular and frequent Ministerial meetings shall be held; and in particular special meetings shall be convened at the request of either side. Officials may meet in subordinate groups. Membership of the Conference and of sub-groups shall be small and flexible. When the Conference meets at Ministerial level the Secretary of State for Northern Ireland and an Irish Minister designated as the Permanent Irish Ministerial Representative shall be joint Chairmen. Within the framework of the Conference other British and Irish Ministers may hold or attend meetings as appropriate: when legal matters are under consideration the Attorneys-General may attend. Ministers may be accompanied by their officials and their professional advisers: for example, when questions of security policy or security cooperation are being discussed, they may be accompanied by the Chief Constable of the Royal Ulster Constabulary and the Commissioner of the Garda Siochana; or when questions of economic or social policy or cooperation are being discussed, they may be accompanied by officials of the relevant Departments. A Secretariat shall be established by the two Governments to service the Conference on a continuing basis in the discharge of its functions as set out in this Agreement.

Article 4

(a) In relation to matters coming within its field of activity, the Conference shall be a framework within which the United Kingdom Government and the Irish Government work together

    (i) for the accommodation of the rights and identities of the two traditions which exist in Northern Ireland; and

    (ii) for peace, stability and prosperity throughout the island of Ireland by promoting reconciliation, respect for human rights, cooperation against terrorism and the development of economic, social and cultural cooperation.

(b) It is the declared policy of the United Kingdom Government that responsibility in respect of certain matters within the powers of the Secretary of State for Northern Ireland should be devolved within Northern Ireland on a basis which would secure widespread acceptance throughout the community. The Irish Government support that policy.

(c) Both Governments recognise that devolution can be achieved only with the cooperation of constitutional representatives within Northern Ireland of both traditions there. The Conference shall be a framework within which the Irish Government may put forward views and proposals on the modalities of bringing about devolution in Northern Ireland, in so far as they relate to the interests of the minority community.

C. POLITICAL MATTERS

Article 5

(a) The Conference shall concern itself with measures to recognise and accommodate the rights and identities of the two traditions in Northern Ireland, to protect human rights and to prevent discrimination. Matters to be considered in this area include measures to foster the cultural heritage of both traditions, changes in electoral arrangements, the use of flags and emblems, the avoidance of economic and social discrimination and the advantages and disadvantages of a Bill of Rights in some form in Northern Ireland.

(b) The discussion of these matters shall be mainly concerned with Northern Ireland, but the possible application of any measures pursuant to this Article by the Irish Government in their jurisdiction shall not be excluded.

(c) If it should prove impossible to achieve and sustain devolution on a basis which secures widespread acceptance in Northern Ireland, the Conference shall be a framework within which the Irish Government may, where the interests of the minority community are significantly or especially affected, put forward views on proposals for major legislation and on major policy issues, which are within the purview of Northern Ireland Departments and which remain the responsibility of the Secretary of State for Northern Ireland.

Article 6

The Conference shall be a framework within which the Irish Government may put forward views and proposals on the role and composition of bodies appointed by the Secretary of State for Northern Ireland or by departments subject to his direction and control including:

the Standing Advisory Commission on Human Rights;

the Fair Employment Agency;

the Equal Opportunities Commission;

the Police Authority for Northern Ireland;

the Police Complaints Board.

D. SECURITY AND RELATED MATTERS

Article 7

(a) The Conference shall consider:

(i) security policy;

(ii) relations between the security forces and the community;

(iii) prisons policy.

(b) The Conference shall consider the security situation at its regular meetings and thus provide an opportunity to address policy issues, serious incidents and forthcoming events.

(c) The two Governments agree that there is a need for a programme of special measures in Northern Ireland to improve relations between the security forces and the community, with the object in particular of making the security forces more readily accepted by the nationalist community. Such a programme shall be developed, for the Conference's consideration, and may include the establishment of local consultative machinery, training in community relations, crime prevention schemes involving the community, improvements in arrangements for handling complaints, and action to increase the proportion of members of the minority in the Royal Ulster Constabulary. Elements of the programme may be considered by the Irish Government suitable for application within their jurisdiction.

(d) The Conference may consider policy issues relating to prisons. Individual cases may be raised as appropriate, so that information can be provided or inquiries instituted.

E. LEGAL MATTERS, INCLUDING THE ADMINISTRATION OF JUSTICE

Article 8

The Conference shall deal with issues of concern to both countries relating to the enforcement of the criminal law. In particular it shall consider whether there are areas of the criminal law applying in the North and in the South respectively which might with benefit be harmonised. The two Governments agree on the importance of public confidence in the administration of justice. The Conference shall seek, with the help of advice from experts as appropriate, measures which would give substantial expression to this aim, considering *inter alia* the possibility of mixed courts in both jurisdictions for the trial of certain offences. The Conference shall also be concerned with policy aspects of extradition and extraterritorial jurisdiction as between North and South.

F. CROSS-BORDER COOPERATION ON SECURITY, ECONOMIC, SOCIAL AND CULTURAL MATTERS

Article 9

(a) With a view to enhancing cross-border cooperation on security matters, the Conference shall set in hand a programme of work to be undertaken by the Chief Constable of the Royal Ulster Constabulary and the Commissioner of the Garda Siochana and, where appropriate, groups of officials in such areas as threat assessments, exchange of information, liaison structures, technical cooperation, training of personnel, and operational resources.

(b) The Conference shall have no operational responsibilities; responsibility for police operations shall remain with the heads of the respective police forces, the Chief Constable of the Royal Ulster Constabulary maintaining his links with the Secretary of State for Northern Ireland and the Commissioner of the Garda Siochana his links with the Minister for Justice.

Article 10

(a) The two Governments shall cooperate to promote the economic and social development of those areas of both parts of Ireland which have suffered most severely from the consequences of the instability of recent years, and shall consider the possibility of securing international support for this work.

(b) If it should prove impossible to achieve and sustain devolution on a basis which secures widespread acceptance in Northern Ireland, the Conference shall be a framework for the promotion of cooperation between the two parts of Ireland concerning cross-border aspects of economic, social and cultural matters in relation to which the Secretary of State for Northern Ireland continues to exercise authority.

(c) If responsibility is devolved in respect of certain matters in the economic, social or cultural areas currently within the responsibility of the Secretary of State for Northern Ireland, machinery will need to be established by the responsible authorities in the North and South for practical cooperation in respect of cross-border aspects of these issues.

G. ARRANGEMENTS FOR REVIEW

Article 11

At the end of three years from signature of this Agreement, or earlier if requested by either Government, the working of the Conference shall be reviewed by the two Governments to see whether any changes in the scope and nature of its activities are desirable.

H. INTERPARLIAMENTARY RELATIONS

Article 12

It will be for Parliamentary decision in Westminster and in Dublin whether to establish an Anglo-Irish Parliamentary body of the kind adumbrated in the Anglo-Irish Studies Report of November 1981.[1] The two Governments agree that they would give support as appropriate to such a body, if it were to be established.

I. FINAL CLAUSE

Article 13

This Agreement shall enter into force on the date on which the two Governments exchange notifications of their acceptance of this Agreement.

THE SOUTH PACIFIC NUCLEAR FREE ZONE TREATY

Adopted by the South Pacific Forum at its meeting in Rarotonga on 6 August 1985, and signed (subject to ratification) on the same day by representatives of the Governments of New Zealand, Australia, Cook Islands, Fiji, Kiribati, Niue, Tuvalu and Western Samoa.

PREAMBLE

The Parties to this Treaty

United in their commitment to a world at peace;

Gravely concerned that the continuing nuclear arms race presents the risk of nuclear war which would have devastating consequences for all people;

Convinced that all countries have an obligation to make every effort to achieve the goal of eliminating nuclear weapons, the terror which they hold for humankind and the threat which they pose to life on earth;

[1]Cmnd. 8414

Believing that regional arms control measures can contribute to global efforts to reverse the nuclear arms race and promote the national security of each country in the region and the common security of all;

Determined to ensure, so far as lies within their power, that the bounty and beauty of the land and sea in their region shall remain the heritage of their peoples and their descendants in perpetuity to be enjoyed by all in peace;

Reaffirming the importance of the Treaty on the Non-Proliferation of Nuclear Weapons (NPT) in preventing the proliferation of nuclear weapons and in contributing to world security;

Noting, in particular, that Article VII of the NPT recognises the right of any group of States to conclude regional treaties in order to assure the total absence of nuclear weapons in their respective territories;

Noting that the prohibitions of emplantation and emplacement of nuclear weapons on the seabed and the ocean floor and in the subsoil thereof contained in the Treaty on the Prohibition of the Emplacement of Nuclear Weapons and Other Weapons of Mass Destruction on the Seabed and the Ocean Floor and in the Subsoil Thereof apply in the South Pacific;

Noting also that the prohibition of testing of nuclear weapons in the atmosphere or under water, including territorial waters or high seas, contained in the Treaty Banning Nuclear Weapon Tests in the Atmosphere, in Outer Space and Under Water applies in the South Pacific;

Determined to keep the region free of environmental pollution by radioactive wastes and other radioactive matter;

Guided by the decision of the Fifteenth South Pacific Forum at Tuvalu that a nuclear free zone should be established in the region at the earliest possible opportunity in accordance with the principles set out in the communique of that meeting;

Have agreed as follows:

Article 1: Usage of terms

For the purposes of this Treaty and its Protocols:
  (a) 'South Pacific Nuclear Free Zone' means the areas described in Annex 1 as illustrated by the map attached to that Annex;
  (b) 'territory' means internal waters, territorial sea and archipelagic waters, the seabed and subsoil beneath, the land territory and the airspace above them;
  (c) 'nuclear explosive device' means any nuclear weapon or other explosive device capable of releasing nuclear energy, irrespective of the purpose for which it could be used. The term includes such a weapon or device in unassembled and partly assembled forms, but does not include the means of transport or delivery of such a weapon or device if separable from and not an indivisible part of it;
  (d) 'stationing' means emplantation, emplacement, transportation on land or inland waters, stockpiling, storage, installation and deployment.

Article 2: Application of the treaty

(1) Except where otherwise specified, this Treaty and its Protocols shall apply to territory within the South Pacific Nuclear Free Zone.

(2) Nothing in this Treaty shall prejudice or in any way affect the rights, or the exercise of the rights, of any State under international law with regard to freedom of the seas.

Article 3: Renunciation of nuclear explosive devices

Each Party undertakes:
  (a) not to manufacture or otherwise acquire, possess or have control over any nuclear explosive device by any means anywhere inside or outside the South Pacific Nuclear Free Zone;
  (b) not to seek or receive any assistance in the manufacture or acquisition of any nuclear explosive device;
  (c) not to take any action to assist or encourage the manufacture or acquisition of any nuclear explosive device by any State.

Article 4: Peaceful nuclear activities

Each Party undertakes:
  (a) not to provide source or special fissionable material, or equipment or material especially designed or prepared for the processing, use or production of special fissionable material for peaceful purposes to:
    (i) any non-nuclear-weapon State unless subject to the safeguards required by Article III.1 of the NPT, or

(ii) any nuclear-weapon State unless subject to applicable safeguards agreements with the International Atomic Energy Agency (IAEA).
Any such provision shall be in accordance with strict non-proliferation measures to provide assurance of exclusively peaceful non-explosive use;
  (b) to support the continued effectiveness of the international non-proliferation system based on the NPT and the IAEA safeguards system.

Article 5: Prevention of stationing of nuclear explosive devices

(1) Each Party undertakes to prevent in its territory the stationing of any nuclear explosive device.
(2) Each Party in the exercise of its sovereign rights remains free to decide for itself whether to allow visits by foreign ships and aircraft to its ports and airfields, transit of its airspace by foreign aircraft, and navigation by foreign ships in its territorial sea or archipelagic waters in a manner not covered by the rights of innocent passage, archipelagic sea lanes passage or transit passage of straits.

Article 6: Prevention of testing of nuclear explosive devices

Each Party undertakes:
  (a) to prevent in its territory the testing of any nuclear explosive device;
  (b) not to take any action to assist or encourage the testing of any nuclear explosive device by any State.

Article 7: Prevention of dumping

(1) Each Party undertakes:
  (a) not to dump radioactive wastes and other radioactive matter at sea anywhere within the South Pacific Nuclear Free Zone;
  (b) to prevent the dumping of radioactive wastes and other radioactive matter by anyone in its territorial sea;
  (c) not to take any action to assist or encourage the dumping by anyone of radioactive wastes and other radioactive matter at sea anywhere within the South Pacific Nuclear Free Zone;
  (d) to support the conclusion as soon as possible of the proposed Convention relating to the protection of the natural resources and environment of the South Pacific region and its Protocol for the prevention of the pollution of the South Pacific region by dumping, with the aim of precluding dumping at sea of radioactive wastes and other radioactive matter by anyone anywhere in the region.
(2) Paragraph 1 (a) and 1 (b) of this Article shall not apply to areas of the South Pacific Nuclear Free Zone in respect of which such a Convention and Protocol have entered into force.

Article 8: Control system

(1) The Parties hereby establish a control system for the purpose of verifying compliance with their obligations under this Treaty.
(2) The control system shall comprise:
  (a) reports and exchange of information as provided for in Article 9;
  (b) consultations as provided for in Article 10 and Annex 4 (1);
  (c) the application to peaceful nuclear activities of safeguards by the IAEA as provided for in Annex 2;
  (d) a complaints procedure as provided for in Annex 4.

Article 9: Reports and exchanges of information

(1) Each Party shall report to the Director of the South Pacific Bureau for Economic Cooperation (the Director) as soon as possible any significant event within its jurisdiction affecting the implementation of this Treaty. The Director shall circulate such reports promptly to all parties.
(2) The Parties shall endeavour to keep each other informed on matters arising under or in relation to this Treaty. They may exchange information by communicating it to the Director, who shall circulate it to all Parties.
(3) The Director shall report annually to the South Pacific Forum on the status of this Treaty and matters arising under or in relation to it, incorporating reports and communications made under paragraphs 1 and 2 of this Article and matters arising under Articles 8(2)(d) and 10 and Annex 2(4).

Article 10: Consultation and review

Without prejudice to the conduct of consultations among Parties by other means, the Director, at the request of any Party, shall convene a meeting of the Consultative Committee established by Annex 3 for consultation and cooperation on any matter arising in relation to this Treaty or for reviewing its operation.

Article 11: Amendment

The Consultative Committee shall consider proposals for amendment of the provisions of this Treaty proposed by any Party and circulated by the Director to all Parties not less than three months prior to the convening of the Consultative Committee for this purpose. Any proposal agreed upon by consensus by the Consultative Committee shall be communicated to the Director who shall circulate it for acceptance to all Parties. An amendment shall enter into force thirty days after receipt by the depositary of acceptances from all Parties.

Article 12: Signature and ratification

(1) This Treaty shall be open for signature by any Member of the South Pacific Forum.

(2) This Treaty shall be subject to ratification. Instruments of ratification shall be deposited with the Director who is hereby designated depositary of this Treaty and its protocols.

(3) If a Member of the South Pacific Forum whose territory is outside the South Pacific Nuclear Free Zone becomes a Party to this Treaty, Annex 1 shall be deemed to be amended so far as required to enclose at least the territory of that Party within the boundaries of the South Pacific Nuclear Free Zone. The delineation of any area added pursuant to this paragraph shall be approved by the South Pacific Forum.

Article 13: Withdrawal

(1) This Treaty is of a permanent nature and shall remain in force indefinitely, provided that in the event of a violation by any Party of a provision of this Treaty essential to the achievement of the objectives of the Treaty or of the spirit of the Treaty, every other Party shall have the right to withdraw from the Treaty.

(2) Withdrawal shall be effected by giving notice twelve months in advance to the Director who shall circulate such notice to all other Parties.

Article 14: Reservations

This Treaty shall not be subject to reservations.

Article 15: Entry into force

(1) This Treaty shall enter into force on the date of deposit of the eighth instrument of ratification.

(2) For a signatory which ratifies this Treaty after the date of deposit of the eighth instrument of ratification, the Treaty shall enter into force on the date of deposit of its instrument of ratification.

Article 16: Depositary functions

The depositary shall register this Treaty and its Protocols pursuant to Article 102 of the Charter of the United Nations and shall transmit certified copies of the Treaty and its Protocols to all Members of the South Pacific Forum and all States eligible to become Party to the Protocols to the Treaty and shall notify them of signatures and ratifications of the Treaty and its Protocols.

IN WITNESS WHEREOF the undersigned, being duly authorised by their Governments, have signed this Treaty.

DONE at Rarotonga, this sixth day of August, 1985, in a single original in the English language.

Annex 1

South Pacific Nuclear Free Zone

A. *(Specifies the area of the SPNFZ geographically by reference to latitude, longitude or other defined marks; this is depicted in the map opposite.)*

B. *(Provides that Australian islands westward of the above area and north of latitude 60 deg. S—i.e. in the Indian Ocean—while included with Area A in the SPNFZ, shall cease to be so if they have become subject to another, similar treaty.)*

Annex 2

IAEA safeguards

Annex 2 concerns the safeguards referred to in Art.8. Each Party to the NFZ will conclude an agreement with the IAEA on all fissionable material used in peaceful nuclear activities within its territory or under its

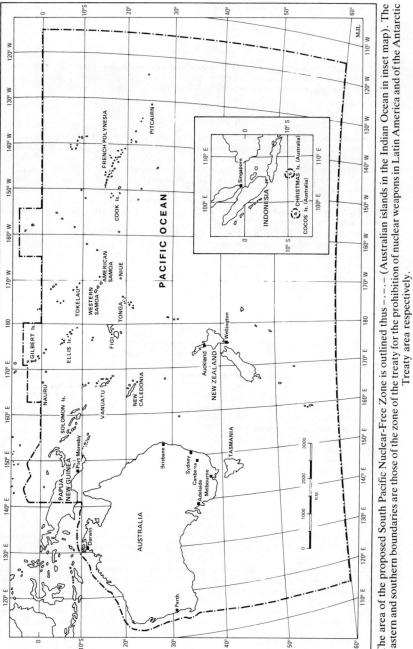

The area of the proposed South Pacific Nuclear-Free Zone is outlined thus —·—·— (Australian islands in the Indian Ocean in inset map). The eastern and southern boundaries are those of the zone of the treaty for the prohibition of nuclear weapons in Latin America and of the Antarctic Treaty area respectively.

jurisdiction or control, with the object of verifying the non-diversion of nuclear material from peaceful activities to nuclear explosive devices.

Annex 3

Consultative committee

Annex 3 establishes a Consultative Committee consisting of one representative of each Party, with advisers. Subject to the provisions of Article 11, decisions of the Consultative Committee shall be taken by consensus or, failing consensus, by a two-thirds majority of those present and voting. . . .

Annex 4

Complaints procedure

(1) A Party which considers that there are grounds for a complaint that another Party is in breach of its obligations under this Treaty shall, before bringing such a complaint to the Director, bring the subject matter of the complaint to the attention of the Party complained of and shall allow the latter reasonable opportunity to provide it with an explanation and to resolve the matter.

(2) If the matter is not so resolved, the complainant Party may bring the complaint to the Director with a request that the Consultative Committee be convened to consider it. Complaints shall be supported by an account of evidence of breach of obligations known to the complainant Party. Upon receipt of a complaint the Director shall convene the Consultative Committee as quickly as possible to consider it.

(3) The Consultative Committee, taking account of efforts made under paragraph 1, shall afford the Party complained of a reasonable opportunity to provide it with an explanation of the matter.

(4) to (8) *(Provide for any special inspection deemed necessary, to which the Party complained against must afford all required facilities and evidence.)*

(9) If the Consultative Committee has decided that the Party complained of is in breach of its obligations under this Treaty, or that the above provisions have not been complied with, or at any time at the request of either the complainant or complained of Party, the Parties shall meet promptly at a meeting of the South Pacific Forum.

DRAFT PROTOCOLS

The draft Protocols involve countries that are not members of the South Pacific Forum.

Under Protocol 1 any such country may apply, in respect of the territories for which it is internationally responsible situated within the South Pacific Nuclear Free Zone, the prohibitions contained in Articles 3, 5 and 6, insofar as they relate to the manufacture, stationing and testing of any nuclear explosive device within those territories, and the safeguards specified in Article 8(2)(c) and Annex 2 of the Treaty.

Under Protocol 2 it may undertake not to contribute to any act which constitutes a violation of the Treaty or its Protocols by Parties to them, and further not to use or threaten to use any nuclear explosive device against: (a) Parties to the Treaty; or (b) any territory within the SPNFZ for which a State subscribing to Protocol 1 is internationally responsible.

This Protocol is open for signature by France, the People's Republic of China, the USSR, the United Kingdom and the USA.

Under Protocol 3 each Party may undertake not to test any nuclear explosive device anywhere within the South Pacific Nuclear Free Zone.

THE GROUP OF FIVE

Extracts from a statement issued by the Group of Five Finance Ministers and Central Bank Governors after their meeting in New York, 21–23 September 1985.

Ministers of finance and central bank governors of France, the Federal Republic of Germany, Japan, the United Kingdom and the United States . . . reviewed economic developments and policies in each of their countries and assessed their implications for economic prospects, external balances, and exchange rates. . . .

The ministers and governors were of the view that significant progress has been made in their efforts to promote a convergence of favourable economic performance among their countries on a path of steady non-inflationary growth. Furthermore, they concluded that their countries are restoring the vitality and responsiveness of their economies.

As a result of these developments, they are confident that a firm basis has been established for a sustained, more balanced expansion among their countries. This sustained growth will benefit other industrial countries and will help ensure expanding export markets for developing countries, thereby contributing importantly to the resolution of problems of heavily indebted developing countries. . . .

These positive economic developments notwithstanding, there are large imbalances in external positions which pose potential problems, and which reflect a wide range of factors. Among these are: the deterioration in its external position which the US experienced from its period of very rapid relative growth; the particularly large impact on the US current account of the economic difficulties and the adjustment efforts of some major developing countries; the difficulty of trade access in some markets; and the appreciation of the US dollar.

The interaction of these factors—relative growth rates, the debt problems of developing countries, and exchange rate developments—has contributed to large, potentially destabilizing external imbalances among major industrial countries. In particular, the United States has a large and growing current account deficit, and Japan, and to lesser extent Germany, large and growing current account surpluses.

The US current account deficit, together with other factors, is now contributing to protectionist pressures which, if not resisted, could lead to mutually destructive retaliation with serious damage to the world economy. . . .

The finance ministers and governors affirmed that each of their countries remains firmly committed to its international responsibilities and obligations as leading industrial nations. They also share special responsibilities to ensure the mutual consistency of their individual policies.

The ministers agreed that establishing more widely strong, non-inflationary domestic growth and open markets will be a key factor in ensuring that the current expansion continues in a more balanced fashion, and they committed themselves to policies toward that end. In countries where the budget deficit is too high, further measures to reduce the deficit substantially are urgently required.

Ministers and governors agreed that it was essential that protectionist pressures be resisted. . . .

The ministers of finance and central bank governors agreed that recent economic developments and policy changes, when combined with the specific policy intentions, provide a sound basis for continued and a more balanced expansion with low inflation. They agreed on the importance of these improvements for redressing the large and growing external imbalances that have developed. In that connection, they noted that further market-opening measures will be important to resisting protectionism.

The ministers and governors agreed that exchange rates should play a role in adjusting external imbalances. In order to do this, exchange rates should better reflect fundamental economic conditions than has been the case. They believe that agreed policy actions must be implemented and reinforced to improve the fundamentals further, and that in view of the present and prospective changes in fundamentals, some further orderly appreciation of the main non-dollar currencies against the dollar is desirable. They stand ready to cooperate more closely to encourage this when to do so would be helpful.

THE COMMONWEALTH ACCORD ON SOUTHERN AFRICA

Signed at Lyford Quay, Nassau, Bahamas, on 20 October 1985, having been unanimously agreed by the participants in the Commonwealth Heads of Government Meeting, 16–22 October, at which 46 countries were represented, 41 of them by their Heads of State or Prime Ministers

1. We consider that South Africa's continuing refusal to dismantle apartheid, its illegal occupation of Namibia, and its aggression against its neighbours constitute a serious challenge to the values and principles of the Commonwealth, a challenge which Commonwealth countries cannot ignore. At New Delhi we expressed the view that 'only the eradication of apartheid and the establishment of majority rule on the basis of free and fair exercise of universal adult suffrage by all the people in a united and non-fragmented South Africa can lead to a just and lasting solution of the explosive situation prevailing in Southern Africa.' We are united in the belief that reliance on the range of pressures adopted so far has not resulted in the fundamental changes we have sought over many years. The growing crisis and intensified repression in South Africa mean that apartheid must be dismantled now if a greater tragedy is to be averted and that concerted pressure must be brought to bear to achieve that end. We consider that the situation calls for urgent practical steps.

2. We, therefore, call on the authorities in Pretoria for the following steps to be taken in a genuine manner and as a matter of urgency:

    (a) Declare that the system of apartheid will be dismantled and specific and meaningful action taken in fulfilment of that intent.

    (b) Terminate the existing state of emergency.

(c) Release immediately and unconditionally Nelson Mandela and all others imprisoned and detained for their opposition to apartheid.

(d) Establish political freedom and specifically lift the existing ban on the African National Congress and other political parties.

(e) Initiate, in the context of a suspension of violence on all sides, a process of dialogue across lines of colour, politics and religion, with a view to establishing a non-racial and representative government.

3. We have agreed on a number of measures which have as their rationale impressing on the authorities in Pretoria the compelling urgency of dismantling apartheid and erecting the structures of democracy in South Africa. The latter, in particular, demands a process of dialogue involving the true representatives of the majority black population of South Africa. We believe that we must do all we can to assist that process, while recognising that the forms of political settlement in South Africa are for the people of that country—all the people—to determine.

4. To this end, we have decided to establish a small group of eminent Commonwealth persons to encourage through all practicable ways the evolution of that necessary process of political dialogue. We are not unmindful of the difficulties such an effort will encounter, including the possibility of initial rejection by the South African authorities, but we believe it to be our duty to leave nothing undone that might contribute to peaceful change in South Africa and avoid the dreadful prospect of violent conflict that looms over South Africa, threatening people of all races in the country, and the peace and stability of the entire Southern Africa region.

5. We are asking the President of Zambia and the Prime Ministers of Australia, The Bahamas, Canada, India, the United Kingdom and Zimbabwe to develop with the Secretary-General the modalities of this effort to assist the process of political dialogue in South Africa. We would look to the group of eminent persons to seek to facilitate the processes of dialogue referred to in paragraph 2(e) above and by all practicable means to advance the fulfilment of the objectives of this Accord.

6. For our part, we have, as an earnest of our opposition to apartheid, reached accord on a programme of common action as follows:

(i) We declare the Commonwealth's support for the strictest enforcement of the mandatory arms embargo against South Africa, in accordance with United Nations Security Council Resolutions 418 and 558, and commit ourselves to prosecute violators to the fullest extent of the law.

(ii) We reaffirm the Gleneagles Declaration of 1977, which called upon Commonwealth members to take every practical step to discourage sporting contacts with South Africa.

(iii) We agree upon, and commend to other governments, the adoption of the following further economic measures against South Africa, which have already been adopted by a number of member countries:

(a) a ban on all new government loans to the Government of South Africa and its agencies;

(b) a readiness to take unilaterally what action may be possible to preclude the import of Krugerrands;

(c) no Government funding for trade missions to South Africa or for participation in exhibitions and trade fairs in South Africa;

(d) a ban on the sale and export of computer equipment capable of use by South African military forces, police or security forces;

(e) a ban on new contracts for the sale and export of nuclear goods, materials and technology to South Africa;

(f) a ban on the sale and export of oil to South Africa;

(g) a strict and rigorously controlled embargo on imports of arms, ammunition, military vehicles and paramilitary equipment from South Africa;

(h) an embargo on all military cooperation with South Africa; and

(i) discouragement of all cultural and scientific events except where these contribute towards the ending of apartheid or have no possible role in promoting it.

7. It is our hope that the process and measures we have agreed upon will help to bring about concrete progress towards the objectives stated above in six months. The heads of Government mentioned in paragraph 5 above, or their representatives, will then meet to review the situation. If in their opinion adequate progress has not been made within this period, we agree to consider the adoption of further measures. Some of us would, in that event, consider the following steps among others:

(a) a ban on air links with South Africa;

(b) a ban on new investment or reinvestment of profits earned in South Africa;

(c) a ban on the import of agricultural products from South Africa;

(d) the termination of double taxation agreements with South Africa;

(e) the termination of all government assistance to investment in, and trade with, South Africa;

(f) a ban on all government procurement in South Africa;

(g) a ban on government contracts with majority-owned South African companies;

(h) a ban on the promotion of tourism to South Africa.

8. Finally, we agree that should all of the above measures fail to produce the desired results within a reasonable period, further effective measures will have to be considered. Many of us have either taken or are prepared to take measures which go beyond those listed above, and each of us will pursue the objectives of this Accord in all the ways and through all appropriate fora open to us. We believe, however, that in pursuing this programme jointly we enlarge the prospects of an orderly transition to social, economic and political justice in South Africa and peace and stability in the Southern Africa region as a whole.

THE UNITED KINGDOM CONSERVATIVE CABINET

(as at 1 January 1985)

Prime Minister, First Lord of the Treasury and Minister for the Civil Service	Rt. Hon. Margaret Thatcher, FRS, MP
Lord President of the Council and Leader of the House of Lords	Rt. Hon. The Viscount Whitelaw, CH, MC
Lord Chancellor	Rt. Hon. The Lord Hailsham of Saint Marylebone, CH, FRS, DCL
Secretary of State for Foreign and Commonwealth Affairs and Minister of Overseas Development	Rt. Hon. Sir Geoffrey Howe, QC, MP
Secretary of State for the Home Department	Rt. Hon. Leon Brittan, QC, MP
Chancellor of the Exchequer	Rt. Hon. Nigel Lawson, MP
Secretary of State for Education and Science	Rt. Hon. Sir Keith Joseph, Bt, MP
Secretary of State for Energy	Rt. Hon. Peter Walker, MBE, MP
Secretary of State for Defence	Rt. Hon. Michael Heseltine, MP
Secretary of State for Scotland	Rt. Hon. George Younger, TD, MP
Secretary State for Wales	Rt. Hon. Nicholas Edwards, MP
Secretary of State for the Environment	Rt. Hon. Patrick Jenkin, MP
Lord Privy Seal and Leader of the House of Commons	Rt. Hon. John Biffen, MP
Secretary of State for Social Services	Rt. Hon. Norman Fowler, MP
Secretary of State for Trade and Industry	Rt. Hon. Norman Tebbit, MP
Secretary of State for Employment	Rt. Hon. Tom King, MP
Minister of Agriculture, Fisheries and Food	Rt. Hon. Michael Jopling, MP
Chief Secretary to the Treasury	Rt. Hon. Peter Rees, QC, MP
Secretary of State for Transport	Rt. Hon. Nicholas Ridley, MP
Secretary of State for Northern Ireland	Rt. Hon. Douglas Hurd, CBE, MP
Chancellor of the Duchy of Lancaster and Minister for the Arts	Rt. Hon. The Earl of Gowrie
Minister without Portfolio	Rt. Hon. The Lord Young of Graffham

THE UNITED KINGDOM CONSERVATIVE CABINET

(as at 31 December 1985 following changes on 2 September)

Prime Minister, First Lord of the Treasury and Minister for the Civil Service	Rt. Hon. Margaret Thatcher, FRS, MP
Lord President of the Council and Leader of the House of Lords	Rt. Hon. The Viscount Whitelaw, CH, MC
Lord Chancellor	Rt. Hon. The Lord Hailsham of Saint Marylebone, CH, FRS, DCL
Secretary of State for Foreign and Commonwealth Affairs and Minister of Overseas Development	Rt. Hon. Sir Geoffrey Howe, QC, MP
Secretary of State for Trade and Industry	Rt. Hon. Leon Brittan, QC, MP
Chancellor of the Exchequer	Rt. Hon. Nigel Lawson, MP
Secretary of State for the Home Department	Rt. Hon. Douglas Hurd, CBE, MP
Secretary of State for Education and Science	Rt. Hon. Sir Keith Joseph, Bt. MP
Secretary of State for Energy	Rt. Hon. Peter Walker, MBE, MP
Secretary of State for Defence	Rt. Hon. Michael Heseltine, MP
Secretary of State for Scotland	Rt. Hon. George Younger, TD, MP
Secretary of State for Wales	Rt. Hon. Nicholas Edwards, MP
Lord Privy Seal and Leader of the House of Commons	Rt. Hon. John Biffen, MP
Secretary of State for Social Services	Rt. Hon. Norman Fowler, MP
Chancellor of the Duchy of Lancaster	Rt. Hon. Norman Tebbit, MP
Secretary of State for Northern Ireland	Rt. Hon. Tom King, MP
Minister of Agriculture, Fisheries and Food	Rt. Hon. Michael Jopling, MP
Secretary of State for Transport	Rt. Hon. Nicholas Ridley, MP
Secretary of State for Employment	Rt. Hon. The Lord Young of Graffham
Secretary of State for the Environment	Rt. Hon. Kenneth Baker, MP
Paymaster General	Rt. Hon. Kenneth Clarke, QC, MP
Chief Secretary to the Treasury	Rt. Hon. John MacGregor, OBE, MP

OBITUARY

Adams, The Rt. Hon. J.M.G.M. (known as Tom), QC (b. 1931), was Prime Minister of Barbados from 1976 until his death. The son of Sir Grantley Adams, a former Premier of the then colony, he won a scholarship to Oxford, worked for the BBC and was called to the Bar in London. Returning to Barbados in 1962, he was active in the Barbados Labour Party, becoming its leader in 1971 after its electoral defeat and leading it to victory at the polls in 1976 and again in 1981. His policies were realistic and successful, alike in the economic, defence and social fields. Shocked by the destruction of democracy in neighbouring Grenada, he welcomed the United States' invasion, but he was as pro-British as he was pro-American. Died 11 March

Ashley, Laura (b. 1925), British fashion and fabric designer, with her husband Bernard created, from the smallest domestic beginnings in Wales in 1953, a business which spanned the world and was valued at £200 million. From the opening of the first Laura Ashley shop in Kensington in 1967 the enterprise was a great success, not only commercially but also in disseminating a particular Laura Ashley style both in fabric and in clothes (later extended to soft-furnishings and wallpaper) which made her name world-famous, a style romantic, simple, almost nostalgic, directly contrary to the prevailing modern trend. Died 17 September

Bailey, Sir Donald (b. 1901), made his name famous by his invention of the Bailey bridge, a structure of rectangular trussed welded-steel modules which could be erected quickly by a small corps of men as a temporary bridge in warfare. Designed in 1940 and commissioned in May 1941, it was in use in November of that year, and by the end of World War II nearly 2,000 Bailey bridges had been indispensable to the land victories of the Allied forces. A technical civil servant from 1928, Bailey became director of the military engineering experimental establishment of the Ministry of Supply and dean of the Royal Military College of Science 1962–66. Died 5 May

Balogh, Lord (b. in Hungary 1905), British economist, was an expert on the problems of development. He was economic adviser to the Indian Planning Board (1955, 1960), the governments or central banks of Malta, Jamaica, Greece, Algeria and Sudan and the Economic Commission for Latin America (1960), and also advised FAO (1957–59). After study in Budapest, Berlin and the USA he worked for a stockbroking firm in London before World War II. He was a lecturer at University College, London (1934–40), then lecturer (1939–45) and Fellow (1945–73) of Balliol College, Oxford, and university reader in economics (1960–73). A supporter of Labour and a friend of Harold Wilson, he became adviser on economic affairs in the Cabinet Office 1964–70, and in 1974 Minister of State at the Department of Energy, then deputy chairman of the British National Oil Corporation. Died 20 January

Biró, Ladislao José (b. in Hungary 1899), gave his name to the ball-point pen which he invented. His first crude pen, using instant-drying printer's ink, was devised before he emigrated to Argentina in 1940. There a company in which he held one-third of the shares was founded to develop the invention; in 1944 the North American rights were sold to a US firm, and thereafter 'biros' entered into universal use. Biró was a prolific inventor, not much interested in business, and also a modernist painter. Died 24 October

Boland, Dr Frederick (b. 1904), was for twenty years the most influential diplomatist of Eire/Republic of Ireland, as permanent head of the department of external affairs (1946–50), ambassador to London (1950–56), permanent representative at the UN (1956–64) and president of the UN General Assembly (1960). Died 4 December

Böll, Heinrich (b. 1917), German novelist, won the Nobel prize for literature in 1972. His writing, which began after he had served in the ranks in World War II, reflected the traumas of Germany's cultural revival after a dozen years of Nazi rule, war and defeat. It combined realism with poetic imagination and a profound humanism which, with his support of dissident writers like his friend Solzhenitsyn, made him a target for bitter communist criticism, though he was widely read in East as well as West Germany and in Soviet Russia. Most of his novels and short stories, from *The Train was on Time* (1949) to *The Lost Honour of Katharina Blum* (1975), were translated into English: the latter was made into a film in 1977. Died 16 July

Braudel, Professor Fernand (b. 1902), was among France's most eminent historians. Best-known of his works, many of which were translated into English, were the masterly *La Méditerranée et le monde méditerranéen* (1949) and *Civilisation matérielle, Economie et Capitalisme XVe–XVIIIe siècle*, both of which reflected his belief in *l'histoire totale* examining the whole range of human activity at a particular epoch, contrasted with *l'histoire événementielle* focusing on political events. After teaching in Algiers 1924–32, Paris 1932–34 and São Paulo 1934–37, he returned to Paris to become director of the Ecole Pratique des Hautes Etudes. In 1949 he was elected to the Collège de France and in 1984 to the Académie Française. Died 28 November

Bryant, Sir Arthur, CH (b. 1899), British historian, was an elegant and persuasive writer of history rather than an academic pundit, though his famous trilogy on Samuel Pepys (1933, '35, '38) was based, as was all his work in its degree, on thorough research. After education at Harrow School and Oxford, he held teaching posts before giving his whole time to writing, following the great success of his first historical book, *King Charles II* (1931). His second, widely-read trilogy was a study of England in Napoleonic times—*The Years of Endurance* (1942), *The Years of Victory* (1942), *The Age of Elegance* (1950). Two volumes of *The Story of England*, on early times and the late Middle Ages, published in 1953 and 1963, won much praise from academic historians who had been inclined to write him off as a popularizer. Among the best-known of his many other works were two volumes based on the World War II diaries of Field Marshal Lord Alanbrooke, *The Turn of the Tide* (1957) and *Triumph in the West* (1959). He also wrote without intermission for many years an essay in *The Illustrated London News*, first weekly then monthly. A devoted patriot and conservative, all his work was instinct with love of his country, its history and its institutions. Died 22 January

Brynner, Yul (b. 1920?), stage and film actor and singer, depended for world fame mainly on two roles, those of the King of Siam in the film *The King and I* (1956) and of a gunman in the film *The Magnificent Seven* (1960) and its sequel. Of Swiss and Mongolian parentage, he spent his childhood in Peking and his youth in Paris, where he attended the Sorbonne and joined the world of theatre and circus. In 1940 he moved to the US and became a stage actor, and for a while a radio commentator. His triumph in the stage musical *The King and I* (1951–54) took him to Hollywood, where he played in some 20 films, apart from those mentioned above, none of great memorability, except perhaps *The Brothers Karamazov* (1958). Having settled in

Switzerland in 1960, he returned to the US in 1972 to play in a television series based on *The King and I* and a New York revival of the original musical, in which he continued to act until his death from lung cancer. Died 10 October

Burnham, Forbes (b. 1923), was President of Guyana from 1980 until his death. Called to the Bar in London in 1948, he had a high reputation as a lawyer while pursuing a political career. With the Indian-race Cheddi Jagan he founded the left-wing anti-colonialist People's Progressive Party (PPP) in 1950, but after forming a short-lived Government, following its electoral victory in 1953, the PPP split, and in 1957 Burnham founded the anti-Jagan, anti-communist People's National Congress (PNC), which formed a coalition Government in 1964. Burnham led Guyana to independence in 1966 and appeared to be a moderate and internationalist statesman, but after the PNC achieved undiluted power in 1968 he became more and more dictatorial, nationalizing foreign firms, imposing state socialism, moving towards a one-party state, controlling the media, offending human rights and rigging elections. In 1980, under a new constitution, he became Executive President. Nevertheless, with his tub-thumping oratory and political cunning he remained popular with a great many Guyanans. Died 6 August

Calvino, Italo (b. in Cuba 1923), Italian novelist and essayist, was a creative influence in European literary culture for close on 40 years. He combined inventive modernism with popular readability, realism with fantasy, contemporary narrative with retold fable, the last his supreme *forte*. An anti-Nazi partisan in World War II, a militant communist until he left the party in 1957, he was on the staff of the Turin publisher Giulio Einaudi when in 1947 he published his first novel (translated in 1956 as *The Path of the Nest of Spiders*). His *Italian Fables* (1956, in English 1959) greatly swelled his fame at home and abroad. The trilogy *Il Visconte Dimezzato* (1952), *Il Barone Rampante* (1957) and *Il Cavaliere Inesistente* (1959), published in English under the general title *Our Forefathers*, well displayed his gifts of fantasy and satirical wit. The most notable of his later works were *Le cosmicomiche* (1965, translated as *Cosmocomics* 1968) and *Se una notte d'inverno un viaggiatore* (1979, translated as *If on a Winter's Night a Traveller*, 1981). Died 19 September

Chagall, Marc (b. 1887), Russian-born artist, lived in France for most of his adult life. A poor Jew from Vitebsk, he managed to enlist in the Académie des Beaux Arts in St Petersburg, and by 1910 he was in Paris, becoming rapidly acquainted, even intimate with the revolutionary artists of the day. Returning to Russia in 1910, for some years after the Revolution of 1917 he worked as a teacher and public artist, but his use of figurative and folkloric elements was not favoured, nor was he sympathetic to notions of art as propaganda or revolutionary theories of art. By 1922 he had left Russia; and after two productive decades, mostly in France, he fled to the USA in 1941, returning to Europe in 1948. Chagall was fond of his apothegm that 'great art picks up where nature ends'. In different phases of his career he remained a great applied artist: murals, theatrical and ballet and opera designs, and perhaps his finest achievement, in very late life, stained glass. As he grew old his painting sweetened and sentimentalized, without losing its radiant colour. But his greatest work, calling on village and folk memory, but marrying the images into a fractured and dislocated space, was done in the earlier decades of the century. Gentle fantasy, melancholy, a tragic sense and feeling of wonder and joy, too, permeated his paintings, sophisticated in execution. His love for his first wife, Bella Rosenfeld, his memories of harsh Russian life, illuminated by familial and community relationships, sent figures spinning into brightly-coloured space. The many exhibitions of his work were crowned by a huge and vastly popular retrospective at the Royal Academy, London, on the eve of his death, which marked for many the end of the era of the ascendancy of the School of Paris in 20th-century art. Of the first-generation heroes of modernism, only Dali (b. 1904) and Henry Moore (b. 1898) were still living. Died 28 March

M.V.

Chernenko, Konstantin (b. 1911), as General Secretary of the Soviet Communist Party and chairman of the Supreme Soviet Presidium, was Russia's head of government from February 1984 (and of state from April 1984) until his death 13 months later. Of peasant parentage, he had a scant education, and it was not until he was 30, after a decade as an active Party member, that he held office as a secretary of the regional party in Krasnoyarsk, his birth place. In 1948 he was sent to Moldavia as head of the propaganda department of the regional central committee, and there he came to the notice of Leonid Brezhnev, whose patronage shaped his future career. In 1956 he became a secretary of the Central Committee in Moscow; in 1960 he succeeded Brezhnev as head of the Secretariat of the Presidium; and in 1965 he was made head of a department of the Central Committee, of which he became a candidate member in 1966 and a full member in 1971; Brezhnev promoted him to a secretaryship of the Central Committee in 1976, candidate membership of the Politburo in 1977 and full membership in 1978. When Brezhnev died in 1982 Chernenko was seen as a natural successor to the general secretaryship but his supporters were out-manoeuvred by those of Yuri Andropov, to whom he was obliged to pay second fiddle, but he recaptured some power during Andropov's illness and was chosen by the Party leaders to succeed him upon his death after 15 months in office. His headship was inevitably a period of standstill in most foreign and domestic

affairs. His health visibly grew worse, his appearances became rare, and he died 10 March

Cruz, Ramon Ernesto (b. 1903), was President of Honduras 1971–72 until overthrown by a military coup. Died 6 August.

de Quay, Dr Jan Eduard (b. 1901), was Prime Minister of the Netherlands 1959–63. A professor at the Roman Catholic University of Tilburg, in 1940 he became leader of the controversial Netherlands Union which supported limited cooperation with the occupying German forces, but the Union was itself banned and de Quay was imprisoned 1942–43. He was Minister of War in 1945 and Governor of North Brabant 1946–54. His centre-right coalition Government was headed by his own Catholic People's Party. Retiring from politics in 1969, he was chairman of the board of the airline KLM 1964–72. Died 4 July

Diplock, Lord (b. 1907), was a Lord of Appeal in Ordinary from 1968, and as such was highly respected for the lucidity and meticulous forensic analysis of his judgments; but to the non-legal public he was most famed for his recommendation, in 1972, of non-jury courts in troubled Northern Ireland—the so-called 'Diplock courts'—and for his chairmanship, 1971–82, of the Security Commission. In this capacity he investigated a number of notorious security cases, including the ministerial sex scandals of 1973, the allegations of spying against the former head of MI5, Sir Roger Hollis, and an outcry in 1981 against phone-tapping and mail interception by police, customs and security services. He had risen rapidly at the Bar after serving in the RAF in World War II, and was appointed a High Court judge in 1956 and a judge of Appeal in 1961. Died 14 October

Douglas-Home, Charles (b. 1937), was editor of *The Times*, London, from 1982 until his death. After a varied early career and progress as a journalist in the *Express* group, in January 1965 he was appointed defence correspondent of *The Times*, a role giving ample play to his talents of balanced judgment and clear discernment of the real issues. He became successively features editor, home editor and foreign editor of *The Times*, then in 1981 deputy editor under a new chief whose methods were not to his taste. His intention to resign was intercepted by the latter's own resignation. Douglas-Home's editorship affirmed the paper's authority, increased its circulation and restored the morale of its staff. Died 29 October

Erlander, Tage (b. 1901), was Prime Minister of Sweden 1946–69, and as such the chief builder of his country's economic success under a Social Democratic regime, and architect of its neutral but basically pro-Western detachment from the major power blocs. Entering Parliament in 1932, he became a junior Minister 1938–44, Minister without Portfolio 1944–45 and Minister of Education 1945–46. His outlook was internationalist and radical; he founded domestic economic policy on cooperation with both sides of industry, notably exemplified in restricted wage-bargaining. Died 21 June

Fender, Percy G.H. (b. 1892), was known as the best county cricket captain who never captained England. He was captain of Surrey 1921–32 and played in Test matches in 1920–21, 1922–23, 1924 and 1929. A fine all-rounder, his total of 19,034 runs, 1,894 wickets and 558 catches in first-class cricket included six achievements of 1,000 runs and 100 wickets in a season. By hitting 100 runs in 35 minutes against Northamptonshire in 1920 he set a world record which was not surpassed for 63 years. Died 15 June

George-Brown, Lord (b. 1914), British politician, was Foreign Secretary 1966–68, after serving for two years as Secretary of State for Economic Affairs. Elected as MP in 1945, he was runner-up to Harold Wilson as leader of the Labour Party after Hugh Gaitskell's death in 1963, and when Wilson formed his Government in the following year he became Deputy Prime Minister as well as deputy leader of the party, retaining the latter post, which he had held since 1960, after he had quarrelled with Wilson and resigned office in 1968. In both his Cabinet posts he met with disappointment from external events—in 1966 when the Government, faced with a balance of payments crisis, adopted deflationary policies which he had strenuously resisted in favour of control of wages and other incomes, and in 1967 when President de Gaulle vetoed Britain's entry into the European Common Market, on which George Brown had set his heart. He lost his Commons seat in 1970, resigned from Labour in 1976, and in 1981 became a founder-member of the Social Democratic Party. Tact and good temper were not his forte, but no one doubted his intense patriotism, his oratorical force or his emotional commitment to the causes he espoused. Died 2 June

Graves, Robert (b. 1895), British poet and author, was known to a worldwide public above all for his historical novels *I, Claudius* and *Claudius the God* (both 1934) and the autobiographical work *Goodbye to All That* (1929) with its scathing recollection of the Western Front in World War I; but he regarded the former two books primarily as means—highly successful, as it proved—of making money to sustain his life as a poet. Some critics held him to be the finest lyrical poet of the twentieth century in the English language. After public school he volunteered immediately for the army when war broke out in 1914, was twice mentioned in despatches for brave service and was all-but mortally wounded. His first books of poetry were published while he was a serving officer. When war ended he went to Oxford University; already married and in ill health he did not take his BA examinations but later graduated with a BLitt awarded for a book of literary criticism. His private life was peculiar; for a time he conducted a *ménage à trois* with his wife Nancy, daughter of the artist William Nicholson, and the American poet Laura Riding, with whom he founded the Seizin Press, largely on the proceeds of his 'official' biography of T.E. Lawrence, *Lawrence and the Arabs* (1927), and with whom he built a house on Majorca; it remained his home for the rest of his life, except a period of exile during the Spanish civil war. The *Claudius* novels were followed by *Count Belisarius* (1938), two books written in partnership with Alan Hodge, whose former wife Beryl he married, and more historical novels—the *Sergeant Lamb* duo (1940–41) and *Wife of Mr Milton* (1943)—*The Golden Fleece* (1944), the highly controversial *King Jesus* (1946) and *The White Goddess*, a statement of poetic experience and faith. In 1961 he was elected Professor of Poetry at Oxford. Eccentric, quarrelsome, often contemptuous of other literary figures, he was at the same time courageous, honourable, generous and humane, and above all a dedicated poet. Died 7 December

Harlech, Lord, KCMG, PC (b. 1918), was British ambassador to the US 1961–65—as David Ormsby-Gore until 1964, when he succeeded to his father's barony. Already an intimate friend of John F. Kennedy, with whom he also had a family connection, he was able to give the President personal advice, and to receive confidences from him, far beyond their official relationship, to particular good effect in the Cuba missile crisis. After military service in World War II he became a Conservative MP in 1950, and held junior ministerial offices in the Foreign Office 1956–61. After the Washington embassy he was deputy leader of his party in the House of Lords 1966–67, President of the British Board of Film Censors from 1965, chairman of Harlech Television from 1967, President of the Pilgrims of Great Britain

1965–77, chairman of the European Movement 1969–75, of the National Commission for Electoral Reform from 1976 and of the Royal Institute for International Affairs 1978–81, President of Shelter (campaign for the homeless), a trustee of the Tate Gallery 1971–78 and a director of Morgan Crucible Co. and the Bank of Wales, posts which indicated not only his interests and ability but also his reformist political stance. Died 26 January

Hoxha, Enver (b. 1908), was the effective ruler of Albania from its inception as a People's Republic in 1946 until his death. The son of a landowner, he embraced communism while a student in Paris in the 1930s. Returning to Albania in 1936, he was reduced by his militant beliefs from intellectual work to keeping a tobacco kiosk which became a focus for communist dissidents. In 1941, during the Italian occupation, he became secretary-general of the Albanian Labour Party, and a little later chief political commissar of the National Liberation Army. After the defeat of the Axis he was simultaneously Prime Minister, Foreign Minister and Minister of Defence, but from 1953 he exercised power through his leadership of the Party as First Secretary. He was an obdurate Stalinist, whose native animus against Yugoslavia became hatred when Tito broke with Stalin in 1948. When Khrushchev succeeded Stalin and attempted a Russian rapprochement with Yugoslavia, Hoxha turned from the USSR, ousting it from Albanian naval bases, abusing Khrushchev at the Moscow meeting of Communist Parties in 1960, and turning to China as Albania's aider and abetter. From 1960 Albania became an anti-Soviet Chinese satellite, but Hoxha opposed Beijing's opening to the West and by 1978 Sino-Albanian friendship had ended in recrimination, leaving Albania doggedly isolated, with religion expunged, capitalist loans forbidden, tourism choked off. Hoxha's regime was ruthless and bloody, but his personal power was never challenged. Died 11 April

Kertész, André (b. 1894), Hungarian-born photographer who became a US citizen in 1944, did not attain world fame until he was nearly 70, when he won the gold medal of the Venice Biennale (1963) and was given (1964) a major exhibition at the Museum of Modern Art in New York. From Budapest he had gone to Paris in 1925, then to New York in 1936, a fortunate haven for a Jew when the holocaust struck. His favourite subjects were human-interest studies of the city streets. Major exhibitions included those at the Tokyo World Exhibition Centre 1970, the Centre Pompidou in 1977 and the National Museum of Photography in Bradford, England, in 1984. Died 27 September

Kimball, Spencer (b. 1895), was president and prophet of the Mormon church (the Church of Jesus Christ of Latter Day Saints) from 1973. His leadership was marked by the admission of blacks to the priesthood, a consequent surge in church membership, his missionary travels round the world and his stern opposition to demands for women's rights. Died 5 November

Koo, Dr Wellington (Ku Wei-chun) (b. 1888), was an outstanding world statesman from World War I until his retirement from diplomacy to become a judge of the International Court of Justice 1957–67 (vice-president 1964–67). Educated in Shanghai, where he was born, and at Columbia University, N.Y., he progressed in public service from the post of secretary to the President of China to that of Minister in the Washington embassy in 1915. As chairman of China's delegation to the Paris peace conference in 1919 he refused to sign the treaty because his country's claim to former German rights in Shantung was not conceded. After serving as delegate to the League of Nations 1920–22 he returned to China, becoming successively Minister of Foreign Affairs, Finance Minister and (1926–

27) Prime Minister. Then he was appointed to the Hague Court of Arbitration, but he also frequently represented China at the League of Nations in the 1930s. He was China's ambassador to London 1941–45 and to Washington 1945–55. Leading China's delegation to the San Francisco conference in 1945, he was the first signatory of the Charter of the UN. When he retired from what was now Taiwan's embassy he continued to advise Chiang Kai-shek and his successor as President of Taiwan. Died November

Kuznets, Professor Simon (b. in Russia 1901), was awarded the Nobel prize for economics in 1971. After study and research at Columbia University, New York, he joined the National Bureau of Economic Research in 1927, and then taught at the University of Pennsylvania 1930–54, with a three-year break for service with the War Production Board during World War II. He was professor of political economy at Johns Hopkins University 1954–60 and of economics at Harvard 1960–71. His chief early work was on business cycles, but his fame and influence stemmed chiefly from his statistical studies—notably in his massive book *National Income and its Composition 1919–1938*—which he demonstrated were the essential foundation of economic theory and from which he deduced a systematic account of economic growth. Died 8 July

Larkin, Philip, CH, CBE (b. 1922), British poet, became the most widely-read of his generation after the publication of *The Less Deceived* in 1955, his fourth collection of poems. His earliest work had been published by small presses, and attracted little attention. His output was small, and he earned his bread as a librarian. He disliked most contemporary poetry, admired Graves and Betjeman, and was in essence a traditionalist, though an original and sophisticated one. He published two novels, *Jill* (1946) and *A Girl in Winter* (1947), and was also a regular newspaper critic of jazz. His last collections of poems were *The Whitsun Weddings* (1964) and *High Windows* (1974). He edited *The Oxford Book of Twentieth Century Verse* (1974), a task which had taken him six years. Died 2 December

Lewis, Saunders (b. 1893), Welsh poet, playwright and nationalist, was a key figure in the cultural and political life of Wales, militantly before World War II and afterwards through the inspiration of his poetry and plays and his devotion to the cause of the Welsh language. He was founder-president of the Welsh Nationalist Party (later Plaid Cymru) 1925–35. In 1937 he and two others were sentenced to 9 months' imprisonment for an act of arson in an attempt to stop the establishment of an aircraft bombing range in Caernafon, and this suspended his career as a university lecturer until 1952 and led to his concentration on writing and drama (notably his plays *Siwan*, *Esther* and *Brad*). His Welsh patriotism was not chauvinistic; he was widely read in European literature, and though the son of a nonconformist minister he was converted to Roman Catholicism. Died 1 September

Lodge, Henry Cabot (b. 1902), American politician and diplomatist, was the grandson of the famous isolationist Senator of the same name. After four years in the Massachusetts legislature he was elected to the US Senate in 1936, where he combined progressive Republicanism with an isolationist leaning. The latter he forsook after Pearl Harbour and his experiences in active war service in North Africa and France, which caused his resignation from the Senate in 1944. Two years later he was re-elected, but surprisingly lost his seat in the Eisenhower landslide election of 1952. Eisenhower appointed him ambassador to the UN, with a seat in the Cabinet. After the presidential election of 1960, when he was Nixon's vice-presidential candidate, he became director-general of the Atlantic Institute 1961–63, before being appointed by President Kennedy

ambassador to Saigon 1963–64. He participated, unsuccessfully, in the 1964 presidential election, and was reappointed to Saigon 1965–67 by President Johnson. Later diplomatic posts included the Bonn embassy and that of the President's special envoy to the Vatican. Died 27 February

Lon Nol, Marshal (b. 1913), was President of Kampuchea 1972–75, after an anti-Sihanouk coup in 1970 which he helped to engineer. Having served under the French colonial administration, after World War II he became successively chief of the national police, governor of Battambang province, chief of staff of the armed forces and (1960–66) commander-in-chief and Minister of Defence. He was Prime Minister 1966–67, first Vice-President 1967–69, and Minister of Defence and chief of staff as well as Prime Minister again, 1969–70. His period of nominal supremacy was marked by growing insurgency which culminated in the victory of the Khmer Rouges. Lon Nol fled, and spent his last years in California. Died 17 November

Lule, Professor Yusufu (b. 1912), was briefly President of Uganda in 1979. An academic teacher educated in Uganda, South Africa and the UK, he was appointed a Minister in the colonial government in 1955 and chairman of the Public Service Commission in 1960, then returned to academic life as principal of Makerere University 1963–70. He was assistant secretary-general in the Commonwealth Secretariat 1970–72 and secretary-general of the Association of African Universities 1972–77. In 1979 he was summoned from retirement in England to lead the anti-Amin Liberation Front, and he became President after Idi Amin's defeat, but was almost immediately replaced by President Binaisa, himself ousted by Milton Obote in 1980. In renewed exile in London, Lule became political leader of the anti-Obote National Resistance Movement. Died 21 January

Luxembourg, HRH the Grand Duchess Charlotte of, GCVO (b. 1896), was sovereign of the Grand Duchy from 1919, after the abdication of her pro-German elder sister, until 1964, when she herself abdicated in favour of her son Prince Jean. She married in 1919 Prince Félix of Bourbon-Parma. After 20 peaceful and prosperous years Luxembourg's neutrality was violated by the German invasion in 1940, and the grand-ducal family escaped only in the nick of time, to spend five years in exile in North America and Britain. In April 1945 Grand Duchess Charlotte returned to a rapturous welcome. Died 9 July

McKell, The Rt. Hon. Sir William, GCMG, PC (b. 1891), was Governor-General of Australia 1947–53. Of working-class origin, he was a trade union official when he was elected to the New South Wales parliament in the Labour interest in 1917. He held state ministerial office 1920–22, 1925–27 and 1930–32, meanwhile qualifying for the Bar, and in 1939, during the NSW Labour Party's long spell in opposition, was elected its leader. Victory in 1941 brought him the state premiership, which he held for six years until Australia's Labour Prime Minister Mr Chifley recommended him as Governor-General, against the convention that the post should not go to an active party politician. His impartiality in office, however, was unquestioned. He was a member of the Malayan Constitutional Commission 1956–57. Died 11 January

Mayer, Sir Robert, CH, KCVO (b. in Germany 1879), having become a British citizen made a fortune in the metal business in the first two decades of the 20th century and thereafter devoted his life to philanthropy, especially in the world of music. He and his wife, the soprano Dorothy Moulton, founded in 1923 and throughout their long lives supported the Children's Concerts with which his name was indelibly associated; in 1954 he founded Youth and Music; and in 1932 he co-founded with Sir Thomas Beecham the London Symphony Orchestra. But his benefactions were extended in many other directions too. His autobiography (1979) was entitled *My First Hundred Years.* Died 9 January

Médici, General Emílio Garrastazú (b. 1905), was President of Brazil 1969–74. His military dictatorship was marked both by draconian suppression of dissent and by a remarkable phase of economic growth. A career soldier, he had been head of the Brazilian military academy, C-in-C Third Army and head of the intelligence service set up by the army to support its rule of the country. Died 9 October

Moch, Jules (b. 1893) French politician, reached a peak of fame in 1947 when, as Minister of the Interior (1947–50), he used strong police and military action to break the menacing insurrectionary strikes fomented by the communists, and another in 1958 when in the same office, having vainly striven to mount a strong defence against the army revolt in Algeria, he called for General de Gaulle's return to power. A Socialist, he held office under Léon Blum's Popular Front Government, 1936–40, but he resigned from the party in 1974 in protest at its electoral alliance with the Communists. In World War II, after imprisonment as an enemy of the Pétain regime, he joined de Gaulle and served with the Free French navy. De Gaulle rewarded him with portfolios in successive post-liberation Governments. As Minister of Defence in the Pléven Administration in 1950 he favoured modest rearmament of West Germany but opposed the projected European Defence Community. Died 1 August

Mota Pinto, Dr Carlos da (b. 1936), was Prime Minister of Portugal for seven months 1978–79. While professor of civil law at Coimbra University he helped found the Popular Democratic Party, later the Social Democratic Party (PSD), after the

1974 revolution, becoming its parliamentary leader but soon leaving it in order to stand as an independent. He was Minister of Commerce and Tourism 1976–77. His short-lived Government was defeated by the Socialist and Communist parties. He returned to the PSD, became its leader and deputy Prime Minister and Minister of Defence 1983–85, but resigned in February 1985 and returned to academic life. Died 7 May

Naipaul, Shiva (b. 1945), West Indian writer, was overshadowed as a novelist by his brother V.S. Naipaul, but he published a number of highly-praised books, among them his novels *Fireflies* (1970) and *A Hot Country* (1983), the travel diary *North of South: an African Journey* (1978) and a study of the Jonestown mass suicide, *Black and White* (1980). His novel *The Chip-Chip Gatherers* (1973) won the Whitbread Award. Born of a Hindu family in Trinidad, he was educated there and at Oxford. Died 13 August

Neves, Tancredo (b. 1910), President-elect of Brazil, died before he could be inaugurated in office. His political career, which began in earnest in 1950, when, already a member of the state parliament of Minas Gerais, he was elected as a Social Democrat to the federal congress, was geared to the alternation of military and democratic government in Brazil; but although he was a consistant advocate of democracy he was tolerated by the military regime of 1964–84. Under President Vargas he became Justice Minister 1953–54, under President Kubitschek president of the Banco do Brazil and the National Economic Development Bank, under President Goulart Prime Minister with amputated powers 1961–62, and under military rule Governor of Minas Gerais 1982–84. In January 1985, in an indirect election for the presidency under a new constitutional order, he defeated the candidate backed by the army. Died 21 April

Ormandy, Eugene, Hon. KBE (b. 1899), Hungarian musician, was conductor of the Philadelphia Orchestra from 1936 to 1980. A precocious virtuoso violinist, he studied under Jeno Hublay and became a professor at the Royal Academy of Music in Budapest at the age of 17. Five years later a defaulting concert tour left him stranded in New York, where he earned his living as a violinist in a cinema orchestra, of which he eventually became assistant conductor; thus finding his *métier*, he gained a growing reputation as a guest conductor with leading orchestras. In 1931 he was appointed conductor of the Minneapolis Orchestra, in 1936 associate conductor, along with Leopold Stokowski, of the Philadelphia Orchestra, and its sole conductor in 1938. Like Stokowski a strict disciplinarian, he perfected an orchestral instrument for sensitive tonal interpretation of a wide range of works, from Bach and Vivaldi to the 20th century. He was a greatly-admired guest conductor of British and other European orchestras. Died 12 March

Penn Nouth, Samdech (b. 1906), was Prime Minister of Kampuchea for five periods, the longest of which was 1952–55, between 1948 and 1969, and Prime Minister of the Royal Government of the National Union of Kampuchea 1970–76. He was ambassador to France 1958–60. A supporter of Prince Sihanouk, he broke with him when the Prince allied himself with the Khmer Rouge. Died in exile 18 May

Porter, Professor Rodney Robert, FRS (b. 1917), British biochemist, shared with Dr G.M. Edelman (USA) the Nobel prize for medicine in 1972. After graduation at Liverpool University and war service 1939–45, he worked successively in the department of biochemistry at Cambridge and the National Institute for Medical Research. In 1960 he became professor of biochemistry at St Mary's Hospital, Paddington, and in 1967 Whitley Professor of Biochemistry at Oxford. He made a number of fundamental discoveries in the field of immunology, notably in the structure and behaviour of antibodies, and received many academic and professional honours, including foreign associateship of the American National Academy of Sciences. Died shortly after retiring from his Oxford chair, 6 September

Prittie, The Hon. Terence (b. 1913), wrote on Israel for the Annual Register 1974–84. After soldiering in World War II he became successively cricket correspondent, correspondent in Germany and diplomatic correspondent of the *(Manchester) Guardian*, and in 1969 director of 'Britain and Israel'. He was as deeply concerned with building mutual understanding with Germany as with Israel, and he enlivened his political perception with idiosyncratic humour. Died 28 May

Ramgoolam, Sir Seewoosagur, GCMG, PC (b. 1900), became Governor-General of Mauritius in 1984 after holding top political office in the island for over 20 years, followed by a spell in opposition—Chief Minister 1961–64, Premier 1964–67, Prime Minister under self-government and independence 1967–82. After qualifying as a doctor in London, he returned to Mauritius and helped to reorganize the colony's Labour Party, of which he became leader. In 1965 he incurred much hostility from the left for his consent to the transfer of the Chagos archipelago (including Diego Garcia) to the British Indian Ocean Territory, and his Governments after the elections of 1967 were all coalitions, opposed by the left-wing Mouvement Militant Mauricien and Parti Socialiste Mauricien, which together swept the board in the 1982 elections, only to lose power in the following year. Died 15 December

Redgrave, Sir Michael (b. 1908), British actor, was born to theatrical parents but had a conventional education at public school and Cambridge. After three years of school-teaching,

however, he joined the Liverpool Playhouse repertory company and in 1936 was recruited to the Old Vic by Tyrone Guthrie. Acclaim from the critics came soon, especially for his Tusenbach in *Three Sisters*, 1938. His distinguished film career began in the same year, with Hitchcock's *The Lady Vanishes*. Thereafter he was recognized on both sides of the Atlantic as a major artist on both stage and screen. Among his most memorable parts were, on the stage, Macbeth, the Emperor in *Anthony and Cleopatra*, Aguecheek, Uncle Vanya, and Orin Manon in *Mourning Becomes Electra*; on the cinema screen, the ventriloquist in Cavalcanti's *The Dead of Night*, Crocker-Harris in *The Browning Version* and leading roles in *Confidential Report*, *The Dambusters* and *The Go-Between*. Despite progressive illness he last appeared in *Close of Play* at the National Theatre in 1979. His three children, Vanessa, Corin and Lynn, all followed him in theatrical careers. Died 21 March

Richter, Dr Charles (b. 1900), American seismologist, perpetuated his name when in 1932 he devised the universally-employed Richter scale of the forces of earthquakes, on which each point registers an intensity 10 times greater than the preceding point. He was for many years until his retirement professor of seismology at the California Institute of Technology. Died 30 September

Romulo, General Carlos (b. 1899), was Foreign Minister of the Philippines 1950–52 and from 1968 onwards. After an early career as a university teacher of English and a Pulitzer Prize journalist he joined the US Army in 1941, fought at Bataan and again in the liberation campaign of 1944–45. He signed the UN Charter on behalf of his country in 1945, and led its delegation to the UN 1945–54 (President of the General Assembly 1949). He was also ambassador to the US 1952–53. Died 15 December

Roy, H.E. Cardinal Maurice (b.

1905), was Roman Catholic Primate of Canada 1956–81. Born in Quebec, he taught at Laval University, P.Q., 1930–46, then became successively Bishop of Trois Rivières in 1946 and Archbishop of Quebec in 1947. During World War II he was Assistant Principal RC Chaplain to the Canadian forces. He was made a Cardinal in 1965 and was president of the Holy See's Council of Laity and the Pontifical Commission for Justice and Peace 1967–77. Died 24 October

Sarkis, Elias (b. 1924), was President of Lebanon 1976–82. A Maronite Christian and an apostle of 'Chehabism'—a strong central state—he was narrowly defeated by Sulaiman Franjieh for the presidency in 1970, and was himself elected in 1976 under the military protection of Syria, disguised as the anti-Palestinian 'Arab Deterrent Force'. His attitude to the Israeli invasion in 1982 was equivocal, for he believed it might counter-balance his indebtedness to Syria. Died 27 June

Sattar, Abdus, (b. 1906), was President of Bangladesh for four months in 1981–82. A lawyer and judge (of the East Pakistan High Court from 1968), he had been a member of Pakistan's second Constituent Assembly in 1954. After the separation of Bangladesh in 1971 he became Minister of Law and Parliamentary Affairs in General Ziaur Rahman's Government 1975–77, and Vice-President 1977–81. His position as acting President after Zia's murder in May 1981 was ratified by an overwhelming popular vote in November, but in the following March he was deposed by Lieut.-General Ershad, who placed the country under military rule. Sattar thereafter led a movement for the return of democratic government. Died 5 October

Spiegel, Sam (b. 1904 in Poland, then part of the Austro-Hungarian Empire), was the most creative and original American film producer of his time. His first job in Hollywood, in 1927, was as a story translator, but he returned to Europe to work for Universal Films as an independent producer. He fled Germany in 1933 and migrated to the US in 1939. His first memorable Hollywood film was *Tales of Manhattan* (1942), followed by Orson Welles's (q.v.) *The Stranger* (1945) and a string of successes, many of them breaking new ground, including *We Were Strangers* (1948), *African Queen* (1951), *On the Waterfront* (1954), *The Bridge on the River Kwai* (1957), *Suddenly Last Summer* (1959), *Lawrence of Arabia* (1962) and *Nicholas and Alexandra* (1971). He was honoured with three Academy Awards (Oscars). Died 31 December

Springer, Axel (b. 1912), German newspaper proprietor, built a huge press empire around two highly profitable papers *Die Welt* and *Bild*, the latter a down-market tabloid with a circulation of over 5 million. The son of a printer, with experience as a reporter, immediately after World War II he set up his own publishing company in Hamburg and by leave of the occupying authorities launched the radio programme guide *Hör Zu* and the evening paper *Hamburger Abendblatt* with great success enhanced by novel sales-promotion methods. In 1952 he founded *Bild*, Germany's first successful mass-circulation tabloid, garish and vulgar but attuned to the taste of the public it aimed to please. A year later he took over the leading quality newspaper *Die Welt*, originally set up under occupation authority. To those early ventures he added a number of magazines and local newspapers. His political stance, which decisively influenced his nominally independent editors, was broadly right-wing, anti-communist, pro-Western and pro-Israel. Died 22 September

Trevelyan, Lord, KG, GCMG (b. 1905), British administrator and diplomat, became the most respected of all figures in the foreign service of his country. Humphrey Trevelyan's career started in the Indian Civil Service in 1929, but he switched to the Political

Department which dealt with the princely states. His Indian service proceeded to the joint secretaryship of the External Affairs department. Upon the end of British rule in 1947 he joined the British foreign service, where he quickly rose through posts in Iraq and Germany to become chargé d'affaires in Peking (1953–55) and ambassador in Cairo (1955–56), where he bore the brunt of Egyptian reaction to the Anglo-French–Israeli operation against the Suez Canal. After briefly serving at the UN, he became ambassador to Iraq (1958–61), Deputy Under-Secretary of State at the Foreign Office 1962 and ambassador in Moscow. Retiring in 1965, he was called back in 1967 to become High Commissioner in Aden when its independence as South Yemen was looming amid actual and threatened violence, a transition which he effected with great firmness and courage. He became a director of important companies, chairman of the British Museum Trustees (1970–79) and of the Royal Institute of International Affairs (1970–77). His books included The Middle East in Revolution (1970), Worlds Apart, based on his experiences of the USSR and communist China, The India We Left (1972) and an autobiography, Public and Private (1980). Died 8 February

Visser't Hooft, Dr Willem Adolph (b. 1900), Netherlands pastor, was the first general secretary of the World Council of Churches (WCC) 1938–66 and its honorary president from 1968. Ordained in the Dutch Reformed Church, he became secretary of the world committee of the YMCA in 1924 and general secretary of the World Student Christian Federation in 1931. While the newly-formed WCC was operating from Geneva during World War II, Visser't Hooft kept open lines with the resistance movements in the Netherlands and Germany. In his leadership of the greatly expanding WCC he worked for the widest ecumenism, drawing in the Eastern Orthodox churches and a number of autonomous Asian and African churches and maintaining links with the Roman Catholic Church. He wrote many books on theology and the ecumenical movement, and one on Rembrandt. Died 4 July

Welles, Orson (b. 1915), American actor, film producer and director, reached a pinnacle of fame very early in life with his production in 1941 of Citizen Kane, of which he wrote much of the script and in which he acted the title role, a film judged then and later as one of the finest ever made. An infant prodigy, Welles was only 16 when he boasted his way into an acting job at the Gate Theatre in Dublin. Returning to the US, he launched a successful stage career as actor and theatre director, but it was a radio triumph, his devastatingly realistic production of H.G. Wells's The War of the Worlds, that took him to Hollywood with a reputation far beyond his 25 years. Nothing later ever matched Citizen Kane, but he produced and/or acted in a number of memorable films, including Jane Eyre (as Rochester), The Third Man (as Harry Lime), his own Macbeth and Othello, The Trial (based on Kafka) and Chimes at Midnight (as Falstaff). On stage he remained deeply impressive in both Othello and King Lear, but many of his later film roles were trivial. Died 10 October

Whitlock, Harold (b. 1903), British athlete, won the gold medal in the 50km walk at the Berlin Olympic Games in 1936, after setting a world record for the 30-mile walk in the previous year. He competed in the 1952 Olympics as Britain's oldest-ever international track athlete. Though never retired from racing, he became a successful coach and race judge. Died December

Zafrulla Khan, Sir Muhammed (b. 1893), was Pakistan's first Foreign Minister in 1947 and its permanent representative at the UN 1961–64 (President of the General Assembly 1962–63). Between 1947 and 1954 he had represented his country at the Security Council and the General Assembly when the Indo-Pakistani dispute over Kashmir was high on the agenda. Under British rule he had served with distinction as a member of the Punjab Legislative Council (1926–35), a delegate to the Round Table conference (1930–32) and to the joint select committee on the Bill that became the Government of India Act 1935, and a member of the Governor-General's Executive Council (1935–41). He was president of the All India Muslim League in 1931. Zafrulla was, however, primarily a lawyer, originally practising in the Lahore High Court 1916–35 and becoming a judge of the Federal Court of India 1941–47. From 1954 to 1961, and from 1964 to 1973, he was a judge at the International Court of Justice at The Hague (President 1970–73). A deeply religious man, he was greatly shocked when the Ahmadiya sect to which he belonged was declared non-Muslim by Mr Bhutto's Government in 1974, and his last years were spent mainly in England. Died 1 September

Zimbalist, Efrem (b. 1890), Russian violinist, made his highly successful debut in Berlin and London in 1907, after studying under Leopold Auer at St Petersburg Conservatory. After playing to immense acclaim in Britain and New York in 1911, he decided to stay in the US, where he married the soprano Alma Gluck. A teacher at the Curtis Institute from 1928, he became its director 1941–68. At the age of 62, though retired from the concert platform, he gave the premiere of Menotti's violin concerto, which was dedicated to him. Died 22 February

CHRONICLE OF PRINCIPAL EVENTS IN 1985

JANUARY

2 President Reagan and Japanese PM Nakasone held talks in Los Angeles.
In UK, *The Times* celebrated its 200th anniversary.

3 It was reported that Israel had masterminded a secret airlift of Ethiopian Jews (Falashas) to Israel during past two months; 4 Jan. airlift ended following revelation.

7 US Secretary of State Shultz and Soviet Foreign Minister Gromyko held talks in Geneva to discuss resumption of arms control negotiations.

10 Sr Daniel Ortega sworn in for a six-year term as President of Nicaragua.
One hundred people reported to have died as result of exceptionally severe winter weather conditions affecting whole of Europe.

11 In West Germany, three US servicemen died when Pershing-II nuclear missile caught fire at army base at Heilbronn.

12 In New Caledonia, separatist leader Eloi Machoro shot dead by security forces; a state of emergency was imposed when rioting broke out; 19 Jan. President Mitterrand paid one-day visit to island and upon his return declared that France would reinforce its military base there to safeguard its strategic presence in S. Pacific; 25 Jan. state of emergency extended to 30 June; 23 reported dead in recent violence.

14 Israeli Cabinet decided upon three-stage withdrawal from occupied Lebanon beginning in February.
In UK, sterling fell to $1.1105 despite rise of Minimum Lending Rate to 12 per cent (see 23 July).
Hun Sen elected PM of Cambodia in succession to Chan Sy who died on 31 Dec. 1984.

15 In Brazil, electoral college elected Tancredo Neves (Democratic Alliance) first civilian President for 21 years but he died on 21 April before taking office; 22 April, José Sarney (Vice-President) sworn in as President.

17 A three-day summit conference at the UN between President Kyprianou of Cyprus and Turkish-Cypriot leader Rauf Denktash failed to reach agreement on future of island.

20 In USA, President Reagan was sworn in for a second term.

22 In UK, Government published White Paper (Cmnd. 9428) on public expenditure for next three years, proposing cuts in 1985–86 and thereafter two years of restraint.

23 In UK, proceedings of the House of Lords broadcast live on television for first time.

25 In S. Africa, President Botha opened new three-chamber Parliament for Whites, Indians and Coloureds in Cape Town.

26 Pope John Paul II began 12-day visit to Venezuela, Ecuador, Peru and Trinidad & Tobago.

FEBRUARY

1 In the Philippines, trial opened in Manila of 25 military men and one civilian charged with complicity in 1983 murder of Benigno Aquino (see 2 Dec.).

4 In USA, President Reagan's military budget called for tripled spending on 'Star Wars' space weapons research.

5 In Gibraltar, frontier gates with Spain reopened after 16 years as talks began in Geneva between British and Spanish Foreign Ministers on future of the Rock.
Libya released four detained Britons following negotiations by Archbishop of Canterbury's envoy Mr Terry Waite.

7 In Poland, four secret police officers, convicted of murder of Fr Jerzy Popieluszko in October 1984, received gaol terms of between 14 and 25 years.

President Reagan and Australian PM Bob Hawke held talks in Washington on proposed US testing of MX nuclear missiles in S. Pacific.

8 Kim Dae Jung returned to S. Korea after two-year exile in USA and was immediately placed under house arrest; accompanying US officials were beaten up by airport security men.

11 In UK, Mr Clive Ponting, former Ministry of Defence official who had leaked documents relating to sinking of Argentine cruiser *General Belgrano* during Falklands war, acquitted on charges under Official Secrets Act.

12 King Fahd of Saudi Arabia began five-day visit to USA.

In first-ever elections for National Assembly in S. Korea, newly-formed New Korea Democratic Party secured 29·2 per cent of vote to become largest party in opposition to ruling Justice Party, which topped the poll.

15 In Moscow, world chess championship abandoned after six months and 48 matches with Anatoly Karpov leading Gary Kasparov 5-3 (see 8 Nov.).

19 In Spain, 145 died when Iberia Boeing 727 crashed at Bilbao.

In Irish Republic, Dail passed emergency law enabling Government to seize up to IR£10 million from a Provisional IRA bank account.

20 Mrs Thatcher, in Washington for talks with President Reagan, addressed a joint session of Congress.

21 Cardinal Glemp, Primate of Poland, began 12-day visit to UK during which he held talks with Archbishop of Canterbury.

25 In Pakistan, 38 former members of banned Pakistan People's Party won seats in elections to National Assembly despite ban by President Zia on political parties in contest; 2 March, Zia announced major constitutional changes increasing power of President (see 30 Dec.).

26 In UK, disruptive action in schools by teachers protesting over pay and conditions began and continued throughout the year.

27 In UK, following breakdown of talks on settlement of pits dispute, National Coal Board reported over 50 per cent of Britain's miners now back at work (see 3 March).

28 In Northern Ireland, eight police officers and one civilian died in mortar bomb attack on Newry police station, Co. Down.

MARCH

1 Sr Julio Sanguinetti took office as Uruguay's first elected President in 12 years.

3 In UK, delegate conference of National Union of Mineworkers voted for an immediate return to work without settlement of year-long strike over pit closures.

120 died and many were injured in earthquake in central Chile.

8 In Lebanon, 80 died in car-bomb explosion in Beirut (see 10 March).

In UK, Secretary of State for Environment announced plans for £9·5 million art gallery, 'Tate in the North', to be built in Liverpool.

10 President Chernenko of the USSR died; his funeral on 13 March was attended by many world leaders (see 11 March, 2 July).

President Karamanlis resigned as President of Greece in protest over proposed constitutional reform (see 30 March).

In southern Lebanon, Shia Muslim suicide bomber rammed Israeli army convoy, killing 12 Israelis, claiming revenge for car-bomb attack on 8 March.

11 In USSR, Mikhail Gorbachev named General Secretary of Communist Party.

12 A major new round of arms limitation talks between USA and USSR opened in Geneva, ending 23 April.

17 President Reagan and Canadian PM Brian Mulroney held summit talks in Quebec.

President Nyerere of Tanzania on official visit to UK (see 27 Oct.).

Iraq warned international airlines to avoid Iranian air space as Gulf war intensified.

18 British embassy in Beirut closed following kidnapping of two Britons and an American journalist and Phalangist revolt against Government of President Gemayel.

19 In UK, Budget day: personal tax thresholds raised by more than inflation; excise duties up; major changes in National Insurance proposed; measures to improve training opportunities for unemployed; PSBR set at £7 billion (2 per cent of GDP).

21 In S. Africa, 18 dead, 36 injured, when police fired on crowd of blacks in Uitenhage on 25th anniversary of Sharpeville massacre; 22 March, President Botha announced judicial commission of inquiry following worldwide condemnation of shootings.
The 300th anniversary of the birth of J. S. Bach.

24 In East Germany, a Soviet guard shot dead an unarmed US army officer; 25 March, US protested and demanded full explanation.

26 HM Queen Elizabeth II and Prince Philip began four-day visit to Portugal.

28 In UK, Government published White Paper on employment, *The Challenge for the Nation* (Cmnd. 9474).
Mr Karoly Nemeth appointed deputy to Hungarian Communist Party leader Janos Kádár.
President Devan Nair resigned as President of Singapore on health grounds (see 30 Aug.).

29 A two-day summit conference of EEC heads of government opened in Brussels; terms were agreed for admission of Spain and Portugal to Community on 1 Jan. 1986 (see 12 June).

30 Judge Christos Sartzetakis sworn in as President of Greece following election by Parliament on 29 March (see 10 March).
In UK, Grand National won by Last Suspect at 50–1.

31 In National Assembly elections in El Salvador, Christian Democrat Party of President Duarte won 33 out of 60 seats.

APRIL

4 Mrs Thatcher began 11-day tour to six S.E. Asian nations.

5 In Jordan, Zeid Refei sworn in at head of 23-man Cabinet following resignation of PM Ahmed Obeidat.

6 In Sudan, President Gaafar Nimairi overthrown in bloodless coup led by Gen. Abdul-Rahman Suwar al-Dahab; 10 April, 15-man military junta named (see 22 April).
In UK, Oxford won University Boat Race by 4¾ lengths.

7 In USSR, Mr Gorbachev announced moratorium on missile deployment in Europe until November and declared willingness to hold summit talks with President Reagan (see 19 Nov.).

11 Enver Hoxha, First Secretary of Albanian Communist Party and leader of his country for over 40 years died; Mr Ramiz Alia subsequently named First Secretary.

12 In Spain, 18 died, 82 injured, in bomb explosion in Madrid; responsibility claimed by Islamic Jihad.

14 Elections in Peru resulted in defeat for ruling Popular Action Party of President Belaúnde Terry; Sr Alan Garcia Perez, leader of social democratic APRA, took over as President in July.

15 President Botha announced that all remaining S. African forces would be withdrawn from southern Angola by 18 April.
President Chadli of Algeria on official visit to Washington.

16 Dr Hastings Banda, Life President of Malawi, began four-day state visit to UK.

17 Mr Rashid Karami resigned as PM of Lebanon in protest over Shia Muslim and Druze militia attacks in West Beirut killing 29 (he stayed on in caretaker capacity).

18 In UK, a new world record for a painting was set at Christie's when Mantegna's *Adoration of the Magi* was sold to the Getty Museum for £7.5 million.

19 President Botha announced that S. African Government would return legislative powers and executive authority to Namibia, insisting that he would continue to negotiate with UN on achievement of internationally-recognized independence for territory in terms of Resolution 435; plan was rejected by Swapo.

The Prince and Princess of Wales began 17-day official visit to Italy.

21 In UK, 15,500 runners participated in London Marathon won by Steve Jones.

22 In Argentina, trial opened of nine former military leaders including Gen. Galtieri and two other former Presidents, charged with crimes against human rights (see 9 Dec.).

In Sudan, General Abdul-Rahman Suwar al-Dahab named Dr Dafaa-Allah as PM to head 15-member interim Cabinet (see 6 April).

23 East German leader Honecker on two-day official visit to Rome—the first visit by an East German head of state to a Nato or EC capital.

26 Following summit talks in Warsaw, Warsaw Pact leaders issued communique announcing that the seven countries had agreed to renew military alliance (originally signed in 1955) for a further 30 years.

28 In USA, raiders stole $25-50 million from Wells Fargo Bank in New York.

30 Canadian PM Brian Mulroney held talks in London with Mrs Thatcher.

MAY

1 In USA, President Reagan signed order imposing financial and trade sanctions against Nicaragua.

In Spain terrorist bombs exploded on two beaches in the Costa Blanca; further bombs exploded in holiday resorts later in the week.

2 The 11th annual seven-nation Western economic summit conference opened in Bonn, ending 4 May; following 8 May summit, President Reagan made 10-day tour of Europe during which he addressed European Parliament (see 5 May).

In UK, Tories suffered extensive losses in county council elections; Liberal–SDP Alliance held balance of power in 27 shire counties.

3 In UK, 27 reported dead in outbreak of Legionnaires disease in Stafford.

5 President Reagan made controversial visit to military cemetery at Bitburg (containing graves of SS officers) and also visited ruins of Belsen concentration camp.

6 In S. Africa, black trade union leader Andries Raditsela died following release from police custody; a second black later reported to have died after detention by police.

8 Ceremonies took place throughout Europe and in USSR to mark 40th anniversary of end of World War II in Europe; HM the Queen attended a special service in Westminster Abbey.

10 Pope John Paul II began visit to Netherlands and Luxembourg; 12 May, police fired shots to disperse anti-papal rioters in Utrecht.

11 In UK, 52 died in fire at Bradford City Football Ground.

HRH Prince Andrew officially opened new airport in Falkland Islands.

13 In India, 84 reported dead in three days of Sikh extremist bomb attacks in three Indian cities including Delhi.

14 US Secretary of State Shultz and Soviet Foreign Minister Gromyko held talks in Vienna on arms control and other matters.

In Sri Lanka, 146 died during Tamil attacks in holy city of Anuradhapura.

16 In UK, Government published White Paper, *Review of Public Order Law* (Cmnd. 9510), proposing new powers on picketing and football crowds.

17 In Japan, 60 died in colliery fire in Hokkaido.

20 In S. Africa, trial of 16 anti-apartheid campaigners accused of treason opened in Natal (see 9 Dec.).

22 In Lebanon, 60 people died in car bomb explosion in Christian sector of Beirut.

25 10,000 died in cyclone which hit southern Bangladesh.

26 25 dead, 40 injured, when explosion destroyed two tankers off Gibraltar.

27 Trial opened in Rome of three Bulgarians and five Turks accused of conspiring to kill Pope John Paul II in May 1981.

29 In Belgium, 38 football supporters died in riot at European Cup Final between Liverpool and Juventus (of Turin) (see 2 June and 16 July).

In USA, President Reagan sent to Congress a far-reaching plan for tax reform.

JUNE

2 In Greece, general election won by ruling Panhellenic Socialist Movement (Pasok) led by PM Andreas Papandreou.
Union of European Football Association (Uefa) announced indefinite ban on English clubs from European competitions following Brussels riot (see 29 May).
3 Chinese PM Zhao Ziyang on a week's official visit to Pakistan.
In UK, Government published four Green Papers (Cmnd. 9517-9520) proposing changes in welfare state (see 16 Dec.).
5 In UK, Government published White Paper, *Airports Policy* (Cmnd. 9542), backing the enlargement of Stansted airport.
In UK, the Derby won by Slip Anchor at 9–4.
6 In India, trial opened in Delhi of Satwant Singh, alleged assassin of Mrs Indira Gandhi.
10 In USA, Claus von Bulow acquitted of charge of attempted murder of his wife following a second trial.
11 President Miguel de la Madrid of Mexico began four-day state visit to UK.
Twenty-three Westerners, gaoled in East Germany and Poland, handed over in W. Berlin in exchange for four E. Europeans convicted of espionage.
12 Spain and Portugal signed treaty of accession to European Community which they would join on 1 Jan. 1986 (see 29 March).
13 In Portugal, coalition Government of PM Mario Soares resigned (see 6 Oct.).
In UK, the National Gallery received a donation of £50 million from Mr Paul Getty, Jr.
14 Lebanese Shia Muslim gunmen hijacked TWA jet with 145 passengers and crew of 8, demanding release of 700 Shia prisoners held by Israel; after the plane had been flown from Beirut to Algiers and back three times some hostages were released, one man having been shot dead; 17 June remaining passengers and crew were removed from plane into custody of Shia Muslim militiamen (see 30 June).
S. African forces killed 15 in dawn raids in Gaborone, Botswana.
19 In China, nine new Ministers with specialist knowledge were appointed to spearhead drive for modernization of China.
In W. Germany, three dead, 42 injured, in bomb attack at Frankfurt airport.
20 In Norway, former diplomat Arne Treholt gaoled for 20 years for spying on behalf of KGB and Iraq.
In UK, Chancellor of Exchequer criticised Bank of England for failure to act quickly to avert £248 million collapse of Johnson Matthey Bank in 1984 (see 17 July, 8 Nov.).
23 Air India Boeing 747 crashed into Atlantic off Irish coast killing all 329 people aboard; a terrorist bomb was the suspected cause.
In Japan, two died in bomb explosion at Tokyo airport.
24 In UK, Scotland Yard announced it had uncovered plans for IRA bombing campaign in seaside resorts.
25 Three-day summit conference of Comecon opened in Warsaw; final communique reaffirmed proposal to open relations between Comecon and EEC.
27 In Zimbabwe, Conservative Alliance of Zimbabwe led by former PM Ian Smith won 15 of 20 white seats in elections for Parliament (see 1 July).
28 A two-day summit conference of EEC heads of government opened in Milan.
30 Thirty-nine US hostages taken from hijacked TWA jet taken to Damascus where they were released, following mediation with Shia Muslim leaders by Syria (see 14 July).

JULY

1 In Zimbabwe, polling began in elections for 80 black seats in Parliament; 6 July, results gave overwhelming victory for Zanu (PF) Party led by PM Robert Mugabe.

2 In USSR, Mr Andrei Gromyko, Foreign Minister for 28 years, named President; Mr Eduard Shevardnadze succeeded him as Foreign Minister.
3 Signor Francesco Cossiga succeeded Alessandro Pertini as President of Italy.
4 In UK, by-election at Brecon and Radnor, previously Tory seat, won by Liberal for Alliance, putting Tories in third place.
   In Guinea, troops put down attempted coup led by former PM Col. Diarra Traore.
7 In UK, Boris Becker, aged 17, of W. Germany became youngest-ever winner of men's singles title at Wimbledon tennis championships.
8 King Juan Carlos of Spain on three-day official visit to France.
   In W. Germany, reporter Gerd Heideman and a book dealer gaoled for forgery and sale of alleged 'Hitler Diaries' in 1983.
11 In New Zealand, one man died when environmental pressure group Greenpeace's ship *Rainbow Warrior* was sunk in Auckland harbour (see 26 Aug., 20, 22 Sept., 4 Nov.).
13 In USA, President Reagan underwent cancer surgery.
   Live Aid, a rock concert beamed worldwide by satellite from USA and UK, raised more than £40 million for African famine relief.
   New Zealand Rugby Football Union cancelled All Blacks' tour of S. Africa in response to interim injunction in New Zealand High Court.
14 In Bolivia, elections for President and 157 seats in Houses of Congress (see 5 Aug.).
16 In Belgium, King Baudouin refused to accept resignation of Government of Mr Martens over handling of Brussels football riot on 29 May (see 13 Oct.).
17 In UK Chancellor announced police investigation of affairs of Johnson Matthey Bank (see 20 June, 8 Nov.).
19 In Italy, 260 died in the Dolomites when a reservoir burst, flooding villages in the valley below.
20 S. African Government declared state of emergency in 36 districts which had suffered severe violence during past year (see 29 July).
   European Community Ministers and central bank governors agreed to major realignment of foreign exchange rates and 8 per cent devaluation of lira.
21 Sandy Lyle became first Briton for 16 years to win British Open Golf Championship.
22 In Zimbabwe, the Spanish ambassador Sr Blanco Briones found murdered.
23 Sterling rose to $1.41 as dollar weakened on world currency markets (see 14 Jan.).
   In India, PM Rajiv Gandhi held talks in Delhi with Sant Harchand Singh Longowal, leader of Sikh community in Punjab, in attempt to seek solution to four-year crisis in Punjab (see 20 Aug.).
25 In UK, a report of the National Federation of Housing Associations, chaired by HRH the Duke of Edinburgh, recommended radical reforms, including abolition of mortgage tax relief.
27 In Uganda, President Milton Obote overthrown in military coup led by Brig. Basilio Olara Okello; coup followed by widespread looting in Kampala; 29 July, Lt.-Gen. Tito Okello sworn in as Chairman of Military Council.
29 In S. Africa, 1,215 reported arrested, 18 dead, since introduction of state of emergency.
30 World Foreign Ministers attended three-day tenth anniversary meeting of signing of Helsinki Final Act of European Security Conference.
31 Mr Paulo Muwanga, former Vice-President, named PM of Uganda (see 25 Aug.).

AUGUST

3 Mr Gerry Adams, MP for West Belfast and President of Sinn Fein, replaced Martin McGuiness as IRA chief of staff.
   In USA, 132 died in air crash at Dallas-Fort Worth.
4 In S. Africa, black miners voted for indefinite strike at gold and coal mines, demanding lifting of state of emergency.

5 Sr Victor Paz Estenssoro elected President of Bolivia by Congress following inconclusive result of July elections (see 14 July).
6 In Japan, 55,000 people took part in ceremonies at Hiroshima marking 40th anniversary of atomic bombing of the city of World War II.
  Former PM Desmond Hoyte became President of Guyana following death in office of President Forbes Burnham.
  In UK, TUC and Labour Party published joint document, *A New Partnership, A New Britain*, setting out policies for the next Labour Government.
7 In UK, BBC and ITV journalists staged one-day strike over BBC Governors' banning of documentary on Northern Ireland extremism, *Real Lives*; an edited version was screened later.
8 Pope John Paul II began a 12-day visit to seven African nations.
  In S. Africa, at least 19 died, 100 injured, in rioting in Indian and black townships around Durban.
12 In Japan, 520 died when Japan Airlines Boeing 747 crashed into mountains; four survived.
15 In S. Africa, President Botha reaffirmed his commitment to apartheid and ruled out possibility of parliamentary representation for blacks.
  Virgin Atlantic Challenger sank off Isles of Scilly after $3\frac{1}{2}$ days at sea in attempt to break record for fastest crossing of Atlantic set by SS *United States* in 1952.
16 President Khamenei received 89 per cent of votes cast in Iranian presidential election; inaugurated for fourth term 4 Sept.
  Australian PM Bob Hawke announced that Australia and Britain had reached agreement on ending remaining legal ties.
17 In Lebanon, 60 died, 100 injured, in car-bomb explosion in Christian East Beirut; 19 Aug., 29 died, 82 injured in Christian revenge car-bomb explosions in Muslim quarter of Beirut; 20 Aug. 44 civilians died in car-bombing in Tripoli, Lebanon.
20 In India, moderate Sikh leader Sant Harchand Singh Longowal assassinated by Sikh extremists in Sherpur (see 23 July).
21 USA accused USSR of using dangerous chemicals to monitor activities of US embassy personnel in Moscow.
22 In UK, 54 died when Boeing 737 caught fire at Manchester airport.
23 Senior W. German counter-espionage official Hans Joachim Tiedge sought political asylum in E. Germany (see 29 Aug.); two female secretaries in government service had disappeared earlier in month (see 17 Sept.).
25 Abraham Waligo replaced Paulo Muwanga as PM of Uganda (see 31 July).
26 Report by M Bernard Tricot exonerated French Government of any blame for sabotage of Greenpeace ship *Rainbow Warrior* (see 11 July); report rejected by New Zealand Government; 27 Aug. French PM Fabius ordered further investigations (see 20, 22 Sept., 4 Nov.).
27 S. African civil rights activist Rev. Allan Boesak arrested on eve of march to prison where Nelson Mandela had been held for 23 years; 28 Aug. five died in widespread clashes between demonstrators and police trying to prevent march.
  In Nigeria, Maj.-Gen. Muhammad Buhari overthrown in military coup; Maj.-Gen. Ibrahim Babangida named President and commander of armed forces.
28 In W. Germany, Chancellor Kohl dismissed head of secret service over Tiedge affair (see 23 Aug.).
29 Miss Benazir Bhutto, leader of banned Pakistan People's Party, placed under house arrest after returning to Pakistan from 19-month exile for funeral of her brother.
  In W. Germany, two former Ministers, Otto Graf Lambsdorff and Herr Hans Friederichs, went on trial for allegedly receiving bribes in so-called 'Flick affair'.
30 In S. Africa, 28 reported dead in three days of violence in townships around Cape Town.
  In France, 43 died in train crash near Argentan-sur-Creuse.
  Salvage experts located wreck of the *Titanic* which sank on Atlantic seabed 375 miles south of Newfoundland in 1912.

SEPTEMBER

1 President Botha announced that South Africa would impose 4-month freeze of repayment of foreign debt following refusal of international bankers to extend credit because of worsening internal political situation.

2 In UK, Cabinet reshuffle, Mr Douglas Hurd became Home Secretary; Mr Leon Brittan moved to Department of Trade and Industry; Mr Norman Tebbit became Conservative Party Chairman.

Former ruler of Kampuchea, Pol Pot, resigned as C-in-C of Khmer Rouge army and was replaced by Son Senn.

4 Kamal Hassan Ali resigned as PM of Egypt and was replaced by Ali Lufti.

5 In Australia, Mr John Howard replaced Mr Andrew Peacock as leader of Opposition Liberal Party.

8 In Norwegian general election, coalition Government led by Mr Kaare Willoch retained power by one seat.

9 President Reagan announced selective US economic sanctions against S. Africa.

In Thailand, four died in abortive military coup; a former PM was among those charged with complicity.

11 President Botha said S. African Government was willing to restore citizenship to some 8 million blacks deprived of it under homelands system but made no new offer on political rights.

13 British Government expelled 25 Soviet diplomats and officials named by Soviet defector Oleg Gordievsky as KGB officers; 14 Sept. USSR expelled 25 Britons from Moscow in retaliation; 16 Sept. Britain expelled six more Russians; 18 Sept. USSR expelled further six Britons and Mrs Thatcher called a halt to tit-for-tat expulsions.

President Mitterrand of France visited European Space Centre in French Guiana and nuclear test site at Mururoa despite protests by New Zealand PM.

14 In general election in Sweden, Socialist Government of Olof Palme returned with reduced majority.

16 Mrs Thatcher began four-day visit to Egypt and Jordan where she visited Palestinian camps.

In China, ten elderly Politburo members and 64 Central Committee members resigned to make way for younger supporters of Deng Xiaoping; 24 Sept. six new Politburo members elected by Central Committee.

17 W. Germany revealed that a secretary in Chancellor Kohl's office had defected to E. Germany (see 23, 28 Aug.).

19 Over 7,000 died in earthquake in Mexico City measuring 7·8 on Richter scale; a further earthquake shook the city the following day.

20 In France, Defence Minister Charles Hernu resigned over *Rainbow Warrior* affair (see 11 July etc.) and was replaced by M Paul Quiles; Admiral Pierre Lacoste was dismissed as head of foreign service; 22 July PM Fabius admitted that French secret service had sunk Greenpeace ship (see 4 Nov.).

25 In Indian Cabinet reshuffle PM Rajiv Gandhi assumed Defence and Technology portfolios; Bali Ram Bhagat became Foreign Minister.

President Barletta of Panama forced by army to resign; Sr Eric Arturo del Valle replaced him.

26 In Hong Kong, 24 members of an enlarged Legislative Council were elected for three-year term in first such elections held in 100 years of colonial rule.

27 In USSR, Nikolai Ryzhkov replaced Nikolai Tikhonov as PM.

Hurricane Gloria caused widespread damage along eastern coast of USA.

29 In Canada, Mr Pierre-Marc Johnson succeeded Mr René Lévesque as leader of Parti Québecois and provincial premier (see 2 Dec.).

30 Four Russian diplomats kidnapped in W. Beirut; one later found murdered.

In UK, Labour Party conference opened in Bournemouth; during it Mr Kinnock made major speech attacking Militant Tendency but conference carried Mr Scargill's resolution calling for reimbursement of union's losses incurred during miner's strike.

OCTOBER

1 Soviet leader Mikhail Gorbachev began four-day official visit to France.

Israeli bombers attacked PLO headquarters in Tunis, killing 60 people, in retaliation for murder in Cyprus of three Israelis by PLO.

6 In general election in Portugal, Social Democrats led by Professor Anibal Cavaco Silva topped poll and he subsequently formed Government; Socialists lost nearly half their support.

In UK, a policeman died in riots in Tottenham district of London, following riots and looting, mainly by blacks, in Handsworth (Birmingham) 9 Sept. and Brixton (S. London) 28 Sept.

7 Palestinian guerrillas hijacked Italian cruise liner *Achille Lauro* in Mediterranean with some 450 people aboard; 9 Oct. surrendered to Egyptian authorities, one US passenger having been murdered (see 10, 12, 17 Oct.).

9 HM Queen Elizabeth II began 3½-week tour of 10 former British colonies in Caribbean including visit to Commonwealth conference (see 16 Oct.).

10 US jets intercepted plane taking *Achille Lauro* hijackers from Egypt to Tunis, forcing it to land at Sicily where Italian authorities arrested terrorists (see 12 Oct.).

12 US protested when Italian authorities released terrorist who they alleged had masterminded *Achille Lauro* hijacking.

13 In Belgian general election Centre-Right coalition led by Mr Wilfried Martens returned to office (see 17 July).

In elections for Sejm in Poland, six million voters abstained in reponse to Solidarity's call for a boycott.

14 Indian PM Rajiv Gandhi on two-day official visit to Britain.

15 In first presidential elections in Liberia since 1980 military coup, General Samuel Doe declared winner amid widespread allegations of irregularities.

16 Commonwealth heads of government meeting opened in Nassau, Bahamas, ending 23 Oct.; 21 Oct. leaders reached agreement on package of measures to pressurize S. Africa into dismantling apartheid (see 10 Dec. and DOCUMENTS).

17 In Italy, Government of Signor Bettino Craxi tendered resignation in aftermath of *Achille Lauro* affair but was asked to stay in office by President Cossiga (see 10, 12 Oct.).

In UK, House of Lords ruled that it was not illegal for doctors to prescribe contraceptive pills to girls under 16 without parental consent.

18 In S. Africa, Benjamin Moloise hanged for murder of a policeman despite worldwide protests and riots in Johannesburg.

In UK, Nottinghamshire miners voted in favour of new breakaway union, Union of Democratic Miners.

24 Mrs Thatcher and President Reagan addressed UN General Assembly which was commemorating 40th anniversary of United Nations.

In UK, three servicemen acquitted at Old Bailey on charges of spying in Cyprus after longest (116 days) and most costly espionage trial in British legal history; four others subsequently also acquitted.

27 Julius Nyerere retired after nearly 24 years as President of Tanzania (since independence) and was succeeded by Ali Hassan Mwinyi.

Prince and Princess of Wales began 10-day visit to Australia, subsequently visiting USA.

In France, nine priceless Impressionist paintings stolen from Marmottan Museum in Paris.

29 United Bermuda Party led by PM Mr John Swan won record 31 seats out of 40 in House of Assembly elections.

NOVEMBER

2 In S. Africa, new emergency restrictions on media coverage of unrest were imposed by Government.

4 In New Zealand, two French secret servicemen pleaded guilty to manslaughter and sabotage in connection with sinking of *Rainbow Warrior* on 11 July; they were gaoled for ten years.

 US Secretary of State Shultz in Moscow for talks with Soviet Foreign Minister Shevardnadze.

 Vitaly Yurchenko, a senior KGB officer who defected to USA in August, claimed at press conference in Soviet embassy in Washington that he had been kidnapped by persons unknown and was now returning voluntarily to USSR.

6 General Jaruzelski resigned as PM of Poland but was named Chairman of Council of State; Prof Zbigniew Messner became PM.

 In UK, state opening of Parliament; Queen's speech foreshadowed new Bills on law and order, privatization and removal of restrictions on Sunday trading.

7 In Colombia, 95 people died when troops stormed Palace of Justice in Bogota to end 24-hour siege by members of M-19 guerrilla movement (see 24 Nov.).

8 Gary Kasparov became youngest-ever world chess champion after defeating reigning champion Anatoly Karpov in a 24-game match in Moscow.

 In UK, Labour MP made allegations in House of Commons of bribery and fraud in affair of Johnson Matthey bank (see 20 June); 28 Nov. it was disclosed that evidence of fraud had been found by investigating detectives.

12 Emir of Qatar on four-day state visit to UK.

13 In Colombia, at least 25,000 believed dead when Nevado del Ruiz volcano erupted swamping town of Armero and surrounding area with ash and mud (see 24 Nov.).

14 In UK, NUM submitted written apology to High Court to purge contempt and end sequestration order imposed upon it during 1984 strike.

15 At Hillsborough Castle, Belfast, Mrs Thatcher and Irish PM Dr FitzGerald signed Anglo-Irish Agreement giving the Republic a consultative role in affairs of N. Ireland for first time since partition (see 17 Dec. and DOCUMENTS).

18 President Mitterrand of France in London for talks with Mrs Thatcher at which both expressed enthusiasm for Channel link.

19 A two-day summit conference between Soviet leader Mikhail Gorbachev and President Reagan opened in Geneva; 21 Nov. a joint statement declared that nuclear war could not be won and must never be fought, and that neither side would seek military superiority.

20 In UK, House of Commons voted against televising of its proceedings.

21 In Papua New Guinea Mr Michael Somare resigned as PM and was succeeded by Mr Paias Wingti.

22 In UK, Liverpool City Council agreed to set legal budget, city having been on verge of bankruptcy because of anti-government campaign by militant Labour councillors.

23 Iran announced that Ayatollah Hosain Ali Montazeri would succeed Ayatollah Khomeini as figurehead leader upon the latter's death.

24 Sixty people died when Egyptian commandos stormed a hijacked Egyptian airliner at Malta airport.

 Colombia announced a national economic emergency following siege of Palace of Justice (see 7 Nov.) and volcano disaster (see 13 Nov.).

 In Rome, 165 Roman Catholic bishops began two-week extraordinary synod to assess impact of reforms of Second Vatican Council in 1965.

26 The Prince of Wales, speaking in Edinburgh, warned that Britain could become a fourth-rate nation unless individuals changed their attitude to jobs and business.

DECEMBER

2 A two-day summit conference of EEC heads of government opened in Luxembourg.
  In Canada, separatist Parti Québecois defeated in provincial elections when Liberals took 99 of 122 seats in legislature (see 29 Sept.).
  In Philippines, General Fabian Ver and 25 others acquitted of complicity in 1983 murder of Benigno Aquino (see 1 Feb.); Aquino's widow claimed killing was ordered by President Marcos.
3 In UK, the Church of England published a report attacking government policies on the inner cities and calling for increased spending on housing and welfare.
4 President Jaruzelski of Poland paid controversial visit to Paris for talks with President Mitterrand.
  In UK, HM The Queen and Prince Philip dined at No 10 Downing Street to mark 250th anniversary of PM's official residence.
5 British Government announced withdrawal from Unesco on 31 December.
  In Australia, report of Royal Commission into British nuclear tests in Australia recommended that UK should pay for clean-up operation on test sites and Australian Government should compensate Aborigines for loss of land.
8 In Guatemala, Christian Democrat Vinicio Cerezo won second round of presidential election ending 15 years of military rule.
9 In Argentina, former President Galtieri and three others acquitted on all charges but two former junta members gaoled for life for human rights violations (see 22 April).
  In S. Africa, Attorney-General withdrew charges against 12 of 16 anti-apartheid campaigners on trial since May (see 20 May).
  In general election in Guyana, victory claimed by ruling People's National Congress amid opposition allegations of malpractice.
  Opec leaders meeting in Geneva agreed to abolish oil production quotas in order to force non-Opec members to restrain output.
10 Commonwealth 'group of eminent persons', formed after Nassau Conference, held first meeting in London to consider task of promoting dialogue in S. Africa.
  In Oslo, Nobel peace prize awarded to Dr Yevgeny Chazov (USSR) and Dr Bernard Lown (USA), co-chairmen of International Physicians for Prevention of Nuclear War amid controversy over Dr Chazov's alleged condemnation of Nobel laureate Andrei Sakharov.
11 Twelfth annual Franco-African summit, attended by 26 countries, opened in Paris.
12 258 US servicemen died when DC-8 crashed after take-off from Gander airport, Newfoundland.
16 In UK, Government White Paper proposed major changes in social security (Cmnd. 9691).
17 In UK, Ulster Unionist MPs staged mass resignation from House of Commons over Anglo-Irish Accord (see 15 Nov.).
19 In France, Palestinian gunman held Assizes Court at Nantes at gunpoint, releasing two friends on trial; the three men surrendered on 20 Dec. at Nantes airport where they had gone with 4 hostages.
23 In S. Africa, five whites died, 48 injured, in bomb explosion on beach near Durban.
25 Fighting broke out between forces of Mali and Burkina Faso along their mutual border.
27 Fourteen died in an Arab terrorist attack at Rome airport (two others died later); three died in similar attack at Vienna airport.
30 In Pakistan, General Zia ended martial law, in operation since he came to power in 1977.

INDEX